Textbook of Sexual Medicine

Textbook of Sexual Medicine

Robert C. Kolodny, M.D.
Associate Director and Director of Training

William H. Masters, M.D.
Co-Director

Virginia E. Johnson, D.Sc. (Hon.)
Co-Director

The Masters & Johnson Institute
St. Louis, Missouri

Little, Brown and Company
Boston

Published November 1979

Copyright © 1979 by Robert C. Kolodny, William H. Masters, and Virginia E. Johnson

First Edition

Library of Congress Catalog Card No. 79-88165

ISBN 0-316-50154-9

Printed in the United States of America

HAL

Preface

The past decade has seen a remarkable degree of public and professional acceptance of sexual health as a legitimate and necessary aspect of modern health-care delivery. Most medical schools now give courses about human sexuality, prestigious journals publish reports of investigations on the subject of sexuality, and hundreds of conferences and workshops are held each year on various aspects of sexual behavior, sexual rehabilitation, and sexual problems. All this is in sharp contrast to the earlier prevailing atmosphere of disinterest, ignorance, or professional disdain.

We decided several years ago that these changes created an obvious place for a textbook oriented primarily toward the needs of clinicians working with patients who have sexual problems. Thus, in the preparation of this book, we incorporated many subjects that we had been asked about in our teaching of physicians and other health-care professionals across the country. The final product, which we believe to be comprehensive and clinically relevant throughout, is a text that we hope will be of equal use to the primary-care provider, the medical or surgical specialist, and the sex therapist. We have deliberately avoided an encyclopedic treatise that would be cumbersome in size, readability, and cost, and for that reason readers will find little mention of data involving animal research, sociologic or cross-cultural aspects of sexuality, and details of general psychotherapeutic theory or technique. On the other hand, the thoroughly referenced chapters of this text provide the reader with an opportunity to acquire a familiarity with our approach to the subject of sexual health. We hope that clinicians and educators will integrate the material presented here—including a substantial amount of previously unpublished data—into their own practices.

Although this book is called a *Textbook of Sexual Medicine*, it is not written for physicians alone. We are often asked by psychologists, social workers, nurses, counselors, and other health-care professionals for information to assist them in working with patients with a wide variety of medical or surgical problems. The detailed discussions of these topics—such as heart disease, drugs, cancer, mutilative surgery, obesity, alcoholism, arthritis, and pulmonary disease—are presented in a fashion that we hope will foster better cooperation and interaction among all members of the health-care team.

We gratefully acknowledge the valuable research assistance of Gail Tullman and Nancy Kolodny in the preparation of this book. Doctors Ira Kodner, Raymond Waggoner, George Murphy, Edward Dietiker, and Mark Schwartz provided considerable help through their critical comments on selected portions of the manuscript. The Washington University School of Medicine's Department of Medical Illustration, directed by Kramer Lewis, supplied proficient technical support. As always, the highly competent editorial services of our friends at Little, Brown and Company were of great assistance—our particular thanks to Christine Ulwick and Jacqueline Cohen. Throughout the many drafts and stages of the writing, Sarah Weems provided expert editorial vigilance, organizational skills, and general enthusiasm. Finally, we are indebted to the countless patients and research subjects who have participated in our work—they are our greatest source of encouragement.

R. C. K.
W. H. M.
V. E. J.

St. Louis

Contents

Textbook of Sexual Medicine

Sexual Anatomy and Physiology

Throughout the medical sciences, it is recognized that a detailed understanding of anatomy and physiology is a prerequisite to considerations of pathology or treatment. This recognition is based on the premise that effective therapy of any disordered body system hinges on an attempt to restore the equilibrium of normal function, although this goal may not always be attainable. Sexual behavior and sexual function are not, of course, only biologic in nature. The interaction of *psyche* and *soma* is nowhere more plainly illustrated than in the area of sexuality, where factors such as ego strength, social learning, personality, and values clearly combine with fundamental mechanisms of physiologic function in a highly complex system. In this chapter, discussion focuses on the biologic components of sexual response, with only brief commentary on pertinent psychological aspects.

Female Sexual Anatomy

The External Genitals

The external genitals of the female consist of the labia majora, the labia minora, the clitoris, and the perineum. Bartholin's glands, which open on the inner surfaces of the labia minora, may be considered functionally within the context of the external genitals, although their anatomic position is not in fact external.

Figure 1-1 presents a schematic depiction of the external genitals of the adult female. The appearance of the genitals varies considerably from one woman to another, including: (1) marked variation in the amount and pattern of distribution of pubic hair; (2) variation in size, pigmentation, and shape of the labia; (3) variation in size and visibility of the clitoris; and (4) variation in the location of the urethral meatus and the vaginal outlet. In the sexually unstimulated state, the labia majora usually meet in the midline, providing mechanical protection for the opening of the urethra and the vagina.

Histologically, the labia majora are folds of skin composed of a large amount of fat tissue and a thin layer of smooth muscle (similar to the muscle fibers present in the male scrotum). Pubic hair grows on the lateral surfaces; both the medial and lateral surfaces have many sweat and sebaceous glands. The labia minora have a core of vascular, spongy connective tissue without fat cells; their surfaces are composed of stratified squamous epithelium with large sebaceous glands.

The clitoris, which is located at the point where the labia majora meet anteriorly, is made up of two small erectile cavernous bodies enclosed in a fibrous membrane surface and ending in a glans or head. Histologically, the tissue of the clitoris is very similar to that of the penis. The

Figure 1-1. The human female external genitalia. (From Masters and Johnson [1].)

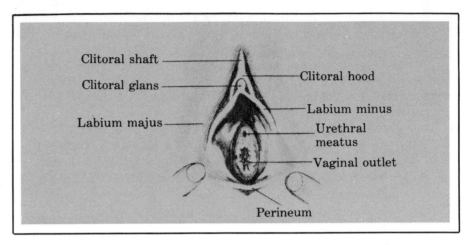

clitoris is richly endowed with free nerve endings, which are extremely sparse within the vagina [1], and is not known to have any function other than serving as a receptor and transducer for erotic sensation in the female.

The Internal Genitals   The internal genitals of the female include the vagina, cervix, uterus, fallopian tubes, and ovaries (Fig. 1-2). These structures may show considerable variation in size, spatial relationship, and appearance as a result of individual differences as well as reproductive history, age, and presence or absence of disease.

The vagina exists functionally more as a potential space than as a balloonlike opening. In the sexually unstimulated state, the walls of the vagina are collapsed together. The opening of the vagina (vaginal introitus) is covered by a thin membrane of tissue called the hymen, which has no known function; rather than being a solid band of tissue blocking the vaginal orifice, the hymen typically has perforations in it that allow menstrual flow to be eliminated from the body at the time of puberty. The walls of the vagina are completely lined with a mucosal surface that is now known to be the major source of vaginal lubrication; there are no secretory glands within the vaginal walls, although there is a rich vascular bed. The vagina is actually a muscular organ, capable of contraction and expansion; it can accommodate to the passage of a baby or can adjust in size to accept a much smaller object.

The cervix is a part of the uterus that protrudes into the vagina. The

Figure 1-2. Female pelvis: normal anatomy (lateral view). (From Masters and Johnson [1].)

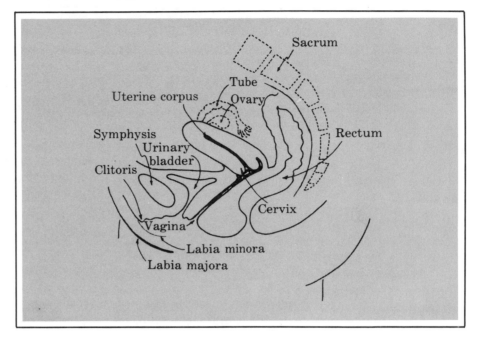

mouth of the cervix (cervical os) provides a point of entry for spermatozoa into the upper female genital tract and also serves as an exiting point for menstrual flow. The endocervical canal (a tubelike communication between the mouth of the cervix and the uterine cavity) contains numerous secretory crypts ("glands") that produce mucus. The consistency of cervical secretions varies during various phases of hormonal stimulation throughout the menstrual cycle: Just prior to or at the time of ovulation, cervical secretions become thin and watery; at other times of the cycle, these secretions are thick and viscous, forming a mucus plug that blocks the cervical os.

The uterus is a muscular organ that is situated in close proximity to the vagina. The lining of the uterus (the endometrium) and the muscular component of the uterus (the myometrium) function quite separately. The myometrium is important in the onset and completion of labor and delivery, with hormonal factors thought to be the primary regulatory mechanism. The endometrium changes in structure and function depending on the hormonal environment. Under the stimulus of increasing estrogenic activity, the endometrium thickens and be-

Figure 1-3. The penis: normal
anatomy (lateral view). (From Masters and Johnson [1].)

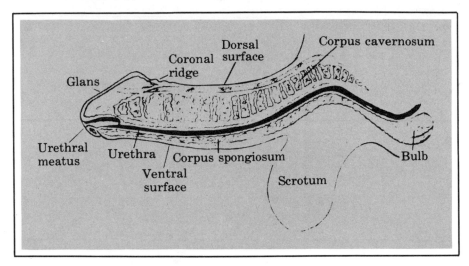

comes more vascular in preparation for the possible implantation of a
fertilized egg. If the fertilized ovum implants, the endometrium participates in the formation of the placenta. When fertilization and implantation do not occur, the greatly thickened endometrium begins to break
down, resulting in menstrual flow as a means of shedding the previously proliferated endometrial tissue, which will regenerate under appropriate hormonal stimulus in the next menstrual cycle. Endometrial
biopsy may be undertaken as part of an infertility evaluation to determine if ovulation has occurred and to observe whether appropriate
progesterone secretion has been present.

The fallopian tubes or oviducts originate at the uterus and open near
the ovaries, terminating in fingerlike extensions called fimbriae. The
fallopian tube is the usual site of fertilization; the motion of cilia within
the tube combined with peristalsis in the muscular wall results in
transport of the fertilized ovum to the uterine cavity.

The ovaries are paired abdominal structures that periodically release
eggs during the reproductive years and also produce a variety of steroid
hormones. Discussion of ovarian structure and function is beyond the
scope of this volume; interested readers are referred to the reference
list at the end of this chapter [2, 3].

Male Sexual Anatomy   The penis consists of three cylindrical bodies of erectile tissue (Figs. 1-3
and 1-4): The paired corpora cavernosa lie parallel to each other and

Figure 1-4. The penis: normal
anatomy (transverse section). (From
Masters and Johnson [1].)

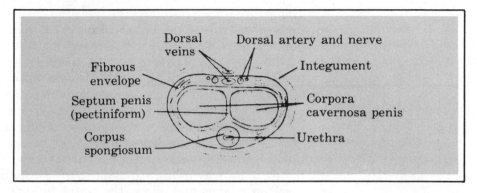

just above the corpus spongiosum, which contains the urethra. The
erectile tissues consist of irregular spongelike networks of vascular
spaces interspersed between arteries and veins. The distal portion of
the corpus spongiosum expands to form the glans penis. Each cylindrical body is covered by a fibrous coat of tissue, the tunica albuginea, and
all three corpora are enclosed in a covering of dense fascia. At the base
of the penis the corpora cavernosa diverge to form the crura, which
attach firmly to the pubis and ischium (the pubic arch). The blood
supply to the penis derives from terminal branches of the internal
pudendal arteries.

Erection occurs as a result of vasocongestion within the spongy tissue of the penis. When the penis is flaccid, the vascular spaces in the
erectile tissue are relatively empty; with arteriolar dilatation, blood
flows into the network of sinuses in the spongy tissue and increased
hydraulic pressure results in enlargement and hardening of the penis.
When the rate of arterial inflow of blood is matched by the rate of
venous return, a state of equilibrium is reached and the erection is
maintained. The role of venous blockade in the process of erection is
uncertain; detumescence occurs as a result of venous outflow exceeding
arterial input.

The vascular events that produce erection are under the control of
neural impulses. Although it has been speculated that parasympathetic fibers in sacral cord roots S2, S3, and S4 mediate erection,
this theory is a matter of some controversy.

The skin that covers the penis is freely movable and forms the foreskin or prepuce at the glans. Inflammation or infection of the foreskin or
glans may cause pain during sexual activity. There is much controversy

and little data surrounding the question of the effect of circumcision on male sexual function. There is also a great deal of confusion in regard to penis size and sexual function. With rare exceptions due to conditions of a true microphallus (see Chap. 9), the marked variation in size of the flaccid penis from man to man is less apparent in the erect state, because a greater percentage volume increase typically occurs during erection in the smaller penis than in a larger one.

The scrotum is a thin sac of skin containing the testicles. Involuntary muscle fibers are an integral part of the scrotal skin; these muscle fibers contract as a result of exercise or exposure to cold, causing the testes to be drawn upward against the perineum. In hot weather, the scrotum relaxes and allows the testes to hang more freely away from the body. These alterations in the scrotum are important thermo-regulators: Since spermatogenesis is temperature-sensitive, eleva-tion of the testes in response to cold provides a warmer environment by virtue of body heat, whereas loosening of the scrotum permits the testes to move away from the body and provides a larger skin surface for the dissipation of intrascrotal heat. The scrotum is divided into two com-partments by a septum.

Although the testes differentiate embryologically as intra-abdominal organs, they ordinarily descend to their scrotal position prior to birth. The testes function as the site of spermatogenesis and also play an important role in the production of sex steroid hormones. Spermatozoa are produced in the seminiferous tubules of the testes, while steroid hormone production occurs in the Leydig cells located in the interstitial tissue. Although architecturally these tissues are admixed within the testis, the two functions are under separate control from the pituitary gland. Hormone synthesis may proceed in a completely normal fashion even if the seminiferous tubules are dysfunctional, but spermato-genesis is generally disrupted if testosterone synthesis is seriously impaired.

The prostate gland, which is normally about the size of a chestnut, consists of a fibrous muscular portion and a glandular portion. The prostate is located directly below the bladder and surrounds the ure-thra as it exits from the bladder. The rectum is directly behind the prostate, permitting palpation of this gland by rectal examination. The prostate produces clear alkaline fluid that constitutes a portion of the seminal fluid; the prostate also is a major site of synthesis of chemical substances, known as prostaglandins, which have a wide variety of metabolic roles. Prostatic size and function are largely androgen-dependent. Cancer of the prostate arises in the glandular portion,

Figure 1-5. Male pelvis: normal anatomy (lateral view). (From Masters and Johnson [1].)

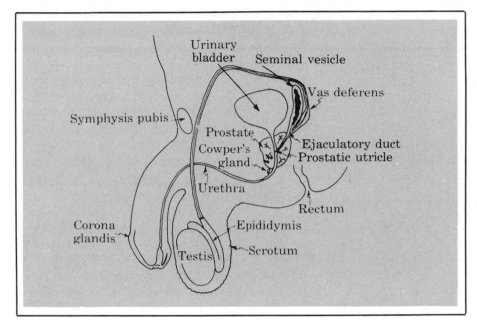

whereas benign prostatic hypertrophy usually results from enlargement of the fibromuscular component of the prostate.

The seminal vesicles (Fig. 1-5) are paired structures that lie against the posterior aspect of the base of the bladder and join with the end of the vasa deferentia (the tubelike structures that convey spermatozoa from the testes) to form the ejaculatory ducts. The ejaculatory ducts open into the prostatic urethra; the major fluid volume of the ejaculate derives from the seminal vesicles. Cowper's glands, which may produce a pre-ejaculatory mucoid secretion, are otherwise of unknown function.

The Sexual Response Cycle

Masters and Johnson introduced the idea of a human sexual response cycle on the basis of extensive laboratory observations [1]. Understanding the anatomic and physiologic changes that occur during sexual functioning is facilitated by consideration of this model. However, it is important to recognize that the various phases of the response cycle are arbitrarily defined, are not always clearly demarcated from one another, and may differ considerably both in one person at different times and between different people. The diagrams of female and male sexual response cycles (Figs. 1-6 and 1-7) are only schematic concep-

Figure 1-6. The female sexual response cycle. (From Masters and
Johnson [1].)

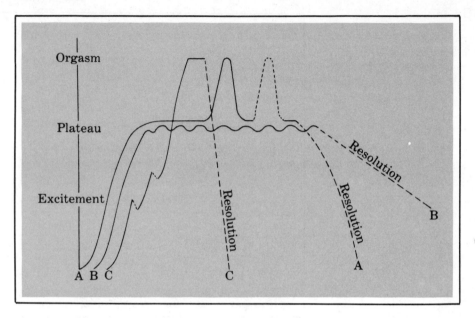

Figure 1-7. The male sexual response
cycle. (From Masters and Johnson
[1].)

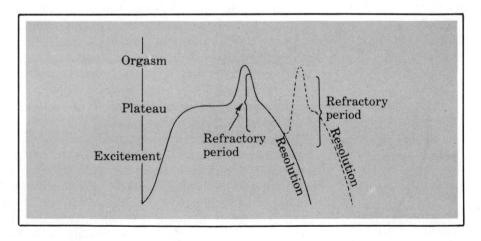

Figure 1-8. Vaginal lubrication.
(From Masters and Johnson [1].)

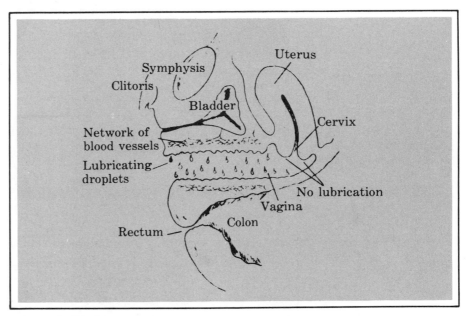

tualizations of commonly observed physiologic patterns. The clinical implications of disruptions of these patterns are discussed in greater detail in Chapters 20 and 21.

Excitement Phase

Excitation occurs as a result of sexual stimulation, which may be either physical or psychic in origin. Stimulation arising in situations without direct physical contact is neither unusual nor unexpected, since activation of many physiologic processes of the body occurs as a result of thought or emotion (for example, salivation and gastric acid production may be initiated by thinking about food; sweating, tachycardia, and palpitations may be precipitated by fear or anger). At times, the excitement phase may be of short duration, quickly merging into the plateau phase; at other times, however, sexual excitation may begin slowly and proceed in a gradual manner over a long time interval.

Sexual excitation in the female is characterized by the appearance of vaginal lubrication, which is produced by vasocongestion in the walls of the vagina leading to a transudation of fluid (Fig. 1-8). It is important to recognize that there are no "secretory glands" producing lubrication within the vagina and that the secretory glands lining the cervix do not

Figure 1-9. Female pelvis: excitement phase. (From Masters and
Johnson [1].)

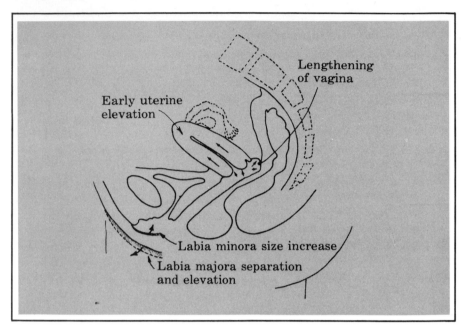

contribute meaningfully to vaginal lubrication. Other genital changes
that occur during excitation in the female include expansion of the
inner two-thirds of the vaginal barrel, elevation of the cervix and the
body of the uterus, and flattening and elevation of the labia majora
(Fig. 1-9). The clitoris increases in size as a result of vasocongestion,
although a true erection does not occur. Erection of the nipples is
characteristic of the excitement phase for the woman, although both
nipples may not achieve full erection simultaneously. In the late excitement phase, surface venous patterns of the breast become more
visible and there may be an increase in the size of the breasts as well.

Sexual excitation in the male (Fig. 1-10) is usually characterized by
penile erection, which occurs as a direct result of vasocongestive
changes within the spongelike tissue of the penis. It is helpful to realize,
however, that physical as well as psychological arousal may be present
without a firm erection, particularly when anxiety or fatigue are present. The normal appearance of the scrotum begins to change as vasocongestion produces a smoothing out of skin ridges on the scrotal sac;
the scrotum also flattens because of an internal thickening of the

Figure 1-10. Male pelvis: excitement phase. Key to abbreviations (also for Figs. 1-14, 1-16, and 1-18): T = testis; E = epididymis; U = urethra; CG = Cowper's gland; P = prostate; PU = prostatic utricle; ED = ejaculatory duct; VD = vas deferens; SV = seminal vesicle; UB = urinary bladder; SP = symphysis pubis; R = rectum. (From Masters and Johnson [1].)

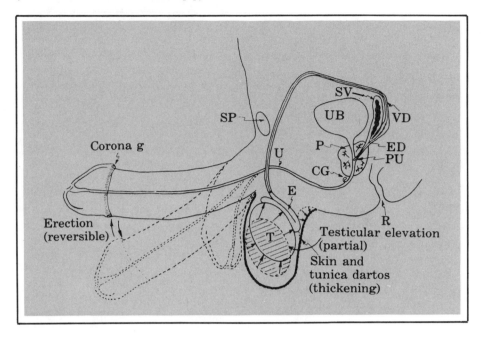

scrotal integument. The testes are partially elevated toward the perineum by shortening of the spermatic cords, mediated by the cremasteric muscles. In some men nipple erection occurs during excitation, but in others this phenomenon is absent throughout the sexual response cycle.

In both men and women, the physical changes of the excitement phase are neither constant nor always ascending. Distractions of either a mental or a physical nature are quite likely to decrease the buildup of sexual tension that is the hallmark of excitation. An extraneous sound, a shift in position, or a muscle cramp, for example, are types of distraction that may occur. In addition, changes of tempo or manner of direct sexual stimulation can also temporarily disrupt sexual arousal. The vasocongestive mechanisms of the excitation phase do not constitute a quantitative appraisal of sexual arousal. In fact, an erection may be diminishing in firmness at just the time that excitation is heightening; likewise, vaginal lubrication may appear to have ceased, although neuromuscular tension is clearly nearing the plateau phase.

Plateau Phase

In the excitement phase, there is a marked increase in sexual tension above baseline (unaroused) levels. The plateau phase represents a

Figure 1-11. Female pelvis: plateau
phase. (From Masters and Johnson
[1].)

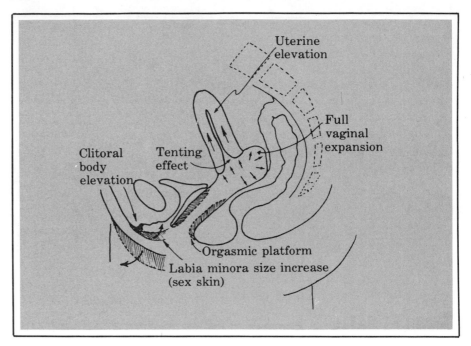

leveling off of the increments in sexual tension that are occurring,
although there is a further intensification if effective stimulation continues. This phase therefore describes a high degree of sexual arousal
that occurs prior to reaching the threshold levels required to trigger
orgasm. The duration of the plateau phase varies widely; it is often
exceptionally brief in men who are premature ejaculators. In women, a
short plateau phase may precede a particularly intense orgasm.

Prominent vasocongestion occurs in the outer third of the vagina in
the plateau phase. This reaction, shown in Figure 1-11, is called the
orgasmic platform. As a result of this vasocongestion, the opening of
the vagina narrows. This narrowing action is one reason why the size of
the penis is relatively unimportant to the physical stimulation received
by the woman during intercourse, since there is actually a "gripping"
action of the outer portion of the vagina around the penis. Other
reasons include the expansion of the inside of the vagina, which decreases direct stimulation received distally from penile thrusting regardless of penis length, and the fact that the inner two-thirds of the
vagina contains few sensory nerve endings, whereas there is a richer

Figure 1-12. The clitoris in the female sexual response cycle. The orgasmic phase is not depicted because of lack of information. (From Masters and Johnson [1].)

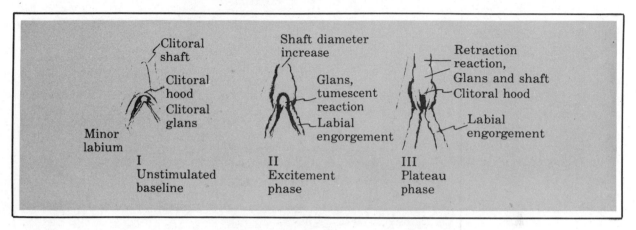

concentration of such sensory endings in the area in which the orgasmic platform forms. During the plateau phase, the inner two-thirds of the vagina undergoes a minor additional expansion in size, and there is a corresponding increase in elevation of the uterus. The rate of vaginal lubrication often slows during this phase as compared to excitation, especially if the plateau phase is prolonged.

Both the shaft and the glans of the clitoris retract against the pubic symphysis during the plateau phase. This change, coupled with the vasocongestion occurring in the labia, makes it difficult to visualize the clitoris in this situation (Fig. 1-12) and also partially masks the location of the clitoris to touch. No loss of clitoral sensation occurs during these changes, however, and stimulation to the general vicinity of the mons pubis or the labia will result in clitoral sensations.

Late in the excitement phase, the areolae begin to become engorged. During the plateau phase, this areolar tumescence becomes so prominent that it masks the antecedent nipple erection that is actually still present (Fig. 1-13). Increases in breast size during the plateau phase are less pronounced in women who have previously nursed; in women who have not breast-fed a child, increases in breast size of 20 to 25 percent above baseline levels are not uncommon.

Late in the excitement phase or early in the plateau phase, a rash resembling measles develops in 50 to 75 percent of women and in a smaller percentage of men. This "sex flush" generally begins in the epigastrium and then spreads rapidly over the breasts and anterior chest wall, but it may also be noted on other parts of the body, including

Figure 1-13. The breasts in the female sexual response cycle. (From
Masters and Johnson [1].)

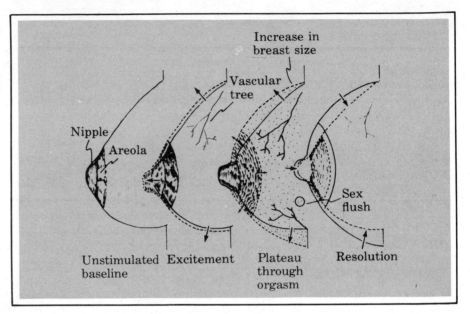

the buttocks, back, extremities, and face. Other extragenital features of
the plateau phase common to both women and men include a generalized myotonia, tachycardia, hyperventilation, and an increase in blood
pressure. These changes are primarily seen during the late plateau
phase.

During the plateau phase in the male (Fig. 1-14), there is a minor
increase in the diameter of the proximal portion of the glans penis,
where there is frequently a visible deepening in color due to venous
stasis. Vasocongestion causes further increases in the size of the testes,
with increments of 50 to 100 percent of baseline volume typically seen.
As sexual tension mounts towards orgasm, the testes continue not only
the process of elevation initiated in the excitement phase but also a
process of anterior rotation so that the posterior testicular surfaces rest
in firm contact with the perineum. Small amounts of fluid from the
male urethra may sometimes appear during the plateau phase; this
fluid is presumed to consist of secretions from Cowper's glands and has
sometimes been observed to carry live spermatozoa.

Orgasm

The specific neurophysiologic mechanisms of orgasm are not presently
known. Nevertheless, it can be postulated that orgasm is triggered by a

Figure 1-14. Male pelvis: plateau phase. (From Masters and Johnson [1].)

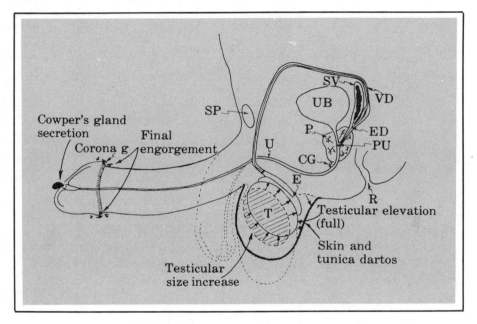

neural reflex arc once the orgasmic threshold level has been reached or exceeded. This speculative model, based on the physiology of other body systems, will be important in the context of later clinical discussion.

Orgasm in the female is marked by simultaneous rhythmic contractions of the uterus, the orgasmic platform (outer third of the vagina), and the rectal sphincter (Fig. 1-15), beginning at 0.8-second intervals and then diminishing in intensity, duration, and regularity. However, orgasm is a total body response, not just a response localized to the pelvis. Electroencephalogram patterns measured during orgasm have shown significant changes in hemispheric laterality [4], as well as changes in rates and types of brain wave activity [5]. Contractions of peripheral muscle groups have also been carefully measured, as well as rates of respiration and heartbeat. Women do not ejaculate during orgasm, and orgasm occurs naturally in women who have had a hysterectomy or in those who have had surgical excision of the clitoris.

The male orgasm is triggered by the buildup of sexual tension to the point where the accessory sex organs begin a series of contractions that cause seminal fluid to pool in the prostatic urethra. This fluid, with its concentration of live sperm cells, is formed from three different sources:

Figure 1-15. Female pelvis: orgasmic
phase. (From Masters and Johnson
[1].)

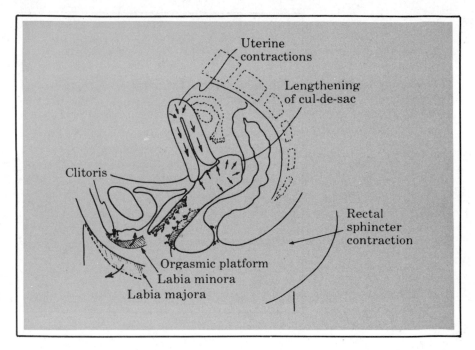

the prostate, the seminal vesicles, and the vas deferens. At this first
stage of the ejaculatory process, the male experiences a sensation of
ejaculatory inevitability when the changing pressure dynamics are
perceived as the start of ejaculation, although the external propulsion
of fluid will be delayed for several seconds. This time lag between onset
of ejaculation and appearance of seminal fluid from the penis is a result
of the distance the ejaculate must travel through the urethra as well as
the interval required for the buildup of sufficient contractile pressure to
push the seminal fluid pool in an anterior fashion. The internal sphincter of the neck of the urinary bladder is tightly closed during ejaculation, ensuring that the fluid bolus moves anteriorly, toward the path of
least resistance. Rhythmic contractions of the prostate, the perineal
muscles, and the shaft of the penis combine to assist the propulsion
process of ejaculation (Fig. 1-16).

Resolution Phase

Women have the potential to be multiorgasmic—that is, to have a series
of identifiable orgasmic responses without dropping below the plateau
phase of arousal (see Fig. 1-6). Men, however, do not share this capacity.
Immediately following ejaculation, the man enters a refractory period

Figure 1-16. Male pelvis: orgasmic phase. (From Masters and Johnson [1].)

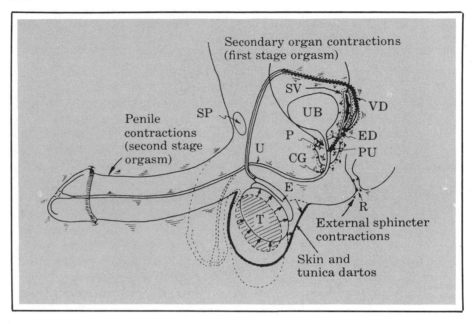

(see Fig. 1-7) during which further ejaculation is impossible, although partial or full erection may sometimes be maintained. This refractory period may last for a few minutes or it may last for many hours; for most men, this interval lengthens with age and is typically longer with each repeated ejaculation within a time span of several hours. There is great variability in the length of the refractory period both within and between individual men. The refractory period is not present in the female sexual response cycle, although most women are not multiorgasmic.

In the resolution phase, the anatomic and physiologic changes that occurred during the excitement and plateau phases reverse. In women, the orgasmic platform disappears as the muscular contractions of orgasm pump blood away from these tissues. The uterus moves back into the true pelvis, the vagina begins to shorten in both width and length, and the clitoris returns to its normal anatomic position (Fig. 1-17). In men, the erection diminishes in two stages: a prompt loss of erection due to penile contractions during orgasm that quickly reduce vasocongestion, and a second stage of detumescence corresponding to a slower process of return to normal vascular flow. The testes decrease in

Figure 1-17. Female pelvis: resolution phase. (From Masters and Johnson [1].)

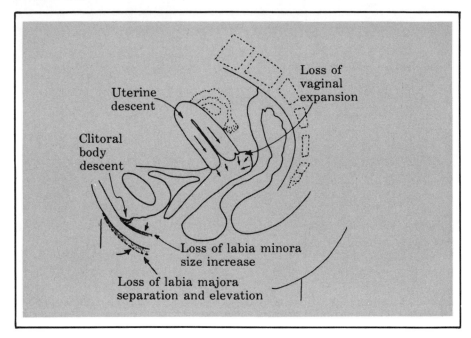

size and descend into the scrotum unless sexual stimulation is continued (Fig. 1-18).

Endocrine Aspects of Sexual Behavior

The importance of hormonal influences on reproduction and sexual behavior has been recognized since the early part of this century. Although it was initially thought that the pituitary gland was the primary locus of control over those processes, it is now known that the brain itself acts as the major regulator, with hormones that are secreted in the hypothalamus controlling the functions of the pituitary [6] (Fig. 1-19). The brain is also a target for the sex steroid hormones manufactured in the gonads: For example, these hormones act on sexual differentiation of the brain during fetal life (see Chap. 2), initiate puberty (see Chap. 4), and play a role in the regulation of sexual behavior.

The hypothalamus produces a decapeptide gonadotropin-releasing hormone that controls the release of luteinizing hormone (LH) and follicle-stimulating hormone (FSH) by the anterior pituitary. Although there has been some question of whether there is a single gonad-

Figure 1-18. Male pelvis: resolution phase. (From Masters and Johnson [1].)

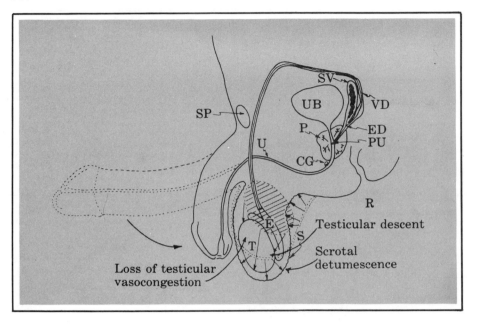

otropin-releasing hormone or separate LH- and FSH-releasing substances, it now appears that a single decapeptide (Fig. 1-20) is the sole regulatory agent [7]. The hypothalamus is controlled by a negative feedback system involving circulating gonadal steroids; high levels of these steroids turn off production of gonadotropin-releasing hormone and in this fashion lower the pituitary secretion of LH and FSH. In contrast, when circulating levels of sex steroid hormones are low, the hypothalamus responds by elaborating increased amounts of gonadotropin-releasing hormone, which stimulates pituitary secretion of LH and FSH. In addition, there is a secondary feedback mechanism wherein concentrations of LH and FSH also contribute to hypothalamic regulation.

In the male, LH controls the production of testosterone by the Leydig cells of the testis, while FSH acts as a stimulus to spermatogenesis. Circulating levels of testosterone exert a negative feedback effect on the hypothalamus. In addition, an unidentified substance known as inhibin that is elaborated in the process of sperm production contributes to the regulation of FSH secretion. If testosterone levels are low, LH levels normally are elevated in an attempt to compensate for this deficiency (see Chap. 6 for specific clinical examples); if low testosterone

Figure 1-19. (A) Changes in anterior pituitary hormone secretion produced by hypothalamic releasing factors or inhibitors. Key to abbreviations: TRF = thyrotropin-releasing factor; CRF = corticotropin-releasing factor; LRF = gonadotropin-releasing factor; PIF = prolactin-inhibiting factor; SRIF = somatostatin; TSH = thyrotropin; PRL = prolactin; GH = growth hormone; LH = luteinizing hormone; FSH = follicle-stimulating hormone; ACTH = corticotropin. Symbols: ↑ = increase; ↓ = decrease. (B) Hypothalamic lesions produce changes in anterior pituitary (adenohypophysis) hormone secretion. (C) The hypothalamic-pituitary portal system. (D) Photomicrograph of the hypothalamic-pituitary portal system after injection with an opaque dye. (From Guillemin [52]. Copyright 1978 by the American Association for the Advancement of Science.)

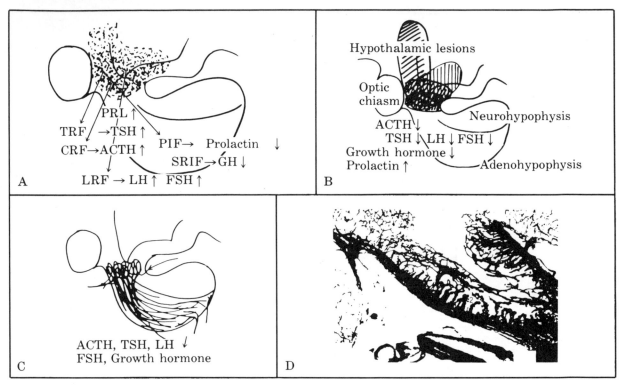

levels are accompanied by low LH concentrations, this points to the possibility of a central (hypothalamic or pituitary) problem. Similarly, in cases of marked deficiencies in spermatogenesis, FSH levels are typically elevated, except when the problem is one of hypothalamic or pituitary dysfunction.

In a normal adult male, testosterone is produced primarily by the testes, with less than 5 percent normally contributed by the adrenal cortex. The average testosterone production rate for adult men is 6 to 8 mg per day. There is a diurnal variation in circulating levels of testosterone, with peak concentrations measured in the morning hours (prior to 10:00 A.M.). Measurement of urinary testosterone levels has now been discarded by most researchers and clinicians in favor of direct measurement of circulating hormone by radioimmunoassay techniques. Typical values for circulating testosterone are listed in Table 1-1.

Testosterone appears to be the major biologic determinant of the sex drive in both sexes, as will be discussed in subsequent chapters. Marked

Figure 1-20. Molecular structure of
the decapeptide gonadotropin-
releasing hormone. (From Schally
[53].)

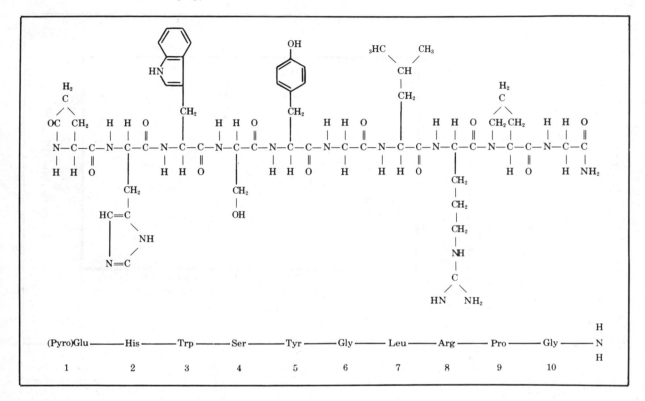

Table 1-1. Typical
Ranges of Serum or
Plasma Testosterone
Concentrations

Group	Testosterone Concentration (ng/dl)
Adult males	385–1,000
Prepubertal children	20–80
Pubertal boys	120–600
Hypogonadal adult males	100–300
Adult females	20–80
Females using oral contraceptives	45–125

Figure 1-21. Hormonal changes in
the normal menstrual cycle.

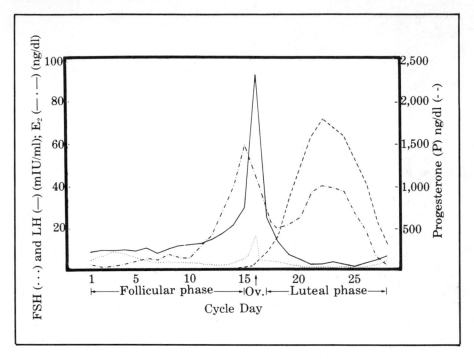

testosterone deficiencies in the male are usually accompanied by depressed libido and impotence, which improve with restoration of normal hormone levels. In addition, since the prostate and seminal vesicles are androgen-dependent, seminal fluid volume is diminished when a severe testosterone deficiency is present. Most men with impotence have normal levels of testosterone, reflecting the fact that most instances of sexual dysfunction are of psychogenic rather than biologic origin.

The precise relationship between hormones and sexual behavior is not clearly understood at present. In a variety of nonprimate animal species, plasma testosterone concentrations increase after coitus or ejaculation [8–12]. In monkeys, however, although access of adult males to receptive females reportedly leads to increased circulating testosterone [13], neither testosterone nor luteinizing hormone increases significantly after coitus or ejaculation [14, 15]. Conflicting results have been reported in regard to humans. Although some studies indicate that testosterone levels do not increase after coitus or masturbation [16, 17], and other reports fail to document a positive correlation between either sexual activity or sexual interest and serum testosterone levels [18–21], there are studies indicating increased testosterone after masturbation [22], during and after coitus [23], and in response to viewing erotic movies [21]. Persky and his colleagues have recently suggested interrelationships between hormone levels and the sexual behavior of couples [24, 25]; in addition, evidence indicating that there may be a seasonal cycle of plasma testosterone in men [26–29] further compounds the methodological difficulties in investigations of this type.

Endocrine regulation in women is somewhat more complex than in men, since women undergo a series of cyclic hormone changes from the onset of menstruation until the time of menopause. A detailed discussion of the nature of the menstrual cycle is beyond the scope of this volume, but the interested reader may wish to consult other reviews [3, 30, 31]. The hormonal changes of a typical menstrual cycle are shown in Figure 1-21.

The normal menstrual cycle is divided into two phases by the occurrence of ovulation: the follicular phase, marked by a proliferative endometrium and increasing levels of estrogen secretion (with low progesterone output), and the luteal phase, occurring after ovulation, marked by a secretory edometrium and high levels of progesterone secretion. FSH rises modestly early in the follicular phase and has a midcycle peak coinciding with the LH surge just prior to ovulation. Estradiol, the most potent of the naturally occurring estrogens, peaks late in the follicular phase (usually one or two days before the LH peak) and is thought to be the trigger for the LH surge. A second estradiol peak occurs in the midluteal phase. LH levels peak abruptly in midcycle and appear to be the direct trigger for ovulation. Progesterone levels begin to rise during the LH surge and reach high levels during the luteal phase. Several days before the end of the cycle, progesterone declines sharply.

Mechanisms of female sexual behavior in animals have been reviewed in detail in two recent surveys [32, 33]. In humans, some evidence indicates that female sexual receptivity and initiatory behavior may be greatest around the time of ovulation [34–37]. Persky and coworkers found a greater frequency of sexual activity throughout the menstrual cycle in women whose periovulatory testosterone levels reached higher peaks than in a group of women with lower peak periovulatory testosterone levels; they also reported that women showed a greater degree of sexual responsiveness and a greater need for affection around the time of ovulation [24]. These findings must be interpreted cautiously since only 11 women were studied and blood

Figure 1-22. Simplified horizontal
cross-section of the rat brain showing dopaminergic, noradrenergic,
and serotonergic neuroregulatory
pathways. (From Barchas, Akil, El-
liot, Holman, and Watson [54].
Copyright 1978 by the American Association for the Advancement of Science.)

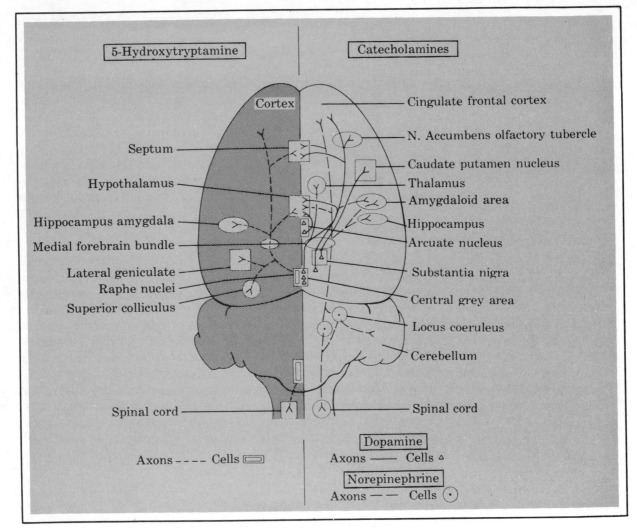

samples were obtained only twice per week. Adams, Gold, and Burt
reported a rise in female-initiated sexual activity at the time of presumed ovulation (hormonal testing was not done in this study) and
found that this behavioral pattern was not present in women using oral
contraceptives [37]. On the other hand, a number of studies fail to
document a midcycle peak in female sexual behavior or arousal [38–40].
Resolution of these differences must await carefully designed studies

that will integrate sequential endocrine data with precise behavioral measures [41].

A possible additional factor in the relationship between human sexual behavior and neuroendocrine changes is olfaction. It is uncertain how important olfaction may be as an occasional mechanism of sexual arousal. In a wide variety of animal species, sex-attractant pheromones—chemical substances that serve as a means of communication between members of the same species—have been identified [42–45]. The finding of similar chemical substances in human vaginal secretions has permitted some speculation about the possible role that pheromones may play in human sexuality [46–50]. Although olfaction may be important in certain aspects of sexual behavior—and situations involving abnormal olfactory acuity are frequently related to endocrine or reproductive disturbances (see Chap. 6)—it is unlikely that a sex-attractant pheromone system is operational in human beings [51].

Our understanding of physiologic control mechanisms related to neuroendocrinology and reproductive behavior is advancing rapidly. New data about the role of peptides in brain and endocrine function [52, 53] and better delineation of neuroregulatory substances such as endorphins, dopamine, and serotonin [54–57] (Fig. 1-22) promise to bring about further progress in understanding human sexuality. However impressive these lines of inquiry may be, we must clearly keep them in perspective as one part of a whole complex picture in which psychosocial factors interact with biologic ones to determine the behaviors, feelings, attitudes, and attributes that make up human sexuality.

References

1. Masters, W. H., and Johnson, V. E. *Human Sexual Response*. Boston: Little, Brown and Co., 1966.
2. Greep, R. O., and Astwood, E. B. (eds.). *Endocrinology (Handbook of Physiology*, Section 7). Washington, D.C.: American Physiological Society, 1973. Vol. 2 *(Female Reproductive System*, Part 1).
3. Speroff, L., Glass, R. H., and Kase, N. G. *Clinical Gynecologic Endocrinology and Infertility*. Baltimore: Williams & Wilkins Co., 1978.
4. Cohen, H. D., Rosen, R. C., and Goldstein, L. Electroencephalographic laterality changes during human sexual orgasm. *Archives of Sexual Behavior* 5:189–199, 1976.
5. Heath, R. G. Pleasure and brain activity in man. *Journal of Nervous and Mental Disease* 154:3–17, 1972.
6. Yen, S. S. C., Naftolin, F., Lein, A., Krieger, D., and Utiger, R. Hypothalamic Influences on Pituitary Function in Humans. In R. O. Greep and M. A. Koblinsky (eds.), *Frontiers in Reproduction and Fertility Control*. Cambridge, Mass.: The M.I.T. Press, 1977. Pp. 108–127.

7. Schally, A. V., and Arimura, A. Physiology and Nature of Hypothalamic Regulatory Hormones. In L. Martini and G. M. Besser (eds.), *Clinical Neuroendocrinology*. New York: Academic Press, 1977. Pp. 1–42.
8. Saginor, M., and Horton, R. Reflex release of gonadotropin and increased plasma testosterone concentration in male rabbits during copulation. *Endocrinology* 82:627–630, 1968.
9. Haltmeyer, G. C., and Eik-Nes, K. B. Plasma levels of testosterone in male rabbits following copulation. *Journal of Reproduction and Fertility* 19:273–277, 1969.
10. Kamel, F., Mock, E. J., Wright, W. W., and Frankel, A. I. Alterations in plasma concentrations of testosterone, LH, and prolactin associated with mating in the male rat. *Hormones and Behavior* 6:277–288, 1975.
11. Katongole, C. B., Naftolin, F., and Short, R. V. Relationship between blood levels of luteinizing hormone and testosterone in bulls, and the effects of sexual stimulation. *Journal of Endocrinology* 50:457–466, 1971.
12. Feder, H. H., Story, A., Goodwin, D., and Reboulleau, C. Testosterone and "5 α-dihydrotestosterone" levels in peripheral plasma of male and female ring doves *(Streptopelia risoria)* during the reproductive cycle. *Biology of Reproduction* 16:666–677, 1977.
13. Rose, R. M., Gordon, T. P., and Bernstein, I. S. Plasma testosterone levels in the male rhesus: Influences of sexual and social stimuli. *Science* 178:643–645, 1972.
14. Phoenix, C. H., Dixson, A. F., and Resko, J. A. Effects of ejaculation on levels of testosterone, cortisol, and luteinizing hormone in peripheral plasma of rhesus monkeys. *Journal of Comparative and Physiological Psychology* 91:120–127, 1977.
15. Goldfoot, D. A., Slob, A. K., Scheffler, G., Robinson, J. A., Wiegand, S. J., and Cordo, J. Multiple ejaculations during prolonged sexual tests and lack of resultant serum testosterone increases in male stumptail macaques *(M. arctoides)*. *Archives of Sexual Behavior* 4:547–560, 1975.
16. Stearns, E. L., Winter, J. S. D., and Faiman, C. Effects of coitus on gonadotropin, prolactin and sex steroid levels in man. *Journal of Clinical Endocrinology and Metabolism* 37:687–691, 1973.
17. Lee, P. A., Jaffe, R. B., and Midgley, A. R. Lack of alteration of serum gonadotropin in men and women following sexual intercourse. *American Journal of Obstetrics and Gynecology* 120:985–987, 1974.
18. Raboch, J., and Stárka, L. Coital activity of men and the levels of plasmatic testosterone. *Journal of Sex Research* 8:219–224, 1972.
19. Brown, W. A., Monti, P. M., and Corriveau, D. P. Serum testosterone and sexual activity and interest in men. *Archives of Sexual Behavior* 7:97–103, 1978.
20. Kraemer, H. C., Becker, H. B., Brodie, H. K. H., Doering, C. H., Moos, R. H., and Hamburg, D. A. Orgasmic frequency and plasma testosterone levels in normal human males. *Archives of Sexual Behavior* 5:125–132, 1976.
21. Pirke, K. M., Kockott, G., and Dittmar, F. Psychosexual stimulation and plasma testosterone in man. *Archives of Sexual Behavior* 3:577–584, 1974.
22. Purvis, K., Landgren, B. -M., Cekan, Z., and Diczfalusy, E. Endocrine effects of masturbation in men. *Journal of Endocrinology* 70:439–444, 1976.

23. Fox, C. A., Ismail, A. A. A., Love, D. N., Kirkham, K. E., and Loraine, J. A. Studies on the relationship between plasma testosterone levels and human sexual activity. *Journal of Endocrinology* 52:51–58, 1972.

24. Persky, H., Lief, H. I., O'Brien, C. P., Strauss, D., and Miller, W. Reproductive Hormone Levels and Sexual Behaviors of Young Couples During the Menstrual Cycle. In R. Gemme and C. C. Wheeler (eds.), *Progress in Sexology*. New York: Plenum Press, 1977. Pp. 293–310.

25. Persky, H., Lief, H. I., Strauss, D., Miller, W. R., and O'Brien, C. P. Plasma testosterone level and sexual behavior of couples. *Archives of Sexual Behavior* 7:157–173, 1978.

26. Kihlström, J. E. A Male Sexual Cycle. In A. Ingelman-Sundberg and N. -O. Lunell (eds.), *Current Problems in Fertility*. New York: Plenum Press, 1971. Pp. 50–54.

27. Southren, A. L., and Gordon, G. G. Rhythms and testosterone metabolism. *Journal of Steroid Biochemistry* 6:809–813, 1975.

28. Baker, H. W. G., Santen, R. J., Burger, H. G., de Kretser, D. M., Hudson, B., Pepperell, R. J., and Bardin, C. W. Rhythms in the secretion of gonadotropins and gonadal steroids. *Journal of Steroid Biochemistry* 6:793–801, 1975.

29. Doering, C. H., Kraemer, H. C., Brodie, H. K. H., and Hamburg, D. A. A cycle of plasma testosterone in the human male. *Journal of Clinical Endocrinology and Metabolism* 40:492–500, 1975.

30. Vollman, R. F. *The Menstrual Cycle*. Philadelphia: W. B. Saunders Co., 1977.

31. Abraham, G. E. The Normal Menstrual Cycle. In J. R. Givens (ed.), *Endocrine Causes of Menstrual Disorders*. Chicago: Year Book Medical Publishers, 1978. Pp. 15–44.

32. Komisaruk, B. R. The Nature of the Neural Substrate of Female Sexual Behavior in Mammals and Its Hormonal Sensitivity: Review and Speculations. In J. B. Hutchison (ed.), *Biological Determinants of Sexual Behavior*. New York: John Wiley & Sons, 1978. Pp. 349–393.

33. Herbert, J. Neuro-Hormonal Integration of Sexual Behavior in Female Primates. In J. B. Hutchison (ed.), *Biological Determinants of Sexual Behavior*. New York: John Wiley & Sons, 1978. Pp. 467–491.

34. Udry, J. R., and Morris, N. M. Distribution of coitus in the menstrual cycle. *Nature* 220:593–596, 1968.

35. Udry, J. R., and Morris, N. M. Effect of contraceptive pills on the distribution of sexual activity in the menstrual cycle. *Nature* 227:502–503, 1970.

36. Cavanagh, J. R. Rhythm of sexual desire in women. *Medical Aspects of Human Sexuality* 3(3):29–39, 1969.

37. Adams, D. B., Gold, A. R., and Burt, A. D. Rise in female-initiated sexual activity at ovulation and its suppression by oral contraceptives. *New England Journal of Medicine* 299:1145–1150, 1978.

38. Hart, R. D. Monthly rhythm of libido in married women. *British Medical Journal* 1:1023–1024, 1960.

39. James, W. H. Coital rates and the pill. *Nature* 234:555–556, 1971.

40. Spitz, C. J., Gold, A. R., and Adams, D. B. Cognitive and hormonal factors affecting coital frequency. *Archives of Sexual Behavior* 4:249–264, 1975.

41. Kolodny, R. C., and Bauman, J. E.   Female sexual activity at ovulation (letter). *New England Journal of Medicine* 300:626, 1979.

42. Michael, R. P., Keverne, E. B., and Bonsall, R. W.   Pheromones: Isolation of male sex attractants from a female primate. *Science* 172:964–966, 1971.

43. Curtis, R. F., Ballantine, J. A., Keverne, E. B., Bonsall, R. W., and Michael, R. P.   Identification of primate sexual pheromones and the properties of synthetic attractants. *Nature* 232:396–398, 1971.

44. Keverne, E. B.   Olfactory Cues in Mammalian Sexual Behavior. In J. B. Hutchison (ed.), *Biological Determinants of Sexual Behavior*. New York: John Wiley & Sons, 1978. Pp. 727–763.

45. Goodwin, M., Gooding, K. M., and Regnier, F.   Sex pheromone in the dog. *Science* 203:559–561, 1979.

46. Comfort, A.   Likelihood of human pheromones. *Nature* 230:432–433, 479, 1971.

47. Preti, G., and Huggins, G. R.   Cyclical changes in volatile acidic metabolites of human vaginal secretions and their relation to ovulation. *Journal of Chemical Ecology* 1:361–376, 1975.

48. Sokolov, J. J., Harris, R. T., and Hecker, M. R.   Isolation of substances from human vaginal secretions previously shown to be sex attractant pheromones in higher primates. *Archives of Sexual Behavior* 5:269–274, 1976.

49. Michael, R. P., Bonsall, R. W., and Warner, P.   Human vaginal secretions: Volatile fatty acid content. *Science* 186:1217–1219, 1974.

50. Doty, R. L., Ford, M., Preti, G., and Huggins, G. R.   Changes in the intensity and pleasantness of human vaginal odors during the menstrual cycle. *Science* 190:1316–1318, 1975.

51. Bauman, J., Kolodny, R. C., Trivedi, L., Webster, S., and Dornbush, R. L.   Aliphatic acid levels in human vaginal secretions and hormonal correlates. Presented at the third annual meeting of the International Academy of Sex Research, Bloomington, Indiana, August 3, 1977.

52. Guillemin, R.   Peptides in the brain: The new endocrinology of the neuron. *Science* 202:390–402, 1978.

53. Schally, A. V.   Aspects of hypothalamic regulation of the pituitary gland: Its implications for the control of reproductive processes. *Science* 202:18–28, 1978.

54. Barchas, J. D., Akil, H., Elliott, G. R., Holman, R. B., and Watson, S. J.   Behavioral neurochemistry: Neuroregulators and behavioral states. *Science* 200:964–972, 1978.

55. Judd, S. J., Rakoff, J. S., and Yen, S. S. C.   Inhibition of gonadotropin and prolactin release by dopamine: Effect of endogenous estradiol levels. *Journal of Clinical Endocrinology and Metabolism* 47:494–498, 1978.

56. Harms, P. G., Ojeda, S. R., and McCann, S. M.   Prostaglandin involvement in hypothalamic control of gonadotropin and prolactin release. *Science* 181:760–761, 1973.

57. Meyerson, B. J., and Malmnäs, C. O.   Brain Monoamines and Sexual Behavior. In J. B. Hutchison (ed.), *Biological Determinants of Sexual Behavior*. New York: John Wiley & Sons, 1978. Pp. 521–554.

2

Biology of Sexual Development: Genetic and Endocrine Factors

The normal sequence and pathologic vicissitudes of sexual development have been studied with great enthusiasm in the past decade. Technologic advances in endocrinology and genetics have clarified many points previously uncertain, but these newer methods of investigation have unleashed a host of additional queries that remain unanswered. It is readily apparent that sexual development is a complex process occurring at many different levels. This chapter focuses primarily upon prenatal biologic components of sexual development, but in order to illuminate our understanding of the overall process it also includes information relating to subsequent behavior and individual psychology in the context of hormonal or genetic syndromes.

Purely biologic aspects of sexuality such as genetic sex, genital sex, and reproductive status have obvious differences from psychosocial aspects of sexuality such as gender identity, sexual behavior, and sexual values. Nevertheless, it is a mistake to regard the biologic and psychosocial domains as divergent or separate—these forces interact as a complex set of vectors that may sometimes have surprising consequences. Readers are urged to read this chapter and the two that follow as a unit to gain a clear picture of the constant interaction of biologic and psychosocial forces from the prenatal to the pubertal stage. Readers are also cautioned against assuming that biologic phenomena—because they may be rather easily quantified—are therefore better understood than behavioral phenomena.

Prenatal Factors in Sexual Differentiation
Normal Genetic Development

When conception occurs, genetic material from each parent is combined in the fertilized egg. At the moment of conception, the X or Y sex chromosome carried by the sperm cell is ordinarily added to the X chromosome contained within the ovum to determine the genetic sex of the developing fetus. Since there is normally a total of 44 other chromosomes that carry genetic material, a 46,XY chromosome pattern is the genetic code for a male and a 46,XX pattern is that for a female. Figure 2-1 shows these chromosome patterns in karyotypes, or photomicrographs, with the various chromosomes grouped according to size and shape.

Information about chromosomal sex can also be obtained by examination of individual cells for the presence of a chromatin mass, or Barr body, which is present in 25 to 50 percent of mucosal cells in females but is absent in normal males or found only in low numbers (see Fig. 2-2). The stainable chromatin mass is usually hemispherical, with one side in

Figure 2-1. (*A*, *B*) Karyotypes of
46,XX (female) and 46,XY (male)
chromosome patterns, respectively.
(From C. C. Snyder, C. D. Scott, and
E. Z. Browne, Jr., Intersexuality:
Diagnosis and Treatment, in C. E.
Horton [ed.], *Plastic and Recon-
structive Surgery of the Genital Area*,
Boston: Little, Brown and Co., 1973.)

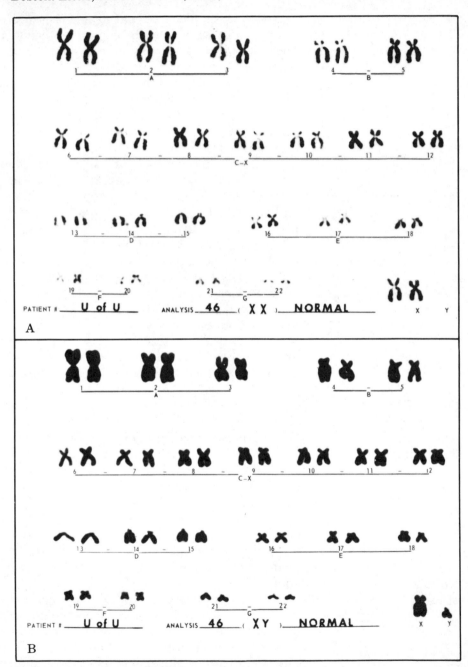

Figure 2-2. (*A*) Nucleus from a cell obtained by buccal smear, showing a dense chromatin mass known as a Barr body. (*B*) Polymorphonuclear neutrophil leukocyte from a female showing a drumstick (magnification × 2200). (*C*) Nucleus from a mucosal cell without a Barr body (× 2200). (*D*) Polymorphonuclear neutrophil leukocyte from a male; no drumstick is seen (× 2200). (From C. C. Snyder, C. D. Scott, and E. Z. Browne, Jr., Intersexuality: Diagnosis and Treatment, in C. E. Horton [ed.], *Plastic and Reconstructive Surgery of the Genital Area*, Boston: Little, Brown and Co., 1973.)

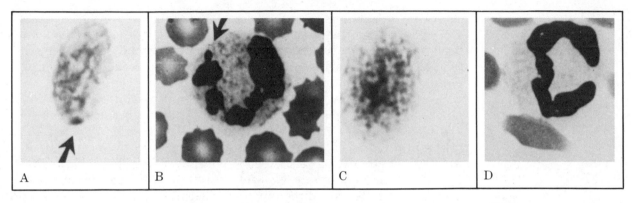

A   B   C   D

apposition to the inner surface of the nuclear membrane. A similar diagnostic body is found in 5 to 15 percent of polymorphonuclear leukocytes in females: This dense chromatin nuclear appendage is termed a "drumstick" (see Fig. 2-2B). The maximum number of Barr bodies or drumsticks in any individual cell is one less than the total number of X chromosomes.

Under ordinary circumstances the genetic programming for biologic sex triggers a series of events that results in normal male or female differentiation. However, there are some circumstances under which the normal sequence of differentiation will not occur or will occur in some manner of disarray. Such an alteration is not unique to the expression of the genetic coding for sex development, because other aspects of genetic programming can also be altered by subsequent events, both prenatally and after birth. For example, exposure of the developing fetus to certain drugs may cause malformations of the limbs, the cardiovascular system, or the nervous system, depending on the drug and the timing and degree of exposure. Likewise, even after childhood a genetically determined characteristic such as height can be influenced adversely by nongenetic events such as chronic illness or inadequate nutrition.

Normal Development of Sexual Anatomy

In the usual sequence of human sexual differentiation, the genetic male and female fetuses are anatomically indistinguishable during the first weeks of development. Primitive gonads begin to organize at approximately the sixth week of gestation [1], at which point they exist in a bipotential state; that is, the primitive gonads may differentiate into either testes or ovaries, depending on subsequent events. Differentiation into functioning testes occurs at approximately eight weeks of gestation, a time when secretion of testosterone by the fetal testis has been shown [2]. In contrast, if the bipotential gonads develop in the female pattern, ovarian differentiation does not occur until approximately the twelfth gestational week.

Subsequent sexual differentiation occurs at three different anatomic sites: the external genitalia, the internal sex structures, and the brain. Detailed research evidence indicates that the direction of this sexual differentiation is determined by the presence or absence of critical amounts of circulating testosterone within the developing fetus [3–7]. In the absence of adequate levels of testosterone, differentiation always occurs in the female direction, regardless of genetic programming. Stated another way, certain hormonal conditions must exist for male development to ensue, even if the sex chromosome pattern is 46,XY.

In the seventh week of intrauterine life, male and female fetuses have identical internal and external sexual anatomy (Figs. 2-3 and 2-4). During normal female differentiation, the primitive müllerian duct system develops into the uterus, fallopian tubes, and the inner one-third of the vagina. This process is not dependent on the presence of ovarian hormones, since it will occur even if ovaries are not present [8]. In the normal process of male differentiation, the presence of a locally acting, müllerian duct–inhibiting substance causes a regression of the müllerian duct system, and circulating androgens lead instead to development of the wolffian duct system, which becomes the vas deferens, seminal vesicles, and ejaculatory ducts. The exact chemical nature of the müllerian duct–inhibiting substance is not known at present, but it is known to be secreted by the fetal testis [2]. By the fourteenth week of gestation, a clear difference in the anatomy of the internal sex structures can be seen (Fig. 2-3).

Current evidence indicates that the fetal testis acquires the capacity to convert C_{21} steroid precursors (progesterone and pregnenolone) to testosterone at an early stage of development [2]. Interestingly, this secretory capacity occurs at precisely the point in fetal development when dramatic histologic changes occur within the developing testis. The exact time when the fetal testes become capable of synthesizing testosterone de novo from cholesterol is not known at present.

The development of the external genitalia in both sexes occurs from an identical embryologic starting point, shown in Figure 2-4. From the undifferentiated genitalia of the 8-week fetus, without the presence of adequate levels of testosterone and dihydrotestosterone during the critical periods of sexual differentiation, a clitoris, vulva, and vagina

Figure 2-3. Stages of internal fetal sex differentiation. (A) The undifferentiated state of the fetus at approximately 7 weeks of development. (B, D) The patterns of female internal differentiation at approximately weeks 14 and 40. (C, E) Male differentiation at weeks 14 and 40. (Modified from J. Money and A. A. Ehrhardt, *Man and Woman, Boy and* *Girl.* Copyright © 1972 by Johns Hopkins University Press, Baltimore.)

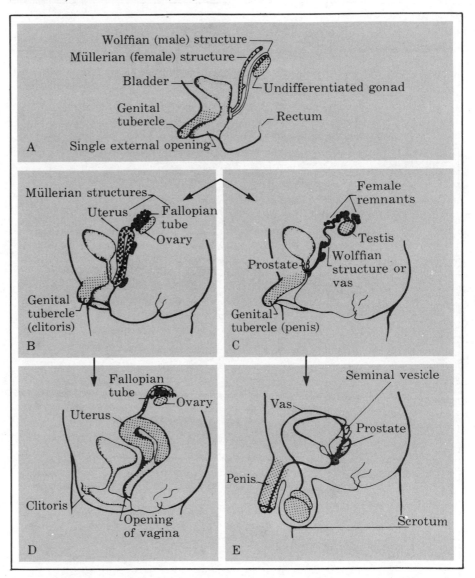

will form. This process of feminization of the external genitalia occurs normally in genetic females and, under certain conditions such as profound androgen deficiency or androgen insensitivity, in genetic males. With effective androgen stimulation, however, the urogenital

Figure 2-4. Stages of fetal differentiation of the external genitals. (*A*,
B) Development of the external
genitalia in the undifferentiated
state at approximately 4 and 7
weeks, respectively. (*C*, *E*, *G*) The
male external genitalia at weeks 9,
11, and 12. (*C₁*, *E₁*, *E₂*, *E₃*, *G₁*) Corresponding schematic transverse sec-
tions through the developing penis.
(*D*, *F*, *H*) The female external
genitalia at weeks 9, 11, and 12.
(From K. L. Moore, *The Developing
Human*, 2nd ed., Philadelphia: W. B.
Saunders Co., 1977.)

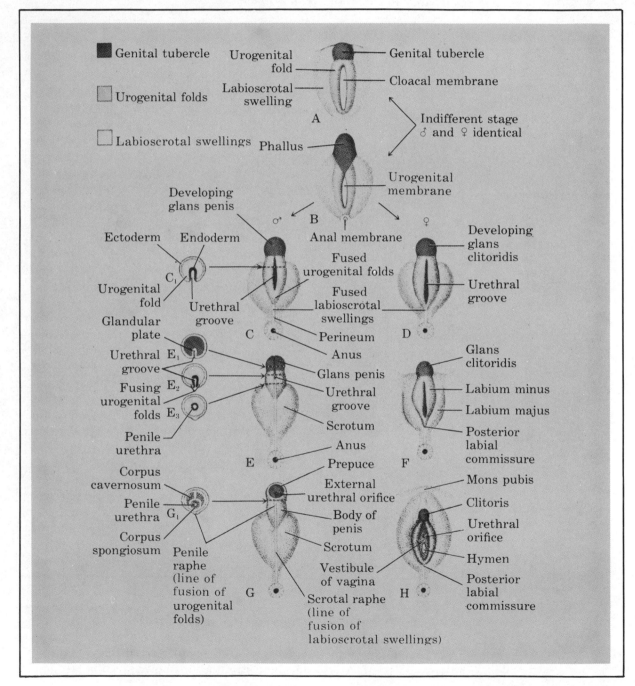

folds that would develop into the labia minora in the female go on to grow anteriorly and meet in the midline, forming the cylindrical shaft of the penis, with the urethra running its length. The line of fusion of the two urogenital folds is visible in the newborn male and persists throughout life as the median (penile) raphe. The genital tubercle, which in the female develops into the clitoris, differentiates into the glans of the penis in the male. The labioscrotal swelling either differentiates into the labia majora in the female or forms the scrotal sac by anterior growth and fusion in the male. The testes form as organs within the abdomen and normally migrate into their scrotal position during the eighth or ninth month (see Fig. 2-5). In approximately 3 percent of male newborns the testes have not descended fully, but descent usually occurs within a month or two.

Normal Development of Brain Centers Related to Sex

Just as hormonal conditions during intrauterine life are critical to the direction of anatomic differentiation of the external genitalia and the internal sex structures, the fetal hormonal environment also plays an important role in the development of the brain and anterior pituitary gland. Pfeiffer documented the first evidence of this phenomenon in 1936 [9], and subsequent studies by numerous investigators [8, 10–14] have confirmed the role of hormones in the sexual differentiation of pituitary and hypothalamic function. At the simplest level, adult functioning of the hypothalamic-pituitary-gonadal system is cyclic in women and noncyclic in men. This characteristic applies to both adult hormone production and adult fertility. A large body of animal studies, skillfully reviewed by others [8, 15, 16], documents the fact that fetal hormones may also influence a variety of behaviors, both sexual and nonsexual. It appears that these patterns (hormone cyclicity, certain aspects of behavior) are programmed by the presence or absence of androgen during a critical period in a fashion analogous to the differentiation of the external genitalia: Without adequate levels of androgen, differentiation occurs in the female direction; with high androgen stimulation, differentiation follows the male pattern.

The pituitary gland develops from two different embryologic sources: ectoderm from the pouch of Rathke and neuroectoderm from the diencephalon. The anlage of the human fetal pituitary gland is present at four to five weeks of gestation; by the seventh week of gestation, basophilic cells can be identified [17]. The first hypothalamic nuclei appear by the eighth week of gestation. Prolactin has been detected in fetal pituitary glands at 10 weeks of gestation, possibly stimulated by high levels of estrogen characteristic of pregnancy acting directly on

Figure 2-5. Embryologic formation of the inguinal canals and descent of the testes. (A) Sagittal section of a 7-week embryo showing the testis before its descent from the dorsal abdominal wall. (B, C) Sagittal sections at approximately 28 weeks. The processus vaginalis and the testis are beginning to pass through the inguinal canal. (D) Frontal section of a fetus about 3 days later, illustrating descent of the testis behind the processus vaginalis. The processus vaginalis has been cut away on the left side to show the testis and the ductus deferens. (E) Sagittal section of a newborn male showing the processus vaginalis communicating with the peritoneal cavity by a narrow canal or stalk. (F) Similar section of a one-month-old male infant after obliteration of the stalk of the processus vaginalis. The extended fascial layers of the abdominal wall now form the coverings of the spermatic cord. (From K. L. Moore, *The Developing Human*, 2nd ed., Philadelphia: W. B. Saunders Co., 1977.)

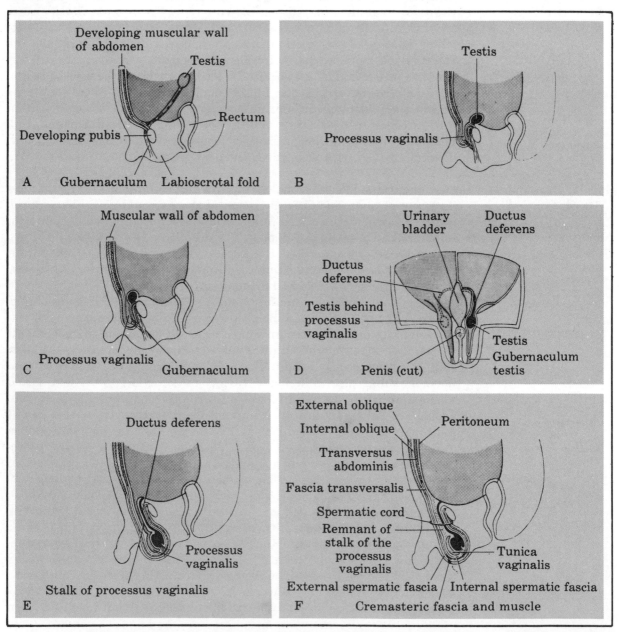

the fetal anterior pituitary [18]. Gonadotropins have been identified in the human fetal pituitary at eight to nine weeks of gestation [19, 20], with some researchers noting a significantly higher pituitary content and concentration of LH and FSH in the female than in the male [17]. It should be noted, however, that certain aspects of the regulatory mechanisms governing the hypothalamic-pituitary-gonadal axis have not matured by the time of birth; the specific role of fetal gonadotropins in relation to fetal gonadal function is not well understood at present. It appears that placental and fetal circulating human chorionic gonadotropin levels—which reach a maximum just before and during testicular development—may be more important in the stimulation of testosterone production than are fetal pituitary gonadotropins [21, 22]. Levels of testosterone in the amniotic fluid of women pregnant with male fetuses are higher than in women pregnant with female fetuses (see Fig. 2-6) [23], and levels of testosterone in male fetuses are higher in the first half of pregnancy than in the latter half [24].

Abnormal Development

Entire books have been written about disorders that result in abnormal sexual development. The objective of this section is to acquaint the reader with examples of the types of problems that may be encountered, rather than to present an encyclopedic discussion of unusual clinical syndromes that may never be seen. In addition, the study of states reflecting the excess or deficiency of certain hormones allows some inferences to be made about the relative contribution of biologic and psychosocial influences on sexual development. Interested readers are referred to the reference list for further detail [1, 8, 25, 26].

Genetic Abnormalities

Klinefelter's Syndrome. The most common sex chromosome disorder is Klinefelter's syndrome, which occurs in approximately 1 in 500 live male births [26, 27]. In this condition, the presence of an extra X chromosome (47,XXY) (see Fig. 2-7) is typically found, although variants and mosaic forms (instances in which certain cell lines in the body possess normal chromosome content, whereas others are abnormal) make up approximately 10 percent of cases. External anatomy is completely normal in the newborn boy with Klinefelter's syndrome, and unless cytogenetic screening is being conducted, the diagnosis is usually not established before early adulthood.

Childhood behavior is typically normal in boys with Klinefelter's syndrome, although there is general agreement that there is a higher rate of associated mental retardation in this group than is found in the general population [28, 29]. In adolescence, problems may occur because

Figure 2-6. Concentrations of 17-
hydroxyprogesterone, testosterone,
and progesterone in human amniotic
fluid as a function of fetal sex and
fetal age. (From Warne, Faiman,
Reyes, and Winter [23].)

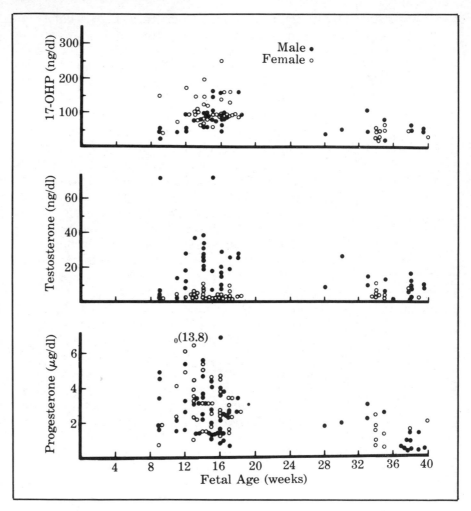

sexual development is often delayed by testosterone deficiency. By
adulthood the presence of small, atrophic testes and associated infertility are frequently coupled with low libido (sexual interest or drive) and
sometimes impotence (see Chap. 6 for additional discussion). Money
observes that men with Klinefelter's syndrome are at risk for an increased incidence of psychopathology of almost any type, including the
sporadic occurrence of gender-identity anomalies; he speculates that
the extra X chromosome found in this condition may predispose to

Figure 2-7. Karyotype of Klinefelter's syndrome (47,XXY). (From C. C. Snyder, C. D. Scott, and E. Z. Browne, Jr., Intersexuality: Diagnosis and Treatment, in C. E. Horton [ed.], *Plastic and Reconstructive Surgery of the Genital Area*, Boston: Little, Brown and Co., 1973.)

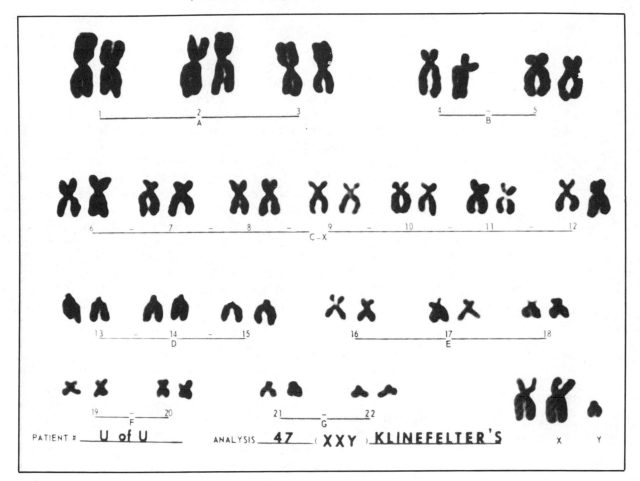

"vulnerability to developmental psychologic deficit or impairment" [8, 26, 28, 30].

An interesting aspect of this syndrome is its effect on adult behavior. Although it is true that studies of prison populations and psychiatric hospitals report a higher percentage of men with Klinefelter's syndrome than is found in the general population [26, 29, 31], the most typical pattern of behavior in 47,XXY men is a tendency toward generalized passivity and lack of ambition, combined with a minor proclivity to sudden outbursts of aggression or violence. This pattern is often reversed dramatically when long-term testosterone replacement therapy is instituted in men with Klinefelter's syndrome who have testosterone deficiency. As a consequence of adequate hormone replacement, many of these men have increased libido and improved potency as well as increased assertiveness and a heightened sense of self-esteem. Since there is ample documentation that in animals testosterone levels are closely correlated with aggressive behavior [32–35], it seems likely that the human model provided by this clinical situation reflects the same general phenomenon.

Turner's Syndrome. When there is only a single X chromosome, the absence of a second sex chromosome leads to failure of formation of normal gonads. Instead, nonfunctioning streaks of fibrous tissue appear in the place of ovaries, and internal and external differentiation occurs in typical female fashion because of the lack of androgen stimulation. The result is a condition known as Turner's syndrome (45,XO), which occurs in approximately 1 in 2,500 live female births [36]. The physical features of this condition, which almost invariably include short stature and amenorrhea (absence of menstrual flow) in adolescence and adulthood, are described in Chapter 6.

The development of girls with Turner's syndrome is normal until the time of puberty, unless the syndrome is complicated with one or more of the congenital anomalies that occur with increased frequency in this disorder. At puberty, the inability of the primitive streak gonads to manufacture estrogens and other sex hormones leads to absent menses, lack of breast development, and poor skeletal growth. Menarche (the onset of menses) can be induced by cyclic estrogen therapy, which will also serve to stimulate breast development, but hormone therapy usually will not significantly improve the short stature that is a hallmark of Turner's syndrome. Being physically different from their peers may cause girls with this syndrome to have problems in self-esteem, and the absence of pubertal hormonal production probably has direct implications for behavioral adjustment as well. The absolute infertility resulting from Turner's syndrome may also be a source of psychosocial problems.

Money and his coworkers [8, 28, 30, 36, 37] have shown that behavior patterns seen in patients with Turner's syndrome may reflect the absence of fetal hormonal stimulation of the brain. For instance, there are typically deficits in space-form perception, directional sense, and motor coordination in these individuals; their personality often exhibits complacency, slowness to take the initiative, and a lack of a normal range of affect. In general, however, females with the 45,XO karyotype are remarkably free of psychopathology.

Girls with Turner's syndrome grow up in what has been traditionally regarded as typically feminine fashion. No increase in tomboyish behavior has been noted; there is less athletic interest and athletic skill than in age-matched girls without this disorder; there is very little aggressive behavior manifested; and great interest in clothing, jewelry, perfume, and hair styling is characteristically seen [8]. In addition, there are no differences between girls with the 46,XX and 45,XO chromosome patterns in terms of childhood sexual behavior, play preferences, and anticipation of romance, marriage, and maternalism.

These findings support the concept that feminine gender identity can develop in a relatively normal fashion despite the absence of prenatal sex steroid hormones as well as the absence of a second X chromosome. Needless to say, the development of gender identity, which will be examined in greater detail in the next chapter, does depend heavily on childhood learning factors, including parental attitudes and role models, peer group interaction, and personality.

Counseling the girl with Turner's syndrome includes two important component parts: hormonal management (and care of associated physical problems) and sensitive attention to psychosocial concerns. These two areas are not independent of one another, since there are many ways in which the biologic factors interact with the psychosocial. The suggestions given here must necessarily be tailored to the needs of the individual patient, taking into account her age and ability to understand facts and prognosis. Truthfulness in explaining the nature, frequency, and consequences of the chromosomal anomaly is of immense importance in dealing with such situations. An obvious reason for this approach is the fact that patients are commonly able to guess when they are receiving deliberate misinformation from a counselor, as a result of body language, facial expression, and verbal inflections; furthermore, patients may overhear conversations between parents, teachers, nurses, or physicians that reveal the truth, and they will consequently imagine an ominous prognosis (even young children), since they have a condition that requires secrecy and deception. Needless to say, if such deception is discovered the patient will be extremely reluctant to trust the same counselor any longer and may generalize this distrust to all health-care professionals, and perhaps to all authority figures, with unfortunate consequences.

While truthfulness is important, how the truth is presented is also a matter of significance. A gentle, sensitive discussion that explains the nature of chromosomes in a matter-of-fact manner, emphasizing the frequency of chromosomal variations from normal—for example, "About one in every hundred babies has some variation in their chromosomes," and "About 40,000 women and girls in this country have a chromosome arrangement like yours" (rather than saying, "This occurs in 1 in 2,500 live female births")—and showing the patient a photograph of a typical karyotype will be helpful in first approaching the subject. When discussing the high probability of infertility, it also helps to explain that the patient can become a mother by adoption, so as not to preclude the possibility of parenthood. As Watson and Money point out [36], this approach allows the patient to incorporate the idea of motherhood by adoption rather than by pregnancy into her fantasies about the future and therefore may increase the chances of preparing her psychologically for acceptance of this role as well as potentially helping her to prepare her spouse or future spouse for this possibility.

The timing and dosage of estrogen therapy in the early adolescent girl with Turner's syndrome will depend partly on the age when the diagnosis is made. For reasons of body image, self-esteem, and peer group acceptance, it is important to hormonally induce menstrual cycles and breast growth reasonably close to the time when girls with normal sex chromosomes are spontaneously developing these signs of puberty—approximately ages 13 to 15 [38]. Regrettably, the use of estrogens to induce puberty also accelerates the cessation of growth in height by causing earlier closure of the growth-ends of the long bones in the body, so that a decision must be made balancing the gains from inducing puberty with the risk of decreasing what is already predestined to be extremely short stature. Typically, women with Turner's syndrome are no taller than five feet, and may often be five or six inches shorter.

Brief mention must be made of the fact that the parents of a girl with a 45,XO karyotype require education and will sometimes need further counseling in order to cope successfully with a situation that may be highly stressful for them. If the parents begin to treat their daughter in an insensitive manner, if they become despondent at the knowledge that she has impaired intelligence or limited social or personal capabilities, serious problems may in fact develop. Not only the initial evaluation but subsequent patient management and follow-up should include attention to the child's perceptions of her parents as well as the parents' feelings of security in dealing with the situation.

Miscellaneous Genetic Syndromes. There has been considerable recent interest in the behavior of men with a 47,XYY genotype, which is estimated to occur in approximately 1 in 1,000 live births [39] but is found with much greater frequency among men in penal institutions [29, 31, 39]. These men tend to be tall and to have abnormalities of the seminiferous tubules [27, 29, 39], but otherwise they show no signs of physical disorders. Reports have indicated that as children, boys with an extra Y chromosome have more difficulties at school, are more immature socially than their age-matched peers, exhibit more impulsive behavior, and have more difficulty in interpersonal relationships [26, 29, 31]. The evidence for an increased incidence of criminality in 47,XYY men has been substantiated in numerous studies [29, 31, 39–41], although the cause of this is not clear. It was first postulated that the higher rate of criminality exhibited by these men was due to aggressive behavior, but further analysis has shown that general aggressiveness is not typically increased in these men and that the crimes they commit are not characteristically those of an aggressive nature [29]. An alternate hypothesis that has received some support is the concept that the antisocial behavior typical of this syndrome occurs because of dysfunction in the intellectual domain. This explanation is supported by preliminary evidence of electroencephalogram differences between XYY men and men with a 46,XY genotype [42]. Evidence concerning the hormonal status of XYY males is inconclusive [43–45].

Whatever the findings of further study in the area of behavioral cytogenetics, it must be emphasized that the relationship between chromosomes and behavior is not a simple one. Regardless of the genetic programming or predisposition to risk for cognitive, emotive, or sexual impairment, the ultimate expression of the genetic makeup will be mediated by numerous other intervening variables. Currently there is, at best, only incomplete comprehension of what these variables are and how they interact.

Hormonal Abnormalities: Two Examples

The Adrenogenital Syndrome. Genetic defects in enzyme systems that control the production of cortisol in the adrenal cortex produce their effects on sexual development by hormonal action before and after birth. This action occurs because the blockage in biochemical steps in the synthesis of cortisol leads to an excessive buildup of other adrenal hormones due to hypersecretion of ACTH; these hormones are usually androgenic (masculinizing) in nature. When this exposure to elevated androgen levels occurs during fetal development in genetic females, the effect may vary from mild clitoral hypertrophy to the formation of

Figure 2-8. Masculinization of the
external genitalia in a female infant
with the adrenogenital syndrome.
Complete fusion of the labia and
clitoral hypertrophy give the appearance of a cryptorchid male.
(From C. J. Migeon, Diagnosis and
management of congenital adrenal
hyperplasia, *Hospital Practice*
12:75–82, 1977.)

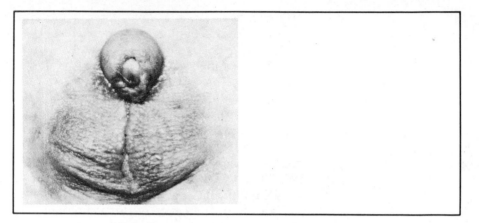

apparently male external genitals, as shown in Figures 2-8 and 2-9. The
exact nature of the effect probably reflects both the timing and the
severity of exposure to excess androgenization in a genetic female;
similarly, in a genetic female with the adrenogenital syndrome the
internal sex structures always differentiate in a normal female fashion,
since there is no müllerian duct–inhibiting substance produced by the
adrenals.

The various types of enzyme defects that have been identified as a
cause of the adrenogenital syndrome, all of which are transmitted as
autosomal recessive traits, are listed in Table 2-1. Partial or complete
defects in C_{21} hydroxylase activity account for more than 90 percent of
the cases of this syndrome [38]. In the less common cases of enzyme
defects that lead to male pseudohermaphroditism, the absence of fetal
testosterone secretion results in external genital ambiguity or frank
female appearance, but since the müllerian duct–inhibiting substance
is unaffected, no uterus or fallopian tubes develop.

With appropriate treatment initiated at an early age—namely, the
use of cortisone, which suppresses the abnormal adrenal androgen
output by suppressing pituitary production of ACTH—subsequent
physical growth and the development of secondary sex characteristics
can be relatively normal, including normal fertility for the majority of
patients [46–50]. However, when treatment is not begun until after age
6, adult height is usually shortened because of premature closure of the
growth-ends of long bones, brought about by the excessive androgen
stimulation. Hormonal therapy constitutes only one aspect of manage-

Figure 2-9. Severe virilization in an untreated female with adrenogenital syndrome. Copious pubic hair has been shaved preparatory to surgery. (From C. C. Snyder, C. D. Scott, and E. Z. Browne, Jr., Intersexuality: Diagnosis and Treatment, in C. E. Horton [ed.], *Plastic and Reconstructive Surgery of the Genital Area*, Boston: Little, Brown and Co., 1973.)

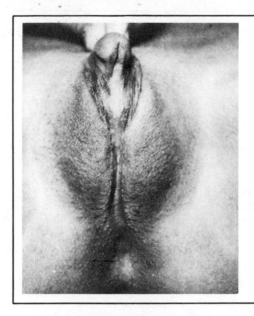

ment of such patients, however, and it may be beneficial to examine certain other aspects in temporal sequence.

When a baby is born with ambiguous external genitals, the labor-room obstetricians, midwives, or nurses involved in the delivery are immediately at a critical point, although they may not realize it. The impact that the first pronouncement of "It's a boy" or "It's a girl" will have on the way in which parents think and feel about their child is profound. For obvious reasons, if this first statement of anatomic gender is later reversed by the health-care team, parents and families may have extraordinary difficulty in adjusting to this new information [51]. It is recommended that whenever there is even slight doubt about the size and shape of the genitals, it is wisest to tell the parents that the sex organs are not quite developed and that several days of testing will be required to analyze the situation. Although it may seem harsh to use a noncommittal statement of this nature, the potential risk of making a declaration that may later be changed is in fact much more cruel to all concerned.

The masculinized external genitals of the baby girl with the adrenogenital syndrome are best treated by surgical revision at the earliest possible age. As long as the parents continue to see a "penis" on their

Table 2-1. Varieties of
Congenital Adrenal
Hyperplasia

Enzyme Defect	Female Virilization	Male Pseudo-hermaphroditism	Hypertension	Comments
C_{21} hydroxylase	Yes	No	No	Commonest form; significant virilism in females unless treated
C_{11} hydroxylase	Yes	No	Yes	Prominent virilism in females
3β-Hydroxysteroid dehydrogenase	$\pm$	Yes	No	Rare
17α-Hydroxylase	No	Yes	Yes	Rare
Cholesterol 20α-hydroxylase	No	Yes	No	Major accumulation of lipids in the adrenal cortex and gonads

daughter—a fact of repeated observation every time the child is diapered or bathed—feelings of ambiguity, guilt, or even revulsion may be activated. Jones and coworkers recommend surgery before 17 months of age [52], while others would aim for an even earlier operation. A surgical procedure to reconstruct the vaginal introitus, if required, may be postponed until after puberty, since operations done in early childhood reportedly have a high rate of stenosis and scarring [53]. Of course, if the diagnosis of the adrenogenital syndrome is not made until later in childhood or adolescence, surgery can still be highly beneficial, depending on the sex the child has been raised in and individual medical and psychological considerations. If a genetic female with masculinized genitals has been reared as a boy, reassignment of gender identity is probably too traumatic after the age of 2½ years.

Another critical point in the adjustment of parents and the adrenogenital child to this disorder is the way in which education and counseling are provided. Rosenbloom presents an outstanding discussion of this topic [54], including a manual suitable for use with parents and older children and a listing of the goals of such an educational program, some of which are summarized here:

1. Understanding how the diagnosis was made.
2. Understanding the effects on sexual development.
3. Understanding why treatment is required.
4. Understanding the goals of treatment.
5. Knowing the effects and signs of overtreatment and undertreatment.
6. Knowing how to adjust treatment dosage when required, including familiarity with injection techniques.
7. Understanding the genetic implications of the disorder.

Depending on the specific enzymatic defect affecting the individual patient, problems such as hypertension or a tendency to lose salt may further complicate management.

A number of investigators have studied the effects of the adrenogenital syndrome on girls who began receiving hormone therapy at an early age, so that the major period of excess androgen exposure was prenatal. These girls have been found to have a high incidence of tomboyishness, a pattern of high energy expenditure in rough outdoor play activities, a decided preference for having boys rather than girls as playmates, and correspondingly low levels of interest in doll-play, caring for infants, attractiveness of physical appearance, or grooming, as well as little rehearsal of adult roles as mother or wife [55, 56]. These girls clearly identify themselves as females, however, and do not fantasize about changing their sex. As Ehrhardt and Baker point out [56], the behavioral differences noted above are best viewed as variations within an acceptable range of feminine behavior in our culture.

In a study of dating, romance, friendship, and sexuality in 17 early-treated adrenogenital females, Money and Schwartz reported that these girls began dating at a later age than their unaffected peers, had difficulty forming close erotic friendships, frequently tended toward bisexual fantasy or experience, and evidenced some inhibition of erotic arousal or expression [57]. This appears to confirm an earlier report that found that 48 percent of women with late-treated adrenogenital syndrome showed homosexual inclinations in dreams and fantasies and 18 percent had actual homosexual experience [58], although another study reports conflicting data [59]. In addition to the effects of prenatal androgen exposure, the history of a chronic condition requiring genital surgery, continuing use of medications, and repeated pelvic examinations during childhood and adolescence may contribute to some of the above findings [57].

Boys with the most common form of the adrenogenital syndrome do not have adverse effects on their sexual development if they are treated hormonally from an early age. If such treatment does not occur, they will typically have precocious puberty (see pp. 85–87) and will have diminished stature as well. No behavioral effects have been noted on boys exposed to high levels of prenatal androgen.

Testicular Feminization Syndrome. A very different situation is presented in another hormonally mediated condition of prenatal development. The testicular feminization syndrome is a rare disorder in which, in a genetic male (46,XY) fetus with normal testicular production of testosterone during the critical period of sexual differentiation, the development of male external genitals does not occur because the tissues of the fetus are insensitive to the testosterone that is produced. As a result, the external genitals develop embryologically in the female direction, with the formation of labia, a vagina, and a clitoris. Since the functioning testes secrete normally acting müllerian duct–inhibiting substance, the internal sex structures do not develop into a true uterus, cervix, and fallopian tubes. The vagina is typically shortened, since the inner one-third of the vagina originates embryologically from the müllerian system. On the other hand, because the testosterone that is secreted is not able to produce any tissue effect, the wolffian ducts do not develop into normal male internal sex structures. At the time of birth, these genetic males usually look like normal females, but they have true functioning testes. Most often, the testes are intra-abdominal or only incompletely descended. Inguinal masses or hernias in an infant girl may signal the possibility of the testicular feminization syndrome, which can be detected by a karyotype demonstrating the 46,XY pattern. Occasionally, the testes descend more completely and can be palpated within the labia; in this instance the diagnosis may also be established at the time of birth. The most common pattern, however, is that the situation is not uncovered until midadolescence, when the failure to begin menstruation (since no uterus is present) calls for diagnostic evaluation.

The testicular feminization syndrome is thought to be genetically transmitted as an X-linked recessive trait [60]. The exact nature of the androgen insensitivity is not understood at present, but it is believed to be the result of a biochemical defect that involves the binding of androgens to nuclear receptors in target tissues. There are a number of

Figure 2-10. Syndrome of testicular feminization. (*A*) A 17-year-old patient who is a genetic male with breast development but no facial, pubic, or axillary hair. (*B, C*) The microscopic and gross appearance of intra-abdominal testes found at laparotomy. The Leydig cells show hyperplasia, but no spermatogenesis is seen. (*D, E, F*) An incomplete form of this syndrome in a 25-year-old patient. Note the clitoral hypertrophy shown in *F*, accompanied by pubic hair; this indicates some degree of androgen end-organ effect. (From Grumbach and Van Wyk [38].)

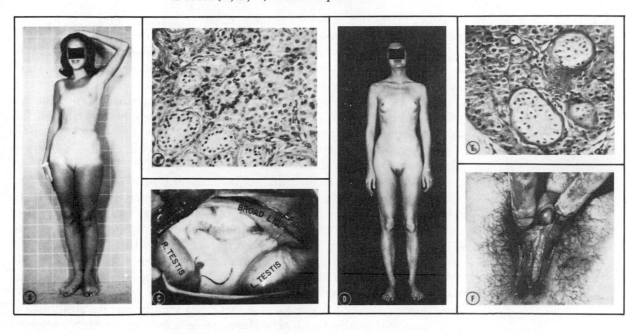

variants of this syndrome in which less severe physical manifestations occur [1, 60–66]. A familial defect in 5α-reductase, an enzyme necessary for the conversion of testosterone to dihydrotestosterone, has been shown to be associated with some of these disorders [1, 62, 63, 67].

Children with the complete testicular feminization syndrome are almost always (and correctly) reared as girls, even when discovery of the diagnosis is made at birth. Although it may sound surprising, these genetic males with testes but with the external appearance of girls go through a remarkably normal childhood when raised in this fashion. At the time of puberty, the functional testes produce testosterone and smaller amounts of estrogen than they would in normal pubertal boys. Since the androgen insensitivity is a lifelong condition, the usual male pubertal changes (e.g., increased muscle mass, deepened voice, growth of facial hair) do not occur. Instead, the combination of estrogen produced in the testes and estrogen that derives from metabolic breakdown of the circulating testosterone is sufficient to stimulate normal female breast growth (Fig. 2-10). The result is often a particularly attractive female appearance. These girls (who happen to be genetic males) are strongly feminine in a broad range of behaviors and attitudes [8].

It is a mistake to attempt to raise these children as boys for a number of reasons. Development of an adequate penis cannot occur either as a result of testosterone treatment (due to the androgen insensitivity) or by current surgical techniques. Muscle mass and body habitus will also remain in a female pattern regardless of subsequent management. Fertility is impossible under any circumstances because of the absence of adequate internal sex structures. Furthermore, at the time of puberty, breast development will occur and will require surgical correction. The failure of pubertal masculinization to occur is likely to have significant behavioral consequences as well.

Management of this disorder requires attention to several important details. In regard to patient or parental education, it is usually best to avoid the use of terms such as "testes" or "male" and instead to talk about a disorder involving the hormones made in the gonads. Stressing the positive aspect of developmental normalcy is helpful when one is introducing the information that menstruation will not occur and that fertility will be impossible. As explanation for these facts, the statement can be truthfully made that the uterus has not developed normally. It may be necessary to remove the testes surgically during childhood if they are within the labia or if they cause a hernia; in such patients, replacement estrogen must be given at the appropriate time (usually around age 13) to induce puberty. Some authorities recommend routine removal of the testes postpubertally, since there may be an increased risk of malignancy. In this instance also, hormone replacement usually must be undertaken. In some patients surgical lengthening of the vagina may be required to permit comfortable intercourse; if the testes are within the labia they sometimes must be removed because of painful intercourse caused by the male partner thrusting against the labia.

A recent study of gender identity among Costa Rican male pseudo-hermaphrodites with decreased dihydrotestosterone production due to a 5α-reductase deficiency indicates that of 18 subjects raised during childhood as girls, all but one changed to a male gender identity during or after puberty, perhaps indicating a predominance of testosterone-mediated effects over social conditioning in the determination of gender identity. In these subjects, with normal fetal and pubertal testosterone levels, there were female-appearing external genitalia at birth, with virilization (including growth of the phallus) occurring during puberty [67a]. Whether this represents a special case or whether it illustrates a general principle of gender identity development remains to be shown.

Figure 2-11. Hypospadias associated with maternal treatment with progestins. Note the relation between the position of the urethral meatus and the time of gestation at which drug exposure began. (From Aarskog [72].)

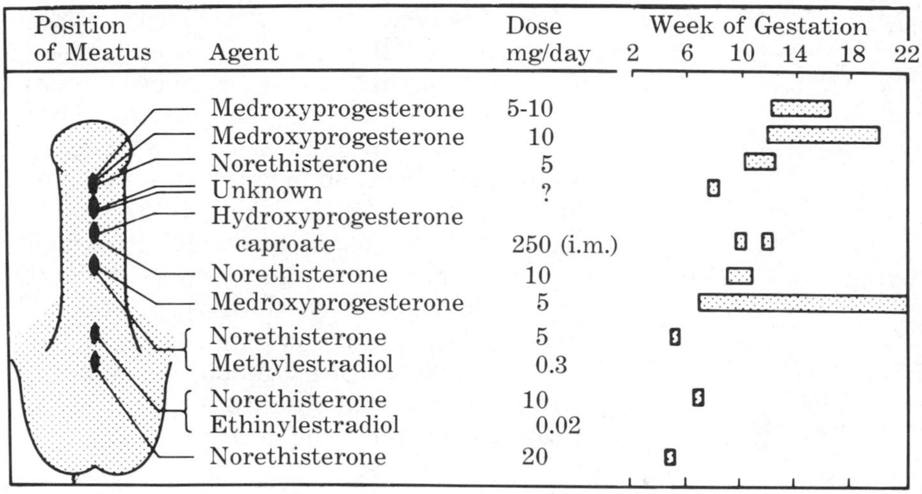

Position of Meatus	Agent	Dose mg/day	Week of Gestation
	Medroxyprogesterone	5-10	
	Medroxyprogesterone	10	
	Norethisterone	5	
	Unknown	?	
	Hydroxyprogesterone caproate	250 (i.m.)	
	Norethisterone	10	
	Medroxyprogesterone	5	
	Norethisterone	5	
	Methylestradiol	0.3	
	Norethisterone	10	
	Ethinylestradiol	0.02	
	Norethisterone	20	

(Week of Gestation axis: 2 6 10 14 18 22)

Effects of Drugs on Prenatal Sexual Development

In animal species and in humans, prenatal exposure to exogenous hormones can lead to alterations in sexual anatomy and postnatal sex role behavior. For example, exposure to significant quantities of androgens during pregnancy may masculinize a female fetus; in rodents and in rhesus monkeys, behavioral masculinization as well as anatomic virilization has been observed under similar circumstances [68–70]. Boys exposed prenatally to exogenous estrogen and progesterone given to their diabetic mothers have been found to have an increased rate of hypospadias and to exhibit less assertiveness or aggressiveness and less athletic ability than control subjects [71]. Recent data suggest that synthetic progestins are causally implicated in many cases of hypospadias, with the location of the urethral meatus apparently related to the timing of progestin exposure (see Fig. 2-11) [72]. In fact, a wide range of congenital anomalies may be associated with fetal exposure to exogenous female hormones [73–77]. The effects of prenatal exposure to diethylstilbesterol (DES) are discussed separately (see pp. 288–289).

Efforts to restrict the use of progesterone or synthetic progestins (not equivalent substances, since progesterone itself is naturally present in high concentrations during pregnancy) in light of the above findings have not been entirely successful, however, as these two substances are claimed to be clinically efficacious in treating threatened or habitual abortion, luteal phase defects, and dysfunctional uterine bleeding, and as progesterone is widely used in the diagnostic approach to amenorrhea [78]. Although comprehensive data about the behavioral and psychosexual consequences of prenatal exposure to progesterone or progestins are lacking at present, companion reports of male and female fetal exposure to medroxyprogesterone acetate indicate insignificant effects on male sex-dimorphic behavior [79] and only subtle effects in the direction of enhancing female sexually dimorphic behavior such as consistent preference for feminine clothing and a lower incidence of being labeled a tomboy during childhood [80]. In summary, the timing, duration, and dosage of certain types of prenatal drug exposure may have a specific impact on the sexual development of the fetus. Avoidance of exogenous sex steroid hormone use during pregnancy except under unusual clinical circumstances seems judicious, given the present evidence.

References

1. Imperato-McGinley, J., and Peterson, R. E.   Male pseudohermaphroditism: The complexities of male phenotypic development. *American Journal of Medicine* 61:251–272, 1976.
2. Siiteri, P. K., and Wilson, J. D.   Testosterone formation and metabolism during male sexual differentiation in the human embryo. *Journal of Clinical Endocrinology and Metabolism* 38:113–125, 1974.
3. Jost, A.   Problems of fetal endocrinology: The gonadal and hypophyseal hormones. *Recent Progress in Hormone Research* 8:379–418, 1953.
4. Jost, A.   A new look at mechanisms controlling sex differentiation in mammals. *Johns Hopkins Medical Journal* 130:38–53, 1972.
5. Reinisch, J. M.   Fetal hormones, the brain, and human sex differences: A heuristic, integrative review of the recent literature. *Archives of Sexual Behavior* 3:51–90, 1974.
6. Luttge, W. G., and Whalen, R. E.   Dihydrotestosterone, androstenedione, testosterone: Comparative effectiveness in masculinizing and defeminizing reproductive systems in male and female rats. *Hormones and Behavior* 1:265–281, 1970.
7. Arai, Y.   Sexual Differentiation and Development of the Hypothalamus and Steroid-Induced Sterility. In K. Yagi and S. Yoshida (eds.), *Neuroendocrine Control*. New York: John Wiley & Sons, 1973. Pp. 27–55.
8. Money, J., and Ehrhardt, A. A.   *Man and Woman, Boy and Girl*. Baltimore: Johns Hopkins University Press, 1972.
9. Pfeiffer, C. A.   Sexual differences of the hypophyses and their determination by the gonads. *American Journal of Anatomy* 58:195–226, 1936.
10. Clayton, R. B., Kogura, J., and Kraemer, H. C.   Sexual differentiation of the brain: Effects of testosterone on brain RNA metabolism in newborn female rats. *Nature* 226:810–812, 1970.
11. Harris, G. W.   Sex hormones, brain development and brain function. *Endocrinology* 75:627–648, 1964.
12. Karsh, F. J., Dierschke, D. J., and Knobil, E.   Sexual differentiation of

pituitary function: Apparent differences between primates and rodents. *Science* 179:484–486, 1973.

13. Gorski, R. A. Gonadal Hormones and the Perinatal Development of Neuroendocrine Function. In L. Martini and W. F. Ganong (eds.), *Frontiers in Neuroendocrinology*. London: Oxford University Press, 1971. Pp. 237–290.

14. Dörner, G. *Hormones and Brain Differentiation.* Amsterdam: Elsevier Scientific Publishing Company, 1976.

15. Friedman, R. C., Richart, R. M., and Vande Wiele, R. L. (eds.). *Sex Differences in Behavior.* New York: John Wiley & Sons, 1974.

16. Goy, R. W., and Goldfoot, D. A. Hormonal Influences on Sexually Dimorphic Behavior. In R. O. Greep (ed.), *Endocrinology (Handbook of Physiology*, Section 7). Washington, D.C.: American Physiological Society, 1973. Vol. 2 (*Female Reproductive System*, Part 1), pp. 169–186.

17. Kaplan, S. L., and Grumbach, M. M. Development of Hormonal Secretion by the Human Fetal Pituitary Gland. In L. Martini and W. F. Ganong (eds.), *Frontiers in Neuroendocrinology*. New York: Raven Press, 1976. Vol. 4, pp. 255–276.

18. Aubert, M. L., Grumbach, M. M., and Kaplan, S. L. The ontogenesis of human fetal hormones: III. Prolactin. *Journal of Clinical Investigation* 56:155–164, 1975.

19. Groom, G. V., Groom, M. A., Cooke, I. D., and Boyns, A. R. The secretion of immuno-reactive luteinizing hormone and follicle-stimulating hormone by the human foetal pituitary in organ culture. *Journal of Endocrinology* 49:335–334, 1971.

20. Siler-Khodr, T. M., Morgenstern, L. L., and Greenwood, F. C. Hormone synthesis and release from human fetal adenohypophyses *in vitro*. *Journal of Clinical Endocrinology and Metabolism* 39:891–905, 1974.

21. Forest, M. G., De Peretti, E., and Bertrand, J. Hypothalamic-pituitary-gonadal relationships in man from birth to puberty. *Clinical Endocrinology* 5:551–569, 1976.

22. Clements, J. A., Reyes, F. I., Winter, J. S. D., and Faiman, C. Studies on human sexual development: III. Fetal pituitary and serum, and amniotic fluid concentrations of LH, CG, and FSH. *Journal of Clinical Endocrinology and Metabolism* 42:9–19, 1976.

23. Warne, G. L., Faiman, C., Reyes, F., and Winter, J. S. D. Studies on human sexual development: V. Concentrations of testosterone, 17-hydroxyprogesterone and progesterone in human amniotic fluid throughout gestation. *Journal of Clinical Endocrinology and Metabolism* 44:934–938, 1977.

24. Reyes, F. I., Boroditsky, R. S., Winter, J. S. D., and Faiman, C. Studies on human sexual development: II. Fetal and maternal serum gonadotropin and sex steroid concentrations. *Journal of Clinical Endocrinology and Metabolism* 38:612–617, 1974.

25. Jones, H. W., and Scott, W. W. *Hermaphroditism, Genital Anomalies and Related Endocrine Disorders.* Baltimore: Williams & Wilkins Co., 1971.

26. Money, J., Annecillo, C., Van Orman, B., and Borgaonkar, D. S. Cytogenetics, hormones and behavior disability: Comparison of XYY and XXY syndromes. *Clinical Genetics* 6:370–382, 1974.

27. Philip, J., Lundsteen, C., Owen, D., and Hirshhorn, K. The frequency of chromosome aberrations in tall men with special reference to 47,XYY and 47,XXY. *American Journal of Human Genetics* 28:404–411, 1976.

28. Money, J. Intellectual Functioning in Childhood Endocrinopathies and Related Cytogenic Disorders. In L. I. Gardner (ed.), *Endocrine and Genetic Diseases of Childhood and Adolescence* (2nd ed.). Philadelphia: W. B. Saunders Co., 1975.

29. Witkin, H. A., Mednick, S. A., Schulsinger, F., Bakkestrøm, E., Christiansen, K. O., Goodenough, D. R., Hirschhorn, K., Lundsteen, C., Owen, D. R., Philip, J., Rubin, D. B., and Stocking, M. Criminality in XYY and XXY men. *Science* 193:547–555, 1976.

30. Money, J. Behavior genetics: Principles, methods and examples from XO, XXY and XYY syndromes. *Seminars in Psychiatry* 2:11–29, 1970.

31. Baker, D., Telfer, M. A., Richardson, C. E., and Clark, G. R. Chromosome errors in men with antisocial behavior: Comparison of selected men with Klinefelter's syndrome and XYY chromosome pattern. *Journal of the American Medical Association* 214:869–878, 1970.

32. Rose, R. M., Holaday, J. W., and Bernstein, I. S. Plasma testosterone, dominance rank and aggressive behavior in male rhesus monkeys. *Nature* 231:366–368, 1971.

33. Hart, B. L. Gonadal androgen and sociosexual behavior of male mammals: A comparative analysis. *Psychological Bulletin* 81:383–400, 1974.

34. Edwards, D. A., and Rowe, F. A. Neural and Endocrine Control of Aggressive Behavior. In B. E. Eleftheriou and R. L. Sprott (eds.), *Hormonal Correlates of Behavior*. New York: Plenum Press, 1975. Vol. 1 (*A Lifespan View*), pp. 275–303.

35. Kling, A. Testosterone and Aggressive Behavior in Man and Non-Human Primates. In B. E. Eleftheriou and R. L. Sprott (eds.), *Hormonal Correlates of Behavior*. New York: Plenum Press, 1975. Vol. 1 (*A Lifespan View*), pp. 305–323.

36. Watson, M. A., and Money, J. Behavior cytogenetics and Turner's syndrome: A new principle in counseling and psychotherapy. *American Journal of Psychotherapy* 29:166–177, 1975.

37. Money, J., and Mittenthal, S. Lack of personality pathology in Turner's syndrome: Relation to cytogenetics, hormones and physique. *Behavior Genetics* 1:43–56, 1970.

38. Grumbach, M. M., and Van Wyk, J. J. Disorders of Sex Differentiation. In R. H. Williams (ed.), *Textbook of Endocrinology* (5th ed.). Philadelphia: W. B. Saunders Co., 1974. Pp. 423–501.

39. Nielsen, J., and Christensen, A. -L. Thirty-five males with double Y chromosome. *Psychological Medicine* 4:28–37, 1974.

40. Hook, E. B. Behavioral implications of the human XYY genotype. *Science* 179:139–150, 1973.

41. Money, J., Wiedeking, C., Walker, P., Migeon, C., Meyer, W., and Borgaonkar, D. 47,XYY and 46,XY males with antisocial and/or sex-offending behavior: Antiandrogen therapy plus counseling. *Psychoneuroendocrinology* 1:165–178, 1975.

42. Volavka, J., Mednick, S. A., Sergeant, J., and Rasmussen, L. Electroen-

cephalograms of XYY and XXY men. *British Journal of Psychiatry* 130:43–47, 1977.

43. Papanicolaou, A. D., Kirkham, K. E., and Loraine, J. A.   Abnormalities in urinary gonadotropin excretion in men with a 47,XYY sex chromosome constitution. *Lancet* 2:608–610, 1968.

44. Nielsen, J., and Johnsen, S. G. Pituitary gonadotrophins and 17-ketosteroids in patients with the XYY syndrome. *Acta Endocrinologica* 72:191–196, 1973.

45. Pelzmann, K. S., and Brodie, H. K. H.   Circulating plasma testosterone in the XYY male. *Life Sciences* 18:1207–1212, 1976.

46. Kirkland, R. T., Keenan, B. S., and Clayton, G. W.   Long-Term Follow-Up of Patients with Congenital Adrenal Hyperplasia in Houston. In P. A. Lee, L. P. Plotnick, A. A. Kowarski, and C. J. Migeon (eds.), *Congenital Adrenal Hyperplasia.* Baltimore: University Park Press, 1977.

47. Klingensmith, G. J., Garcia, S. C., Jones, H. W., Jr., and Migeon, C. J. Linear Growth, Age of Menarche, and Pregnancy Rates in Females with Steroid-Treated Congenital Adrenal Hyperplasia at the Johns Hopkins Hospital. In P. A. Lee, L. P. Plotnick, A. A. Kowarski, and C. J. Migeon (eds.), *Congenital Adrenal Hyperplasia.* Baltimore: University Park Press, 1977.

48. Pang, S., Kenny, F. M., Foley, T. P., and Drash, A. L.   Growth and Sexual Maturation in Treated Congenital Adrenal Hyperplasia. In P. A. Lee, L. P. Plotnick, A. A. Kowarski, and C. J. Migeon (eds.), *Congenital Adrenal Hyperplasia.* Baltimore: University Park Press, 1977.

49. Urban, M. D., Lee, P. A., and Migeon, C. J.   Adult height and fertility in men with congenital virilizing adrenal hyperplasia. *New England Journal of Medicine* 299:1392–1396, 1978.

50. Kirkland, R. T., Keenan, B. S., Holcombe, J. H., Kirkland, J. L., and Clayton, G. W. The effect of therapy on mature height in congenital adrenal hyperplasia. *Journal of Clinical Endocrinology and Metabolism* 47:1320–1324, 1978.

51. Lewis, V. G., and Money, J.   Adrenogenital Syndrome: The Need for Early Surgical Feminization in Girls. In P. A. Lee, L. P. Plotnick, A. A. Kowarski, and C. J. Migeon (eds.), *Congenital Adrenal Hyperplasia.* Baltimore: University Park Press, 1977.

52. Jones, H. W., Jr., Garcia, S. C., and Klingensmith, G. J.   Necessity for and the Technique of Secondary Surgical Treatment of the Masculinized External Genitals of Patients with Virilizing Adrenal Hyperplasia. In P. A. Lee, L. P. Plotnick, A. A. Kowarski, and C. J. Migeon (eds.), *Congenital Adrenal Hyperplasia.* Baltimore: University Park Press, 1977.

53. Sotiropoulos, A., Morishima, A., Homsy, Y., and Lattimer, J. K.   Long-term assessment of genital reconstruction in female pseudohermaphrodites. *Journal of Urology* 115:599–601, 1976.

54. Rosenbloom, A. L.   Education of the Patient and Parent in Congenital Adrenal Hyperplasia. In P. A. Lee, L. P. Plotnick, A. A. Kowarski, and C. J. Migeon (eds.), *Congenital Adrenal Hyperplasia.* Baltimore: University Park Press, 1977.

55. Ehrhardt, A. A., and Baker, S. W.   Fetal Androgens, Human Central

Nervous System Differentiation, and Behavior Sex Differences. In R. C. Friedman, R. M. Richart, and R. L. Vande Wiele (eds.), *Sex Differences in Behavior*. New York: John Wiley & Sons, 1974.

56. Ehrhardt, A. A., and Baker, S. W. Males and Females with Congenital Adrenal Hyperplasia: A Family Study of Intelligence and Gender-Related Behavior. In P. A. Lee, L. P. Plotnick, A. A. Kowarski, and C. J. Migeon (eds.), *Congenital Adrenal Hyperplasia*. Baltimore: University Park Press, 1977.

57. Money, J., and Schwartz, M. Dating, Romantic and Nonromantic Friendships, and Sexuality in 17 Early-Treated Adrenogenital Females, Aged 16–25. In P. A. Lee, L. P. Plotnick, A. A. Kowarski, and C. J. Migeon (eds.), *Congenital Adrenal Hyperplasia*. Baltimore: University Park Press, 1977.

58. Ehrhardt, A. A., Evers, K., and Money, J. Influence of androgen and some aspects of sexual dimorphic behavior in women with the late-treated adrenogenital syndrome. *Johns Hopkins Medical Journal* 123:115–122, 1968.

59. Lev-Ran, A. Sexuality and educational levels of women with the late-treated adrenogenital syndrome. *Archives of Sexual Behavior* 3:27–32, 1974.

60. Madden, J. D., Walsh, P. C., MacDonald, P. C., and Wilson, J. D. Clinical and endocrinologic characterization of a patient with the syndrome of incomplete testicular feminization. *Journal of Clinical Endocrinology and Metabolism* 41:751–760, 1975.

61. Boyar, R. M., Moore, R. J., Rosner, W., Aiman, J., Chipman, J., Madden, J. D., Marks, J. F., and Griffin, J. E. Studies of gonadotropin-gonadal dynamics in patients with androgen insensitivity. *Journal of Clinical Endocrinology and Metabolism* 47:1116–1122, 1978.

62. Fisher, L. K., Kogut, M. D., Moore, R. J., Goebelsmann, U., Weitzman, J. J., Isaacs, H., Jr., Griffin, J. E., and Wilson, J. D. Clinical, endocrinological, and enzymatic characterization of two patients with 5α-reductase deficiency: Evidence that a single enzyme is responsible for the 5α-reduction of cortisol and testosterone. *Journal of Clinical Endocrinology and Metabolism* 47:653–664, 1978.

63. Saenger, P., Goldman, A. S., Levine, L. S., Korthschutz, S., Muecke, E. C., Katsumata, M., Doberne, Y., and New, M. I. Prepubertal diagnosis of steroid 5α-reductase deficiency. *Journal of Clinical Endocrinology and Metabolism* 46:627–634, 1978.

64. Larrea, F., Benavides, G., Scaglia, H., Kofman-Alfaro, S., Ferrusca, E., Medina, M., and Pérez-Palacios, G. Gynecomastia as a familial incomplete male pseudohermaphroditism type 1: A limited androgen resistance syndrome. *Journal of Clinical Endocrinology and Metabolism* 46:961–970, 1978.

65. Amrhein, J. A., Klingensmith, G. J., Walsh, P. C., McKusick, V. A., and Migeon, C. J. Partial androgen insensitivity: The Reifenstein syndrome revisited. *New England Journal of Medicine* 297:350–356, 1977.

66. Meyer, W. J., III, Keenan, B. S., De Lacerda, L., Park, I. J., Jones, H. E., and Migeon, C. J. Familial male pseudohermaphroditism with normal Leydig

cell function at puberty. *Journal of Clinical Endocrinology and Metabolism* 46:593–603, 1978.

67. Dube, J. Y., Chapdelaine, P., Dionne, F. T., Cloutier, D., and Tremblay, R. R. Progestin binding in testes from three siblings with the syndrome of male pseudohermaphroditism with testicular feminization. *Journal of Clinical Endocrinology and Metabolism* 47:41–45, 1978.

67a. Imperato-McGinley, J., Petersen, R. E., Gautier, T., and Sturla, E. Androgens and the evolution of male-gender identity among male pseudohermaphrodites with 5α-reductase deficiency. *New England Journal of Medicine* 300:1233–1237, 1979.

68. Sachs, B. D., Pollak, E. I., Krieger, M. S., and Barfield, R. J. Sexual behavior: Normal male patterning in androgenized female rats. *Science* 181:770–771, 1973.

69. Christensen, L. W., and Gorski, R. A. Independent masculinization of neuroendocrine systems by intracerebral implants of testosterone or estradiol in the neonatal female rat. *Brain Research* 146:325–340, 1978.

70. Young, W., Goy, R., and Phoenix, C. Hormones and behavior. *Science* 143:212–218, 1964.

71. Yalom, I. D., Green, R., and Fisk, N. Prenatal exposure to female hormones. *Archives of General Psychiatry* 28:554–561, 1973.

72. Aarskog, D. Maternal progestins as a possible cause of hypospadias. *New England Journal of Medicine* 300:75–78, 1979.

73. Nora, J. J., Nora, A. H., Blu, J., Ingram, J., Fountain, A. Peterson, M., Lortscher, R. H., and Kimberling, W. J. Exogenous progestogen and estrogen implicated in birth defects. *Journal of the American Medical Association* 240:837–843, 1978.

74. Harlap, S., Prywes, R., and Davies, A. M. Birth defects and oestrogens and progesterones in pregnancy. *Lancet* 1:682–683, 1975.

75. Apold, J., Dahl, E., and Aarskog, D. The VATER association: Malformations of the male external genitalia. *Acta Pediatrica Scandinavica* 65:150–152, 1976.

76. Nora, J. J., and Nora, A. H. Can the pill cause birth defects? *New England Journal of Medicine* 291:731–732, 1974.

77. Wilkins, L. Masculinization of female fetus due to use of orally given progestins. *Journal of the American Medical Association* 172:1028–1032, 1960.

78. Chez, R. A. Proceedings of the symposium "Progesterone, Progestins, and Fetal Development." *Fertility and Sterility* 30:16–26, 1978.

79. Meyer-Bahlburg, H. F. L., Grisanti, G. C., and Ehrhardt, A. A. Prenatal effects of sex hormones on human male behavior: Medroxyprogesterone acetate (MPA). *Psychoneuroendocrinology* 2:383–390, 1977.

80. Ehrhardt, A. A., Grisanti, G. C., and Meyer-Bahlburg, H. F. L. Prenatal exposure to medroxyprogesterone acetate (MPA) in girls. *Psychoneuroendocrinology* 2:391–398, 1977.

3

Childhood Sexuality

Few areas in contemporary scientific investigation have been ignored as assiduously as childhood sexuality. To be certain, difficulties in conducting such studies are numerous, ranging from methodological problems [1] to the question of community acceptance to ethical concerns [2, 3], but these factors do not diminish the impact that absence of reliable information entails.

The poverty of systematic research regarding childhood sexuality is in sharp contrast to the abundance of theoretical pronouncements on this subject. Freud recognized the importance of erotic feelings and behavior in childhood, stating, "It is part of popular belief about the sexual instinct that it is absent in childhood and that it first appears in . . . puberty. This, though a common error, is serious in its consequences and is chiefly due to our ignorance of the fundamental principles of the sexual life" [4]. Since that time, remarkably little advancement in knowledge about normal childhood sexuality has occurred.

The prenatal influences on sexual differentiation discussed in the preceding chapter do not abruptly terminate at birth. In some ways, to paraphrase a cliché, biology blends with destiny. The biologic foundation that has resulted from the interaction of genetic, hormonal, and embryologic forces during prenatal development now sets boundaries on certain aspects of the postnatal evolution of sexuality. These boundaries do not determine specific components of childhood or adult sexual behavior in the ordinary sense, but instead they define a continuum of behavior patterns that may emerge with variable expression. From birth onward, the learned component of sexuality is, generally speaking, of much greater consequence than that determined by biology, but as we shall see, there is an interrelatedness of these factors rather than an artificial dichotomy that regards learning and biology as unconnected.

Hormone Status in Infancy

Testosterone levels in newborn boys are significantly higher than in newborn girls [5], but circulating testosterone concentrations decrease rapidly in boys during the first neonatal week [6]. This change is attributable primarily to the abrupt withdrawal of placental human chorionic gonadotropin [7]. In the second week after birth, testosterone levels increase in boys and continue to rise until 1 to 2 months of age, after which a gradual decline is observed to prepubertal childhood levels by the seventh to twelfth month [7]. Serum LH levels rise rapidly after birth in both boys and girls: At 1 week of age, boys have LH concentrations in the adolescent range; these levels appear to peak at 1 month and subsequently decrease to the childhood range by 4 months of age [8]. Girls show a similar pattern of serum LH changes but do not attain the peak levels exhibited by boys at 1 month [8]. Newborn girls, on the other hand, show a more pronounced serum FSH increase than boys, and while the FSH rise in boys declines by 4 months of age, higher levels of FSH in girls persist until approximately 4 years [8, 9]. The sensitivity of the newborn's pituitary gonadotropin-secreting cells to hypothalamic stimulation has also been shown [10], and normal pituitary prolactin reserve in newborns has been demonstrated recently [11]. However, the precise hormonal explanation of the so-called "witch's milk" phenomenon—spontaneous secretion of milk-like fluid from the newborn's nipples—has not been determined [12].

Freud's Stages of Psychosexual Development

Freud theorized extensively about the nature of childhood sexuality from the perspective of a clinician; his theories were inferential, retrospective, and bound by the culture and times in which he lived. Nevertheless, the monumental significance of his thinking must be acknowledged firmly, although many of the details of his conceptualizations are no longer particularly useful constructs and in some ways were not revolutionary departures from previous literature dealing with sexuality. Freud viewed sexuality as a combination of psychic and biologic drives that are present in all stages of life; his articulate presentation of the centrality of infantile sexuality to personality development was a major accomplishment that changed all subsequent thinking about personality and behavior.

Freud's studies of hysteria and obsessional neurosis led him to believe that childhood sexual traumas were important determinants of adult psychopathology. His self-analysis provided some modification and extension of his thinking, and his writings portray a schema of different stages of psychosexual development that he believed were universal to all children. The *oral stage*, dominant in the first 12 to 18 months of life, is characterized by responses to thirst and hunger that include sucking, swallowing, oral tactile stimulation, and crying. Here Freud posited a connection between somatic processes that are not directly sexual and erotogenic or libidinal gratification. The *anal stage*, from ages 1 to 3, is marked by increasing attention to and mastery of eliminative functions and control over body sphincters. In one sense, this stage represents the first effective assertion of independence by the child and involves conflicting feelings between parental desires and childhood curiosity and possessiveness.* The *phallic stage*, from approximately ages 3 to

*Karl Abraham further subdivided the anal stage into an anal-sadistic phase (marked by

5, focuses erotic interest in the area of the genitals, establishes the conflicts of oedipal impulses, and is associated with the activation of castration anxieties and penis envy in females. When resolution of the initial oedipal conflicts is achieved, the child then enters a *latency stage*, which encompasses the period from about age 6 to the onset of puberty. Instinctual impulses are increasingly controlled by the superego and ego, with the result that during this phase, sexual behavior and interests are quiescent and are sublimated into other activities. The *genital stage* of development, initiated by the biologic forces that trigger puberty, is marked by physical maturation and consequent activation of libidinal drives, complicated by the reemergence of oedipal feelings and the need to assert autonomy from parents. When these problems are resolved, the adolescent makes a final transition into mature, adult genital sexuality.

This brief depiction of Freud's theories about psychosexual development is given primarily as a point of historical interest. Valid objections have been raised to the universality of the oedipal complex, the importance of penis envy, the true nature of "latency," and many other details of this theoretical model. For example, Marmor [13] writes:

This author has never been convinced that the shift to "anal erotogenicity" during the second year is either as clear-cut or as inevitable as Freud believed. Where it does seem to occur, it may well be the consequence of the emphasis on bowel-training which takes place at this time in our culture, and which often becomes the locus for an emotionally laden transaction between child and mother. Moreover, the struggle at this point is not so much over the issue of the child's wish for anal-zone pleasure *per se*, as it is over the child's wish to move its bowels whenever and wherever it wishes.

Further, Stoller, an enthusiastic and eloquent proponent of psychoanalytic thought, observes: "Girls in general just are not masculine in early childhood. Clear-cut femininity is routinely seen by a year or so of age; there is no evidence this is a facade or an imitation of femininity. How can I agree with this statement of Freud's: 'As we all know, it is not until puberty that the sharp distinction is established between the masculine and feminine character'?" [14]. Stoller also identifies the greatest single difficulty with Freud's work: "The theory was drawn up in such a way that most of it cannot be put as propositions to be tested by any scientific procedures yet devised" [14].

---

destructive impulses) and an anal-erotic phase (marked by mastery of bowel control). The many other modifications of Freud's schema for psychosexual development will not be discussed here.

At present there is no unified intrapsychic theory that can adequately explain the process of childhood sexual development. Many workers in the field accept a model that stresses the importance of social learning combined with cognitive forces on the development of sexual identity and sexual behavior.

Infant Sexuality
Infant Sexual Physiology

Apart from theoretical considerations regarding infant sexuality, a number of observations provide an instructive perspective. Personnel in a delivery room or a newborn nursery are familiar with the fact that newborn males have spontaneous erections; newborn females have vaginal lubrication, which may not be so visible a process but which parallels the vasocongestive mechanism that produces erection in the male. These examples of early physiologic function in the sexual apparatus are clearly not learned events but represent an activation of inborn reflex responses in just the same way that an infant does not learn to sweat, to breathe, to digest, or to urinate. The implications of this statement are clear: Sexual functioning is a natural process.

As the newborn grows and is exposed to relationships with others, including parents, as the personality and psyche of the child pass through adolescence and into adulthood, and as cultural taboos and rituals are translated into personal values and attitudes about sex, many complicating variables will potentially exert deleterious effects on the naturalness of sexual function. As a result, sexual problems or sexual dysfunction can appear. Just as the price of civilization over primitive society may be increased cardiovascular mortality or a higher incidence of peptic ulcer disease, so the complexities of civilization lead inexorably to sexual difficulties.

Infant Masturbation

Freud defined infantile sexuality in the broadest possible sense, regarding *sensual* as equivalent to *sexual* [15]. Erikson [16], Brown [17], and others have theorized extensively about the meanings of childhood sexuality. However, the veracity of highly interpretative approaches that regard behavior such as thumb-sucking as a sexual act is as yet unproved. More reliability can be placed on the series of confirmed observations from numerous sources that indicate the frequent occurrence of masturbation during the first year of life in both boys and girls. Although it might be fair to ask whether genital touching by an infant simply represents body exploration and the identification of the contours of the physical self, this limited explanation appears unwarranted since a number of authors document the specific occurrence of orgasm resulting from infant masturbation. For example, Kinsey and his co-workers reported that orgasm during masturbation occurred in nine males less than 1 year old: "The behavior involves a series of gradual physiologic changes, the development of rhythmic body movements with distinct penis throbs and thrusts, an obvious change in sensory capacities, a final tension of muscles . . . a sudden release with convulsions, including rhythmic contractions—followed by the disappearance of all symptoms" [18]. Bakwin described masturbation in three infant females that appeared to result in the physiologic manifestations of orgasm, including abrupt general relaxation and sweating [19]. Havelock Ellis cites a paper by West written in 1895, titled "Masturbation in Early Childhood," and one written by Townsend in 1896 on "Thigh-Friction in Children Under One Year" [20].

Certainly masturbation to the point of orgasm is not a frequent behavior in infancy, but as the child grows, it is likely that identification of genital stimulation as a source of pleasurable sensations leads to repetitive and volitional attention to erotic gratification. As children become able to verbalize their feelings and needs (typically between the ages of 2 and 4), quite specific explanations of the pleasing physical and emotional sensations accruing from genital manipulation can be elicited or may be spontaneously volunteered. The child is quick to sense parental attitudes of disapproval toward genital play and may be confused by parental encouragement to be aware of his or her body but to exclude the genitals from such awareness. The contradictory messages that the child learns in such a situation may be among the earliest recognizable common determinants of adult sexual problems.

Early Parent-Child Bonding

From the outset, the relationship and interaction that a child has with his or her parents is imbalanced: Prior to the baby's birth, the father is an observer only, without direct physical contact with the growing child. Although in some families the father is present at his child's birth (whether in a hospital setting or at home), more typically the father does not share this experience with his wife or with the newborn. It is regrettably all too common that in most modern societies, this imbalance is perpetuated during infancy and childhood, with the father spending significantly less time and having fewer varieties and actual instances of physical contact with the child than does the mother. The consequences of this discrepancy of parental contact with the child are not known, but feedback from parent to child and from child to parent may prove to be important sources for learning adaptive social behaviors.

Precise information about the erotic components of early parent-child interaction is quite sparse, but at least one facet of this interaction—lactation and nursing—must be recognized as possessing sexual components. It is not uncommon for women to become sexually aroused during nursing, and such arousal may precipitate reactions ranging from pleasure to guilt and fear. While many men regard nursing as simply a natural means of providing nutrition, some men may be upset because they interpret the act of nursing as a sexual stimulus to their wife or to their child; others find the act (or even the mere idea) of nursing to be sexually stimulating to themselves. Nursing in the presence of others similarly produces, in those others, varied reactions that presumably have nothing to do with the actual act of feeding a child, since publicly bottle-feeding an infant provokes no cries of impropriety. The sexual symbolism of the breast and the act of suckling are not easily separated from our evolutionary heritage as mammals.

Principles of Gender Identity Formation and Sex Role Development

Although in an important sense the sexual identity of an infant is determined prior to birth by chromosomal factors (the sex genotype) and physical appearance of the genitals (the sex phenotype), postnatal factors can greatly influence the way in which developing children perceive themselves sexually. The way people feel about their individuality as males or females, including ambivalence in their self-perceptions, is their *gender identity*, which must be distinguished from their *gender role*, defined as the way in which gender identity is portrayed to others or evidenced to self. Money and Ehrhardt explain these concepts concisely: "Gender identity is the private experience of gender role, and gender role is the public expression of gender identity" [21]. Although these two terms describe different components of sexuality, they are overlapping parts of the same process.

The ways in which gender identity and gender role develop in children are complex and are subject to semantic confusion. This confusion stems partly from the fact that to many people, masculinity and femininity are perceived as opposite ends of a continuum. By this reasoning, it is feminine to be passive and masculine to be aggressive, or feminine to be interested in language and art but masculine to be interested in science and mathematics. The truth is, of course, that there is no such mutual exclusivity. There are many traits, behaviors, and interests that are shared by boys and girls, men and women. There also may be clustering around certain traits, behaviors, or interests, but this clustering represents a differential rate of distribution related, in most instances, to societal and parental approval.

Spence and Helmreich have studied masculinity and femininity in great detail, discarding what they term the bipolar conception that perceives one set of characteristics (such as "feminine" sensitivity) as precluding the appearance of the opposite set ("masculine" competitiveness) [22]. These authors observe:

A frequent conviction, at least among nonprofessionals, is that sex-role behaviors are not merely correlated with psychological characteristics and sexual proclivities but that they also have causal interconnections. Parents, particularly of boys, often insist that their children behave according to traditional sex-role standards (such as playing only with the "right" kind of toys) lest they grow to resemble the opposite sex psychologically or to become sexual deviants. Similarly, attempts of the schools to develop a unisexual nonacademic curriculum have occasionally led to resistance from some segments of the community because of the corrupting influence such a curriculum may have on the character structure of their participants; boys who are taught to cook, for example, will be robbed of their masculinity, while girls who participate in "male" sports or manual arts training are likely to be "masculinized."

In many ways, masculinity and femininity are culturally defined traits, just as sex roles are, by and large, culturally defined [22–27]. Biologic differences between the sexes generally have little to do with the social distinctions derived in various societies; because boys and girls are reinforced differently by their parents even as newborns, social learning is a far more important determinant of sex role development than is biology [28].

Money and Ehrhardt provide dramatic documentation of the importance of learning in the process of gender identity formation with several case histories of sex reassignment in infancy [21]. In one instance, a normal 7-month-old baby boy with an identical twin brother underwent circumcision by electrocautery which, due to severe burning, resulted in destruction of the penis. After extensive medical and psychological consultation, this child was subsequently raised as a girl and underwent surgery for female genital construction (at the time of normal puberty, hormone replacement therapy will be needed and will have to be maintained). The childhood development of this (genetically male) girl has been remarkably feminine and is very different from the behavior exhibited by her identical twin brother. The normality of her development can be viewed as a substantial indication of the plasticity of human gender identity and the relative importance of social learning and conditioning in this process.

The earliest (and probably most important) establishment of gender identity occurs in the first three years of life. The core gender identity is ordinarily sufficiently developed by the age of 18 months that sex reassignment after this time is usually not recommended, since it is likely to create more future problems and ambivalence than the condition it is intended to correct. As children develop verbal skills, which permit identification of self in a new dimension as well as provide increasing detail to their perceptions of how other people react to them, the use of pronouns such as "he" or "she" and other nuances of language give an increasing solidarity to the earliest impressions of gender identity. At the same developmental stage, usually between 18 months and 3 years, children become more aware of how they are dressed and how others dress, which provides an additional source of information about gender as it is defined within a given culture or society.

By age 3—and sometimes even sooner—children develop an awareness of sex roles within their family and in the world around them. Parental attitudes and interaction with their children are important positive or negative reinforcers of the information processing and sex role identification that occur during this period. Maccoby and Jacklin suggest that cognitive processes are even more critical determinants of how children construct their views of sex-appropriate behavior [29]. Within the same society, sex roles may exhibit discernible changes from one generation to the next, and the child may benefit from opportunities for exposure to different sex role models. It is interesting to note that in our society, the tomboyish girl is typically thought to be "cute," whereas the effeminate boy (often negatively labeled a "sissy") is frequently a source of great parental concern.

Perceptions of others influence the child's developing sexuality in many ways. The child often models behaviors that have been observed; although such imitation may begin strictly as an exercise in curiosity, the new behavior may be maintained (or the particular type of behavior may be dropped) because of reinforcement from others or gratification deriving from the behavior itself. The child who initiates hugging of a parent or sibling may do so for the warmth and physical contact implicit in the act, or he or she may be motivated by the approving and reassuring responses the hug elicits from significant others. As the behavior is repeated, the original motivating factors may become secondary and the ritualistic significance assumes greater importance, frequently serving as a means of nonverbal communication.

The psychology of sex differences has been extensively and expertly reviewed by others [29–31]. Although it is apparent that biologic differences exist in newborn boys and girls apart from differences in their reproductive systems (for example, boys are taller and heavier than girls), there are also differences in the ways in which parents treat their children. Typically, mothers engage in more physical exertional play with their sons than with their daughters and concern themselves more with the physical safety of daughters than of sons [30]. Tasch [32] reported that fathers engage in more rough-and-tumble play with their sons than with their daughters; girls are likely to have more visual and physical contact with their mothers than boys do during infancy [33, 34]. Boys characteristically receive more pressure from both parents than girls do to refrain from what is perceived as inappropriate sex-role behavior [29]. It should be recognized, however, that part of the process of differential treatment of children by their parents may depend on factors other than sex, including the way in which the infant or child reacts, personality variables, birth order, attractiveness, and physical health. Despite these factors, it appears that the most important determinant of differential treatment is attributable to the parents' preconceptions of the ideal boy or the ideal girl [30].

Sex role development ultimately depends on many factors beyond parental input alone. Complex contributions to the process of socialization, including learning about sex roles, are made by schools, churches, and general exposure to the culture. Throughout this process, the pervasive presence of sex-role stereotypes—consensual expectations about the fashion in which males and females behave—is likely to have strong and continuing impact on children's behavior or their feelings about their behavior. Sex-role stereotyping exists in both subtle and blatant forms: Nuances about correct occupational choices may be implied by the language used to describe the occupation (e.g., nurses are referred to generically by the pronoun "she", physicians by the masculine pronoun); and relations between the sexes are frequently depicted with a stereotyped portrayal of women as emotional and nurturing while men are shown as self-reliant, independent, and decisive. Sex-role stereotypes are ubiquitous, existing in books for children [35], television, movies, and even the Sunday comics [36]. Clearly, sex roles in the United States are now evolving away from the traditional stereotypes—in part because of the women's movement and in part for economic reasons that have sanctioned the propriety of a married woman's working outside the home. In spite of these changes, there is still a remarkable degree of parental rigidity in child-rearing practices vis-à-vis sex roles, indicating how powerfully we are influenced by our own upbringing.

An interesting clinical and research question arises when childhood behavior appears that is widely divergent from what is generally perceived as appropriate sex-role behavior. Because some studies of adult males who are transsexuals, transvestites, or homosexuals indicate that they recall their childhood as marked by a preference for stereotypically feminine activities, clothes, toys, and games [37–39], a number of authors suggest that behavioral intervention or psychotherapy is needed to prevent a high rate of similar outcomes in boys showing prominent degrees of feminine behavior and interests during childhood [38–47]. In contrast, there is far less concern with tomboyishness in girls—Green observes that "it can be considered a normal passing phase" and is much more common than pronounced femininity in boys [44]—and, as previously mentioned, the tomboyish girl is often considered "cute" while the effeminate boy is a cause of parental (and clinical) alarm.

Although prospective studies are currently underway to determine the actual outcome of atypical sex-role behavior in childhood [37], without such information it appears difficult both pragmatically and ethically [48] to justify intervention in these cases unless the child is distressed by the situation or other psychiatric problems exist. For situations in which parents are discomfited by their otherwise "normal" child's sex-role behavior, it may be more appropriate, at least until more is known in this area, to provide treatment for the parents. Admittedly, it may be found that there are certain patterns of childhood atypical sex-role behavior that place the child at high risk for subsequent sexual difficulties or psychopathology; then, of course, it will be necessary to intervene in timely fashion. Present evidence makes it justified to place the child whose atypical sex-role behavior is accompanied by a strong, persistent wish to become a person of the opposite sex in this category (see Chap. 18).

Childhood Sex Behavior

Most of the data about childhood sexuality have been obtained by indirect study using methods such as interviews with parents, retrospective surveys of adult recollections of childhood experiences, and information gathered during clinical interviews with children. The hazards of accepting these sources as either accurate or representative of normal childhood experience cannot be stressed strongly enough. Field studies by anthropologists using techniques of direct observation have documented conclusive evidence from numerous cultures indicating that sexual activity during childhood is commonplace and assumes forms commensurate with the proscriptions and prescriptions of the particular culture [21, 49]. Thus, as Marmor points out, sexual latency is neither a psychically nor an organically determined stage of development but, *when it occurs*, reflects the repressions of a culture that strongly depicts sex to the child as dirty, sinful, or shameful [13]. In some cultures, the sexual activity of children is strongly sanctioned rather than disapproved [21, 49]. In some instances, cultural approval extends to or even mandates homosexual activity or the observation of adult sexual practices by children.

Kinsey reported data on the cumulative incidence of masturbation in children before the age of puberty, but the consistency of his data, collected primarily by interviewing adults, has been questioned [50]. At present, no real knowledge of the relative or absolute frequencies with which boys and girls engage in various sexual practices at different ages is available. Nevertheless, some general observations about childhood sexuality are in order.

Most children experiment with their sexuality in various ways. They look at themselves, touch themselves, and discover their genitals as a source of pleasurable sensations. Often they extend this exploratory behavior to looking at and touching the genitals of other children, with an obvious reason for attraction toward the opposite sex being simple curiosity about the nature of the anatomic differences that may exist. Similarly, curiosity about the genitals of same-sex persons can be viewed as a function of knowledge-seeking: "How different am I from others who are like me?"

When children have no knowledge of the procreative aspects of sex, they quite reasonably may assume a mystery that has not yet been explained to them, since they experience sensations in their genitals that are different from those involved in urination. Children also are sensitive to ways in which their parents react differently to their genital anatomy compared to other parts of the body. This discrepancy in parental attitudes is another mystery to be solved—a mystery that is heightened as the child grows older and observes the same differential attitudes in teachers and other adults.

When children are discovered in sex play, either solitary or with others, negative parental attitudes may be difficult to understand but easily perceived. Although a causative relationship has not been proved, it is interesting to note that in many cases of adult sexual problems there is historical evidence of sharply negative parental reactions to the discovery of masturbation or other aspects of childhood sexual activity. Sometimes these reactions include ominous predictions that continued participation in sex will lead to dire consequences later on. At other times, the objection is put in a hygienic context, at least as perceived by the child: The statement "That's dirty" may be interpreted in a variety of ways. Moral sanctions are generally used by parents with children at a somewhat older age (beginning at approximately age seven or eight), and the moral prohibitions of the home may be reinforced by other institutions in the child's life.

It also appears that many parents react in different ways to sexual play of their school-age children. Girls are often cautioned strongly against repetitions of such episodes, especially when the involvement has been in typical childhood heterosexual situations. In contrast, boys frequently receive mixed messages from their parents; they may be admonished or even punished for such activity, but there is a hint of biologic determinism in the attitude that "boys will be boys" that may be directly or indirectly conveyed to them. This tacit permission to boys to follow their sexual curiosity or urges is only rarely found directed to school-age girls in our society, and it becomes an even broader point of divergence as puberty arrives and adolescent behavior patterns pertaining to sexuality are somewhat more openly sanctioned.

Many parents are unaware of the fact that homosexual play among children, as well as heterosexual play, is a normal part of growing up. As long as aggressive or coercive behavior is not involved, it is unlikely that isolated instances of childhood sexual activity are abnormal. Parents who react to the discovery of childhood sex play in a punitive or frightened fashion are probably telling more about their own insecurities about sex than showing concern for their child's welfare. Instead, a matter-of-fact parental approach that incorporates understanding and age-appropriate sex education (while maintaining the parents' prerogative of setting limits) is likely to be effective in helping the healthy psychosexual growth of the child.

Children's sexual attitudes and sexual values derive from many different sources. That parents' attitudes towards sex are important determinants of their children's views has been demonstrated by McNab [51], who administered tests of sex attitudes to 91 males, 81 females, and their natural parents and found a strong correlation between the scores of parents and their children. Parental attitudes toward sex most likely influence the growing child in other ways as well. Whether or not sex is a topic of discussion in the home and how it is discussed may convey implicit attitudes to observant children. Parental attitudes toward nudity—pertaining to themselves or to their children—also probably contribute to how children feel about sex. The presence or absence of visible physical contact demonstrating affection between parents (e.g., the child seeing the father and mother hug and kiss or hold hands with one another) may also be regarded as significant input into the child's developing system of sexual values.

Of course, children develop their sexual attitudes partly on the basis of their own experience, their feelings about themselves and their bodies, and a wide range of other variables including peer group attitudes. Sexual values and attitudes develop in childhood only within the framework of the child's ability to conceptualize, so that as age and cognitive skills progress, the child's sexual values and attitudes will undergo changes as well. Nevertheless, the early patterns of the child's sexual attitudes and values, as precursors of more highly defined adult conceptualization and beliefs, may be prominent elements in the formation of adult sexual behavior.

Sex Education for Children

When the role of sex education for children is considered, there is often more rhetoric than reason or fact. Controversies abound about the proper locus of sex education (home, school, or church), ignoring evidence that for many children the information received from parents about sex and sexuality is minimal or incorrect; these children often rely on information furtively gleaned from their peers as authoritative when, of course, it is often anything but that [52–54]. Another source of controversy is embodied in the fear that sex education encourages children to experiment in their sexual behavior, a belief that has no support in actual data.

There are legitimate questions about the usefulness or propriety of compulsory sex education in the schools; for example, many teachers who were assigned to present such courses had no professional training in sex education and had few curricular resources to draw upon. Fortunately, this problem has been largely overcome in recent years as a growing number of competent sex educators have appeared on the scene, and a number of model curricula are now available for use at various age levels [55–60]. It is also legitimate to question whether sex education teachers should advocate particular values related to sexuality, yet this is not a major question in school courses on other subjects—social studies teachers are generally not accused of propagandizing for a particular political point of view, and competent sex education teachers avoid such pitfalls as well.

It is important to realize that sex education is not confined to topics such as reproduction, contraception, and venereal disease; children need to receive information about interpersonal relationships, falling in love, parenting, and other areas that are included in many courses on sex education. However, school instruction alone cannot be an effective substitute for sex education in the home; the role is complementary rather than exclusionary. Needless to say, the pediatrician or family physician is a potential supplementary source of sex education and may undertake this role either during direct patient contact or by more visible activity in the community at large.

Sexual Abuse of Children

Sexual abuse has recently been termed the most underreported and undiagnosed type of child abuse [61]. Although in most states physicians who treat sexually abused children are legally required to report such cases, in actual practice this is only infrequently done [62]. Incest accounts for a large percentage of cases of sexual abuse of children, but other forms of sexual abuse occur, including child molestation by adults or teenagers who are not family members, rape, forced participation of children in the production of pornographic materials, and instances of child prostitution involving boys as well as girls. Children of any age may be victimized by sexual abuse—the very young as well as the older child.

While no reliable statistics exist on the incidence of child sexual abuse, increasing attention is being given to this problem [61–70]. Since a history of sexual abuse may not be given by either the child or parent on initial interview because of fear or embarrassment, the clinician must be alerted to the possibility of abuse by signs and symptoms such as vaginal or penile discharge or trauma, lesions of the mouth or perineum, trauma to the anal region, painful urination or defecation, the presence of *Trichomonas* or gonorrhea, and evidence of syphilis [61, 65]. In children with these signs or symptoms, the presence of spermatozoa in vaginal smears or in smears obtained from other orifices is strong evidence of the likelihood of sexual abuse and must be followed up vigorously.

Several reports indicate an increased frequency of sexual abuse of children by alcoholics. Rada found that 52 percent of 203 child-molesters were rated as alcoholic; he suggested that the use of alcohol may lower the usual inhibitions of the child-molester and thus facilitate the commission of an act that is less likely to occur in the sober state [68]. Browning and Boatman believe that many cases of father-daughter incest occur when the mother is depressed or emotionally withdrawn [70], a view shared by others [64, 66, 69]. However, further studies are required to develop accurate information about the psychological status of adults who abuse children sexually and who sometimes were themselves abused as children.

The effects of sexual abuse on the child are not well documented at present. While clinicians can attest to dramatic instances of conflicted, guilt-ridden adults who present such histories, there are also many instances of child sexual abuse that have little discernible impact on subsequent life. It is certainly reasonable to assume that children involved in an isolated episode of sexual abuse may be less at risk for ensuing difficulties either sexually or emotionally than those involved in chronically abusive situations. It also appears that if parental reactions to situations of child sexual abuse are supportive, calm, and objective, the potential traumas to the child may be minimized [67].

References

1. Anthony, E. J., Green, R., and Kolodny, R. C. *Childhood Sexuality*. Boston: Little, Brown and Co., in press.
2. Mann, J., and Jonsen, A. R. Ethics of Sex Research Involving Children and the Mentally Retarded. In W. H. Masters, V. E. Johnson, and R. C. Kolodny (eds.), *Ethical Issues in Sex Therapy and Research*, Vol. 2. Boston: Little, Brown and Co., in press.
3. Rosen, A. C., Rekers, G. A., and Bentler, P. M. Ethical issues in the treatment of children. *Journal of Social Issues* 34(2):122–136, 1978.
4. Freud, S. Infantile Sexuality. In J. Strachey (ed.), *The Standard Edition of the Complete Psychological Works of Sigmund Freud*. London: The Hogarth Press, 1953. Vol. 7, p. 173.
5. Forest, M. G., and Cathiard, A. M. Pattern of testosterone and androstenedione during the first month of life: Evidence for testicular activity at birth. *Journal of Clinical Endocrinology and Metabolism* 41:977–980, 1975.
6. Forest, M. G., Sizonenko, P. C., Cathiard, A. M., and Bertrand, J. Hypophyso-gonadal function in humans during the first year of life. *Journal of Clinical Investigation* 53:819–828, 1974.
7. Forest, M. G., De Peretti, E., and Bertrand, J. Hypothalamic-pituitary-gonadal relationships in man from birth to puberty. *Clinical Endocrinology* 5:551–569, 1976.
8. Winter, J. S. D., Faiman, C., Hobson, W. C., Prasad, A. V., and Reyes, F. I. Pituitary-gonadal relations in infancy: I. Patterns of serum gonadotropin concentrations from birth to four years of age in man and chimpanzee. *Journal of Clinical Endocrinology and Metabolism* 40:545–551, 1975.
9. Penny, R., Olambiwonnu, N. O., and Frasier, S. D. Serum gonadotropin concentrations during the first four years of life. *Journal of Clinical Endocrinology and Metabolism* 38:320–321, 1974.
10. Delitala, G., Meloni, T., Masala, A., Alagna, S., Devilla, L., and Corti, R. Effect of LRH on gonadotropin secretion in newborn male infants. *Journal of Clinical Endocrinology and Metabolism* 46:689–690, 1978.
11. Delitala, G., Meloni, T., Masala, A., Alagna, S., Devilla, L., and Corti, R. Dynamic evaluation of prolactin secretion during the early hours of life in human newborns. *Journal of Clinical Endocrinology and Metabolism* 46:880–882, 1978.
12. Hiba, J., Del Pozo, E., Genazzani, A., Pusterla, E., Lancranjan, I., Sidiropoulos, D., and Gunti, J. Hormonal mechanism of milk secretion in

the newborn. *Journal of Clinical Endocrinology and Metabolism* 44:973–976, 1977.

13. Marmor, J. "Normal" and "deviant" sexual behavior. *Journal of the American Medical Association* 217:165–170, 1971.

14. Stoller, R. J. Overview: The impact of new advances in sex research on psychoanalytic theory. *American Journal of Psychiatry* 130:241–251, 1973.

15. Freud, S. Three Essays on the Theory of Sexuality. In J. Strachey (ed.), *The Standard Edition of the Complete Psychological Works of Sigmund Freud.* London: The Hogarth Press, 1953. Vol. 7, pp. 125–245.

16. Erikson, E. H. *Childhood and Society* (2nd ed.). New York: W. W. Norton, 1963.

17. Brown, N. O. *Life Against Death.* New York: Vintage Books, 1961.

18. Kinsey, A. C., Pomeroy, W. B., and Martin, C. E. *Sexual Behavior in the Human Male.* Philadelphia: W. B. Saunders Co., 1948.

19. Bakwin, H. Erotic feelings in infants and young children. *Medical Aspects of Human Sexuality* 8(10):200–215, 1974.

20. Ellis, H. *Studies in the Psychology of Sex.* New York: Random House, 1942 (reissue of 1905 work). Vol. 1, part 3, p. 179; vol. 2, part 1, p. 155.

21. Money, J., and Ehrhardt, A. A. *Man and Woman, Boy and Girl.* Baltimore: Johns Hopkins University Press, 1972.

22. Spence, J. T., and Helmreich, R. L. *Masculinity & Femininity: Their Psychological Dimensions, Correlates and Antecedents.* Austin, Tex.: University of Texas Press, 1978.

23. Bem, S. L. The measurement of psychological androgyny. *Journal of Consulting and Clinical Psychology* 42:155–162, 1974.

24. Bem, S. L. Sex-role adaptability: One consequence of psychological androgyny. *Journal of Personality and Social Psychology* 31:635–643, 1975.

25. Bem, S. L., Martyna, W., and Watson, C. Sex typing and androgyny: Further explorations of the expressive domain. *Journal of Personality and Social Psychology* 34:1016–1023, 1976.

26. Ellis, L. J., and Bentler, P. M. Traditional sex-determined role standards and sex stereotypes. *Journal of Personality and Social Psychology* 25:28–34, 1973.

27. Scanzoni, J. H. *Sex Roles, Life Styles, and Child Bearing.* New York: The Free Press, 1975.

28. Marlowe, L. *Social Psychology: An Interdisciplinary Approach to Human Behavior.* Boston: Holbrook Press, 1975. Pp. 102–104.

29. Maccoby, E. E., and Jacklin, C. M. *The Psychology of Sex Differences.* Stanford, Calif.: Stanford University Press, 1974.

30. Kagan, J. Psychology of Sex Differences. In F. A. Beach (ed.), *Human Sexuality in Four Perspectives.* Baltimore: Johns Hopkins University Press, 1976. Pp. 88–114.

31. Lee, P. C., and Stewart, R. S. (eds.). *Sex Differences: Cultural and Developmental Dimensions.* New York: Urizen Books, 1976.

32. Tasch, R. J. The role of the father in the family. *Journal of Experimental Education* 20:319–361, 1952.

33. Cramer, B. Sex differences in early childhood. *Child Psychiatry and Human Development* 1:133–151, 1971.

34. Goldberg, S., and Lewis, S.   Play behavior in the year-old infant: Early sex differences. *Child Development* 40:21–33, 1969.
35. Weitzman, L. J., Eiffer, D., Kokada, E., and Ross, C.   Sex-role socialization in picture books for pre-school children. *American Journal of Sociology* 77:1125–1150, 1972.
36. Brabant, S.   Sex role stereotyping in the Sunday comics. *Sex Roles* 2:331–337, 1976.
37. Green, R.   One-hundred ten feminine and masculine boys: Behavioral contrasts and demographic similarities. *Archives of Sexual Behavior* 5:425–446, 1976.
38. Rekers, G. A., Rosen, A. C., Lovaas, O. I., and Bentler, P.   Sex-role stereotypy and professional intervention for childhood gender disturbance. *Professional Psychology* 9:127–136, 1978.
39. Newman, L. E.   Treatment for the parents of feminine boys. *American Journal of Psychiatry* 133:683–687, 1976.
40. Rekers, G. A., Lovaas, O. I., and Low, B.   The behavioral treatment of a "transsexual" preadolescent boy. *Journal of Abnormal Child Psychology* 2:99–116, 1974.
41. Rekers, G. A., Yates, C. E., Willis, T. J., Rosen, A. C., and Taubman, M.   Childhood gender identity change: Operant control over sex-typed play and mannerisms. *Journal of Behavior Therapy and Experimental Psychiatry* 7:51–57, 1976.
42. Rekers, G. A.   Atypical gender development and psychosocial adjustment. *Journal of Applied Behavior Analysis* 10:559–571, 1977.
43. Rekers, G. A.   Sexual Problems: Behavior Modification. In B. B. Wolman, J. Egan, and A. O. Ross (eds.), *Handbook of Treatment of Mental Disorders in Childhood and Adolescence*. Englewood Cliffs, N.J.: Prentice-Hall, 1978. Pp. 268–296.
44. Green, R.   *Sexual Identity Conflict in Children and Adults*. New York: Basic Books, 1974.
45. Stoller, R.   Psychotherapy of extremely feminine boys. *International Journal of Psychiatry* 9:278–280, 1970–71.
46. Green, R., and Fuller, M.   Group therapy with feminine boys and their parents. *International Journal of Group Psychotherapy* 23:54–68, 1973.
47. Lebovitz, P. S.   Feminine behavior in boys: Aspects of its outcome. *American Journal of Psychiatry* 128:1283–1289, 1972.
48. Kolodny, R. C.   Ethical Issues in the Prevention of Sexual Problems. In C. B. Qualls, J. P. Wincze, and D. H. Barlow (eds.), *The Prevention of Sexual Disorders*. New York: Plenum Press, 1978. Pp. 183–196.
49. Ford, C. S., and Beach, F. A.   *Patterns of Sexual Behavior*. New York: Harper & Row, 1951.
50. Broderick, C. B.   Preadolescent sexual behavior. *Medical Aspects of Human Sexuality* 2(1):20–29, 1968.
51. McNab, W. L.   Sexual attitude development in children and the parents' role. *Journal of School Health* 46:537–542, 1976.
52. Kirkendall, L. A., and Calderwood, D.   The family, the school and peer groups: Sources of information about sex. *Journal of School Health* 35:290–297, 1965.

53. Kravetz, J. H., and Smith, S. A.   Sex education: Too little—too late. *Fertility and Sterility* 24:202–207, 1973.
54. Thornburg, H. D.   Age and first sources of sex information as reported by 88 college women. *Journal of School Health* 40:156–158, 1970.
55. Schiller, P.   *Creative Approach to Sex Education and Counseling.* New York: Association Press, 1973.
56. Kilander, H. F.   *Sex Education in the Schools.* New York: The Macmillan Co., 1970.
57. Rosenzweig, N., and Pearsall, F. P. (eds.).   *Sex Education for the Health Professional.* New York: Grune and Stratton, 1978.
58. Broderick, C. B., and Bernard, J. (eds.).   *The Individual, Sex and Society: A SIECUS Handbook for Teachers and Counselors.* Baltimore: Johns Hopkins University Press, 1969.
59. Karlin, M. S.   *Administering and Teaching Sex Education in the Elementary School.* West Nyack, N.Y.: Parker Publishing Co., 1975.
60. Levin, A. L., and Lynch, B. H.   *Human Sexuality in Family Life Education.* Dubuque, Iowa: Kendall Hunt Publishing Co., 1976.
61. Herjanic, B., and Wilbois, R. P.   Sexual abuse of children: Detection and management. *Journal of the American Medical Association* 239:331–333, 1978.
62. James, J., Womack, W. M., and Stauss, F.   Physician reporting of sexual abuse of children. *Journal of the American Medical Association* 240:1145–1146, 1978.
63. Summit, R., and Kryso, J.   Sexual abuse of children: A clinical spectrum. *American Journal of Orthopsychiatry* 48:237–251, 1978.
64. Peters, J. J.   Children who are victims of sexual assault and the psychology of offenders. *American Journal of Psychotherapy* 30:398–421, 1976.
65. Terrell, M. E.   Identifying the sexually abused child in a medical setting. *Health and Social Work* 2(4):113–130, 1977.
66. Finkelhor, D.   Psychological, cultural and family factors in incest and family sexual abuse. *Journal of Marriage and Family Counseling* 4:41–49, October 1978.
67. Weeks, R. B.   Counseling parents of sexually abused children. *Medical Aspects of Human Sexuality* 10(8):43–44, 1976.
68. Rada, R. T.   Alcoholism and the child molester. *Annals of the New York Academy of Sciences* 273:492–496, 1976.
69. Nakashima, I. I., and Zakus, G. E.   Incest: Review and clinical experience. *Pediatrics* 60:696–701, 1977.
70. Browning, D. H., and Boatman, B.   Incest: Children at risk. *American Journal of Psychiatry* 134:69–72, 1977.

4

Puberty and Adolescent Sexuality

Adolescence is often regarded as a time of turmoil—a time when physical maturation induced by awakening endocrine forces has added to it a wide variety of psychosocial tasks demanding to be mastered. The teenager is expected to develop and accept emotional independence and autonomy from his or her parents as part of the process Erikson calls the search for a sense of personal identity [1]. Simultaneously, the adolescent must develop skills in peer group interaction, a workable set of ethical precepts, competence in intellectual function, and a sense of social and personal responsibility. As if all this were not enough, the adolescent must also cope with a variety of issues relating to sexuality, such as how to deal with new or more powerful sexual feelings, whether to participate in various types of sexual behavior, how to recognize love, how to prevent unwanted pregnancy, and how to define age-appropriate sex roles. Despite the seeming impossibility of standing up to this barrage of developmental demands, most adolescents succeed remarkably well in emerging from their teenage years intact, if not unscarred. In this chapter, after discussion of the physical and hormonal changes of puberty, selected aspects of adolescent sexual behavior and sexual concerns will be considered.

Puberty

During childhood, circulating levels of testosterone and estrogen are low in both boys and girls and principally reflect the synthesis of sex steroid hormones occurring in the adrenal cortex. LH and FSH levels are also low during childhood, probably as a result of an inhibitory feedback of minimal amounts of gonadal sex steroid hormone production, since circulating gonadotropin levels in agonadal children are elevated throughout childhood [2]. Gonadotropin levels in children do not exhibit pulsatile episodic fluctuations of the type found in adulthood [3], but mildly increased gonadotropin levels can be detected in both boys and girls at approximately ages 10 to 12 [4].

Puberty can be defined as a transition period that takes the individual from biologic immaturity to maturity. During this period of developmental transition, dramatic physical changes of many types occur, the most visible ones being the acceleration in skeletal growth (the adolescent growth spurt) and the development of secondary sex characteristics. There is great variability both in the ages at which these processes begin and end and in the sequence in which they occur.

Changes in Body Size

As a result of the interaction of hormonal stimulus and genetic and environmental factors, children experience a marked increase in the velocity of their skeletal growth during puberty. In girls, the maximum growth rate occurs at an average age of 12.14 ± 0.88 years (mean ± S.D.), whereas in boys the major portion of the adolescent growth spurt does not occur until some two years later (14.06 ± 0.92 years) [5, 6]. Because of this sex difference in the timing of the adolescent growth spurt, it is common for girls to be taller than boys of the same age from about age 11 to age 14. In midadolescence, however, onset of the male peak growth velocity coincident with the usual deceleration in further height changes in girls results in boys attaining, on average, a greater height [7].

Marshall notes that the adolescent growth spurt does not start at the same time in all parts of the body. For example, growth of the foot typically begins about four months earlier than growth in the lower leg, with the result that the feet may temporarily appear to be disproportionately large [7]. This differential growth rate may at times cause problems of body image and self-esteem for the adolescent who has no knowledge of the fact that things will soon return to more harmonious relative proportions.

It is important to realize that failure to develop an "early" growth spurt in adolescence is not predictive of the final height that will be attained. A boy who is shorter than his peers at age 13 or 14 may go on to become as tall as or taller than his age-mates by age 17 or 18; however, the psychosocial ramifications of being among the shortest in a class seem to be somewhat greater for boys than for girls. Girls who are considerably taller than their male classmates may either be somewhat ostracized socially or resort to dating and interacting with older boys.

Sexual Maturation in Girls

The first physical sign of the onset of pubertal changes in girls typically is modest development of the breasts. This change is followed by the appearance of pubic hair, which usually precedes the onset of menstruation (menarche). The exact timing of these changes is subject to considerable variation, but some clinically useful guidelines may be derived from the detailed studies of Marshall and Tanner on children in England [5–9]. These workers have developed a descriptive method of staging pubertal development. The various stages of breast development (shown in Fig. 4-1) are as follows:

Stage 1 (B1) Infantile or childhood pattern.
Stage 2 (B2) Early pubertal breast development, sometimes referred to as a "breast bud." A small mound of breast tissue causes a visible elevation.

Figure 4-1. Stages of female breast development during puberty. (From J. M. Tanner, *Growth at Adolescence*, 2nd ed., Oxford: Blackwell Scientific Publications, 1962.)

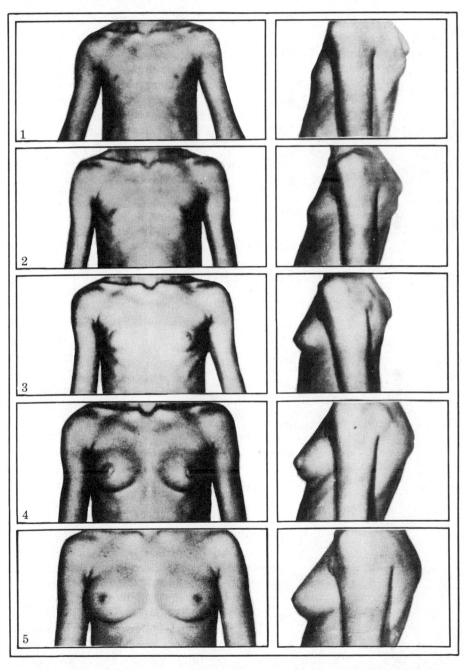

Stage 3 (B3) The areola and the breast undergo more definite pronouncement in size, with a continuous rounded contour.

Stage 4 (B4) The areola and nipple enlarge further and form a secondary mound projecting above the contour of the remainder of the breast.

Stage 5 (B5) The adult breast stage. The secondary mound visible in
the preceding stage has now blended into a smooth contour of the breast.

Breast development may begin normally as early as age 8 or as late as
age 13 [9].

Pubic hair development (shown in Fig. 4-2) has also been described in
five stages:

Stage 1 (PH1) Infantile pattern. No true pubic hair present, although
there may be a fine downy hair distribution.

Stage 2 (PH2) Sparse growth of lightly pigmented hair, longer than
the fine down of the previous stage, appearing on the
mons or the labia.

Stage 3 (PH3) The pubic hair becomes darker, coarser, and curlier.
Distribution is still minimal.

Stage 4 (PH4) The pubic hair is adult in character, but not yet as
widely distributed as in most adults.

Stage 5 (PH5) The pubic hair is distributed in the typical adult female
pattern, forming an inverse triangle.

Marshall reported that in the United Kingdom the average age at
menarche is 13.0 years, with a standard deviation of approximately one
year [7]. Zacharias and Wurtman reported that the mean age at
menarche in the United States, based on a retrospective study of 6,217
student nurses, was 12.65 ± 1.2 (S.D.) years [10]. In extensive data
collected by the National Center for Health Statistics, the median age
at menarche for whites was found to be 12.80 and for blacks, 12.52 years
[11]. There is now general agreement that the age at menarche, which
has been consistently decreasing on a decade-by-decade basis for the
last century, is influenced significantly by socioeconomic factors, climate, heredity, family size, and nutritional status [10]. It currently
appears that the decreasing age at menarche has leveled off in this
country and in England, perhaps as a reflection of more uniform nutritional status during childhood and adolescence.

Most commonly, menarche occurs after the adolescent girl has

Figure 4-2. Stages of female pubic hair development during puberty. Infantile pattern (stage 1) is not shown. Although stage 2 appears to have more hair density than stage 3, there is actually longer and curlier hair in the latter stage. (From J. M. Tanner, *Growth at Adolescence*, 2nd ed., Oxford: Blackwell Scientific Publications, 1962.)

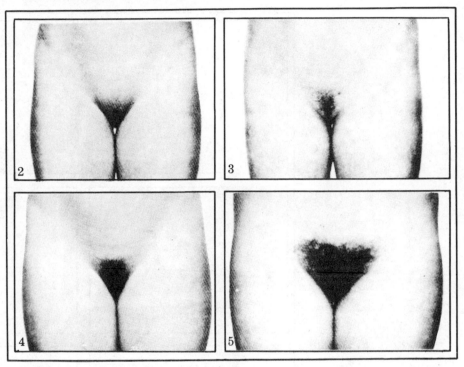

reached stage 4 of breast development. However, approximately 25 percent of girls experience menarche while in B3, and 5 percent do so while in B2 [9]. The adolescent growth spurt for girls typically occurs during B2 or B3; it is exceptionally rare for menarche to occur before the peak growth spurt [5].

The first year after menarche is frequently characterized by irregular menstrual cycles that are anovulatory in nature [12]. However, the very first menstrual cycle—or any subsequent cycle—can be an ovulatory one, so that contraceptive use is required by young adolescents who are coitally active.

Sexual Maturation in Boys

Testicular volume in prepubertal boys is 1 to 3 ml, whereas in adult men testicular volume is 12 to 25 ml; this volume change is almost entirely a reflection of growth during puberty [7]. Similarly, pubertal development is associated with rising levels of testosterone production, which stimulates growth of the male accessory sex organs (the prostate,

Figure 4-3. Stages of male genital
development during puberty. (From
J. M. Tanner, *Growth at Adolescence*,
2nd ed., Oxford: Blackwell Scientific
Publications, 1962.)

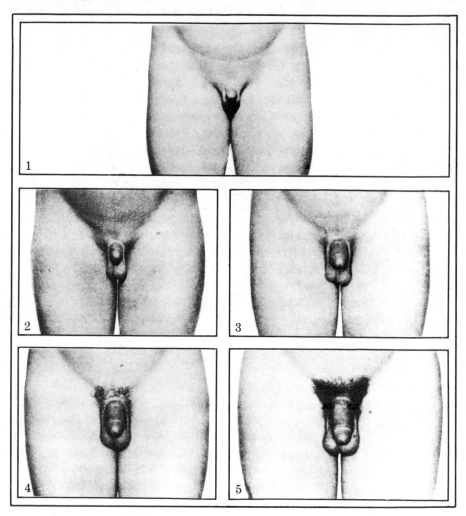

seminal vesicles, and epididymis) and leads to their development of
adult function.

Tanner described five stages in the development of the male genitalia
during puberty (shown in Fig. 4-3):

Stage 1 (G1)   Infantile, existing from birth until pubertal testicular
development begins.

Stage 2 (G2)   Enlargement of the testes and scrotum, with reddening of the scrotum and change in texture of the scrotal skin.

Stage 3 (G3)   Penis increases in length and, to a lesser degree, in circumference; there is additional growth of the testes and scrotum.

Stage 4 (G4)   Further increase in size of the penis and testes; scrotum has darkened; glans penis more fully developed.

Stage 5 (G5)   Adult size and shape of genitalia.

Boys reach G2 at a mean age (± S.D.) of 11.64 ± 1.07 years, and they reach G5 by 14.92 ± 1.10 years, according to Marshall and Tanner [6]. These authors have described a staging sequence for pubic hair development similar to that previously outlined for girls. Boys vary considerably in age at the time of reaching a particular stage, with wide variation also observed between the duration of stages in each individual. The usual sequence of genital development from G2 to G5 spans an average of three years, but in some normal boys it may range from a duration as short as one year to a length of five and one-half years [9]. Most boys experience their maximum adolescent growth spurt during G3.

Other physical changes that occur in boys as a result of increasing testosterone secretion during puberty include development of facial and axillary hair growth and deepening of the voice due to enlargement of the larynx and thickening of the vocal cords. Gynecomastia is a common finding in adolescent boys, probably affecting 40 to 50 percent. This gynecomastia, which is presumably caused by interconversion of testosterone to estrogen, typically regresses within one to two years, but severe cases may persist much longer [13, 14].

Hormonal Correlates of Pubertal Development in Girls

The exact factors regulating the onset of puberty in humans are not known at present. Hansen and coworkers have shown that premenarcheal girls have a pattern of 20- to 40-day cyclicity in their nocturnal excretion of FSH and LH, suggesting that a cyclic hypothalamic-pituitary-ovarian interaction occurs before the onset of menstruation [15]. There is also evidence that puberty in girls is more closely related to weight than to age: It appears that a critical body weight for height must be attained in order for menarche to occur [16–19]. Boyar and coworkers have documented a sleep-associated increase in plasma LH and FSH in prepubertal children prior to the onset of clinically apparent puberty, a phenomenon they have described as the initial central nervous system phase of puberty [20, 21].

Figure 4-4. The changing sensitivity
of hypothalamic regulatory mechanisms involving circulating sex steroid hormones from fetal life to
adulthood. (From M. M. Grumbach,
G. D. Grave, and F. E. Mayer [eds.],
Control of the Onset of Puberty, New
York: John Wiley & Sons, 1974.)

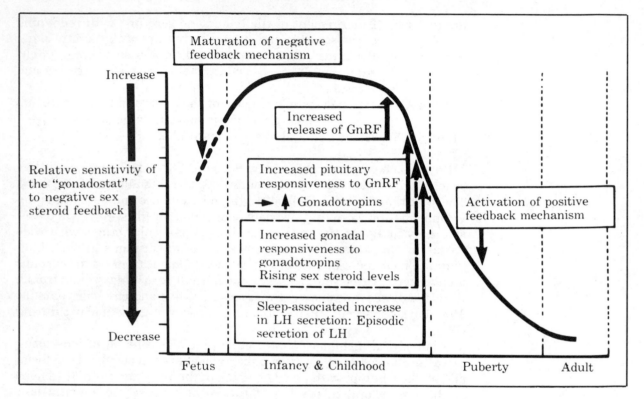

It is likely that in late childhood an interaction between the central
nervous system and the maturing hypothalamus, involving a change in
hypothalamic sensitivity to circulating sex steroid hormones, actually
initiates the onset of puberty [22, 23]. As shown schematically in Figure
4-4, a decreasing sensitivity of the hypothalamic sex steroid receptors
(the "gonadostat") leads sequentially to increased hypothalamic secretion of gonadotropin-releasing factor (GnRF), increased secretion of
FSH and LH by the pituitary, increased gonadal responsiveness to
pituitary stimulation, and modestly increasing sex steroid hormone
levels [24].

The hormonal changes associated with puberty have been documented extensively [12, 20, 25–35]. Pituitary gonadotropin levels (LH
and FSH) are higher in postmenarcheal girls than in those before
menarche [25, 28]. Plasma estrone and estradiol levels rise in girls in a

manner that is well correlated with pubertal stage, but plasma testosterone levels do not increase markedly above prepubertal levels [31–33, 35].

Hormonal Correlates of Pubertal Development in Boys

The initiation of pubertal mechanisms in boys is presumed to follow the general scheme depicted in Figure 4-4 and discussed in the preceding section. A prepubertal sleep-associated increase in LH and testosterone is found in boys approaching the onset of puberty [21, 36], and there is also evidence of increasing testicular responsiveness to gonadotropin stimulation as a sequential step in the onset of puberty [35]. Evidence for the important role of the central nervous system in this process includes the dramatic alterations in the timing of puberty that may occur in association with diseases of the hypothalamus or proximal brain structures.

Hormonal studies of male puberty clearly show that testosterone levels correlate strongly with pubertal development, using the genital growth criteria of Tanner. At stages G1 and G2, boys and girls show little difference in plasma testosterone levels, since these values primarily reflect adrenal androgen synthesis. However, as shown in Figure 4-5, at subsequent stages of genital development a wide difference in circulating testosterone is shown. Gonadotropin levels also increase during puberty, but the changes are of a much smaller magnitude than the tenfold to twentyfold increases typically seen in circulating testosterone levels.

Increasing testosterone secretion during male puberty is responsible for the greater muscle mass that the average late-adolescent boy has in contrast to the late-adolescent girl. The reason for this difference is that testosterone facilitates the incorporation of nitrogen from protein into muscle. Testosterone increases also correlate strongly with increasing testicular volume [37, 38].

Precocious Puberty

Precocious puberty is generally regarded as sexual development occurring before age 8 in girls or before age 10 in boys [39, 40]. Premature sexual and reproductive development, including the appearance of adult secondary sex characteristics, usually occurs in a sequence similar to that of normal puberty, although there are numerous exceptions to this general observation—for example, menarche may sometimes precede breast development. Precocious puberty is also accompanied by acclerated physical growth and development: increased height, increased muscle development, premature epiphyseal closure, and early cessation of growth [39].

Figure 4-5. Plasma testosterone
levels in childhood and adolescence
when plotted by chronological age
(*A*) and by pubertal stages (*B*). (From
Gupta [31].)

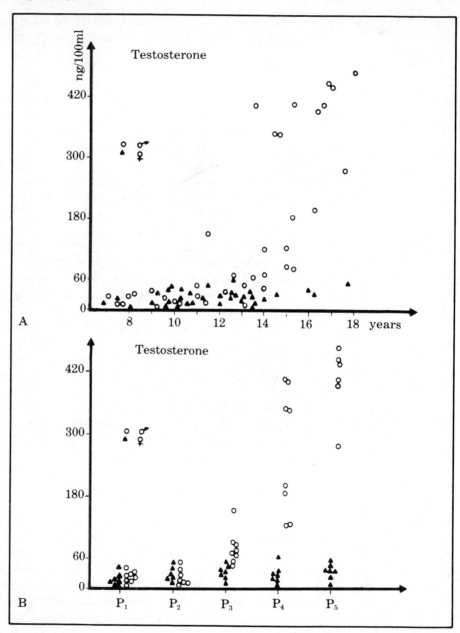

True sexual precocity occurs in a sex ratio of approximately 8 : 1 (girls to boys); 80 percent of the cases in girls and 40 percent of those in boys are of unknown origin [39]. Cerebral lesions account for the majority of nonidiopathic cases; such cases can also occur rarely with juvenile hypothyroidism (see Chap. 6) or with McCune-Albright syndrome, which is also characterized by fibrous bone dysplasia and cutaneous pigmentation and occurs almost exclusively in girls [40]. Treatment of patients with cerebral lesions may require neurosurgical intervention; other patients may be managed by the use of antigonadotropic agents such as medroxyprogesterone acetate or the use of the antiandrogen, cyproterone acetate, an experimental drug discussed in Chapter 13 [41, 42]. Management should also take into account the psychological needs of the affected child and family (siblings as well as parents may be concerned, uncomprehending, and at times very cruel).

Children with precocious puberty will typically be considerably taller than their chronological peers as a result of accelerated skeletal growth. Of course, once their age-mates reach puberty, children with precocious puberty will appear somewhat shorter due to their earlier cessation of growth. As Ehrhardt and Meyer-Bahlburg point out, adults will often give these children more responsibilities than would normally be accorded to someone of their age [43]. The discrepancy between physical appearance and cognitive capabilities or social skill attainment may at times create problems. However, many children with precocious puberty with otherwise normal health may benefit from acceleration in school to allow them to interact with children of a more similar physical age [44]. Sex education should be provided to all children with precocious puberty to give them an understanding of their situation; parents should be made aware of the general observation that precocious puberty does not usually precipitate precocious sexual behavior in either girls or boys [43].

Delayed Puberty

Adolescents who develop much more slowly than their peers from the viewpoint of sexual and physical development are considered to have delayed puberty. Although there is no consensus as to specific ages at which this diagnosis can be made, boys who have no testicular growth by age 14 and who have not experienced a skeletal growth spurt by age 16 may be considered delayed; girls who have not begun breast growth by age 14 or who have not experienced a skeletal growth spurt by age 15 may be considered delayed. If a girl has shown normal physical and sexual development but has not experienced menarche, the diagnosis of delayed puberty does not apply.

The majority of instances of delayed puberty are considered to be constitutional [45]. Other causes include endocrine disorders affecting the hypothalamic-pituitary-gonadal axis (see Chap. 6), hypothyroidism, growth hormone deficiency, chromosomal disorders, or severe chronic illness. It is not presently known if there is any sex difference in the incidence of delayed puberty.

Delayed sexual maturation in girls has not been reported to cause serious psychosocial problems for the majority of affected individuals. Late-maturing girls are much more likely to be well accepted by their peers than are very early-maturing girls, who may be perceived in a threatening way by peers as well as by adults. In contrast, boys with delayed puberty are handicapped in a number of important ways [46]. Their lack of muscle development and short stature creates a gap between their athletic prowess and that of other boys of the same age. Because they are usually shorter than girls in their class and also appear childlike (i.e., no facial hair growth, high-pitched voice), they are handicapped in heterosexual and heterosocial situations; their classmates of both sexes may joke about their size or lack of development, thus making it even more awkward for these boys to begin dating or to attempt sexual interaction. Leadership roles during junior and senior high school years more typically go to early-maturing boys than to boys with delayed adolescence. A long-term study of a group of late-maturing boys found that at age 33 even though differences in size and physique had disappeared, late-maturing boys had lower levels of occupational attainment than did early-maturing boys [47]; another study found that late-maturing boys married at later ages, had fewer children, and earned less money than early-maturing boys [48].

Both boys and girls with delayed puberty may have problems with self-esteem and body-image as a result of the discrepancy in physical appearance between themselves and their friends and classmates. These problems may lead to difficulties in school performance; other areas of behavior may be affected as well, if the adolescent tries to overcompensate for his or her physical shortcomings. Parents may tend to have overprotective postures toward children with delayed puberty, further compounding the difficulties faced by the adolescent.

Adolescent Sexual Behavior

The sexual behavior of contemporary adolescents is the subject of considerable speculation but far less study. It is clear that the incidence of teenage pregnancy has increased and that younger adolescent girls are becoming pregnant in larger numbers; the rising frequency of venereal disease among adolescents is also well known. However, reliable data about patterns of adolescent sexual behavior are not available.

The pubertal adolescent must contend with the combined physical and psychosocial ramifications of growth and development. Although not yet an adult in the legal or economic sense, the adolescent is clearly no longer a child, as becomes quickly apparent as parents, teachers, and peers begin to place greater pressures and expectations on the young teenager. There is a push for the adolescent to develop self-responsibility and independence, but contradictory restrictions are often imposed to limit the dimensions of such development. The teenager is caught in the middle of a seemingly insoluble system; as a result, perhaps, adolescent abuse of drugs and alcohol has reached astonishing levels in the past few years.

The methodological problems involved in doing research about adolescent sexuality create difficulties in interpreting what little is known. Nevertheless, information from several sources [49–56] may be examined. In 1948 Kinsey and his coworkers reported that masturbation was the usual source of the male's first ejaculation, with approximately two-thirds of adolescents reporting this experience [49]. Less frequently, nocturnal ejaculation or coitus was the first source of orgasm. By age 15, 82 percent of boys had masturbated to orgasm, whereas only 8.4 percent had experienced orgasm during heterosexual petting and 38.8 percent had experienced premarital intercourse [49]. In contrast, only 3 percent of the females studied by Kinsey had had coital experience by age 15; by this same age, 20 percent had masturbated to orgasm and 4 percent had experienced orgasm during heterosexual petting [50].

In 1972 Kantner and Zelnick reported that 14 percent of girls had coitus by age 15, 21 percent by age 16, 27 percent by age 17, 37 percent by age 18, and 46 percent by age 19 [51]. In 1973 Sorenson reported that 30 percent of the girls in his sample had experienced intercourse by age 15, and 57 percent were no longer virgins at age 19 [52]. Miller and Simon found that 7 percent of girls between ages 13 and 15 had experienced intercourse, with a corresponding incidence of 9 percent for boys of the same age; for the group aged 16 to 19, 22 percent of females and 21 percent of males reported coital experience [53]. In a second survey encompassing a national probability sample of young unmarried women, conducted in 1976, Zelnick and Kantner found that the prevalence of sexual activity among teenage women had increased by 30 percent above their previous survey performed five years earlier: By age 19, 55 percent of unmarried teenage women had experienced sexual intercourse [54]. Vener and Stewart also found evidence of a trend toward earlier sexual experience for both sexes in their survey of a Michigan community: In 1970, 11 percent of females aged 13 to 15 had had coital experience, but by 1973 the incidence had risen to 17 percent (the corresponding incidence figures for males in the same age group were 25 percent and 33 percent, respectively); for girls aged 16 to 19, the incidence of coitus rose from 25 percent to 33 percent between 1970 and 1973 [55].

Most of the information about age at first intercourse has been obtained through cross-sectional studies, looking simultaneously at adolescents of all ages. In an important investigation of the psychological aspects of the transition from virginity to nonvirginity during adolescence, Jessor and Jessor conducted a four-year longitudinal study of 432 high school students and 205 college students [56]. In their sample, 21 percent of tenth-grade males had experienced intercourse at least once, with increases to 28 and 33 percent in the eleventh and twelfth grades, respectively. Interestingly, a larger fraction of females at each grade level were experienced in intercourse: 26, 40, and 55 percent for tenth, eleventh, and twelfth grades, respectively. Eighty-two percent of males and 85 percent of females were no longer virgins by the fourth year of college. On the basis of detailed assessment of personality, perceived environment (including items about perceptions of parents and friends), and behavior, the Jessors suggested that a transition-proneness may be predictable in adolescents who "tend to have higher values on and expectations for independence, to value and expect achievement less, to be more tolerant of deviance and less religious, to have friends whose views agree less with those of their parents and who influence them more than do their parents, to have parents who disapprove less of deviant behavior and friends who approve more and provide more models for deviant behavior, and finally, to have engaged more in general deviance and less in conventional activity related to church and school" [56].

It is important to realize that chronological age does not determine sexual behavior. Increasing amounts of pubertal hormones may provide the biologic catalyst for the initiation or pursuit of certain behaviors, but there are relevant influences from the socioeconomic, cultural, and religious backgrounds of adolescents that most likely contribute to sexual behavior as well. In addition, it appears that the wide discrepancies noted between adolescent male and female sexual activity more than a quarter of a century ago no longer hold so clearly. For example, although the exact mechanism of change is not yet precisely identified, the advent of the modern contraceptive era has been associated with an increasing participation of teenage girls in coital activity. Similarly, changing attitudes toward female sexuality accompanied by increasing media attention may account for an apparently greater degree of experimentation with masturbation by teenage girls.

Sexual activity during adolescence can take many different directions. Sorenson identifies a variety of reasons for which adolescents may choose to be sexually active: for physical pleasure, as a means of communication, to search for a new experience, as an index of personal maturity, to conform to peers, to challenge parents or society, as reward or punishment, as an escape from loneliness, and as an escape from other pressures [52]. When sexual activity is motivated primarily by negative forces (such as the wish to get even with parents for setting social or behavioral limits such as curfews or rules about alcohol use), the potential for adverse effects may be greater than in most circumstances.

Unfortunately, the literature of psychiatry is replete with warnings that sexual behavior by adolescents may disrupt ego development and psychological maturation [57]. Adolescents who follow through on their sexual feelings are often derogatorily described as "acting out," with the implication that they have fallen prey to impulsive behavior that indicated poorly integrated personality controls. Cross-cultural evidence and clinical acumen both indicate, however, that harmful psychological effects do not generally ensue from responsible adolescent sexual relationships or from casual sexual activity that is uncoercive, as long as adequate contraceptive practices are followed. On the other hand, as Gadpaille has observed, "Unless anyone, no matter what age, engages in sex primarily because of genuine erotic urge and arousal, there is some suggestion that emotional conflict is being expressed" [58].

Problems of
Adolescent
Body-Image and
Sexuality

Adolescents who appear to be physically different from their peers may have problems of body-image that alter their sexual attitudes or behavior. The 16-year-old boy who is quite short in stature may refrain from dating activity; the teenager with severe acne may overcompensate by exaggerating the importance of sexual participation or may avoid heterosexual situations assiduously out of embarrassment; the early adolescent girl with ample breast development may have difficulty in resolving the discrepancy between her own sexual values and practices and the perceptions of her that others may have. Little research has been done to document the importance of body-image problems during adolescence as they relate to sexuality, but it is clear that some adolescents have major feelings of sexual inadequacy because they perceive themselves as unattractive. In some instances, as with the adolescent boy with gynecomastia, sexual orientation or gender identity may be questioned by the teenager who improperly understands the physiologic processes affecting his or her body. This confusion may be influenced by the reactions of peers to perceived physical differences as well. Many boys are worried about the size of their penis, seeing others in locker rooms who seem larger and more developed, but except in rare circumstances in which a microphallus is present, penile size is normal. Girls may worry similarly about the size of their breasts and the timing of their development; it is important to recognize the possibility that poor self-esteem, rather than concerns about one's body, may be the most significant element behind such doubts when they persist over time.

Concerns About Sexual Normality in Adolescence

In trying to understand and become integrated into the society around them, adolescents may experience considerable anxiety when they believe themselves to be very different from their peers or from the world of adults to whom they relate most closely. This general tendency is magnified in the developmental task of recognizing and adapting to one's sexuality during adolescence: Cultural prohibitions toward childhood sexual behavior carry over into the teenage years, and lack of accurate factual knowledge often means that the adolescent's frame of reference for perceiving himself or herself as a sexual being is a matrix comprising primarily myth and misconception. Questions arise concerning the conflict between biologic and cultural demands which frequently are not verbalized because the adolescent is embarrassed to show ignorance or is afraid of the possible answer.

The physician is in a unique position to indicate an awareness of the developmental normality of sexual feelings and behavior during puberty and the postpubertal years and to provide information or counseling about sexuality when it is requested. Needless to say, the physician must be both comfortable and knowledgeable about sexuality for such discussions to have a positive effect on adolescent patients and must recognize the necessity for individualizing answers to suit the needs and circumstances of each adolescent: Broad generalizations may be more confusing than helpful in many cases, whereas at other times a listening, supportive stance alone may be valuable.

Adolescents are often concerned about masturbation, wondering if there are adverse physical or emotional effects, if it is an unusual or abnormal activity, if other people can tell that they have masturbated, and if masturbation will impair their subsequent sexual functioning. Myths about masturbation causing acne, insanity, or sterility still abound and of course have no truth whatsoever. Masturbation is rarely problematic behavior in an adolescent, except when it is done in public or when preoccupation with masturbation is so compulsive that it interferes with other components of life. It appears that masturbatory experience is almost universal among adolescent boys and also occurs in a large majority of adolescent girls, with no evidence indicating that masturbation leads to later difficulties in sexual function. Instead, there is clinical evidence that adolescents who repress their sexual feelings so strongly that they never masturbate may have subsequent difficulty in adapting to adult sexuality and may risk emotional disturbances as well [58]. Guilt about the morality of masturbation is another frequently encountered problem that must be dealt with on an individual basis, taking into consideration the religious background and beliefs of the adolescent.

Adolescents may also be concerned about possible homosexuality. It is common for adolescents to have relatively isolated homosexual experiences, which usually do not indicate a pattern of adult sexual orientation. Adolescents who have major difficulty in heterosexual socialization and avoid dating members of the opposite sex may be afraid that this is "proof" of their homosexual character, a false perception that is frequently reinforced by parental and peer attitudes that mistake the origins of lack of enthusiastic participation in teenage social activities. Boys or girls who, as part of the normal process of achieving autonomy from their parents, form emotional attachments of admiration for other adults of the same sex (for example, a teacher or coach) may be confused by the strength of their feelings and believe them to indicate a homosexual predisposition. Concern about homosexuality may also be mobilized by the common occurrence of impaired sexual function in early attempts at intercourse or lack of arousal during other heterosexual activity—situations in which inexperience, anxiety, embarrassment, and guilt may understandably combine to limit physical response patterns.

Other areas that may cause distress to adolescents are the presence, frequency, and content of sexual fantasies, ambivalence about participation in intercourse, confusion about love, and concerns over sexual adequacy. It is safe to say that adolescents who have completed puberty and are not aware of any sexual fantasies or dreams have either repressed or denied these feelings. Sexual fantasy is not only a reflection of normal biologic forces; it is also a natural response to the largely unavoidable erotic content of books, movies, art, music, and advertisements that surround the adolescent in contemporary society. Fantasy that includes or focuses on types of behavior that might be vilified in real life (for example, rape or incest) is not indicative of psychopathology and may often be a useful safety valve for sexual impulses that are socially objectionable.

Just as some adolescents choose to participate in coital activity, for the reasons previously cited, others decide to refrain from intercourse or are never faced with having to make the decision due to lack of opportunity. Reasons for choosing not to have intercourse include fear of pregnancy or venereal disease, not being in love, wishing to preserve later options, self-perception of lack of psychological readiness, and religious, cultural, or personal values. In addition, adolescent girls may be concerned about losing their reputation or being less acceptable for marriage as a result of premarital intercourse. The adolescent who chooses to refrain from intercourse does not typically refrain from all sexual activity, of course. Teenage boys or girls may find that they are subjected to considerable pressure from their more sexually experienced peers to experiment with intercourse or to demonstrate their maturity. Support in the appropriateness of their personal choice should be offered when such pressures from peers or worries about normality occur.

The prevalence and significance of symptoms of sexual dysfunction during adolescence have not been studied systematically. Certain types of problems would appear to warrant careful, prompt evaluation and treatment—for example, dyspareunia (pain associated with intercourse) and vaginismus (involuntary constriction of the outer third of the vagina with attempts at vaginal penetration)—but the requirements are less clear with other problems. At what point therapeutic intervention should be established for the teenage boy who ejaculates too rapidly or for the adolescent girl who is nonorgasmic cannot be inferred from current knowledge about adult sexual dysfunction. Empirically, it might be surmised that sexual dysfunctions are more easily treated if they are not of long duration. Furthermore, the existence of such problems over a period of years during adolescence and young adulthood might lead to other difficulties, including poor self-esteem, depression, and avoidance of sexual activity. On the other hand, a fairly substantial number of cases in which sexual difficulties are present during adolescence may reflect inexperience, lack of knowledge, anxiety, and psychological immaturity more than anything else. In such circumstances, the problem may resolve itself more or less spontaneously. No definitive recommendation can be offered for such cases, but sex counseling or sex therapy can be considered for those teenagers who appear to have major distress associated with an adolescent problem of sexual functioning.

Teenage Pregnancy

In the United States in 1975, 13,000 babies were born to girls less than 15 years old [59]. Each year, at least one million teenagers become pregnant [60] and approximately 300,000 adolescents obtain abortions [61]. Unwanted teenage pregnancies pose a variety of problems for reasons that are both biomedical and socioeconomic: There are increased maternal and infant health risks associated with teenage pregnancy [62–67] along with a "dismal pattern of lost educational opportunity, unstable family life, poor employability and welfare dependence" [68].

The high number of unwanted teenage pregnancies is primarily attributable to lack of use, or to sporadic use, of contraception. Shah, Zelnick, and Kantner found that 70 percent of 15- to 19-year-old girls did not think they could become pregnant and 30 percent had trouble obtaining contraceptives [69]. That few teenage girls use contraception in their earliest coital exposures is well established [52, 60, 65, 68] and is probably a reflection of several factors, including lack of information about contraception, lack of availability of contraceptives, emotional stigmatization associated with the acknowledgment of sexual intent, and misinformation about reproductive risks [52, 68–75]. However, even teenagers with ready access to contraceptives do not always use them regularly, and teenage girls with unwanted pregnancies often continue to be sporadic in the subsequent use of contraceptives [76–78]. Adolescent boys generally show a lack of interest in contraceptive practices [79–82] that appears to be related to several variables, including (1) aesthetic distaste for condom use and its perceived "artificiality," (2) the disruptive nature of coital withdrawal, (3) lack of perceived responsibility for contraception, (4) misinformation about contraceptive risks, and (5) a cultural and emotional double standard about the male role in reproductive behavior.

Efforts to develop satisfactory programs for the prevention of teenage pregnancy have grown considerably in the last decade [60, 66, 68, 70, 71, 83–85]. The essential features of effective intervention strategies are summarized by Fielding: "sex education that starts early in school, availability of contraception for teenagers without parental knowledge or consent, 'free' (government-supplied) contraception and family-planning counseling, and education to enhance parental understanding of the prevalence of sexual activity among teenagers and of the need for a realistic attitude toward the prevention of pregnancy" [68]. The importance of education and counseling for parents is underscored by the observation from an abortion clinic that "the first two repeaters in our clinic were two 13-year-old girls whose mothers refused to allow them to use a birth control method despite their daughters' insistence that they wanted it" [78].

Attempts to determine which teenage girls are at highest risk for unwanted pregnancy are inconclusive to date [79, 86, 87] but need to be pursued. Health-care providers must play an active role in educating and counseling teenagers in regard to the full dimensions of this problem, but legal obstacles remain in some states to the administration of contraceptive care to minors without the consent of their parents [68]. It is hoped that a combination of forces, including comprehensive health-care delivery and legislative change, can reduce the number of unwanted teenage pregnancies significantly below current epidemic levels.

References

1. Erikson, E. H. *Childhood and Society* (2nd ed.). New York: W. W. Norton, 1963.
2. Winter, J. S. D., and Faiman, C. Serum gonadotropin levels in agonadal children and adults. *Journal of Clinical Endocrinology and Metabolism* 35:561–564, 1972.
3. Johanson, A. Fluctuations of gonadotropin levels in children. *Journal of Clinical Endocrinology and Metabolism* 39:154–159, 1974.
4. Johanson, A. J., Guyda, H., Light, C., Migeon, C. J., and Blizzard, R. M. Serum luteinizing hormone by radioimmunoassay in normal children. *Journal of Pediatrics* 74:416–424, 1969.
5. Marshall, W. A., and Tanner, J. M. Variation in the pattern of pubertal changes in girls. *Archives of Disease in Childhood* 44:291–303, 1969.
6. Marshall, W. A., and Tanner, J. M. Variation in the pattern of pubertal changes in boys. *Archives of Disease in Childhood* 45:13–23, 1970.
7. Marshall, W. A. Growth and sexual maturation in normal puberty. *Clinics in Endocrinology and Metabolism* 4:3–25, 1975.
8. Tanner, J. M. *Growth at Adolescence* (2nd ed.). Oxford: Blackwell Scientific Publications, 1962.
9. Tanner, J. M. Sequence and Tempo in the Somatic Changes in Puberty. In M. M. Grumbach, G. D. Grave, and F. E. Mayer (eds.), *Control of the Onset of Puberty.* New York: John Wiley & Sons, 1974.
10. Zacharias, L., and Wurtman, R. J. Age at menarche: Genetic and environmental influences. *New England Journal of Medicine* 280:868–875, 1969.
11. U.S. Department of Health, Education, and Welfare. *Age at Menarche in*

the United States. DHEW Publication No. (HRA) 74-1615. Washington, D.C.: U.S. Department of Health, Education, and Welfare, 1973. P. 3.

12. Apter, D., Viinikka, L., and Vihko, R. Hormonal pattern of adolescent menstrual cycles. *Journal of Clinical Endocrinology and Metabolism* 47:944–954, 1978.

13. Knorr, D., and Bidlingmaier, F. Gynecomastia in male adolescents. *Clinics in Endocrinology and Metabolism* 4:157–171, 1975.

14. Nydick, M., Bustos, J., Dale, J. H., and Rawson, R. W. Gynecomastia in adolescent boys. *Journal of the American Medical Association* 178:449–454, 1961.

15. Hansen, J. W., Hoffman, H. J., and Ross, G. T. Monthly gonadotropin cycles in premenarcheal girls. *Science* 190:161–163, 1975.

16. Frisch, R. E., and Revelle, R. Height and weight at menarche and a hypothesis of critical body weights and adolescent events. *Science* 169:397–399, 1970.

17. Frisch, R. E., and McArthur, J. W. Menstrual cycles: Fatness as a determinant of minimum weight for height necessary for their maintenance or onset. *Science* 185:949–951, 1974.

18. Frisch, R. E. Fatness and the onset and maintenance of menstrual cycles. *Research in Reproduction* 9(6):1, 1977.

19. Frisch, R. E. Menarche and fatness: Reexamination of the critical body composition hypothesis. *Science* 200:1509–1513, 1978.

20. Boyar, R. M., Wu, R. H. K., Roffwarg, H., Kapen, S., Weitzman, E. D., Hellman, L., and Finkelstein, J. W. Human puberty: 24-hour estradiol patterns in pubertal girls. *Journal of Clinical Endocrinology and Metabolism* 43:1418–1421, 1976.

21. Boyar, R. M., Finkelstein, J. W., Roffwarg, H. P., Kapen, S., and Weitzman, E. D. Synchronization of augmented luteinizing hormone secretion with sleep during puberty. *New England Journal of Medicine* 287:582–586, 1972.

22. Kulin, H. E., Grumbach, M. M., and Kaplan, S. L. Changing sensitivity of the pubertal gonadal hypothalamic feedback mechanism in man. *Science* 166:1012–1013, 1969.

23. Schönberg, D. K. Dynamics of hypothalamic-pituitary function during puberty. *Clinics in Endocrinology and Metabolism* 4:57–88, 1975.

24. Grumbach, M. M., Roth, J. C., Kaplan, S. L., and Kelch, R. P. Hypothalamic-Pituitary Regulation of Puberty in Man: Evidence and Concepts Derived from Clinical Research. In M. M. Grumbach, G. D. Grave, and F. E. Mayer (eds.), *Control of the Onset of Puberty.* New York: John Wiley & Sons, 1974.

25. Sizonenko, P. C., Burr, I. M., Kaplan, S. L., and Grumbach, M. M. Hormonal changes in puberty: II. Correlation of serum luteinizing hormone and follicle stimulating hormone with stages of puberty and bone age in normal girls. *Pediatric Research* 4:36–45, 1970.

26. Jenner, M. R., Kelch, R. P., Kaplan, S. L., and Grumbach, M. M. Hormonal changes in puberty: IV. Plasma estradiol, LH, and FSH in prepubertal children, pubertal females, and in precocious puberty, premature thelarche, hypogonadism, and in a child with a feminizing ovarian tumor. *Journal of Clinical Endocrinology* 34:521–530, 1972.

27. Bidlingmaier, F., Wagner-Barnack, M., Butenandt, O., and Knorr, D.

Plasma estrogens in childhood and puberty under physiologic and pathologic conditions. *Pediatric Research* 7:901–907, 1973.

28. Angsusingha, K., Kenny, F. M., Nankin, H. R., and Taylor, F. H. Unconjugated estrone, estradiol and FSH and LH in prepubertal and pubertal males and females. *Journal of Clinical Endocrinology and Metabolism* 39:63–68, 1974.

29. Gupta, D., Attanasio, A., and Raaf, S. Plasma estrogen and androgen concentrations in children during adolescence. *Journal of Clinical Endocrinology and Metabolism* 40:636–643, 1975.

30. Ducharme, J. -R., Forest, M. G., De Peretti, E., Sempé, M., Collu, R., and Bertrand, J. Plasma adrenal and gonadal sex steroids in human pubertal development. *Journal of Clinical Endocrinology and Metabolism* 42:468–476, 1976.

31. Gupta, D. Changes in the gonadal and adrenal steroid patterns during puberty. *Clinics in Endocrinology and Metabolism* 4:27–56, 1975.

32. Korth-Schutz, S., Levine, L. S., and New, M. I. Serum androgens in normal prepubertal and pubertal children and in children with precocious adrenarche. *Journal of Clinical Endocrinology and Metabolism* 42:117–124, 1976.

33. Lee, P. A., Xenakis, T., Winer, J., and Matsenbaugh, S. Puberty in girls: Correlation of serum levels of gonadotropins, prolactin, androgens, estrogens, and progestins with physical changes. *Journal of Clinical Endocrinology and Metabolism* 43:775–784, 1976.

34. Lee, P. A., Plotnick, L. P., Migeon, C. J., and Kowarski, A. A. Integrated concentrations of follicle stimulating hormone and puberty. *Journal of Clinical Endocrinology and Metabolism* 46:488–490, 1978.

35. Swerdloff, R. S. Physiological control of puberty. *Medical Clinics of North America* 62:351–366, 1978.

36. Judd, H. L., Parker, D. C., and Yen, S. S. C. Sleep–wake patterns of LH and testosterone release in prepubertal boys. *Journal of Clinical Endocrinology and Metabolism* 44:865–869, 1977.

37. Burr, I. M., Sizonenko, P. C., Kaplan, S. L., and Grumbach, M. M. Hormonal changes in puberty: I. Correlation of serum luteinizing hormone with stages of puberty, testicular size, and bone age in normal boys. *Pediatric Research* 4:25–35, 1970.

38. Knorr, D., Bidlingmaier, F., Burenandt, O., Fendel, H., and Ehrt-Wehle, R. Plasma testosterone in male puberty: I. Physiology of plasma testosterone. *Acta Endocrinologica* 75:181–194, 1974.

39. Bierich, J. R. Sexual precocity. *Clinics in Endocrinology and Metabolism* 4:107–142, 1975.

40. Barnes, N. D., Cloutier, M. D., and Hayles, A. B. The Central Nervous System and Precocious Puberty. In M. M. Grumbach, G. D. Grave, and F. E. Mayer (eds.), *Control of the Onset of Puberty*. New York: John Wiley & Sons, 1974.

41. Rager, K., Huenges, R., Gupta, D., and Bierich, J. R. The treatment of precocious puberty with cyproterone acetate. *Acta Endocrinologica* 74:399–408, 1973.

42. Angeli, A., Boccuzzi, G., Bisbocci, D., Fonzo, D., Frajria, R., De Sanctis, C., and Ceresa, F. Effect of cyproterone acetate therapy on gonadotropin

response to synthetic luteinizing hormone-releasing hormone (LRH) in girls with idiopathic precocious puberty. *Journal of Clinical Endocrinology and Metabolism* 42:551–560, 1976.

43. Ehrhardt, A. A., and Meyer-Bahlburg, H. F. L. Psychological correlates of abnormal pubertal development. *Clinics in Endocrinology and Metabolism* 4:207–222, 1975.
44. Money, J. Counseling: Syndromes of Statural Hypoplasia and Hyperplasia, Precocity and Delay. In L. I. Gardner (ed.), *Endocrine and Genetic Diseases of Childhood and Adolescence* (2nd ed.). Philadelphia: W. B. Saunders Co., 1975.
45. Prader, A. Delayed adolescence. *Clinics in Endocrinology and Metabolism* 4:143–155, 1975.
46. Clausen, J. A. The Social Meaning of Differential Physical and Sexual Maturation. In S. E. Dragastin and G. H. Elder, Jr. (eds.), *Adolescence in the Life Cycle*. New York: John Wiley & Sons, 1975.
47. Ames, R. Physical maturing among boys as related to adult social behavior. *California Journal of Educational Research* 8:69–75, 1957.
48. Peskin, H. Pubertal onset and ego functioning. *Journal of Abnormal Psychology* 72:1–15, 1967.
49. Kinsey, A. C., Pomeroy, W. B., and Martin, C. E. *Sexual Behavior in the Human Male*. Philadelphia: W. B. Saunders Co., 1948.
50. Kinsey, A. C., Pomeroy, W. B., Martin, C. E., and Gebhard, P. H. *Sexual Behavior in the Human Female*. Philadelphia: W. B. Saunders Co., 1953.
51. Kantner, J. F., and Zelnick, M. Sexual experience of young unmarried women in the United States. *Family Planning Perspectives* 4:9–18, 1972.
52. Sorenson, R. C. *Adolescent Sexuality in Contemporary America*. New York: World Publishing Co., 1973.
53. Miller, P. Y., and Simon, W. Adolescent sexual behavior: Context and change. *Social Problems* 22:58–76, 1974.
54. Zelnick, M., and Kantner, J. F. Sexual and contraceptive experience of young unmarried women in the United States, 1976 and 1971. *Family Planning Perspectives* 9:55–71, 1977.
55. Vener, A. M., and Stewart, C. S. Adolescent sexual behavior in middle America revisited: 1970–1973. *Journal of Marriage and the Family* 36:728–735, 1974.
56. Jessor, S. L., and Jessor, R. Transition from virginity to nonvirginity among youth: A social-psychological study over time. *Developmental Psychology* 11:473–484, 1975.
57. Mathis, J. L. Adolescent sexuality and societal change. *American Journal of Psychotherapy* 30:433–440, 1976.
58. Gadpaille, W. J. *Cycles of Sex*. New York: Charles Scribner's Sons, 1975.
59. Moore, K. A., and Waite, L. J. Early childbearing and educational attainment. *Family Planning Perspectives* 9:220–225, 1977.
60. Green, C. P., and Potteiger, K. *Teenage Pregnancy: A Major Problem for Minors*. Washington, D.C.: Zero Population Growth, 1977.
61. National Center for Disease Control. *Abortion Surveillance: Annual Summary, 1975*. Atlanta: Center for Disease Control, 1977.
62. Anderson, G. D. Comprehensive management of the pregnant teenager. *Contemporary Ob/Gyn* 7:75–80, 1976.

63. Efiong, E. I., and Banjoko, M. O. Obstetric performance of Nigerian primigradivae aged 16 and under. *British Journal of Obstetrics and Gynaecology* 82:228–233, 1975.

64. Nortman, D. Parental age as a factor in pregnancy outcome. *Reports on Population/Family Planning*, No. 16, August 1974.

65. Hunt, W. B. Adolescent fertility: Risks and consequences. *Population Reports*, Series J, No. 10, July 1976.

66. Andrews, B. F. Problems of teenage mothers, their infants, and influence of family planning. *Pediatric Research* 9:257, 1975.

67. Oppel, W. C. Teen-age births: Some social, psychological, and physical sequelae. *American Journal of Public Health* 61:751–756, 1971.

68. Fielding, J. E. Adolescent pregnancy revisited. *New England Journal of Medicine* 299:893–896, 1978.

69. Shah, F., Zelnick, M., and Kantner, J. F. Unprotected intercourse among unwed teenagers. *Family Planning Perspectives* 7:39–41, 1975.

70. Furstenberg, F. F., Jr. The social consequences of teenage parenthood. *Family Planning Perspectives* 8:148–164, 1976.

71. Jaffe, F. S., and Dryfoos, J. G. Fertility control service for adolescents: Access and utilization. *Family Planning Perspectives* 8:167–175, 1976.

72. Presser, H. B. Guessing and misinformation about pregnancy risk among urban mothers. *Family Planning Perspectives* 9:111–115, 1977.

73. Kantner, J., and Zelnick, M. Contraception and pregnancy: Experience of young unmarried women in the United States. *Family Planning Perspectives* 5:21–35, 1973.

74. Reichelt, P., and Werley, H. Contraception, abortion and venereal disease: Teenagers' knowledge and the effect of education. *Family Planning Perspectives* 7:83–88, 1975.

75. Zelnick, M., and Kantner, J. F. Contraceptive patterns and premarital pregnancy among women aged 15–19 in 1976. *Family Planning Perspectives* 10:135–142, 1978.

76. Dickens, H. O., Mudd, E. H., Garcia, C. -R., Tomar, K., and Wright, D. One hundred pregnant adolescents: Treatment approaches in a university hospital. *American Journal of Public Health* 63:794–800, 1973.

77. Jekel, J. F., Klerman, L. V., and Bancroft, D. R. Factors associated with rapid subsequent pregnancies among school-age mothers. *American Journal of Public Health* 63:769–773, 1973.

78. Selstad, G. M., Evans, J. R., and Welcher, W. H. Predicting contraceptive use in postabortion patients. *American Journal of Public Health* 65:708–713, 1975.

79. Brunswick, A. F. Adolescent health, sex, and fertility. *American Journal of Public Health* 61:711–729, 1971.

80. Finkel, M. I., and Finkel, D. J. Sexual and contraceptive knowledge, attitudes, and behavior of male adolescents. *Family Planning Perspectives* 7:256–260, 1975.

81. Middleman, R. R. Services for males in a family planning program. *American Journal of Public Health* 62:1451–1453, 1972.

82. Scales, P. Males and morals: Teenage contraceptive behavior amid the double standard. *Family Coodinator* 26:211–221, 1977.

83. Arnold, C. B., and Cogswell, B. E. A condom distribution program for

adolescents: The findings of a feasibility study. *American Journal of Public Health* 61:739–750, 1971.

84. Muller, C. Fertility control and the quality of human life. *American Journal of Public Health* 63:519–523, 1973.

85. Zapka, J. M., and Mazur, R. M. Peer sex education training and evaluation. *American Journal of Public Health* 67:450–454, 1977.

86. Abernathy, V. Illegitimate conception among teenagers. *American Journal of Public Health* 64:662–665, 1974.

87. Campbell, B. K., and Barnlund, D. C. Communication style: A clue to unplanned pregnancy. *Medical Care* 15:181–186, 1977.

5   Geriatric Sexuality

It is difficult for many people to think of men and women late in life as having sexual feelings, sexual needs, or sexual relationships. Our cultural stereotypes undoubtedly play a large part in this misperception, which may be reinforced by the common tendency of the young to deny the inevitability of aging. In many instances, circumstances such as impaired health or loss of a spouse create a physical or social basis for abstention from sexual activity, but these problems may also accentuate the continued existence of sexual interest. Health-care professionals are not immune to cultural biases about aging and have done little to deal with the multitude of problems that may arise concerning sexuality and aging. This chapter provides pertinent background about the physiologic and psychosocial aspects of geriatric sexuality in a way that may be applicable to clinical and educational programs dealing with the elderly.

Biologic Aspects of Aging Relevant to Sexuality

Aging in the Woman

The aging process brings about a normal cessation of the fertility and the hormonal cyclicity that typify the second through the fifth decades of a woman's life. From age 30 on, there is most likely a gradual decline in female reproductive capability, brought about by a combination of diminishing fertility [1] and a higher rate of abortion or miscarriage [2, 3]. Likewise, disturbances of the menstrual cycle appear to increase with advancing age [4]. Just as the onset of menses marks the transition from childhood to puberty in reproductive terms, the menopause typically signals an end to procreative status and thus a transition to another phase in the biopsychosocial life cycle. The cessation of menses does not always mean that absolute infertility is inevitable; Snaith and Williamson reported 15 pregnancies that occurred after the menopause was presumably reached and amenorrhea had existed for 18 months or longer [5].

Although there is ample documentation of the fact that age at menarche has decreased significantly over the preceding century, there is no agreement as to any corresponding change in the timing of the menopause. Most studies indicate that the menopause occurs at approximately 48 to 51 years of age in a wide variety of populations, but there is great individual variability, particularly on the earlier side of these ages. Since the life expectancy of women is now greater than 75 years [6], the postmenopausal phase of the life cycle is typically 25 years or longer. Understanding the physiologic concomitants of the postmenopausal years is essential in providing health-care services to this large number of women.

There is considerable confusion, even among researchers, over the exact mechanisms that control the onset of the menopause and characterize the events associated with alterations in hormonal secretion that occur during this period [7]. At present, it appears that diminishing ovarian sensitivity to the pituitary gonadotropins results in decreased production of estrogens, which reduces the frequency of ovulation during menstrual cycles in the years shortly before the menopause. The hypothalamic response to diminished estrogen secretion is to increase the output of gonadotropin-releasing factor, causing increased production of LH and FSH. However, the ovaries are unable to elaborate greater amounts of estrogens even in response to this powerful stimulus, with the result being that a steady state is reached in which circulating levels of gonadotropins are quite high, but ovarian synthesis of estrogens and progesterone is typically lower than the amounts produced during the reproductive years [8]. Eventually, the atrophic ovary entirely ceases production of estrogens, although urinary estrogens and serum estrogens are still present in small amounts, reflecting peripheral conversion of steroid precursors as well as adrenal synthesis of estrogens.

Many women experience the menopause without any recognizable symptoms accompanying these changes in their hormonal environment. On the other hand, there are unquestionably a large number of symptoms that are related to the menopause, including vasomotor instability ("hot flashes"), atrophic changes in the breasts, genitals, and skin, and psychological symptoms ranging from irritability to depression. It is not clear to what extent these symptoms occur because of the changing state of hormone equilibrium, the existence of a relative or absolute estrogen deficiency, or the psychosocial programming that leads many women to expect such symptoms to accompany the menopause [6, 9]. Each of these elements may be considered as an important determinant of at least some of the manifestations of the menopause. Several attempts to correlate postmenopausal symptomatology with plasma estrogen levels or vaginal cytology to determine the maturation index (sometimes used as a means of assessing estrogenic activity) have failed to indicate a correlation [9, 10].

Physiologically, the postmenopausal years may evidence the consequences of chronic estrogen deficiency in several ways. Atrophy of the vaginal mucosa accompanied by diminished vaginal lubrication is probably the most frequently encountered problem. Either or both of these changes may cause dyspareunia, which can be corrected by the use of locally applied estrogen creams or the use of systemic estrogen replacement therapy. Accompanying these changes and most likely to be accentuated in the sexually inactive postmenopausal woman is an actual shrinkage in size of the vaginal barrel and loss of elasticity to the walls of the vagina [11, 12]. Of course, decreased tissue elasticity is one manifestation of aging in general and is observed in many parts of the body [13]. The combination of decreased tissue elasticity and estrogen deficiency accounts for changes that occur in the breast with aging: Breast drooping is primarily a manifestation of mechanical factors, whereas there is an actual decrease in breast tissue mass brought about by lowered estrogen stimulation. (The aging breast does not necessarily lose the capacity for lactation, in spite of the changes just mentioned. In some cultures, perimenopausal women serve as wet-nurses [14].)

Aging does not decrease libido or the capacity to be orgasmic for women if general health is good. In *Human Sexual Response,* Masters and Johnson studied 34 women during their postmenopausal years (ranging in age from 51 to 78). They reported that these women were highly functional from a sexual perspective, although some differences were noted in their sexual response patterns as compared to women during their reproductive years. For example, the vasocongestive increase in breast size typically seen during sexual excitement in younger women was reduced or absent postmenopausally. The sex flush occurred less frequently and assumed a more limited distribution in older women. Generalized myotonia was decreased; the vagina was less expansive during sexual stimulation; and vaginal lubrication was decreased in amount and required a longer time to develop. Masters and Johnson pointed out that such changes were accentuated by lack of regularity in sexual activity during the postmenopausal years. They also noted that painful uterine contractions during orgasm appeared most frequently in aging women [11].

In addition to the effects of estrogen deficiency on the genitals and breasts, it is known that other physiologic systems are also affected. For instance, estrogens prevent the deterioration of protein synthesis in the skin and improve microcirculation in the skin, thus lessening epidermal atrophy and preserving skin elasticity [9]. Estrogens also have been shown to delay or prevent the development of post-menopausal osteoporosis in women [9, 15, 16]; the presumed mechanism of such an effect is by decreasing bone loss rather than by increasing formation of new bone.

In light of these findings, it would appear that estrogen replacement therapy in the symptomatic postmenopausal woman would be a widely accepted clinical practice. However, recent evidence purporting to link estrogen therapy with the development of endometrial or breast cancer has reactivated an argument that has been simmering for many years [6, 9, 15, 17–21]. For reasons beyond the scope of this discussion, it is important to recognize that the statistical inferences or associations that have been reported indicating that women who have used estrogen have a higher risk for the development of endometrial carcinoma are methodologically biased [22] and do not prove causality [9, 15, 22]. Until adequate and carefully controlled prospective studies are conducted, it appears impossible to ascertain the actual facts. The preponderance of current evidence indicates that there is significant clinical value in the use of estrogen replacement therapy for women who are symptomatic during their postmenopausal years. Therefore, in a manner consistent with sound patient management, the risks of endometrial carcinoma should be explained to each woman who might be considered for estrogen replacement therapy, and attention should be given to possible medical contraindications to the use of estrogens, including impaired liver function, porphyria, history of breast cancer or endometrial cancer, and history of thromboembolic disease or cerebrovascular disorders. When estrogen replacement therapy is employed, the lowest effective maintenance dosage should be found for each patient and regular periodic gynecologic examinations should be carried out. There is no present agreement as to whether or not cyclical estrogen replacement therapy is needed in women who have had a hysterectomy, but in postmenopausal women with an intact uterus it is advisable to follow a cyclical dosage pattern.

Aging in the Man

The normal pattern of reproductive aging in the human male is fundamentally different from the pattern that occurs with aging in the female, since there is no finite cessation of fertility correlated with age. Although spermatogenesis diminishes with increasing age from the fifth decade on [23, 24], there is persistent sperm production in men in their ninth decade [25]. Likewise, although there is a gradual reduction in circulating levels of testosterone [26–29] from about age 60 onward (see Fig. 5-1), there is usually not as pronounced a decrease in sex steroid hormone levels in men as in women. However, there is an even greater decrease in the amount of free testosterone in circulation (presumably the pool of hormone that is directly available for tissue uptake), because there is a concomitant progressive rise in the concen-

Figure 5-1. Male serum testosterone
levels in association with aging.

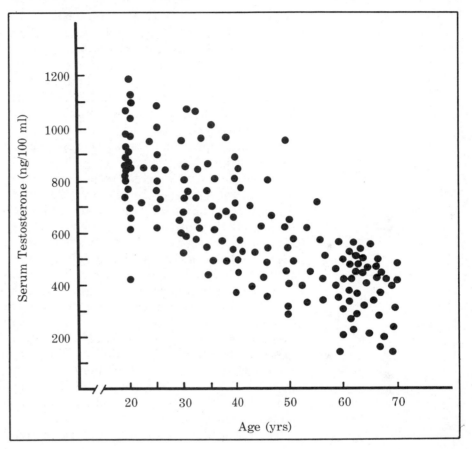

tration of sex steroid-binding globulin after age 50 [29]. Similarly,
age-related changes in pituitary gonadotropins show a gradually increasing pattern after age 40 [30].

A small subgroup of men aged 60 or older manifest a syndrome that
may be called the male climacteric. This condition is characterized by
the following features, which appear in variable combinations: listlessness; weight loss or poor appetite, or both; depressed libido, usually
accompanied by loss of potency; impaired ability to concentrate; weakness and easy fatigability; and irritability. Typically, men with the male
climacteric syndrome exhibit positive findings in at least four of these
categories. Needless to say, these symptoms are primarily nonspecific

and could be attributable to such diverse etiologies as depression, severe chronic anemia, or a malignancy of the gastrointestinal tract. For this reason, in order to establish accurately the diagnosis of the male climacteric it is necessary to find a markedly subnormal plasma testosterone level (below 325 ng per 100 ml) *and* to see remission of symptoms within two months of the institution of testosterone replacement therapy. If the testosterone level is not low or if a man meeting the symptom checklist criteria with a low testosterone level does not show significant improvement with hormone replacement, a careful evaluation must be carried out.

The physiology of sexual response is altered in aging men as compared to younger men in several different ways, as demonstrated by Masters and Johnson by direct laboratory observation [11]. It typically requires both a longer time and more direct genital stimulation for the aging male to achieve erection; furthermore, there is a modest decrease in the firmness of the erection generally found in men over the age of 60 as compared to younger men. The intensity of the ejaculatory experience is usually diminished in aging men, which may partially correspond to the reduced volume of the ejaculate and may also reflect changes in the prostate gland and nerve supply to the genital area. There is usually less of a physical need to ejaculate; many men find that in their sixties, seventies, and eighties, sexual activity can be both stimulating and satisfying without ejaculating at each coital opportunity. Finally, the refractory period—the time interval after ejaculation, when the male is physiologically unable to ejaculate again—tends to lengthen with increasing age.

The effect of disorders of the prostate gland on sexual functioning is discussed in Chapter 9.

Sexual Behavior in the Elderly

Only limited behavioral data regarding sexuality in aging men and women are currently available. There is some disagreement in the findings reported by Kinsey and his colleagues [31, 32], Masters and Johnson [11, 33], Pfeiffer and coworkers [34–38], and Martin [39], but such points of divergence may reflect the different populations studied by these researchers as well as differences that are primarily intergenerational in nature.

Kinsey, Pomeroy, Martin, and Gebhard reported that the menopause had little direct effect on the sexual response of the human female. Although both the surgically induced and natural menopause were associated with decreased levels of sexual activity, it was felt that this decrease was primarily related to the male spouse's declining interest in sex [32]. Kinsey's data indicated that frequency of sexual activity in the male begins to decrease in the late teenage years or early twenties and declines steadily into old age [31]. In contrast, according to these workers, a less prominent decline is seen in female sexual activity with aging [32].

Pfeiffer and coworkers studied 261 white men and 241 white women between the ages of 45 and 71 from the middle and upper socioeconomic classes of a southeastern state [36, 37]. They found that more than 75 percent of men aged 61 to 71 were currently engaging in coital activity with a frequency of once a month or more; 37 percent of men aged 61 to 65 and 28 percent of men aged 66 to 71 had intercourse on at least a once-a-week basis. In contrast, they reported that 61 percent of women aged 61 to 65 and 73 percent of women between the ages of 66 and 71 were not participating in coitus. In their overall sample, there was a corresponding disparity in current levels of sexual interest between men and women: Although only 6 percent of men indicated no current interest in sex, 33 percent of women stated that they had no sexual desire. In the age range of 66 to 71 the difference was even more dramatic, with 50 percent of the women stating they had no sexual interest, whereas only 10 percent of the men described themselves in this category.

Among the subjects who had stopped having intercourse, women primarily attributed the reason for this cessation to their husbands (36 percent cited death of their spouse as the primary reason, 20 percent believed that their husband's illness was the principal factor, 12 percent cited divorce or separation, and 22 percent believed that impotence or loss of interest in sex by their husband accounted for the cessation of intercourse). Men, on the other hand, primarily attributed the cessation of sexual activity to themselves, with 40 percent citing impotence as the major problem, 17 percent indicating that their own illness was the reason, and 14 percent attributing the cessation to their own loss of sexual interest [36].

The very different picture of sexuality in the aging woman that is described by Pfeiffer and colleagues as compared to the reports of Kinsey [32] and Masters and Johnson [11, 33] must be interpreted cautiously. Methodological differences in these studies include the fact that Pfeiffer's data were obtained by a written questionnaire with only a small number of items inquiring about sexuality, whereas Kinsey and Masters and Johnson employed in-depth personal interviews, which are likely to yield more reliable and detailed information. The differences may also be attributable to peculiarities of the sample that Pfeiffer and coworkers selected for study, particularly the fact that their subjects were "non-metropolitan residents of one of the southeastern states of the U.S." [37], whereas Kinsey's sample was national and Masters and Johnson's study population was regional and more metropolitan in nature.

Masters and Johnson [11] reported interviews with 152 women between the ages of 51 and 80. In addition to their biologic findings (summarized in the preceding section), they emphasized the psychic component of aging:

It has become increasingly evident that the psyche plays a part at least equal to, if not greater than, that of an unbalanced endocrine system in determining the sex drive of women during the postmenopausal period of their lives. If endocrine factors alone were responsible for sexual behavior in postmenopausal women (whether menopause occurs by surgical or natural means), there should be a relatively uniform response to the physiologic diminution and ultimate withdrawal of the sex hormones. However, there is no established reaction pattern to sex-steroid withdrawal [11].

These workers also noted that many women became more interested in sex postmenopausally. This interest may result in part from a lack of concern about pregnancy; Masters and Johnson observed that in future generations of women who will have had reliable contraceptives available during their reproductive years, this phenomenon may no longer continue to be of major importance. They also noted that since most problems associated with child-rearing are likely to have ended by the menopausal years, some women may seek new outlets for the attention and energy that they previously devoted to mothering. Finally, these authors cited "the Victorian concept that older women should have no innate interest in any form of sexual activity" as a cultural bias that combines with present sociologic patterns to make continued sexual activity with a partner more difficult for older women who are widows or whose husbands are physically incapacitated.

Martin [39] has recently presented new data that confirm the basic findings of Kinsey and coworkers from three decades earlier. Analyzing information gathered from 628 men between the ages of 20 and 95, he found that coital activity decreased during each five-year interval after age 34, with weekly coital frequency dropping from 2.2 between ages 30 and 34 to 0.7 at ages 60 to 64, 0.4 from ages 65 to 74, and 0.3 at ages 75 to 79. Martin points out that these statistics may represent optimum rates of sexual functioning for males in their middle and later years because his sample was made up primarily of men in good health with financial security and stable marital patterns. His data also substantiate Kinsey's findings and those of Masters and Johnson indicating that coital frequency in early marriage and the overall quantity of sexual activity between age 20 and age 40 correlate significantly with frequency patterns of sexual activity during aging.

Clinical Considerations It is important to recognize that there is great diversity among aging persons with respect to their sexual values, sexual interest, and sexual capabilities. Although it is certainly true that sexual interest and capability can be maintained into the seventh, eighth, and ninth decades of life if a person enjoys a reasonable state of health and the availability of an interested and interesting partner, it is also necessary to examine conditions in which aging sexuality may be altered. Such situations fall primarily into the following categories: general sexual disinterest, sexual boredom, impaired physical sexuality, cultural inhibition, and attrition by disuse.

General sexual disinterest reflects a situation in which attitudes toward sex that were formulated many years earlier in the life cycle accorded only marginal importance to the sexual aspect of a relationship. With advancing years, sex is seen as an unnecessary indulgence, an aesthetically unappealing activity, or a meaningless function since it no longer has reproductive potential. People in this category often evidenced little enthusiasm for sex in their younger years and report that their sexual relationships were neither physically nor emotionally satisfying. At times, the claim of general disinterest in sex is only a coverup for anxiety about sexual inadequacy or accommodation to disinterest or dysfunction by a partner.

Sexual boredom has not been adequately studied. It is interesting to speculate as to whether the declining rates of sexual activity that are assumed to be due to aging alone are not in part attributable to the lack of innovation or exploration in sexual practices that seems to affect many long-term relationships. Even when people realize that boredom is a significant factor in their sex lives, they infrequently institute changes in the sexual habits they have developed in areas such as time, place, or types of sexual activity (including the use of different positions for intercourse, variation of sources of erotic stimulus, or change in sex-role patterns). Boredom may combine with other elements of aging such as diminished sense of self-esteem, cultural inhibitions, or changes in health status to lead to sexual dysfunction in either men or women.

Impairments of a physical nature, discussed at length in subsequent chapters in this text, frequently disrupt sexual capability by either direct or indirect means. Alterations in blood flow to the genitals or disturbance of pelvic innervation are obvious examples of direct suppression of sexual function. More commonly encountered problems of chronic illness, such as fatigue or shortness of breath, also set limitations on the possible range of sexual functioning. In addition to the actual physical impairment, patients' reactions to their altered health status play a central role in determining what, if any, changes occur in their sexual lives. Since physicians infrequently offer constructive suggestions concerning sexual functioning to geriatric patients with health problems, the assumption is often made by patients and their spouses that sexual activity should be avoided or is likely to be problematic. The actual fact is that individualized recommendations, taking into account the physical limitations and personal preferences of patients, can often facilitate a gratifying return to or continuation of sexual participation.

Cultural attitudes that denigrate the aged and glamorize the vitality of an idealized concept of youth, health, and physical attractiveness are so prevalent that it is no wonder many aging individuals feel that it is abnormal to express sexual needs. People who are sensitive to these cultural pressures may feel guilty or embarrassed about experiencing sexual excitation. In some instances, the impact of cultural dictates is so strong that married couples in their geriatric years avoid sexual contact in order to preserve their conformity to imagined normative behavior. This is problematic in many ways, not the least of which is that opportunities for exchange of affection and intimacy are likely to be lessened if sexual contact is omitted in any and all forms. Fortunately, a shift toward a greater degree of openness and accuracy in discussing sexuality and aging has already begun and may be expected to have a subsequent effect on sexual behavior that has previously been limited by such cultural misperceptions.

One of the most critical variables in regard to the maintenance of sexual functioning during aging is the fact that prolonged abstention from sexual activity imposes a considerably greater physiologic handicap than would be true at younger ages. The instances of sexual attrition due to atrophy from disuse ("use it or lose it") are encountered frequently in the geriatric years. The aging woman who abstains from sexual intercourse experiences a greater degree of shrinkage in the size of her vagina than does a woman of the same age who has continued sexual activity [11]; the male in a similar situation of prolonged abstention often finds that with an attempted return to sexual activity he is unable to have erections. Although masturbation may help to maintain the function of vaginal lubrication, it does not provide sufficient opposition to the effects of aging on vaginal size or facility of erection [11]. The principle underlying the concept of disuse atrophy is not unique to sexual functioning, by any means—it applies in many physiologic systems. The point to keep in mind is simply that the effects of disuse are magnified and dramatized in the context of the aging person.

In addition to the general categories considered above that may contribute to sexual distress during the geriatric years, attention should be directed to the lack of preparation that our culture provides for aging. As a result, many people are surprised by the gradual alterations in sexual functioning that normally occur with aging, with the result that these relatively minor changes are taken as evidence that loss of sexual capability is imminent. The man who at age 65 finds that it takes longer to attain an erection may attribute this change to failing potency, whereas it is simply a physiologic change of aging no more or less surprising than the fact that he probably does not have the same physical strength that he had at age 25. A woman who observes that her husband does not ejaculate at each coital opportunity and considers this a reflection of diminishing attractiveness or responsiveness on her part is not informed about the natural sequence of sexual physiology associated with aging. Similarly, the man who infers that diminished vaginal lubrication by his partner indicates that she is less aroused or less interested in sex is making an erroneous assumption based on false expectations for indefinite preservation of sexual function in a manner identical to early adult patterns. Brief preventive counseling for men and women during their forties or fifties could be expected to alter significantly the number of persons who eventually experience sexual difficulty during their geriatric years because of lack of adequate information and unrealistic expectations.

There is also a discomfiting tendency to equate sexual activity with coital activity. The emotional needs of the aging individual—retaining a sense of identity and self-worth and combating loneliness, for example—may be quite fully met by sexual activity that does not always or typically lead to intercourse. The need to hold and to be held, the need to relate to another person, the need to express feelings and be the recipient of others' communicated feelings, neither atrophies nor ends with aging.

Before concluding this chapter, mention must be made of one other aspect of sexuality in the geriatric years. Many of our elderly are placed in nursing homes for a variety of reasons ranging from economic to medical to psychological. In few such institutions are there sanctioned opportunities for privacy for sexual purposes, yet it would be foolish to imagine that people's sexual needs are ended by their placement in such homes [40]. Wasow and Loeb noted that residents in nursing homes generally believe that sexual activity is appropriate for persons in their situation but "most of them were not currently personally involved because of the lack of opportunity" [41]. These authors go on to say:

To be old is to be sexually oppressed. The old values inhibit, then the younger generations disapprove, and finally society sets up many formal barriers to accessibility of sexual partners. Sexual behavior for the aged, though not physiologically impossible nor affectionately dismissible, is culturally and psychologically restricted. The news should be spread around that sexuality for the aged is a good thing, for those who want it.

Although economic and political considerations may create difficulties in altering such long-standing policies, it is interesting to note that social and sexual isolation has changed significantly at university dormitories throughout the nation—perhaps the time is ripe as well for reevaluation of institutions that care for the elderly in regard to lessening current restrictive practices.

References

1. Talbert, G. B.   Effect of maternal age on reproductive capacity. *American Journal of Obstetrics and Gynecology* 102:451–477, 1968.
2. Francis, W. J. A.   Reproduction at menarche and menopause in women. *Journal of Reproduction and Fertility* [Suppl.] 12:89–98, 1970.
3. Woolf, C. M.   Stillbirths and parental age. *Obstetrics and Gynecology* 26:1–8, 1965.
4. Treloar, A. E., Boynton, R. E., Benn, B. G., and Brown, B. W.   Variation of the human menstrual cycle through reproductive life. *International Journal of Fertility* 12:77–126, 1967.
5. Snaith, L., and Williamson, M.   Pregnancy after the menopause. *Journal of Obstetrics and Gynaecology of the British Commonwealth* 54:496–498, 1947.
6. Rogers, J.   Estrogens in the menopause and postmenopause. *New England Journal of Medicine* 280:364–367, 1969.
7. Sherman, B. M., West, J. H., and Korenman, S. G.   The menopausal transition: Analysis of LH, FSH, estradiol, and progesterone concentrations during menstrual cycles of older women. *Journal of Clinical Endocrinology and Metabolism* 42:629–636, 1976.
8. Greenblatt, R. B., College, M. L., and Mahesh, V. B.   Ovarian and adrenal steroid production in the postmenopausal woman. *Obstetrics and Gynecology* 47:383–387, 1976.
9. Van Keep, P. A., Greenblatt, R. B., and Albeaux-Fernet, M.   *Consensus on Menopause Research.* Baltimore: University Park Press, 1976.

10. Stone, S. C., Mickal, A., and Rye, P. H. Postmenopausal symptomatology, maturation index, and plasma estrogen levels. *Obstetrics and Gynecology* 45:625–627, 1975.
11. Masters, W. H., and Johnson, V. E. *Human Sexual Response*. Boston: Little, Brown and Co., 1966.
12. Lang, W. R., and Aponte, G. E. Gross and microscopic anatomy of the aged female reproductive organs. *Clinical Obstetrics and Gynecology* 10:454–465, 1967.
13. Gutman, E., and Hanzlikova, V. *Age Changes in the Neuromuscular System*. Bristol, England: Scientechnica Ltd., 1972.
14. Slome, C. Nonpuerperal lactation in grandmothers. *Journal of Pediatrics* 49:550–552, 1956.
15. Shoemaker, E. S., Forney, J. P., and MacDonald, P. C. Estrogen treatment of postmenopausal women: Benefits and risks. *Journal of the American Medical Association* 238:1524–1530, 1977.
16. Recker, R. R., Saville, P. D., and Heany, R. P. Effect of estrogens and calcium carbonate on bone loss in postmenopausal women. *Annals of Internal Medicine* 87:649–655, 1977.
17. Ryan, K. J. Cancer risk and estrogen use in the menopause. *New England Journal of Medicine* 293:1199–1200, 1975.
18. Ziel, H. K., and Kinkle, W. D. Increased risk of endometrial carcinoma among users of conjugated estrogens. *New England Journal of Medicine* 293:1167–1170, 1975.
19. Weiss, N. S., Szekely, D. R., and Austin, D. F. Increasing incidence of endometrial cancer in the United States. *New England Journal of Medicine* 294:1259–1262, 1976.
20. Mack, T. M., Pike, M. C., Henderson, B. E., Pfeffer, R. I., Gerkins, V. R., Arthur, M., and Brown, S. E. Estrogens and endometrial cancer in a retirement community. *New England Journal of Medicine* 294:1262–1267, 1976.
21. Smith, D. C., Prentice, R., Thompson, D. J., and Hermann, W. L. Association of exogenous estrogen and endometrial carcinoma. *New England Journal of Medicine* 293:1164–1167, 1975.
22. Greenblatt, R. B., and Stoddard, L. D. The estrogen-cancer controversy. *Journal of the American Geriatrics Society* 26:1–8, 1978.
23. MacLeod, J., and Gold, R. Z. The male factor in fertility and infertility: VII. Semen quality in relation to age and sexual activity. *Fertility and Sterility* 4:194–209, 1953.
24. Sasano, N., and Ichijo, S. Vascular patterns of the human testis with special reference to its senile changes. *Tohoky Journal of Experimental Medicine* 99:265–272, 1969.
25. Talbert, G. B. Aging of the Reproductive System. In C. E. Finch and L. Hayflick (eds.), *Handbook of the Biology of Aging*. New York: Van Nostrand Reinhold, 1977.
26. Vermeulen, A., and Verdonck, L. Radioimmunoassay of 17β-hydroxy-5α-androstan-3-one, 4-androstene-3, 17-dione, dehydroepiandrosterone, 17-hydroxyprogesterone and progesterone and its application to human male plasma. *Journal of Steroid Biochemistry* 7:1–10, 1976.

27. Lewis, J. G., Ghanadian, R., and Chisholm, G. D. Serum 5α-dihydrotes-testosterone and testosterone changes with age in men. *Acta Endocrinologica* 82:444–448, 1976.

28. Vermeulen, A., Rubens, R., and Verdonck, L. Testosterone secretion and metabolism in male senescence. *Journal of Clinical Endocrinology and Metabolism* 34:730–735, 1972.

29. Stearns, E. L., MacDonnell, J. A., Kaufman, B. J., Padua, R., Lucman, T. S., Winter, J. S. D., and Faiman, C. Declining testicular function with age: Hormonal and clinical correlates. *American Journal of Medicine* 57:761–766, 1974.

30. Isurugi, K., Fukutani, K., Takayasu, H., Wakabayashi, K., and Tamaoki, B. Age-related changes in serum luteinizing hormone (LH) and follicle-stimulating hormone (FSH) levels in normal men. *Journal of Clinical Endocrinology and Metabolism* 39:955–957, 1974.

31. Kinsey, A. C., Pomeroy, W. B., and Martin, C. E. *Sexual Behavior in the Human Male.* Philadelphia: W. B. Saunders Co., 1948.

32. Kinsey, A. C., Pomeroy, W. B., Martin, C. E., and Gebhard, P. H. *Sexual Behavior in the Human Female.* Philadelphia: W. B. Saunders Co., 1953.

33. Masters, W. H., and Johnson, V. E. *Human Sexual Inadequacy.* Boston: Little, Brown and Co., 1970.

34. Pfeiffer, E., Verwoerdt, A., and Wang, H. -S. Sexual behavior in aged men and women: I. Observations on 254 community volunteers. *Archives of General Psychiatry* 19:753–758, 1968.

35. Pfeiffer, E., Verwoerdt, A., and Wang, H. -S. The natural history of sexual behavior in a biologically advantaged group of aged individuals. *Journal of Gerontology* 24:193–198, 1969.

36. Pfeiffer, E., Verwoerdt, A., and Davis, G. C. Sexual behavior in middle life. *American Journal of Psychiatry* 128:1262–1267, 1972.

37. Pfeiffer, E., and Davis, G. C. Determinants of sexual behavior in middle and old age. *Journal of the American Geriatrics Society* 20:151–158, 1972.

38. Palmore, E. (ed.). *Normal Aging II.* Durham, N. C.: Duke University Press, 1974.

39. Martin, C. E. Sexual Activity in the Ageing Male. In J. Money and H. Musaph (eds.), *Handbook of Sexology.* New York: Elsevier/North Holland Biomedical Press, 1977. Pp. 813–824.

40. Comfort, A. Sexuality in old age. *Journal of the American Geriatrics Society* 22:440–442, 1974.

41. Wasow, M., and Loeb, M. B. Sexuality in nursing homes. *Journal of the American Geriatrics Society* 27:73–79, 1979.

6 Endocrine Factors in Sexual Dysfunction

The science of endocrinology has changed rapidly in the last decade as the availability of new laboratory techniques for the measurement and isolation of a wide range of hormones and neurotransmitters has increased general knowledge of normal physiologic regulatory dynamics and the pathophysiology underlying endocrine disorders. Despite these technical advances, traditional textbooks of endocrinology devote little attention to the sexual consequences of endocrine disease. This is surprising in view of the fact that endocrine causes are found quite frequently among the organic conditions producing sexual problems, as clinicians quickly realize who encounter patients with diabetes, thyroid dysfunction, pituitary lesions, and gonadal disorders. Thus, the primary objective of this chapter is to provide a cohesive discussion of the spectrum of sexual difficulties seen in association with endocrine problems.

Hypogonadism

Male Hypogonadism

Moderate to severe impairment of testicular function leads to decreased production of testosterone, faulty spermatogenesis, or both. A variety of disorders may result in hypogonadism, including conditions that affect the testis indirectly by exerting a principal action on the hypothalamus or pituitary. Generally, conditions that cause such secondary hypogonadism are marked by decreased levels of LH, FSH, or both gonadotropins and are therefore grouped under the term *hypogonadotropic hypogonadism*. In contrast, when the functional integrity of the hypothalamus and pituitary is intact, the normal response to diminished testicular function is increased secretion of gonadotropins, leading to a state known as *hypergonadotropic hypogonadism*. Examples of male hypogonadism are shown in the following lists:

Hypergonadotropic Hypogonadism	*Hypogonadotropic Hypogonadism*
Klinefelter's syndrome	Kallmann's syndrome
Anorchism	Isolated FSH deficiency
Male Turner's syndrome	Isolated LH deficiency
Orchitis (mumps, gonorrhea)	Hypopituitarism
Sequelae of irradiation	Hemochromatosis
Myotonic dystrophy	Suprasellar tumors
	Prader-Willi syndrome
	Delayed puberty

Figure 6-1. Three men with Klinefelter's syndrome. The patient in (B) shows mild gynecomastia; a testicular biopsy from this patient, shown in (C), reveals a severe degree of hyalinization of the seminiferous tubules and Leydig cell hyperplasia, an uncharacteristic feature. (From M. M. Grumbach and J. J. Van Wyk, Disorders of Sex Differentiation, in R. H. Williams [ed.], *Textbook of Endocrinology*, 5th ed., Philadelphia: W. B. Saunders Co., 1974.)

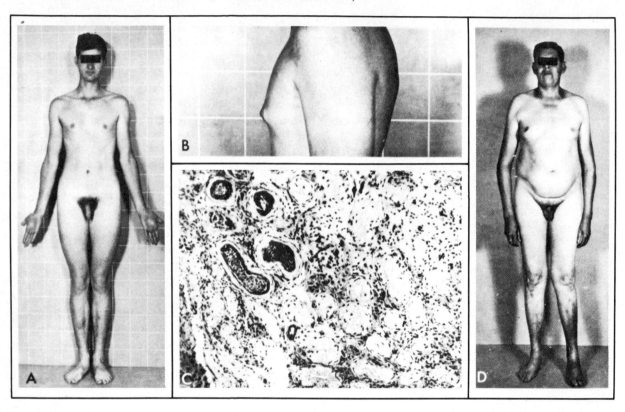

Klinefelter's Syndrome. Klinefelter's syndrome is usually the result of an abnormal 47,XXY chromosome pattern, although many variations of the chromosomal makeup may be found. The classic picture is that of a tall person with long limbs (sitting height is usually less than half of the standing height), poor muscle development, gynecomastia, sparse facial and body hair, and small, firm testes (Fig. 6-1) [1–4]. Testosterone levels are usually subnormal (80 percent of cases) [5, 6], and infertility with azoospermia is the rule. Microscopic examination of the testis usually shows cessation or severe disruption of spermatogenesis, with fibrosis and hyalinization of the seminiferous tubules and abnormal architecture of the Leydig cells. Alterations in testicular histology have been found prepubertally in boys with Klinefelter's syndrome, and reduced numbers of spermatogonia are present from the neonatal period on [6]. Rarely, a pure XXY karyotype in peripheral blood leukocytes may be associated with spermatogenesis [7–9], but this picture is more likely to be seen in mosaic forms of the disorder. Mosaic patients show a greater degree of variability in the physical features of Klinefelter's syndrome, as well.

In those men with Klinefelter's syndrome and normal testosterone levels, LH concentrations are normal but FSH is almost invariably elevated. In most men with Klinefelter's syndrome, however, elevated levels of both LH and FSH are typically seen [6, 10]. When testosterone levels are normal or near normal in men with Klinefelter's syndrome, sexual functioning is often not impaired. More usually, though, men with Klinefelter's syndrome have low sex drive and varying degrees of impotence.

This disorder occurs in approximately 1 in 500 live male births [11], but the diagnosis is rarely made until after childhood. A higher frequency of this disorder is found in mental institutions, and there is generally agreed to be an increased rate of both mental retardation and behavioral disturbances in these men. Patients with Klinefelter's syndrome may present as young adults for evaluation of infertility or sexual dysfunction. One report found that 20 percent of adult men with azoospermia had chromatin-positive Klinefelter's syndrome [12], although in our experience the frequency appears to be less than 10 percent. Patients with Klinefelter's syndrome may also be seen in late adolescence with a problem of delayed sexual maturation. In any case, the diagnosis is made by detecting an extra Barr body on buccal smear or an extra X chromosome on formal karyotyping.

The infertility associated with Klinefelter's syndrome is irreversible, but the low libido and impotence will usually respond promptly to androgen replacement therapy when a testosterone deficiency is present. A dose of 300 to 400 mg of testosterone cypionate or its equivalent given by intramuscular injection on a monthly basis is usually effective. Becker found that facial and body hair increased, musculature improved, body contour became more masculine, and erections and ejaculations improved in 105 adults with Klinefelter's syndrome treated with long-term testosterone administration [13]. Since there is an increased frequency of diabetes mellitus in men with Klinefelter's syndrome [2, 6], failure of impotence to ameliorate despite increasing libido during testosterone therapy should lead to evaluation of glucose tolerance.

Testosterone replacement may produce behavioral changes beyond the area of sexuality alone in men with Klinefelter's syndrome, particularly in those whose prior behavior patterns were marked by a general motif of passivity. The induction of a greater element of assertive or aggressive behavior or both in such a situation may be striking; in light of this possibility, it is wise to discuss the types of changes that may occur with the spouse as well as with the patient, and to titrate the testosterone replacement schedule carefully to a dosage level that will lead to satisfactory sexual function without untoward behavioral consequences. When counseling is undertaken in such situations, it is helpful to include an endocrinologist as a consultant in a team approach.

Conditions of Male Pseudohermaphroditism. The disorders characterized by male pseudohermaphroditism, which range from the syndrome of testicular feminization to other manifestations of defective androgen receptors, biochemical abnormalities in the synthesis or conversion of testosterone, and absence of the müllerian duct-inhibiting factor, are discussed in Chapter 2. A recent report suggests that androgen insensitivity may be present in men with normal phenotypic development [14]. Three men with severe oligospermia or azoospermia were found to have elevated circulating levels of testosterone and LH, accompanied by reduced androgen-binding capacity in the fibroblasts of the genital skin, raising the possibility that partial androgen resistance may contribute to infertility in otherwise normal men. It is thus apparent that defects in the action of androgen may be expressed quite variably, with a wide spectrum of clinical consequences.

Anorchism. Congenital absence of the testes is a rare condition that may occur as a result of prenatal testicular torsion. Acquired (functional) anorchism may result from surgery, trauma, or infection, but often the etiology is unknown. In all instances, puberty fails to develop, sexual infantilism persists, and somatic growth may be somewhat stunted. Sex chromosome patterns show a normal XY karyotype; LH and FSH are markedly elevated by late adolescence or early adulthood. Since testosterone production occurs only in the adrenal cortex, circulating levels of testosterone are extremely low. Testosterone secretion does not increase with exogenous stimulation, and laparotomy reveals no testicular tissue either in the scrotum, in other sites intra-abdominally, or along the course of embryologic migration.

In one series of 21 cases of anorchism, 16 adolescents received testosterone replacement therapy beginning at a mean age of 13.6 years [15]. This therapy produced a normal pubertal growth spurt, normal de-

Figure 6-2. Normal and anorchic
twin brothers at (A) 12.5 years of age
and (B) 17.4 years (after the anorchic
twin had received testosterone therapy for several years). (From
Aynsley-Green, Zachmann, Illig,
Rampini, and Prader [15].)

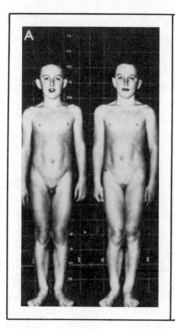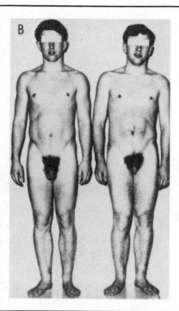

velopment in genital size, normal development of secondary sex characteristics, and normal appearance of libido (see Fig. 6-2).

Psychological counseling for these patients should be routinely
undertaken, and consideration might be given to the implantation of
Silastic testicular prostheses after sexual maturation has occurred by
hormone therapy, to aid in the cosmetic and psychological adjustment
to this condition.

Male Turner's Syndrome. The combination of decreased testicular function with somatic features similar to those found in female Turner's
syndrome (see Table 6-1) is regarded as the male Turner's syndrome
[16]. The majority of these patients have a normal 46, XY chromosome
pattern, although various chromosomal abnormalities have been observed in approximately 20 percent of affected males [17]. The testes
may be undescended and abnormal sperm production is usual, resulting in infertility. Testosterone production typically is decreased and
gonadotropin levels are elevated. Treatment consists of androgen re-

placement therapy, which fosters pubertal development and maintains libido and sexual function.

Miscellaneous Conditions of Hypergonadotropic Hypogonadism. Mumps orchitis during the pubertal or postpubertal years can cause permanent damage to the seminiferous tubules, with a microscopic pattern sometimes resembling that of Klinefelter's syndrome. Infertility is common but androgen output of the testes most often is not impaired, although in severe cases disruption of testicular hormone synthesis may occur [18]. FSH levels are characteristically elevated. Orchitis resulting from gonorrhea may present a similar picture.

Irradiation of the testes does not affect testosterone production but significantly influences sperm production, since irradiation affects rapidly dividing cells in the body. Unless large doses of radiation are received, spermatogenesis typically recovers three to six months later. FSH levels increase during the period of suppressed spermatogenesis, but LH levels remain normal. Similarly, drugs used in the treatment of malignancy frequently affect spermatogenesis and may result in increased FSH output [19].

Hypogonadism may also be associated with neurologic disease such as myotonic dystrophy, familial cerebellar ataxia, or spinal cord damage (see Chapters 10 and 14).

Kallmann's Syndrome. The syndrome of hypogonadotropic hypogonadism and anosmia (absent sense of smell) was initially described by Kallmann and coworkers [20]. Color blindness is a frequent but variably associated feature of this condition; cryptorchidism is also a common feature [21]. The characteristic gonadotropin deficiency results in failure of pubertal testicular development and therefore produces a eunuchoid habitus. The disorder appears to be familial and may affect both males and females [21–23].

Kallmann's syndrome is caused by a hypothalamic disorder, since pituitary gonadotropin release can be achieved by the use of exogenous gonadotropin-releasing factor [24]. Gonadal response to stimulation by LH or FSH is usually subnormal (see Fig. 6-3). Other aspects of hypothalamic-pituitary function are normal.

Men with this syndrome are infertile and most typically are unable to ejaculate. Their history will usually reveal the lack of nocturnal ejaculation. Impotence is present in the great majority of cases, and low or absent libido is a frequent associated finding. Gynecomastia is not typical but may occur. Treatment with gonadotropin-releasing factor or

Figure 6-3. Four-day HCG stimulation test in six men with Kallmann's syndrome. The open circles refer to one man with bilateral cryptorchidism and Kallmann's syndrome. The shaded area shows the response range seen in five normal men. (From Santen and Paulsen [25].)

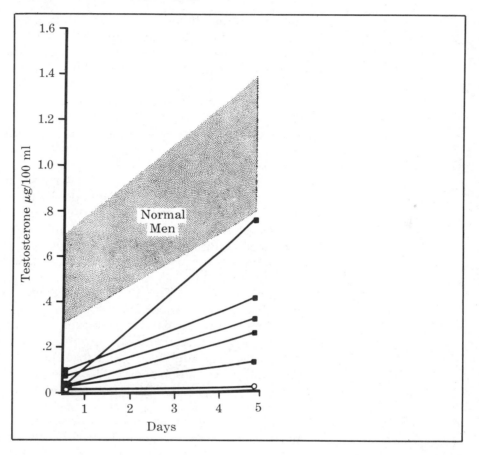

pituitary gonadotropins will result in sexual maturation and, at least in some cases, initiation of spermatogenesis [25, 26]. If fertility is not a goal of treatment, testosterone replacement therapy can also be used to instigate sexual maturation and to support improved libido and potency.

Miscellaneous Conditions of Hypogonadotropic Hypogonadism. An isolated deficiency of LH results in a clinical picture of the so-called fertile eunuch, showing inhibited somatic sexual maturation, impotence, and low libido, but spermatogenesis that is normal or only modestly diminished. Testosterone therapy improves the sexual difficulties and also facilitates the development of adult male secondary sex characteristics. An isolated FSH deficiency, which is a rare disorder, is associated with abnormal spermatogenesis but normal steroidogenesis [27–29].

In hypopituitarism, there is failure of pituitary gonadotropin secretion due to the underlying pathology, which results in atrophy of the testes, cessation of spermatogenesis, and a marked decrease in testosterone synthesis. Typically, such patients are impotent and infertile and exhibit low libido. This condition will be discussed more fully later in this chapter.

Female
Hypogonadism

Failure of ovarian function does not result in decreased libido or impaired sexual function in the female. In fact, it is unclear at present what behavioral alterations, if any, characteristically occur as a consequence of female hypogonadism. Diminished ovarian function as a result of aging is discussed in Chapter 5, while other disorders of ovarian function are considered in Chapters 2 and 8.

Turner's Syndrome. The association of short stature, sexual infantilism, a female phenotype, and a variety of somatic abnormalities with a 45,XO chromosome pattern (sometimes referred to as X-chromosome monosomy, meaning that the second sex chromosome is missing) describes a group of females with a disorder known as Turner's syndrome [30–32]. This condition represents one end of a spectrum of disorders of female hypogonadism that are collectively referred to as *gonadal dysgenesis.*

In classic Turner's syndrome, many somatic defects occur; their frequencies are summarized in Table 6-1. Some of these abnormalities are shown in Figures 6-4 to 6-6. The short stature of these patients is striking and is almost invariably present, the average adult height being 55 inches (with a range of 48 to 58 inches) [33]. The external genitalia are female but are characteristically immature. The vagina may be shallow, the uterus is small, and the gonads consist of fibrous streaks of connective tissue. LH and FSH levels are usually elevated at the time that puberty would normally occur, although the absence of functioning ovaries precludes normal pubertal development. Fourteen cases of Turner's syndrome with spontaneous sexual development have been reported; in a recent report of such a case, describing a 45,XO girl with menarche, pubarche, and thelarche at age 12, ovulation was induced by the use of clomiphene citrate [34]. With very rare exceptions, amenorrhea and infertility are hallmarks of this condition.

Turner's syndrome with a 45,XO chromosome pattern occurs in ap-

Table 6-1. Frequency of Abnormalities in Turner's Syndrome (Karyotype 45,XO)*

Feature	Approximate Frequency (%)
Short stature	99
Primary amenorrhea	98
Lack of breast development	95
Sexual infantilism	95
Retarded bone age	90
Cubitus valgus	80
Shield chest	80
Short 4th metacarpal	80
Low hairline on neck	60
Webbed neck	60
Renal abnormalities	60
Congenital heart disease	40
Lymphedema	40
Hypertension	30
High-arched palate	30
Coarctation of the aorta	15

*Based on data from references 30–32, supplemented by unpublished observations.

proximately one in 2,500 live female births [11], but the XO karyotype has been identified in five percent of spontaneous abortions [35]. There is no correlation between advanced maternal age and the frequency of Turner's syndrome [30, 35]. Diabetes and disorders of the thyroid both occur with increased frequency in this condition [32].

Normal female gender identity develops in girls with Turner's syndrome, as documented by careful studies of childhood, adolescent, and adult behavior [36]. Although the endocrine literature suggests a higher than expected association between Turner's syndrome and mental retardation, a more accurate picture is presented in the psychology literature. Verbal abilities in patients with Turner's syndrome are normal as measured by the Wechsler verbal intelligence quotient [37]. However, nonverbal intelligence may be affected, as shown particularly by space-form blindness, poor directional sense, and difficulties with calculations [11, 38]. In general, patients with Turner's syn-

Figure 6-4. A patient with Turner's
syndrome, showing shield-shaped
chest, short stature, and widespread
nipples. (From C. C. Snyder, C. D.
Scott, and E. Z. Browne, Intersexuality: Diagnosis and Treatment, in
C. E. Horton [ed.], *Plastic and Reconstructive Surgery of the Genital Area,*
Boston: Little, Brown and Co., 1973.)

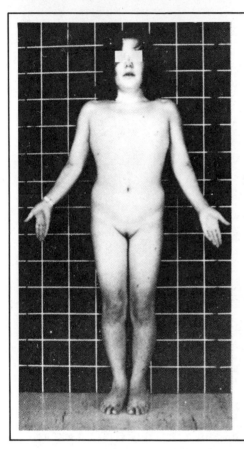

drome are remarkably free of psychiatric disturbance. Frequently,
there is a tendency toward "inertia of emotional arousal"—complacency and slowness in asserting initiative—which may be a positive factor in allowing these individuals to cope with their short
stature and frequent lack of physical attractiveness [39].

When estrogen therapy is provided for patients with Turner's syndrome during adolescence and is continued during adult life, there is
normal breast development. However, in patients with a small vagina,
coitus may precipitate discomfort. Although libido is normal in some
women with Turner's syndrome, more typically it is moderately to
severely depressed. This depressed libido may be a reflection of psy-

Figure 6-5. Webbing of the neck and low posterior hairline in a woman with Turner's syndrome. (From R. S. Wilroy, Jr., Gonadal Dysgenesis. In J. R. Givens [ed.], *Gynecologic Endocrinology*. Copyright © 1977 by Year Book Medical Publishers, Inc., Chicago. Used by permission.)

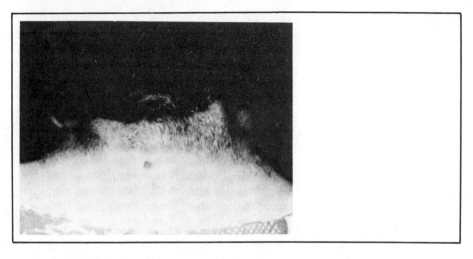

Figure 6-6. High-arched palate in Turner's syndrome. (From R. S. Wilroy, Jr., Gonadal Dysgenesis. In J. R. Givens [ed.], *Gynecologic Endocrinology*. Copyright © 1977 by Year Book Medical Publishers, Inc., Chicago. Used by permission.)

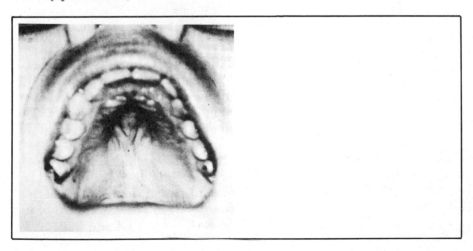

chosocial factors rather than a biologic influence alone. Some women with Turner's syndrome report normal orgasmic responsiveness, although it appears that orgasmic dysfunction is common in this group of patients.

Management of the patient with Turner's syndrome is discussed in Chapter 2. It should be remembered that many variant forms of Turner's syndrome exist, with markedly different somatic and endocrine features. Interested readers may consult references 30 to 33 for a discussion of these conditions.

Kallmann's Syndrome. Women as well as men can be affected by Kallmann's syndrome, a disorder of hypogonadotropic hypogonadism with anosmia. Typically, pubertal development is delayed and significant breast growth and menstruation occur only after estrogen therapy is begun. Libido is not depressed, since it is supported by androgens in the female, and orgasmic capacity is generally normal. The olfactory bulbs may be absent. The pituitary gland is normal, and the defect is thought to be in the hypothalamus. Ovulation can be induced successfully in some women with Kallmann's syndrome, and pregnancy is occasionally possible [22].

Premature Menopause. When menopause occurs spontaneously below the age of 35, it is sufficiently unusual to be considered premature. When cessation of menses before this age is accompanied by elevated gonadotropin levels and evidence of estrogen deficiency, this diagnosis can be confirmed. The cause of this disorder is not known, although in some instances associated chromosomal anomalies have been uncovered, and in other cases autoimmune mechanisms have appeared to be the cause, with the demonstration of circulating autoantibodies that reacted to various components of ovarian tissue [40, 41]. Treatment is required under the conditions previously outlined for treatment of the menopausal or postmenopausal woman (see Chap. 5).

Diabetes Mellitus
Male Sexual
Dysfunction in
Diabetes

Impotence. For almost two hundred years, it has been recognized that diabetes mellitus is frequently associated with impotence. Estimates of the frequency of impotence among men with diabetes have usually ranged from 40 to 60 percent, with general consensus on the fact that approximately one out of every two men with clinically apparent diabetes is sexually dysfunctional [42–45]. The significance of this fact is more apparent when it is realized that there are at least two million men with diabetes in the United States—thus one million men in this country alone are impotent as a result of the complications of this metabolic disorder.

The impotence associated with diabetes can occur at any age, although most published studies report a tendency for a slightly lower prevalence of this problem in diabetics in their twenties or thirties (probably 25 to 30 percent of diabetics in this age group are impotent), compared with a prevalence rate of impotence of 50 to 70 percent in men over age 50 who have diabetes. This difference may be attributable in part to changes in circulation secondary to accelerated arteriosclerosis, which occurs more noticeably in the aging diabetic population.

NATURAL HISTORY. The most frequently observed pattern of impaired sexual function in men with diabetes begins several years or more after the diabetes is discovered. The earliest manifestation is a mild to moderate decrease in firmness of the erection, although this change often is not noticed by either the man or his sexual partner since vaginal intromission is usually possible. Attention may be called to the alteration in sexual function either by sporadic episodes of impotence or by diminished responses to erotic stimuli during sexual activity. Gradual deterioration in the quality of the erection (i.e., decreased firmness) as well as in the durability of the erection occurs over a period of 6 to 18 months [45]. The ability to ejaculate or to be aware of orgasmic sensations is not lost, however, and libido is usually unimpaired.

A less common pattern of impotence associated with diabetes may precede the actual diagnosis of this disorder. In such circumstances, the impotence is a manifestation of a general catabolic state and is typically accompanied by other highly noticeable symptoms, such as excessive hunger (polyphagia), excessive thirst (polydipsia), excessive urination (polyuria), pruritus, and weight loss. This form of diabetic impotence is characterized by an abrupt onset, can occur at any age, and may be marked by loss of libido. When the diagnosis is made and sufficient metabolic control is established to correct the catabolic state, the loss of potency (as well as the alteration in libido) quickly reverses. It is not known if the occurrence of this type of impotence is a prognostic sign for the subsequent development of further potency problems.

PATHOGENESIS. Although it was first believed that a specific hormonal defect in the diabetic male involving the hypothalamic-pituitary-gonadal axis was the primary cause of impotence [43], it is now known that usually such a problem does not exist. Measurement of levels of circulating testosterone and pituitary gonadotropins has not shown differences between impotent diabetic men and diabetic men with unimpaired sexual functioning, nor do these hormone levels in diabetics differ from an age-matched nondiabetic population [45]. Exceptions to this usually normal state of hormonal support can occur, particularly when the diabetes is a manifestation of hemochromatosis (an iron deposition disease that frequently causes damage to the testes and pituitary gland, thus resulting in hypogonadism), when diabetes is complicated by renal failure, or when diabetes occurs as a result of severe liver disease, as with alcoholic cirrhosis.

It is now reasonably certain that the impotence of diabetes mellitus is caused principally by diabetic neuropathy, a process of microscopic damage to nerve tissue that occurs throughout the body of the diabetic [44]. Although the exact cause of this neuropathy is not known, current experimental evidence suggests that it is the result of an abnormal accumulation in nerve fibers of chemical substances called polyols, which produce segmental demyelination and defective myelin synthesis, a process that results primarily from hyperglycemia. Investigators have found that autonomic nerve fibers in the corpora cavernosa of the penis in diabetic men with impotence examined at the time of autopsy showed morphologic abnormalities of varying degrees [46]. In addition, clinical study of a series of men with diabetes revealed a much higher rate of abnormal cystometrograms, indicating neurogenic bladder dysfunction, in diabetics with impotence (37 of 45 men) than in nonimpotent diabetic subjects (3 of 30 men) [44]. In most reports, a higher percentage of impotent diabetic men have been found to have evidence of peripheral neuropathy* on clinical examination than age-matched diabetic men without impotence.

In some diabetic men, macrovascular or microvascular changes resulting from diabetes may be important causes of impotence. The small blood vessel disease that produces many of the complications of diabetes (e.g., retinopathy and nephropathy) is known as diabetic microangiopathy. This abnormality is characterized by a thickening of the basement membranes of capillaries, a process that may be due to genetic factors as well as to increased carbohydrate content. Since the process of penile erection reflects a dynamic state of circulatory responses, it is possible that disease involving the network of small blood vessels in the body of the penis would result in impairment of erectile capacity. Obviously, large vessel damage such as that produced by

---

*Peripheral neuropathy may be manifested by absent deep tendon reflexes, pain or paresthesias, impaired motor strength, and decreased tactile or vibratory sensations in the extremities, particularly the legs and feet.

major arteriosclerotic lesions would also compromise the process of erection severely.

EVALUATION. Most impotence associated with diabetes mellitus is not curable by known methods. However, there are important considerations to keep in mind in assessing this problem and determining details of management. Above all, one should remember that impotence occurring in a man with diabetes is not necessarily caused by the diabetes. Diabetic men who are experiencing potency problems must be evaluated thoroughly to determine whether or not the distress is primarily psychogenic or whether it is caused by an organic process apart from the diabetes itself. Diabetics are just as susceptible as others to the psychic stresses of life; therefore, causes of impotence such as depression and anxiety should be considered. Diabetic men with impotence that is psychogenic will respond just as well to competent psychotherapy as nondiabetic men. Another significant factor is that the medications being used by the man with diabetes may be the triggering mechanism for loss or impairment of erectile capacity. Since drug-induced impotence is usually reversible when the offending pharmacologic agent is either discontinued or reduced in dosage, the prognosis in such instances is good (for further discussion of this point, see Chapter 13).

Diabetics have an increased risk for many other diseases, including infection, various forms of endocrine disease (especially disorders of the thyroid and adrenal cortex), and cardiovascular disease. Since such associated pathology at times may be the major etiologic factor in sexual dysfunction, the presence or absence of these conditions must be assessed by a careful medical history, physical examination, and laboratory evaluation.

TREATMENT. When impotence is an early symptom of diabetes, it is usually a reflection of poor metabolic control. In these instances, careful attention to appropriate dietary management and the use of insulin or oral hypoglycemic agents will frequently produce relatively rapid amelioration of the disturbed potency. If impotence persists despite good metabolic control, consideration should be given to whether this problem is the result of anxieties (fears of performance, for example, as discussed in further detail in Chapters 19 and 20) that may remain even though the metabolic status of the individual has improved considerably. One should note that these anxieties may have come about only *after* the beginning of sexual dysfunction; in such cases, it is important to tell the patient that the impotence began as a manifestation of a specific health problem but is being perpetuated by the psychological *reaction* to that problem. Brief counseling to assist in anxiety reduction, coupled with a supportive approach to participation in sexual activity, will frequently be enough to overcome this pattern of impotence.

If impotence is present early in the course of diabetes even when control of the blood sugar appears good, the chances are that the prognosis for reversal of the sexual problem is much poorer. Nevertheless, either in this situation or in dealing with impotence that occurs years after the onset of diabetes, when underlying organic factors such as neuropathy, vascular disease, or hormonal disturbances cannot be identified, diabetic men will often respond to sex therapy.

In deciding whether or not impotence in the diabetic may be amenable to psychotherapeutic reversal, the following points may apply:

1. *Is the history suggestive of a primary organic etiology?* If a man can attain full erections with masturbation or in response to certain types of erotic stimuli (e.g., fellatio, reading erotic material), it is likely that the impotence is primarily psychogenic. Similarly, the man who reports the presence of firm morning or nocturnal erections is not impotent as a result of diabetes. The impotence associated with diabetic neuropathy or vascular disease rarely is abrupt in its onset. Such points can be of assistance in deciding if referral for sex therapy is indicated.

2. *Are there indicators of significant personality or interpersonal factors that may be contributing to the sexual dysfunction?* The presence of depressive symptoms—including decreased libido; sleep or appetite disturbances; crying; feelings of worthlessness, helplessness, or hopelessness; loss of interest in work; and impaired capacity to perform ordinary social functions—may signal the existence of an intrapsychic process requiring prompt therapeutic intervention. Impotence or other disturbances in sexual function frequently accompany such difficulties. Guilt, anxiety, poor self-esteem, phobias, thought disorders, and a wide range of other intrapsychic processes may also indicate a nonphysical cause for sexual disturbances. Likewise, marital conflict, difficulties at work, financial pressures, problems in child-rearing, and a host of other interpersonal factors may point to important mechanisms underlying the occurrence of sexual problems.

3. *Can evidence be found supporting the existence of neuropathy or vascular damage as a cause of impotence?* Although not all diabetic men who are impotent should be subjected to extensive (and expensive) testing to determine the cause of their problem, for those men who are strongly motivated to reverse this difficulty, specific diagnostic evalua-

tion is in order. The most promising single test for such an assessment is the monitoring of nocturnal penile tumescence patterns (see Chap. 20), which can either be done on an outpatient basis or be conducted in a sleep research laboratory. If normal patterns of erection occur during sleep, it can be assumed that there is no organic basis for the impotence. In such cases, sex therapy is likely to work approximately 70 to 80 percent of the time. Since the nocturnal penile tumescence pattern cannot identify the pathologic process impairing erection, further study on an individualized basis may be undertaken using cystometrograms, nerve conduction velocity measures or other electrophysiologic techniques, or selective arteriography to delineate the difficulty more precisely. At times, vascular obstruction causing impotence can be corrected by one of several surgical approaches. At present, there is no known cure for impotence due to diabetic neuropathy.

Although the majority of impotent diabetic men cannot undergo medical or psychotherapeutic reversal of their problem, there are important points in patient management that need to be considered. Whenever possible, counseling should include the spouse or sexual partner of the diabetic man with impotence. Frequently, impotence is mistakenly assumed to mean that a man finds his partner less attractive or less sexually stimulating. At other times, a wife may believe that impotence reflects a homosexual tendency on her husband's part or that it indicates that he is having an affair. Such interpretations or assumptions are obviously apt to be detrimental to the trust and closeness of the relationship, both sexually and otherwise. Receiving accurate information about the occurrence of impotence in diabetes usually helps people understand their sexual relationship. Giving the nondiabetic partner an opportunity to learn about the disease and its complications is an important preparatory step in helping a couple seek viable sexual options that can be satisfying to them. When counseling is available for the couple, rather than for the diabetic patient alone, an important opportunity for ventilation, including the expression of guilt or anger, is provided.

The physician providing such counseling services should recognize that patients with diabetes are confronted with a variety of emotional consequences resulting from this disease. While they are often encouraged to lead a "normal" life, diabetics are reminded of their problem constantly by the need to adhere to a special diet, to follow schedules of insulin or drug use, to check urine specimens for glucose, to have an awareness of the symptoms of hypoglycemia or severe hyperglycemia, and to attempt to prevent the numerous (and frightening) complications of this disorder. When sexual dysfunction occurs within this matrix, it may be a particularly devastating reminder of how different a man is from his nondiabetic friends.

Impotence does not merely signal a loss of a particular phase of sexual gratification, since for many men the ability to function sexually is an important source of ego strength and self-esteem. Recognition of this facet of a man's reaction to sexual dysfunction is a necessary component of providing effective patient management and may point to the need for more intensive psychotherapy.

The couple should be told that usually impotence associated with diabetes is not a constant, unchanging condition. Just as symptoms in many chronic illnesses remit or exacerbate from time to time, the severity of impairment of erectile functioning is likely to vary considerably. If a couple stops having sexual contact because of frustration over their inability to have intercourse, they will, needless to say, miss those occasions when intercourse may be possible. Furthermore, it should be stressed that impotence does not mean inability to be aroused or to obtain gratification from sexual activity. More than 95 percent of impotent diabetic men are able to ejaculate normally, and even when ejaculation does not occur, the emotional as well as physical gratification that is produced by sexual intimacy should not be lightly neglected.

In providing counseling services to the diabetic man and his partner, consideration must be given to the personal, cultural, and religious factors that are important to the couple's sexual value system. Suggestions about the appropriateness of noncoital activity such as oral-genital play cannot be made on a routine basis to all couples. Stressing the opportunities of sharing, loving, and intimacy that are available rather than sounding like an engineer of sexual performance is an important facet of providing such counseling.

SURGICAL APPROACHES TO TREATMENT. Recently there has been increasing experience with the surgical implantation of penile prosthetic devices to provide a more satisfactory solution to the sexual problems facing men with organic impotence that is irreversible by other treatment modalities. (A discussion of the different types of devices that are currently available is presented in Chapter 9.)

For selected diabetic men, this approach may be extremely beneficial. It is likely to be of the most usefulness in cases where (1) the man has invested a major portion of his self-esteem in his ability to function sexually; (2) significant depression occurs as a consequence of diabetic impotence; (3) sexual dysfunction is materially affecting the quality or stability of a marriage or long-term relationship; (4) there is no major loss of libido or impairment in the ability to ejaculate; and (5) there are no medical contraindications to surgery.

It is necessary to realize that whichever prosthetic device is utilized, a totally physiologic sexual response pattern will not occur, so that some men may be disappointed by the postsurgical results. Furthermore, because of the difficulties of wound-healing and greater susceptibility to infection that accompany diabetes mellitus, there may be a higher rate of operative and postoperative risk associated with this surgery than in nondiabetic patients. Nevertheless, this approach may be warranted in carefully selected patients and may contribute to a resolution of one of the most difficult problems confronting persons with this chronic disease.

Retrograde Ejaculation. Retrograde ejaculation is a condition in which seminal fluid flows backwards into the bladder at the time of orgasm, rather than being propelled in a forward fashion through the distal urethra. This disorder is found in 1 to 2 percent of diabetic men. The cause of the problem in these men is an autonomic neuropathy that has progressed to involvement of the neck of the urinary bladder [47, 48]. Normally the neck of the bladder closes tightly during orgasm and ejaculation, with the result that pressure posterior to the prostatic urethra is so high that the seminal fluid moves anteriorly, in the direction of least resistance. In affected diabetic men, because the internal sphincter of the bladder does not close effectively there is more resistance in the forward direction (resistance created normally by the walls of the urethra) and less resistance backwards into the bladder, since the distance is considerably shorter. Seminal fluid therefore mixes freely with urine in the bladder and is expelled from the body with urination. The diagnosis is established by finding numerous sperm cells in a postcoital urine specimen after having demonstrated the absence of an ejaculate or spermatozoa in a condom used during intercourse.

Diabetic men with this condition may or may not be impotent. If they are not impotent, there is a high probability that erective dysfunction will occur in the future, since the underlying neuropathy is likely to worsen. However, diabetics with retrograde ejaculation still experience orgasm, although the sensations associated with the passage of seminal fluid through the distal urethra are absent, so that a man with this condition may describe an altered set of orgasmic sensations. Rhythmic contractions of the prostate and seminal vesicles occur in a normal fashion.

For obvious reasons, retrograde ejaculation may be a cause of infertility. One potential solution to this problem is to perform artificial insemination, using an aliquot of seminal fluid and sperm cells obtained by centrifugation of the first postcoital urine specimen. If such an approach is taken, it is advisable to alkalinize the urine prior to ejaculation (the usual acidity of urine is spermicidal) by having the man ingest sodium bicarbonate [48].

Sexual Dysfunction in Diabetic Women

It is telling to note that, in spite of the detailed research information concerning impotence in diabetic men, nothing appeared in the literature until 1971 reporting prevalence data for sexual dysfunction in diabetic women. Despite the fact that hundreds of publications described the reproductive problems of women with diabetes, no one seemed curious enough to ascertain whether or not parallel difficulties existed in the realm of sexual functioning.

A survey was done in 1971 comparing 125 sexually active diabetic women with a group of 100 sexually active nondiabetic women, all subjects being between the ages of 18 and 42 [49]. There was a marked similarity between these two groups of women in terms of age, religion, education, marital status, age at menarche, incidence of dysmenorrhea, parity, frequency of coital activity, self-estimation of sexual interest, and history of psychiatric care (Table 6-2). However, 35.2 percent of the diabetic women reported being completely nonorgasmic in the preceding year, whereas only 6 percent of the nondiabetic women reported complete absence of orgasmic response during the same time period.

Interestingly, the nonorgasmic women without diabetes had never experienced orgasm from any type of sexual play—suggesting that they had a psychogenic variety of dysfunction—whereas most of the diabetic women who were nonorgasmic at the time of the study had previously been orgasmic, often on a regular basis, and had subsequently developed a pattern of sexual dysfunction. This fact, coupled with the time sequence of the sexual dysfunction, was strongly suggestive of an organic basis for the problem.

Natural History. For diabetic women whose sexual dysfunction is not lifelong, the onset of orgasmic difficulties is gradual and progressive, usually developing over a period of six months to one year. Most typically, the time of onset is four to eight years after the diagnosis of diabetes is made (Fig. 6-7). Many women recall that they first experienced a gradual decrease in the frequency of orgasmic response, sometimes accompanied by a noticeable lessening of the intensity of orgasm

Characteristic	Diabetics (N = 125)	Nondiabetics (N = 100)
Age (years)		
Mean	32.6	32.9
Median	32.0	33.0
Mode	30.0	34.0
Age at menarche (years)	12.8	12.3
Marital status		
Single	30%	24%
Married	64%	70%
Divorced	4%	6%
Widowed	2%	0%
Contraception		
None	49%	30%
Rhythm	16%	18%
IUD	1%	4%
Diaphragm	18%	14%
Jelly or foam	8%	3%
Oral agent	8%	31%
Education (years)	13.1	13.9
Dysmenorrhea	6%	10%
Parity	1.5	2.1
Frequency of coitus (times per week)	2.1	2.2
Sexual interest[a]	2.9	2.8
History of psychiatric care	6%	3%
Orgasmic dysfunction	35.2%	6.0%

Table 6-2. Characteristics of Study Groups in a Survey of Sexual Dysfunction in Diabetic Females. (From Kolodny [49].)

[a]Self-estimation of sexual interest based on a scale of 0 to 5, with 0 indicating no interest and 5 indicating maximal interest in sexual activity.

as subjectively perceived. Sexual interest usually is not diminished, but a minority of women complain that it seems to require longer periods of direct sexual stimulation for them to reach high levels of arousal, whether engaged in masturbatory or coital activity. Vaginal lubrication is not significantly altered in most diabetic women with sexual dysfunc-

Figure 6-7. Relationship of the duration of diabetes mellitus to the incidence of orgasmic dysfunction in 125 female diabetics aged 18 to 42. (From Kolodny [49].)

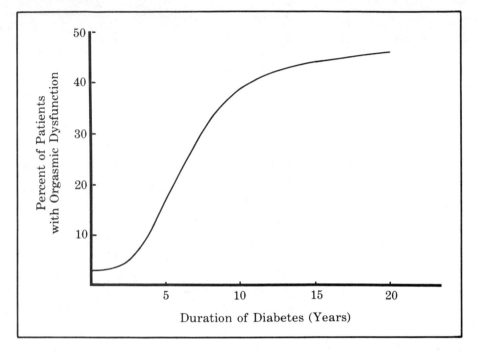

tion, and in the previously cited series only 4 of 125 diabetic women complained of dyspareunia (painful intercourse), including two diabetic women who were orgasmic.

Pathogenesis. Although there is no definitive research evidence pinpointing the specific etiology of sexual dysfunction in diabetic women, mechanisms similar to those operating in the male diabetic might be expected. In this regard, the correlation between orgasmic dysfunction and duration of diabetes suggests that either neuropathic or microvascular changes or both may be implicated, since both of these complications of diabetes occur at greater rates with disease of longer chronicity. The importance of vascular changes as the major pathogenic mechanism is suspect, however, since microvascular impairment would most likely manifest itself by impaired vaginal lubrication, since lubrication is highly dependent on patterns of vaginal vasocongestion.

Further study in this area has established the fact that in at least some diabetic women with sexual dysfunction, evidence of other autonomic nervous system impairment can be found by careful evaluation [50]. Since independent investigations have previously demonstrated that even mild neuropathic changes in diabetes can significantly raise stimulatory threshold levels—thus requiring greater afferent stimuli to trigger the appropriate response—it is theoretically possible that most diabetic women do not "lose" the capacity to be orgasmic but simply require higher levels of stimulus to set off the orgasmic reflex. Studies with a small number of diabetic women who have experienced orgasmic difficulty that was overcome by the use of a vibrator have indicated that this may be the case [51].

An element of possible etiologic importance in the sexual dysfunction of some women with diabetes is the greater susceptibility to infection that is a prominent clinical feature of diabetes mellitus [52]. This problem, thought to be caused by a combination of factors including decreased leukocyte phagocytosis [53] and elevated tissue concentrations of glucose that provide an optimal growth medium for many microbial organisms, is particularly relevant to infections in the vaginal area or urinary tract. Although acute vaginitis can be extremely uncomfortable, psychologically as well as physically, chronic infection remains a greater cause of sexual problems. This is so because the tissue changes that occur with chronic infection—particularly the moniliasis that seems most troublesome for the diabetic woman—produce tissue tenderness, malodorous discharge, pruritus, and decreased vaginal lubrication. This last change may result from pH differences associated with such vaginal infections, from alterations in osmotic pressure gradients within the vaginal mucosa, and from inflammation and swelling in the vaginal walls, causing impairment in capillary permeability.

It is also possible that for some women, fear of the complications of pregnancy associated with diabetes or concern about the increased risk of congenital defects in their children [54–56] may predispose to the development of psychogenic sexual difficulties, particularly when viewed in the context of a chronic, life-threatening disease which, for some individuals, may require major psychosocial adjustment. It seems unlikely that this attitude is of primary importance in most cases, however, since such psychogenic dysfunction might be expected to be accompanied by diminished libido and a higher occurrence of dyspareunia, and it might also be typified by a pattern of more abrupt onset, particularly in association with pregnancy.

Management. EVALUATION. Many of the same principles that apply to management of sexual dysfunction in men with diabetes are relevant to the approach to women with diabetes who are experiencing sexual problems. One should remember that the coexistence of sexual dysfunction and diabetes does not always imply that the two are causally related; indeed, the predominance of psychosocial factors in the etiology of female sexual dysfunction, compared to primary organic components, is helpful to keep in mind. A detailed medical and psychosocial history will provide part of the data base for a systematic approach to differential diagnosis, which can be supplemented by information from the physical examination and the laboratory. Information pertaining to drug use, medical problems, contraceptive and reproductive history, marital conflicts, other interpersonal difficulties, self-esteem, and attitudes toward sexuality will be of assistance in formulating both an accurate diagnosis and an individual plan of management.

It is necessary to be sure that vaginal infection is not a contributing factor to the woman's sexual dysfunction; such a conclusion can be reached only with the use of vaginal cultures, since not all infections are either symptomatic or recognizable by visual inspection or microscopic examination. When infection is found, followup cultures at the conclusion of a treatment regimen are mandatory, since many infections in diabetics are recalcitrant to treatment. Particular care should be exercised in looking for monilial infections, which are frequently present in diabetics, since they may not be detected by routine vaginal culture alone. If the woman complains of dyspareunia, urethritis, cystitis, or vaginal abscesses may be implicated.

Dyspareunia associated with diabetes may be due to a variety of causes (see Chap. 8); after infection, the most common causes are poor vaginal lubrication, atrophic (estrogen-deficient) vaginitis, and, infrequently, diabetic neuritis. Poor vaginal lubrication in diabetic women may result from impaired microcirculation in the vagina, estrogen deficiency, or chronic infection, but it should be kept in mind that this condition may also be a side effect of the use of antihistamines. Evaluation of vaginal cytology and circulating estrogen levels can be done to determine if an estrogen deficiency exists, but the decision of whether to use systematic estrogen replacement therapy or local estrogen-containing creams must be made on an individual basis. When estrogen deficiency is not present, the problem can be effectively managed by the use of artificial lubricants.

A number of other endocrine disorders occur more frequently in diabetics than in nondiabetics. These conditions include Addison's disease, Cushing's syndrome, hypothyroidism, hypopituitarism, and multiple endocrine adenomatosis [57]. Since these disorders may produce sexual dysfunction through different mechanisms than diabetes does, it is important to consider them in the process of differential diagnosis. In contrast to the situation in which sexual dysfunction is caused by diabetes, these diseases generally produce decreased libido and difficulty associated with sexual arousal.

TREATMENT. Counseling the sexually dysfunctional woman with diabetes is best approached by working with her together with her spouse or partner whenever possible. Since current evidence supports the idea that careful metabolic control of hyperglycemia and glycosuria will provide some protection against the development of complications of diabetes [58], such counseling might be considered as a routine approach to the care of all newly diagnosed cases of diabetes in women. Whether or not the development of neuropathy can be prevented or at least delayed, it is clear that controlling blood sugar levels and urinary glucose concentrations will be important in diminishing the frequency and severity of infections that a diabetic will experience. It is also possible that at least some women with orgasmic dysfunction resulting from diabetes will experience improvement in their sexual responsiveness when their metabolic control is improved. Nevertheless, it is important to recognize that the complications of diabetes are not necessarily preventable; a person with diabetes must therefore be helped in understanding that the occurrence of complications does not mean that she or he neglected a proper medical regimen.

In the counseling approach, it is important to be supportive but not unrealistic. Empathy, education, and elucidation of available options are frequently helpful in aiding the diabetic woman and her partner to cope with their sexual situation, but they will not magically restore the ability to be orgasmic. As previously discussed, the counselor should first attempt to eliminate possible correctable conditions causing the sexual dysfunction, such as drug effects, infection, or other physical disease. The counselor should also be prepared to recognize personality patterns or psychoneuroses significantly contributing to the change in sexual function, and to make appropriate referral for psychotherapy in those instances in which such therapy may be beneficial.

Once these things have been accomplished—and from the perspective of an adequate data base—the following points may be useful:

1. Inability to be orgasmic does not alter a woman's reproductive capacity.
2. Inability to be orgasmic does not equate with inability to enjoy sex.
3. Limitations to orgasmic responsiveness are not necessarily due to

emotional problems; physical factors can be the primary or sole source of this limitation.

4. Intimacy, sharing, and gratification—sexually and nonsexually—within a relationship do not depend on being orgasmic.

5. One's femininity or attractiveness is not reduced by not being orgasmic.

6. The husband or sexual partner of the diabetic woman who is sexually dysfunctional may need reassurance in knowing that he is not the cause of the problem.

Although some of these points may seem so obvious that they do not need to be made, often they are of great importance in helping a couple (or an individual) deal with their problems. Giving both the woman with diabetes and her sexual partner an opportunity for ventilation and a supportive, receptive attitude toward sexuality within the scope of their sexual value system can make it easier for them to adjust to the sexual sequelae of this chronic disorder.

Disorders of the Thyroid Gland

Thyroid disease has been widely assumed to be a frequent cause of sexual problems in both men and women, as well as a common cause of male sterility. Although disorders of the thyroid are not rare by any means, they are also not as prevalent as some would believe. In a series of 700 impotent men evaluated at the Masters & Johnson Institute, only 4 had clinically significant disorders of the thyroid. Similarly, a series of 800 nonorgasmic women revealed only 9 patients with thyroid disease. Finally, of 210 men with oligospermia or azoospermia, only 3 had thyroid abnormalities.

In spite of these statistics, there is a significant assocation between thyroid disease and sexual problems. This association is demonstrated in a dramatic and convincing fashion in the clinical evaluation of patients with either hypothyroidism or hyperthyroidism.

Hypothyroidism

Whether primary (due to a defect in the thyroid gland itself) or secondary (due to disorders of the pituitary or hypothalamus), hypothyroidism is a disease that affects most systems of the body. Characteristic symptoms include weakness, easy fatigability, dry or coarse skin, intolerance to cold, slow speech, impaired memory, weight gain, constipation, and muscular aching. Physical signs, which vary widely from person to person, include facial edema, a coarse, husky voice, bradycardia, cardiomegaly, slowed deep tendon reflexes, especially during the relaxation phase, and polyneuropathies.

The patient with a deficiency of thyroid hormone frequently experiences disruptions in sexual functioning, although the literature is quite incomplete on systematic data in this regard. (Part of the reason for this discrepancy is undoubtedly the fact that many of these patients were not asked about their sex life.) Approximately 80 percent of men with hypothyroidism experience depressed libido, and 40 to 50 percent of these patients are also impotent to varying degrees. Likewise, approximately 80 percent of hypothyroid women describe difficulty in becoming sexually aroused. In one series of 75 women with hypothyroidism, 28 reported being nonorgasmic [59].

Juvenile hypothyroidism in its untreated state is usually associated with a general retardation of body growth and development. When the hormone deficiency is severe in both duration and degree, the result in either boys or girls is usually a failure of progression of pubertal development. Rarely, primary hypothyroidism may be associated with sexual precocity, including early breast development, maturation of the vaginal mucosa, vaginal bleeding, and galactorrhea in girls, and testicular and penile enlargement in boys [60]. These changes are reversible by the administration of thyroxine and may reflect an excess secretion of TRF (thyrotropin-releasing factor) from the hypothalamus, which causes elevated levels of circulating prolactin and possibly the pituitary gonadotropins, FSH and LH. The more typical delay in sexual maturation caused by hypothyroidism also is reversible with adequate replacement of thyroid hormone.

The decreased libido frequently seen in either men or women with hypothyroidism is largely a manifestation of the chronic disease process affecting all body systems, with decreased energy and initiative as common features. In addition, synthesis of testosterone in both the testes and the adrenal cortex is diminished in hypothyroidism, and the percentage of testosterone that is bound to protein in the blood, thus making it theoretically less available to body tissues, is increased. Alterations in the metabolism of both androgens and estrogens occur in both men and women with thyroid deficiencies, with all of these changes reversing promptly with restoration to euthyroid status.

Women with hypothyroidism may have menorrhagia ($\cong 35\%$), sometimes of marked severity, or may have amenorrhea ($\cong 10\%$), sometimes accompanied by galactorrhea and elevated prolactin levels. Fertility is often impaired in women with moderate to severe hypothyroidism, and men with this disorder frequently have depressed sperm production. Pregnancies in women with untreated hypothyroidism exhibit an increased rate of abortion.

Hyperthyroidism

Excess quantities of circulating thyroid hormone produce a condition of hyperthyroidism, or thyrotoxicosis, which may be due to a number of causes. Graves' disease, which occurs with a striking female preponderance (the sex ratio is approximately 7:1), is typified by goiter, thyrotoxicosis, and exophthalmos. Excess thyroid hormone may also result from autonomously functioning thyroid adenomas, from a toxic multinodular goiter, from chronic ingestion of large amounts of thyroid hormone (thyrotoxicosis factitia), or from a TSH-producing tumor of the pituitary.

The clinical manifestations of hyperthyroidism are dramatic when severe. The skin is unusually warm and moist, due to cutaneous vasodilation and excessive sweating; tachycardia at rest is typically observed, and palpitations are often noted (approximately 10 percent of such patients evidence cardiac arrhythmias, particularly atrial fibrillation); the patient appears nervous, hyperkinetic, and may exhibit marked lability in affect. Weakness, fatigue, tremor, hypersensitivity to heat, weight loss accompanied by an increased appetite, and increased gastrointestinal motility are also typical features. Eye signs, including a characteristic stare, lid retraction, lid lag on downward gaze, strabismus, and infrequent blinking; hyperreflexia; and the presence of a goiter on clinical examination complete the picture that is often seen when hyperthyroidism is overtly manifest.

Sexual functioning and sexual behavior may be affected in divergent ways by hyperthyroidism. Increased libido is seen in 10 to 20 percent of patients, particularly those with milder disease, but may sometimes be accompanied by impotence in the male. More frequently, libido is unaltered (50 percent of cases) or is diminished (30 to 40 percent of cases). In cases of thyrotoxicosis occurring during adolescence, a mistaken diagnosis of psychiatric illness may be made as a result of hypersexual behavior, which is sometimes the first manifestation of this disorder. In adults it may be difficult at times to distinguish clinically between mania and hyperthyroidism.

Impotence occurs in about 40 percent of the men with hyperthyroidism; the pathogenesis of this dysfunction is not yet clearly understood. The physiologic significance of a number of changes in androgen and estrogen metabolism associated with this disorder is not known at present. Liver damage is sometimes associated with hyperthyroidism [61], and muscle atrophy or myopathy [62] is also an associated feature; these conditions may contribute to the sexually dysfunctional state as well. Finally, gynecomastia can occur with hyperthyroidism [63], although the mechanism of this phenomenon is not known.

In women, the menstrual cycle is usually disrupted by hyperthyroidism, with menstrual flow characteristically reduced or the woman becoming amenorrheic. The overall cycle length can be either lengthened or shortened, or it may simply become very erratic. Ovulation is typically unimpaired, but this is not universally true. Orgasmic response and sexual arousal patterns may be heightened in some women (5 to 10 percent) with hyperthyroidism, but in most there is either no change (70 to 80 percent) or a mild decrease in responsiveness noted (approximately 15 percent). In light of this diversity, it is likely that these changes result from the overall effects of the illness more than from specific hormonal, circulatory, or neurologic alterations.

The alterations in sexual functioning that occur with hyperthyroidism are reversible as the metabolic derangement is brought under control. This may be accomplished by the use of radioactive iodide (^{131}I), by the use of drugs such as propylthiouracil or methimazole, or by surgery. Regardless of the treatment modality, all patients with "corrected" hyperthyroidism are at risk for the subsequent development of a hypothyroid state.

In general, the problem in diagnosing disorders of the thyroid gland is not with the typical cases in which symptomatology is as described in the preceding sections, but with atypical cases. Instances of "apathetic thyrotoxicosis" can present as flat affect, fatigue, insomnia, and congestive heart failure [64]; the similarity of rampant hyperthyroidism to a manic state has already been mentioned; confusion is also easily possible with occult malignancy, chronic cardiovascular disease, or senility. An index of suspicion for disorders of the thyroid is a prerequisite for making the diagnosis. Use of the laboratory in this regard is relatively simple and economical, but is not without its pitfalls, including alterations in laboratory tests of thyroid function produced by any one of a large number of drugs. In particular, estrogen usage increases levels of thyroxine-binding globulin and may therefore lead to elevated serum thyroxine levels; in contrast, androgens and high doses of corticosteroids depress thyroxine-binding globulin and may therefore lead to low total serum thyroxine [65].

Disorders of the Adrenal Cortex
Adrenocortical Insufficiency

Destruction or atrophy of the adrenal cortex produces a deficiency of cortisol and aldosterone. This disorder, known as Addison's disease, may be due to a variety of etiologies. Idiopathic adrenocortical atrophy, which may actually represent an autoimmune disease, is the most common form of this disorder today. Infectious destruction of the adrenal cortex, most commonly from tuberculosis or histoplasmosis, metastatic carcinoma involving both adrenals, surgical removal (sometimes done in the treatment of breast cancer), hemorrhage, amyloidosis, and congenital defects may also be responsible for the primary forms of adrenocortical insufficiency. Secondary forms of this disorder are caused by either hypopituitarism, isolated ACTH deficiency (a limited form of pituitary dysfunction), or suppression of the hypothalamic-pituitary axis, particularly as a result of long-term suppression with exogenous steroid therapy or as a consequence of an encroachment on the pituitary by a tumor or cyst.

The typical signs and symptoms of Addison's disease commonly include weakness, weight loss, hypotension, fasting hypoglycemia, and hyperpigmentation. Poor appetite, nausea and abdominal pain, easy fatigability, personality changes, and a heightened sense of smell are also typical features. The hyperpigmentation may be confused with a suntan, but it is typically present over areas that are not exposed to the sun. Hyperpigmentation may also be evident in the gums or other mucous membranes.

In women, the menstrual cycle is usually not altered in Addison's disease, since ovarian and gonadotropin function are not disturbed unless a hypopituitary state is present. However, since adrenocortical androgen production is markedly diminished, there is frequently a significant decrease in libido. Vaginal lubrication is unaltered unless a hypopituitary state is present or unless a vaginal infection occurs (there is an increased frequency of moniliasis associated with Addison's disease); typically, patterns of female sexual arousal are intact. Approximately 30 to 40 percent of women with adrenocortical insufficiency, however, report a diminished orgasmic capacity or loss of orgasmic response. It is not clear whether this change, which sometimes reverses with cortisone replacement, is primarily androgen-dependent or whether it is simply a reflection of a response to chronic illness.

Women who have adrenocortical insufficiency will sometimes continue to experience depressed sexual interest and impairment in orgasmic functioning despite adequate restoration of corticosteroid support. In such cases, a trial of low-dose oral androgen replacement therapy often reverses the sexual problems. This finding may reflect the fact that replacement of corticosteroids (e.g., prednisone or cortisone) does not replace the lost adrenocortical androgen synthesis, since these drugs are only weakly androgenic. Nevertheless, in women with adrenal insufficiency in whom alterations in libido or sexual function do not occur, no purpose is served ordinarily by using androgen supplementation. Women with adrenocortical insufficiency will often note decreased growth of body hair as a result of their androgen deficiency.

Men with Addison's disease usually experience a diminished interest in sex and a decrease in initiatory sexual behaviors. This change does not reflect a lowering of circulating levels of testosterone (since more than 90 percent of testosterone in the male is testicular in origin) but appears to be an effect of the weakness, debility, and mental changes that occur in this disease. When secondary adrenal insufficiency occurs, the disruption of pituitary or hypothalamic function often extends to disturbances of gonadotropin secretion, so that both testosterone synthesis and spermatogenesis may be significantly diminished. In these instances, cortisone replacement will not correct the associated impotence, which requires androgen for reversal (see also the section on hypopituitarism later in this chapter). Approximately 35 percent of men with Addison's disease are impotent, whereas closer to 80 percent of men with secondary forms of adrenocortical insufficiency are impotent for the reasons mentioned above.

Usually the dramatic improvements in general well-being, energy level, and physical strength that occur with adequate treatment of Addison's disease are sufficient to reverse the associated sexual problems in the male. When this reversal does not occur, evaluation of the possibility of associated endocrine disorders, such as diabetes mellitus or thyroid disease, may be beneficial, since there is an increased incidence of these disorders with primary adrenocortical insufficiency.

Counseling for either men or women with sexual disturbances due to adrenal insufficiency can usually be minimal, since these problems respond well to adequate medical management. Attention to determining the followup status of both libido and sexual functioning one to two months after corticosteroid therapy is begun is important in this regard, since some patients may require further diagnostic testing or more detailed and directive counseling. Ordinarily, however, a supportive and educational approach will be all that is required.

Hypercortisolism

Hypercortisolism, the result of excess production of cortisol, is also known as Cushing's syndrome. The patient's appearance is typically altered by a pattern of trunkal obesity, wherein the extremities are usually not affected and the gain in weight is primarily due to the accumulation of adipose tissue, often causing a "buffalo hump." Easy bruisability, florid facies, hypertension, diabetes mellitus, weakness, edema, purple striae on the abdomen, and alterations of personality are also common features.

Cushing's syndrome may be the result of an adrenal tumor (either adenoma or carcinoma, usually unilateral) in which tumor cells produce cortisol independently of regulation from pituitary ACTH levels; it may also result from the excess secretion of ACTH by the pituitary gland (this is known as Cushing's disease, in contrast to Cushing's syndrome); or it can occur when there is ectopic production of ACTH by tumors (usually carcinomas) of nonpituitary origin. Tumors of the lung, pancreas, and thymus are most frequently implicated in ectopic ACTH production [66], while other sources include gastric carcinoid, prostatic carcinoma, apudoma of the esophagus, carcinoma of the cervix, salivary gland adenocystic carcinoma, pheochromocytoma, and liver tumors [67].

Amenorrhea is a common feature of Cushing's syndrome, occurring in approximately 80 percent of women with this disorder; almost all women with Cushing's syndrome experience a disruption of their menstrual cycles with oligomenorrhea. The ovaries in Cushing's syndrome are histologically unaffected [68], and the specific cause of these menstrual disturbances is not known. About two-thirds of women with this disorder exhibit an increased production of adrenal androgen [69] and therefore develop physical signs of mild to moderate virilism, including hirsutism, clitoral hypertrophy, deepening of the voice and, occasionally, temporal hair recession [70]. Libido in women with Cushing's syndrome is variably affected, being slightly diminished or normal in most women but being either markedly increased or decreased in about 10 to 20 percent of women. It is difficult to sort out all the factors that may be influencing libido under conditions of cortisol and androgen excess, since the following negative components may be offsetting the behavioral stimulus of excess androgen levels:

1. Nonspecific effects of chronic illness.
2. Diminished physical attractiveness and loss of self-esteem associated with altered body image.
3. Frequent occurrence of diabetes mellitus.
4. Predisposition to vaginal infections.
5. Medications used to control high blood pressure.
6. Muscle weakness and vertebral bone pain.
7. Changes in psychological status, including psychosis and depression.

Orgasmic function has not been carefully assessed in women with Cushing's syndrome, but in a series of 23 patients, 7 women (30 percent) reported being nonorgasmic [71]. In 4 of these women, the orgasmic dysfunction was reversed after appropriate medical or surgical management of the underlying disease.

Men with Cushing's syndrome characteristically report diminished libido or difficulty in erective function, or both. In one report, 100 percent of the male patients with Cushing's syndrome had such disruption of sexual function [70]. In another series, 8 of 11 men with this syndrome were impotent and all reported noticeable decreases in libido [71]. These changes are usually correctable when the disease is controlled medically or surgically, but impotence may persist if the diabetes brought about by Cushing's syndrome does not improve significantly with treatment. In addition to the possible effect of diabetes or antihypertensive drugs on sexual function, the role of lowered potassium levels must be considered, along with the fact that gynecomastia and other feminizing signs may occur. In some patients, decreased testosterone levels have been documented [69]. Testicular histology in patients with Cushing's syndrome may reflect atrophy, disrupted spermatogenesis, and fibrosis of the tubules; Leydig cells have sometimes been found to be absent in these patients [70]. The matter is further complicated by the fact that some authors have proposed a psychosomatic basis for Cushing's disease [72].

Other Disorders of the Adrenal Gland

Feminizing Adrenocortical Tumors

A feminizing adrenocortical tumor is a rare condition that usually occurs in men between the ages of 20 and 45. The tumor, which may be either an adenoma or a carcinoma, produces large quantities of estrogens that lead to feminization. Almost all male patients with this disorder have gynecomastia, and the testes are typically atrophic, with suppression of both testosterone production and spermatogenesis. Libido is usually diminished, and potency disorders are common. The tumor may metastasize; treatment consists of surgical excision.

Hyperaldosteronism

Hyperaldosteronism is a spectrum of disorders presenting a situation of excess aldosterone in circulation; this condition may be either primary (due to adrenocortical tumor or hyperplasia) or secondary (due to the nephrotic syndrome, cirrhosis, malignant hypertension, or other extra-adrenal disease). The usual presentation of primary hyperaldosteronism is with hypertension and hypokalemia. The hypokalemia frequently leads to paresthesias and muscle weakness, as well as postural hypotension. Impotence occurs in approximately 30 to 40 percent of men, presumably as a result of the neurologic consequences of depleted body potassium stores. Libido may be decreased in either men or women with this disorder, although in some patients it is not significantly altered. Twenty percent of women with primary hyperaldosteronism experience reduction or loss of orgasmic responsiveness. In secondary forms of hyperaldosteronism, the sexual consequences, if any, are those resulting from the underlying disease process.

Pheochromocytoma

A pheochromocytoma is a tumor of the adrenal medulla that produces large amounts of catecholamines, either continuously or in an episodic fashion. The usual manifestations of this disorder include hypertension, excessive sweating, headache, palpitations, tachycardia, and psychic changes. Sexual dysfunction is not a common accompaniment to this condition, but rarely the location of such a tumor in the bladder or within the pelvis can cause a massive outpouring of catecholamines in association with sexual arousal, leading to an attack of flushing, weakness, palpitations, or, occasionally, syncope.

Disorders of the Pituitary

The pituitary gland is a small organ located in the base of the skull in close anatomic proximity to the optic chiasm (the crossing of the optic nerves). Hormones secreted by the anterior pituitary gland play an important role in the control of other endocrine glands. Although it is now known that the pituitary gland is not the "master gland" of endocrine regulation in the body, since most primary regulatory mechanisms occur in the hypothalamus, the pituitary gland has a large number of important endocrine roles. Only those disorders of the pituitary that are associated prominently with sexual problems will be considered here.

Hypopituitarism

The most dramatic and complete expression of a deficiency in pituitary function occurs after the surgical removal or destruction through irradiation of the pituitary gland. Such procedures have been undertaken in the treatment of metastatic carcinoma or severe diabetic retinopathy as well as for the removal of pituitary tumors. Depending on the completeness of such surgery or the damage to pituitary tissue produced by irradiation, subsequent pituitary function can range from absolute deficiency to moderate impairment. Complete pituitary deficiency, in its untreated state, is not compatible with survival because of the severe disruption of adrenocortical and thyroid function that it produces. When replacement of cortisone and thyroid hormone is properly instituted, patients who have had hypophysectomies (removal of the pituitary) are usually able to lead relatively normal lives.

Hypopituitarism can also result from tumors of the pituitary, most commonly chromophobe adenomas; from tumors in close proximity to the pituitary, such as craniopharyngiomas, which may exert mechanical pressure on the pituitary tissue and thus produce damage; from pituitary infarction, most often associated with massive postpartum uterine hemorrhage (Sheehan's syndrome); and from granulomas and infiltrations, which may be either infectious or noninfectious in nature.

Pituitary tumors produce significant hormonal deficiencies in approximately 60 percent of cases. Hypogonadism is typically the first sign of hypopituitarism, occurring much earlier than signs of thyroid hormone deficiency or cortisol deficits. Common manifestations of pituitary tumors include loss of vision, headaches, sleep or appetite disturbances, and disruptions of reproductive and sexual function. These tumors can also produce excessive amounts of some pituitary hormones.

Lundberg and Wide studied 65 adult males (mean age, 44.1 years) with pituitary tumors and found that 76 percent had decreased or absent libido and potency [73]. In approximately 32 percent of their patients, sexual dysfunction was the initial symptom of the tumor, but only 1 out of 20 of these men sought medical evaluation because of this symptom. There was a marked difference in the frequency of sexual problems in men with small intrasellar tumors compared to men with larger tumors that extended into the suprasellar region: Sexual dysfunction was found in 52.3 percent of the former group and in 88.1 percent of the latter group. Although 14 of 36 patients had hyperprolactinemia, only 40 percent of the patients with sexual problems had elevated serum prolactin levels. However, most of the men with pituitary tumors and sexual dysfunction had low serum FSH and LH concentrations, and only 1 of 32 men with sexual disturbances had a normal testosterone level (see Fig. 6-8).

Snyder and his colleagues recently described gonadal function in 50 men with untreated pituitary adenomas [74]. They found evidence of significant hypogonadism (mean [±S.E.M.] serum testosterone = 243 ± 25 ng per 100 ml), although mean basal LH and FSH concentrations were normal. Only 14 of their 50 patients could produce a semen specimen; four of these men were found to have normal total sperm counts despite subnormal testosterone concentrations. Libido was impaired in 38 of their 50 patients, but only 9 of 33 men with subnormal testosterone

Figure 6-8. Serum testosterone concentrations in 40 men with pituitary
tumors. (From P. O. Lundberg and L.
Wide, Sexual function in males with
pituitary tumors, *Fertility and
Sterility* 29:175–179, 1978. Reproduced with the permission of the authors and the publisher, The American Fertility Society.)

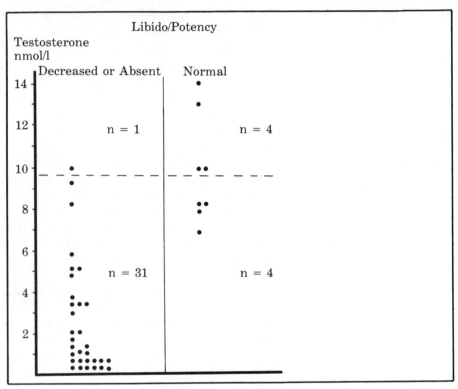

levels had small testes. Hyperprolactinemia was found in 14 of the 50
men; interestingly, 11 men had normal LH responses to GnRH stimulation despite having low serum testosterone levels, and 24 percent of the
men with pituitary adenomas had elevated basal FSH levels or exaggerated FSH responses to GnRH [74].

Carter and coworkers studied a series of 22 men with prolactin-
secreting pituitary tumors and hypogonadism and found that 20 of
them (91 percent) complained of impotence and decreased libido [75].
The median pretreatment serum prolactin level in this group was
880 ng per milliliter, and following surgery or radiation therapy all
prolactin levels remained elevated. Men who were then treated with
bromocryptine (a dopamine agonist) developed decreased serum prolactin levels, increased testosterone levels, and improved potency. Two
patients who received testosterone replacement therapy without
bromocryptine had no improvement of the impotence. Interestingly, in

most of the patients in this series, LH and FSH levels were either low or low-normal, while human chorionic gonadotropin stimulation revealed a normal capacity of Leydig cells to increase testosterone production despite the existence of hyperprolactinemia. As the authors point out, this indicates that the hyperprolactinemia may cause or coexist with diminished GnRH secretion, which subsequently leads to disturbed LH output and reduced testosterone secretion. Destruction of pituitary or hypothalamic tissue as a result of mechanical tumor compression does not appear to be the primary factor, since testosterone levels rose promptly after bromocryptine therapy had begun. Hyperprolactinemia in men may also be associated with disrupted spermatogenesis, which can be corrected by bromocryptine therapy [76–78]. Bromocryptine therapy has recently been reported as effective in reducing the size of a pituitary tumor (see Fig. 6-9) and in improving potency despite the persistence of low levels of circulating testosterone [79].

An elevated serum prolactin level is an early diagnostic indicator of the existence of a pituitary adenoma; in fact, 20 to 30 percent of otherwise unexplained secondary amenorrhea and one-third of cases of galactorrhea-amenorrhea now appear to be attributable to prolactin-secreting pituitary tumors [80–82]. Newer techniques such as polytomography that allow detection of pituitary microadenomas in cases in which standard x-rays of the pituitary and sella turcica show no abnormality also contribute to improved diagnostic acumen [83]. In light of such rapidly increasing information correlating pituitary tumors, hypogonadism, and hyperprolactinemia, and because of the therapeutic potential of bromocryptine, patients with amenorrhea, galactorrhea, or impotence associated with low testosterone should have serum prolactin levels measured routinely.

Prolactin-secreting pituitary tumors have been reported to regress during long-term bromocryptine therapy [84], and intermittent bromocryptine therapy as well as continuous therapy can be used to induce ovulation in hyperprolactinemic patients [85, 86]. Gemzell and Wang note that the risk of developing complications during pregnancy is significantly higher in women with untreated pituitary macroadenomas (35.7%) than in women with untreated microadenomas (5.5%) or treated adenomas (7.1%); furthermore, the women with pituitary adenomas had generally uncomplicated obstetric courses [86].

In Sheehan's syndrome, which is the most common cause of pituitary deficiency after tumor and hypophysectomy, destruction of pituitary tissue occurs as a result of infarction and subsequent necrosis precipitated by the circulatory shock accompanying severe postpartum hem-

Figure 6-9. (A) EMI brain scan (before and after intravenous injection of iothalamate meglumine) of a 27-year-old man with impotence, 3 years after discovery of a locally invasive pituitary adenoma treated initially by surgery and radiation therapy (total dose, 4,500 rads external megalovoltage irradiation). A large tumor with suprasellar and right lateral extension is seen. (B) EMI brain scan of the same patient after 3 months of bromocryptine therapy: Potency and libido were normal, and there appears to have been complete regression of the tumor mass. (From McGregor, Scanlon, Hall, Cook, and Hall [79]. Reprinted, by permission, from the *New England Journal of Medicine.*)

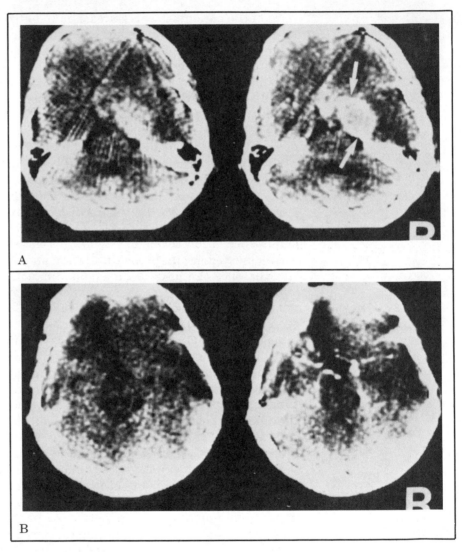

orrhage. The first sign of this problem is usually failure of lactation; recovery from the bleeding is extremely slow and appears never to be complete. Amenorrhea is common; if menstruation returns, there is usually severe oligomenorrhea. Infertility problems are also frequent. Evidence of hypothyroidism or adrenal insufficiency occurs early, but the diagnosis may not be made for years.

Hemochromatosis, a disease of iron deposition in many body tissues, affects the pituitary gland in approximately 60 percent of cases [87]. Decreased pituitary prolactin reserve and hypogonadotropic hypogonadism have been reported specifically as a result of hemochromatosis [88]. This disorder may also lead to direct testicular damage [89], although there is some disagreement as to this point [90]. Sexual disturbances in men with hemochromatosis can result from impaired pituitary function, from the usually associated diabetes, from testicular damage, or from liver impairment by iron deposition. Seventy to 80 percent of men with hemochromatosis report impotence and depressed libido. Other infiltrative processes (Hand-Schüller-Christian disease, amyloidosis) and granulomatous disease (sarcoidosis, eosinophilic granuloma, tuberculosis, and syphilis) can produce hypopituitarism infrequently.

Obliteration of pituitary gonadotropin production due to hypophysectomy or other disorders results in severe atrophy of the gonads in both sexes. Spermatogenesis halts almost completely and testosterone synthesis in both the testes and the adrenals is essentially obliterated. In men, libido and potency decrease with an almost invariable consistency, usually within a matter of weeks following the hypophysectomy. Frequently, the ability to ejaculate is lost; if the capacity for ejaculation persists, it is noted that the volume of seminal fluid may be greatly decreased, since this is an androgen-sensitive phenomenon. Facial hair growth ceases and body hair decreases with time. There is often weakness, easy fatigability, weight loss, and decreased muscle mass due to the lack of anabolic support of androgens. These alterations are easily reversible with the administration of adequate exogenous testosterone, except for the atrophy of the testes and lack of sperm production, which require gonadotropin stimulation. Instead of using exogenous testosterone replacement, the same effects can be obtained by the use of injections of human chorionic gonadotropin (HCG), which stimulates the Leydig cells to produce testosterone in a normal fashion. It is possible in many instances to restore fertility, if desired, by a treatment regimen using a combination of exogenous HCG and FSH, although spermatogenesis will develop and persist for only as long as this treatment is continued. Money and Clopper observe that postpubertal males who have had hypophysectomies in childhood generally demonstrate some degree of erotic inertia [91].

Ordinarily, treatment by gonadotropins of the secondary hypogonadism that results from hypopituitarism is unwarranted, since it requires frequent injections (usually at least three times weekly), is extremely expensive, and may lead to problems of antibody formation directed against the injected hormones.

Hypopituitarism in the female leads to infertility due to anovulation, amenorrhea or oligomenorrhea, and estrogen deficiency. The estrogen deficiency results in atrophy of the vaginal mucosa and breast tissue (the role of prolactin deficiency in the postpubertal woman in support of breast tissue mass is not well understood at present). Most women with pituitary deficiency experience a drop in libido, but this is primarily a result of the androgen deficiency that occurs because of the decreased functioning of the adrenal cortex. However, the reduced androgen levels are clearly not the only determinant of lowered libido, since both chronic disease and debility, and the specific medical and psychological complications of the underlying disease producing hypopituitarism, will also be important factors in determining levels of sexual interest. In one series of six women with panhypopituitarism who received hormone replacement for five to seven years, all showed depressed libido, but in half these women, neither androgen nor estrogen therapy was successful in completely restoring premorbid levels of sexual functioning [92].

Orgasmic response is frequently impaired in women with hypopituitarism. In a series of 18 women with pituitary deficiencies resulting from chromophobe adenoma (N = 7), Sheehan's syndrome (N = 4), hypophysectomy (N = 4), craniopharyngioma (N = 2), and sarcoidosis (N = 1), six women were nonorgasmic and an additional seven women noted a significant decrease in their orgasmic frequency [71]. It is not known whether or not the prolactin deficiency that many of these women had may have contributed to their sexual problems. All of the 18 women described lowered libido in comparison to previous levels of sex drive. Similarly, Schorr and Sutherland reported on changes in female sexuality after hypophysectomy in women with metastatic breast cancer [93]. These workers found that while neither mastectomy nor oophorectomy had a significant influence on sexual functioning, following hypophysectomy there was a sharp reduction of sexual desire, activity, and gratification. After hypophysectomy, none of their patients retained their preoperative degree of libido, with 26 of 30 patients claiming no sexual interest whatever.

Conditions of Pituitary Hyperfunction

Acromegaly. Acromegaly is the result of a pituitary tumor (generally an eosinophilic or mixed-cell adenoma) that produces excess amounts of growth hormone. Commonly, this disorder presents with headache, visual disturbances, a coarsening of facial features, thickening of the skull and prominence of the jaw (prognathism), and enlargement of the hands and feet, which often leads to a change in hat, ring, or shoe size. The occurrence of excess production of growth hormone by a tumor prior to puberty results in gigantism, with excessive growth of the long bones in the body in a symmetrical fashion due to the fact that the epiphyseal plates are not yet fused.

Almost all body tissues are affected by acromegaly. The skin becomes thickened and coarse; arthritic symptoms are common, due to bony overgrowth; peripheral neuropathy and paresthesias, particularly in the hands, are not unusual; and enlargement of many body organs, including the heart, thyroid, liver, spleen, and kidneys, occurs in the majority of patients. Impaired glucose tolerance is present in more than half of acromegalics, and overt diabetes develops in approximately 15 to 20 percent [57].

Women with acromegaly commonly note menstrual irregularities or amenorrhea, which may reflect both an alteration in gonadotropin secretion due to the pituitary tumor and the frequent occurrence of thyroid dysfunction associated with acromegaly. Body-image problems are often accompaniments of this disorder in women as well and may contribute to the diminished libido reported by 30 to 50 percent of female patients. Data on orgasmic response in acromegaly are not currently available. Galactorrhea occurs in 10 to 20 percent of women with acromegaly, and prolactin levels are sometimes elevated as a result either of mechanical disruption of normal hypothalamic inhibitory control or of excess production by tumor cells [94].

In men with acromegaly, diminished libido occurs in approximately 70 percent of patients, although early in the course of the disease there is sometimes a paradoxical increase in sex drive. Impotence is a common finding in acromegalic men, affecting 30 to 40 percent of patients [95]. The impotence may be caused by one or more of the following: diabetes, secondary hypogonadism resulting from disruption of gonadotropin secretion, thyroid disorders, neuropathy, or—speculatively—hyperprolactinemia. Treatment of acromegaly, by either surgery, irradiation, or medical means (e.g., use of medroxyprogesterone, bromocryptine or other ergot derivations, or chlorpromazine), is difficult and will not always reverse the associated sexual problems. Careful evaluation to assess the possible need for testosterone replacement therapy, treatment of thyroid disorders, control of diabetes or hyperprolactinemia, and psychological counseling may be beneficial when the primary approach to treatment is not successful in restoring sexual health.

**Miscellaneous
Endocrine Problems
Relating to Sexuality**
Galactorrhea

The occurrence of inappropriate lactation may be due to a wide variety of causes, which are listed below:

Pituitary tumor
Amenorrhea-galactorrhea syndrome
Chiari-Frommel syndrome
Drug-induced
   Oral contraceptives
   Phenothiazines
   Benzodiazepines
   Reserpine
   Alpha-methyldopa
   Antidepressants
   Haloperidol
   Isoniazid
Chest wall lesions
   Herpes zoster
   Post-thoracotomy
Hypothyroidism
Destructive lesions of the hypothalamus
   Sarcoidosis
   Hand-Schüller-Christian disease
Empty-sella syndrome
Head trauma
Precocious puberty
Idiopathic

There is currently much confusion in the literature in describing the incidence of galactorrhea in women during the reproductive years, with estimates ranging from as low as 1 percent of ovulatory women and 3.6 percent of anovulatory women to 22 percent or higher [96]. These differences are attributable to sampling techniques, the specific methods used to detect breast secretions, and the precise way in which galactorrhea is defined. Galactorrhea occurring in association with the use of oral contraceptives is common and is not cause for alarm.

Elevated secretion of prolactin is now known to be an important cause of galactorrhea, although it is not found in all cases nor does the prolactin level correlate with the amount of galactorrhea that occurs

[97]. In one series of 50 women with inappropriate lactation, 38 percent had elevated serum prolactin levels and all had amenorrhea [98]. The frequent occurrence of amenorrhea in association with galactorrhea is usually accompanied by hyperprolactinemia [99]. Conventional medical treatment, using clomiphene citrate or estrogens, generally fails to correct the abnormalities. Instead, the use of drugs such as L-dopa or bromocryptine is often effective in restoring ovarian function and controlling the galactorrhea [82, 96, 100].

An interesting phenomenon that is not generally known is the fact that some women have brief episodes of galactorrhea shortly after vigorous sexual activity, typically when orgasm has occurred. This may be due to elevations in circulating prolactin that occur as a result of breast manipulation [98, 101, 102] and that are associated with orgasm [103]. This type of galactorrhea is unlikely to be a reflection of underlying pathology, although if it changes from a transient to a more persistent pattern or is associated with other symptoms that might be indicative of intracranial tumor (e.g., headaches, visual changes, alterations in the sense of smell), diagnostic studies would be warranted. Galactorrhea from a wide variety of causes may be more evident during or immediately after sexual activity, as well.

Gynecomastia

Enlargement of the male breast due to an increase in glandular tissue rather than to accumulation of adipose tissue or tumor is a common occurrence that may sometimes be associated with endocrine disease. Some of the causes of this condition are given in the following list:

Normal puberty
Hypogonadism
  Klinefelter's syndrome
  Reifenstein's syndrome
Liver disease
Chronic renal failure
Hemodialysis
Refeeding after starvation or malnutrition
Drug ingestion
  Estrogens
  Androgens
  Human chorionic gonadotropin
  Digoxin
  Spironolactone
  Reserpine

Clomiphene citrate
Cimetidine
Tumors
   Testicular
   Adrenal
   Pituitary
   Bronchogenic carcinoma
   Hodgkin's disease
Leprosy
Hypothyroidism or hyperthyroidism
Idiopathic

It should be noted that approximately 40 to 60 percent of adolescent boys exhibit gynecomastia, a phenomenon that is presumably due to the increased levels of estrogens reaching the breast tissue as a result of interconversion from rising androgen levels associated with pubertal development [104]. Although this type of gynecomastia will usually regress within one or two years, it is sometimes a matter of major embarrassment and stigmatization for the affected teenager, who may request surgical correction of this condition. Body-image problems occurring during adolescence may serve as precursors of later psychosexual difficulties in some instances. A recent report claims that 36 percent of 306 normal adult men had gynecomastia, usually ≤ 4 cm in diameter [105]. This finding is not substantiated by our own data, where gynecomastia was detected in only 7.2 percent of 685 men between the ages of 21 and 40 and 9.4 percent of men aged 41 to 60 [106].

Gynecomastia can be a result of drug treatment with a number of different pharmacologic agents ranging from digitalis to spironolactone to phenothiazines or reserpine. Male breast enlargement may also occur during treatment of hypogonadism with testosterone or related androgens or with human chorionic gonadotropin. Drug-induced gynecomastia is usually reversible upon cessation of the drug, but this is not always the case.

Prolactin levels may be elevated in gynecomastia and presumably provide the mechanism of action for the occurrence of breast enlargement in conditions such as those resulting from the use of phenothiazines. However, in many men with gynecomastia, serum prolactin levels are completely normal [107].

When gynecomastia leads to problems with a man's body-image, self-esteem, or sexual identity, referral to a qualified psychotherapist is indicated. In certain instances it may be most efficacious to reduce breast size by surgery under these circumstances, but this decision should be made in collaboration with a careful psychological assessment of the problem.

Hypoglycemia

Symptoms of low blood sugar usually occur when plasma glucose levels drop below 50 mg per 100 ml. Common symptoms include weakness, tremulousness, poor coordination, tachycardia, sweating, anxiety, and altered alertness. The mechanisms that underlie the development of hypoglycemia are extremely varied, but it is safe to say that there is a major degree of overestimation of the occurrence of hypoglycemia by laymen, with many instances of simply not feeling well being self-diagnosed as due to low blood sugar levels.

Although sexual difficulties may frequently accompany some disorders that lead to hypoglycemia (e.g., liver disease, Addison's disease, hypopituitarism), present evidence does not support the general association of sexual difficulties with low blood sugar. It is interesting to note that a recent study showed that 60 percent of patients who *think* they have hypoglycemia have sexual problems, which raises the possibility that these patients seek organic reasons to explain predominantly psychological problems [108]. Clinical experience in treating sexual difficulties supports this observation and reveals a rate of hypoglycemia of less than 0.1 percent.

A Closing Note

Advances are occurring rapidly in the field of endocrinology as highly specific radioimmunoassay techniques and sophisticated hormone isolation procedures developed in the past decade have brought about considerable research and clinical interest. It is likely that additional progress will be made in delineating the interrelationships between hormones and behavior as further attention becomes focused on matters of psychoneuroendocrinology. Such progress is likely to shed even more light on our understanding of human sexuality in health and illness.

1. Klinefelter, H. F., Jr., Reifenstein, E. C., Jr., and Albright, F.   Syndrome characterized by gynecomastia, aspermatogenesis without a-Leydigism, and increased excretion of follicle-stimulating hormone. *Journal of Clinical Endocrinology and Metabolism* 2:615–627, 1942.
2. Zuppinger, K., Engel, E., Forbes, A. P., Mantooth, L., and Claffey, J.   Klinefelter's syndrome, a clinical and cytogenic study in twenty-four cases. *Acta Endocrinologica* [Suppl. 113] 54:5–48, 1967.
3. Barr, M. L.   The natural history of Klinefelter's syndrome. *Fertility and Sterility* 17:429–441, 1966.

4. Becker, K. L. Clinical and therapeutic experiences with Klinefelter's syndrome. *Fertility and Sterility* 23:568–578, 1972.

5. Stewart-Bentley, M., and Horton, R. Leydig cell function in Klinefelter's syndrome. *Metabolism* 22:875–884, 1973.

6. Hsueh, W. A., Hsu, T. H., and Federman, D. D. Endocrine features of Klinefelter's syndrome. *Medicine* (Baltimore) 57:447–461, 1978.

7. Foss, G. L., Bell, E. T., Lewis, F. J. W., Loraine, J. A., and Pollard, B. R. Effect of clomiphene on spermatogenesis and hormone excretion in a patient with Klinefelter's syndrome. *Journal of Reproduction and Fertility* 13:315–320, 1967.

8. Foss, G. L., and Lewis, F. J. W. A study of four cases with Klinefelter's syndrome showing motile spermatozoa in their ejaculate. *Journal of Reproduction and Fertility* 25:401–408, 1971.

9. Futterweit, W. Spermatozoa in seminal fluid of a patient with Klinefelter's syndrome. *Fertility and Sterility* 18:492–496, 1967.

10. Fukutani, K., Isurugi, K., Takayasu, H., Wakabayashi, K., and Tamaoki, B. Effects of depot testosterone therapy on serum levels of luteinizing hormone and follicle-stimulating hormone in patients with Klinefelter's syndrome and hypogonadotropic eunuchoidism. *Journal of Clinical Endocrinology and Metabolism* 39:856–864, 1974.

11. Money, J. Human behavior cytogenics: Review of psychopathology in three syndromes—47,XXY; 47,XYY; and 45,X. *Journal of Sex Research* 11:181–200, 1975.

12. Halbrecht, I. Nuclear sex determination in azoospermic adults and in newborns with hypospadias. *Fertility and Sterility* 11:112–117, 1960.

13. Becker, K. L. Clinical and therapeutic experiences with Klinefelter's syndrome. *Fertility and Sterility* 23:568–578, 1972.

14. Aiman, J., Griffin, J. E., Gazak, J. M., Wilson, J. D., and MacDonald, P. C. Androgen insensitivity as a cause of infertility in otherwise normal men. *New England Journal of Medicine* 300:223–227, 1979.

15. Aynsley-Green, A., Zachmann, M., Illig, R., Rampini, S., and Prader, A. Congenital bilateral anorchia in childhood: Clinical, endocrine and therapeutic evaluation of 21 cases. *Clinical Endocrinology* (Oxford) 5:381–391, 1976.

16. Nielson, J., Friedrich, U., Holm, V., Petersen, G. B., Stabell, I., Simonsen, H., and Johansen, K. Turner phenotype in males. *Clinical Genetics* 4:58–63, 1973.

17. Chaves-Carballo, E., and Hayles, A. B. Ullrich-Turner syndrome in the male. *Mayo Clinic Proceedings* 41:843–854, 1966.

18. Steinberger, E. The etiology and pathophysiology of testicular dysfunction in man. *Fertility and Sterility* 29:481–491, 1978.

19. Vilar, O. Effect of Cytostatic Drugs on Human Testicular Function. In R. E. Mancini and L. Martini (eds.), *Male Fertility and Sterility*. New York: Academic Press, 1974. P. 423.

20. Kallmann, R. J., Schoenfeld, W. A., and Barrera, S. E. The genetic aspects of primary eunuchoidism. *American Journal of Mental Deficiency* 48:203–236, 1944.

21. Santen, R. J., and Paulsen, C. A. Hypogonadotropic eunuchoidism: I.

Clinical study of the mode of inheritance. *Journal of Clinical Endocrinology and Metabolism* 36:47–54, 1973.

22. Tagatz, G., Fialkow, P. J., Smith, D., and Spadoni, L. Hypogonadotropic hypogonadism associated with anosmia in the female. *New England Journal of Medicine* 283:1326–1329, 1970.

23. Males, J. L., Townsend, J. L., and Schneider, R. A. Hypogonadotropic hypogonadism with anosmia—Kallmann's syndrome. *Archives of Internal Medicine* 131:501–507, 1973.

24. Antaki, A., Somma, M., Wyman, H., and Van Campenhout, J. Hypothalamic-pituitary function in the olfactogenital syndrome. *Journal of Clinical Endocrinology and Metabolism* 38:1083–1089, 1974.

25. Santen, R. J., and Paulsen, C. A. Hypogonadotropic eunuchoidism: II. Gonadal responsiveness to exogenous gonadotropins. *Journal of Clinical Endocrinology and Metabolism* 36:55–63, 1973.

26. Paulsen, C. A. The Testes. In R. H. Williams (ed.), *Textbook of Endocrinology* (5th ed.). Philadelphia: W. B. Saunders Co., 1974. Pp. 323–367.

27. Maroulis, G. B., Parlow, A. F., and Marshall, J. R. Isolated follicle-stimulating hormone deficiency in man. *Fertility and Sterility* 28:818–822, 1977.

28. Rabinowitz, D., Cohen, M., and Rosenman, E. Germinal aplasia of the testis associated with FSH deficiency of hypothalamic origin (abstract). *Clinical Research* 22:346A, 1974.

29. Stewart-Bentley, M., and Wallack, M. Isolated FSH deficiency in a male (abstract). *Clinical Research* 24:96A, 1975.

30. Goldberg, M. B., Scully, A. L., Solomon, I. L., and Steinbach, H. L. Gonadal dysgenesis in phenotypic female subjects. *American Journal of Medicine* 45:529–543, 1968.

31. Wilroy, R. S. Gonadal Dysgenesis. In J. R. Givens (ed.), *Gynecologic Endocrinology*. Chicago: Year Book Medical Publishers, 1977. Pp. 93–102.

32. Engel, E., and Forbes, A. P. Cytogenic and clinical findings in 48 patients with congenitally defective or absent ovaries. *Medicine* (Baltimore) 44:135–164, 1965.

33. Grumbach, M. M., and Van Wyk, J. J. Disorders of Sex Differentiation. In R. H. Williams (ed.), *Textbook of Endocrinology* (5th ed.). Philadelphia: W. B. Saunders Co., 1974. Pp. 423–501.

34. Lisker, R., Jiménez, R., Larrea, F., Mutchinick, O., Ruz, L., Medina, J. M., and Pérez-Palacios, G. Cytogenic and endocrine studies in a 45,X female subject with spontaneous sexual development. *American Journal of Obstetrics and Gynecology* 133:149–153, 1979.

35. Carr, D. H. Chromosome studies in spontaneous abortions. *Obstetrics and Gynecology* 26:308–326, 1966.

36. Ehrhardt, A. A., Greenberg, N., and Money, J. Female gender identity and absence of fetal gonadal hormones: Turner's syndrome. *Johns Hopkins Medical Journal* 126:237–248, 1970.

37. Money, J. Two cytogenic syndromes: Psychologic comparisons: I. Intelligence and specific-factor quotients. *Journal of Psychiatric Research* 2:223–231, 1964.

38. Alexander, D., Ehrhardt, A. A., and Money, J. Defective figure drawing,

geometric and human, in Turner's syndrome. *Journal of Nervous and Mental Disease* 142:161–167, 1966.

39. Watson, M. A., and Money, J. Behavior cytogenics and Turner's syndrome: A new principle in counseling and psychotherapy. *American Journal of Psychotherapy* 29:166–177, 1975.

40. Adamopoulos, D. A., Loraine, J. A., and Ginsburg, J. Endocrinological findings in two patients with premature ovarian failure. *Lancet* 1:161–164, 1971.

41. Ross, G. T., and Vande Wiele, R. L. The Ovaries. In R. H. Williams (ed.), *Textbook of Endocrinology* (5th ed.). Philadelphia: W. B. Saunders Co., 1974. Pp. 408–409.

42. Rubin, A., and Babbott, D. Impotence and diabetes mellitus. *Journal of the American Medical Association* 168:498–500, 1958.

43. Schöffling, K., Federlin, K., Ditschuneit, H., and Pfeiffer, E. F. Disorders of sexual function in male diabetics. *Diabetes* 12:519–527, 1963.

44. Ellenberg, M. Impotence in diabetes: The neurologic factor. *Annals of Internal Medicine* 75:213–219, 1971.

45. Kolodny, R. C., Kahn, C. B., Goldstein, H. H., and Barnett, D. M. Sexual dysfunction in diabetic men. *Diabetes* 23:306–309, 1974.

46. Faerman, I., Glover, L., Fox, D., Jadzinsky, M. N., and Rapaport, M. Impotence and diabetes: Histological studies of the autonomic nervous fibers of the corpora cavernosa in impotent diabetic males. *Diabetes* 23:971–976, 1974.

47. Ellenberg, M., and Weber, H. Retrograde ejaculation in diabetic neuropathy. *Annals of Internal Medicine* 65:1237–1246, 1966.

48. Bourne, R. B., Kretzschmar, W. A., and Esser, J. H. Successful artificial insemination in a diabetic with retrograde ejaculation. *Fertility and Sterility* 22:275–277, 1971.

49. Kolodny, R. C. Sexual dysfunction in diabetic females. *Diabetes* 20:557–559, 1971.

50. Brooks, M. H. Effects of diabetes on female sexual response. *Medical Aspects of Human Sexuality* 11(2):63–64, 1977.

51. Kolodny, R. C. Unpublished observation, 1977.

52. Younger, D., and Hadley, W. B. Infection and Diabetes. In A. Marble, P. White, R. Bradley, and L. P. Krall (eds.), *Joslin's Diabetes Mellitus* (11th ed.). Philadelphia: Lea & Febiger, 1971. Pp. 621–636.

53. Bagdade, J. D., Root, R. K., and Bulger, R. J. Impaired leukocyte function in patients with poorly controlled diabetes. *Diabetes* 23:9–15, 1974.

54. Day, R. E., and Insley, J. Maternal diabetes mellitus and congenital malformation: Survey of 205 cases. *Archives of Disease in Childhood* 51:935–938, 1976.

55. Gabbe, S. G. Review: Congenital malformations in infants of diabetic mothers. *Obstetrical and Gynecological Survey* 32:125–132, 1977.

56. Rowland, T. W., Hubbell, J. P., Jr., and Nadas, A. S. Congenital heart disease in infants of diabetic mothers. *Journal of Pediatrics* 83:815–820, 1973.

57. Kozak, G. P. Diabetes and Other Endocrine Disorders. In A. Marble, P. White, R. Bradley, and L. P. Krall (eds.), *Joslin's Diabetes Mellitus* (11th ed.). Philadelphia: Lea & Febiger, 1971. Pp. 666–694.

58. Cahill, G. F., Jr., Etzwiler, D. D., and Freinkel, N. "Control" and diabetes (editorial). *New England Journal of Medicine* 294:1004, 1976.
59. Kolodny, R. C. Unpublished observation, 1978.
60. Barnes, N. D., Hayles, A. B., and Ryan, R. J. Sexual maturation in juvenile hypothyroidism. *Mayo Clinic Proceedings* 48:849–856, 1973.
61. Dooner, H. P., Paradia, J., Aliaga, C., and Hoyl, C. The liver in thyrotoxicosis. *Archives of Internal Medicine* 120:25–32, 1967.
62. Ramsay, I. D. Muscle dysfunction in hyperthyroidism. *Lancet* 2:931–934, 1966.
63. Becker, K. L., Winnacker, J. L., Matthews, M. J., and Higgins, G. A., Jr. Gynecomastia and hyperthyroidism: An endocrine and histological investigation. *Journal of Clinical Endocrinology* 28:277–285, 1968.
64. Thomas, F. B., Mazzaferri, E. L., and Skillman, T. G. Apathetic thyrotoxicosis: A distinctive clinical and laboratory entity. *Annals of Internal Medicine* 72:679–685, 1970.
65. Cryer, P. E. *Diagnostic Endocrinology.* New York: Oxford University Press, 1976. P. 39.
66. Imura, H., Matsukura, S., Yamamoto, H., Hirata, Y., Nakai, Y., Endo, J., Tanaka, A., and Nakamura, M. Studies on ectopic ACTH-producing tumors: II. Clinical and biochemical features of 30 cases. *Cancer* 35:1430–1437, 1975.
67. Schwartz, T. B., and Ryan, W. G. *The Year Book of Endocrinology 1978.* Chicago: Year Book Medical Publishers, 1978. P. 234.
68. Iannaccone, A., Gabrilove, J. L., Sohval, A. R., and Soffer, L. J. The ovaries in Cushing's syndrome. *New England Journal of Medicine* 261:775–780, 1959.
69. Smals, A. G. H., Kloppenborg, P. W. C., and Benraad, T. J. Plasma testosterone profiles in Cushing's syndrome. *Journal of Clinical Endocrinology and Metabolism* 45:240–245, 1977.
70. Soffer, L. J., Iannaccone, A., and Gabrilove, J. L. Cushing's syndrome: A study of fifty patients. *American Journal of Medicine* 31:129–146, 1961.
71. Kolodny, R. C. Unpublished observation, 1978.
72. Gifford, S., and Gunderson, J. G. Cushing's disease as a psychosomatic disorder: A report of ten cases. *Medicine* (Baltimore) 49:397–409, 1970.
73. Lundberg, P. O., and Wide, L. Sexual function in males with pituitary tumors. *Fertility and Sterility* 29:175–179, 1978.
74. Snyder, P. J., Bigdeli, H., Gardner, D. F., Mihailovic, V., Rudenstein, R. S., Sterling, F. H., and Utiger, R. D. Gonadal function in fifty men with untreated pituitary adenomas. *Journal of Clinical Endocrinology and Metabolism* 48:309–314, 1979.
75. Carter, J. N., Tyson, J. E., Tolis, G., Van Vliet, S., Faiman, C., and Friesen, H. G. Prolactin-secreting tumors and hypogonadism in 22 men. *New England Journal of Medicine* 299:847–852, 1978.
76. Saidi, K., Wenn, R. V., and Sharif, F. Bromocriptine for male infertility. *Lancet* 1:250–251, 1977.
77. Segal, S., Polishuk, W. Z., and Ben-David, M. Hyperprolactinemic male infertility. *Fertility and Sterility* 26:1425–1427, 1976.
78. Sheth, A. R., Joshi, L. R., Moodbidri, S. B., and Rao, S. S. Serum prolactin levels in fertile and infertile men. *Andrologie* 5:297–298, 1973.

79. McGregor, A. M., Scanlon, M. F., Hall, K., Cook, D. B., and Hall, R.   Reduction in size of a pituitary tumor by bromocriptine therapy. *New England Journal of Medicine* 300:291–293, 1979.

80. Kleinberg, D. L., Noel, G. L., and Frantz, A. G.   Galactorrhea: A study of 235 cases, including 48 with pituitary tumors. *New England Journal of Medicine* 296:589–600, 1977.

81. Jacobs, H. S.   Prolactin and amenorrhea. *New England Journal of Medicine* 295:954–956, 1976.

82. Reichlin, S.   The prolactinoma problem. *New England Journal of Medicine* 300:313–315, 1979.

83. Wiebe, R. H., Hammond, C. B., and Handwerger, S.   Prolactin-secreting pituitary microadenoma: Detection and evaluation. *Fertility and Sterility* 29:282–286, 1978.

84. Nillius, S. J., Bergh, T., Lundberg, P. O., Stahle, J., and Wide, L.   Regression of a prolactin-secreting pituitary tumor during long-term treatment with bromocriptine. *Fertility and Sterility* 30:710–712, 1978.

85. Coelingh Bennink, H. J. T.   Intermittent bromocriptine treatment for the induction of ovulation in hyperprolactinemic patients. *Fertility and Sterility* 31:267–272, 1979.

86. Gemzell, C., and Wang, C. F.   Outcome of pregnancy in women with pituitary adenoma. *Fertility and Sterility* 31:363–372, 1979.

87. Stocks, A. E., and Martin, F. I. R.   Pituitary function in haemochromatosis. *American Journal of Medicine* 45:839–844, 1968.

88. Levy, C. L. and Carlson, H. E.   Decreased prolactin reserve in hemochromatosis. *Journal of Clinical Endocrinology and Metabolism* 47:444–446, 1978.

89. Walsh, C. H., Wright, A. D., Williams, J. W., and Holder, G.   A study of pituitary function in patients with idiopathic hemochromatosis. *Journal of Clinical Endocrinology and Metabolism* 43:866–872, 1976.

90. Bezwoda, W. R., Bothwell, T. H., Van der Walt, L. A., Kronheim, S., and Pimstone, B. L.   An investigation into gonadal dysfunction in patients with idiopathic haemochromatosis. *Clinical Endocrinology* 6:377–385, 1977.

91. Money, J., and Clopper, R. R.   Postpubertal psychosexual function in post-surgical male hypopituitarism. *Journal of Sex Research* 11:25–38, 1975.

92. Reichlin, S.   Relationship of the pituitary gland to human sexual behavior. *Medical Aspects of Human Sexuality* 5(2):146–154, 1971.

93. Schorr, M., and Sutherland, A. M.   The role of hormones in human behavior: III. Changes in female sexuality after hypophysectomy. *Journal of Clinical Endocrinology and Metabolism* 20:833–841, 1960.

94. Franks, S., Jacobs, L. S., and Nabarro, J. D. N.   Prolactin concentrations in patients with acromegaly: Clinical significance and response to surgery. *Clinical Endocrinology* (Oxford) 5:63–69, 1976.

95. Daughaday, W. H.   The Adenohypophysis. In R. H. Williams (ed.), *Textbook of Endocrinology* (5th ed.). Philadelphia: W. B. Saunders Co., 1974. Pp. 31–79.

96. Kemmann, E., Buckman, M. T., and Peake, G. T.   Incidence of galac-

torrhea (letter to editor and reply). *Journal of the American Medical Association* 236:2747, 1976.

97. Tolis, G., Somma, M., Van Campenhout, J., and Friesen, H. Prolactin secretion in sixty-five patients with galactorrhea. *American Journal of Obstetrics and Gynecology* 118:91–101, 1974.

98. Archer, D. F., Nankin, H. R., Gabos, P. F., Maroon, J., Nosetz, S., Wadhwa, S. R., and Josimovich, J. B. Serum prolactin in patients with inappropriate lactation. *American Journal of Obstetrics and Gynecology* 119:466–472, 1974.

99. Zárate, A., Canales, E. S., Jacobs, L. S., Maneiro, P. J., Soria, J., and Daughaday, W. H. Restoration of ovarian function in patients with the amenorrhea-galactorrhea syndrome after long-term therapy with L-dopa. *Fertility and Sterility* 24:340–344, 1973.

100. Boyd, A. E., and Reichlin, S. Galactorrhea-amenorrhea, bromergocryptine, and the dopamine receptor (editorial). *New England Journal of Medicine* 293:451–452, 1975.

101. Kolodny, R. C., Jacobs, L. S., and Daughaday, W. H. Mammary stimulation causes prolactin release in women. *Nature* 238:284–286, 1972.

102. Noel, G. L., Suh, H. K., and Frantz, A. G. Prolactin release during nursing and breast stimulation in postpartum and nonpostpartum subjects. *Journal of Clinical Endocrinology and Metabolism* 38:413–423, 1974.

103. Noel, G. L., Suh, H. K., Stone, J. G., and Frantz, A. G. Human prolactin and growth hormone release during surgery and other conditions of stress. *Journal of Clinical Endocrinology and Metabolism* 35:840–851, 1972.

104. Lee, P. A. The relationship of concentrations of serum hormones to pubertal gynecomastia. *Journal of Pediatrics* 86:212–215, 1975.

105. Nuttal, F. Q. Gynecomastia as a physical finding in normal men. *Journal of Clinical Endocinology and Metabolism* 48:338–340, 1979.

106. Kolodny, R. C. Unpublished data, 1979.

107. Turkington, R. W. Serum prolactin levels in patients with gynecomastia. *Journal of Clinical Endocrinology and Metabolism* 34:62–66, 1972.

108. Ford, C. V. Hypoglycemia, hysteria, and sexual function. *Medical Aspects of Human Sexuality* 11(7):63–74, 1977.

7

Sex and Cardiovascular Disease

In order to pay more than lip service to the phrase "quality of life," health-care professionals must consider the consequences of the impact of acute or chronic illness across broad dimensions of life. In few areas is the effect of disease on sexual function as pronounced as that seen in regard to the patient with cardiovascular problems, but relatively little attention has been devoted to this topic until recent years. This chapter summarizes available research data and suggests guidelines for practical management of the sexual rehabilitation of patients with a variety of heart problems.

Myocardial Infarction

Previous studies indicate that there is a substantial occurrence of impotence and diminished libido in men after myocardial infarction. Klein and coworkers studied 20 men who were interviewed between 3 and 48 months postinfarct, and found that only 25 percent reported a return of sexual activity to preinfarct levels [1]. Tuttle, Cook, and Fitch reported that two-thirds of the men they interviewed through a work evaluation clinic after recuperation from a heart attack had a significant decrease in coital frequency, to levels less than half their prior patterns [2]. Singh and coworkers stated that 24.2 percent of their sample of men interviewed after myocardial infarction abstained from sexual activity because of either medical advice, chest pain or dyspnea, generalized weakness, or fear of recurrence of infarction [3]. Furthermore, of those men who continued sexual activity, frequency of intercourse was markedly diminished in 46.4 percent. Weiss and English reported that 10 of 31 postcoronary subjects were impotent [4]; observation of a more recent series of 81 men less than 60 years old, who were studied one to two years postinfarction, reveals that 18 (22.2 percent) reported impotence and 48 (59.3 percent) described a significant reduction in libido [5].

The literature on the sexual function of women who have experienced myocardial infarctions is notably absent. Abramov has described a higher rate of prior sexual dissatisfaction in women hospitalized for heart attacks as compared to women hospitalized for other illnesses [6], but this report is methodologically and conceptually inadequate. In a preliminary series of 14 women interviewed one year after a myocardial infarct, 3 described diminished libido and none reported loss of orgasmic responsiveness, although the frequency of intercourse decreased for 10 of the 14 women [5].

The reasons underlying the development of sexual difficulties after a myocardial infarction are infrequently of organic origin. The occasional patient who experiences sexual problems as a result of drug therapy or chest pain precipitated by mild exertion is in the minority. For larger numbers of coronary patients, sexual distress arises out of a combination of misconception, anxiety, avoidance, depression, and poor self-esteem. The situation is frequently worsened by a lack of adequate counseling by physicians in regard to the postinfarction return to sexual activity.

For most men experiencing their first myocardial infarction, the initial realization is one of the threat to life itself. This reminder of one's own mortality often comes unexpectedly and is dramatized by the high technology of the modern coronary care unit. As the initial hours of hospitalization pass and the chest pain is relieved by medications, the patient's thoughts often begin to turn to what changes the heart attack will lead to in his life. At this point, concern about his job ("Can I go back to work?" "Will I have to change my work habits?") and about his sexuality ("Will I be able to have sex?" "How will my sex life be affected?") are common. Fears that the heart attack will produce major curtailment of sexual activity typically begin to surface at this time. It is not unusual to find patients on a coronary care unit deeply depressed [7]; one reason for this depression is misperception of how life will be altered by the heart attack. In a sense, the depressive reaction represents a mourning for the loss of intactness that the coronary victim feels so acutely.

Numerous worries about continued sexual functioning are voiced by heart patients. These concerns include (1) fear that the excitement and exertion of sexual activity will lead to sudden death; (2) fear that medical advice will preclude sexual activity or will greatly change the nature of participation in sexual relationships; (3) fear that the heart attack will create physical difficulties in sexual function; (4) concern that the heart attack is a "warning" of the aging process and therefore signals an impending deterioration of sexual capacity; and (5) concern that excitement and orgasm may precipitate another infarct. With such formidable worries, it is no wonder that a large percentage of coronary patients have sexual difficulties following their heart attacks. The situation is confounded further by the fact that in the past, few physicians or nurses have discussed specific recommendations for sexual rehabilitation with patients or their spouses. This omission of professional counsel is sometimes interpreted by patients as an unspoken prohibition, particularly since there is much detailed discussion about return to work, physical exertion, and dietary habits. Failure of health-care professionals to specifically endorse a timely return to sexual activity may also be taken to imply verification of the risky nature of postcoronary sex. More realistically, the failure of health-care professionals to actively address the subject of resumption of sexual activity for the postcoronary patient stems from lack of an adequate data base from which physiologically factual recommendations can be made, professional unfamiliarity with routinely advising patients about sex, and lack of specific education in sex-counseling techniques.

In the past, when advice was given it was typically to abstain from sexual activity for periods ranging from three to six months to allow the myocardium ample time to heal. However, the net effect of such a prohibition may be more stressful than the situation being avoided [8]. Fortunately, the availability of increasing knowledge of the cardiovascular dynamics of sexual activity allows for a more sensible approach to management.

Physiologic Data   Laboratory observations of cardiovascular and respiratory patterns in healthy subjects during sexual activity, including intercourse and orgasm, have demonstrated marked increases in heart rate, blood pressure, and respiratory rate. Masters and Johnson found that blood pressure increases by 30 to 80 mm Hg (systolic) and 20 to 50 mm Hg (diastolic), while heart rate may increase to 140 to 180 beats per minute during orgasm [9]. However, these measurements cannot be assumed to apply to people with heart disease or to sexual activity occurring in a home environment as opposed to a laboratory setting.

Hellerstein and Friedman studied 48 middle-age men with arteriosclerotic heart disease and 43 middle-age coronary-prone men without evidence of heart damage [10]. They found that the overall level of sexual activity in their postcoronary patients declined significantly during the first year after myocardial infarction. As part of this study, the researchers monitored electrocardiographic tracings of a subsample of these men for 24- to 48-hour periods of their home lives, during which sexual activity took place. In this subsample, the mean age was 47.5 years, average body weight was 76.5 kg (169 lb), and physical fitness was judged to be low. The mean peak heart rate at the time of orgasm was 117.4 beats per minute (with a range of 90 to 144). In the two 1-minute intervals preceding the peak heart rate, average rates were 87.0 and 101.2 beats per minute. As Hellerstein and Friedman pointed out, "The equivalent oxygen cost of the average maximal rate during sexual activity is less than that of performing a standard single Master 2-step test" [10]. In fact, the mean maximal heart rate observed during typical everyday work activity was 120.1 beats per minute, actually higher than the rate during orgasm.

These scientists assessed equivalent blood pressure changes in the same men by monitoring blood pressure response to bicycle stress testing at an exercise rate that duplicated the heart rate measured during home sexual activity. They found that equivalent blood pressure measured at maximal heart rate was 162/89 mm Hg, hardly an alarming blood pressure elevation.

Evidence of cardiac ischemia as judged by ST-T wave depression was no more frequent in subjects monitored during sexual activity than during ordinary work. Likewise, the occurrence of ectopic premature beats was comparable in coitus and in the pursuit of ordinary occupational activities.

The authors concluded that conjugal sexual activity in middle-age men imposes only modest physiologic cost, with maximal cardiac stress lasting no more than 10 to 15 seconds. They compared the equivalent oxygen cost to "climbing a flight of stairs, walking briskly, or performing ordinary tasks in many occupations" [10].

Studies published by Stein on a group of 22 men aged 46 to 54 who were evaluated 12 to 15 weeks after their first myocardial infarction substantiate the above findings [11]. The mean peak heart rate during sexual activity in these men was 127 beats per minute (with a range of 120 to 130). When 16 of these men participated in a four-month exercise training program, a decrease in mean peak heart rate during coitus to 120 beats per minute was observed, although no such change occurred with the passage of time in the other 6 men who did not undergo exercise training.

Rehabilitation and Counseling

The physiologic facts outlined in the preceding section clearly depict the cardiovascular cost of marital sex for the man recovering from a heart attack. Needless to say, these data do not pertain to all heart patients and most specifically must be amended to fit the biomedical profile of each patient, since the existence of concurrent illnesses, use of medications, and other physical limitations may all be relevant to the specific recommendations that should be made.

There is no current information about the cardiovascular cost of extramarital coitus. Since it may be presumed that a greater level of stress occurs in such situations, several authors suggest that there are higher cardiac risks attendant to sex with an unfamiliar partner. Ueno, in a frequently cited study performed in Japan, reported that 34 of 5,559 cases of endogenous sudden death (0.6 percent) occurred during coitus [12]. Eighteen of the 34 deaths were thought to be cardiac in origin, and

27 of these deaths occurred during or after extramarital coitus. However, there are no reliable data to indicate the actual magnitude of risk involved, and it is likely that other factors, including alcohol use, may have complicated the picture.

Similarly, no studies have been published that document the cardiovascular responses to sexual activity, including intercourse and orgasm, for the postcoronary woman. Although the close similarity in sexual physiology between healthy women and men noted in a laboratory setting [9] may pertain to cardiac patients, it is unclear at present whether or not the situation is in fact parallel. However, pending reports of significant differences in cardiovascular patterns between men and women who have had coronaries, it presently appears warranted to apply the same physiologic data to both sexes.

The approach to advising the coronary patient about a return to sexual activity is predicated on knowledge of the medical, physiologic, and social dynamics of each case. Whenever possible, the spouse of the cardiac patient should be included in such a discussion; if this is not done, the spouse may not believe or understand the suggestions that were given and may decide to "protect" his or her partner by a pattern of sexual avoidance or abstinence. The spouse's attitudes and behavior toward the resumption of sex appear to be critical variables in the overall rehabilitation process [13]. If the spouse (woman or man) is not given a chance to ventilate fears and to ascertain factual answers to questions, the likelihood of introducing an additional strain into the posthospitalization period increases.

Adequate advice cannot be given without knowledge of the previous sexual patterns of the patient. This information should be obtained by private interview (without the spouse present), since it is unlikely that certain types of historical material will be discussed as openly during a conjoint session. The interviewer should ascertain the past frequency of intercourse and noncoital orgasmic outlets, the range of positions used during intercourse, the presence or absence of sexual dysfunctions, and general characteristics of the marital and sexual relationships. This limited amount of knowledge will assist in individualizing the suggestions that are given to the needs of each patient or couple. It is reasonable to expect a good prognosis for attaining a sexual pattern comparable in frequency and quality to that before the heart attack if there are no complicating medical circumstances, but one cannot expect that a person who has had little or no sexual activity for years will suddenly begin functioning with any degree of regularity. If a person who has recently had a myocardial infarction previously had difficulty in sexual functioning, this fact must be considered in advising that person.

For the patient with a first heart attack and no significant medical complications (including absence of cardiac failure or arrhythmias), if exercise can be tolerated to the extent of raising the heart rate to approximately 110 to 120 beats per minute without precipitating angina or severe shortness of breath, sexual activity almost invariably can be resumed. This means that many postcoronary patients can return to sexual activity two to four weeks after discharge from the hospital. Exercise tolerance can be ascertained by formal testing (such as the use of a calibrated bicycle ergometer, a submaximal treadmill test, or a Master 2-step test), or it can be monitored in other ways, including measures of heart rate before and at the end of walking up one or two flights of stairs or walking up and down the hospital corridor. Needless to say, such testing should only be carried out with due precautions taken for the possibility of adverse reaction, and maximal physical exertion should not be elicited without a gradual exposure to increasing exercise over time. The patient who can participate in moderate exercise without tachycardia is probably able to participate in sex without major problems.

Patients who fall into this category should be advised on the following points:

1. The patient should not attempt to prove anything sexually by athletic prowess or marathon sessions. He or she should proceed gradually, especially as sexual activity is being reestablished after the coronary; this means the use of comfortable positions for intercourse combined with moderate degrees of exertion during intravaginal thrusting or other aspects of sexual activity. (A recent study showed no significant difference in heart rate or blood pressure in healthy men using the male-on-top compared to the male-on-the-bottom position for having intercourse [14]. Nevertheless, positions that require isometric exertion should be avoided, since these positions are more likely to increase heart rate or to precipitate arrhythmias in patients with coronary disease.)
2. The patient should avoid sexual activity shortly after consuming food or drink, since this will only disrupt circulatory efficiency and divert blood flow to the gut. Alcohol decreases cardiac index and stroke index in patients with heart disease even when taken in small

amounts [15] and thus may impose a greater risk during sexual activity.
3. If symptoms of chest pain, chest tightness, or dyspnea occur during sex, the patient should slow down or terminate the activity. The physician should be notified of this symptom promptly.
4. Patients and their spouses should be urged to communicate freely and directly with each other about their physical and emotional feelings regarding sex.

Occasionally the wife of a man who has had a heart attack may not believe the physiologic facts about his resuming sexual activity. One authority suggests that allowing her to watch her husband exercise vigorously under controlled and monitored conditions often alleviates the attendant anxieties that she may have harbored [16]. Nevertheless, it must be recognized that early myocardial recuperation from an uncomplicated infarct is not complete during the first three to eight weeks after the injury: According to one report, a majority of patients who were showing satisfactory recovery clinically had elevated left ventricular end-diastolic pressure [17]. The point that applies here is that the patient's status, rather than a numerical response to physiologic testing, must be the final guide to management.

The cardiac patient who experiences angina with mild exertion or with emotional stress alone may be managed in several different ways. Long-range management may benefit the most from a carefully supervised physical exercise program designed to increase cardiac work-load capacity. The patient's functional cardiac status may be changed dramatically by such a program, with improvement in self-esteem a likely and valuable by-product that relates very directly to sexuality. For other patients (or for those who are participating in exercise programs), the use of nitroglycerin or long-acting nitrate preparations or the use of antianginal medications such as beta-adrenergic blocking agents presents viable options. Long-acting nitrate preparations should be taken approximately 30 minutes before anticipated sexual activity, whereas beta-blocking agents are usually used on a regular four-times-a-day schedule. In some patients with severe coronary artery disease, bypass surgery will offer the most effective therapeutic approach and may significantly improve exercise tolerance.

Hellerstein and Friedman suggest that when doubt exists about the sexual advice that should be given to an individual patient, monitoring the electrocardiogram during sexual activity in the patient's home by a Holter monitoring device may be a useful diagnostic approach [10].

Other Aspects of Cardiovascular Disease and Sexual Function

A variety of cardiovascular conditions other than heart attacks may be associated with sexual problems. Most of these conditions share common features that derive from the pathophysiology of the underlying cardiac disturbance; for example, both disorders of myocardial function and mechanical disorders of the heart valves may lead to congestive heart failure. Similarly, a significant component of the sexual difficulties that occur in heart patients arises from the general observation that myocardial function that is adequate at rest may be unable to compensate appropriately during physical exertion, leading to ischemia (usually manifested by chest pain), reduced cardiac output (manifested by weakness, fatigability, or, when severe, syncope), or disturbances of heart rate and rhythm (resulting in palpitations, dyspnea, and angina). The physical limitations that influence the heart patient's sexual capabilities are often compounded by anxieties, misconceptions, and other psychological problems, as discussed in the preceding section.

Angina Pectoris

Patients with ischemic heart disease have an imbalance of regional myocardial perfusion in relation to the demand for myocardial oxygenation. This imbalance is typically transient and is precipitated by conditions imposing an increased rate of myocardial metabolic activity such as exercise, anger, anxiety, or postural changes. Although angina usually presents as chest pain or discomfort, the location of pain may be entirely extrathoracic (neck, jaw, shoulder, or arm pain is sometimes observed to be independent of chest pain in these patients) or may include variable distributions of pain or discomfort patterns.

Patients who experience anginal attacks during sexual activity may benefit from the prophylactic use of nitroglycerin, the use of long-acting nitrate preparations, or the use of beta-blocking agents such as propranolol. These patients are also well advised to embark upon carefully supervised physical exercise programs to increase their exercise tolerance. In some instances, the use of a sitting or standing position for sexual activity may reduce the frequency or severity of anginal attacks, presumably by reducing left ventricular dilatation that occurs during recumbency [18]. Since smoking lessens the duration or degree of exertion required to precipitate ischemic pain and raises the heart rate as well, it is useful to advise anginal patients to avoid cigarettes, avoid alcohol use, and not to attempt sexual activity postprandially.

For patients whose angina is so severe that the preceding suggestions do not produce significant relief, and in whom appropriate attention has been given to associated abnormalities (such as hyperthyroidism, plasma lipid abnormalities, obesity, hypertension, or anemia) that may exacerbate anginal symptoms, consideration of bypass surgery or the use of a carotid sinus nerve stimulator is in order. Discussion of these treatment modalities is beyond the scope of this chapter.

Congestive Heart Failure

When heart function is impaired in such a way that the rate of cardiac output is insufficient to keep up with peripheral tissue demands, a state of heart failure has occurred. The causes that precipitate heart failure are numerous; Braunwald lists ten categories to consider [19]:

1. Pulmonary embolism.
2. Infection.
3. Anemia.
4. Thyrotoxicosis and pregnancy.
5. Arrhythmias.
6. Myocarditis.
7. Bacterial endocarditis.
8. Physical, dietary, environmental, and emotional excesses.
9. Systemic hypertension.
10. Myocardial infarction.

The clinical manifestations of congestive heart failure include dyspnea, orthopnea (dyspnea while lying down), weakness and fatigue, and peripheral edema. Medical management centers on identification and treatment of both the precipitating cause and the underlying cardiac abnormality. Typical management programs include dietary restriction of sodium, reduction of fluid intake, use of cardiac glycosides to improve myocardial contractility, use of diuretics, and reduction of the cardiac work-load. Sexual activity should be prohibited in patients with poorly controlled congestive heart failure, since tachycardia will only aggravate the underlying abnormalities. However, the compensated patient who is able to tolerate moderate physical exertion (for example, climbing one to two flights of stairs) can most likely be permitted to resume sexual activity. Coital positions that avoid the development of orthopnea might be advised for such patients. Research data about sexual functioning of patients with congestive heart failure are not presently available.

Disorders of the Mitral Valve

Mitral stenosis, which is typically rheumatic in origin, may cause distress during sexual intercourse by precipitating increased pulmonary capillary pressure, leading to dyspnea and cough [20]. This problem may occur with minimal degrees of mitral stenosis; with increasing severity of this condition, sexual activity may be precluded because of the attendant shortness of breath. Atrial fibrillation or other disturbances of atrial rhythm may further complicate the capacity of the person with mitral stenosis to function sexually. Although surgery is the treatment of choice for symptomatic patients with mitral stenosis resulting in an effective mitral opening of less than 1.5 cm² [20] and generally produces significant physiologic improvement [21], 92 percent of a group of patients undergoing open mitral commissurotomy demonstrated psychological problems that hindered the actual recovery achieved by the operation [21]. Sexual problems, depression, and difficulties with self-esteem were among the variables that correlated significantly with impaired psychological adjustment to open-heart surgery [21].

Although there is not firm agreement on this point, it appears that many women who have undergone closed mitral valvuloplasty may have subsequent pregnancy (with full-term delivery) with no greater risk to their postoperative course than for women who do not bear children after such surgery [22]. Needless to say, the altered cardiovascular dynamics of pregnancy require careful medical management of such patients.

Mitral insufficiency may be caused by rheumatic heart disease, a congenital anomaly, rupture of the papillary muscles or chordae tendineae, or valvular destruction due to bacterial endocarditis [20]. Prominent symptoms include fatigue, dyspnea on exertion, and orthopnea. Weakness and debility may be pronounced, although many cases of rheumatic origin are relatively asymptomatic. Sexual problems arise from the weakness and dyspnea that may accompany severe mitral insufficiency. Mitral valve replacement is likely to improve hemodynamic status and sexual functioning, although difficulties in achieving sexual satisfaction may persist postoperatively in a significant number of patients [21].

Disorders of the Abdominal Aorta

Vascular problems that impinge on the blood supply to the penis hamper the efficiency of the vasocongestive changes that lead to erection in the male. The Leriche syndrome, a thrombotic obstruction of the aortic bifurcation, is an example of such a situation [23]. The manifestations of this disorder are intermittent claudication (pain in the legs and buttocks with walking), impotence, symmetrical atrophy of the musculature in the lower extremities, and absence of the femoral pulses. These patients can be helped significantly by surgical repair of the aortic obstruction and by attention to medical management of lipid abnormalities. Potency is typically restored following such surgery.

Surgical dissection of the aorta and common iliac arteries can also produce sexual difficulties, however. Hallböök and Holmquist [24] reported that 10 of 31 men who underwent extensive surgery on the lower part of the abdominal aorta were unable to ejaculate, while 4 of the remaining 21 men were impotent. Presumably, these abnormalities occur because of damage to nerves that supply the internal bladder sphincter. Similar disturbances were noted in a report by May and coworkers [25].

A Closing Note

The complicated nature of cardiovascular illness has not been reflected by many multidisciplinary studies of patients with such problems from the viewpoint of sexual functioning. The data base that currently exists is only fragmentary and, in many regards, conjectural. While the interrelatedness of personality, environment, heredity, economics, and medical factors may be broadly acknowledged, relatively little definitive information linking these variables is available at the present time.

Many patients with cardiovascular disease use drugs to control hypertension, plasma lipid patterns, impaired myocardial contractility, or fluid abnormalities. Each of these classes of pharmacologic agents may impair sexual function (see Chap. 13), but little systematic research has been done regarding this aspect of practical patient management. Indeed, little is known of the sexual consequences of untreated hypertension or arteriosclerosis [26]. Cardiac bypass surgery, valve repairs, and the use of a variety of artificial cardiac pacemakers are other examples of areas that require investigation. Therefore, the reader is reminded of the limitations of scope in our present knowledge and is advised to consider carefully the recommendations and statements of sexual prognosis given to each patient who falls into this general category of illnesses.

In real life, as opposed to textbooks, many patients with heart disease have concurrent illnesses (diabetes, renal disease, arthritis, anemia), experience multiple episodes of myocardial infarction or coronary insufficiency, and have courses complicated by congestive heart failure, pulmonary embolus, pericarditis, arrhythmias, shock, or other conditions. These patients are likely to have more difficulties with all aspects of rehabilitation and require highly individualized approaches to management. This chapter provides only a starting point for the health-care professional who is interested in this subject.

References

1. Klein, R. F., Dean, A., Willson, L. M., and Bogdonoff, M. D.   The physician and postmyocardial infarction invalidism. *Journal of the American Medical Association* 194:123–128, 1965.
2. Tuttle, W. B., Cook, W. L., and Fitch, E.   Sexual behavior in postmyocardial infarction patients. *American Journal of Cardiology* 13:140–153, 1964.
3. Singh, J., Singh, S., Singh, S., Singh, A., and Malhotra, R. P.   Sex life and psychiatric problems after myocardial infarction. *Journal of the Association of Physicians of India* 18:503–507, 1970.
4. Weiss, E., and English, O. S.   *Psychosomatic Medicine* (3rd ed.). Philadelphia: W. B. Saunders Co., 1957. P. 216.
5. Kolodny, R. C.   Unpublished data, 1978.
6. Abramov, L. A.   Sexual life and sexual frigidity among women developing acute myocardial infarction. *Psychosomatic Medicine* 38:418–425, 1976.
7. Cassem, N. H., and Hackett, T. P.   Psychiatric consultation in a coronary care unit. *Annals of Internal Medicine* 75:9–14, 1971.
8. Green, A. W.   Sexual activity and the postmyocardial infarction patient. *American Heart Journal* 89:246–252, 1975.
9. Masters, W. H., and Johnson, V. E.   *Human Sexual Response.* Boston: Little, Brown and Co., 1966.
10. Hellerstein, H. K., and Friedman, E. H.   Sexual activity and the postcoronary patient. *Archives of Internal Medicine* 125:987–999, 1970.
11. Stein, R. A.   The effect of exercise training on heart rate during coitus in the post-myocardial infarction patient. *Circulation* 55:738–740, 1977.
12. Ueno, M.   The so-called coition death. *Japanese Journal of Legal Medicine* 17:333–340, 1969.
13. Puksta, N. S.   All about sex . . . after a coronary. *American Journal of Nursing* 77:602–605, 1977.
14. Nemec, E. D., Mansfield, L., and Kennedy, J. W.   Heart rate and blood pressure responses during sexual activity in normal males. *American Heart Journal* 92:274–277, 1976.
15. Gould, L., Zahir, M., DeMartino, A., and Gomprecht, R. F.   Cardiac effects of a cocktail. *Journal of the American Medical Association* 218:1799–1802, 1971.
16. Bicycling for sex. *Emergency Medicine* 9:181–182, November 1977.
17. Rahimtoola, S. H., DiGilio, M. M., Sinno, M. Z., Loeb, H. S., Rosen, K. M., and Gunnar, R. M.   Cardiac performance three to eight weeks after acute myocardial infarction. *Archives of Internal Medicine* 128:220–228, 1971.
18. Goldstein, R. E., and Epstein, S. E.   Medical management of patients with angina pectoris. *Progress in Cardiovascular Diseases* 14:360–398, 1972.
19. Braunwald, E.   Heart Failure. In G. W. Thorn, R. D. Adams, E. Braunwald, K. J. Isselbacher, and R. G. Petersdorf (eds.), *Harrison's Principles of Internal Medicine* (8th ed.). New York: McGraw-Hill Book Co., 1977. Pp. 1178–1187.
20. Braunwald, E.   Valvular Heart Disease. In G. W. Thorn, R. D. Adams, E. Braunwald, K. J. Isselbacher, and R. G. Petersdorf (eds.), *Harrison's Prin-*

ciples of Internal Medicine (8th ed.). New York: McGraw-Hill Book Co., 1977. Pp. 1243–1261.

21. Heller, S. S., Frank, K. A., Kornfeld, D. S., Malm, J. R., and Bowman, F. O. Psychological outcome following open-heart surgery. *Archives of Internal Medicine* 134:908–914, 1974.

22. Wallace, W. A., Harken, D. E., and Ellis, L. B. Pregnancy following closed mitral valvuloplasty: A long-term study with remarks concerning the necessity for careful cardiac management. *Journal of the American Medical Association* 217:297–304, 1971.

23. Leriche, R., and Morel, A. The syndrome of thrombotic obliteration of the aortic bifurcation. *Annals of Surgery* 127:193–206, 1948.

24. Hallböök, T., and Holmquist, B. Sexual disturbances following dissection of the aorta and the common iliac arteries. *Journal of Cardiovascular Surgery* 11:255–260, 1970.

25. May, A. G., DeWeese, J. A., and Rob, C. G. Changes in sexual function following operation on the abdominal aorta. *Surgery* 65:41–47, 1969.

26. Mudd, J. W. Impotence responsive to glyceryl trinitrate. *American Journal of Psychiatry* 134:922–925, 1977.

8

Gynecologic Disorders and Sex

Gynecologic disorders are frequently associated with changes in sexual function or sexual behavior. In addition, disorders affecting the genitals or the reproductive system may have indirect repercussions on female sexuality by affecting body-image or self-esteem, by altering reproductive status, or by leading to physical discomfort. Since it is not possible to provide detailed discussion of the entire range of gynecologic conditions in one textbook chapter, certain topics have been selected for discussion because of their clinical relevance or elucidation of principles of management, while other topics have been deliberately omitted. The sexual problems associated with gynecologic malignancies and with breast cancer are discussed in Chapter 11.

Congenital Anomalies
Congenital Absence of the Vagina

Congenital absence of the vagina (vaginal agenesis) is a rare disorder thought to occur in approximately 1 in 4,000 female births [1]. In most instances, the vagina is hypoplastic rather than being completely absent; in these cases, the abnormality involves absence of the inner two-thirds of the vagina, and a blind-ending vagina of 1 to 4 cm in depth may be found. Less frequently, there may be only a mild depression or dimple of skin at the normal location of the vaginal introitus, or there may be no indication of the vagina at all. The clitoris and labia, because of their separate embryologic origin, are typically normal in females with this disorder; as a result, the diagnosis is not usually made until after puberty, when either primary amenorrhea or inability to accomplish coitus leads to medical evaluation [2].

When congenital absence of the vagina occurs in association with a variety of anatomic abnormalities of the uterus, it is called the Rokitansky-Kuster-Hauser syndrome [3]. The uterus may be relatively normal anatomically but not communicating with the vagina, or the uterus may be of rudimentary size or shape. Urologic abnormalities are frequently associated with vaginal agenesis [3, 4]; in one series, 47 percent of patients in whom evaluation of the urinary tract was undertaken had anomalies present [4]. In a literature review of 534 reported cases of congenital absence of the vagina, Griffin and coworkers found 71 instances of ectopic kidneys, 70 cases of renal agenesis, and 19 abnormalities of the renal pelvis or ureters, among other anomalies [3]. In the same review, 12 percent of patients were found to have skeletal abnormalities and 4 percent had congenital heart disease.

Fertility may be preserved in some patients in whom the uterus and fallopian tubes are reasonably normal, if reconstructive surgery is undertaken before damage occurs due to backup of menstrual flow.

Measurement of serum gonadotropins and progesterone has confirmed the occurrence of normal ovarian function, as has the demonstration of normal ovarian follicles obtained by laparoscopy [5]. Nevertheless, most women with this disorder will have a functional state of infertility despite optimal medical and surgical management.

Congenital absence of the vagina is differentiated from the testicular feminization syndrome by the presence of a normal female sex chromosome pattern and the presence of ovaries. The anatomic configuration of the uterus may be determined by laparotomy, laparoscopy, pelvic pneumography, or ultrasonographic techniques.

Treatment can be either surgical or nonsurgical. Although the first modern operative approach to vaginal agenesis by Baldwin utilized an isolated loop of bowel for creating an artificial vagina, operative morbidity and mortality with this approach are higher than desirable. Instead, the method of McIndoe, using a single large skin graft around a rubber mold [6, 7], has led to far lower operative risk and better cosmetic results [8]. Alternatively, a nonsurgical approach for the development of an artificial vagina has been found to be highly efficacious [9–11]: In this technique, a series of dilators are applied to the vaginal dimple with uniform pressure over a period of time to create an invagination of increasing depth.

Following the successful creation of an artificial vagina by either surgical or nonsurgical means, the physiology and anatomy of vaginal response to sexual arousal are almost equivalent to the response patterns of the normal vagina. Specifically, vaginal lubrication occurs with excitation, the vagina dilates relatively normally, and an orgasmic platform forms, leading to normal orgasmic responsiveness [12]. However, in spite of the relative anatomic normalcy that may be brought about by proper treatment, it is not unusual for women with this problem to have psychological difficulties that may require in-depth attention.

Congenital Anomalies of the Uterus

A variety of anatomic abnormalities involving the uterus are encountered clinically (Fig. 8-1). Congenital absence of the cervix in combination with an otherwise normal vagina and uterus is extremely rare; this configuration leads to retained menstrual secretions postpubertally and requires operative intervention [13]. More frequently seen are conditions of uterine duplication, which may have varying effects on reproductive capacity but infrequently cause alterations in sexual function. Dyspareunia may sometimes be attributable to anomalies of the uterus; in most cases the diagnosis can only be established by

Figure 8-1. Cogenital uterine abnormalities. (A) Double uterus and double vagina; (B) double uterus with single vagina; (C) bicornuate uterus; (D) bicornuate uterus with a rudimentary left horn; (E) septate uterus; (F) unicornuate uterus. (From K. L. Moore, *The Developing Human*, 2nd ed., 1977. Courtesy of W. B. Saunders Co., Philadelphia.)

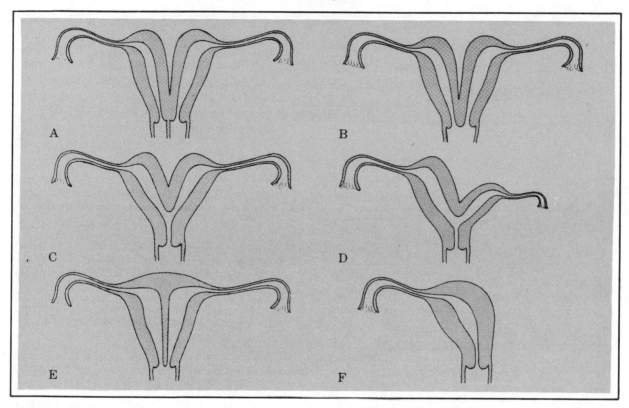

hysterosalpingogram, since uterine palpation by physical examination may not reveal the anomaly. Surgical correction of uterine duplication can often be achieved, improving fertility and symptoms of dysmenorrhea.

Gynecologic Infections and Sexuality

Gynecologic infections may arise for many different reasons. In some instances, infection occurs because of the overgrowth of microbial flora ordinarily present within the female genitourinary tract (Table 8-1); in other instances, infection is a result of sexual transmission of a pathogen, trauma, altered resistance to infection, surgery, or other factors. Regardless of the origin, if gynecologic infection leads to local pain, burning, or itching, it may understandably contribute to sexual difficulties by inducing withdrawal, distraction, or avoidance. In addition, the psychological impact of genitourinary infection on sexuality should not

Table 8-1. Normal Flora
of the Vagina*

Lactobacillus species

Staphylococcus aureus

Staphylococcus epidermidis

Fecal streptococci

Streptococcus viridans

Anaerobic streptococci

Neisseria species (other than *N. gonorrhoeae* and *N. meningitidis*)

Diphtheroids

Corynebacterium species

Hemophilus vaginalis

Coliform bacilli

Proteus species

Mima polymorpha

Clostridium species

Bacteroides species

Fusobacterium species

Mycoplasma

Candida species

*Note that several of the organisms listed may be pathogens. Source: Adapted from C. J. Wilkowskie and P. E. Hermans, Antimicrobial agents in the treatment of obstetric and gynecologic infections, *Medical Clinics of North America* 58:711–727, 1974, and C. M. Corbishley, Microbial flora of the vagina and cervix, *Journal of Clinical Pathology* 30:745–748, 1977.

be disregarded: Both the affected woman and her partner may be uncertain of the origin of the infection and may make faulty inferences with interpersonal ramifications.

Urinary Infections

The incidence of urinary tract infections such as cystitis or urethritis in women is clearly related to sexual activity; the close anatomic proximity of the urethral meatus to the vagina creates a ready path for ascending infection to occur. Although bacterial transmission during coitus is undoubtedly the most common route for such infections, pathogens may also be inadvertently introduced into the genitourinary area, including the female urethra, by manual or oral stimulation or by the use of objects such as vibrators or dildos during sexual activity.

Bacteriuria in women is often preceded by colonization of the vaginal introitus with fecal bacteria [14]. Postmenopausal women or women with estrogen deficiencies are highly susceptible to urinary tract or vaginal infections arising from coitus because of diminished vaginal lubrication and atrophic tissue changes in the urethral and vaginal mucosa.

Buckley and coworkers recently reported that sexual intercourse leads to asymptomatic transient increases in bacteria counts in urine specimens [15]. The increased bacteria counts were attributable to both pathogens and nonpathogens, but since the urethra of a woman with recurrent urinary tract infections is more often colonized with coliform bacteria [16], it is not clear at present what the precise correlation is between coitus and urethritis or cystitis [17]. The most probable mechanism of bacterial entrance into the bladder during intercourse occurs as a result of the inward urethral milking that accompanies coital thrusting.

Vulvar Infections The vulva may become infected for a variety of reasons, including venereal diseases, parasitic diseases such as pediculosis pubis or scabies, and a vulvovaginitis such as is commonly encountered with *Monilia* or *Trichomonas*. These disorders must be differentiated from noninfectious inflammatory reactions of the vulva that may produce similar symptoms (particularly itching) and may be impossible to distinguish by physical examination alone. A Bartholin's gland cyst, which typically appears as a mass on the posterior half of the labium, may become secondarily infected and develop abscess formation. These lesions may be quite painful, producing dyspareunia and at times a secondary reaction of vaginismus; treatment is ideally total excision of the cyst, including the abscess, since incomplete excision may lead to recurrence [13].

Condylomata acuminata (venereal warts) are papular, moist, soft, pedunculated lesions that may occur singly or in numbers on the labia and perineum. Clusters of these lesions, which range in color from pink to red or dark gray, often have a cauliflower appearance. These warts are produced by a virus and may be sexually transmitted (the male may have condylomata at the prepuce, the glans, or the coronal ridge of the penis; both sexes may develop lesions of the fingers or tongue), but there is no evidence that these usually painless lesions are always venereal.

Herpes genitalis is caused by infection with the herpes simplex virus, type 2. The characteristic lesion is a cluster of tiny vesicles on the labia, on the clitoral hood, and, in 75 percent of cases, on the cervix. The vesicles may ulcerate to form larger round or oval lesions surrounded by diffuse erythema and inflammation; external lesions, or vesicles within the urethral meatus or vaginal introitus, may cause dyspareunia, intense pruritus, and burning. During acute infections, fever, inguinal lymphadenopathy, and local pain are common. Recurrent lesions are common and may occur at intervals of weeks to months; such lesions may thus pose a chronic obstacle to sexual activity and be the source of considerable anxiety as well as physical discomfort.

Transmission of this infection is highly venereal; treatment is often unsatisfactory, with symptomatic therapy that is variable in its results. The use of photodynamic tricyclic dyes applied to the labia, followed by exposure to fluorescent light, inactivates the virus and rapidly resolves the lesions, but the theoretical risks of this procedure include potentiating the oncogenic properties of the herpes virus [18, 19]. Because there is also evidence suggesting an association between herpes virus type 2 infections and cervical carcinoma [20, 21], recurrent herpes virus infections may involve a greater oncogenic risk than their treatment by photodynamic inactivation.

Herpetic lesions of the labia or vagina may also result from herpes simplex type 1, although this variety typically accounts for fewer than 10 percent of cases. Herpes simplex type 1 infections of the genitals may be more likely following oral-genital contact. Herpes genitalis infection during pregnancy can cause congenital malformations via transplacental infections and may also lead to abortion, premature labor, or infection of the neonate via exposure to the cervix or vagina during passage through the birth canal [22, 23]. Approximately half of infected neonates die or undergo serious sequelae involving the central nervous system and eyes.

Vaginitis

Vaginitis may be caused by either infection or inflammation. Atrophic vaginitis, attributable to diminished estrogen support of the vaginal mucosa, is discussed in Chapter 5. The most common infectious causes of vaginitis are *Trichomonas*, *Candida albicans*, *Hemophilus vaginalis*, and *Mycoplasma*. Whatever the causative pathogen, it should be recognized that infection involving the vagina may produce a variety of symptoms that interfere with sexual enjoyment. The physical discomfort associated with many forms of vaginitis, including pruritus, burning, and mucosal tenderness, may make sexual activity undesirable. At times, vaginitis may be the cause of dyspareunia, which becomes most problematic with chronic vaginitis that is recalcitrant to treatment. In addition, some women or their sexual partners prefer to avoid sexual activity for aesthetic reasons due to the vaginal discharge or malodorous nature of some vaginal infections. Furthermore, anxieties related to vaginal infection frequently add to the adverse impact of vaginitis on sexual function.

Trichomonas vaginalis, an ordinary microbial inhabitant of the vagina, may produce highly symptomatic vaginitis with pruritus of the labia and vagina, burning, and dyspareunia. A profuse, watery, frothy discharge that ranges in color from grayish-white to yellowish-brown is typically seen. Trichomoniasis is venereally transmitted, although the male carrier infrequently has any symptoms; for this reason, it is often advisable to treat both sex partners simultaneously to avoid a back-and-forth transmission of infection, which may occur if the woman alone receives therapy. Metronidazole (Flagyl), an oral trichomonacide, is the treatment of choice.

Monilial vaginitis, caused by the yeast *Candida albicans*, frequently occurs in association with diabetes, pregnancy, or Addison's disease, and in women using broad-spectrum antibiotic therapy or oral contraceptives. Moniliasis is accompanied by intense pruritus and a thick, white, cheesy discharge that may have a patchlike distribution on the cervix and vaginal walls. Microscopic examination of a drop of the discharge mixed with 10% potassium hydroxide solution will demonstrate budding yeast cells and pseudohyphae. Alternatively, culture of the discharge on Nickerson's medium may be used to identify the infection. Treatment approaches include the use of miconazole nitrate (Monistat cream), nystatin vaginal tablets (Mycostatin), or candicidin (Vanobid) vaginal tablets or ointment.

Recent data suggest that all sexually active patients with genital yeast infections should be screened for other sexually transmitted diseases. Thin, Leighton, and Dixon found that 35.3 percent of women attending a venereal disease clinic had genital yeast infections [24]. Oriel and coworkers found a 26 percent incidence of genital yeast infections in women seen in their venereal disease clinic; in 81 percent of these cases, *Candida albicans* was isolated as the infective organism [25]. The symptomatic presentation of a genital yeast infection may mask the coexistence of a venereal disease such as gonorrhea or syphilis, which will be detected only by appropriate cultures or serologic testing.

Hemophilus vaginitis is caused by *Hemophilus vaginalis*, a small gram-negative bacillus, which is now known to be responsible for more than 90 percent of cases that were formerly called nonspecific bacterial vaginitis [13]. This infection is characterized by an odoriferous dirty-white discharge accompanied by burning and itching; it is often easily confused with trichomoniasis. The recent finding of *H. vaginalis* in the urethra of 79 percent of male sex partners of infected women and the correlation of recurrent infection with sexual re-exposure suggests the possibility of a venereal transmission [26]. A gram-stain of the vaginal discharge reveals large epithelial cells with gram-negative bacilli on their surfaces. Treatment with ampicillin (2 gm per day for one week) or metronidazole (1 gm per day for one week) is usually effective [26].

Vaginal infections due to mycoplasmas are of uncertain significance. McCormack and colleagues showed that vaginal colonization with mycoplasmas is related to sexual activity: Women they studied without a prior history of sexual activity were virtually free of mycoplasmas, whereas 37.5 percent of women with a single sex partner and 75 percent of women having three or more coital partners showed vaginal colonization with mycoplasmas [27]. Mycoplasmas may cause nonspecific urethritis and may also contribute to fertility problems [28, 29], but further study is required to establish the precise sequelae of such infections [30, 31].

Vaginitis may also arise from inflammatory rather than infectious causes. Allergic vaginitis may develop as a sensitivity reaction to the chemical constituents of substances that come in contact with the vaginal mucosa, including vaginal contraceptive foams or jellies, solutions used for douching, and bath oil or bubble bath. Allergic vaginitis is usually marked by pruritus, a vaginal discharge, and erythema of the vaginal mucosa. Radiation vaginitis may occur after local irradiation used in the treatment of cervical carcinoma or after radiation therapy of other malignancies. Atrophy of the vaginal lining and diminished vaginal lubrication are common; therapy with locally applied estrogen creams and the use of artificial lubrication usually prevent dyspareunia. If sexual activity is not resumed on a regular basis, vaginal stenosis and adhesions may occur.

Gonorrhea and
Syphilis

There is considerable interest today in the public health implications of venereal disease. It is beyond the scope of this text to offer a thorough discussion of the diagnostic problems, natural history, complications, and treatment of the spectrum of venereal diseases, but a few brief observations will be offered.

From a gynecologic viewpoint, gonorrhea presents a significant problem for several reasons. Approximately 75 percent of infected women are asymptomatic carriers [32], making diagnosis difficult unless appropriate cultures are obtained. Endocervical and anal cultures should be obtained in all cases of suspected gonorrhea in women, plating the material promptly on Thayer-Martin medium. Although gonorrhea confined to the cervix or urethra does not pose a serious health threat, infection can extend into the uterus (causing endometritis), into the fallopian tubes (causing salpingitis), or into the peritoneal cavity (causing peritonitis), or it can be widely disseminated (causing arthritis, skin lesions and, rarely, endocarditis or meningitis) [23, 33]. Pelvic inflammatory disease of gonococcal origin may lead to tubal scarring and occlusion and altered tubal motility, with resultant infertility. Gonorrhea may also be manifested by lesions of the pharynx arising from oral-genital contact and primary infection may involve the rectum, as well. Because uncomplicated gonorrhea usually does not produce pain or dysuria in infected women, the risk of transmission via continued sexual activity is substantial.

Syphilis results from infection with the spirochete *Treponema pallidum*. Transmission occurs by direct skin contact with an actively infected partner; after an incubation period of 10 to 90 days, a chancre develops, located most typically on the vulva. This indurated ulcer is usually single and clearly defined, but it may sometimes occur on the cervix, in the rectum, or elsewhere on the body. The chancre is followed by the appearance of nontender lymphadenopathy within a few days. Dark-field microscopic examination of material from a suspected lesion should be carried out to establish the early diagnosis, since it may take several weeks to establish a positive serologic test for syphilis. If untreated, syphilis passes through secondary and tertiary stages marked by widely varying systemic involvement that may include the skin, central nervous system, kidneys, liver, and cardiovascular system [23].

Although neither gonorrhea nor syphilis causes direct disruption of sexual responsiveness, either infection may produce an emotional toll on the involved woman which must be considered when treatment is offered. Health-care professionals must be careful to avoid judgmentalism in patient care and should be sensitive to the potential stigmatization that may accompany the diagnosis of a venereal disease. If the female patient is made uncomfortable by persons providing diagnostic or treatment services, she is less likely to complete an adequate course of treatment, to attain necessary followup evaluation, or to cooperate in identifying her sexual partners who have also been exposed to infection. In addition, the impact of an episode of venereal disease on some patients is so strong that they may be troubled by guilt (seeing the venereal disease as retribution for "improper" sexual behavior) or they may be so frightened that they withdraw from sexual activity entirely—hardly a solution that is likely to be beneficial to their overall health. Patients should be educated in the basic facts about venereal disease, including means of prevention, and such education should include the entire age range of sexually active persons, even the very young.

Disorders of the Clitoris

The clitoris is frequently the object of great attention in matters sexual but is often virtually overlooked from the standpoint of medical care. The entire range of pathologic processes that can affect other body organs can of course afflict the clitoris; thus, infection, tumor, inflammation, scarring, and atrophy are possible within this specialized organ. To be practical, we shall mention here only a few selected points in regard to abnormalities of the clitoris.

Clitoral hypertrophy may be a reflection of excessive androgen stimulation, regardless of the source, but it may also sometimes be encountered in women who masturbate with great frequency, applying repeated and prolonged mechanical stimulation directly to the clitoral glans. This observation is not meant to induce a retreat to the ancient (and usually fallacious) medical concept that masturbation can be detected by examination of the genitalia—the few cases we have seen in which masturbation led to marked clitoral hypertrophy all involved multiple daily episodes of self-stimulation over a long period of time, usually in association with a vibrator applied directly to the clitoris. In some cases of injudicious use of vibrators or other objects as a source of clitoral stimulation, irritation, laceration, or abrasion of the clitoris may ensue and may be quite painful until healed.

There has been considerable discussion in recent years of the possible role of clitoral adhesions or phimosis as a cause of impaired female sexual responsivity. If this entity occurs with any significant frequency in the general population, it has not been apparent from patients or research subjects seen at the Masters & Johnson Institute, where only two cases have been detected in more than 2,000 consecutive examinations. Similarly, claims that clitoral sensations—and therefore female sexual arousal—are enhanced by clitoral circumcision have not been substantiated by any carefully conducted research that has been published to date. However, because some women's magazines have described clitoral circumcision as a magical way of transforming female sexuality, there are many patients requesting such operations with the expectation that they will experience a new set of sexual feelings and responses.

Clitoral pain may occur under a variety of circumstances, but not all women are able to name the locus of their discomfort accurately. Although infection is undoubtedly the commonest source of clitoral pain, the specific etiology and type of presentation may vary widely. In some circumstances, discrete lesions of the clitoris are observed, such as those found with herpes genitalis; in other instances, a more generalized vulvitis extends to involve the clitoris as well, as is frequently seen in the patient with monilial infection. Irritation is probably the second most common origin of clitoral pain, sometimes accompanied or exacerbated by secondary infection; the irritation may relate to sexual practices (e.g., biting or scratching the clitoris or using mechanical devices that induce irritation) but may also be a reflection of other types of problems, including chafing from tightly fitting undergarments or chemical irritation from soap, perfume, or detergents. Neuritis may sometimes affect the clitoris, causing either a constant or intermittent pattern of pain: This condition is most apt to be encountered in diabetic women, who may be given some degree of relief by low doses of phenothiazines.

Women who complain of clitoral tenderness only at the time of high levels of sexual arousal probably have no pathology present at all—their reaction is a very normal reflection of the fact that the tip of the clitoris characteristically becomes extremely sensitive to direct stimulation during peak phases of the female sexual response cycle. Furthermore, since there is no lubrication produced at or immediately adjacent to the clitoris, manual stimulation of the clitoris may be painful unless some vaginal lubrication is brought to the clitoral area. One additional factor often of clinical relevance is that many men pursue the objective of clitoral stimulation in a rough or overly persistent fashion. In either event, the woman may experience discomfort and seek medical attention to explain "her" problem.

Dyspareunia

Pain during or after coitus lessens sexual enjoyment and, over time, may lead to behavioral and attitudinal changes that seriously alter a sexual relationship. While the preponderance of cases of dyspareunia may reflect psychological rather than physical factors, it is the task of the physician to assess the situation adequately and to make a reasonably thorough attempt to identify any possible organic pathologic condition. Table 8-2 lists the conditions that should be considered in this evaluation; obviously, an accurate diagnosis can be made only after completion of a careful pelvic and rectal examination.

Many cases of dyspareunia are primarily attributable to difficulty with vaginal lubrication. Although there are a number of organic processes that may cause this problem, such as use of antihistamines,

Table 8-2. Differential
Diagnosis of Dys-
pareunia

Condition	Typical Pattern of Pain	Comments
Abscess of labium or vagina	Localized; sharp, burning or searing	
Adhesions	Deep pain exacerbated by thrusting and deep penetration	Pelvic inflammatory disease, endometriosis, postsurgical
Anorectal disease	Localized or diffuse	Inflammatory bowel disease, severe hemorrhoids, rectovaginal fistulae
Atrophic vaginitis	External, introital, or vaginal pain, either sharp or low grade	Estrogen deficiency: postmenopausal, hypopituitarism, uremia, untreated Turner's syndrome
Bartholin's gland cyst	External or introital pain	
Behçet's syndrome	Varied	Labial and/or vaginal ulcerations usually accompanied by oral lesions, ocular inflammation, and arthralgia or polyarthritis; rare
Broad ligament lesions	Deep pain exacerbated by thrusting; may persist for hours after coitus	Varices, tears, endometriosis
Cervicitis		Infrequently a cause of dyspareunia; increased incidence in oral contraceptive users
Clitoral phimosis Clitoral neuritis Clitoriditis	External burning pain	Infrequent
Condyloma accuminata	External or introital burning	
Congenital deformities	Varied	Shortened vaginal barrel may occur with syndrome of testicular feminization, Turner's syndrome or the Rokitansky-Kuster-Hauser syndrome; uterine anomalies are rarely associated with dyspareunia
Cystitis	Anterior pain associated with vaginal thrusting	
Cystocele	Anterior vaginal pain	
Dermatologic lesions of the vulva	External burning	
Endometritis	Deep pain	
Endometriosis	Usually deep pain with thrusting, but may vary considerably	Pain often most severe premenstrually; tender nodularity in cul-de-sac is almost pathognomonic; dysmenorrhea and infertility are common accompaniments

Condition	Typical Pattern of Pain	Comments
Episiotomy, poorly healed	Introital pain, usually sharp	
Herpes genitalis	Burning pain, external and/or internal	Venereal transmission
Hymeneal remnants or intact hymen	Introital distress worsened by thrusting	
Hysteria	Dramatic patterns frequently related	See Chapter 12
Inadequate vaginal lubrication	Burning and pain with insertion or thrusting	Consider drugs (antihistamines, phenothiazines), Sjögren's syndrome, diabetes, vaginitis, and psychological factors
Lacerations, abrasions, or excoriations	Varied	
Leukoplakia	External	
Myometritis	Deep pain induced by thrusting	Infrequent
Ovarian cyst	Deep pain	Infrequent
Pelvic inflammatory disease	Lower abdominal pain induced by thrusting	Suspect gonorrhea
Psychogenic	Varied	
Radiation vaginitis	Varied	
Urethral caruncle Urethral diverticulum Urethritis Urethrocele	Introital burning exacerbated by active thrusting	
Uterine retroversion	Induced by deep thrusting	Fixed retroversion is principal problem
Vaginismus	Difficulty with penetration; pain at introitus or more generalized	See Chapter 21
Vaginitis (atrophic, infectious, chemical, radiation)	Burning	
Vulvitis (infectious, chemical)	External burning	

Sjögren's syndrome, atrophic vaginitis, radiation vaginitis, and diabetes mellitus, the usual causes relate to lack of sexual arousal. A woman who is apprehensive or who feels rushed or otherwise pressured during sexual activity is unlikely to become easily aroused and thus may have relatively little vaginal lubrication at the time coitus is attempted; in addition, a woman already worried about the possible occurrence of pain during intercourse from previous experiences may be so anxious and tense that the situation is appreciably worsened by the lack of spontaneous lubrication. In some cases, penile insertion into the vagina is accomplished comfortably, but if vaginal lubrication ceases while a pattern of active thrusting is maintained, discomfort may result.

Dyspareunia due to endometriosis can assume a variety of different patterns. Coital pain that occurs with deep penile thrusting is the commonest pattern observed in association with endometriosis: This pain can frequently be reproduced during a pelvic examination by pressure on the uterus or by movement of the cervix, since these maneuvers put tension on the broad ligaments and uterosacral ligaments, which are a common location for endometrial implants. If endometrial lesions are located within the vagina or near the introitus, pain may occur upon penile insertion, but this is a relatively infrequent finding. Dyspareunia is often most severe premenstrually in cases of endometriosis, since the lesions are hormonally responsive and become highly vascular and edematous; in fact, it may be advisable to perform a pelvic examination premenstrually in a woman whose complaint of dyspareunia is not explained on a random pelvic examination but whose history is suggestive of endometriosis (dysmenorrhea, pelvic pain, and infertility are common features of this disorder). The finding of tender nodularity in the cul-de-sac is the hallmark of endometriosis, but culdoscopic examination and biopsy may be required to make the diagnosis definitively [34]. Fixed uterine retroversion is also commonly seen in endometriosis but may result from nonspecific adhesions as well.

Unfortunately, many women with dyspareunia receive only a cursory pelvic examination and an abbreviated explanation that "it's all in your head." In cases where no organic pathologic condition is detected, the physician should provide reassurance and education and should acquire sufficient historical data to decide whether referral for sex counseling or sex therapy is indicated. Often, simple suggestions related to coital positioning, communication between sexual partners, and the use of artificial lubrication may lead to significant improvement in the patient's sexual distress. Recognition of the instances in which dyspareunia is a symptom of marital or emotional conflict will similarly allow an opportunity for the provision of appropriate treatment services.

Polycystic Ovary Syndrome

In 1935, Stein and Leventhal described a series of women with amenorrhea, enlarged, polycystic ovaries, and varying degrees of obesity and hirsutism [35]. Although it is now clear that this condition, which is often referred to as the Stein-Leventhal syndrome, is marked by a wider degree of clinical heterogeneity than was first believed, these investigators were remarkably astute in discovering that bilateral ovarian wedge resections are often successful in restoring cyclic ovarian function, including ovulation.

Although the precise etiology of the polycystic ovary syndrome remains unclear [13], it is now known that hormonal mechanisms play an important role in this disorder. The polycystic ovary generally produces excessive amounts of androgens, including Δ^4-androstenedione, dehydroepiandrosterone, and testosterone [36–38]; in addition, the adrenals frequently also produce elevated quantities of androgens in women with the polycystic ovary syndrome. The hallmark of this syndrome is anovulation, usually (but not always) accompanied by secondary amenorrhea. Occasionally, oligomenorrhea or menometrorrhagia is found. Hirsutism is observed in the majority of women with the disorder, and obesity is a frequent finding as well, although neither of these features is essential to making the diagnosis. Hirsutism, of course, can occur independently of polycystic ovary disease (for a detailed review of this subject, see reference 39). Frank virilization is unusual in women with the Stein-Leventhal syndrome, although a slight degree of clitoral enlargement is occasionally seen [13].

Recently, preliminary evidence has been presented suggesting that women with the polycystic ovary syndrome have heightened libido and an increased willingness to initiate, pursue, and dominate sexual activity as compared to control groups of women with strong career or athletic interests [40]. This finding is consistent with clinical observation of patients with the polycystic ovary syndrome in our infertility program, from which it appears that many women with this disorder have heightened libido and actively pursue their sexual interests. On the other hand, the combination of obesity and hirsutism that affects many women with the polycystic ovary syndrome may create problems of body-image and physical attractiveness; furthermore, the associated infertility may itself predispose to the occurrence of sexual problems (see Chapter 15).

Although appropriate medical therapy (clomiphene or human menopausal gonadotropins to induce ovulation) or surgery (wedge resection) will generally correct the infertility, the other features of this disorder may remain prominent, posing a difficult management problem. Electrolysis is often the best solution for the patient particularly concerned about hirsutism.

Hysterectomy and Sexuality

Removal of the uterus may be undertaken for a number of medical reasons, including the presence of benign or malignant tumors, recurrent refractory dysfunctional bleeding, pelvic infections, cystocele, the pelvic congestion syndrome, endometriosis, and uterine prolapse. Whatever the primary indication, hysterectomy may be accompanied by alterations in sexuality that occur for a variety of biologic and psychosocial reasons.

In some instances, sexual problems that occur following hysterectomy may be simply a continuation or a further evolution of previously existing difficulties. The woman who has associated her sexuality primarily with the ability to reproduce may experience decreased libido and impaired sexual responsiveness after hysterectomy because she expects to, because she places little value on nonreproductive sex, or because she is misinformed. In other instances, women who have been experiencing dyspareunia as a result of the underlying pelvic pathologic condition leading to their surgery may be so negatively conditioned to sexual activity that they abstain postoperatively or avoid sexual contact, worrying about persistence or recurrence of their discomfort. Women who believe that their sexual functioning will abruptly end at the menopause may also encounter sexual difficulties after hysterectomy if they are already in their middle or late forties, or if they perceive the cessation of monthly menstruation as equivalent to being menopausal.

In some cases, the opposite reaction occurs. The woman who is relieved of significant dysmenorrhea or who is freed from symptoms of dyspareunia as a result of surgery may find her sexual responsiveness facilitated. Similarly, women who were fearful of unwanted conception or of the risk of developing cervical or endometrial cancer may experience increased libido and an improvement in sexual satisfaction after hysterectomy. Women who were troubled by abnormal menstrual flow or dysfunctional bleeding may likewise be relieved by surgery, with a resultant improvement in general health, correction of anemia due to chronic blood loss, and a fostered sense of body-image or self-esteem.

Drellich and colleagues have summarized additional relevant considerations regarding the impact of hysterectomy:

The uterus is seen as necessary for the fulfillment of roles ordinarily construed as feminine in the individual's personal life and as a member of society. It is valued as a childbearing organ; a cleansing instrument; a sexual organ; a source of strength, youth, and feminine attractiveness; and a regulator of general body health and well-being. Anxieties surrounding the imminent loss of this valued organ are responsible for delays in treatment and irrational preoperative fears and, at times, may contribute to a prolonged postoperative invalidism which is out of proportion to the actual tissue impairment. These emotional reactions derive from the patient's beliefs about the effects of the loss of the uterus upon their bodies, their lives, and their total adjustment [41].

In light of these attitudes, it is not surprising that women who have had hysterectomies develop an increased incidence of depression or other psychiatric abnormalities in comparison with women who have had other types of major surgery, such as cholecystectomy [42]. Interestingly, the occurrence of psychiatric referral after hysterectomy is higher among women in whom no pelvic pathology was found.

Women who have undergone oophorectomy (removal of their ovaries) concomitantly with excision of the uterus may develop postmenopausal symptoms regardless of their age. Of these difficulties, diminished vaginal lubrication and atrophic changes in the vaginal mucosa are most likely to produce coital discomfort or otherwise hamper sexual function. Although it does not appear that estrogen is required for orgasmic responsivity, sexual arousal may be impaired in the presence of estrogen deficiency, although libido is typically unaltered. The use of local estrogen creams may reverse the vaginal problems that occur as a result of hormone deficiency; the controversy regarding systemic estrogen replacement therapy is discussed in Chapter 5.

Dennerstein and coworkers studied 89 patients who had undergone hysterectomy and oophorectomy, finding that 37 percent described deterioration of their sexual relationships after surgery while 34 percent had improved sexual responsiveness [43]. Preoperative anxieties about subsequent diminished sexuality correlated significantly with the development of postoperative sexual difficulties; postoperative estrogen replacement therapy did not improve libido, ability to reach orgasm, ease of vaginal lubrication, or enjoyment of sex, although estrogen use appeared to reduce the occurrence of dyspareunia. Utian also found that estrogen replacement therapy was not efficacious in ameliorating lowered libido following hysterectomy and oophorectomy [44].

Hysterectomy without removal of the cervix is now an obsolete procedure that should be utilized only when the technical aspects of surgery require this approach [13, 45]. The formerly held concept that the cervix is a significant source of vaginal lubrication during sexual arousal has now been refuted by extensive study [46]; in addition to this fact, leaving the cervix intact after hysterectomy places the patient at continued risk for the development of cervical carcinoma.

Complications resulting from hysterectomy procedures include those of infectious or traumatic origin and difficulties in wound healing. Unless complications such as vaginal vault abscess, pelvic cellulitis, prolapse of the fallopian tube, and formation of vesicovaginal or rectovaginal fistulas are properly identified and treated, sexual problems may be compounded. It is easy to imagine how bleeding from the vaginal cuff precipitated by coitus might badly frighten both the woman and her sexual partner; for this reason, care should be taken in postoperative followup to determine that proper tissue healing has occurred before the resumption of sexual activity. The presence of excessive granulation tissue may predispose to such vaginal bleeding.

Radical and superradical surgical procedures used in the treatment of malignancy are considerably more likely to disturb sexual function for organic reasons than are simple hysterectomy techniques. In a small number of patients, vaginal reconstructive surgery may be possible after total pelvic exenteration, with reportedly good results. However, because pelvic exenteration procedures involve severance of the pelvic nerve supply, normal anatomic and physiologic responsiveness is lost and the artificial vagina is not as functional as in instances where surgery is done to correct vaginal agenesis. Exenteration procedures are also complicated by the need for urinary diversion or colostomy or both, creating additional problems of body-image and self-esteem.

The reaction of the husband or sexual partner of the woman who has had a hysterectomy appears to be an important determinant of subsequent sexual adjustment. If the husband equates removal of the uterus with loss of libido or diminished femininity, he may inadvertently avoid sexual interaction with his wife. Men who do not understand the nature of female anatomy or the functional results of hysterectomy surgery may harbor many misconceptions regarding sex after such an operation. Men who appear indifferent to uterine removal may actually feel anxious or guilty about subsequent coital activity with their partner. For these reasons, it is important to include the husband in both preoperative and postoperative counseling sessions

Figure 8-2. Disorders of pelvic support. (*A*) Uterine prolapse; (*B*) cystocele; (*C*) rectocele. (From Green [13].)

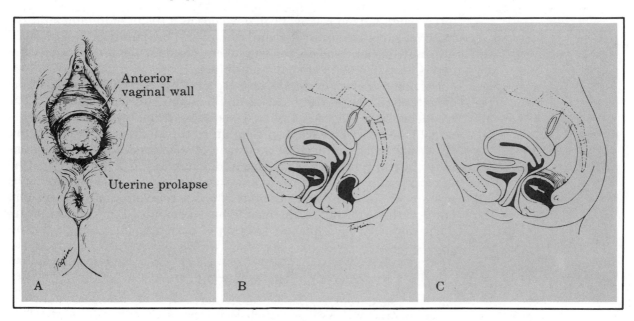

that explain the details of surgery and the ways in which hysterectomy may actually enhance a woman's sexual activity.

When simple hysterectomy is performed for necessary medical reasons, whatever the age of the woman, the probability is that her sexual functioning will improve significantly following recuperation from the operation, in comparison to what it was in the months before surgery. If health-care professionals take the time that is necessary to assuage fears and doubts regarding such operations and provide a reasonable amount of factual information to both the woman and her sexual partner, few sexual difficulties will ensue postoperatively. As with other types of surgery that may have an impact on sexuality, such counseling should be a routine part of preoperative, postoperative, and followup care.

Disorders of Pelvic Support

Normal variations in the anatomic position of the uterus are unlikely to impede sexual function, although it is not unusual for women to have some anxiety upon being told of such a variant. The fact that 20 percent or more of all women have retroversion of the uterus indicates the frequency with which such a situation is encountered [13]. Dyspareunia does not usually occur with simple uterine retroversion; on the other hand, when a fixed retroversion develops as a result of inflammation or infection, dyspareunia is more common. The posteriorly positioned uterus, whether fixed or freely movable, does not elevate from the true pelvis in response to sexual stimuli [46].

Uterine prolapse, cystocele, or rectocele (Fig. 8-2) usually result from obstetric trauma to the muscles and ligaments of pelvic support. The frequency and degree of sexual sequelae from these disorders are difficult to describe except in relation to the severity of the anatomic abnormality. In the surgical treatment of such conditions, care must be taken by the gynecologist to avoid undue narrowing of the introitus and vagina, which may lead to permanent coital disability [47]. Colporrhaphy procedures, used in the treatment of pelvic relaxation, involve a tightening of the walls of the vagina and have been noted to result in severe dyspareunia in a significant fraction of patients [48].

References

1. Bryan, A. L., Nigro, J. A., and Counseller, V. S. One hundred cases of congenital absence of the vagina. *Surgery, Gynecology and Obstetrics* 88:79–86, 1949.
2. David, A., Carmil, D., Bar-David, E., and Serr, D. M. Congenital absence of the vagina: Clinical and psychologic aspects. *Obstetrics and Gynecology* 46:407–409, 1975.
3. Griffin, J. E., Edwards, C., Madden, J. D., Harrod, M. J., and Wilson, J. D. Congenital absence of the vagina: The Mayer-Rokitansky-Kuster-Hauser syndrome. *Annals of Internal Medicine* 85:224–236, 1976.
4. Fore, S. R., Hammond, C. B., Parker, R. T., and Anderson, E. E. Urologic and genital anomalies in patients with congenital absence of the vagina. *Obstetrics and Gynecology* 46:410–416, 1975.
5. Karam, K. S., Salti, I., and Hajj, S. N. Congenital absence of the uterus: Clinicopathologic and endocrine findings. *Obstetrics and Gynecology* 50:531–535, 1977.
6. McIndoe, A. H., and Banister, J. B. An operation for the cure of congenital absence of the vagina. *Journal of Obstetrics and Gynaecology of the British Empire* 45:490–494, 1938.
7. McIndoe, A. Discussion of treatment of congenital absence of the vagina with emphasis on long-term results. *Proceedings of the Royal Society of Medicine* 52:952–954, 1959.
8. Garcia, J., and Jones, H. W. The split thickness graft technique for vaginal agenesis. *Obstetrics and Gynecology* 49:328–332, 1977.
9. Frank, R. T. The formation of an artificial vagina without operation. *American Journal of Obstetrics and Gynecology* 35:1053–1055, 1938.
10. Thompson, J. D., Wharton, L. R., and TeLinde, R. W. Congenital absence of the vagina: An analysis of thirty-two cases corrected by the McIndoe operation. *American Journal of Obstetrics and Gynecology* 74:397–404, 1957.
11. Cali, R. W., and Pratt, J. H. Congenital absence of the vagina. *American Journal of Obstetrics and Gynecology* 100:752–763, 1968.

12. Masters, W. H., and Johnson, V. E.   The Artificial Vagina: Anatomy and Physiology. In W. H. Masters and V. E. Johnson, *Human Sexual Response.* Boston: Little, Brown and Co., 1966. Pp. 101–110.
13. Green, T. H., Jr.   *Gynecology—Essentials of Clinical Practice.* Boston: Little, Brown and Co., 1977.
14. Stamey, T. A., and Timothy, M. M.   Studies of introital colonization in women with recurrent urinary infections: I. The role of vaginal pH. *Journal of Urology* 114:261–263, 1975.
15. Buckley, R. M., Jr., McGuckin, M., and MacGregor, R. R.   Urine bacterial counts after sexual intercourse. *New England Journal of Medicine* 298:321–324, 1978.
16. Cox, C. E., Lacy, S. S., and Hinman, F., Jr.   The urethra and its relationship to urinary tract infection: II. The urethral flora of the female with recurrent urinary infection. *Journal of Urology* 99:632–638, 1968.
17. Kunin, C. M.   Sexual intercourse and urinary infections. *New England Journal of Medicine* 298:336–337, 1978.
18. Juel-Jensen, B. E.   Antiviral Compounds with Special Reference to Genital Herpes. In R. D. Catterall and C. S. Nicol, *Sexually Transmitted Diseases.* London: Academic Press, 1976. Pp. 170–177.
19. Berger, R. S., and Papa, C. M.   Photodye herpes therapy—Cassandra confirmed? *Journal of the American Medical Association* 238:133–134, 1977.
20. Catalano, L. W., and Johnson, L. D.   Herpesvirus antibody and carcinoma *in situ* of the cervix. *Journal of the American Medical Association* 217:447–450, 1971.
21. Rawls, W. E., Adam, E., and Melnick, J. L. An analysis of seroepidemiological studies of herpesvirus type 2 and carcinoma of the cervix. *Cancer Research* 33:1477–1482, 1973.
22. Hanshaw, J. B. *Herpesvirus hominis* infections in the fetus and the newborn. *American Journal of Diseases of Children* 126:546–555, 1973.
23. Evans, T. N.   Sexually transmissible diseases. *American Journal of Obstetrics and Gynecology* 125:116–133, 1976.
24. Thin, R. N., Leighton, M., and Dixon, M. J.   How often is genital yeast infection sexually transmitted? *British Medical Journal* 2:93–94, 1977.
25. Oriel, J. D., Partridge, B. M., Denny, M. J., and Coleman, J. C.   Genital yeast infections. *British Medical Journal* 4:761–764, 1972.
26. Pheifer, T. A., Forsyth, P. S., Durfee, M. A., Pollock, H. M., and Holmes, K. K.   Nonspecific vaginitis: Role of *Haemophilus vaginalis* and treatment with metronidazole. *New England Journal of Medicine* 298:1429–1433, 1978.
27. McCormack, W. M., Almeida, P. C., Bailey, P. E., Grady, E. M., and Lee, Y. -H.   Sexual activity and vaginal colonization with genital mycoplasmas. *Journal of the American Medical Association* 221:1375–1377, 1972.
28. Gnarpe, H., and Friberg, J.   Mycoplasma and human reproductive failure: I. The occurrence of different Mycoplasmas in couples with reproductive failure. *American Journal of Obstetrics and Gynecology* 114:727–731, 1972.
29. Lee, Y. -H., and McCormack, W. M.   Clinical implications of the genital mycoplasmas in obstetrics and gynecology. *Journal of Reproductive Medicine* 13:123–127, 1974.
30. Idriss, W. M., Patton, W. C., and Taymore, M. L.   On the etiologic role of

Ureaplasma urealyticum (T-mycoplasma) infection in infertility. *Fertility and Sterility* 30:293–296, 1978.

31. Rehewy, M. S. E., Jaszczak, S., Hafez, W. S. W., Thomas, A., and Brown, W. J. *Ureaplasma urealyticum* (T-mycoplasma) in vaginal fluid and cervical mucus from fertile and infertile women. *Fertility and Sterility* 30:297–300, 1978.

32. Fiumara, N. J. The diagnosis and treatment of gonorrhea. *Medical Clinics of North America* 56:1105–1113, 1972.

33. Kraus, S. J. Complications of gonococcal infection. *Medical Clinics of North America* 56:1115–1125, 1972.

34. Kistner, R. W. Management of endometriosis in the infertile patient. *Fertility and Sterility* 26:1151–1166, 1975.

35. Stein, I. F., and Leventhal, M. L. Amenorrhea associated with bilateral polycystic ovaries. *American Journal of Obstetrics and Gynecology* 29:181–191, 1935.

36. Greenblatt, R. B., and Mahesh, V. B. The androgenic polycystic ovary. *American Journal of Obstetrics and Gynecology* 125:712–726, 1976.

37. Stahl, N. L., Teeslink, C. R., and Greenblatt, R. B. Ovarian, adrenal, and peripheral testosterone levels in the polycystic ovary syndrome. *American Journal of Obstetrics and Gynecology* 117:194–200, 1973.

38. DeVane, C., Czekala, N., Judd, H., and Yen, S. S. C. Circulating gonadotropins, estrogens, and androgens in polycystic ovarian disease. *American Journal of Obstetrics and Gynecology* 121:496–500, 1975.

39. Muller, S. A. Hirsutism. *American Journal of Medicine* 46:803–817, 1969.

40. Gorzynski, G., and Katz, J. L. The polycystic ovary syndrome: Psychosexual correlates. *Archives of Sexual Behavior* 6:215–222, 1977.

41. Drellich, M. G., Bieber, I., and Sutherland, A. M. The psychological impact of cancer and cancer surgery: VI. Adaptation to hysterectomy. *Cancer* 9:1120–1126, 1956.

42. Daly, M. J. Psychological Impact of Surgical Procedures on Women. In A. M. Freedman, H. I. Kaplan, and B. J. Sadock (eds.), *Comprehensive Textbook of Psychiatry*. Baltimore: Williams & Wilkins, 1975. Pp. 1477–1480.

43. Dennerstein, L., Wood, C., and Burrows, G. D. Sexual response following hysterectomy and oophorectomy. *Obstetrics and Gynecology* 49:92–96, 1977.

44. Utian, W. H. Effect of hysterectomy, oophorectomy and estrogen therapy on libido. *International Journal of Obstetrics and Gynaecology* 13:97–100, 1975.

45. Amias, A. G. Sexual life after gynaecological operations: I. *British Medical Journal* 2:608–609, 1975.

46. Masters, W. H., and Johnson, V. E. *Human Sexual Response*. Boston: Little, Brown and Co., 1966.

47. Amias, A. G. Sexual life after gynaecological operations: II. *British Medical Journal* 2:680–681, 1975.

48. Jeffcoate, T. N. A. Posterior colpoperineorrhaphy. *American Journal of Obstetrics and Gynecology* 77:490–502, 1959.

9

Sex and Urologic Illness

Problems of genitourinary function are frequently accompanied by changes in sexual function or sexual behavior. This association arises not only from the specific pathophysiology of genitourinary disorders, but also as a result of the psychological impact of attention being drawn to the organs of reproduction and elimination. Many patients harbor misunderstandings of the effects urologic illness may have on sex, further complicating the picture from the viewpoint of clinical management. In this chapter, discussion is focused on urologic problems that may influence male sexuality. The sexual problems associated with testicular tumors are discussed in Chapter 11.

Congenital Anomalies of the Penis

Penile Agenesis and Retroscrotal Penis

Disturbances of normal embryologic development of the male external genitalia may result in a variety of anatomic defects. Agenesis of the penis is a rare condition that may be associated with other anomalies of the genitourinary and lower intestinal tracts; at least 36 cases have been described in the literature [1]. This problem requires a prompt decision to rear the newborn child as a girl [2], with the use of surgery to remove the testes and create an artifical vagina, and (beginning in adolescence) the use of estrogen therapy to foster development of a female habitus and secondary sex characteristics, since there is currently no satisfactory procedure for the surgical construction of a fully functional penis.

The development of penile tissue in a retroscrotal location (Fig. 9-1) may initially simulate the appearance of penile agenesis. Fifteen cases of retroscrotal penis have been reported in the literature [3]. In these cases, associated anomalies of the urinary tract may be present; the penis may be anatomically normal but malpositional or may reflect varying degrees of impaired development. In some instances it is possible to reposition the penis in an anterior fashion by surgery.

Double Penis

Diphallic male genitalia—the existence of two more or less well-formed penises—is a rare anomaly that has been estimated to occur once in 5.5 million births [4]. Wilson cited 108 case reports in a review article written in 1973 [5]. Surgery should be undertaken only after urologic investigation has identified the patency of the urethra and the anatomy of the genitourinary system, since typically only one penis contains a functional and patent urethra.

Figure 9-1. (*A, B*) An infant with
retroscrotal penis. A true penis is not
present. There is a mass of erectile
tissue covered by ectopic scrotal skin
posterior to the scrotum. (From Kernahan [3].)

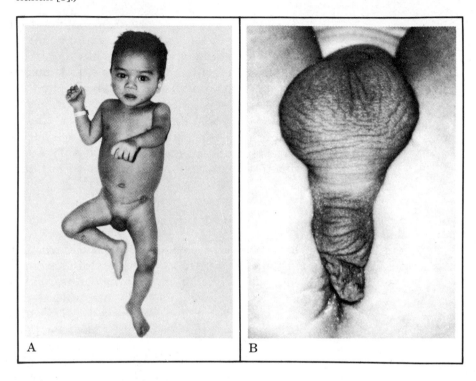

A

B

Micropenis

Although many parents express anxiety about the size of their child's
penis, true micropenis is an unusual disorder. A micropenis is properly
formed embryologically, with the abnormality being a matter of size
rather than shape (see Fig. 9-2). The urethral meatus is properly positioned, there is a distinct glans and shaft to the penis, and the testes
may be of normal size. The etiology of micropenis is unknown, although
it appears to be sometimes associated with a defect in androgen secretion during the second or third trimester of pregnancy [6]. In some
cases, micropenis occurs in the context of other disorders, which are
characterized by abnormalities of the hypothalamus or pituitary (e.g.,
anencephaly, congenital absence of the pituitary, the Prader-Willi syndrome, Kallman's syndrome, and Meckel's syndrome) or abnormalities
of the testes or chromosomes [6], while in other instances micropenis
occurs in an otherwise healthy baby.

In light of the potential psychological impact that this condition may
have on the growing child, it is frequently advisable to treat this

Figure 9-2. Appearance of the external genitalia in a 3-year-old boy with micropenis and undescended testes. (From Walsh, Wilson, Allen, Madden, Porter, Neaves, Griffin, and Goodwin [6].)

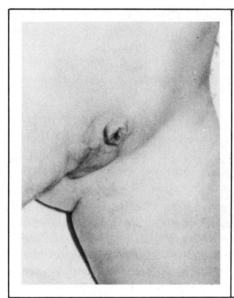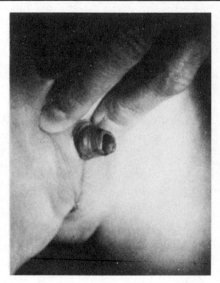

condition in children with topical 1 percent testosterone cream for a period of three to six months, which will usually produce moderate growth in phallic size [1]. If a satisfactory response to this approach does not occur, parenteral testosterone therapy for a period of three months may be considered, since this treatment has been reported to produce penile growth with only transient effects on skeletal growth patterns and minor degrees of virilization [7]. It is important to avoid excessive androgen therapy during childhood, however, since premature epiphyseal closure may limit subsequent growth of the long bones. Recently, Money and Mazur reported the successful use of a juvenile-sized flexible plastic prosthetic phallus for a 9-year-old boy with micropenis [8]. This device allowed the child to urinate while standing and significantly enhanced his self-esteem.

When the condition of micropenis persists into adulthood, it is typically a reflection of an underlying hormonal disorder, since the normal pubertal surge of testosterone leads to phallic growth. If a testosterone deficiency is documented, parenteral replacement therapy may correct the problem. However, most adult men who express concern over the size of their penis are anatomically normal. In some instances the penis may appear to be small because of obesity or because of conditions that produce scrotal swelling, thus foreshortening the visible portion of the penile shaft. Except in instances of true micropenis, it is unlikely that penile size will adversely affect sexual functioning, although men or women who are preoccupied about penile size may well develop sexual difficulties because of this concern.

Hypospadias

Hypospadias is the abnormal occurrence of the urethral opening on the ventral aspect (undersurface) of the penis or on the perineum. This congenital anomaly has been estimated to occur in approximately 1 in 125 newborn males [9]. In most cases the defect is minimal, with the urethral opening located on the glans of the penis or at the coronal ridge; approximately 13 percent of men have penile, scrotal, or perineal hypospadias (Table 9-1). There may be a ventral curvature in the penis (chordee) associated with the abnormal location of the urethral orifice (Fig. 9-3), caused by a fibrous band of tissue. In some cases the positioning of the penis is further distorted by a degree of penile torsion.

Hypospadias occurs when the normal embryologic patterns of genital development are altered or interrupted. This alteration may result from delayed onset of androgen secretion by the fetal testis, inadequate production of androgen by the fetal testis, target organ insensitivity to androgen action, or exposure to progestational or estrogenic drugs during fetal development [10, 11]. There is recent evidence that a relative testosterone deficiency may persist in adulthood in patients with severe forms of hypospadias [12].

If hypospadias of a moderate or severe degree is untreated, both sexual function and sexual behavior may be affected. Problems may

Table 9-1. Types of Hypospadias by Location of Urethral Meatus

Type of Hypospadias	Percentage of Occurrence
Glandular	50.0
Anterior penile	31.5
Posterior penile	10.0
Penoscrotal	4.0
Scrotal	4.0
Perineal	0.5

Figure 9-3. Distal hypospadias and chordee in an adult male (arrow points to urethral meatus). (From Horton and Devine [14].)

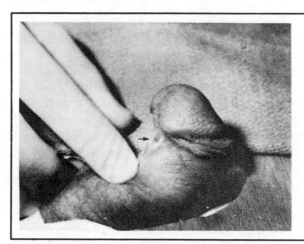

arise because of the psychological reaction to the appearance of the anatomic defect as well as for physical reasons. Boys with hypospadias may have to urinate in a sitting position due to the malposition of the urethral opening, and this may lead to ridicule from their classmates as well as create childhood problems with self-esteem, masculinity, and body-image. Adolescents or adults with hypospadias may avoid sexual activity for similar reasons. In addition, erectile function may be impaired because of hypoplastic development of the penis, the presence of chordee, associated genitourinary anomalies, or testosterone deficiency. Ventral curvature was noted in 8 of 23 males with untreated glandular or coronal hypospadias, in 21 of 35 males with untreated distal penile hypospadias, and in all cases of midpenile or more severe hypospadias in a recent study [13].

An extensive literature exists describing surgical approaches for the correction of hypospadias and chordee [14–17]. Whenever possible, a one-stage repair is advisable [15–17], eliminating the need for multiple operations. Surgery involves removal of fibrous chordee (correcting the ventral curvature of the penis) and repositioning of the urinary meatus. Neonates with hypospadias should not be circumcised, since the tissue of the prepuce is utilized in the reconstructive surgery [14]. Although there is no firm agreement on the age at which such procedures are best undertaken, it is often advisable to operate on patients with hypospadias between 2 and 4 years of age to minimize the psychological trauma attendant upon such surgery and to correct the anatomic problem prior to school age. Operations during infancy are technically more difficult because of the small size of the penis.

The results of surgery are successful in straightening the penis, allowing normal erectile function, and permitting a normal voiding pattern in 70 to 80 percent of patients [13, 14]. Surgery is usually not required for the correction of glandular hypospadias. Kenawi found that sexual function after treatment for hypospadias was disturbed only when incomplete or incorrect surgery was performed [13]. However, Farkas and Hynie [18] found that of 130 patients who had hypospadias repairs during childhood, 17 percent had disturbances of erection, and a majority of patients abstained from sexual intercourse or had intercourse only rarely. In contrast, a recent detailed longitudinal study of pubertal development, age at initiation of sexual activity, and sexual function in males with hypospadias showed few differences from the normal population [19]. It is likely that as surgical techniques improve, all but the most severe cases of hypospadias can be corrected so that relatively normal sexual function is attainable.

Epispadias

Epispadias occurs in 1 in 30,000 males and is marked by the opening of the urethra on the dorsal (upper) surface of the penis. Epispadias may be uncomplicated, but more often it is associated with exstrophy of the bladder and a ventral wall defect in the abdomen. Usually surgery must correct urinary incontinence, the malpositioning of the urethra, and the frequently associated dorsal chordee that makes intercourse difficult or impossible [20]. Some form of urinary diversion may also be required, further complicating the picture. Except in cases of isolated epispadias, which are very rare, surgical correction is unlikely to provide normal sexual function.

Congenital Anomalies of the Testes
Cryptorchidism

The testes normally descend into the scrotum in the latter months of intrauterine development. However, in 3 percent of full-term males and in 30 percent of premature male infants, the testes are cryptorchid (undescended) [1]. In the majority of these cases the testes descend normally within the first few months of life, but at 1 year of age approximately 0.8 percent of males still have undescended testes. The term *cryptorchidism* derives from the Greek *cryptos* or "hidden"; possible locations of undescended or incompletely descended testes are shown in Figure 9-4.

Cryptorchid testes may be either unilateral or bilateral. Although the defect is usually isolated, abnormalities of the urinary tract have been found in 13 percent of patients with this problem, and cryptorchidism may also be associated with genetic abnormalities such as the male Turner's syndrome, Prader-Willi syndrome, or Reifenstein's syndrome [1].

By age 5, alteration of the histologic pattern of tissue in the undescended testis is observable [21, 22]. If the testes remain bilaterally cryptorchid after puberty, infertility results even though testosterone production is usually normal or only mildly impaired. In unilateral cryptorchidism, fertility may be normal. However, studies of the fertility status of men who have undergone orchiopexy for a unilateral undescended testis show a persistence of impaired spermatogenesis a decade or more after surgery, although testosterone levels are normal [23]. Surgery is advisable if cryptorchid testes cannot be stimulated to descend by treatment with human chorionic gonadotropin (HCG); the reason for this, in addition to concerns about fertility potential, is that there is a markedly increased risk of carcinoma in an intra-abdominal testis [24, 25].

Surprisingly little psychological research has been done on the subject of cryptorchidism. Cytryn and coworkers studied 27 cryptorchid boys aged 3 to 17 years and reported an increased incidence of confusion of body-image and gender identity [26]. A more recent study of 10 bilaterally cryptorchid patients who were evaluated three to ten years following corrective surgery showed that "absence of the testes from the scrotum during the time of sex assignment, early sex-typing, and gender-identity formation does not usually lead to serious and permanent damage to gender role and gender identity" [27]. However, in the same study the authors noted that cryptorchid subjects tended toward later onset of masturbation and other types of sexual activity than did anatomically normal males. Raboch and coworkers found that adult men with cryptorchidism had histories of first ejaculation slightly later than a control group and also had a lower rate of nocturnal emission during puberty [28]. Similarly, in adulthood the frequency of sexual activity of cryptorchid men was somewhat lower than that of normal controls.

If cryptorchid boys become alarmed as a result of frequent examinations of their genitalia or because of the failure of the testes to

Figure 9-4. Sites of cryptorchid and
ectopic testes. (A) Locations of cryptorchid testes, numbered in order of
frequency. (B) Positions of ectopic
testes. (From K. L. Moore, *The Developing Human*, 2nd ed., 1977. Courtesy of W. B. Saunders Co., Philadelphia.)

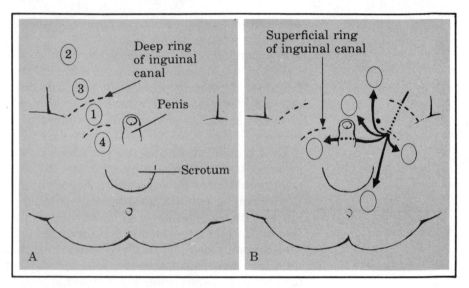

descend with hormone therapy, it is quite possible that psychosexual
difficulties may result. The parents of the cryptorchid child must be
provided with information about the nature of this disorder and given
reassurance about the prognosis for sexual potency in later life. Parents should also be discouraged from repeated examinations of their
boy's scrotum to check the position of the testes; such evidence of
parental concern, no matter how well intended, may be traumatic or
confusing to the child.

Ectopic Testis

After passage through the inguinal canal, the descending testis may
deviate from normal positioning within the scrotum, thus resulting in
an ectopic location of the male gonad. Ectopic testes are rare; their
possible locations are shown in Figure 9-4. Surgery is generally indicated when the diagnosis is made, since orchiopexy performed prior to
puberty usually results in normal testicular function.

Anorchism

Congenital bilateral anorchism (absence of the testes) is a rare disorder
that is discussed in Chapter 6. Strong consideration should be given to
the surgical implantation of prosthetic testes, thus minimizing disorders of body-image and psychosexual development. Either a silicone
rubber prosthesis or artificial testes consisting of a silicone rubber
capsule filled with silicone gel may be employed; the latter approach

offers a more natural-feeling prosthesis [29]. Recently, there has been a case report of successful testicular transplantation in identical twins, one of whom was anorchic [30].

Sexual Aspects of Genitourinary Infections

Orchitis

Acute inflammation of the testes may occur as a result of hematogenous spread of any infection. Mumps orchitis, the most common form of this disorder, may also be caused by a descending infection, since the mumps virus is excreted in the urine. Twenty percent of postpubertal males with mumps infections develop orchitis, with bilateral involvement in one-quarter of this group [31]. Symptoms of orchitis include pain and swelling of the testes and fever, sometimes accompanied by chills. Approximately half the testes affected by mumps orchitis become atrophic, although testosterone production usually remains unimpaired. It has recently been noted that Leydig cell function is impaired during the acute phases of mumps orchitis and, in some individuals, may continue to show altered testosterone secretion on a long-term basis [32]. In other cases of orchitis, spermatogenesis is only transiently affected.

Orchitis may produce dyspareunia in the male, since vasocongestion occurring during sexual arousal of the already inflamed testis typically produces pain; pain may also be caused by elevation and rotation of the testis and pressure derived from coital thrusting.

Urethritis and Cystitis

Although almost every type of infectious agent can cause infection of the lower urinary tract, bacterial infection is the most common cause of urethritis and cystitis. Urethritis is typically classified as either gonococcal or nongonococcal; in approximately 90 percent of cases of nongonococcal urethritis, no etiologic agent is identified by routine screening and culture methods, and the infection is termed *nonspecific urethritis* [33]. Special testing in an extensive study isolated *Chlamydia trachomatis* from the urethra of 42 percent of men with nongonococcal urethritis [34]; trichomoniasis and candidiasis are also frequent causes of this disorder.

Urethritis typically produces dysuria (pain or burning on urination), urinary urgency, and urinary frequency. Patients with gonococcal urethritis usually have a urethral discharge, whereas most patients with nongonococcal urethritis have no discharge [35]. The presence of pus at the urethral meatus is strongly suggestive of gonorrhea. In contrast, cystitis (which is often accompanied by urethritis) is marked by suprapubic pain or tenderness.

Needless to say, urethritis and cystitis may be sexually transmitted diseases. In some cases, urethritis may result from hypertrophy of the prostate or may spread from chronic prostatitis. Nevertheless, many men react negatively to the occurrence of urinary tract symptoms, including urethral discharge, initially using denial as a way of coping with their fear or guilt. Such men may avoid diagnostic or treatment services and may thus expose their sexual partners to the risk of infection, or they may withdraw from sexual activity as a means of hiding their abnormality.

Urethritis does not ordinarily interfere with sexual function except when the inflammation of the urethral mucosa is extensive. In spite of this fact, some men develop potency problems on a psychogenic basis as a consequence of their infection. The incidence of urethritis from all causes is considerably higher in homosexual men than in heterosexuals, reflecting the increased exposure to enteric bacteria from anal intercourse. Likewise, the occurrence of urethritis is increased in sexually active men with hypospadias as compared to normals; in this situation, microbial organisms from the vaginal environment may be "scooped up" into the urethral meatus during coital thrusting.

Prostatitis

Chronic bacterial prostatitis is the most common cause of recurrent urinary tract infections in men [36]. This disorder is usually caused by gram-negative bacilli, with *Escherichia coli* predominating (80 percent of patients) and the remainder of cases attributed to *Klebsiella, Proteus mirabilis, Pseudomonas,* and *Enterobacteriaceae.* Although acute bacterial prostatitis is marked by fever, chills, perineal pain, rectal discomfort, dysuria, urinary frequency, and urinary urgency, chronic bacterial prostatitis is often less well defined. Chronic bacterial prostatitis may manifest as low back pain, perineal aching, or urethral discharge, but in many cases there are no symptoms except during exacerbation, when cystitis or evidence of prostatic obstruction may arise.

Treatment of bacterial prostatitis is complicated by the fact that currently available antibiotic drugs cannot cross the prostatic epithelium into prostatic fluid, so that the prostate functions as a reservoir of infection [36]. Although Meares and Stamey have stated that bacterial prostatitis is not associated with sexual complaints or problems [37], other authors have reported that sexual difficulties occur frequently. Davis and Mininberg observed loss of libido and painful erection or ejaculation occurring with acute prostatitis, and these authors reported that chronic prostatitis "is frequently associated with sexual dysfunction" [38]. They also noted that chronic prostatitis may be accompanied by decreased libido, premature ejaculation, bloody ejaculation (hemospermia), and frequent, painful nocturnal emissions.

In chronic prostatitis, the persistent nidus of infection and inflammation in prostatic tissue predisposes to spasmodic, painful contraction of the prostate during orgasm. These spasmodic prostatic contractions may be referred as pain to either the rectum, the testis, or the glans of the penis. The sometimes sharp and usually disquieting pain of this disorder may be experienced with prostatic congestion that occurs during sexual excitation, particularly if there is a prolonged period of such congestion; however, the most severe pain occurs coincidentally with the onset of orgasm (the stage of ejaculatory inevitability) or immediately postejaculation. Although not all men with chronic prostatitis experience such discomfort, the occurrence of these symptoms may well lead to a pattern of avoidance of sexual activity or the onset of secondary impotence.

Sexual Function after Prostatectomy

Surgical intervention to correct benign prostatic hypertrophy or carcinoma of the prostate is frequently required for the aging male. In one report, the incidence of benign prostatic hypertrophy was estimated to progress from 30 percent of men between the ages of 41 and 50 to 75 percent of men aged 80 or older [39]. Although cancer of the prostate is virtually unknown among men under age 40, it accounts for 15.2 percent of all cancers among white males and 21.8 percent of all cancers among black males in the United States [40].

Benign prostatic hypertrophy may require surgery when it leads to bladder outlet obstruction, depending on the severity of symptoms (such as urinary hesitancy, frequency, or urgency; nocturia; hematuria; and acute urinary retention). However, the effects of prostate surgery on sexual function have been greatly misunderstood by most patients, who fear a total loss of sexual capability as a result of such an operation. This fear is further highlighted when it is placed in the following context: There is no indication that benign prostatic hypertrophy diminishes sexual functioning [41].

Four different surgical approaches are utilized in the treatment of benign prostatic hypertrophy (Fig. 9-5). The *transurethral approach* is used for smaller prostatic adenomas; in this approach an endoscopic resection is carried out, which offers the relative advantages of low operative mortality and morbidity and a comparatively short hospital

Figure 9-5. Four surgical approaches to prostatectomy. (From Glenn [24].)

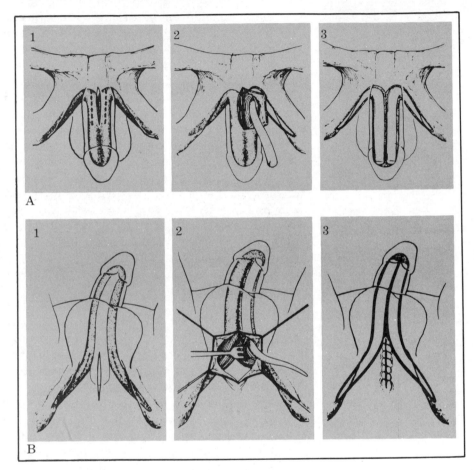

stay [24, 41, 42]. The transurethral resection does not interfere with the nerve fibers that control erection, nor does it cause disruption of blood flow to the penis; the occurrence of postoperative organic impotence in patients undergoing this procedure is unusual. Finkle and Prian reported that only 5 percent of men who had transurethral prostatectomies experienced loss of potency [43]; such cases appear to be primarily attributable to psychogenic factors. However, about 90 percent of men experience retrograde ejaculation after transurethral prostatectomy because of damage to the internal sphincter of the bladder.

The *suprapubic approach* to prostatectomy was historically the first to be generally employed [24]. This technique requires an incision in the anterior wall of the bladder and dissection of mucosa surrounding the bladder neck; as a result, most men (75 to 80 percent) undergoing this type of prostatectomy experience irreversible postoperative retrograde ejaculation. Only about 10 to 20 percent of men become impotent following a suprapubic prostatectomy, however [41, 43]. The *retropubic approach* offers a low mortality rate and good surgical exposure [24, 41]. There does not appear to be any difference in the rate of potency disorders occurring postoperatively in men undergoing this type of surgery as compared with the approaches already mentioned [41–43].

In contrast, the *perineal approach* to prostatectomy is marked by a considerably higher rate of postoperative impotence. When the perineal approach is used for simple prostatectomy for the treatment of benign prostatic hypertrophy, the ensuing rate of impotence is approximately 40 to 50 percent [44]. When a radical perineal prostatectomy is performed for the treatment of prostatic carcinoma, because of the wide dissection that is carried out, including seminal vesiculectomy, there is a 98 percent or greater incidence of impotence postoperatively due to damage to the nerve pathways that control erection. In the unusual case of a man whose potency persists after a radical perineal prostatectomy, an incomplete operation was probably performed, leaving a portion of the prostatic capsule (and a portion of the periprostatic nerve plexus) intact.

A number of considerations should be mentioned in regard to the alterations in sexual function or sexual behavior that occur following prostatectomy. To begin, the operation performed for the treatment of benign prostatic hypertrophy is not a true prostatectomy, since the tissue that is removed is actually periurethral adenomatous tissue, and the body of the prostate is left undisturbed [24, 42, 44]. Nevertheless, potency may be impaired postoperatively for a number of reasons. For men undergoing a transurethral resection or a suprapubic or retropubic prostatectomy, it appears that the majority of cases of impotence are psychogenic rather than organic. This reaction may be attributable to the man's fear of surgery involving his genitourinary functioning, coupled with ignorance as to the anatomy and physiology of such approaches; it may also be a psychological reaction to the alteration in ejaculation that commonly occurs following surgery. In some instances, prostatectomy provides a convenient excuse for the already aging man to avoid sexual activity; similarly, in some situations the unwillingness of the man's sex partner to participate in coitus postoperatively (often stemming from fear or ignorance about the medical and surgical facts) is the primary factor in the occurrence of impotence. In addition, there is increasing evidence that the preoperative explanation given to the prostatectomy patient is an important determinant of subsequent sexual function. Zohar and colleagues found that men who were given a reassuring, factual preoperative discussion explaining the anticipated results of surgery did not develop impotence postoperatively, whereas five out of eight patients who were not given such an explanation became impotent after their prostatectomy [45]. It appears to be advisable to offer preoperative counseling to both the man and his sexual partner, so that factual information can be accurately presented to both of them.

Further substantiation of the persistence of normal erectile function after transurethral resections is available. Madorsky and coworkers studied nocturnal penile tumescence patterns preoperatively and postoperatively in a sleep research laboratory and found that not a single subject had complete loss of penile tumescence patterns postoperatively, indicating that both the innervation and the blood supply of the penis remained reasonably intact following the transurethral procedure [46]. For unknown reasons, however, about half of the subjects experienced some degree of decreased quality in their postoperative nocturnal erections.

When postprostatectomy impotence does occur, evaluation of the situation may be facilitated by monitoring nocturnal penile tumescence to differentiate organic from psychogenic impairment. Men who have organic impotence resulting from a prostatectomy may wish to consider the possibility of implantation of a penile prosthetic device to permit active participation in coitus; men with psychogenic impotence as a result of urologic surgery will often respond well to psychotherapy. For reasons that are both medicolegal and related to patient management, it is mandatory to obtain a preoperative sex history to determine baseline levels of sexual functioning, since frequently men in the age group undergoing prostatic surgery may have had sexual difficulties prior to their operation. Interestingly, in some patients sexual function will improve following prostatectomy, although the precise mechanism for this change is unknown.

When bilateral orchiectomy or exogenous estrogen therapy is employed in the treatment of inoperable prostatic carcinoma, libido is typically suppressed and impotence occurs in the overwhelming majority of patients. Current research involving the use of radiation, antineoplastic chemotherapy, and low-dose estrogen therapy may lead to the development of treatment methods for advanced prostatic carcinoma that offer palliation without obliterating sexual function [42].

Peyronie's Disease

Peyronie's disease is a fibrous induration of the penis that leads to penile curvature. In some cases the curvature is apparent in the flaccid penis, but the usual pattern is for the curvature to be detected only when the penis is partially or fully erect. The most common location of the fibrous induration is on the dorsal surface of the penis; other locations, including multiple sites of involvement, are sometimes seen, however [47]. Men with Peyronie's disease may experience painful erections or impotence, although some men with this disorder are not hampered in their sexual functioning. The disease typically occurs in men over the age of 40, but it may be seen at any age.

Although some cases of Peyronie's disease remit spontaneously, perhaps as a result of resolving vasculitis that does not progress to the stage of fibrous plaque formation [47], treatment is problematic. The use of local steroid injections or low dosage radiation therapy [48] has been tried, with variable results. Surgical management is difficult; Poutasse advises selecting only patients whose disease has been stabilized and in whom the penile curvature is severe enough to interfere with sexual activity [47]. A portion of the fibrous plaque is removed and, when necessary, the dorsal vein of the penis must be cut to permit penile lengthening if this vessel has become inelastic. In some instances, a dermal graft may be used to replace the diseased tunica albuginea.

Priapism

The term *priapism* refers to a persistent state of penile erection that is usually independent of sexual arousal. Although it may be impossible to determine the etiology of priapism, the most common causes include sickle cell anemia, polycythemia, and leukemia. In these cases, altered microvascular blood flow dynamics occur as a result of sludging of blood; the resulting venous stasis blocks normal mechanisms of penile detumescence. Priapism may also result from venous obstruction due to malignancy [49–51], from spinal cord injuries, from penile trauma resulting in hematoma formation, and from local reflex stimuli such as those associated with phimosis, urethral polyps, urethral calculi, or prostatitis [51–53]. In some instances, priapism may be drug-induced; thioridazine [54], heparin, testosterone, and hydralazine have been reported to cause this disorder [51].

Priapism is an emergency, since venous drainage to the corpora cavernosa must be restored and damage to erectile tissue must be minimized [55]; if the disorder is not brought under control, ischemic changes may occur in penile tissue [51, 53]. Treatment modalities range from the application of ice packs and sedation to the use of a variety of surgical shunt approaches [51, 53, 56]. Therapeutic defibrination by the use of proteolytic enzyme given intravenously has also been reported to be successful [57]. Anesthetic blocks, corporal aspiration of trapped blood, and use of low-molecular-weight dextran have also been advocated [51]. However, there is no single approach that will alleviate the priapism while guaranteeing successful restoration of the erectile mechanism.

Retrograde Ejaculation Retrograde ejaculation occurs when seminal fluid is propelled posteriorly into the bladder rather than anteriorly through the distal urethra. The diagnosis is usually made by demonstrating large numbers of spermatozoa in the centrifuged sediment of a urine specimen produced promptly after sexual activity leading to orgasm. The man affected by this disorder usually is aware of orgasm occurring but notices the absence of the sensation of fluid spurting through the distal urethra; this difference from normal ejaculation is distressing to some patients, but is of no concern to others. The retrograde deposition of semen produces a functional state of infertility.

Normally during ejaculation the bladder neck closes and blocks backward passage of seminal fluid. Conditions that alter the anatomic integrity of the bladder neck or that interfere with its neurologic tone may thus produce retrograde ejaculation. The most common causes of this disorder are prostatectomy, diabetes mellitus with neuropathy, bladder surgery or trauma, sympathectomy, spinal cord injury, use of drugs that produce sympathetic blockade (especially guanethidine), and extensive pelvic dissection (e.g., rectal excision, retroperitoneal lymph node dissection).

Stewart and Bergant have recently reported the use of a sympathomimetic medication, phenylpropanolamine, to correct retrograde ejaculation in a diabetic male by improving smooth muscle function in the region of the bladder neck [58]. Several techniques have been devised for the recovery and preservation of spermatozoa for artificial insemination from patients with retrograde ejaculation [59, 60]. In addition, surgical reconstruction of the bladder neck has been reported to reverse retrograde ejaculation [61]. Finally, Schramm described a case of conception occurring with retrograde ejaculation following voiding of a postejaculate specimen directly into the vagina [62]. Despite these approaches to treatment, most cases of retrograde ejaculation are not correctable by current methods, and achieving a pregnancy is difficult at best.

The psychosexual impact of retrograde ejaculation varies widely from patient to patient. In some instances, the underlying pathology produces erectile dysfunction as well as retrograde ejaculation (as commonly seen in patients with diabetes or spinal cord injuries). In most cases, however, erectile function is normal, and libido is typically unimpaired. If the man attaches great importance to his ability to procreate, it is common for potency problems to arise as a secondary reaction to retrograde ejaculation. At times, the female sex partner may be more concerned than the affected male by the absence of an external ejaculate. Counseling efforts should be educative and support-ive, stressing the fact that pleasurable sexual function is possible if other limiting medical problems do not exist concurrently.

Urologic Trauma

Injury to the pelvis, the penis, or the testes can interfere with normal erectile and ejaculatory function. In some instances, penile trauma is intentionally self-inflicted—a situation that may be encountered in cases related to transsexualism or other types of psychiatric illness [63]—while other self-inflicted injuries are unintentional and may vary from gunshot wounds to lacerations or severe ischemia [64]. A recent review of the literature on male genital self-mutilation reported 53 cases; 87 percent of these patients were believed to be psychotic [65]. Several reports indicate that surgical repair may be undertaken suc-cessfully in cases of complete or nearly complete amputation of the penis [66, 67]. Engelman and coworkers noted that preservation of urination, erectile and ejaculatory function, and even partial skin sen-sation was possible when the time lapse between injury and surgery is less than six hours [67].

Various devices such as rubber bands, rings, or straps may be used to constrict the penis to foster the maintenance of an erection by occlud-ing venous drainage. Unfortunately, this type of constriction can lead to penile ischemia or gangrene. The use of mechanical suction devices such as vacuum cleaners has also been associated with severe penile injuries sustained during masturbation [68]. A common type of penile injury, usually mild, is entrapment of penile skin in a zipper [69]. In-juries to the penis or urethra may occur because of intraurethral insertion of a foreign object as a source of sexual stimulation.

Traumatic rupture of the corpora cavernosa can occur from the ap-plication of a sudden external force to the erect penis; this is a rare disorder that may sometimes occur during sexual intercourse as a result of a sudden shift in coital position or upon attempts at penile insertion in the female astride position. Most patients with this condition respond to conservative management with good recovery; occasionally, persistent penile angulation on erection or other deformities make attempts at coitus painful or impossible, requiring surgical treatment [70].

Urethral damage can also lead to impotence. Chambers and Balfour reported that 8 of 19 patients became impotent after pelvic fracture with urethral damage [71]. In 35 patients with rupture of the membranous urethra, impotence occurred in 73 percent [72]. Netto and Freire found that 8 of 42 patients were impotent after urethral injury [73]; one of their patients underwent implantation of a penile prosthetic device with good results.

Sphincterotomy

There is considerable disagreement in the literature describing the effects of sphincterotomy (a procedure used to improve bladder emptying in spinal cord injury patients) on sexual function. Kiviat found that 33 percent of his patients developed postoperative impotence [74], while Nanninga and coworkers found a 14 percent rate of erectile dysfunction in 43 patients [75] and Morrow and Scott reported "complete, permanent loss of erectile function" in 8.2 percent of patients and diminished erectile function in an additional 16.8 percent [76]. Most investigators point out that temporary postoperative impotence is more common than permanent impotence [74–77]; additional data are required to delineate the precise risks of sphincterotomy procedures in terms of compromising sexual function and to develop appropriate approaches to counseling patients undergoing this type of surgery.

Implantable Penile Prostheses

Although most cases of impotence are attributable to psychogenic factors, significant numbers of men are impotent because of irreversible organic causes. In the past decade, increasing interest in sexual function coupled with advancing technology has led to the development of a variety of penile prosthetic devices that are implanted surgically in men with organic impotence to facilitate their participation in coital function. Candidates for such surgery include men with impotence resulting from diabetes, penile or pelvic trauma, vascular or neurologic disorders, and various types of operations (for example, impotence due to prostatectomy, cystectomy, colectomy, or aneurysm repair).

Different types of penile prostheses are available for the treatment of impotence. The basic difference involves whether a fixed rod prosthesis

Figure 9-6. Three pairs of Small-Carrion penile prostheses. (From Small [83].)

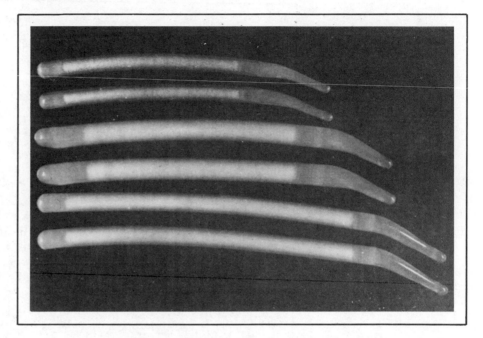

is used or whether an inflatable prosthetic device is employed. Fixed rod devices made of different materials, such as Silastic (silicone rubber), acrylic, or polyethylene, have been used by a number of surgeons (see Fig. 9-6) [78–87]. These devices have the advantage of relative simplicity of surgical technique of insertion (see Fig. 9-7), but they result in a perpetual state of semierection once insertion has been carried out, potentially creating both psychological distress and physical discomfort. The inflatable penile prosthesis (Fig. 9-8) produces an erection only when it is desired; the appearance of the penis in both the flaccid and erect states is completely normal. Although the surgical insertion of this device is technically more difficult than implantation of the fixed rod, there appears to be a reduced risk of tissue erosion or perforation because of the more favorable pressure dynamics. Both the patient and his sexual partner seem to indicate a greater degree of acceptance of the inflatable device.

Pearman initially approached the implantation of the Silastic penile prosthesis by placement of the device between Buck's fascia and the tunica albuginea, but later changed to a position between the under-

Figure 9-7. Surgical placement of the Small-Carrion prosthesis. (A) By penile incision: (1) A midline incision is made in the dorsum of the penis through the Colles' fascia. (2) Both outer layers are retracted laterally to avoid injury to midline nerves and vessels beneath Buck's fascia. The tunica albuginea is opened with an incision through Buck's fascia. (3) Both silicone rods are in place, filling each corpus nearly completely. (B) By perineal incision: (1) A midline incision is made at the level of the bulbous urethra. (2) After identifying the crus of the penis and the overlying ischiocavernous muscle, the tunica albuginea is opened longitudinally. When dilatation of the erectile tissue is complete, the silicone rod is inserted. (3) Both rods are seated securely. (From Melman [84].)

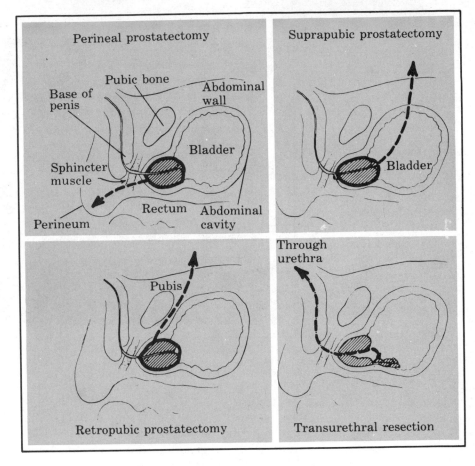

surface of the tunica albuginea and the corpora cavernosa [80]. Insertion is accomplished through a longitudinal incision in the midline at approximately the midshaft of the penis. Complications with this procedure have included aseptic necrosis, lymphatic edema, hemorrhage, and herniation of the tunica albuginea [80]. The Small-Carrion penile prosthesis consists of two partially foam-filled silicone rods [81, 82], which are available in different lengths and widths. The device is implanted by a perineal approach, except in patients with Peyronie's disease, in whom a penile shaft incision is made. Severe wound infection with extrusion of the prosthesis was reported in 2 of 75 patients by Small [81] and in 4 of 61 patients by Gottesman and colleagues [82], but in

Figure 9-8. An inflatable penile prosthesis. (Courtesy of American Medical Systems Inc.)

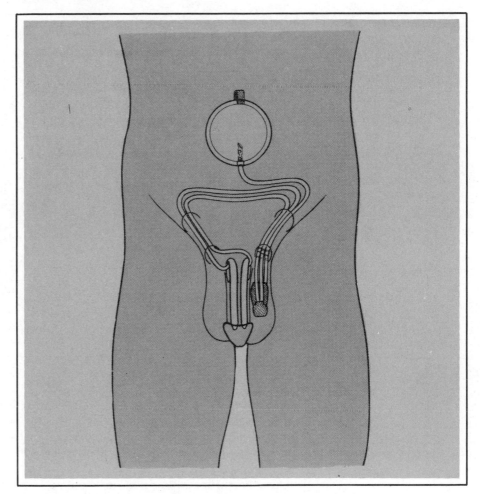

general the rate of complications has been lower than with the Silastic
rod. Recently, Small reported an overall complication rate of less than
0.5 percent in a series of 260 patients [83], but this appears to be a
significant underreporting of the situation since others have found
complication rates that are considerably higher. For example, Kramer
and coworkers noted that 20 of 76 patients who underwent insertion of
the Small-Carrion prosthesis at Duke University had postoperative
complications, including 7 men who lost one or both prostheses by
spontaneous extrusion or surgical removal [88].

Figure 9-9. An inflatable penile prosthesis after implantation. (A) Fluid is
in the reservoir; the penis is flaccid.
(B) Fluid is in the penile cylinders;
the penis is erect. (Courtesy of
American Medical Systems Inc.)

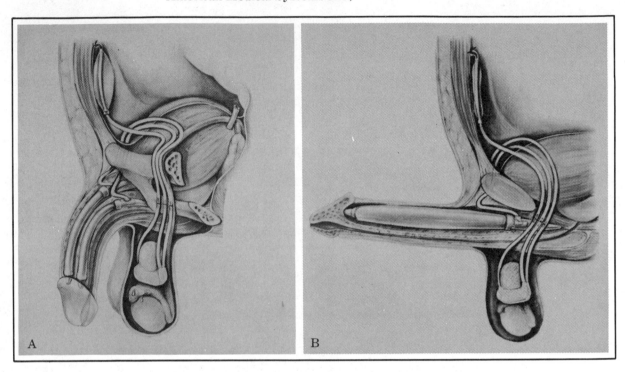

The inflatable penile prosthesis requires more time to implant and is
a more expensive device [86, 89]. Since 1973, when Scott, Bradley, and
Timm reported their initial experience with five patients [90], this
method has been increasingly used [84, 86, 91–93]. The inflatable prosthesis consists of two tapered inflatable cylinders, which are placed
within the tunica albuginea adjacent to the corpora cavernosa. These
cylinders, which come in varied sizes, are connected by tubing to a
simple pump that is placed low in the scrotum, outside the tunica
vaginalis. A fluid storage reservoir is implanted in the prevesical space
(Fig. 9-9). The patient activates the pump by compressing the bulb in
the scrotum; radiopaque fluid is then transferred from the fluid reservoir to the penile cylinders, causing the cylinders to expand and producing penile tumescence. The erection is released by pressing a valve
in the lower portion of the scrotal bulb, which allows fluid to be
evacuated from the penile cylinders back to the reservoir. The operating room protocol for this type of surgery has been described in detail
[94].

The major complications with the inflatable penile prosthesis have been caused by mechanical failure of the cylinders or tubing system. Since the introduction of this device, manufacturing improvements have reportedly lowered the incidence of such problems, which initially required surgical intervention in a significant number of cases [86, 93]. The rate of postoperative infection has not been unusually high; the operation now appears to be an accepted mode of treatment for organic impotence.

Further study is needed to become fully informed about patient acceptance of penile prosthetic devices and to assess the psychological impact of this type of surgery. Although some authors advocate the use of such a therapeutic approach for men with psychogenic impotence, it seems wisest to exercise considerable caution in this regard; such patients should probably be given an intensive exposure to sex therapy before considering operative techniques to cure their impotence. In addition, it should be recognized that diabetic men may be predisposed to a higher rate of surgical and postoperative complications with this procedure due to microvascular problems and impaired immunity (see Chap. 6) [95]; thus penile implants should be undertaken in this population only when the potential risks as well as benefits have been carefully described to the patient.

References

1. DiGeorge, A. M.   Male Genital Disorders. In V. C. Vaughan, R. J. McKay, and W. E. Nelson (eds.), *Textbook of Pediatrics* (10th ed.). Philadelphia: W. B. Saunders Co., 1975. Pp. 1367–1370.
2. Young, H. H., II, Cockett, A. T. K., Stoller, R., Ashley, F. L., and Goodwin, W. E.   The management of agenesis of the phallus. *Pediatrics* 47:81–87, 1971.
3. Kernahan, D. A.   Congenital Anomalies of the Scrotum. In C. E. Horton (ed.), *Plastic and Reconstructive Surgery of the Genital Area*. Boston: Little, Brown and Co., 1973. Pp. 175–181.
4. Adair, E. L., and Lewis, E. L.   Ectopic scrotum and diphallia. *Journal of Urology* 84:115–117, 1960.
5. Wilson, J. S. P.   Diphallus. In C. E. Horton (ed.), *Plastic and Reconstructive Surgery of the Genital Area*. Boston: Little, Brown and Co., 1973. Pp. 163–174.
6. Walsh, P. C., Wilson, J. D., Allen, T. D., Madden, J. D., Porter, J. C., Neaves, W. B., Griffin, J. E., and Goodwin, W. E.   Clinical and endocrinological evaluation of patients with congenital microphallus. *Journal of Urology* 120:90–95, 1978.
7. Guthrie, R. D., Smith, D. W., and Graham, C. B.   Testosterone treatment for micropenis during early childhood. *Journal of Pediatrics* 83:247–252, 1973.
8. Money, J., and Mazur, T.   Microphallus: The successful use of a prosthetic

phallus in a 9-year-old boy. *Journal of Sex and Marital Therapy* 3:187–196, 1977.

9. Sweet, R. A., Schrott, H. G., Kurland, R., and Culp, O. S. Study of the incidence of hypospadias in Rochester, Minnesota, 1940–1970, and a case-control comparison of possible etiologic factors. *Mayo Clinic Proceedings* 49:52–58, 1974.

10. Walsh, P. C., Curry, N., Mills, R. C., and Siiteri, P. K. Plasma androgen response to hCG stimulation in prepubertal boys with hypospadias and cryptorchidism. *Journal of Clinical Endocrinology and Metabolism* 42:52–59, 1976.

11. Aarskog, D. Clinical and cytogenic studies in hypospadias. *Acta Paediatrica Scandinavica* [Suppl.] 203:1–62, 1970.

12. Raboch, J., Pondelickova, J., and Starka, L. Plasma testosterone values in hypospadiacs. *Andrologia* 8:255–258, 1976.

13. Kenawi, M. M. Sexual function in hypospadiacs. *British Journal of Urology* 47:883–890, 1976.

14. Horton, C. E., and Devine, C. J., Jr. Hypospadias. In C. E. Horton (ed.), *Plastic and Reconstructive Surgery of the Genital Area*. Boston: Little, Brown and Co., 1973. Pp. 235–381.

15. Broadbent, R. T., Woolf, R. M., and Toksu, E. Hypospadias: One-stage repair. *Plastic and Reconstructive Surgery* 27:154–159, 1961.

16. Des Prez, J. D., Persky, L., and Kiehn, C. L. One-stage repair of hypospadias by island flap technique. *Plastic and Reconstructive Surgery* 28:405–411, 1961.

17. Devine, C. J., Jr., and Horton, C. E. A one-stage hypospadias repair. *Journal of Urology* 85:166–172, 1961.

18. Farkas, L. G., and Hynie, J. Aftereffects of hypospadias repair in childhood. *Postgraduate Medicine* 47(4):103–105, 1970.

19. Avellán, L. The development of puberty, the sexual debut and sexual function in hypospadiacs. *Scandinavian Journal of Plastic and Reconstructive Surgery* 10:29–44, 1976.

20. Williams, D. I. Epispadias: I. In C. E. Horton (ed.), *Plastic and Reconstructive Surgery of the Genital Area*. Boston: Little, Brown and Co., 1973. Pp. 223–228.

21. Mancini, R. E., Rosemberg, E., Cullen, M., Lavieri, J. C., Vilar, O., Bergada, C., and Andrada, J. A. Cryptorchid and scrotal human testes: I. Cytological, cytochemical and quantitative studies. *Journal of Clinical Endocrinology and Metabolism* 25:927–942, 1965.

22. Mengel, W., Hienz, H. A., Sippe, W. G., II, and Hecker, W. C. Studies on cryptorchidism: A comparison of histological findings in the germinative epithelium before and after the second year of life. *Journal of Pediatric Surgery* 9:445–450, 1974.

23. Lipshultz, L. I., Caminos-Torres, R., Greenspan, C. S., and Snyder, P. J. Testicular function after orchiopexy for unilateral undescended testis. *New England Journal of Medicine* 295:15–18, 1976.

24. Glenn, J. F. The Male Genital System. In D. C. Sabiston, Jr. (ed.), *Davis-Christopher Textbook of Surgery* (11th ed.). Philadelphia: W. B. Saunders Co., 1977. Pp. 1758–1793.

25. Lattimer, J. K., Smith, A. M., Dougherty, L. J., and Beck, L.   The optimum time to operate for cryptorchidism. *Pediatrics* 53:96–99, 1974.
26. Cytryn, L., Cytryn, E., and Rieger, R. E.   Psychological implications of cryptorchism. *Journal of the American Academy of Child Psychiatry* 6:131–165, 1967.
27. Meyer-Bahlburg, H. F. L., McCauley, E., Schenck, C., Aceto, T., Jr., and Pinch, L.   Cryptorchidism, Development of Gender Identity, and Sex Behavior. In R. C. Friedman, R. M. Richart, and R. L. Vande Wiele (eds.), *Sex Differences in Behavior*. New York: John Wiley & Sons, 1974. Pp. 281–299.
28. Raboch, J., Mellan, J., and Starka, L.   Adult cryptorchids: Sexual development and activity. *Archives of Sexual Behavior* 6:413–420, 1977.
29. Lattimer, J. K., Vakili, B. F., Smith, A. M., and Morishima, A.   A natural feeling testicular prosthesis. *Journal of Urology* 110:81–83, 1973.
30. Silber, S. J.   Transplantation of a human testis for anorchia. *Fertility and Sterility* 30:181–187, 1978.
31. Marcy, S. M., and Kibrick, S.   Mumps. In P. D. Hoeprich (ed.), *Infectious Diseases*. New York: Harper & Row, 1977. Pp. 621–627.
32. Adamopoulos, A., Lawrence, D. M., Vassilopoulos, P., Contoyiannis, P. A., and Swyer, I. M.   Pituitary-testicular interrelationships in mumps orchitis and other viral infections. *British Medical Journal* 1:1177–1180, 1978.
33. Kaufman, R. E., and Wiesner, P. J.   Nonspecific urethritis. *New England Journal of Medicine* 291:1175–1177, 1974.
34. Holmes, K. K., Handsfield, H. H., Wang, S. P., Wentworth, B. B., Turck, M., Anderson, J. B., and Alexander, E. R.   Etiology of nongonococcal urethritis. *New England Journal of Medicine* 292:1199–1205, 1975.
35. Jacobs, N. F., Jr., and Kraus, S. J.   Gonococcal and nongonococcal urethritis in men: Clinical and laboratory differentiation. *Annals of Internal Medicine* 82:7–12, 1975.
36. Stamey, T. A.   Chronic bacterial prostatitis. *Hospital Practice* 6(4):49–55, 1971.
37. Meares, E. M., and Stamey, T. A.   Bacteriologic localization patterns in bacterial prostatitis and urethritis. *Investigative Urology* 5:492–518, 1968.
38. Davis, J. E., and Mininberg, D. T.   Prostatitis and sexual function. *Medical Aspects of Human Sexuality* 10(8):32–40, 1976.
39. Flocks, R. H.   Benign prostatic hyperplasia. *Hospital Medicine* 5(11):72–81, 1969.
40. Owen, W. L.   Cancer of the prostate: A literature review. *Journal of Chronic Diseases* 29:89–114, 1976.
41. Madorsky, M., Drylie, D. M., and Finlayson, B.   Effect of benign prostatic hypertrophy on sexual behavior. *Medical Aspects of Human Sexuality* 10(2):8–22, 1976.
42. Basso, A.   The prostate in the elderly male. *Hospital Practice* 12(10):117–123, 1977.
43. Finkle, A. L., and Prian, D. V.   Sexual potency in elderly men before and after prostatectomy. *Journal of the American Medical Association* 196:125–129, 1966.
44. Nelson, B. J.   How to prevent impotence after prostatectomy. *Sexual Medicine Today* 2(3):4–41, 1978.

45. Zohar, J., Meiraz, D., Maoz, B., and Durst, N.   Factors influencing sexual activity after prostatectomy: A prospective study. *Journal of Urology* 116:332–334, 1976.

46. Madorsky, I. L., Ashamalla, M. G., Schussler, I., Lyons, H. R., and Miller, G. H., Jr.   Postprostatectomy impotence. *Journal of Urology* 115:401–403, 1976.

47. Poutasse, E. F.   Peyronie's Disease. In C. E. Horton (ed.), *Plastic and Reconstructive Surgery of the Genital Area*. Boston: Little, Brown and Co., 1973. Pp. 621–625.

48. Duggan, H. E.   Effect of X-ray therapy on patients with Peyronie's disease. *Journal of Urology* 91:572–573, 1964.

49. Smith, M. J. V., and Benacorti, A. F.   Malignant priapism due to clear cell carcinoma: A case report and review of the literature. *Journal of Urology* 92:297–299, 1964.

50. Narayana, A. S., and Young, J. M.   Short case report: Malignant priapism. *British Journal of Urology* 49:326, 1977.

51. LaRocque, M. A., and Cosgrove, M. D.   Priapism. *Medical Aspects of Human Sexuality* 10(6):69–70, 1976.

52. LaRocque, M. A., and Cosgrove, M. D.   Priapism: A review of 46 cases. *Journal of Urology* 112:770–773, 1974.

53. Becker, L. E., and Mitchell, A. D.   Priapism. *Surgical Clinics of North America* 45:1522–1534, 1965.

54. Appell, R. A., Shield, D. E., and McGuire, E. J.   Short case report: Thioridazine-induced priapism. *British Journal of Urology* 49:160, 1977.

55. Tynes, W. V., II. Priapism. In C. E. Horton (ed.), *Plastic and Reconstructive Surgery of the Genital Area*. Boston: Little, Brown and Co., 1973. Pp. 627–633.

56. Cosgrove, M. D., and LaRocque, M. A.   Shunt surgery for priapism: Review of results. *Urology* 4:1–4, 1974.

57. Bell, W. R., and Pitney, W. R.   Management of priapism by therapeutic defibrination. *New England Journal of Medicine* 280:649–650, 1969.

58. Stewart, B. H., and Bergant, J. A.   Correction of retrograde ejaculation by sympathomimetic medication: Preliminary report. *Fertility and Sterility* 26:1073–1074, 1974.

59. Fuselier, H. A., Jr., Schneider, G. T., and Ochsner, M. G.   Successful artificial insemination following retrograde ejaculation. *Fertility and Sterility* 27:1214–1215, 1976.

60. Donnelly, J. D.   Retrograde ejaculation. *Medical Aspects of Human Sexuality* 9(1):51–52, 1975.

61. Abrahams, J. I., Solish, G. I., Boorjian, P., and Waterhouse, R. K.   The surgical correction of retrograde ejaculation. *Journal of Urology* 114:888–890, 1975.

62. Schramm, J. D.   Retrograde ejaculation: A new approach to therapy. *Fertility and Sterility* 27:1216–1218, 1976.

63. Money, J., and De Priest, M.   Three cases of genital self-surgery and their relationship to transexualism. *Journal of Sex Research* 12:283–294, 1976.

64. Rosenblum, R.   Self-inflicted injuries to the penis or urethra. *Medical Aspects of Human Sexuality* 8(3):197–209, 1974.

65. Greilsheimer, H., and Groves, J. E.   Male genital self-mutilation. *Archives of General Psychiatry* 36:441–446, 1979.

66. Best, J. W., Angelo, J. J., and Milligan, B.   Complete traumatic amputation of the penis. *Journal of Urology* 87:134–138, 1962.

67. Engelman, E. R., Polito, G., Perley, J., Bruffy, J., and Martin, D. C.   Traumatic amputation of the penis. *Journal of Urology* 112:774–778, 1974.

68. Mannion, R.   Penile laceration (letter). *Journal of the American Medical Association* 224:1763, 1973.

69. Mofenson, H. C., and Greensher, J.   Penile trauma in boys. *Medical Aspects of Human Sexuality* 9(8):68–73, 1975.

70. Farah, R. N., Stiles, R., Jr., and Cerny, J. C.   Surgical treatment of deformity and coital difficulty in healed traumatic rupture of the corpora cavernosa. *Journal of Urology* 120:118–120, 1978.

71. Chambers, H. L., and Balfour, J.   The incidence of impotence following pelvic fractures with associated urinary tract injury. *Journal of Urology* 80:702–703, 1963.

72. Gibson, G. R.   Impotence following fractured pelvis and ruptured urethra. *British Journal of Urology* 42:86–88, 1970.

73. Netto, N. R., Jr., and Freire, J. G. C.   Sexual alterations following urethral damage. *International Surgery* 60:621–622, 1975.

74. Kiviat, M. D.   Transurethral sphincterotomy: Relationship of site of incision to postoperative potency and delayed hemorrhage. *Journal of Urology* 114:399–401, 1975.

75. Nanninga, J. B., Rosen, J. S., and O'Conor, V. J., Jr.   Transurethral external sphincterotomy and its effect on potency. *Journal of Urology* 118:395–396, 1977.

76. Morrow, J. W., and Scott, M. B.   Erections and sexual function in postsphincterotomy bladder neck patients. *Journal of Urology* 119:500–503, 1978.

77. Schoenfeld, L., Carrion, H. M., and Politano, V. A.   Erectile impotence: Complication of external sphincterotomy. *Urology* 4:681–685, 1974.

78. Beheri, G. E.   Surgical treatment of impotence. *Plastic and Reconstructive Surgery* 38:92–97, 1966.

79. Loeffler, R. A., Sayegh, E. S., and Lash, H.   The artificial os penis. *Plastic and Reconstructive Surgery* 34:71–74, 1964.

80. Pearman, R. O.   Insertion of a Silastic penile prosthesis for the treatment of organic sexual impotence. *Journal of Urology* 107:802–806, 1972.

81. Small, M. P.   Small-Carrion penile prosthesis: A new implant for management of impotence. *Mayo Clinic Proceedings* 51:336–338, 1976.

82. Gottesman, J. E., Kosters, S., Das, S., and Kaufman, J. J.   The Small-Carrion prosthesis for male impotency. *Journal of Urology* 117:289–290, 1977.

83. Small, M. P.   The Small-Carrion penile prosthesis: Surgical implant for the management of impotence. *Sexuality and Disability* 1:282–291, 1978.

84. Melman, A.   Development of contemporary surgical management for erectile impotence. *Sexuality and Disability* 1:272–281, 1978.

85. Melman, A., and Hammond, G.   Placement of the Small-Carrion penile prosthesis to enable maintenance of an exdwelling condom catheter. *Sexuality and Disability* 1:292–298, 1978.

86. Lange, P. H., and Smith, A. D. A comparison of the two types of penile prostheses used in the surgical treatment of male impotence. *Sexuality and Disability* 1:307–311, 1978.

87. Finney, R. P. New hinged silicone penile implant. *Journal of Urology* 118:585–587, 1977.

88. Kramer, S. A., Anderson, E. E., Bredael, J., and Paulson, D. F. Complications of Small-Carrion penile prosthesis. *Urology* 13:49–51, 1979.

89. Ambrose, R. B. Treatment of organic erectile impotence: Experience with the Scott procedure. *Journal of the Medical Society of New Jersey* 72:805–807, 1975.

90. Scott, F. B., Bradley, W. E., and Timm, G. W. Management of erectile impotence: Use of implantable inflatable prosthesis. *Urology* 2:80–82, 1973.

91. Furlow, W. L. Surgical management of impotence using the inflatable penile prosthesis: Experience with 36 patients. *Mayo Clinic Proceedings* 51:325–328, 1976.

92. Malloy, T. R., and Voneschenbach, A. C. Surgical treatment of erectile impotence with inflatable penile prosthesis. *Journal of Urology* 118:49–51, 1977.

93. Furlow, W. L. Diagnosis and treatment of male erectile failure. *Diabetes Care* 2:18–25, 1979.

94. Schuster, K. Operating room protocol in implantation of the inflatable penile prosthesis. *Mayo Clinic Proceedings* 51:339–340, 1976.

95. Sotile, W. M. The penile prosthesis and diabetic impotence: Some caveats. *Diabetes Care* 2:26–30, 1979.

10 Sex and Chronic Illness

Long-term disruptions of normal health have a significant impact on numerous facets of life. Coping with chronic illness involves not only appropriately managing the physical or metabolic condition but also dealing with the complex psychosocial issues that may arise. A good example of the interplay between the physical effects of chronic illness and the behaviors and emotions that are associated with such illness is the influence on sexuality that such illness may have. Although the relationship between chronic illness and sex will vary considerably from person to person for reasons ranging from severity of health impairment to variables of age, personality, previous sexual health, and social circumstances, it is helpful to understand the ways in which certain types of chronic illness will be likely to influence sexual functioning.

A broad perspective on some general principles related to the impact of chronic illness on sexuality is in order. In some instances of chronic illness, specific features of anatomy or physiology will be altered to such a degree that sexual functioning is impaired. This is the case, for example, when a demyelinating disease such as multiple sclerosis affects the neurophysiology of transmission of afferent and efferent impulses through the central nervous system, causing impotence or impairment of female orgasm [1, 2]. Illnesses that interfere with vascular supply to the pelvis, thus restricting the vasocongestive changes that are an important part of sexual response for both men and women, also produce *direct* impairments of sexual function. In contrast to these examples are a large number of conditions that may impede sexuality via *indirect* mechanisms. A person with chronic obstructive lung disease may be too hypoxic to tolerate the increased oxygen demands of sexual excitation; a person with chronic arthritis may find it difficult to participate in coitus due to limitations of movement and position; and an extremely obese person may have mechanical difficulties of access to the genitals for the initiation of intercourse. Any disease that produces weakness, listlessness, and easy fatigability is likely to affect the sex drive of a man or a woman, just as it would reduce their desire to engage in other forms of physical exertion. Illnesses that involve such disparate symptoms as pain, fever, malaise, poor appetite, skin rashes, or similar problems are quite likely to diminish interest in sex or to interfere with sexual function.

Although the physical consequences of illness are easily recognized, it is also necessary to be cognizant of some of the social elements that are typically affected by illness. The sick person is excused from most social obligations and is not blamed for his or her condition; family, friends, and colleagues are usually generous in extending this attitude toward illness in general—and of course, the more chronic the illness, the more problematic this process may become for all parties involved. The perception of illness by the patient and by surrounding persons may greatly influence subsequent behavior and functioning. There may be particular motivations, situational factors, or adaptive needs that also influence the way in which the patient copes with chronic illness, and cultural or ethnic values and sex-role patterns may also be important variables [3]. All these elements may be relevant to the sexual effects of chronic illness in circumstances of widely varied natures. For example, some women and men will successfully invoke the presence of illness or symptoms of illness as a means of avoiding unwanted sexual activity, although they recognize that there is no actual limitation on their sexual status. Others will use the existence of illness in a manipulative fashion to obtain something that they want sexually. The psychodynamics and social dynamics in such situations are intricate and can only be briefly alluded to here.

In the assessment of the effects of chronic illness on sexual function, the following areas should be scrutinized:

1. Antecedent sexual history.
2. Nature and severity of the illness.
3. Concurrent illness(es).
4. Drugs, surgery, or other treatment modalities being used.
5. Social circumstances.
6. Personality variables.
7. Sex partner's reaction to the illness.
8. Coping abilities.
9. Attitudes toward sex.

An understanding of the defenses and coping behaviors of the patient provides an insight that is helpful in the clinical management of sexual problems associated with any type of chronic illness. It is also useful to recognize that many health-care professionals insulate themselves from the emotional frustrations of dealing with certain types of chronic illness by the mobilization of their own defense mechanisms and cognitive means of adaptation. For example, physicians are likely to interact less directly and for shorter periods of time with terminally ill patients; pessimism and impatience may color the physician's relationship with alcoholic or obese patients. Denial is undoubtedly a prominent factor in many mistaken diagnoses, particularly in regard to iatrogenic sexual problems; incorrectly attributing sexual difficulties to aging may be more a matter of projection than a carefully reasoned diagnostic conclusion. In reading the following sections, it may be useful to consider the physician's reactions to the topic of sex and chronic illness in addition to the factual material that is discussed.

Chronic Renal Failure

Chronic renal failure is a life-threatening condition that affects most body systems. In the United States, uremia is usually treated by maintenance hemodialysis in anticipation of kidney transplantation. Advances in medical technology over the past decade and the increased availability of equipment, personnel, and financial resources have combined to improve survival statistics for uremia significantly; however, this disorder remains a serious and debilitating illness with numerous complications.

Sexual Function: Uremia, Dialysis, Transplantation

Untreated chronic renal failure produces major changes in the sexuality of both men and women. The severity of uremia is generally proportional to the degree of diminished libido and inability to function normally [4]. Ninety percent of men with uremia and 80 percent of uremic women report a decrease in libido compared to pre-illness levels, and 80 percent of men report difficulty in obtaining or maintaining erections. Although less reliable data are available regarding the sexual function of women with uremia, it appears that approximately three-quarters of these women experience difficulty in becoming sexually aroused and approximately half report reduced frequency or intensity of orgasm or loss of their orgasmic responsiveness [5–7].

The initiation of hemodialysis does not typically improve the sexual function of uremic patients despite the metabolic enhancement that occurs: In a questionnaire study of 536 patients with chronic renal failure, Levy found that hemodialysis was associated with an actual worsening of sexual functioning in 35 percent of men and 25 percent of women, whereas only 9 percent and 6 percent, respectively, experienced improvement after beginning hemodialysis [6]. Because libido may improve during hemodialysis, the associated deterioration of sexual functioning is an even greater problem. Steele and coworkers reported that 7 of 17 couples in which one spouse was on maintenance hemodialysis did not engage in intercourse at all, and 6 of the 17 couples had intercourse less than once a month [7]. Only 2 of the 17 couples reported having intercourse at least once a week, although the majority of patients and their spouses indicated that they would prefer to have more frequent intercourse.

A small percentage of men who have uremia or are on dialysis experience inability to ejaculate or difficulty in ejaculating; this problem is more frequently seen in men who are using drugs such as guanethidine or alpha-methyldopa to control hypertension. About one-fifth of women who have uremia or are on dialysis experience dyspareunia, which can understandably interfere with both arousal and orgasmic response.

Successful kidney transplantation does not resolve all the sexual difficulties associated with chronic renal failure. Although Levy reported that women who had successful transplants returned to their pre-illness levels of sexual function, a significant percentage of men did not [6]. Others have observed patients in whom posttransplantation sexual function continued to be impaired [8–10], although libido typically improves significantly. Salvatierra and coworkers found that a sizable number of men experienced improved sexual functioning to pre-illness levels after transplantation [11], but Procci, Hoffman, and Chatterjee noted that the frequency of intercourse following successful transplantation remained significantly below pre-illness levels for both men and women [12].

Etiologic Factors. HORMONAL STATUS. The complex metabolic effects of uremia and dialysis are not fully understood as yet; there is considerable controversy regarding some of the mechanisms that may be operating [13]. In women, severe renal failure usually leads to amenorrhea or hypomenorrhea and infertility. Detailed investigations of the hormonal status of uremic women on dialysis have not been conducted, but the clinical findings cited above and the frequent observation of diminished breast tissue mass, decreased vaginal lubrication, and atrophic vaginitis may be indicative of an estrogen deficiency. After beginning maintenance hemodialysis, many women develop hypermenorrhea [14]. A full-term pregnancy is extremely rare in women on chronic hemodialysis [4], but following successful transplantation, fertility improves dramatically and relatively uneventful pregnancies are possible.

Men with uremia typically develop testicular atrophy and impaired spermatogenesis [4, 13, 15], and these conditions are not improved by hemodialysis [16]. Markedly decreased testosterone levels are also usually found in men both with uremia and during dialysis, even when the uremia is well controlled [13, 15–17]. Although most reports have documented increases in circulating LH and FSH concentrations in these men, in some patients normal LH and FSH levels seem to indicate that a relative hypothalamic suppression may occur in chronic renal failure [17]. Similarly, there is contradictory evidence regarding the Leydig cell reserve of the testes, with some researchers showing a normal capacity for testosterone synthesis and others documenting diminished capacity [15–18]. Testosterone levels return to normal within a few months after successful transplantation [16], probably accounting for the improved libido observed in this situation. The administration of testosterone during uremia or hemodialysis does not improve problems of erective or ejaculatory function, although libido may be increased.

Gynecomastia is found in a small percentage of men with chronic renal failure, but it occurs much more frequently in patients on hemodialysis [4, 13, 19]. It is not clear whether this problem is caused by elevated prolactin levels or whether it may be more comparable to the "refeeding gynecomastia" that is seen with resumption of feeding after starvation [13].

NEUROLOGIC FACTORS. Neurologic disturbances occur with increased frequency in uremia and hemodialysis [20, 21]. Uremic neuropathy affecting the pelvic autonomic nervous system undoubtedly contributes to the presence of sexual dysfunction in both men and women, although this mechanism is likely to be a primary etiologic factor in a relatively small percentage of cases. Elevation of the vibrotactile threshold has been found in men on maintenance dialysis [21], which also may be a significant contributor to the impairment of sexual arousal seen in patients with chronic renal failure. The metabolic encephalopathy of uremia would be expected to affect libido and may be another component of the overall disturbances of sexual function that are encountered.

CONCURRENT ILLNESS AND DRUG USE. The underlying disease process that leads to chronic renal failure may affect sexual functioning independently of the kidney damage. Diseases that may be included in this category are diabetes mellitus, systemic lupus erythematosus, polyarteritis nodosa, scleroderma, amyloidosis, sarcoidosis, heavy metal poisoning, and tuberculosis. In addition, complications of chronic renal failure such as anemia, calcium abnormalities, and other electrolyte disorders may contribute to weakness, depressed libido, and impaired neuromuscular function. The altered immune response system that is associated with uremia predisposes to infection, resulting in frequent vaginal infections that may cause dyspareunia or decreased vaginal lubrication.

Many uremic patients and patients on hemodialysis are hypertensive, requiring medications to control their elevated blood pressure. As discussed at length in Chapter 13, these drugs may adversely affect sexual functioning, further complicating the picture.

PSYCHOSOCIAL FACTORS. The stress of a life-threatening illness exerts its impact not only on the patient but on the family as well. In addition to the fear of death, there are financial pressures, stresses related to medical management (and to the anticipation of transplant surgery), disruptions in work, and sometimes psychological changes. The spouse of the patient with chronic renal failure is typically burdened with providing health care (i.e., attention to diet, drugs, dialysis, and all the complications of uremia) and assuming additional family roles; resentment is a common reaction to these major responsibilities as time drags on and things only seem to worsen. It is no wonder, then, that marital discord is a prevalent situation for hemodialysis patients and their spouses and may relate to their sexual difficulties [7, 22, 23].

Depression is frequently seen in dialysis patients, occurring perhaps as a result of physical limitations, dependence on a machine, loss of mastery over their own life, and other problems cited previously. Steele and coworkers [7] reported finding a strong relationship between the severity of depression in hemodialysis patients and severity of sexual dysfunction. Approximately half of dialysis patients have been reported to be depressed [7, 24, 25]. Since depression typically diminishes libido and disturbs normal sexual functioning, it is likely to be a major etiologic factor in the sexual problems of dialysis patients and may account partially for the worsening of sexual function reported after the initiation of hemodialysis.

Management

At present, there are no certain cures for most of the organic complications of chronic renal failure. Although hormonal replacement has generally been of little usefulness in improving sexual functioning, one recent report suggests that in uremic men, clomiphene citrate in doses of 100 mg per day for prolonged periods restores circulating testosterone levels to normal and results in increased libido, normal potency, and a general sense of well-being [17]. Another possible management strategy is suggested by the preliminary finding that impaired sexual functioning and low testosterone in dialysis patients may sometimes be corrected by the dialytic administration of zinc when a zinc deficiency is present [26]. Both of these approaches require further substantiation before they can be recommended, however. In women with chronic renal failure, careful attention to possible vaginal infections is indicated, and in patients of both sexes, evaluation of drugs being used may alleviate the severity of sexual problems in at least some instances.

It appears that the most useful approach to management at the present time would be to provide counseling services that identify the existence of problems and permit different levels of intervention. Physicians working on a renal dialysis unit or serving in such a counseling capacity will need to recognize the typical defense mechanisms used by such patients, including denial, projection, displacement, and reaction formation [27], and will have to be skilled in diagnosing depression, detecting the possibility of suicide attempts, and dealing with family dynamics as well. An ideal approach would be the availability of a multidisciplinary team integrating the requisite medical knowledge with appropriate psychosocial skills. Patients could then be referred for individual psychotherapy when necessary, but frequently a group therapy setting could be extremely appropriate. In this latter format, strong consideration could be given to forming groups comprising dialysis patients and their spouses.

In some situations it may be possible to determine that a sexual dysfunction is purely psychogenic in nature (see Chapters 20 and 24). If this is the case, for example, after successful renal transplantation, a program of sex therapy is likely to be effective. Patients with anxieties about sexual functioning are less likely to respond well to sex therapy alone while long-term dialysis is going on, since they are under too many diverse sources of stress. In these instances, limited sex therapy should be combined with psychotherapy that focuses on other aspects of the patient's reaction to his or her illness.

Until more information is available, it is important to realize that the sexual problems of dialysis patients are founded on both physical and emotional factors. Although it may not always be possible to correct the physical or metabolic aspects of sexual dysfunction, sensitive counseling can lessen patients' anxiety, raise their self-esteem, introduce or reinforce their view of sexual options that may be available, and assist in their overall ability to cope.

Alcoholism and Sex

Chronic abuse of alcohol frequently leads to deterioration of sexual functioning in both men and women. Although currently there are no adequate prevalence statistics describing this problem, clinical observation indicates that approximately 50 percent of alcoholic men and 25 percent of alcoholic women experience disturbances of their sexuality [28]. Alcoholic men with significant liver damage ranging from alcoholic hepatitis to end-stage cirrhosis have been reported to have an even greater frequency of sexual problems (in one study, 78 percent of men were found to have impaired potency and libido [29]), but alcoholics with little or no detectable hepatic impairment may also have sexual difficulties.

Chronic alcoholic men typically display a reduction in libido as compared to their previous levels of sexual desire, even if allowances are made for age differences. About 40 percent of alcoholic men are impotent and approximately 5 to 10 percent have retarded or inhibited ejaculation. After abstention from alcohol use for months or even years, sexual functioning returns to normal in only about half of the cases [30].

Alcoholic women exhibit a greater heterogeneity in patterns of sexual behavior and sexual function. Libido appears to remain intact more often than in alcoholic men, but this may reflect insufficient information distinguishing between participation in sexual activity and true sexual desire. Thirty to 40 percent of alcoholic women report difficulties in becoming sexually aroused, and approximately 15 percent of female alcoholics experience either loss of orgasmic responsiveness or significant reduction in the frequency or intensity of orgasm [28]. In a recent study, 35 of 62 alcoholic women were described as having inadequate sexual response of various degrees [31].

Organic Factors

The sexual problems of alcoholic men may be caused in part by the direct gonadal effects of alcohol. There is evidence that alcohol decreases the production rate of testosterone [32, 33], causes a relative or absolute shift toward greater estrogenicity [33–35], increases the percentage of circulating testosterone bound to protein, thus making free, biologically active testosterone less available to tissues [35, 36], and impairs spermatogenesis as well [29, 36, 37]. These changes have been observed in men with and without significant liver damage. In fact, studies of normal, nonalcoholic men after four weeks of daily alcohol intake showed decreases in circulating testosterone [38].

It appears that alcohol exerts its effects on gonadal function in a number of ways. Hepatic 5α-testosterone reductase activity—important as a major enzymatic pathway for testosterone breakdown—is increased by long-term alcohol ingestion in both animals and man [39]. An abnormality of hypothalamic or pituitary function in regard to gonadal regulation has also been demonstrated [34, 40]. Finally, the possible occurrence of nutritional deficiencies in the chronic alcoholic may also contribute to the hormonal disruptions that have been described. The result in its classic form is a clinical picture of alcoholic hypogonadism marked by testicular atrophy, gynecomastia, diminished libido, impotence, and sterility. However, not all alcoholic men with sexual problems exhibit this syndrome. Despite the fact that detailed information is available on the hormonal abnormalities in alcoholic men, testosterone replacement therapy has not been found to restore normal potency, although it may—in some cases—improve libido.

There are no data presently available on the hormonal status of alcoholic women. Since it appears that women are more susceptible to chronic advanced liver disease and other alcohol-related disorders than are men [41], it is quite likely that the endocrine system is affected in a parallel fashion. Van Thiel has observed that alcoholic women seem to age prematurely and undergo early menopause [36], but whether this finding reflects nutritional deficits or other nonspecific effects of chronic illness more than ovarian failure is not known. Ryback has described two cases of alcoholism causing amenorrhea and the experimental blocking of estrus in rats given alcohol [42].

In addition to the associated endocrine disturbances, chronic alcoholism leads to other medical complications that may affect sexual functioning and libido. In a group of alcoholics with impaired liver function tests, 29 percent of the men and 57 percent of the women were found to have peripheral neuropathy [41]. Anemia is also frequently observed in chronic alcoholics [43, 44]. In chronic alcoholics who develop cirrhosis, changes in physical appearance may occur when ascites or peripheral edema develops, and these physical changes may also lead to discomfort during sexual activity. An additional factor in the impaired sexual functioning of the alcoholic man or woman is the persistently high concentration of alcohol in the bloodstream. This chemical alteration is likely to exert a powerful suppressing effect on the sex reflex pathways of the central nervous system, perhaps by altering neurotransmitter metabolism [45].

Finally, an intriguing recent investigation of autoimmune phenomena in alcoholic men deserves mention. Van Thiel and coworkers studied 40 men who had histories of alcohol abuse ranging from five to 40 years [46]. Testicular atrophy was found in 65 percent of the group, reduced facial hair in 55 percent, and a female escutcheon in 50 percent; 17 of 22 men in this group were impotent. Antitesticular antibodies were demonstrated in the serum of 15 percent of men studied, while autoantibodies to sperm were found in 17.5 percent, frequencies that were significantly higher than those observed in a control population of 450 nonalcoholic hospitalized men. Furthermore, antibody production toward other potential autoantigens (e.g., adrenal, parathyroid, pancreas, parietal cells, thyroglobulin) was not found to be increased in the test group, indicating a high degree of specificity for this autoimmune phenomenon. The investigators postulated that alcoholic damage to testicular tissue may lead to leaking of testicular antigens across the testicular blood barrier, inducing autoantibody formation by lymphocytes. The significance of autoimmune processes in alcoholics requires further investigation but supports the complexity of pathophysiologic mechanisms underlying the occurrence of sexual problems.

Psychosocial Factors

Despite the numerous organic causes of diminished sexual interest and function in alcoholics, there are many clinical instances in which these variables do not sufficiently explain the sexual problems that exist. Perhaps the best example of this situation is the persistence of sexual problems in the otherwise healthy alcoholic who has successfully abstained from alcohol use for months or years. A number of psychosocial factors may be relevant, including fears of performance, marital discord, poor self-esteem, guilt, depression, or sexual problems antedating the abuse of alcohol.

The importance of the pattern of transient sexual difficulties leading to goal-setting, lack of spontaneity, being a spectator in one's own bedroom, and further fears of performance has been described in detail by Masters and Johnson [47]. Alcohol is the precipitating agent in a large percentage of cases of impotence that originate in this fashion, although the alcohol use may be short-lived rather than chronic. What is less widely recognized is the fact that women who experience sexual difficulties (either impaired arousal or loss of orgasm) may also become worried, begin deliberately to try to "make something happen" sexually, and watch themselves to monitor their responsiveness (usually producing the opposite effect to that desired). These women may become trapped in a cycle wherein performance anxieties create physical and emotional tension, loss of spontaneity, and impaired sexual sensations. This pattern may explain the sexual difficulties of some alcoholics. Needless to say, without direct therapeutic intervention during other aspects of rehabilitation from alcoholism, sexual problems arising from this set of conditions would not disappear.

A variation on the theme stated above appears to apply to some alcoholics, namely, people who begin drinking heavily as a means of coping with preexisting feelings of sexual inadequacy or fears of performance. Many of these people are not sexually dysfunctional but perceive themselves to be inadequate for a number of reasons. Alcohol may indeed help to obliterate these feelings of inadequacy, whether or not a dysfunction is present, because the importance of sexual pleasure or participation is replaced by the importance of alcohol use. Once the alcoholic stops drinking, the earlier feelings of sexual inadequacy commonly return, often reinforced and magnified by guilt over the period of alcoholism, the abandonment of responsibilities toward family or job, and other concomitant problems. It is important to identify such difficulties early in the process of treatment of the alcoholic and to deal with them promptly by appropriate techniques, including sex therapy, marriage counseling, or psychotherapy in a group or individual format.

Numerous articles have been written about marital discord in couples in which one spouse is an alcoholic; the interested reader is referred to references 48 to 52. The importance of difficulties in the marital relationship such as poor communication, hostility, distrust, immaturity, and lack of problem-solving abilities should be recognized as significant contributors to the development or persistence of sexual problems. It is not uncommon for the wife of an alcoholic man to withdraw from sexual activity as a means of demonstrating her resentment of his drinking and a way of protecting herself from the physical abuse, lack of tenderness, and altered physical attractiveness that are sometimes present. Although at times the husband of an alcoholic woman may also withdraw sexually (sometimes directing his sexual attentions extramaritally), a frequently encountered pattern is one in which the husband makes increasing sexual demands on his wife, exacting a form of payment for her alcoholic transgressions. In either circumstance, or in many other dyadic patterns that have been encountered clinically, the presence of a coercive element in the sexual relationship may continue as a negative factor even when drinking has been stopped.

As a man or a woman who has been abusing alcohol begins a period of rehabilitation and abstention, poor self-esteem, guilt, and depression are commonly seen, singly or in combination [53]. Each of these psychological variables can be closely related to the presence of sexual difficulties. Elements of treatment must be directed toward such problems because failure to diminish their intensity may lead to a return to drinking, since alcohol may lessen the psychic pain of such feelings. Just as these factors may create sexual problems, persistent sexual difficulties may lead to loss of self-esteem, guilt emanating from a number of sources, or a reactive depression. Careful evaluation must sometimes be undertaken to ascertain the direction of such causal relationships.

Management

It may be possible that the generally unsatisfactory treatment results obtained in dealing with alcoholism are due in part to lack of attention to the sexual rehabilitation of the alcoholic. For the reasons discussed above, persistent sexual difficulties may pose a psychological stress of such intensity at a time of increased vulnerability that the recovering alcoholic chooses to return to drinking as the easiest way out. The negative attitude of many health-care professionals toward alcoholism undoubtedly contributes further to the treatment problem, but this attitude may be attributed in part to frustrating success rates in the rehabilitation of alcoholics. Treatment programs for alcoholism might benefit from the following approaches:

1. Whenever possible, include the spouse or sexual partner of the alcoholic in the program.
2. Identify the existence of sexual problems by careful interviewing or the use of a questionnaire.
3. Provide needed amounts of sex education to help allay anxieties.
4. Allow ample opportunity for ventilation of feelings.
5. Identify physical, marital, or psychological elements that are contributing to the existence of a sexual problem.
6. Use a short-term approach to sex counseling to suggest ways of dealing with specific difficulties.
7. When satisfactory resolution of the sexual problems is not obtained by these approaches, refer the couple for sex therapy.

Formal sex therapy is probably not likely to be as useful during the early months of abstention from alcohol abuse as it is after 6 to 12 months of abstention. This period of time will allow for equilibration of the medical situation, adequate restoration of nutritional status, and the resolution of many important issues that would be distractions from the necessary focus on sexuality during an intensive therapy program to correct the sexual difficulties that have persisted.

Sexual Function after Ileostomy, Colostomy, or Ileal Conduit Surgery

Little attention has been given to the sexual adjustment of a person undergoing surgery that alters the anatomy of the lower gastrointestinal tract or the urinary tract by creating an artificial opening on the abdomen and diverting the normal flow of intestinal contents or urine. There are three different types of ostomy surgery. In an ileostomy, the colon (and usually the rectum) is removed and the small intestine is fashioned into an anterior stomal opening in the abdominal wall. This type of surgery is done most frequently because of inflammatory disease of the bowel. In colostomy surgery, a portion of the colon is opened and brought through the abdominal wall. There may be either one or two stomas in such surgery (only one of which is functional) depending

Table 10-1. Estimated
Occurrence of Disturbed
Male Sexual Function
after Ostomy Surgery

Type of Surgery	Impotence (%)	Retrograde Ejaculation (%)	Loss of Ability to Ejaculate (%)
Ileostomy and removal of rectum	15	<5	10
Colostomy and removal of rectum due to cancer	40	50	40
Colostomy and removal of rectum due to other causes	20	30	20
Ileal conduit done in childhood	20	60	30
Ileal conduit done in adulthood	80	20	70

on the indications and the techniques used, and the location of the colostomy may vary as well. The usual reason for colostomy is cancer of the colon or rectum, but this procedure is sometimes used to control inflammatory disease of the bowel or highly symptomatic diverticular disease. Surgery for the construction of an ileal conduit is performed to divert the flow of urine to an abdominal stoma because of impaired bladder function or need for removal of the bladder due to conditions such as birth defects, cancer, neurologic problems, or injury.

The sparse research literature on patients who have had ostomies indicates that sexual dysfunction occurs most commonly in older men who undergo such surgery [54–57]. Impotence may be expected more commonly in this group because of nerve damage that occurs during dissection of the rectum or bladder in the extensive surgery usually required for cancer removal. In some men the ability to ejaculate is lost, whereas in others retrograde ejaculation occurs (see pages 220–221) because of damage to the innervation of the bladder sphincter. The ability to ejaculate may sometimes be lost while normal erective function remains.

Estimated rates of impotence, retrograde ejaculation, and loss of ability to ejaculate following such surgery are listed in Table 10-1. These estimates are derived from a review of the literature, discussions with surgeons, and interviews with men who have had ostomies. They should be regarded as general approximations only rather than predictive statements, since many important determinants of postsurgical

Figure 10-1. Extensive formation of perineal fistulas in a woman with severe regional enteritis. (Courtesy of Ira J. Kodner, M.D., Waldheim Department of Surgery, The Jewish Hospital of St. Louis.)

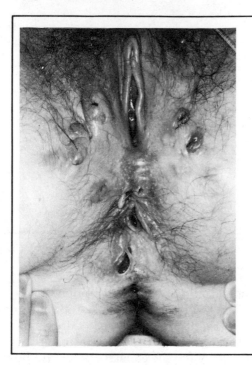

sexual functioning and adjustment are psychosocial rather than medical. These estimates do not differentiate between sexual problems due to organic sequelae of surgery and those due to psychogenic causes.

There are few satisfactory descriptions of the sexual difficulties of women who have had ostomies. In one study, 5 of 40 women (12.5 percent) aged 16 to 49 who had undergone ileostomies because of ulcerative colitis experienced dyspareunia [56]; 2 women also reported the loss of pelvic sensations of sexual arousal or orgasm. In another report, 21 percent of women reported dyspareunia or lack of vaginal sensations after abdominoperineal resection for cancer of the colon [58]. Burnham and coworkers reported that one-third of women who had ileostomies and rectal excision had painful intercourse [57]. The actual occurrence of dyspareunia is probably somewhat higher than the above figures indicate, in part because of the formation of fistulas or abscesses in the perineal area or within the vagina itself as complications of virulent inflammatory bowel disease (Fig. 10-1) and in part because of vaginal scarring resulting from the surgery itself.

There are a number of important factors to keep in mind regarding the diverse group of people who require ostomy surgery. Cancer of the rectum or colon usually occurs in persons over the age of 50, whereas the group undergoing surgery because of inflammatory bowel disease is typically considerably younger, including many patients in their teens and twenties. In addition to this age differential, there is often a marked difference in the duration of presurgical illness. Inflammatory bowel disease is treated surgically only after prolonged attempts at medical control of the disease do not succeed, whereas the time frame of presurgical illness with cancer is usually quite short. It is more likely that the younger person with inflammatory bowel disease was severely incapacitated by his or her illness.

The time just before and shortly after surgery is apt to be a difficult period of psychological adjustment to the body alteration that has occurred. While much emphasis may be placed on discussions and instruction about care of the stoma, diet, and physical activity, neither physicians nor nurses have routinely incorporated discussion of the impact of the ostomy on the patient's sexuality, and this obvious omission is taken by some patients as an ominous sign. Because anxieties or fears about sexual capabilities are important causes of sexual dysfunction [47], the stage may be set inadvertently for problems to develop.

Patients who have had ostomy surgery are apt to question their sexual attractiveness and, if they are married or have a current sexual partner, will usually worry about how this person will accept them in their sexual interaction. Reassurances given by the partner may be suspected as well-meant but untrue; concern over stomal odors or appearance may seem overwhelming; and postoperative depression may contribute to poor self-esteem and general pessimism. Unmarried patients will have similar concerns and will also be worried about how they will be able to establish future sexual relations. In either group of patients, peer counselors who have themselves had ostomy surgery and have learned to live with it comfortably may be of help. An often overlooked possibility for peer counseling in a slightly different context is to have the spouse or sexual partner of the ostomy patient talk with his or her counterpart in a couple that has already lived through the impact of such surgery.

Problems may be encountered after discharge from the hospital if sexual activity is attempted before the ostomate has regained a reasonable degree of physical strength. If significant sexual anxieties are not aired and reduced through discussion or counseling, there is also a greater likelihood of problems being present. Medications that may affect sexual function or the presence of genital abnormalities (infection or scarring) may also contribute to early difficulties with the resumption of sexual activity. Advice on the timing of a return to sexual function must be based on such individual considerations, combined with knowledge of the type of surgery, the underlying disorder, concurrent diseases, and the patient's recuperative powers.

At times, sexual difficulties that appear to be organic in origin are present during the first postoperative months but then resolve. Psychological adjustment may also be facilitated by the passage of time, but if sexual problems are reinforced by repeated failures that lead to increasing fears of performance, the chances become greater that the problems will persist. A reasonable approach to this situation is to incorporate appropriate amounts of sex counseling into postoperative care (both prior to discharge from the hospital and during followup visits over the first six months after surgery) and to refer patients with sexual difficulties that persist beyond this time for formal evaluation. Men who are experiencing impotence after having an ostomy are good candidates for evaluation of nocturnal penile tumescence patterns to ascertain whether the problem is psychogenic or organic (see Chap. 20). Unfortunately, there is no current diagnostic screening test to make a similar determination in women.

People react in different ways to having an ostomy. Some will want to be sure that their sexual partner does not see the ostomy site or appliance, whereas others will have a strong desire to have their partner become familiar with its appearance. Whatever is most comfortable psychologically for both partners is likely to work well for them. During sexual activity, some ostomates will want to wear an article of clothing such as a slip or a T-shirt that covers the ostomy site, while others will prefer to be unclothed and to wear either a dressing or nothing at all. Again, whatever is mutually comfortable and acceptable is also sensible. Some people with ostomies are so worried about how their partner will react to their operation that they become preoccupied with obtaining "proof" of their acceptability; they may demand that the partner touch and look at the ostomy or even incorporate contact with the ostomy into sexual play. This attitude may create problems for the partner, who does not equate his or her feelings for the ostomate with feelings for the ostomy. In such circumstances, pointing out that people are always making aesthetic choices in their sexual participation (for example, few people feel much sexual attraction for an elbow) may help to alleviate the worry that *not* paying attention to the ostomy is detracting from something.

Practical management of the sexual adjustment of the ostomate can be facilitated by the following suggestions:

1. Initiate discussions about sexuality during the hospitalization period.
2. Find out about the patient's prior sexual history.
3. Determine what the patient's current expectations and attitudes toward sex are.
4. When possible, include the spouse or sexual partner of the ostomate in at least one discussion about resumption of sexual activity.
5. Consider the use of written materials (the United Ostomy Association publishes booklets* entitled *Sex and the Male Ostomate*; *Sex, Pregnancy, and the Female Ostomate*; and *Sex, Courtship and the Single Ostomate*) or the possibility of a visit by someone from the local ostomy association as a way of reducing doubts and anxieties.
6. Point out the existence of noncoital sexual options.
7. Refer patients for appropriate counseling if they seem to be depressed or if sexual problems persist despite a supportive approach.

There are many practical suggestions about sex that can be given to ostomy patients on the basis of their individual needs. For example, if a woman is very worried about her husband's reaction to physical contact with the ostomy (or if her husband is concerned initially with hurting the ostomy stoma), a rear-entry or female-on-top position might be suggested for intercourse. Such recommendations are based merely on common sense. Some general reminders about personal cleanliness, avoiding intake of food that creates bowel problems, and emptying the appliance prior to sexual activity may also help to answer unspoken questions.

Finally, male ostomates should be informed that even if impotence occurs because of their operation, there are surgical procedures for the implantation of a penile prosthesis that can correct the problem (see Chapter 9). Women of childbearing age should also be told that an ostomy does not ordinarily interfere with their ability to become pregnant or to deliver a healthy child [59].

Obesity

Excessive body weight is both a culturally and a conditionally defined state [60]. In our society, obese persons generally are regarded as

---

*These booklets may be obtained by writing to the United Ostomy Association, 1111 Wilshire Boulevard, Los Angeles, California 90017.

unattractice, underachieving, and unable to control impulsive behavior [61, 62]. Although some individuals are sexually attracted to heavy persons, at times with an almost fetish-like fascination [63], it is far more common to find that obesity is an undesired trait in a sex partner and may actually constitute a deterrent to the activation of sexual feelings. While obesity is most accurately regarded as a symptom rather than a disease, as shown by its clinical and experimental heterogeneity [64], a discussion of sex and obesity appears logically situated in a chapter about chronic illness because many obese persons contend with being overweight on a lifelong basis.

While present evidence indicates that only a minuscule fraction of cases of obesity are attributable to disease states, certain genetic or hormonal conditions characteristically lead to excessive body fat. Some of these disorders are associated with concomitant hypogonadism, such as is found in the Prader-Willi syndrome [65], the Laurence-Moon-Biedl syndrome [66], and Cushing's disease [67]. Even in obese persons with no causative endocrinopathy or genetic disorder, alterations in sex hormone status have been reported. Amatruda and coworkers studied plasma testosterone and binding of testosterone in 22 obese men [68]. They found that men who were 176 to 199 percent of ideal body weight had a mean (±S.D.) plasma testosterone level significantly below a control group of nonobese men (less than 120% of ideal body weight): 424 ± 136 compared to 572 ± 137 ng per 100 ml. Men who were 200 percent or more of ideal body weight had an even lower mean (±S.D.) plasma testosterone (211 ± 65 ng/100 ml) and also had a decreased mean free testosterone index. All patients in their series had normal testicular size and normal patterns of masculinization; only 2 of 22 men complained of low libido and none had gynecomastia or impotence. Circulating levels of LH and FSH were within the normal range. Schneider and coworkers recently reported finding elevated serum and urinary estrogen levels in obese men, although no signs of feminization were detected [69]. Although these investigators also found low serum testosterone levels in their study subjects, they found normal free testosterone fractions and normal gonadotropin status.

Obese women have been noted to have a higher rate of menstrual dysfunction than women of normal weight [70]. The combination of obesity, hirsutism, and oligomenorrhea or amenorrhea is commonly seen by clinicians and is known to be frequently associated with high plasma androgen levels and low testosterone-binding globulin [71]. Weight loss by massively obese women can restore spontaneous menses and lead to a reduction in plasma androgen levels [72]. This situation may reflect, in part, an increase in adrenocortical activity in obesity [73] or it may be due to subtle changes in hypothalamic regulation, which controls both appetite and endocrine function.

It is apparent that obesity does not interfere with sexuality in many persons. On the other hand, obesity may influence sexuality via several different mechanisms. Appraisal of these possibilities is called for in the obese patient who complains of dissatisfaction with sex. First, obesity may be associated with a number of medical conditions that increase the risk of sexual problems. Altered insulin secretory dynamics and insulin antagonism [64] are both characteristic of obesity; diabetes occurs in obese persons more frequently than in people who are not overweight. Since diabetes is associated with a high rate of sexual problems (see Chap. 6), impotent obese men or anorgasmic obese women should undergo careful glucose-tolerance testing. The common finding of high blood pressure in the obese [60] frequently leads to use of antihypertensive drugs, which have a wide range of possible sexual sequelae (see Chapter 13) in this population of patients. In addition, since excessive weight may lead to accelerated deterioration of joint surfaces [74], obese persons may have difficulty in mechanical positioning for coitus.

Second, obesity frequently leads to a number of psychological problems that might potentially be associated with sexual difficulties. Many obese persons have problems with their body-image and self-esteem [75–77]. In addition, difficulties in interpersonal effectiveness and an increased occurrence of depression—possibly related to a state of "learned helplessness" in regard to the obesity—are likewise apt to be impediments to sexuality. It is clear that such problems lead to the avoidance of sexual activity by a substantial number of obese persons who fear being rejected or appearing grotesque or foolish to others. In some cases, the revulsion toward his or her body is so strong that the obese person abstains from masturbatory activity. In other instances, obese persons may marry at the first opportunity in an attempt to validate or upgrade their self-esteem, even when the available partner is deficient in qualities that are important to them.

Third, there may be mechanical difficulties with coital activity in the massively obese. These problems relate primarily to positioning for coitus: At times, the abdominal girth may be so large (along with commensurate adiposity in the thighs and buttocks) that intravaginal coitus is impossible. This problem is particularly apparent in the sexual relations of two severely obese partners. In such instances, substitute patterns of sexual activity may have been devised by the couple, including oral-genital sex, manual stimulation of the genitals, and intramammary coitus. Coital positions that require one person to be on top of the other may be problematic because of the excessive weight burden on the "underneath" partner or because the person attempting to straddle the obese partner may be quite uncomfortable.

Excessive body weight may become an interpersonal issue in a marriage under a varied set of circumstances. The common denominator of these situations seems to be dissatisfaction on the part of one spouse with his or her partner's physical appearance; such dissatisfaction may appear years after marrying, in the case of a person with a lifelong history of obesity, or it may occur with the onset of obesity some time after the marriage. The spouse of the obese person may pressure and cajole his or her mate about losing weight in a number of ways, including withdrawal from physical intimacy and closeness, and pursuit of extramarital affairs. Each of these reactions, of course, runs the risk of reinforcing patterns of overeating as a defense mechanism against rejection, loneliness, and frustration.

Neill and his colleagues suggest that when obesity is present during mate selection, subsequent interactions within the marriage may reinforce the meaning of obesity for the couple and might exert a protective and stabilizing effect on both the individuals and the marriage [78]. This conclusion is supported by evidence from these workers that intestinal bypass surgery and subsequent weight reduction lead to a high incidence of sexual and marital problems for both spouses of a marriage in which one person is massively obese [78]. However, there is other conflicting evidence regarding the overall psychosocial consequences of intestinal bypass surgery and weight loss. Solow, Silberfarb, and Swift found that affect, self-esteem, interpersonal and vocational effectiveness, and body-image all improved substantially in massively obese people after such surgery [79]. They attributed these changes to reduced self-consciousness and a reduced sense of hopelessness and helplessness; however, while interpersonal relations were described as improved by 24 of 29 patients, sex was reported to be more enjoyable by only 14. Abram and his colleagues found a less optimistic picture after intestinal bypass surgery [80]: Twenty-four percent of patients in their series developed psychiatric difficulties after hospital discharge.

On balance, it appears that following significant weight reduction, the dynamics of interpersonal relations may shift in varying degrees: The formerly obese person may become more assertive, more self-confident, and more likely to question the value of a marriage to a partner who is perceived as inadequate in certain dimensions. In view of this, it seems advisable to incorporate marital and sexual counseling into programs aimed at dramatic weight loss to resolve potential problem areas.

Neurologic Disorders

Sexual behavior and sexual function are both dependent on a complex hierarchy of integrated functions involving the nervous system. For this reason, a variety of neurologic disorders may lead to alterations in sexuality. The particular problems of sexual functioning in the spinal cord–injured are discussed in Chapter 14. A brief survey of other chronic neurologic disorders that may affect sexuality is presented in this section.

Intracranial Disorders

Temporal Lobe Lesions. Temporal lobe lesions have frequently been associated with alterations of sexuality. Gastant and Collomb found that two-thirds of 36 men with temporal lobe epilepsy were impotent and usually had low libido [81]. Similarly, Hierons and Saunders described a series of 15 men with temporal lobe damage who were impotent, but noted that these men all had normal libido [82]. On the other hand, disorders of the temporal lobe may be associated with hypersexuality [83–85], with priapism [86], and with aberrations of sexual behavior, including exhibitionism, fetishism, and transvestism [87–90].

Currier and coworkers described three patients who experienced occasional sexual activity or sensations in association with seizures [91]. These authors suggested that the temporal lobes serve as repositories of "connections for and memories related to sexual experiences and sexual intercourse" and also postulated that the postictal confusional stage of temporal lobe seizures may cause release of sexual behavior "as a response to activation of temporal lobe sexual connections with the limbic system and hypothalamus during the seizure" [91]. In animals, haloperidol (a blocker of dopamine transmission) diminishes hypersexuality associated with temporal lobe seizures [83].

Klüver-Bucy Syndrome. The Klüver-Bucy syndrome, first produced by bilateral temporal lobe ablation in rhesus monkeys, consists of hypersexuality, psychic blindness (visual agnosia), strong oral tendencies, hypermetamorphosis (excessive reaction to all visual stimuli), and a decrease in both aggression and fear [92]. This rare disorder may arise in humans because of temporal lobe damage from degenerative disorders, trauma, or encephalitis and has been reported as successfully treated with carbamazepine [93].

Epilepsy. Epilepsy and sexuality have been historically linked in many contexts. Until the early twentieth century, it was generally believed that epilepsy was caused by excessive masturbation [94, 95]. Still earlier, ancient physicians regarded "untimely intercourse" as a cause of epilepsy, and some even advised castration as a treatment of seizure disorders [96]. Although the sexual behavior and sexual functioning of most epileptics is quite normal, there are a number of factors that may operate singly or in combination to cause disturbances in their sexuality. Drugs used in the management of epilepsy may produce a degree of sedation that lowers libido and interferes with the normal reflexes of sexual responsivity. Although no systematic investigation of this aspect of anticonvulsive drug regimens has been conducted to date, our clinical experience has shown that in some cases, reducing the dosage of drugs such as diphenylhydantoin or phenobarbitol to levels that permit improved sexual function may also lower the convulsive threshold. Undesirable side effects associated with these drugs, including severe gingival hyperplasia and hirsutism, may create difficulty in matters of personal appearance and attractiveness and thus present impediments to sexual behavior [96]. In addition, many patients with epilepsy have difficulty with social stigmatization, feelings of inferiority, and a sense of anxiety or helplessness surrounding their vulnerability to the sudden occurrence of a seizure. These psychological problems may be associated with low libido or a sense of sexual inadequacy; and the avoidance of sexual activity by some epileptics may be a defense against the triggering of a seizure by increased neuromuscular excitability. Rarely, injuries sustained during a seizure or a hypoxic-hypotensive crisis during a series of prolonged seizures may cause severe mental and physical changes that overshadow the loss of sexual functioning.

Brain Injury. Brain injury of many varieties may produce alterations in patterns of sexual behavior. Weinstein observes that these changes "are often abnormal by reason of the circumstances in which they occur, rather than through their intrinsic nature" [97]. The sexual manifestations of brain injury include inappropriate behavior in public places (disrobing or masturbation, for example), delusions or hallucinations of a sexual nature, sexual aggression or violent sexual behavior, and unmasking of bluntness and stereotype. It is not unusual to see perseverative sexual behavior in such patients, although it must be emphasized that most brain-injured patients do not exhibit a marked degree of sexual interest at all.

Stroke. Patients who have had strokes have not been very carefully studied from the viewpoint of their sexual functioning. Ford and Orfirer reported on 105 stroke patients less than 60 years old and noted that 60 percent of this group did not experience loss of libido following their cerebrovascular accident [98]. However, the same authors reported that for a majority of their patients, the partner's concerns about sexual activity precipitating further neurological sequelae resulted in a lessening of sexual opportunities. It should be understood that these findings are not directly applicable to all stroke victims, many of whom are well above age 60 and may have been affected by a number of factors preceding their stroke that account for impairment of their sexual functioning. Among these are lack of a sexual partner, pre-existing illness or drug use that has created sexual problems, loss of interest in sex, and misinformation about sexuality and the process of aging. Furthermore, the physical consequences of a stroke may include serious limitations on sexual functioning, although many strokes produce only modest or moderate neurologic impairment.

Kalliomaki and coworkers, also studying patients under the age of 60, noted that decreased libido after a stroke is more common in right-side paralysis than in left-side paralysis [99], a fact substantiated by a more recent study [100]. Goddess, Wagner, and Silverman found that poststroke diminished libido is common if the dominant hemisphere is damaged but unlikely if the stroke affects only the nondominant hemisphere; in addition, they reported that prestroke patterns of sexual activity are excellent predictors of sexual behavior following the occurrence of a stroke [100].

Strokes may result in a variety of physical manifestations, including hemiplegia, sensory deficits, blindness, dizziness, dysphasia, and dysarthria. Loss of sphincter control is an obvious source of sexual problems for some stroke patients. Although direct sexual problems such as impotence, ejaculatory incompetence, and anorgasmia may occur because of neurologic damage, these are relatively unusual phenomena; most often, sexual problems after a stroke reflect a combination of mechanical difficulties (such as poor motor strength or lack of coordination or maneuverability) and emotional factors. Depression frequently occurs in the wake of a stroke, as the victim feels overwhelmed and relatively helpless in adjusting to his or her disabilities; the clinician must be particularly cognizant of this possibility, for the potential improvement, sexually and otherwise, once proper treatment of the depression has been instituted is high.

It is difficult to offer any generalizations about the advice that should be given to stroke patients regarding their resumption of sexual activity or whether any limitations should be put on continuing sexual participation. The theoretical risk is highest in patients whose stroke was due to intracranial hemorrhage, since the possibility of recurrence of a bleed as a result of the elevated blood pressure associated with high levels of sexual arousal is of unknown magnitude. As a practical matter, it seems that this risk is quite small in most cases. Until adequate research data are available to answer this question, however, the clinician must proceed largely by guesswork and inference.

Careful attention to attitudinal and interpersonal needs in the lives of stroke patients can be of benefit to the process of their sexual rehabilitation, if this is a goal that they desire. It must be emphasized that some stroke patients are uninterested in sex and do not need to be gratuitously "given" a problem by an overzealous counselor. On the other hand, some patients harbor anxieties about their sexual capabilities and may misconstrue the neurologic limitations of their condition, believing that sexual functioning is automatically impaired. Drugs that may be required for the treatment of hypertension, which is commonly seen in stroke patients, may cause difficulties with sexual functioning or lowering of libido, but these effects are often reversible with proper management (see Chap. 13). Limitations on verbal communications caused by a stroke may present particular problems in regard to expressing sexual preferences or needs and may lead to withdrawal and frustration. Despite these obstacles, when the stroke patient has a reasonably healthy and interested partner, it is often possible to achieve a surprisingly satisfactory level of sexual functioning.

Headaches. Sexual activity has been related to recurrent headaches in a small population of patients. Although the stereotype of a headache as an excuse to avoid sexual contact has a humorous ring, for some patients this association is a very real source of distress. While undoubtedly a significant proportion of individuals with headaches occurring during sex are reacting in a psychosomatic fashion to anxiety, guilt, or tension, in other instances a different explanation may exist. Sicuteri and coworkers discussed the possible interrelationship between serotonin, sex, and migraine headaches without presenting any convincing evidence [101]. Paulson described three patients with headaches related to orgasm whose symptoms were relieved by the use of propranolol, a beta-adrenergic blocking agent [102], and also postulated that headaches associated with sexual stimulation may be a result of either low spinal fluid pressure, severe myotonia, sudden changes in cerebral blood pressure, or vascular predisposition as well as to a variety of emotional factors. We have only rarely encountered headaches precipitated by sexual activity in our clinical population, and in these instances the headaches were quite infrequent. Appropriate management appears to depend both on the frequency and severity of the headaches and on adequate neurologic evaluation.

Multiple Sclerosis

Multiple sclerosis is a demyelinating disease of uncertain etiology, which most typically affects young adults between the ages of 20 and 40. This puzzling disorder is usually characterized clinically by periods of exacerbation and remission that become progressively more disabling over a period of years. Although diagnosis in the early stages of illness may be difficult, certain typical features occur frequently enough to lead to a high index of suspicion when encountered in this age group. The most frequent manifestations include visual impairment (sudden blindness, double vision, eye pain), tremor, ataxia, sensory alterations, paraplegia, scanning speech, and bladder dysfunction. The inappropriate cheerfulness ("la belle indifférence") that is observed in some patients with this disease is neither pathognomonic of multiple sclerosis nor typical.

There is no known cure for multiple sclerosis, although some patients respond positively to therapy with adrenocorticotropin [103]. Since the average duration of this disease is more than 20 years, with marked uncertainty about functional health status from month to month, it is easy to see that adjusting to multiple sclerosis can be an arduous psychological task.

Sexual dysfunction is a prominent symptom of this disorder. Ivers and Goldstein reported that 26 percent of men with multiple sclerosis were impotent [104], while Vas noted that 47 percent of male patients without major neurologic disability had some impairment of erection [1]. Lundberg found that 13 of 25 women with mild cases of multiple sclerosis (involving little or no physical disability) were experiencing sexual problems [105]. Nine women reported decreased libido and nine women had difficulty with their orgasmic response, while five women had dyspareunia and three noted lack of vaginal lubrication.

Lilius and coworkers administered a written questionnaire to 302 men and women with multiple sclerosis and found substantial evidence of sexual difficulties [106]. Sixty-four percent of the men and 39 percent of the women in their series reported either having an unsatisfactory sex life or having stopped participation in sexual activity. The overall physical condition of these two groups was judged to be poor in contrast to those who reported a satisfactory sex life. Eighty percent of the men reported difficulties with erection and a diminished frequency of sexual intercourse, and 56 percent described diminished libido. General weakness, spasticity, and loss of penile sensations were cited by some men as reasons for sexual difficulties, but impotence was the primary difficulty. Forty-eight percent of women reported decreased or absent interest in intercourse, while 49 percent of women described diminished or absent clitoral sensitivity and 57 percent described difficulty in attaining orgasm. Of 53 women with sexual dissatisfaction or cessation of sexual activity, the main problem was cited as loss of orgasm (33 percent), loss of libido (27 percent), spasticity (12 percent), husband's disinterest (9 percent), weakness (9 percent), dryness of the vagina (5 percent), and lack of sexual partner (5 percent) [106].

Although the patients with multiple sclerosis surveyed by Lilius and colleagues were primarily in an advanced stage of the disease, it is important to realize that sexual difficulties may be among the first manifestations of this disorder. This symptom can present problems in differential diagnosis, since the dysfunction may remit after a period of weeks or months, only to return at a later time. Because episodic sexual dysfunction is generally regarded as psychogenic in origin and because people early in the course of multiple sclerosis may appear to be in excellent overall health, clinicians should be alert to this diagnostic difficulty. A family history of multiple sclerosis, the occurrence of optic neuritis, or the presence of symptoms or signs of diffuse neurologic involvement (nystagmus, cerebellar ataxia, Babinski signs, personality changes, vertigo, incontinence) should occasion careful neurologic evaluation.

Hartings and coworkers have described a group counseling format for multiple sclerosis patients to help them identify behavioral, psychological, and social adaptations necessitated by this disease [107]. This approach may be particularly valuable in helping the young, unmarried person with multiple sclerosis to acknowledge the sexual difficulties that he or she is having and to consider means of dealing with them. For men with significant potency problems resulting from this disorder, the use of a surgically implanted penile prosthesis may greatly enhance self-esteem and may also assist socialization (see Chap. 9). Patients with sexual difficulties due to spasticity may be helped by pharmacologic management, although this treatment may serve to create further erectile distress. Some women with multiple sclerosis may benefit from the use of artificial lubrication. A major point to be stressed in counseling both men and women with this disorder is that the fluctuating course of neurologic symptoms is important to keep in mind. If sexual activity is given up entirely as a result of disappointment with one's level of performance or gratification (particularly when these factors are narrowly judged in terms of coitus or coital orgasm), subsequent intervals of symptom remission—when sexual activity and satisfaction may be quite similar to premorbid levels—will be unknowingly missed.

Other Neuromuscular Conditions

An extensive catalogue of the disorders that may create sexual difficulties because of limitation of movement, spasticity, or weakness is not likely to yield many practical suggestions. Nevertheless, several additional neuromuscular illnesses will be mentioned briefly because of their unique features.

Cerebral Palsy. Cerebral palsy covers a variety of conditions of diverse etiologies that result in disturbance of motor function. In some cases, the predominant manifestations are spasticity, rigidity, and weakness; usually these symptoms affect all four extremities (but the legs more so than the arms). In other cases the defect is primarily choreopathic in nature, while in still other varieties, the manifestations are predominantly those of cerebellar ataxia. Mental retardation may sometimes be associated with these disorders, but in many cases intelligence is normal. Persons with cerebral palsy may have major difficulties in adolescent socialization for a number of reasons, including their appearance during ambulation or other motor functions, speech impediments, and skeletal deformities. Anxiety can precipitate reflex spasticity, which may further limit both social and sexual exploration. In some instances, counseling of the mildly cerebral palsied may help to facilitate sexual adjustment and to provide guidance in matters related to genetics and reproduction [108]. Typically, libido is unimpaired.

Muscular Dystrophy. The syndromes of muscular dystrophy are all disabling to one degree or another, but for most, the primary effect on sexual functioning occurs through weakness of the skeletal musculature. In one form of this disorder, myotonic dystrophy, the typical manifestations begin in early adult life. Muscle atrophy is accompanied by the inability to relax a muscle normally after contraction (myotonia); cataracts, frontal baldness at an early age (in affected men and women both), and gonadal insufficiency are common features. Atrophy of the testes, testosterone deficiency, and impaired spermatogenesis are typical of the affected male [109]. Impotence and infertility are common findings. The myotonia, which may create difficulties during sexual activity, is symptomatically improved by the use of quinine; testosterone replacement therapy will often improve the impotence.

Myasthenia Gravis. Occasionally patients with myasthenia gravis, a disease characterized by muscular weakness and easy fatigability that is most symptomatic with repetitive muscular exertion, are unable to sustain sexual activity for any length of time due to the mechanical effort involved. Such patients may benefit from the use of anticholinesterase agents (neostigmine, pyridostigmine bromide, or ambenonium chloride) taken prior to sexual involvement. In addition, these patients may encounter fewer difficulties if sexual activity is begun after a period of resting and if the tempo of their sexual participation permits intervals of little or no exertion on their part. For some patients with myasthenia, coitus is less difficult than attempting oral stimulation of their partner: The tongue is frequently severely affected by this disorder.

Poliomyelitis. Poliomyelitis is a viral disorder that results in various types of paralysis in only a small percentage of cases. Spinal damage is caused by lesions in the anterior horn cells, which affect motor function but do not abolish sensation. Autonomic nerve involvement may produce ileus or bladder dysfunction, and in such cases impotence may result. However, most people with paralysis resulting from poliomyelitis are not physiologically impaired in their sexual functioning except to the extent that paralysis or motor weakness limits physical activity or hinders the mechanical aspects of sexual positioning. On the other hand, because of the assumption that paraplegia must be associated with impotence or other sexual problems, there may be psychosocial difficulties for the person who is confined to a wheelchair as a result of paralytic polio.

Arthritis and Connective Tissue Disorders

Chronic arthritis of any etiology may have adverse effects on sexual functioning. The most common sexual problem encountered by arthritic patients is a mechanical limitation on coital positioning, which is usually a result of hip disease; this difficulty is more apt to be troublesome in women than in men and is most pronounced in the presence of bilateral hip involvement. In addition to other mechanical problems that may occur because of joint contractures or swollen, painful joints, the patient with rheumatoid arthritis also may be limited sexually by nonspecific symptoms including weakness and easy fatigability, vasomotor disturbances, numbness and tingling of the hands and feet, and muscular atrophy. Although limitation of motion early in the course of rheumatoid arthritis is usually due to pain and inflammation, later in the progression of the disease it may be a result of fibrosis of the joint capsule, shortening of muscles, or fibrous ankylosis. Characteristically, stiffness in rheumatoid arthritis is greatest in the morning upon awakening and subsides somewhat with moderate activity: Many patients with arthritis report that joint symptoms are least troublesome in late morning or early afternoon. For persons who notice a significant time variation in the severity of symptomatology, it can be helpful to plan sexual activity to coincide with the optimal time of day. Similarly, since a large number of patients with arthritis benefit from the application of heat to affected joints, the use of a hot bath, shower, or compress immediately prior to sexual activity may minimize the difficulties that are encountered. In fact, it is quite appropriate for patients to incorporate such "treatments" into sensual play with their partner by bathing together and sharing the intimacy of the moment.

When physical limitations on coital positioning are mild to moderate, couples will often benefit from simple suggestions about how to minimize discomfort occasioned by excessive weightbearing of a joint or the need for an extensive range of joint motion. For example, when hip abduction or external rotation is difficult for the woman with arthritis, a rear-entry coital position may be employed; when it is the male who has moderate hip disease, a lateral coital position or the female-astride position may be useful. In severe cases of mechanical limitation, corrective surgery, including use of joint prostheses, may be required to restore an adequate opportunity for sexual functioning.

Herstein and coworkers recently reported a followup study of the sexuality of 58 patients seen an average of 14.5 years from the onset of juvenile rheumatoid arthritis [110]. They found that while the sexual activity of most patients was quite similar to that of the nonarthritic population, 38 percent of patients expressed a need for sex counseling; they also noted that limitations on sexual activity were more closely correlated with the activity of the disease rather than with the severity of joint deformity.

Sjögren's Syndrome. A variety of sexual difficulties may be associated with problems affecting certain populations of people with arthritis. Sjögren's syndrome, which consists of chronic arthritis accompanied by dry eyes (keratoconjunctivitis sicca) and dry mouth (xerostomia), is often marked by impairment of vaginal lubrication, which may cause dyspareunia. Fewer than 10 percent of patients with Sjögren's syndrome are men, and this disorder is typically seen in middle-aged women [111].

Reiter's Syndrome. Reiter's syndrome consists of a subacute or chronic arthritis accompanied by nongonococcal urethritis, conjunctivitis, and mucocutaneous lesions; this disorder affects men in the third and fourth decades and is believed to be infectious in origin. Although Reiter's syndrome has been observed following bacillary dysentery, the specific etiologic agent is still a matter of controversy. The urethral discharge may be asymptomatic or dysuria may be noted; the urethral meatus is often erythematous. Skin lesions are frequently present on the glans penis, beginning as small vesicles but quickly changing to superficial ulcerations; although these lesions are usually painless, when they are located along the penile shaft they may cause discomfort during sexual activity. It is important to obtain urethral cultures for gonorrhea in men with urethritis accompanied by arthritis, since *gonococcal arthritis* requires prompt treatment with penicillin.

Behçet's Syndrome. Arthritis may be associated with inflammatory bowel disease (most commonly in patients with ulcerative colitis) but usually subsides following ostomy surgery. In Behçet's syndrome, marked by ulcerated lesions of the mouth and the genitalia accompanied by ocular inflammation, there is often a recurring pattern of acute inflammatory arthritis [112]. Although the oral and genital ulcerations seen in Behçet's syndrome are usually painful and recalcitrant to treatment, they characteristically heal spontaneously after several weeks and do not usually result in scarring. These lesions may occur anywhere along the penis or scrotum in men or on the labia or vaginal interior in women. Central nervous system involvement is seen in approximately a quarter of patients, and thrombophlebitis is also frequently encountered, sometimes contributing further to the sexual difficulties that may be associated with this disorder. *Degenerative joint disease*, typically occurring later in life than rheumatoid arthritis, is characterized by aching, pain, and joint stiffness but only a minimal degree of morning stiffness; the underlying condition is destruction of joint cartilage and hypertrophy of bone. Limitation of motion of the hips is most likely to limit sexual functioning for mechanical reasons in persons who have degenerative joint disease. Weight loss may be beneficial to overweight persons with this disorder, and general treatment measures such as the local application of heat and individualized physical therapy may further improve the capacity for functioning in some patients.

Systemic Lupus Erythematosus. Systemic lupus erythematosus (SLE) is a chronic disease of unknown etiology that involves a multitude of immunologic abnormalities. This disorder affects women far more frequently than men (the sex ratio is 9:1) and occurs principally during the reproductive years. The major clinical manifestations of SLE include arthritis and arthralgias, fever, skin rash, lymphadenopathy, renal involvement, anorexia, nausea or vomiting, myalgia, and anemia. Fifteen to 20 percent of patients give false-positive results to a serologic test for syphilis.

The impact of SLE on sexual function varies from patient to patient. As with any chronic illness that involves a multiplicity of symptoms, libido may be severely depressed in this disorder. The skin changes that occur, frequently involving a facial rash, may lead to alterations in body-image. Arthritic symptoms may contribute to difficulty in the mechanical aspects of coitus. Ulcers affecting the mucous membranes of either the mouth or the vagina may create pain upon any sexual contact; dyspareunia may also result from decreased vaginal lubrication, which occurs in approximately one-fifth of patients with SLE as a part of Sjögren's syndrome. Central nervous system manifestations are common in lupus patients, with convulsive disorders, psychosis, and emotional lability frequently seen. Iatrogenic problems arising from the use of corticosteroids to treat this disorder may cause sexual difficulties by altering the patient's appearance (the moon facies and trunkal obesity of the cushingoid patient), increasing the rate of vaginal infections, and producing amenorrhea. The antihypertensive drugs sometimes used in this disorder may cause sexual problems (see Chap. 13). If SLE results in severe renal damage, uremia may occur, with its attendant sexual difficulties. Counseling of the patient with SLE must be approached on an individual basis.

Chronic Obstructive Pulmonary Disease

A major source of disability due to chronic illness in the adult population is attributable to emphysema and chronic bronchitis. These two conditions are usually combined in the same patient—although one or the other may predominate in clinical importance—so that it is convenient to consider the process of chronic obstructive pulmonary disease as an appropriate diagnostic term. The pulmonary abnormalities include increased resistance to airflow and inflammation, hypersecretion, and alveolar collapse or destruction. Patients with chronic obstructive pulmonary disease severe enough to produce dyspnea with moderate exertion sometimes experience difficulty during sexual activity due to hypoxia. In patients with further progression of the disease, especially those who become dyspneic at rest or with only minimal exertion, significant limitations on sexual activity are characteristically found.

Although Kass and coworkers reported that only 17 of 100 men with chronic obstructive pulmonary disease were impotent [113], Agle and Baum found that 19 of 23 men participating in a rehabilitation program for COPD complained of low libido and impaired erectile function; 39 percent of these men reported total impotence for one or more years [114]. It is likely that the different findings in these two investigations are primarily a reflection of a difference in severity of impairment of lung function in the two groups studied.

Patients with a major degree of disability from chronic obstructive pulmonary disease characteristically have major anxieties about dyspnea itself and a fear of suffocation, hence they are likely to avoid physical activity whenever possible [114, 115]. In addition, many patients with severe pulmonary impairment are depressed [116], which may also contribute to decreased libido or sexual dysfunction. Poor self-esteem, alcoholism, reduced muscle strength, easy fatigability, and impaired cognition due to persistent hypoxia are other possible contributors to sexual problems that the patient with chronic lung disease may face. In addition, Narayan and Ferranti have recently found that peripheral sensory and motor nerve conduction is impaired in patients with respiratory insufficiency and severe chronic hypoxemia, posing one further potential mechanism for sexual difficulty [117].

As a practical matter, patients with chronic obstructive lung disease so severe that it interferes with sexual functioning cannot always be helped. Since reducing hypoxia is sometimes beneficial in allowing patients to tolerate physical activity, the home use of carefully controlled oxygen therapy (preferably with nasal prongs rather than a mask) may improve the patient's capacity for sexual responsiveness and may also provide an important degree of anxiety reduction. Unfortunately, oxygen therapy is not without attendant risks and is not suitable for all patients. Similarly, reducing the amount of physical exertion required during sexual activity is beneficial to many patients; this may be accomplished by the use of positions that minimize physical work and by the cooperation of an understanding partner. The use of a waterbed is one possible way of facilitating sexual activity, since active movement by the healthy partner produces a fluid wave which then propels the inactive person passively, with the net effect of creating motion without requiring a significant increase in work capacity or oxygen consumption. Attention to matters of hydration, postural drainage, and appropriate pharmacologic management may also sometimes improve sexual functioning in patients with chronic obstructive lung disease.

References

1. Vas, C. J.   Sexual impotence and some autonomic disturbances in men with multiple sclerosis. *Acta Neurologica Scandinavica* 45:166–182, 1969.
2. Smith, B. H.   Multiple sclerosis and sexual dysfunction. *Medical Aspects of Human Sexuality* 10(1):103–104, 1976.
3. Mechanic, D.   Illness behavior, social adaptation, and the management of illness: A comparison of educational and medical models. *Journal of Nervous and Mental Disease* 165:79–87, 1977.
4. Bailey, G. L.   The sick kidney and sex (editorial). *New England Journal of Medicine* 296:1288–1289, 1977.
5. Kolodny, R. C.   Unpublished observations, 1978.
6. Levy, N. B.   Sexual adjustment to maintenance hemodialysis and renal transplantation. *Transactions; American Society for Artificial Internal Organs* 19:138–143, 1973.
7. Steele, T. E., Finkelstein, S. H., and Finkelstein, F. O.   Hemodialysis patients and spouses: Marital discord, sexual problems, and depression. *Journal of Nervous and Mental Disease* 162:225–237, 1976.
8. Thurm, J. A.   Effect of chronic renal disease on sexual function. *Medical Aspects of Human Sexuality* 10(8):81–82, 1976.
9. Abram, H. S., Hester, L. R., Sheridan, W. F., and Epstein, G. M.   Sexual function in patients with chronic renal failure. *Journal of Nervous and Mental Disease* 160:220–226, 1975.
10. Levy, N. B.   Uremic sex (letter). *New England Journal of Medicine* 297:725–726, 1977.
11. Salvatierra, O., Fortmann, J. L., and Belzer, F. O.   Sexual function in males before and after renal transplantation. *Urology* 5:64–66, 1975.
12. Procci, W. R., Hoffman, K. I., and Chatterjee, S. N.   Sexual functioning of renal transplant recipients. *Journal of Nervous and Mental Disease* 166:402–407, 1978.
13. Feldman, H. A., and Singer, I.   Endocrinology and metabolism in uremia and dialysis: A clinical review. *Medicine* (Baltimore) 54:345–376, 1974.
14. Rice, G. G.   Hypermenorrhea in the young hemodialysis patient. *American Journal of Obstetrics and Gynecology* 116:539–543, 1973.
15. Holdsworth, M. B., Atkins, R. C., and de Kretser, D. M.   The pituitary-testicular axis in men with chronic renal failure. *New England Journal of Medicine* 296:1245–1249, 1977.
16. Lim, V. S., and Fang, V. S.   Gonadal dysfunction in uremic men: A study of the hypothalamo-pituitary-testicular axis before and after renal transplantation. *American Journal of Medicine* 58:655–662, 1975.
17. Lim, V. S., and Fang, V. S.   Restoration of plasma testosterone levels in uremic men with clomiphene citrate. *Journal of Clinical Endocrinology and Metabolism* 43:1370–1377, 1976.
18. Chen, J. C., Vidt, D. G., Zorn, E. M., Hallberg, M. C., and Wieland,

R. G.   Pituitary-Leydig cell function in uremic males. *Journal of Clinical Endocrinology and Metabolism* 31:14–17, 1970.

19. Freeman, R. M., Lawton, R. L., and Fearing, M. O.   Gynecomastia: An endocrinologic complication of hemodialysis. *Annals of Internal Medicine* 69:67–72, 1968.

20. Raskin, N. H., and Fishman, R. A.   Neurologic disorders in renal failure: Part I. *New England Journal of Medicine* 294:143–148, 1976.

21. Edwards, A. E., Kopple, J. D., and Kornfeld, C. M.   Vibrotactile threshold in patients undergoing maintenance hemodialysis. *Archives of Internal Medicine* 132:706–708, 1973.

22. McKevitt, P. M.   Treating sexual dysfunction in dialysis and transplant patients. *Health and Social Work* 1:133–157, 1976.

23. Brown, T. M., Feins, A., Parke, R. C., and Paulus, D. A.   Living with long-term home dialysis. *Annals of Internal Medicine* 81:165–170, 1974.

24. Kaplan De-Nour, A., and Czaczkes, J. W.   The influence of the patient's personality on adjustment to chronic dialysis: A predictive study. *Journal of Nervous and Mental Disease* 162:323–333, 1976.

25. Gordon-Foster, F., Cohn, G. L., and McKegney, F. P.   Psychobiologic factors and individual survival on chronic renal hemodialysis: A two-year follow-up: Part I. *Psychosomatic Medicine* 35:64–82, 1973.

26. Antoniou, L. D., Shalhoub, R. J., Sudhakar, T., and Smith, J. C., Jr. Reversal of uraemic impotence by zinc. *Lancet* 2:895–898, 1977.

27. Reiner, M. L.   Counseling the hemodialysis patient. *Osteopathic Physician* 44(2):39–50, 1977.

28. Kolodny, R. C., and Masters, W. H.   Unpublished observation, 1977.

29. Van Thiel, D. H., Sherins, R. J., and Lester, R. Mechanism of hypogonadism in alcoholic liver disease (abstract). *Gastroenterology* 65:A-50/574, 1973.

30. Lemere, F., and Smith, J. W.   Alcohol-induced sexual impotence. *American Journal of Psychiatry* 130:212–213, 1973.

31. Browne-Mayers, A. N., Seelye, E. E., and Sillman, L.   Psychosocial study of hospitalized middle-class alcoholic women. *Annals of the New York Academy of Sciences* 273:593–604, 1976.

32. Southren, A. L., Gordon, G. G., Olivo, J., Rafii, F., and Rosenthal, W. S.   Androgen metabolism in cirrhosis of the liver. *Metabolism: Clinical and Experimental* 22:695–702, 1973.

33. Gordon, G. G., Olivo, J., Rafii, F., and Southren, A. L.   Conversion of androgens to estrogens in cirrhosis of the liver. *Journal of Clinical Endocrinology and Metabolism* 40:1018–1026, 1975.

34. Van Thiel, D. H., Lester, R., and Sherins, R. J.   Hypogonadism in alcoholic liver disease: Evidence for a double defect. *Gastroenterology* 67:1188–1199, 1974.

35. Chopra, I. J., Tulchinsky, D., and Greenway, F. L.   Estrogen-androgen imbalance in hepatic cirrhosis. *Annals of Internal Medicine* 79:198–203, 1973.

36. Van Thiel, D. H.   Testicular atrophy and other endocrine changes in alcoholic men. *Medical Aspects of Human Sexuality* 10(6):153–154, 1976.

37. Van Thiel, D. H., Gavaler, J., and Lester, R.   Ethanol inhibition of vita-

min A metabolism in the testes: Possible mechanism for sterility in alcoholics. *Science* 186:941–942, 1974.

38. Gordon, G. G., Altman, K., Southren, A. L., Rubin, E., and Lieber, C. S. Effect of alcohol (ethanol) administration on sex-hormone metabolism in normal men. *New England Journal of Medicine* 295:793–797, 1976.

39. Rubin, E., Lieber, C. S., Altman, K., Gordon, G. G., and Southren, A. L. Prolonged ethanol consumption increases testosterone metabolism in the liver. *Science* 191:563–564, 1976.

40. Kent, J. R., Scaramuzzi, R. J., Lauwers, W., Farlow, A. F., Hill, M., Penardi, R., and Hillard, J. Plasma testosterone, estradiol, and gonadotrophins in hepatic insufficiency. *Gastroenterology* 64:111–115, 1973.

41. Morgan, M. Y., and Sherlock, S. Sex-related differences among 100 patients with alcoholic liver disease. *British Medical Journal* 1:939–941, 1977.

42. Ryback, R. S. Chronic alcohol consumption and menstruation (letter). *Journal of the American Medical Association* 238:2143, 1977.

43. Straus, D. J. Hematologic aspects of alcoholism. *Seminars in Hematology* 10:183–194, 1973.

44. Cumming, R. L. C., and Goldberg, A. Alcohol and the hematopoietic system. *Clinics in Endocrinology and Metabolism* 7:447–461, 1978.

45. Littleton, J. Alcohol and neurotransmitters. *Clinics in Endocrinology and Metabolism* 7:369–384, 1978.

46. Van Thiel, D. H., Gavaler, J. S., Smith, W. I., and Rabin, B. S. Testicular and spermatozoal autoantibody in chronic alcoholic males with gonadal failure. *Clinical Immunology and Immunopathology* 8:311–317, 1977.

47. Masters, W. H., and Johnson, V. E. *Human Sexual Inadequacy.* Boston: Little, Brown and Co., 1970.

48. Bullock, S. C., and Mudd, E. H. The interrelatedness of alcoholism and marital conflict: II. The interaction of alcoholic husbands and their nonalcoholic wives during counseling. *American Journal of Orthopsychiatry* 29:519–527, 1959.

49. Bailey, M. B. Alcoholism and marriage: A review of research and professional literature. *Quarterly Journal of Studies on Alcohol* 22:81–97, 1961.

50. Bowen, M. Alcoholism as viewed through family systems theory and family psychotherapy. *Annals of the New York Academy of Sciences* 233:115–122, 1974.

51. Janzen, C. Family treatment for alcoholism: A review. *Social Work* 23:135–141, 1978.

52. Orford, J., Oppenheimer, E., Egert, S., Hensman, C., and Guthrie, S. The cohesiveness of alcoholism-complicated marriages and its influence on treatment outcome. *British Journal of Psychiatry* 128:318–339, 1976.

53. Pottenger, M., McKernon, J., Patrie, L. E., Weissman, M. M., Ruben, H. L., and Newberry, P. The frequency and persistence of depressive symptoms in the alcohol abuser. *Journal of Nervous and Mental Disease* 166:562–570, 1978.

54. Dlin, B. M., Perlman, A., and Ringold, E. Psychosexual response to ileostomy and colostomy. *American Journal of Psychiatry* 126:374–381, 1969.

55. Stahlgren, L. H., and Fergusson, L. K.   Influence on sexual function of abdomino-perineal resection for ulcerative colitis. *New England Journal of Medicine* 259:873–875, 1958.

56. Grüner, O. P. N., Naas, R., Fretheim, B., and Gjone, E.   Marital status and sexual adjustment after colectomy: Results in 178 patients operated on for ulcerative colitis. *Scandinavian Journal of Gastroenterology* 12:193–197, 1977.

57. Burnham, W. R., Lennard-Jones, J. E., and Brooke, B. N.   Sexual problems among married ileostomists. *Gut* 18:673–677, 1977.

58. Druss, R. G., O'Connor, J. F., and Stern, L. O.   Psychologic response to colectomy. *Archives of General Psychiatry* 20:419–427, 1969.

59. Barwin, B. N., Harley, J. MacD. G., and Wilson, W.   Ileostomy and pregnancy. *British Journal of Clinical Practice* 28:256–258, 1974.

60. Mann, G. V.   The influence of obesity on health. *New England Journal of Medicine* 291:178–185, 1974.

61. Allon, N.   The Stigma of Overweight in Everyday Life. In G. A. Bray (ed.), *Obesity in Perspective*. Washington, D. C.: DHEW Publication No. (NIH) 75-708, 1973. Pp. 83–102.

62. Kiell, N. (ed.).   *The Psychology of Obesity*. Springfield, Ill.: Charles C Thomas, Publisher, 1973.

63. Davis, L.   Fat men are good in bed. *Forum: The International Journal of Human Relations* 8(3):93–96, 1978.

64. Bray, G. A., Davidson, M. B., and Drenick, E. J.   Obesity: A serious symptom. *Annals of Internal Medicine* 77:797–805, 1972.

65. Zellweger, H., and Schneider, H. J. Syndrome of hypotonia-hypomentia-hypogonadism-obesity (HHHO) or Prader-Willi syndrome. *Archives of Diseases in Children* 115:588–598, 1968.

66. Klein, D., and Ammann, F.   The syndrome of Laurence-Moon-Bardet-Biedl and allied diseases in Switzerland. *Journal of Neurological Science* 9:479–513, 1969.

67. Soffer, L. J., Iannoccone, A., and Gabrilove, J. L.   Cushing's syndrome: A study of fifty patients. *American Journal of Medicine* 31:129–146, 1961.

68. Amatruda, J. M., Harman, S. M., Pourmotabbed, G., and Lockwood, D. H.   Depressed plasma testosterone and fractional binding of testosterone in obese males. *Journal of Clinical Endocrinology and Metabolism* 47:268–271, 1978.

69. Schneider, G., Kirschner, M. A., Berkowitz, R., and Ertel, N. H.   Increased estrogen production in obese men. *Journal of Clinical Endocrinology and Metabolism* 48:633–638, 1979.

70. Rogers, J., and Mitchell, G. W.   The relation of obesity to menstrual disturbances. *New England Journal of Medicine* 247:53–55, 1952.

71. Hosseinian, A. H., Kim, M. H., and Rosenfield, R. L.   Obesity and oligomenorrhea are associated with hyperandrogenism independent of hirsutism. *Journal of Clinical Endocrinology and Metabolism* 42:765–769, 1976.

72. Glass, A. R., Dahms, W. T., Abraham, G., Atkinson, R. L., Bray, G. A., and Swerdloff, R. S.   Secondary amenorrhea in obesity: Etiologic role of weight-related androgen excess. *Fertility and Sterility* 30:243–244, 1978.

73. Schteingart, D. E., and Conn, J. W.   Characteristics of the increased

adrenocortical function observed in many obese patients. *Annals of the New York Academy of Sciences* 131:388–403, 1965.

74. Julkunen, H., Heinanen, O. P., and Pyorala, K.   Hyperostosis of the spine in an adult population: Its relation to hyperglycemia and obesity. *Annals of Rheumatic Disease* 30:605–612, 1971.

75. Stunkard, A., and Mendelson, M.   Obesity and the body image: I. Characteristics of disturbances in the body image of some obese persons. *American Journal of Psychiatry* 123:1296–1300, 1967.

76. Stunkard, A., and Burt, V.   Obesity and the body image: II. Age at onset of disturbances in the body image. *American Journal of Psychiatry* 123:1443–1447, 1967.

77. Kalucy, R. S., and Crisp, A. H.   Some psychological and social implications of massive obesity. *Journal of Psychosomatic Research* 18:465–473, 1974.

78. Neill, J. R., Marshall, J. R., and Yale, C. E.   Marital changes after intestinal bypass surgery. *Journal of the American Medical Association* 240:447–450, 1978.

79. Solow, C., Silberfarb, P. M., and Swift, K.   Psychosocial effects of intestinal bypass surgery for severe obesity. *New England Journal of Medicine* 290:300–304, 1974.

80. Abram, H. S., Meixel, S. A., Webb, W. W., and Scott, H. W.   Psychological adaptation to jejunoileal bypass for morbid obesity. *The Journal of Nervous and Mental Disease* 162:151–157, 1976.

81. Gastant, H., and Collomb, J.   Étude de comportement sexuel chez les épileptiques psychomoteurs. *Annales Medico-Psychologiques* 112:657–696, 1954.

82. Hierons, R., and Saunders, M.   Impotence in patients with temporal-lobe lesions. *Lancet* 2:761–763, 1966.

83. Andy, O. J., and Velamati, S.   Temporal lobe seizures and hypersexuality. *Applied Neurophysiology* 41:13–28, 1978.

84. Terzian, H., and Ore, G. D.   Syndrome of Klüver and Bucy reproduced in man by bitemporal removal of temporal lobes. *Neurology* 5:373–380, 1955.

85. Blumer, D.   Hypersexual episodes in temporal lobe epilepsy. *American Journal of Psychiatry* 126:1099–1106, 1970.

86. Penfield, W., and Jasper, H.   *Epilepsy and the Functional Anatomy of the Human Brain.* Boston: Little, Brown and Co., 1954. Pp. 393, 413.

87. Epstein, A. W.   Relationship of fetishism and transvestism to brain and particularly to temporal lobe dysfunction. *Journal of Nervous and Mental Disease* 133:247–253, 1961.

88. Hooshmand, H., and Brawley, B. W.   Temporal lobe seizures and exhibitionism. *Neurology* 19:1119–1124, 1969.

89. Hunter, R., Logue, V., and McMenemy, W. H.   Temporal lobe epilepsy supervening on longstanding transvestism and fetishism. *Epilepsia* 4:60–65, 1963.

90. Mitchell, W., Falconer, M. A., and Hill, D.   Epilepsy fetishism relieved by temporal lobectomy. *Lancet* 2:626–630, 1954.

91. Currier, R. D., Little, S. C., Suess, J. F., and Andy, O. J.   Sexual seizures. *Archives of Neurology* 25:260–264, 1971.

92. Klüver, H., and Bucy, P. C.   Psychic blindness and other symptoms

following bilateral temporal lobectomy in rhesus monkeys. *American Journal of Physiology* 119:352–353, 1937.

93. Hooshmand, H., Sepdham, T., and Vries, J. K. Klüver-Bucy syndrome: Successful treatment with carbamazepine. *Journal of the American Medical Association* 229:1782, 1974.

94. Temkin, O. *The Falling Sickness*. Baltimore: Johns Hopkins University Press, 1971.

95. Haller, J. S., Jr., and Haller, R. M. *The Physician and Sexuality in Victorian America*. New York: W. W. Norton & Co., 1974.

96. Money, J., and Pruce, G. Psychomotor Epilepsy and Sexual Function. In J. Money and H. Musaph (eds.), *Handbook of Sexology*. New York: Elsevier/North Holland Biomedical Press, 1977. Pp. 969–977.

97. Weinstein, E. A. Sexual disturbances after brain injury. *Medical Aspects of Human Sexuality* 8(10):10–30, 1974.

98. Ford, A. B., and Orfirer, A. P. Sexual behavior and the chronically ill patient. *Medical Aspects of Human Sexuality* 1(2):51–61, 1967.

99. Kalliomaki, J. L., Markkanen, T. K., and Mustonen, V. A. Sexual behavior after cerebral vascular accidents. *Fertility and Sterility* 12:156–158, 1961.

100. Goddess, E. D., Wagner, N. N., and Silverman, D. R. Poststroke sexual activity of CVA patients. *Medical Aspects of Human Sexuality* 13(3): 16–30, 1979.

101. Sicuteri, F., Del Bene, E., and Fonda, C. Sex, migraine, and serotonin interrelationships. *Monographs in Neural Sciences* 3:94–101, 1976.

102. Paulson, G. W. Headaches associated with orgasm. *Medical Aspects of Human Sexuality* 11(5):7–16, 1975.

103. Poskanzer, D. C., and Adams, R. D. Multiple Sclerosis and Other Demyelinating Diseases. In G. W. Thorn, R. D. Adams, E. Braunwald, K. J. Isselbacher, and R. G. Petersdorf (eds.), *Harrison's Principles of Internal Medicine* (8th ed.). New York: McGraw-Hill Book Co., 1977. Pp. 1900–1906.

104. Ivers, R. R., and Goldstein, N. P. Multiple sclerosis: A current appraisal of symptoms and signs. *Mayo Clinic Proceedings* 38:457–466, 1963.

105. Lundberg, P. O. Sexual dysfunction in patients with multiple sclerosis. *Sexuality and Disability* 1:218–222, 1978.

106. Lilius, H. G., Valtonen, E. J., and Wikström, J. Sexual problems in patients suffering from multiple sclerosis. *Journal of Chronic Diseases* 29:643–647, 1976.

107. Hartings, M. F., Pavlou, M. M., and Davis, F. A. Group counseling of MS patients in a program of comprehensive care. *Journal of Chronic Diseases* 29:65–73, 1976.

108. Steinbock, E. A., and Zeiss, A. M. Sexual counseling for cerebral palsied adults: Case report and further suggestions. *Archives of Sexual Behavior* 6:77–83, 1977.

109. Harper, P., Penny, R., Foley, T. P., Migeon, C. J., and Blizzard, R. M. Gonadal function in males with myotonic dystrophy. *Journal of Clinical Endocrinology and Metabolism* 35:852–856, 1972.

110. Herstein, A., Hill, R. H., and Walters, K. Adult sexuality and juvenile rheumatoid arthritis. *Journal of Rheumatology* 4:35–39, 1977.

111. Gilliland, B. G., and Mannik, M. Rheumatoid Arthritis. In G. W. Thorn, R. D. Adams, E. Braunwald, K. J. Isselbacher, and R. G. Petersdorf (eds.), *Harrison's Principles of Internal Medicine* (8th ed.). New York: McGraw-Hill Book Co., 1977. Pp. 2050–2061.

112. Chajek, T., and Fainaru, M. Behçet's disease: A report of 41 cases and a review of the literature. *Medicine* 54:179–196, 1975.

113. Kass, I., Updegraff, K., and Muffly, R. B. Sex in chronic obstructive pulmonary disease. *Medical Aspects of Human Sexuality* 6(2):33–42, 1972.

114. Agle, D. P., and Baum, G. L. Psychological aspects of chronic obstructive pulmonary disease. *Medical Clinics of North America* 61:749–758, 1977.

115. Dudley, D. L., Martin, C. J., and Holmes, T. H. Dyspnea: Psychologic and physiologic observations. *Journal of Psychosomatic Research* 11:325–339, 1968.

116. Dudley, D. L., Wermuth, C., and Hague, W. Psychosocial aspects of care in the chronic obstructive pulmonary disease patient. *Heart and Lung* 2:389–393, 1973.

117. Narayan, M., and Ferranti, R. Nerve conduction impairment in patients with respiratory insufficiency and severe chronic hypoxemia. *Archives of Physical Medicine and Rehabilitation* 59:188–192, 1978.

Sex and the Oncology Patient

If there has often been a relative neglect by health-care professionals of the sexual problems of patients with chronic illness, the lack of attentiveness to the sexuality of people with a malignancy is even more striking. It is often both comfortable and convenient for the physician to "forget" that oncology patients continue to have sexual needs and sexual feelings or easy to assume that such patients are no longer interested in sex. In addition, the physician who is questioned about sexual problems by a patient with a malignancy will find that relatively little research has been done in this area and thus will have few guidelines or sources of information to follow. This chapter presents an analysis of the types of sexual difficulties that oncology patients may face, accompanied by a more detailed look at the sexual effects of the medical or surgical management of certain types of malignancies.

Sexual Problems Associated with Malignancy

There is no simple way of summarizing the numerous factors associated with malignancy that may undermine sexual functioning for a variety of reasons. It is obvious that certain physical effects of malignancy—such as anemia, anorexia, muscle atrophy, and neurological impairment—are all likely to produce severe weakness and debility that may make sexual function difficult or impossible. Indeed, many of the methods used to treat malignancy—drugs, surgery, and radiation—may themselves precipitate sexual problems under certain circumstances.

For example, Weinstein and Roberts reported on the effects of surgery for rectal carcinoma on subsequent sexual function in 44 patients [1]. They noted that with an anterior rectal resection, in which the distal rectum was left intact following tumor removal, sexual functioning was undisturbed in both men and women. However, after abdominoperineal resections (including a wide excision of the entire rectum and its mesentery along with surrounding lymphatic tissue), all men who attempted intercourse were unable to obtain erections, although three women were able to participate in coitus and experience orgasm without difficulty. The authors attributed this difference to the fact that the pudendal nerves, left undisturbed by this surgery, constitute important components of female sexual responsivity, while in men the neurologic damage that occurs produces irreversible impotence.

In other instances, tumors may produce hormonal changes that alter sexual functioning. For example, feminization may occur in association with primary liver cancer, due to high levels of estrogen produced by hepatic interconversion [2]; and ectopic ACTH production by neoplasms (especially carcinoma of the lung, thymus, and pancreas) may lead to Cushing's syndrome [3]. Neurologic deficits may be frequently encountered with certain types of malignancy [4], posing yet another possible source of sexual problems.

However, psychological factors relating to the diagnosis of malignancy are also of major importance to the genesis of sexual difficulties and in many ways, far more complex and less predictable than the physical effects of this group of disorders. The discovery of malignancy is itself a highly traumatic event, immediately raising quite legitimate fears about survival. Although the reaction each patient (and his or her spouse, family, or sex partner) experiences is partly related to the particular type of malignancy and its prognosis, it is fair to say that the most common pattern of response includes simultaneous activation of anxiety, anger, and a sense of despair [5, 6]. This initial phase of reaction often includes a strong element of denial, which may go on to blend into a process of depersonalization wherein the cancer patient perceives himself or herself as apart from the body that betrayed them.

These early reactions to the diagnosis of malignancy are not surprising in light of the horrific mystery that surrounds our very use of the words "cancer" and "malignancy" in everyday life. Susan Sontag has written at length about this phenomenon:

Punitive notions of disease have a long history, and such notions are particularly active with cancer. There is the "fight" or "crusade" against cancer; cancer is the "killer" disease; people who have cancer are "cancer victims." Ostensibly, the illness is the culprit. But it is also the cancer patient who is made culpable. Widely believed psychological theories of disease assign to the luckless ill the ultimate responsibility both for falling ill and for getting well. And conventions of treating cancer as no mere disease but a demonic enemy make cancer not just a lethal disease but a shameful one [7].

Patients with a malignancy are caught in a bitter dilemma: While one source of fear is their knowledge of internal disarray, of neoplastic cells growing and upsetting the equilibrium and architecture of their body, this fear is coupled with an equally portentous fear of multilation, pain, and loss of physical strength resulting from treatment. No matter what scientific or prognostic evidence is available to address and assuage such dilemmas, the traumas attendant on the diagnosis of malignancy are undeniably present.

The patient during treatment often experiences physical discomfort and indignity, whether this results from surgery or from other forms of therapeutic intervention. For instance, the hair loss that frequently accompanies vincristine therapy [8] is likely to add one further dimension to problems of body-image the patient may be experiencing; the nausea and vomiting accompanying radiation therapy or chemotherapy are apt to provoke strong feelings of repulsion and a sense of loss of control of one's body. Grinker describes some additional aspects of the problems that may occur:

The dread of exposing oneself to one's spouse as crippled, damaged, incomplete or dying may cause sexual inhibition or abstinence. Intimacy and sexual bodily functions may be affected by shame and embarrassment. Mutilation (e.g., mastectomy) may make exposure and nudity extremely painful. Self-disgust may be displaced and projected onto the partner.... There may be an increase in the need for contact and reassurance or, on the other hand, outrage that the partner displays any interest in sex. In fact, normal interests may be seen as an invasion of the rights of the "damaged" person whose injury often (especially in "cured" cancers) may be more narcissistic than real. Lack of self-esteem and a relative feeling of emotional poverty in survivors may prevent the resumption of their previous relationships [6].

The impact of cancer on marital relationships has been a generally neglected topic, but there is evidence that cancer patients of both sexes experience an increased desire for physical closeness accompanied by a lowered interest in coitus [9].

Depression is a frequent accompaniment of malignancy [5, 6, 9, 10], although in this context depression may be viewed as a rather normal reaction [10]. While the patient is likely to overcome such a depression once it appears that a cure of the malignancy has been obtained, there may be a host of residual problems, including fear of recurrence, altered body-image, guilt, poor self-esteem, and marital conflict, that continue to influence the sexuality of patients following treatment of a malignancy. The management of each patient must include appropriate assessment of these potential problem areas combined with counseling individualized to suit the particular coping abilities each person has. Sensitivity, honesty, and empathy are the hallmarks of a successful approach to this aspect of patient care.

Mastectomy and Sex   Recent statistics from the National Cancer Institute indicate that breast cancer accounts for the highest annual incidence of female cancer (26 percent) and the largest proportion of annual cancer deaths in women (19 percent) [11]. Approximately 90,000 new cases of breast cancer occur each year, with a 65 percent five-year survival rate noted for breast cancer patients [11]. It has been estimated that a 20-year-old white female has an 8.24 percent probability of developing breast cancer in her lifetime; for nonwhite females, the probability is 5.42 percent [12].

There are a number of current controversies in the diagnosis and treatment of breast cancer that are beyond the scope of this discussion. The first issue is the value of mammography as a mass screening aid in the detection of breast cancer [13–15]; the second controversy is over the correct surgical approach to the patient with breast cancer, highlighted by the question of whether radical mastectomy should be employed for all breast cancer patients or if a simple mastectomy or "lumpectomy" (excision of the tumor and some surrounding tissue, leaving the breast relatively intact) might not be suitable in many cases of localized tumors [16–22]. The type of operation utilized to treat breast cancer may have important implications for the postoperative sexual adjustment of the patient, but little research data is currently available on which to base a conclusion in this regard.

Although it has been said that when breast cancer is discovered, a woman's first concern is for survival [23], in fact many conflicting emotions occur simultaneously. Fear of mutilation, anxiety about rejection by husband or sexual partner, and other feelings may arise quickly when the diagnosis of a breast tumor is made; as Bard and Sutherland point out, there is no uniform response pattern and no reliable way of predicting from past responses to stressful situations how a particular woman will cope with this news [24].

In our culture and in others, the breast is generally regarded as a symbol of femininity and attractiveness. The breast may function both as a source of nutrition and mother-infant bonding and as a source of sexual excitation. In the latter role, the breast not only receives afferent sexual stimuli for the woman but also may serve as a source of sexual arousal for the man. For these reasons, it is apparent that the surgical removal of one or both breasts may create numerous problems in subsequent psychosocial adaptation.

Witkin has effectively described one perspective of this situation:

It almost goes without saying that the difficulties the woman might have in accepting and accommodating to the loss of a breast arise in large measure from her fears of how others will respond. The pain of rejection increases with intimacy, and the woman's greatest fears revolve around the man with whom she is most intimate. What many women fear is not only rejection in the form of aversion or denial but also rejection in the form of pity; for whereas empathy and concern imply an awareness of the woman's feelings of loss and fear, pity implies a belief that the woman has *really* been diminished, and involves not a sharing of her feelings but a reinforcement of her fantasies of incompleteness and worthlessness [25].

Necessarily, one aspect of a woman's reaction to mastectomy depends on her concept of her own femininity and sexuality. A second component is her perception of her husband's or sexual partner's responses, while a third factor that must be recognized is the skill and sensitivity with which the health-care team provides information, support, and specific suggestions for postoperative rehabilitation.

The chronology of events leading up to mastectomy is such that many patients are uncertain as to whether they will have a simple breast biopsy or whether they will awaken from anesthesia after a more extensive surgical procedure. Polivy studied women's feminine self-concept in patients the day before surgery, six days after surgery, and 6 to 11 months later for women who underwent either breast biopsy alone or mastectomy [26]. She demonstrated that immediately after surgery, there was no change (from presurgery levels) in mastectomy patients' body-image or total self-image. Several months after surgery, however, body-image and self-image were diminished. In contrast, biopsy patients showed a decline in self-image immediately after surgery. Polivy attributed this difference to the fact that biopsy patients, once having discovered that they did not have cancer or need a mastectomy, no longer needed denial mechanisms and thus showed an immediate drop in self-image, whereas denial continued to operate in mastectomy patients during their period of hospitalization [26].

A pilot study conducted by the Masters & Johnson Institute recently examined the experiences of women who had previously undergone mastectomy in an attempt to develop a systematic data base about the impact of such surgery on sexual behavior and attitudes [27]. Only 4 out of 60 women reported having had discussions of how mastectomy might affect their sexuality with a physician or nurse prior to surgery or during their hospitalization for mastectomy; in sharp contrast was the fact that almost half the women queried indicated a desire to have had such discussions, but thought this to be an inappropriate topic since no health-care professional brought it up.

During the three-month period immediately after surgery, there were numerous changes noted in sexual behavior as compared to pre-mastectomy frequencies [27]. Forty-nine percent of the overall sample resumed intercourse within one month after hospital discharge, although a third of the women had not resumed intercourse as long as six months after hospitalization. The percentage of women experiencing orgasm during half or more of coital opportunities decreased following mastectomy from 61 percent to 45 percent, whereas the frequency of women never or rarely having coital orgasm rose from 17 percent prior to mastectomy to 40 percent in the first three months postmastectomy. The frequency of intercourse also decreased for women after mastectomy surgery: While 52 percent of subjects reported intercourse at least once a week before their illness, only 35 percent of the women reported continuing this coital rate during the first three months of recuperation. Women who frequently initiated intercourse prior to their mastectomy generally avoided such behavior after surgery; more than half of this group preferred to wait for their husband's or partner's initiation of sexual activity.

The frequency of breast stimulation as a part of sexual activity declined substantially in women after mastectomy [27]. This finding indicates both avoidance of the remaining breast by the husband or sexual partner and a marked preference on the part of some women who have had mastectomy not to receive breast stimulation. Breast and nipple stimulation decreased as a major source of sexual arousal for many women after their mastectomy and remained low an average of eight years following surgery. The number of women who never used the female-superior position for coitus tripled after mastectomy, indicating that the direct visual realization of the missing breast, which is most apparent in this position, was problematic for the woman, her partner, or both.

Although the role of the husband or sexual partner of the woman who has had a mastectomy has been widely recognized to be important in her process of psychosocial adjustment following surgery [23–27], the actual behavior of both husbands and patients indicated potential problems with acceptance. Thirty-eight percent of men had not viewed the incision site of the mastectomy within the first three months postoperatively [27]. Complete nudity during sexual activity decreased considerably on the woman's part, although this change may have reflected self-consciousness as well as lack of partner acceptance. Since other studies with cancer patients indicate that both patients and their spouses often experience increased desire for physical closeness but diminished interest in intercourse [9], it is not clear whether the husbands and wives are reacting similarly to the perceived needs of the situation or whether alternative explanations exist for such behavioral and attitudinal changes.

Wellisch and his colleagues found that while most men reported a good overall adjustment to their wife or sexual partner's mastectomy, a subgroup of men has marked difficulty in this regard [28]. These investigators noted that sexuality was often negatively affected after the mastectomy and identified the following points as being critical to the process of adjustment: (1) involvement of the men in the decision-making process regarding surgery; (2) frequency of hospital visits; (3) resumption of sexual activity ("problematic at best and traumatic at worst"); and (4) the man viewing his partner's body after surgery [28]. They suggested that an inhospital desensitization program during postoperative recovery with the man viewing the operative site and assisting in changes of dressings might facilitate the development of comfort and involvement [28].

The entire adjustment to mastectomy is not simply psychological. Depending on the type of operation performed, various complications may arise that place physical limitations on recuperation. For example, following radical mastectomy approximately 10 percent of patients develop troublesome and persistent lymphedema [29]. If metastatic disease is present, other therapeutic approaches may be combined with surgery—including radiation therapy, chemotherapy, hormone therapy, or endocrine ablative procedures—in each case involving the possibility of further complications that may create sexual problems. If women are treated by androgen administration, for instance, virilization and increased libido may occur; women treated by oophorectomy or hypophysectomy (removal of the pituitary) to induce remission will characteristically become estrogen-deficient and will usually have decreased vaginal lubrication and vaginal atrophy, which frequently cause dyspareunia.

As with all women undergoing operative procedures that may have an impact on sexuality, the attitudes and support offered by the health-care team are likely to play an important role in subsequent developments. Proper fitting of a breast prosthesis should be done in every applicable case. In addition, awareness of the possibility of reconstructive surgery of the breast after mastectomy offers the potential of minimizing psychological problems in the rehabilitation process [30]. Such reconstruction is a realistic endeavor in the case of women who have undergone less extensive surgery than the classic radical mastectomy with pectoral muscle excision and who have received early and adequate treatment for their cancer. Although it was previously a technically difficult process that required numerous admissions to the hospital, the advent of procedures such as the one-stage reconstruction operation using a silicone gel prosthesis has improved the situation considerably [31]. An example of the results attainable by two-stage

Figure 11-1. A 41-year-old woman 12 years after a modified radical mastectomy (right side) and 7 years after a Halsted radical mastectomy for intraductal carcinoma (left side). Results of two-stage bilateral breast reconstruction are shown (first stage: insertion of custom-made inflatable implants; second stage: bilateral areola-nipple reconstruction from labia majora grafts). (From Birnbaum and Olsen [31].)

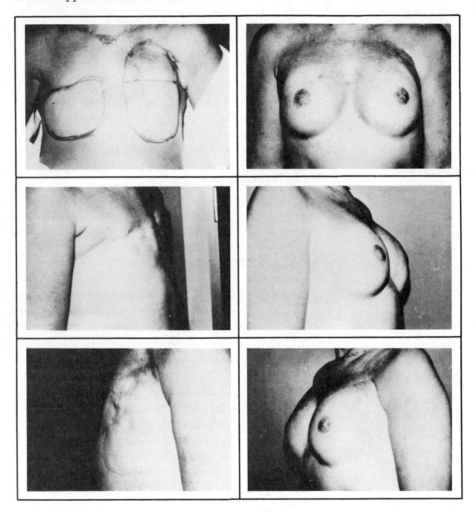

breast reconstruction with the use of inflatable implants is shown in Figure 11-1. Such operations can be performed after the chest wall tissue becomes freely movable (usually about six months after the mastectomy) or at the same time as the mastectomy is done; and it is possible to create an areola by using a skin graft from the vulva [32]. However, it is interesting to note that many men are quite negative in their attitudes toward breast reconstructive surgery [28]; this matter obviously requires careful discussion and airing of feelings.

Despite the provision of adequate amounts of information and support, some women (and their partners) will have initial sexual difficulties as a result of anxiety, self-consciousness, depression, poor self-esteem, or medical complications. An opportunity for discussion with a volunteer who has previously had a mastectomy, from an organization such as Reach to Recovery, is often of great benefit in the rehabilitation process. Nevertheless, it is important to be alert to patients who require referral for psychotherapy or who might benefit from sex therapy if their difficulties persist.

In the absence of any unique medical complications, the mastectomy patient will be physically able to resume sexual activity on discharge from the hospital. Determining her psychological readiness for such interaction, however, hinges upon many factors that must be assessed before giving instructions to any patient. Among these factors are the presence or absence of clinically significant depression, the prior pattern of sexual activity, the nature of the relationship between husband and wife, and the overall coping abilities of the patient. Encouraging the resumption of sexual activity too early may be psychologically devastating to both wife and husband; the physician should exercise careful judgment in this situation, rather than following rigid lines of instruction.

Gynecologic Oncology and Sex

Gynecologic tumors are not generally considered from the viewpoint of interfering with sexual function, although the clinician is apt to be faced with this aspect of patient care fairly frequently. In this diverse group of disorders, sexual problems may arise because of incapacitating illness; as a result of dyspareunia caused by mechanical factors, tissue necrosis, secondary infection, or surgical intervention; or as a consequence of cosmetic or psychological considerations. In each instance, an individualized assessment and approach to management are required; it is not always possible to resolve the sexual difficulty in a satisfactory manner.

Tumors of the Vulva

Epidermoid carcinoma (squamous cell carcinoma) of the vulva occurs primarily in postmenopausal women and comprises 90 percent or more of vulvar malignancies. In many patients with epidermoid carcinoma, leukoplakia of the vulva (tissue changes resulting in a distinctive premalignant microscopic appearance, and characterized grossly by grayish-white patchy lesions that may be erythematous and edematous) precedes the development of vulvar cancer. Adenocarcinoma, basal

Figure 11-2. Extent of a simple vulvectomy. (From R. Anderson and
L. A. Ballard, Jr., Tumors of the
Vulva, in C. E. Horton [ed.], *Plastic
and Reconstructive Surgery of the
Genital Area*, Boston: Little, Brown
and Co., 1973.)

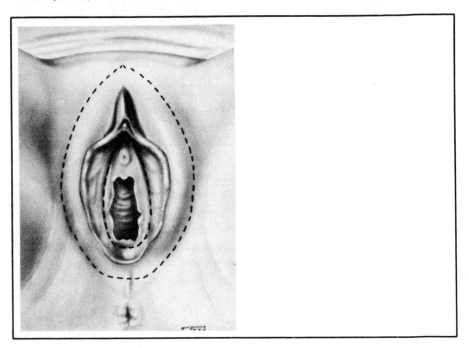

cell carcinoma, and malignant melanoma are less frequent causes of
vulvar malignancy.

Although leukoplakia or noninvasive carcinoma in situ may be
treatable by a simple vulvectomy (Fig. 11-2), the majority of vulvar
malignancies must be treated by radical vulvectomy, including regional
lymph node dissection (Fig. 11-3). Following such surgery, split-
thickness skin grafts are commonly used (Fig. 11-4); nevertheless, there
may be residual difficulties with dyspareunia, although the vagina
itself may not have been altered surgically. In some instances, postoperative introital stenosis may complicate the situation; this condition
can usually be remedied by simple surgical corrective techniques [33].
Younger patients undergoing split-thickness skin grafts after vulvectomy have sometimes been able to have successful vaginal deliveries
with episiotomies [34]; orgasmic responsiveness and physiologic aspects of sexual arousal are usually unimpaired by vulvectomy, even if
the surgery includes excision of a portion of the clitoris, which may
sometimes be involved by tumor.

Figure 11-3. Extent of a radical vulvectomy, showing (*above*) the area of
lymph node dissection (*shaded area*)
and (*below*) the perivulvar incision.
(From R. Anderson and L. A. Ballard, Jr., Tumors of the Vulva, In C.
E. Horton [ed.], *Plastic and Reconstructive Surgery of the Genital Area*,
Boston: Little, Brown and Co., 1973.)

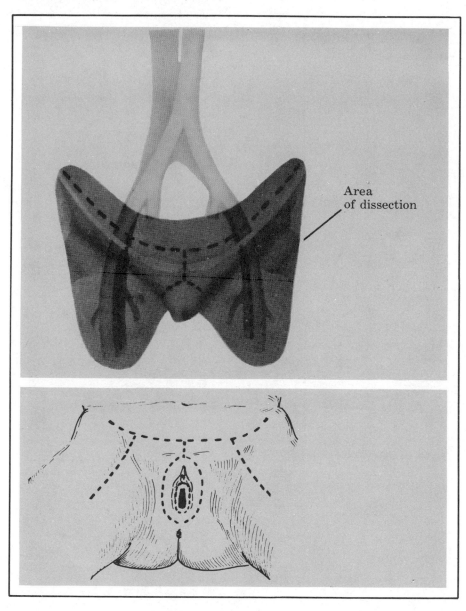

Area
of dissection

Figure 11-4. Skin graft of the post-vulvectomy defect. (*A*) Granulations ready for grafting; (*B*) 5 days after the graft; (*C*) result after healing. (From McGregor [34].)

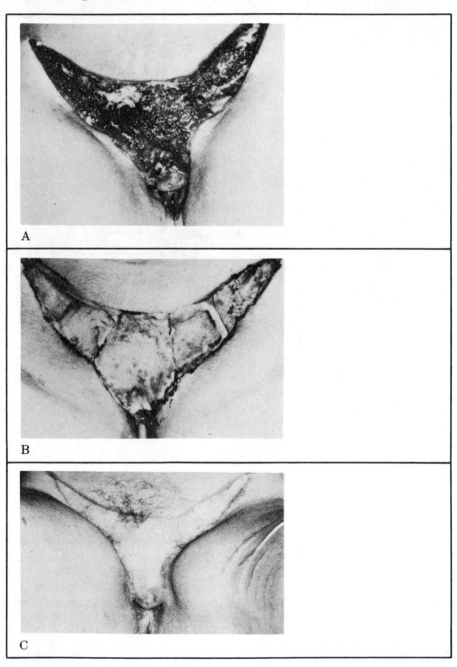

Tumors of the Vagina

Carcinoma of the vagina is a relatively infrequent occurrence, although other primary cancers may extend or metastasize to the vagina. Dyspareunia is typically a late symptom of vaginal carcinoma; early symptoms may include vaginal bleeding or discharge.

The use of radiation therapy in the treatment of vaginal carcinoma is problematic for several reasons: Tumors located in the outer half of the vagina are difficult to treat by radium implants; the bladder and rectum may be involved by postradiation complications because of their anatomic proximity; cure rates are discouragingly low. For these reasons, extensive pelvic surgery is often employed to treat vaginal cancers. Among such operations, the radical Wertheim hysterectomy with vaginectomy and pelvic lymphadenectomy may sometimes be used, although extensive lesions typically require pelvic exenteration procedures.

The outlook for continued sexual functioning after major vaginal surgery for malignancy is poor. Although noncoital function may continue to be a viable option, depending on the woman's subsequent health, intercourse may be precluded by the extent of surgery. If radiation therapy has been employed, radiation vaginitis, radiation proctitis, or fistula formation may also complicate the situation. In addition, the reaction of both the woman and her sexual partner to the illness itself as well as to posttreatment alterations of genital anatomy may lead to sexual difficulties. Nevertheless, in some instances postoperative vaginal anatomy may permit the resumption of coitus; in such circumstances it is often advisable to suggest the use of an artificial lubricant, since vaginal lubrication is likely to be significantly impaired as a result of scarring and changes in patterns of blood flow to the remaining vaginal mucosa. Evaluation of women undergoing such operations must be done on an individual basis. Women who are able to continue coitus may complain of diminished sexual arousal and loss of orgasmic responsiveness, although no studies are currently available describing the frequency of this outcome. Consideration should be given to the surgical creation of a neovagina whenever possible, with attention paid to postoperative use of dilators to prevent stenosis and appropriate use of antibiotic and hormone-containing creams.

Tumors of the Cervix and Uterus

Benign or malignant tumors of the uterus or cervix infrequently cause dyspareunia or interfere with the physiology of sexual excitation. Fibroids (benign smooth muscle tumors) produce such changes in association with their anatomic location and their size in only a small proportion of cases, although they may cause symptoms as a result of mechanical pressure, degeneration, or torsion. Polyps arising from the endometrium, the endocervix, or the cervix only rarely lead to sexual difficulty.

Carcinoma of the cervix is the second most common form of cancer in women (second only to breast cancer) and has received extensive discussion in the literature. This disorder is rare in women who have never had sexual intercourse, and both early marriage and early childbearing also appear to be epidemiologically associated with its occurrence [35]. The possible etiologic role of herpes virus, type 2, has been mentioned previously (see Chap. 8).

A detailed discussion of the natural history, staging, pathology, and treatment modalities for carcinoma of the cervix is beyond the scope of this chapter. However, it should be recognized that both radiation therapy and surgical approaches are commonly employed (sometimes together). Superradical surgical procedures are sometimes used when the bladder or rectum has been invaded by carcinoma; total pelvic exenteration and anterior exenteration (sparing the rectum but removing all other pelvic structures, including the bladder and vagina) are not compatible with continued coital function. Even when less drastic surgical measures are used, there may be profound effects on sexual function as a result of organic changes. The Wertheim hysterectomy removes the upper third of the vagina along with the uterus, so that the length of the vagina is reduced considerably and the functional elasticity of the vagina may be further decreased by scarring. The resumption of coitus in this circumstance must be done carefully, but undue delay postoperatively will only increase the fibrosis that occurs.

Fear may be a significant factor in coital difficulty following either radiation or surgery in the treatment of carcinoma of the cervix. In some instances, this may be related to either fear of recurrence of the malignancy [36] or to the man's fear of injuring his sexual partner or, rarely, to the man's fear of contracting cancer himself. Other psychological reactions may also limit sexual interest and sexual responsiveness; in each case, an adequate pretreatment sexual history will be useful in subsequent patient counseling.

Abitbol and Davenport studied the occurrence of sexual dysfunction after therapy for cervical carcinoma in 75 patients [37]. They found that the effects of radiation therapy were more deleterious than the effects of surgery: 22 of 28 women treated by radiation described either complete cessation of sexual activity (25 percent) or a marked decrease in frequency of sexual activity (53.6 percent), as compared with 2 of 32 women (6.3 percent) undergoing surgical treatment for cervical carcinoma. One-third of the women who received combined surgical and radiation therapy reported much less frequent sexual activity, but, interestingly, none described complete cessation. In almost every instance of sexual dysfunction reported in this study, significant vaginal and pelvic anatomic distortion was noted. The authors pointed out that even the women 65 years of age or older expressed interest in continuing sexual activity.

Malignancies involving the body of the uterus are also common; they generally require surgical removal for definitive therapy, although adjunctive radiation may be used preoperatively to reduce tumor size and eliminate secondary infection. For additional consideration of the sexual implications of hysterectomy, see Chapter 8.

Ovarian Tumors

Five percent of all cancers in women occur in the ovary [38]. Ovarian carcinoma is particularly problematic because diagnosis is often not made until relatively late in the course of the disease. Ovarian cysts and other benign tumors are also common clinical abnormalities. In general, ovarian tumors do not interfere with sexual function; exceptions to this observation include the following situations: (1) rupture of an ovarian cyst may cause acute abdominal pain or intra-abdominal hemorrhage; (2) torsion of an ovary containing a cyst or tumor may lead to chronic intermittent abdominal pain and dyspareunia; (3) rarely, ovarian tumors such as arrhenoblastomas and hilus cell tumors produce androgens and consequently lead to a state of defeminization followed by masculinization, including hirsutism, temporal baldness, clitoral hypertrophy, deepening of the voice, breast atrophy, and a masculine pattern of muscle development; and (4) ovarian carcinoma may lead to ascites, with resultant mechanical difficulties, or to a variety of endocrine abnormalities, with metabolic effects that disrupt sexual responsiveness or interest. In addition, certain types of ovarian tumors—in particular, the Stein-Leventhal (polycystic ovary) syndrome—may be accompanied by infertility, amenorrhea, obesity, and hirsutism, providing a number of features that are likely to lower a woman's self-esteem and body-image and focus anxieties on her reproductive problems.

Women with ovarian cancers that have metastasized may be treated with antineoplastic chemotherapy following surgery. Although the use of chemotherapy may significantly improve survival, the symptoms of the primary disease process and the side effects of chemotherapy both pose exceedingly difficult management problems. The physician working with patients in this category should be aware of the fact that despite their metastatic disease and fear of death, some patients may continue to desire sexual activity and may require counseling both to assist in dealing with physical problems that may arise (recurrent ascites, or cystitis and urethritis resulting from drug use, for example) and to provide reassurance and "permission" that it is all right to be sexual. If high doses of testosterone therapy are also employed, it should be recognized that libido may be increased even in the face of widespread disease.

Diethylstilbestrol
and Genital Tract
Abnormalities

Clear cell adenocarcinoma of the vagina, previously a rare form of malignancy, is currently being seen with increasing frequency in teenagers and young women who were exposed prenatally to diethylstilbestrol (DES), a synthetic hormone that was formerly used in women with problem pregnancies or threatened abortion [39, 40]. This malignancy is extremely rare prior to age 14 and peaks in incidence at approximately age 19; the cumulative risk for this type of cancer, through age 24, for diethylstilbestrol-exposed female subjects is estimated to be between 0.14 and 1.40 per thousand [41]. In addition, a substantial number of DES-exposed females have been found to have a condition of benign cervical and vaginal histologic changes, termed adenomatosis; a multi-institutional project found that 34 percent of 1,275 females who had been exposed to DES *in utero* had such abnormalities [42], although there is no current agreement as to whether such changes may predispose to the subsequent development of malignancy. Schwartz and Stewart [43] examined the psychological effects of DES exposure and noted that mothers who had received DES often experienced guilt and anxiety upon discovery of their daughters' condition; they also suggested that patients responded best when informed of their problem by their mothers and when the relationship between mother and daughter was good.

Further study of diethylstilbestrol has shown that males exposed *in utero* to this drug have an increased incidence of genital tract abnormalities. For example, 35 of 308 DES-exposed men had abnormalities of the testes, including 26 men with hypoplastic testes (17 of whom had a history of cryptorchidism) and 9 with capsular induration of the testes [44]. These abnormalities were significantly more frequent than those found among age-matched control subjects whose mothers did not receive DES. In addition, there were 4 cases of microphallus among the DES-exposed group and 64 cases of epididymal cysts; similarly, semen evaluation showed a reduction in sperm count and sperm motility in these men, raising the question of whether impaired fertility may be one additional consequence of DES exposure. Although preliminary evidence indicating a possible association between *in utero* DES exposure and testicular cancer has been obtained [44], there are a large number of methodological problems that must be satisfactorily addressed before a definitive answer may be obtained to the question of possible carcinogenicity of male *in utero* DES exposure.

Testicular Tumors

Testicular neoplasms may occur at any age but are most commonly encountered during the third and fourth decades. The frequency of testicular malignancy is considerably greater in cryptorchid testes than in descended testes, perhaps reflecting the adverse effects of prolonged exposure to a higher temperature than is present within the scrotum. Seminomas are the most common testicular neoplasms (accounting for 40 to 50 percent of the total), followed in frequency by teratocarcinomas (20 to 25 percent), embryonal carcinomas (15 to 20 percent), teratomas (1 to 5 percent), and interstitial cell tumors (1 to 5 percent) [45]. Although these tumors are relatively rare, accounting for only 1.5 percent of malignancies in males [46], they are of particular concern because of both their high mortality rate and their potentially serious impact on reproduction and sexuality.

The clinical presentation of patients with testicular neoplasms is extremely variable. Although most patients seek evaluation because of their discovery of a testicular mass, in other instances the presenting symptoms may be occasioned by metastatic disease, or the diagnosis may be made as part of an evaluation for infertility or a routine physical examination [46, 47]. Only half the patients present with testicular pain [47]; it is important for the physician to maintain a high index of suspicion about the possibility of a neoplasm in association with any testicular swelling or mass [46].

Surgical removal is generally indicated for testicular tumors; the ten-year survival rate for patients with seminoma treated by orchiectomy and irradiation to the lymphatic drainage areas is 90 percent [48]. Survival statistics are dramatically lower for other varieties of testicular neoplasms [49], although improvements are being slowly made with the use of a number of chemotherapeutic agents.

In cases of nonseminomatous testicular cancer, a high retroperitoneal lymphadenectomy is typically part of the treatment regimen. Kedia and coworkers reported that 49 of 52 men undergoing this procedure subsequently developed loss of ejaculation, although they continued to be orgasmic and to experience normal erectile function [50]. There was no evidence of retrograde ejaculation, since neither sperm nor fructose was found in urine specimens immediately after masturbation. Although two patients subsequently regained the ability to ejaculate—presumably due to regeneration of nerve fibers—it appears that there is a high risk of infertility following retroperitoneal lymphadenectomy. Patients wishing to retain the option of reproduction after such surgery might wish to consider freezing a number of preoperative semen specimens in a sperm bank, for subsequent use in artificial insemination.

In a retrospective questionnaire survey of patients following treatment for a variety of testicular tumors, Bracken and Johnson noted that only 12 of 37 married patients desired children after retroperitoneal lymphadenectomy, and in 7 of these 12 cases, successful pregnancy ensued [51]. However, these investigators found that 9 of 44 men experienced diminished libido after bilateral retroperineal lymphadenectomy and 6 men reported decreased sexual performance. Sexual function was affected in only 1 of 29 patients with seminoma treated by orchiectomy and radiation therapy.

Although these reports seem to indicate that impotence is a relatively uncommon occurrence in men following treatment for testicular neoplasms, such cases are not unusual in clinical practice. The precise explanation for impotence in this context is not always readily apparent; it occasionally may reflect a state of hypogonadism brought about by a combination of factors: orchiectomy, radiation therapy, and repeated courses of chemotherapy. When patients complain of diminished libido and impotence following treatment, measurement of their serum testosterone levels may show a marked deficiency. Since there is no evidence that testosterone replacement therapy will produce recurrence of tumor cells or accelerate tumor growth, we have treated several patients in this category with quite successful restoration of potency and libido following hormonal support.

Brief mention must be made of the emotional impact of a testicular neoplasm and its subsequent surgical removal. Many patients feel a strong sense of guilt related to their previous sexual practices and may entertain fallacious notions of causality that blame the occurrence of malignancy on masturbation, venereal disease, or an "overactive" sex life. These patients are likely to regard their illness as a form of punishment, leading them to markedly alter their subsequent sexual behavior. Other patients, with no such view of their illness, perceive their loss of one testis as making them "less than a man." These men (or boys) are likely to harbor high levels of anxiety about their sexual capabilities and often slip into a pattern of watching themselves during sexual interaction to see if they are functioning properly ("spectatoring," discussed in more detail on pages 480–481), thus placing themselves in a precarious position because of the distraction and loss of spontaneity that ensues. Similarly, the man who equates virility with fertility may be dismayed by loss of his ability to ejaculate or by infertility produced by drug effects or radiation therapy and may go on to develop impotence as a result of his anxieties related to reproduction.

It is important to include appropriate sexual counseling, both pre- and postoperatively, in the management of males being treated for testicular neoplasms. Ascertaining the specific types of anxieties that such patients (and their spouses) may have and addressing these anxieties in a factual, sensitive manner is often sufficient to reduce the sexual problems that such patients may face. Consideration may be given to the use of a biologically inert testicular prosthesis in unmarried men concerned about their physical appearance in future sexual relationships. Finally, it would be helpful for primary care physicians to instruct male patients in techniques of self-examination of the testes to detect masses or other lesions, since time of diagnosis is a crucial variable in treating testicular malignancies.

Cancer Chemotherapy   The chemical management of malignancy has advanced considerably in the past two decades, with notable results being attained in selected situations. However, the use of antineoplastic drugs is accompanied by a variety of undesirable side effects, some of which are chronic as well as acute. That remarkably little is known about the sexual effects such treatment regimens may produce reflects a combination of factors that include little research having been done in this area as well as reluctance on the part of physicians to inquire about the sexuality of cancer patients. Somewhat more information is available about the effects on fertility resulting from chemotherapy.

Cyclophosphamide has been reported to cause amenorrhea [52, 53] and to lead to ovarian failure due to direct destruction of ova and primary follicles [54–56]. Siris and coworkers found that cyclophosphamide was associated with aberrant pubertal development in two of nine leukemic girls [57]. In adult males, cyclophosphamide has been reported to be associated with diminished spermatogenesis and destruction of germinal cells of the testes [58, 59], while this drug may sometimes cause testicular atrophy in prepubertal or pubertal boys [60–62]. Penso and his colleagues found that plasma testosterone levels were entirely normal in seven male patients who were treated with cyclophosphamide prior to or during puberty, but spermatogenesis was severely affected in five of the seven boys one to four years after treatment [63]. In addition, cyclophosphamide causes a high incidence of urinary problems, including hemorrhagic cystitis and bladder fibrosis [64, 65].

Chlorambucil, which is sometimes used in the treatment of lymphomas, has been shown to produce gonadal toxicity in a variety of circumstances. Guersy and colleagues found that chlorambucil caused azoospermia in 17 of 21 adolescents or young men who had received this drug before or during puberty; they noted that azoospermia was a constant (and irreversible) feature in boys who received a total dose of more than 25 mg per kilogram of this drug [66]. Other workers have documented the severe alterations of spermatogenesis that occur in adults given chlorambucil [67]; recovery of spermatogenesis after the cessation of therapy appears to be a highly variable phenomenon [68]. Levels of circulating testosterone and luteinizing hormone are generally normal in men receiving chlorambucil, although FSH levels are sometimes elevated [69].

Vinblastine, used primarily in the treatment of malignant lymphomas, has been associated with diminished spermatogenesis but not with alterations of libido or potency [70]. Hormone levels are not affected by use of vinblastine, and Leydig cells remain morphologically normal [70]. Although *vincristine* may cause neurotoxicity [71] and hair loss [72], it is not known to affect testicular function directly [73]. *Cytosine arabinoside* has been found to produce gonadal toxicity in boys treated for acute lymphoblastic leukemia [61], and a variety of other drugs, including *busulphan* [74] and *procarbazine* [73], may also affect spermatogenesis. A recent study documented the development of gynecomastia, elevated gonadotropins, and lowered serum testosterone levels in pubertal boys who had received combination chemotherapy (mechlorethamine, vincristine, procarbazine, and prednisone) for Hodgkin's disease [73].

Additional studies of the toxicity of oncologic chemotherapy agents are needed to evaluate adequately the possible impact these drugs may have on sexual and reproductive function. It is a matter of regret that despite the widespread clinical use of these powerful medications, relatively little attention has been focused on issues so closely related to their use.

A Concluding Note on Patient Management

It is impossible to separate the emotional responses to cancer from the biomedical facts of each situation. To point out the life-threatening nature of malignancy and the concomitant reactions of uncertainty, anxiety, fear of death, fear of mutilation, anger, guilt, and diminished self-esteem is simply to acknowledge the obvious. However, health-care professionals have been reluctant to accept the idea that the terminally ill person may have sexual needs or sexual problems [75], leaving the patient without an adequate ally or resource to turn to for advice. The physician who works with people who have malignancies can help to change this anachronistic situation by letting patients know that it is permissible to talk about sexual concerns, no matter how mundane or out of place they may seem. The physician can also interact with other members of the health-care team (nurses, psychologists, social workers, clergy) in bringing to their awareness the sexual problems of patients.

It is important to recognize that illness may provide a welcome relief from the need for sexual interaction for some persons. Others will continue to participate in sex out of fear of losing their spouse's support or from fear of the spouse's turning to extramarital sex to release tension. More typically, the person affected by malignancy may want closeness and reassurance from his or her spouse or sexual partner: Even if coital activity is undesirable or physically precluded, hugging, touching, and intimacy that includes sexual contact may continue to be an important facet of life.

The following points of patient management are applicable:

1. Remember that the diagnosis of a malignancy does not put an end to the patient's sexuality.
2. Be informed about the nature of the tumor, including its anatomy, natural history, and prognosis with treatment.
3. Understand the problems that may arise in conjunction with cancer therapy, including surgery, radiation therapy, and chemotherapy.
4. Let the patient know that someone is interested in their sexual concerns.
5. Obtain a sexual history to determine pre-illness patterns of sexual behavior and responsiveness.
6. Discuss the potential limitations on sexual function resulting from surgery, drugs, or radiation therapy with each patient in a factual but positive manner.
7. Offer posttherapy counseling to each patient and his or her spouse or sexual partner regarding resumption of sexual activity. Be certain to individualize advice; be sensitive to the needs and values of each patient.

8. In patient followup, routinely inquire about sexual problems.
9. Be aware of the resource persons available for consultation or referral.

References

1. Weinstein, M., and Roberts, M. Sexual potency following surgery for rectal carcinoma: A followup of 44 patients. *Annals of Surgery* 185:295–300, 1977.
2. Kew, M. C., Kirschner, M. A., Abrahams, G. E., and Katz, M. Mechanism of feminization in primary liver cancer. *New England Journal of Medicine* 296:1084–1088, 1977.
3. Gomez-Uria, A., and Pazianos, A. G. Syndromes resulting from ectopic-hormone producing tumors. *Medical Clinics of North America* 59:431–440, 1975.
4. Walton, J. N. *Brain's Diseases of the Nervous System* (8th ed.). Oxford: Oxford University Press, 1977. Pp. 864–977.
5. Peck, A. Emotional reactions to having cancer. *American Journal of Roentgenology, Radium Therapy and Nuclear Medicine* 114:591–599, 1972.
6. Grinker, R. R. Sex and cancer. *Medical Aspects of Human Sexuality* 10(2):130–139, 1976.
7. Sontag, S. *Illness as Metaphor*. New York: Farrar, Straus & Giroux, 1978. P. 57.
8. Simister, J. M. Alopecia and cytotoxic drugs. *British Medical Journal* 2:1138, 1966.
9. Leiber, L., Plumb, M. M., Gerstenzang, M. L., and Holland, J. The communication of affection between cancer patients and their spouses. *Psychosomatic Medicine* 38:379–389, 1976.
10. Plumb, M. M., and Holland, J. Comparative studies of psychological function in patients with advanced cancer—I. Self-reported depressive symptoms. *Psychosomatic Medicine* 39:264–276, 1977.
11. Silverberg, E. Cancer statistics, 1978. *CA; Cancer Journal for Clinicians* 28:17–32, 1978.
12. Seidman, H., Silverberg, E., and Bodden, A. Probabilities of eventually developing and of dying of cancer. *CA; Cancer Journal for Clinicians* 28:33–46, 1978.
13. Strax, P., Venet, L., and Shapiro, S. Value of mammography in reduction of mortality from breast cancer in mass screening. *American Journal of Roentgenology, Radium Therapy and Nuclear Medicine* 117:686–689, 1973.
14. Bailar, J. C., III. Mammography: A contrary view. *Annals of Internal Medicine* 84:77–84, 1976.
15. Carbone, P. C. A lesson from the mammography issue. *Annals of Internal Medicine* 88:703–704, 1978.
16. Crile, G., Jr. Management of breast cancer: Limited mastectomy. *Journal of the American Medical Association* 230:95–98, 1974.
17. Anglem, T. J. Management of breast cancer: Radical mastectomy. *Journal of the American Medical Association* 230:99–105, 1974.

18. Crile, G., Jr. Management of breast cancer: Limited mastectomy (in rebuttal to Dr. Anglem). *Journal of the American Medical Association* 230:106–107, 1974.
19. Anglem, T. J. Management of breast cancer: Radical mastectomy (in rebuttal to Dr. Crile). *Journal of the American Medical Association* 230:108–109, 1974.
20. Marx, J. L. The continuing breast cancer controversy. *Science* 186:246–247, October 1974.
21. Robinson, G. N., Van Heerden, J. A., Payne, W. S., Taylor, W. F., and Gaffey, T. A. The primary surgical treatment of carcinoma of the breast: A changing trend toward modified radical mastectomy. *Mayo Clinic Proceedings* 51:433–442, 1976.
22. Crile, G., Jr. Results of conservative treatment of breast cancer at 10 and 15 years. *Annals of Surgery* 181:26–39, 1975.
23. Kent, S. Coping with sexual identity crises after mastectomy. *Geriatrics* 30:145–146, October 1975.
24. Bard, M., and Sutherland, A. M. Psychological impact of cancer and its treatment: IV. Adaptation to radical mastectomy. *Cancer* 8:656–672, 1955.
25. Witkin, M. H. Sex therapy and mastectomy. *Journal of Sex and Marital Therapy* 1:290–304, 1975.
26. Polivy, J. Psychological effects of mastectomy on a woman's feminine self-concept. *Journal of Nervous and Mental Disease* 164(2):77–87, February 1977.
27. Frank, D., Dornbush, R. L., Webster, S. K., and Kolodny, R. C. Mastectomy and sexual behavior: A pilot study. *Sexuality and Disability* 1:16–26, 1978.
28. Wellisch, D. K., Jamison, K. R., and Pasnau, R. O. Psychosocial aspects of mastectomy: II. The man's perspective. *American Journal of Psychiatry* 135:543–546, 1978.
29. Grabois, M. Rehabilitation of the postmastectomy patient with lymphedema. *CA; Cancer Journal for Clinicians* 26:75–79, 1976.
30. Chong, G. C., Masson, J. K., and Woods, J. E. Breast restoration after mastectomy for cancer. *Mayo Clinic Proceedings* 50:453–458, 1975.
31. Birnbaum, L., and Olsen, J. A. Breast reconstruction following radical mastectomy, using custom designed implants. *Plastic and Reconstructive Surgery* 61:355–363, 1978.
32. Snyderman, R. K. Reconstruction of the breast after mastectomy. *CA; Cancer Journal for Clinicians* 27:360–362, 1977.
33. Jimerson, G. K. Management of postoperative introital and vaginal stenosis. *Obstetrics and Gynecology* 50:719–722, 1977.
34. McGregor, I. A. Skin Grafts to the Vulva. In C. E. Horton (ed.), *Plastic and Reconstructive Surgery of the Genital Area*. Boston: Little, Brown and Co., 1973. Pp. 605–612.
35. Green, T. H., Jr. *Gynecology—Essentials of Clinical Practice*. Boston: Little, Brown and Co., 1977.
36. Amias, A. G. Sexual life after gynaecological operations: I. *British Medical Journal* 2:608–609, 1975.

37. Abitbol, M. M., and Davenport, J. H. Sexual dysfunction after therapy for cervical carcinoma. *American Journal of Obstetrics and Gynecology* 119:181–189, 1974.

38. Barber, H. R. K., Kwon, T.-H., Buterman, I., and Kakarla, R. Current concepts in the management of ovarian cancer. *Journal of Reproductive Medicine* 20:41–50, 1978.

39. Herbst, A. L., Ulfelder, H., and Poskanzer, D. C. Adenocarcinoma of the vagina: Association of maternal stilbestrol therapy with tumor appearance in young women. *New England Journal of Medicine* 284:878–881, 1971.

40. Herbst, A. L., Poskanzer, D. C., Robboy, S. J., Friedlander, L., and Scully, R. E. Prenatal exposure to stilbestrol: A prospective comparison of exposed female offspring with unexposed controls. *New England Journal of Medicine* 292:334–339, 1975.

41. Herbst, A. L., Cole, P., Colton, T., Robboy, S. J., and Scully, R. E. Age-incidence and risk of diethylstilbestrol-related clear cell adenocarcinoma of the vagina and cervix. *American Journal of Obstetrics and Gynecology* 128:43–50, 1977.

42. O'Brien, P. C., Noller, K., Robboy, S. J., Barnes, A. B., Kaufman, R., Tilley, B., and Townsend, D. E. Vaginal epithelial changes in young women enrolled in the national cooperative diethylstilbestrol-adenosis (DESAD) project. Cited in U.S. DHEW Publication No. (NIH) 79-1688, *DES Task Force Summary Report*. [See ref. 44.]

43. Schwartz, R. W., and Stewart, N. B. Psychological effects of diethylstilbestrol exposure. *Journal of the American Medical Association* 237:252–254, 1977.

44. U.S. Department of Health, Education, and Welfare. *DES Task Force Summary Report*. DHEW Publication No. (NIH) 79-1688. Pp. 59–64.

45. Sulak, M. H. Cancer of the urogenital tract: Classification of different pathologic types. *Journal of the American Medical Association* 213:91–93, 1970.

46. Markland, C. Special problems in managing patients with testicular cancer. *Urologic Clinics of North America* 4:427–451, 1977.

47. Patton, J. F., Hewitt, C. B., and Mallis, N. Diagnosis and treatment of tumors of the testis. *Journal of the American Medical Association* 117:2194–2198. 1959.

48. Berkson, J., and Gage, R. P. Calculation of survival rates for cancer. *Mayo Clinic Proceedings* 25:270–286, 1950.

49. Rubin, P. Cancer of the urogenital tract: Testicular tumors. *Journal of the American Medical Association* 213:89–90, 1970.

50. Kedia, K. R., Markland, C., and Fraley, E. F. Sexual function after high retroperitoneal lymphadenectomy. *Urologic Clinics of North America* 4:523–528, 1977.

51. Bracken, R. B., and Johnson, D. E. Sexual function and fecundity after treatment for testicular tumors. *Urology* 7:35–38, 1976.

52. Fosdick, W. M., Parsons, J. L., and Hill, D. F. Preliminary report: Long-term cyclophosphamide therapy in rheumatoid arthritis. *Arthritis and Rheumatism* 11:151–161, 1968.

53. Fries, J. F., Sharp, G. C., McDevitt, H. O., and Holman, H. R. Cyclophos-

phamide therapy in connective tissue disease (abstract). *Clinical Research* 18:134, 1970.

54. Miller, J. J., III, and Cole, L. J. Changes in mouse ovaries after prolonged treatment with cyclophosphamide. *Proceedings of the Society for Experimental Biology and Medicine* 133:190–193, 1970.

55. Miller, J. J., III, Williams, G. F., and Liessring, J. C. Multiple late complications of therapy with cyclophosphamide, including ovarian destruction. *American Journal of Medicine* 50:530–535, 1971.

56. Warne, G. L., Fairley, K. F., Hobbs, J. B., and Martin, F. I. R. Cyclophosphamide-induced ovarian failure. *New England Journal of Medicine* 289:1159–1162, 1973.

57. Siris, E. S., Leventhal, B. G., and Vaitukaitis, J. L. Effects of childhood leukemia and chemotherapy on puberty and reproductive function in girls. *New England Journal of Medicine* 294:1143–1146, 1976.

58. Miller, D. G. Alkylating agents and human spermatogenesis. *Journal of the American Medical Association* 217:1662–1665, 1971.

59. Fairley, K. F., Barrie, J. U., and Johnson, W. Sterility and testicular atrophy related to cyclophosphamide therapy. *Lancet* 1:568–569, 1972.

60. Hyman, L. R., and Gilbert, E. F. Testicular atrophy in a prepubescent male after cyclophosphamide therapy. *Lancet* 2:426–427, 1972.

61. Arneil, G. C. Cyclophosphamide and the prepubertal testis. *Lancet* 2:1259–1260, 1972.

62. Lendon, M., Hann, I. M., Palmer, M. K., Shalet, S. M., and Jones, P. H. M. Testicular histology after combination chemotherapy in childhood for acute lymphoblastic leukaemia. *Lancet* 2:439–441, 1978.

63. Penso, J., Lippe, B., Ehrlich, R., and Smith, F. G., Jr. Testicular function in prepubertal and pubertal male patients treated with cyclophosphamide for nephrotic syndrome. *Journal of Pediatrics* 84:831–836, 1974.

64. Liedberg, C. F., Rausing, A., and Langeland, P. Cyclophosphamide hemorrhagic cystitis. *Scandinavian Journal of Urology and Nephrology* 4:183–190, 1970.

65. Johnson, W. W., and Meadows, D. C. Urinary-bladder fibrosis and telangiectasia associated with long-term cyclophosphamide therapy. *New England Journal of Medicine* 284:290–294, 1971.

66. Guersy, P., Lenoir, G., and Broyer, M. Gonadal effects of chlorambucil given to prepubertal and pubertal boys for nephrotic syndrome. *Journal of Pediatrics* 92:299–303, 1978.

67. Richter, P., Calamera, J. C., Morgenfeld, M. C., Kierzenbaum, A. L., Lavieri, J. C., and Mancini, R. E. Effect of chlorambucil on spermatogenesis in the human with malignant lymphoma. *Cancer* 25:1026–1030, 1970.

68. Cheviakoff, S., Calamera, J. C., Morgenfeld, M. C., and Mancini, R. E. Recovery of spermatogenesis in patients with lymphoma after treatment with chlorambucil. *Journal of Reproduction and Fertility* 33:155–157, 1973.

69. Kolodny, R. C. Unpublished data, 1978.

70. Vilar, O. Effect of Cytostatic Drugs on Human Testicular Function. In R. E. Mancini and L. Martini (eds.), *Male Fertility and Sterility*. New York: Academic Press, 1974. Pp. 423–440.

71. Watkins, S. M., and Griffin, J. P. High incidence of vincristine-induced neuropathy in lymphomas. *British Medical Journal* 1:610–612, 1978.

72. O'Brien, R., Zelson, J. H., Schwartz, A. D., and Pearson, H. A. Scalp tourniquet to lessen alopecia after vincristine (letter). *New England Journal of Medicine* 283:1469, 1970.

73. Sherins, R. J., Olweny, C. L. M., and Ziegler, J. L. Gynecomastia and gonadal dysfunction in adolescent boys treated with combination chemotherapy for Hodgkin's disease. *New England Journal of Medicine* 299:12–16, 1978.

74. Calabresi, P., and Parks, R. E., Jr. Alkylating Agents, Antimetabolites, Hormones, and Other Antiproliferative Agents. In L. S. Goodman and A. Gilman (eds.), *The Pharmacological Basis of Therapeutics* (5th ed.). New York: Macmillan Publishing Co., 1975. P. 1266.

75. Wasow, M. Human sexuality and terminal illness. *Health and Social Work* 2:105–121, 1977.

Psychiatric disorders are frequently associated with alterations in sexual behavior and sexual function. Most clinicians are well aware that many depressed patients experience loss of libido, but they may be less cognizant of the impact other varieties of psychiatric problems may have on sexuality. Recognizing that there is considerable controversy in contemporary thinking regarding both the nosology and the etiology of psychiatric illness, the purpose of this chapter is to examine the patterns of sexual effects of psychiatric illness while deliberately refraining from addressing a number of theoretical and diagnostic issues that have already been closely scrutinized by other authors.

Affective Disorders

Affect may be defined as the emotions accompanying a state of being, an action, or a thought. The emotions or feelings that affect comprises may be sustained, episodic, or transient: The human condition is generally marked by shifts of mood, a changing balance between pleasure and pain, and a certain degree of relativism in the values attached to these feelings. Affect undeniably influences both behavior and psychomotor function; it is from this perspective that an examination of the clinical manifestations of mood disorders and their impact on sexuality is undertaken.

Depression

While both the family practitioner and the office psychiatrist are apt to encounter depression in their patients more frequently than other psychiatric disturbances, the term *depression* is confusing since it may be used in many different ways. First, it may be used descriptively to apply to mood alone. However, depressed mood (as distinct from sadness) is usually only one of the symptoms of a depressive syndrome. The American Psychiatric Association's *Diagnostic and Statistical Manual of Mental Disorders* (DSM-II) distinguishes between "depressive neurosis," "involutional melancholia," and "manic-depressive illness" [1], thus confusing a severity assessment with an etiologic assumption and a phenomenologically descriptive term. A useful schema of classification skirts these issues to focus on the syndrome as it may or may not be accompanied by other conditions. In this modern schema, primary affective disorders are those occurring in persons without a previous history of psychiatric disorder (other than depression or mania), while secondary affective disorders are those appearing in patients with another preexisting psychiatric illness [2]. The diagnostic classification of affective disorders by this system is independent of the severity or etiology of the mood disorder. In other nosologic approaches, a distinction is drawn between psychotic and neurotic depression on the basis of psychopathologic manifestations such as hallucinations, delusions, and ideas of reference [3–7] or between endogenous and reactive depression, with reactive depressions characterized as those arising in relation to external stress events such as bereavement or illness, and endogenous depressions characterized as those that appear independently of environmental triggering mechanisms and have a characteristic symptom cluster [8]. Finally, the relatively recent distinction between unipolar affective disorders (a category that includes patients who have had only depressive episodes) and bipolar affective disorders (patients who have been manic, whether depression occurs or not) has been gaining in acceptance and may be used descriptively in combination with the classification of primary and secondary affective disorders [2, 7, 8]. While it is beyond the scope of this chapter to dwell further upon these nosologic matters, it is pertinent to note that the boundary between normal affect and depression is not always clearly delineated: The clinician should routinely maintain a high index of alertness to the possibility of depression in his or her patients.

Depression that appears to be unduly persistent or pervasive in a person's life is likely to be characterized by other features in addition to the mood disturbance alone. Anhedonia, the inability to experience pleasure, is often a prominent contrapuntal theme interwoven with the sense of gloom, loneliness, and despondency that marks the clinical syndrome of depression. The depressed person typically exhibits a loss of appetite and physical energy; sleep disturbances—insomnia or hypersomnia—are common; and the ability to concentrate is often impaired. Speech, memory, and motor activity may each be affected by depression, and psychosomatic symptoms of a widely varied nature may appear for the first time or become more prominent as depression heightens. Impaired self-esteem, a sense of hopelessness and helplessness, and guilt are also commonly seen. Depression is frequently attended by suicidal ideation and in its more dramatic dimensions may precipitate suicide attempts or actual suicide.

Current epidemiologic evidence indicates that approximately 15 to 20 percent of the general adult population will experience depressive episodes sometime during their lives [8–10]. Depression occurs more frequently in women than in men [11, 12] and, although it is now apparent that depression can occur at any age, the preponderance of cases are seen during adulthood.

The clinical course of depression characteristically resolves in a matter of months. The older literature, indicating a mean duration of depressive episodes of six to eight months, probably requires revision in light of the more recent trend toward diagnosing depression in milder cases [8]. Murphy and his colleagues found, in a longitudinal study of patients with primary affective disorders, that 16 percent remained chronically depressed over a five-year period, 24 percent had no recurrence of depression, and 60 percent experienced further depressive episodes with durations varying from two weeks to one year [13]. On the other hand, Lundquist found that two-thirds of depressed patients had only a single episode [14]. There is no current method of accurately predicting which patients are most vulnerable to relapses.

The sexual impact of depression varies considerably from person to person and is not always a reflection of the severity of the depression as measured by other criteria. Some depressed persons who continue to function reasonably well in certain aspects of life show a complete loss of interest in sex; others who have difficulty with many facets of their lives continue to function sexually much as they had done before becoming depressed. The explanation for this degree of variability is not known, but it should be recognized that factors such as the sexual behavior of the partner or spouse and the patient's attitudes toward sex (recreation or obligation, habit or occasional event) will certainly play a part, in concert with the overall depressive symptomatology, in the patient's sexual relationships and sexual behavior.

The majority of depressed patients experience a significant reduction of libido. This is in fact the hallmark of depression from a sexual viewpoint, since many depressed persons, although uninterested in sex—and frequently not deriving much gratification from sexual activity—continue to be able to function sexually in a physiologic sense. It is common to find that the depressed patient has few sexual fantasies or thoughts about sex; it is also common to find a significant decrease in initiatory sexual behavior, although the sexual receptivity of depressed persons is somewhat less affected. Mechanisms of sexual arousal (erectile function in the male and vaginal lubrication in the female) are more likely to be intact than to be impaired, but often the perception of sexual arousal is negatively affected.

While approximately 70 percent of depressed patients have impaired libido, sexual dysfunction per se occurs in fewer than one-third of depressed patients. Woodruff and his colleagues found that impotence occurred in 23 percent of men with a primary affective disorder [15]. Tamburello and Seppecher noted that the capacity for erectile response in depression was only slightly diminished from predepressive levels [16]. In a series of 40 consecutive male patients with unipolar depression, impotence was reported by 11 men (27.5 percent) [17]. No studies of sexual responsivity in depressed women have been conducted to date, but it is our clinical impression that only a minority of these women become anorgasmic. Whether depression occurs more frequently in women who are sexually dysfunctional than in those with normal sexual function is an important question that cannot be answered on the basis of present data. Evidence that a socially conditioned cognitive set against assertiveness (a sense of "learned helplessness") is a common pattern among women and may be related to the increased occurrence of depression in females [18, 19] may prove relevant in this regard, since learned helplessness may also delimit sexual responsivity.

When sexual dysfunction occurs as a result of depression, its existence may be masked by a variety of behavioral and relationship problems. For instance, the depressed person may withdraw from social interaction with others, creating a situation that itself lessens opportunities for sexual activity and emotional intimacy; sometimes this withdrawal may be misjudged by the spouse or sexual partner as a sign of diminishing affection or sexual attractiveness. When sexual difficulty is recognized, it may be mistakenly attributed to coexisting problems that are, in fact, simply other manifestations of the underlying depression—for example, impotence may be correlated with somatic complaints, impaired sexual arousal may be linked to insomnia, and low libido may be explained as a reaction to a specific stress event that may have actually triggered the depression.

Depression may be accompanied by changes in sexual behavior that are unusual for the affected person. Although the frequency of these changes is undoubtedly less than that seen in manic patients, exhibitionism, pedophilia, homosexuality, incest, and sexual delusions may sometimes be encountered in association with depression. In addition, depression is quite common in transsexual patients. The depressed individual may initiate an affair to stimulate both mood and sexual performance.

It should be recognized that depression can occur as a result of prior sexual problems, although typically it is a mild depression that dissipates dramatically with successful resolution of the sexual difficulty [20]. Since these cases of depression are likely to be recalcitrant to pharmacologic management, it is important for clinicians to differentiate between instances of secondary depression triggered by the frustrations and lowered self-esteem that often accompany sexual difficulties and situations in which sexual problems occur as a result of the onset of depression. More typically, sexual difficulties associated with depression are secondary to the affective disorder and will resolve only when the depression responds to treatment or remits in the course of time.

Increasing evidence has been gathered in recent years in the search for possible biochemical or neuroendocrine explanations for depression. There are some data suggesting a possible genetic basis for depression [21–24], and a mounting literature describes a number of theories relating affective disorders to catecholamine levels and a variety of other hormonal abnormalities [25–38]. The most compelling of these hypotheses suggests that depression is frequently associated with an absolute or relative deficiency of catecholamines—particularly norepinephrine—at functionally important adrenergic receptor sites in the brain [25, 26]. Other investigators have found a relative deficiency of serotonin in depressed patients and theorized a causal mechanism to this biochemical abnormality [39]. Reports of altered growth hormone secretory dynamics [35, 36, 38] and altered thyroid and gonadal function in depressed patients have been less thoroughly documented [34, 37, 38], but the general inference is clearly that an underlying biochemical abnormality or predisposition may be present. Since the hypothalamus and limbic systems are obviously important in the control of functions that are frequently disturbed in depression—including appetite, sleep, mood regulation, and libido—further progress in this area of investigation may provide additional insights into the clinical management of depressed patients.

Patients with depression usually experience improvement both in libido and in their enjoyment of sexual activity when their mood lifts during a course of appropriate drug therapy. However, about 5 percent of depressed patients treated with tricyclic agents develop a paradoxic sexual response consisting of a deterioration of sexual functioning despite obvious clinical amelioration of most other symptoms (see Chap. 13). In such cases, libido usually improves but sexual function either remains disrupted or may actually worsen: In fact, many of these patients had relatively little disruption of their libido or sexual functioning associated with the depression itself. There is no current explanation of this phenomenon.

The medical management of depression must be individualized to suit the needs of each patient. While chemotherapy and electroconvulsive therapy (ECT) both offer highly effective results [2, 8], psychotherapy may be a useful adjunct to the social reintegration of the depressed patient and may be necessary to bolster self-esteem and improve residual problems of anxiety. Sex therapy is certainly indicated for patients who continue to experience sexual difficulties after the resolution of a depressive phase; in selected cases of mildly depressed patients not significantly impaired in cognitive function, sex therapy may be judiciously employed during the acute depressive episode.

Mania

The clinical features of mania typically include inappropriate and sustained elation or euphoria, hyperactivity, flight of ideas, accelerated speech, and impulsive behavior. Patients who are hypomanic evidence these same features but in a less florid fashion. The manic patient often has a heightened sense of self-esteem and a tendency to grandiosity and exaggeration; in 10 to 20 percent of patients, delusional thinking, hallucinations, and ideas of reference may be seen [2, 8]. Poor judgment is a characteristic finding in mania—not infrequently, patients may deplete their financial resources by making unusual purchases, may resign from their jobs, or may embark on a variety of new and poorly conceived projects simultaneously.

Sexual behavior in mania is often profoundly affected. Both manic men and women have a strong tendency to hypersexual behavior [40, 41], which may sometimes be an early manifestation of this disorder [42]. Ordinary social and sexual inhibitions may be shattered during a bout of mania, with patients of either sex undertaking multiple, often impulsively chosen sexual partners, disrobing in public settings, or engaging in masturbatory activity in inappropriate locales. Hospitalized manic patients may disrupt the psychiatric ward by such display activity or by direct attempts at engaging in overt sexual interaction with hospital staff members or fellow patients.

Tsuang reported a 30 percent rate of hypersexuality in manic patients and a 15 percent rate of diminished sexual drive [42]. Winokur and his colleagues found decreased libido in 13 percent of 61 hospitalized manic patients, whereas 65 percent demonstrated hypersexuality [43]. Spalt noted that married patients with bipolar affective disorder tend to have a greater number of extramarital affairs than unipolar patients [44]. However, there has been relatively little systematic study of the details of sexual behavior or sexual function during mania.

In our limited experience, impotence has been occasionally observed in manic men, although this is certainly not a usual finding. Recent evidence that lithium carbonate, quite useful in the treatment and prophylaxis of mania, may be associated with lowered levels of circulating testosterone [45] is concordant with our own clinical observations and may partially explain the fact that a substantial number of men notice a relative suppression of their libido while using lithium. Studies of the effect of lithium on the hypothalamic-pituitary-ovarian axis have not been conducted to date.

Sex therapy is contraindicated in cases of uncontrolled mania, but in certain instances it may be reasonably attempted. In hypomanic patients without delusional thinking or in patients well controlled by chemotherapy, sex therapy may have a role. In cases of these types, regardless of the underlying sexual difficulty, a great deal of therapeutic attention must generally be given to matters of communication, since marriages in which one person has recurrent bouts of mania—frequently associated with depressive episodes as well—may be severely strained.

Schizophrenia

Defining schizophrenia is no easy matter, for a variety of diagnostic criteria and labels have been employed by different authorities. Following the descriptions of Woodruff and his colleagues [2], we use the term *schizophrenia* to refer to a chronic disorder marked at least intermittently by delusions and hallucinations, thought disorders, and blunted affect; while we use the term *schizophreniform* to refer to an illness in which the symptoms tend to be episodic and of acute onset, affective symptoms are prominent, and the prognosis is considerably better than in schizophrenia. In patients with schizophreniform disorders, sexual behavior and sexual functioning are generally undisturbed between acute episodes of illness; during exacerbations, the schizophreniform patient is likely to be somewhat confused as well as contending with affective problems, with these two features contributing prominently to the occurrence of sexual difficulties. Sex therapy during exacerbations is not advisable.

There is considerable disagreement about the sexual status of schizophrenic patients. As Arieti points out, this may be due to the fact that a change has been noted in the sexual behavior of schizophrenics in the United States over the past 15 years:

Whereas until approximately 15 years ago sexual activity and acting out were relatively rare in schizophrenics, recently they have become a common occurrence both in hospitalized and nonhospitalized patients. Sexual activity of the schizophrenic used to be so limited compared to that of normal people as to induce even psychiatrists of such high quality as Sandor Rado to believe that the schizophrenic was not interested in sexual pleasure or in any pleasure at all; he was suffering from anhedonia. Other psychiatrists interpreted this lack of sexual activity to be part of the schizophrenic withdrawal, and, in prepsychotic states, to be part of the schizoid personality, which seriously limited interpersonal contacts of any kind. . . . Now, at least in the United States, the beginning of a schizophrenic episode is often characterized by increased sexual behavior [45].

Arieti goes on to observe that promiscuity is common in schizophrenic men and women and overt displays of seductiveness are frequently seen. It is not certain that this statement would hold true of narrowly defined schizophrenics. To the extent that it may be so, this changing pattern may be in part related to changing social and environmental stimuli; in addition, increased sexual activity by the schizophrenic may be a way of maintaining contact with the real world [45].

Berardi and Garske have recently demonstrated that nonparanoid schizophrenic outpatient men show evidence of higher sexual arousal on exposure to visual slides with sexual content than do nonschizophrenic men [46]. These workers postulated that lessened ego defensiveness in schizophrenia accounted for this difference, which also would seem to refute the idea that anhedonia is a prominent feature of schizophrenia.

Sexual dysfunction is not a common feature of schizophrenia, although incidental coexistence of these disorders may occur. Reports of the incidence of sexual dysfunction in schizophrenia may understandably be underestimates because of the existence of greater problems. When sexual dysfunction occurs in schizophrenia, sex therapy is generally not indicated for a variety of reasons. Most important, the risk of acute decompensation precipitated by the stresses and intensity of sex therapy is constantly present, even with patients who appear to be in relatively good control. In addition, the disordered thinking, interpersonal difficulties, and impaired contact with reality that are hallmarks of schizophrenia are likely to reduce significantly the possible effectiveness of this treatment approach. In selected cases of paranoid schizophrenia, if the therapists adequately define the paranoid ideation and refrain from treading on this area of the patient's thinking, sex therapy may be conducted with a minimum degree of difficulty. Patients with schizophreniform disease are far more likely to be amenable to sex therapy during remission.

The phenothiazines have significantly improved the management of schizophrenia (for a discussion of the sexual effects of this class of drugs, see Chap. 13) but at the same time have created a number of problems. Some patients who were previously institutionalized have now been discharged on drug maintenance and may be particularly vulnerable to sexual abuse. In at least some instances, this group of schizophrenic patients may turn to prostitution as a source of economic support; in other cases, they may become the victims of sexual assault. Although no formal studies of this aspect of schizophrenia have been conducted to date, it is obviously a matter requiring attention.

Hysteria

Hysteria is a disorder that primarily affects females and is characterized by a multiplicity of somatic symptoms without an underlying organic pathologic condition; its onset is usually before age 30. Symptoms are typically recounted by the hysteric patient in a dramatic fashion but often are not explainable by anatomic and physiologic principles. Because hysteric patients seek repeated medical attention, being firmly convinced of the physical origins of their distressful symptoms, they are frequently hospitalized and undergo a significantly greater number of surgical procedures than age-matched healthy controls [2]. Conversion symptoms may occur in virtually any psychiatric illness and are therefore much more frequent than is the disorder of hysteria; it is important to distinguish between these phenomena.

The word *hysteria* derives from the Greek word for uterus: In ancient times, hysteria was thought to be caused by a wandering uterus [47]. According to Vieth, sweet-smelling substances were inserted into the vagina to induce the wandering uterus to return to its proper anatomic location in the belief that this would ameliorate symptoms [48]. There is no present agreement as to the etiology of hysteria, but many authors believe that sexual conflicts may play a causative role [47, 49].

Perley and Guze documented a characteristic pattern of symptoms that occur in hysteria [50]; they found that 52 percent of hysteric women complain of dyspareunia, 24 percent are nonorgasmic, 44 percent exhibit sexual indifference or low libido, and 48 percent report both dysmenorrhea and irregular menses. Perhaps for this reason, gynecologic surgery accounts for a high percentage of the unnecessary operations that such patients undergo [2]. Purtell and coworkers also documented a high incidence of sexual problems in hysterics, noting that 86 percent of this group had sexual difficulties (including 73 percent claiming no sexual pleasure and 63 percent with dyspareunia) as compared to 29 percent of a control group [51]. Among the conversion symptoms that may be noted in hysteric women are complaints of total vaginal anesthesia or vaginal paresthesias; burning pains in the rectum, mouth, or vagina are also frequently described [50].

Most authorities are reluctant to make the diagnosis of hysteria in men except in cases in which the hysteric symptoms appear in the context of personal injury litigation [2, 49]; Weintraub points out that hysteria must be differentiated from malingering, in which patients are consciously feigning disease to obtain financial gain [47]. Additional difficulties in properly making the diagnosis of hysteria are reviewed elsewhere [2, 47, 52, 53]. An intriguing thesis currently gaining recognition is the idea that hysteria and sociopathy may be interrelated [53–56]. If this is the case, cultural conditioning in regard to sex roles may lead to different behavioral manifestations of the same underlying process.

Marital difficulties and divorce are quite common among women with hysteria [57], although sexual problems are not invariably seen in this context [58]. In some cases, women with hysteria function rather normally sexually; in other instances, while dyspareunia, anorgasmia, or low libido may be present—singly or in combination—the woman and her spouse reach some degree of accommodation in their interpersonal lives and are able to sustain their marriage without difficulty. The frequent occurrence of depression in hysteric patients [59] poses another obvious threat to marital stability.

Hysteric patients are often observed to be seductive. Nemiah notes, in this regard,

At the same time, they show a narcissistic preoccupation and concern with themselves and, behind the seductiveness, an underlying passive-dependent need for help, protection, and nurturance. Motivated by these various needs, these patients attempt to obtain gratification from others through threats of suicide or other measures that play upon the guilt of those around them. Although it is easy to respond to this behavior with a variety of judgmental or otherwise harmful attitudes, it should be remembered that no matter how exaggerated, dramatic, or contrived the patient's behavior may appear, it is, like the accompanying symptoms, the expression of underlying psychological conflicts [49].

The management of patients with hysteria is frustrating and problematic. Sex therapy is unlikely to provide a cure for the sexual difficulties mentioned above, although symptom improvement may occur. Few hysterics referred to a psychiatrist stay under such care for any length of time [2]. Physicians should be extremely cautious in recommending surgery or hospitalization for hysteric patients, while at the same time recognizing that organic illness may occur and necessarily requires appropriate diagnostic evaluation and treatment.

Antisocial Personality

Antisocial personality (sociopathy) is a condition marked by various manifestations of dyssocial behavior: There is characteristically a history from childhood or adolescence onward of delinquent or criminal behavior accompanied by lack of remorse, pathologic lying, irresponsibility, and difficulty in maintaining interpersonal relationships [1, 2, 60, 61]. The *Diagnostic and Statistical Manual* of the American Psychiatric Association notes that the antisocial personality is "incapable of significant loyalty to individuals, groups, or social values ... grossly selfish, callous, irresponsible, impulsive and unable to feel guilt or to learn from experience or punishment" [1]. The sociopath is characteristically glib, self-assured, and charming, creating an illusion that is apt to be betrayed by subsequent behavior. Even then, the sociopath skillfully rationalizes such behavior in a most convincing way.

Although sociopathy is more common in males than in females [2, 56, 60, 61], the point has been made that antisocial and hysteric personality disorders may be in actuality sex-typed forms of a single condition [53]. Diagnostic distinction between the two may reflect more about cultural biases in the perception of masculine and feminine roles than differences in the underlying psychopathology of these disorders.

In contrast to the hysteric, the sociopath is typically quite proficient sexually. Sexual promiscuity is often a prominent feature of sociopathy, usually manifesting itself during adolescence and persisting into adulthood. Sociopaths frequently employ their sexual prowess to endear themselves to their sexual partners in order to attain material gains; once this has been achieved, the sociopath is likely to move on to other things, deserting the "loved one" with no explanation. The emotional poverty of sociopathy seems to be marked not only by lack of guilt over such behavior but also by a specific incapacity to experience love.

It is interesting to note that sociopaths frequently marry, although marital difficulties (including physical abuse) and a high divorce rate are characteristic of this disorder. Robins found that 81 percent of adult sociopaths had marital problems and that 72 percent had histories of alcohol abuse [56]. Woodruff and his coworkers noted that 46 percent of sociopaths who had married subsequently divorced [57]; the sociopath's decision to marry may be precipitous [60] or may be exercised on multiple occasions, even if a preceding marriage has not been legally ended!

Although sexual prowess and charm are often high among sociopaths, sex for them is characteristically a shallow means to an end rather than a gratifying experience on its own merits. Cleckley notes that sociopaths generally have impersonal sex lives that are poorly integrated into the rest of their existence [61]; our clinical experience has borne out this general observation. While sociopaths may profess marked motivation for treatment in a sex therapy program (in our experience, only presenting as the partner of a dysfunctional individual) and while they may actually be "stellar performers" in the early phases of therapy, they are generally unable to sustain sufficient regard for the needs or feelings of their partner to attain a particularly significant result; in fact, their poor judgment, poor reliability, and selfishness may create traumatic situations for their partner in a psychotherapeutic environment.

The natural history of sociopathy is varied. Although some sociopaths never improve, many others undergo remission in their twenties or thirties for reasons that are not presently understood [2, 60]. Even after remission, although a greater personal stability may result, there is a tendency for interpersonal difficulties to persist [60, 61].

Other Psychiatric Conditions

The sexual aspects of certain psychiatric conditions are discussed elsewhere in this text—transsexualism is dealt with in Chapter 18, alcoholism is discussed in Chapter 10, and drug addiction is mentioned in Chapter 13. In this section, brief mention is made of a number of other psychiatric disorders that may be associated with sexual problems.

Personality Disorders

Passive-Aggressive Personality. The passive-aggressive personality is characterized by the use of passive interpersonal behavior as a means of expressing hostility [60]. The person with a passive-aggressive personality typically exhibits disinterest, withdrawal, inefficiency, negativism, and procrastination as a means of accomplishing discomfort in others. For obvious reasons, these behavioral traits frequently lead to sexual difficulties. The passive-aggressive is usually unwilling to be the sexual initiator but may complain of too little sexual interest on the part of his or her partner; alternately, the passive-aggressive person may alter the tempo or style of sexual activity in a manner that is likely to diminish its quality, and then is resentful that things "didn't work out right." Offit observes that "Sexually, the most dangerous passive-aggressive games involve the use or non-use of birth control devices. Forgetting them, not liking them, suffering them, using them improperly: all kinds of pain can be inflicted on others without taking any share of real responsibility" [62]. In conjoint sex therapy, the passive-aggressive will often resort to tears and obstructionism and requires frequent confrontation and insight into alternate means of expressing feelings more directly.

Obsessive-Compulsive Personality. The obsessive-compulsive personality is characterized by having an "excessive concern with conformity and adherence to standards of conscience" [1]. A person with this pattern tends toward rigidity, inhibition, and self-doubt. While it is obvious that the perfectionistic, controlled qualities of the obsessive-compulsive personality may be assets in certain walks of life—the airline pilot or the research scientist may benefit from a singlemindedness of purpose and adherence to strict procedural format—it is also clear that such a person is liable to miss a great deal of the warmth and spontaneity potentially available in sex. Many obsessive-compulsive persons have high levels of sexual anxiety or guilt, making them frequent victims of sexual dysfunction; occasionally, the person whose obsession or compulsion is directed primarily toward sexual performance becomes constrained by an overriding concern for sexual variety, perfectionism, or accomplishment. One such patient seen at the Masters & Johnson Institute brought with him a detailed diary describing his sexual experiences with 432 women over an 18-year interval, which he expected the therapists to read and analyze.

If the obsessional or compulsive concerns of a person's life become personally distressing or interfere with day-to-day functioning, then the diagnosis of obsessive-compulsive neurosis can be properly made. Obsessional fears may be interrelated with sexual avoidance or sexual aversion (see Chap. 22); obsessional thoughts or images which repetitively intrude into consciousness may be overtly and disturbingly sexual; infrequently, when a delusional theme coexists with obsessive-compulsive neurosis, the patient may be convinced that a particular thought or behavior (or failure to have the thought or behavior) will produce dire consequences. Because of the extreme rigidity of their behavior patterns, these patients often respond poorly to sex therapy.

Asthenic and Cyclothymic Personalities. The asthenic personality is characterized by concern with weakness, fatigue, lack of enthusiasm, and somatic complaints. Such people are likely to have low libido and to claim little, if any, satisfaction from sexual activity. The cyclothymic personality, in contrast, is characterized by alternating periods of high and low moods; such persons tend to be extroverted and fun-loving, but become worried and frustrated during their relatively brief depressions. Sexual problems may recur sporadically in this group but generally abate during times of mood upswings—in fact, enthusiasm for sexual activity may alternate inexplicably with sexual disinterest, much to the consternation of the patient's partner or spouse.

The diagnostic utility of personality disorders is currently a matter of discussion in psychiatric circles, since they are difficult to define clearly and there are relatively few indicators of etiology, prognosis, or specific treatment modalities that pertain to each of these categories [60]. Nevertheless, since personality disorders appear to require interpersonal circumstances to become apparent, it is obvious that they may be relevant to diagnostic and treatment issues in sex therapy. Such a correlation is supported by the findings of Kupfer and his colleagues, who reported that chronic anxiety, impulsiveness, and obsessiveness were significantly associated with the occurrence of sexual dysfunction among patients in an outpatient psychiatric clinic [63]. Further research on the frequency of sexual problems in patients with personality disorders appears needed.

Organic Brain
Syndromes

Organic brain syndromes are frequently accompanied by changes in sexuality. In addition to temporal lobe lesions and the Klüver-Bucy syndrome, described in Chapter 10, chronic brain syndromes resulting from diverse conditions such as Alzheimer's disease, neurosyphilis, intracranial neoplasms, advanced arteriosclerosis, and metabolic imbalance are likely to impair cognition, memory, affect, and judgment. Patients with Huntington's disease—a genetically transmitted form of progressive degeneration of the basal ganglia and cerebral cortex—are likely to show clinical manifestations, including choreatic movement, emotional disturbances, and intellectual deterioration, between ages 35 and 45; and they are reported to have a high rate of abnormal sexual behavior such as exhibitionism, voyeurism, hypersexuality, and low libido [64].

Psychiatric Conditions
Unassociated with
Sexual Problems

It is important to recognize that there are a number of psychiatric conditions that do not appear to be associated with an increased frequency of sexual problems. For example, most patients with anxiety neurosis are relatively free of sexual difficulties. Although it has been postulated that lack of female coital orgasmic responsiveness may precipitate psychological symptoms analogous to anxiety neurosis [65], Maurice and Guze found only one case of mild anxiety neurosis in 16 nonorgasmic women [66]. Similarly, the great majority of patients with phobic neurosis are able to function sexually without difficulty. Exceptions to this statement obviously include patients who are phobic about some aspect of sexual activity (see Chap. 22 for examples). In fact, data from several earlier studies indicate that sexual problems are not more common in neurotic patients than in the general population [67–69].

Psychosomatic Disorders

Pseudocyesis. Two unusual psychosomatic disorders will be mentioned briefly. Pseudocyesis is a condition of false pregnancy, accompanied by amenorrhea, increasing abdominal girth, other signs and symptoms of pregnancy, and the belief of being pregnant. Although some authors have considered this to be a variant of hysteria [70], it does not fit easily into any diagnostic category. In a recent literature review, Murray and Abraham found that 512 cases of pseudocyesis had been reported in the English literature, including only 17 since 1960 [71]. Although it has been postulated that a strong desire for pregnancy, especially among older women, and a fear of pregnancy, particularly in younger women, may be associated with this syndrome, the precise etiology remains elusive. It is of interest that a wide variety of physiologic manifestations may occur during pseudocyesis, including breast enlargement and galactorrhea, morning nausea and vomiting, weight gain, and a number of neuroendocrine changes [72, 73]. Brown and Barglow have postulated that biochemical changes associated with depression may be a cause of pseudocyesis [74], although no firm support for this theory has been offered.

Anorexia Nervosa. Another unusual psychosomatic disorder that has been correlated with both sexual problems and neuroendocrine alterations is anorexia nervosa. This condition, which predominantly affects young females, is characterized by an obsessive refusal to eat, prominent weight loss, and problems of body-image. The etiology of anorexia nervosa is unknown, although Bliss cites several factors that may apply: Some patients develop anorexia as a counterphobic protection against obesity, others seem to fear a fantasized pregnancy, and a third group is composed of those attaching symbolic significance to food and eating [75]:

Like ascetics, these patients select semistarvation to attain a sense of control over their sordid body, its impulses and carnal desires. Mastery over a masturbatory, homosexual, or heterosexual conflict may be achieved by this tactic. For others, semistarvation serves as a form of self-punishment and purification, often to expiate guilts. Some perceive cachexia as a form of inconspicuousness or anonymity. It is associated with a return to childhood, infantile dependency, and repudiation of responsibility, feminine contours, and sexuality [75].

Amenorrhea is a characteristic accompaniment of anorexia nervosa; low testosterone levels have been reported in males with this disorder [76]. Pituitary responsiveness to stimulation with gonadotropin-releasing factor is diminished, and hypothyroid-like alterations in testosterone metabolism in females with anorexia nervosa have also been described [77–79]. Recent studies indicate that women with anorexia nervosa with partial or full recovery of their ideal weights continue to show abnormalities in their circadian LH secretory pattern and do not always regain normal menstrual cycling [80]. The sexual behavior of patients with anorexia nervosa is frequently severely constrained. Both low libido and lack of orgasmic responsiveness are typical; negative attitudes toward sex and masturbation are also characteristic. These findings are not surprising in view of the fact that an underlying disorder of body-image is implicit in most cases.

A Concluding Note

This chapter is far from exhaustive in its discussion of sexuality and psychiatric illness. There are many gaps in our current knowledge due to insufficient data, problems of nosology, and missing etiologic information. Along with the need to gather such knowledge is a parallel need to divorce contemporary thinking from outmoded theories and speculations that create erroneous connections between sexual problems and mental disorders. This need is dramatically highlighted by a report from Pinderhughes and coworkers that indicated that psychiatrists believed "that sexual activity could have been a contributing factor in 83 percent of psychiatric conditions," and that in 45 percent of psychiatric conditions, patients' recovery might be hampered or endangered by sexual activity [81]. There is clearly a great deal of misinformation still present in professional circles.

References

1. Committee on Nomenclature and Statistics, American Psychiatric Association. *Diagnostic and Statistical Manual of Mental Disorders* (3rd ed.) (DMS-II). Washington, D.C.: American Psychiatric Association, 1968.
2. Woodruff, R. A., Goodwin, D. W., and Guze, S. B. *Psychiatric Diagnosis*. New York: Oxford University Press, 1974.
3. Beck, A. T. Depressive Neurosis. In S. Arieti and E. B. Brody (eds.), *American Handbook of Psychiatry* (2nd ed.). New York: Basic Books, Inc., 1974. Vol. 3 (*Adult Clinical Psychiatry*), pp. 61–90.
4. Arieti, S. Affective Disorders: Manic-Depressive Psychosis and Psychotic Depression: Manifest Symptomatology, Psychodynamics, Sociological Factors, and Psychotherapy. In S. Arieti and E. B. Brody (eds.), *American Handbook of Psychiatry* (2nd ed.). New York: Basic Books, Inc., 1974. Vol. 3 (*Adult Clinical Psychiatry*), pp. 449–490.
5. Nemiah, J. C. Depressive Neurosis. In A. M. Freedman, H. I. Kaplan,

and B. J. Sadock (eds.), *Comprehensive Textbook of Psychiatry—II* (2nd ed.). Baltimore: Williams & Wilkins Co., 1975. Pp. 1255–1264.

6. Huston, P. E. Psychotic Depressive Reaction. In A. M. Freedman, H. I. Kaplan, and B. J. Sadock (eds.), *Comprehensive Textbook of Psychiatry—II* (2nd ed.). Baltimore: Williams & Wilkins Co., 1975. Pp. 1043–1055.

7. Akiskal, H. S., Bitar, A. H., Puzantian, V. R., Rosenthal, T. L., and Walker, P. W. The nosological status of neurotic depression: A prospective three- to four-year follow-up examination in light of the primary-secondary and unipolar-bipolar dichotomies. *Archives of General Psychiatry* 35:756–766, 1978.

8. Klerman, G. L. Affective Disorders. In A. M. Nicholi, Jr. (ed.), *The Harvard Guide to Modern Psychiatry*. Cambridge, Mass.: The Belknap Press of Harvard University Press, 1978. Pp. 253–281.

9. Blumenthal, M. D., and Dielman, T. E. Depressive symptomatology and role function in a general population. *Archives of General Psychiatry* 32:985–991, 1975.

10. Barrett, J., Hurst, M. W., DiScala, C., and Rose, R. M. Prevalence of depression over a 12-month period in a nonpatient population. *Archives of General Psychiatry* 35:741–744, 1978.

11. Weissman, M. M., and Klerman, G. L. Sex differences and the epidemiology of depression. *Archives of General Psychiatry* 34:98–111, 1977.

12. Dohrenwend, B. P., and Dohrenwend, B. S. Sex differences and psychiatric disorders. *American Journal of Sociology* 81:1447–1454, 1976.

13. Murphy, G. E., Woodruff, R. A., Jr., Herjanic, M., and Super, G. Variability of the clinical course of primary affective disorder. *Archives of General Psychiatry* 30:757–761, 1974.

14. Lundquist, G. Prognosis and course in manic depressive psychosis. *Acta Psychiatrica Neurologica Scandinavica* (Suppl.) 35:1–95, 1945.

15. Woodruff, R. A., Murphy, G. E., and Herjanic, M. The natural history of affective disorders: I. Symptoms of 72 patients at the time of index hospital admission. *Journal of Psychiatric Research* 5:255–263, 1967.

16. Tamburello, A., and Seppecher, M. F. The Effects of Depression on Sexual Behavior: Preliminary Results of Research. In R. Gemme and C. C. Wheeler (eds.), *Progress in Sexology*. New York: Plenum Press, 1977. Pp. 107–128.

17. Kolodny, R. C. Unpublished observation, 1978.

18. Miller, W. R., and Seligman, M. E. P. Depression and learned helplessness in man. *Journal of Abnormal Psychology* 84:228–238, 1975.

19. Abramson, L. Y., Seligman, M. E. P., and Teasdale, J. D. Learned helplessness in humans: Critique and reformulation. *Journal of Abnormal Psychology* 87:49–74, 1978.

20. Kaplan, H. S. *The New Sex Therapy*. New York: Brunner/Mazel Publications, 1974. Pp. 474–500.

21. Allen, M. G. Twin studies of affective illness. *Archives of General Psychiatry* 33:1476–1478, 1976.

22. Johnson, G. F. S., and Leeman, M. M. Analysis of familial factors in bipolar affective illness. *Archives of General Psychiatry* 34:1074–1083, 1977.

23. Winokur, G., and Pitts, F. N., Jr. Affective disorder: VI. A family history study of prevalences, sex differences and possible genetic factors. *Journal of Psychiatric Research* 3:113–123, 1965.

24. Mendlewicz, J., and Fleiss, J. L. Linkage studies with X-chromosome markers in bipolar (manic-depressive) and unipolar (depressive) illnesses. *Biological Psychiatry* 9:261–294, 1974.

25. Akiskal, H. S., and McKinney, W. T. Overview of recent research in depression: Integration of ten conceptual models into a comprehensive clinical frame. *Archives of General Psychiatry* 32:285–305, 1975.

26. Ettigi, P. G., and Brown, G. M. Psychoneuroendocrinology of affective disorder: An overview. *American Journal of Psychiatry* 134:493–501, 1977.

27. Sachar, E. J. Twenty-four-hour cortisol secretory patterns in depressed and manic patients. *Progress in Brain Research* 42:81–91, 1975.

28. Sachar, E. J., Hellman, L., Roffwarg, H. P., Halpern, F. S., Fukushima, D. K., and Gallagher, T. F. Disrupted 24-hour patterns of cortisol secretion in psychotic depression. *Archives of General Psychiatry* 28:19–24, 1973.

29. Mendels, J., Frazer, A., Fitzgerald, R. G., Ramsey, T. A., and Stokes, J. W. Biogenic amine metabolites in the cerebrospinal fluid of depressed and manic patients. *Science* 175:1380–1382, 1972.

30. Ashcroft, G., Blackburn, I., Eccleston, D., Glen, A. I. M., Hartley, W., Kinloch, N. E., Lonergan, M., Murray, L. G., and Pullar, I. A. Changes on recovery in the concentration of L-tryptophan and the biogenic amine metabolites in the cerebrospinal fluid of patients with affective illness. *Psychological Medicine* 3:319–325, 1973.

31. Mendels, J., and Frazer, A. Brain biogenic amine depletion and mood. *Archives of General Psychiatry* 30:447–451, 1974.

32. Carroll, B. J., Curtis, G. C., and Mendels, J. Neuroendocrine regulation in depression: I. Limbic system-adrenocortical dysfunction. *Archives of General Psychiatry* 33:1039–1044, 1976.

33. Carroll, B. J., Curtis, G. C., and Mendels, J. Neuroendocrine regulation in depression: II. Discrimination of depressed from nondepressed patients. *Archives of General Psychiatry* 33:1051–1058, 1976.

34. Hollister, L. E., Davis, K. L., and Berger, P. A. Pituitary response to thyrotropin-releasing hormone in depression. *Archives of General Psychiatry* 33:1393–1396, 1976.

35. Langer, G., Heinze, G., Reim, B., and Matussek, N. Reduced growth hormone responses to amphetamine in "endogenous" depressive patients: Studies in normal, "reactive" and "endogenous" depressive, schizophrenic, and chronic alcoholic subjects. *Archives of General Psychiatry* 33:1471–1475, 1976.

36. Brambilla, F., Smeraldi, E., Sacchetti, E., Negri, F., Cocchi, D., and Müller, E. E. Deranged anterior pituitary responsiveness to hypothalamic hormones in depressed patients. *Archives of General Psychiatry* 35:1231–1238, 1978.

37. Sheard, M. H. Endocrines and Neuropsychiatric Disorders. In B. E. Eleftheriou and R. L. Sprott (eds.), *Hormonal Correlates of Behavior*. New York: Plenum Press, 1975. Vol. 1 (*A Lifespan View*), pp. 341–368.

38. Gruen, P. H.   Endocrine changes in psychiatric diseases: Neuroendocrine studies of affective disorders. *Medical Clinics of North America* 62:285–296, 1978.
39. Coppen, A., Prange, A. J., Jr., and Whybrow, P. C.   Abnormalities of indoleamines in affective disorders. *Archives of General Psychiatry* 26:474–478, 1972.
40. Clayton, P. J., Pitts, F. N., Jr., and Winokur, G.   Affective disorders: IV. Mania. *Comprehensive Psychiatry* 6:313–322, 1965.
41. Allison, J. B., and Wilson, W. P.   Sexual behavior of manic patients: A preliminary report. *Southern Medical Journal* 53:870–874, 1960.
42. Tsuang, M. T.   Hypersexuality in manic patients. *Medical Aspects of Human Sexuality* 9(11):83–89, 1975.
43. Winokur, G., Clayton, P. J., and Reich, T.   *Manic Depressive Illness*. St. Louis: C. V. Mosby Co., 1969. Pp. 61–74.
44. Spalt, L.   Sexual behavior and affective disorders. *Diseases of the Nervous System* 36:644–647, 1975.
45. Arieti, S.   Sexual Problems of the Schizophrenic and Preschizophrenic. In N. Sandler and G. L. Gessa (eds.), *Sexual Behavior: Pharmacology and Biochemistry*. New York: Raven Press, 1975. Pp. 277–282.
46. Berardi, A. L., and Garske, J. P.   Effects of sexual arousal on schizophrenics: A comparative test of hypotheses derived from ego psychology and arousal theory. *Journal of Clinical Psychology* 33:105–109, 1977.
47. Weintraub, M. I.   Hysteria: A clinical guide to diagnosis. *Clinical Symposia* 29(6), 1977.
48. Vieth, I.   *Hysteria—The History of a Disease*. Chicago: University of Chicago Press, 1965.
49. Nemiah, J. C.   Psychoneurotic Disorders. In A. M. Nicholi, Jr. (ed.), *The Harvard Guide to Modern Psychiatry*. Cambridge, Mass.: The Belknap Press of Harvard University Press, 1978. Pp. 173–197.
50. Perley, M. J., and Guze, S. B.   Hysteria—The stability and usefulness of clinical criteria. *New England Journal of Medicine* 266:421–426, 1962.
51. Purtell, J. J., Robins, E., and Cohen, M. E.   Observations on clinical aspects of hysteria. *Journal of the American Medical Association* 146:902–909, 1951.
52. Lewis, W. C.   Hysteria: The consultant's dilemma. Twentieth century demonology, pejorative epithet, or useful diagnosis? *Archives of General Psychiatry* 30:145–151, 1974.
53. Warner, R.   The diagnosis of antisocial and hysterical personality disorders: An example of sex bias. *Journal of Nervous and Mental Disease* 166:839–845, 1978.
54. Cloninger, C. R., and Guze, S. B.   Psychiatric illness and female criminality: The role of sociopathy and hysteria in the antisocial woman. *American Journal of Psychiatry* 127:303–311, 1970.
55. Guze, S. B., Woodruff, R. A., and Clayton, P. J.   Hysteria and antisocial behavior: Further evidence of an association. *American Journal of Psychiatry* 127:957–960, 1971.
56. Robins, L.   *Deviant Children Grown Up*. Baltimore: Williams & Wilkins Co., 1966.

57. Woodruff, R. A., Jr., Guze, S. B., and Clayton, P. J. Divorce among psychiatric out-patients. *British Journal of Psychiatry* 121:289–292, 1972.

58. Prosen, H. Sexuality in females with "hysteria." *American Journal of Psychiatry* 124:687–692, 1967.

59. Bibb, R. C., and Guze, S. B. Hysteria (Briquet's syndrome) in a psychiatric hospital: The significance of depression. *American Journal of Psychiatry* 129:224–228, 1972.

60. Winokur, G., and Crowe, R. R. Personality Disorders. In A. M. Freedman, H. I. Kaplan, and B. J. Sadock (eds.), *Comprehensive Textbook of Psychiatry—II* (2nd ed.). Baltimore: Williams & Wilkins Co., 1975. Pp. 1279–1297.

61. Cleckley, H. *The Mask of Sanity* (4th ed.). St. Louis: C. V. Mosby Co., 1964.

62. Offit, A. K. *The Sexual Self*. New York: Ballantine Books, 1977. P. 63.

63. Kupfer, D. J., Rosenbaum, J. F., and Detre, T. P. Personality style and sexual functioning among psychiatric outpatients. *Journal of Sex Research* 13:257–266, 1977.

64. Dewhurst, K., Oliver, J. E., and McKnight, A. L. Sociopsychiatric consequences of Huntington's disease. *British Journal of Psychiatry* 116:255–258, 1970.

65. Fink, P. J. Correlations between 'actual' neurosis and the work of Masters and Johnson. *Psychoanalytic Quarterly* 39:38–51, 1970.

66. Maurice, W. L., and Guze, S. B. Sexual dysfunction and associated psychiatric disorders. *Comprehensive Psychiatry* 11:539–543, 1970.

67. Winokur, G., Guze, S. B., and Pfeiffer, E. Developmental and sexual factors in women: A comparison between control, neurotic and psychotic groups. *American Journal of Psychiatry* 115:1097–1100, 1959.

68. Raboch, J., and Bartak, V. The sexual life of frigid women. *Psychiatrie, Neurologie und Medizinische Psychologie* (Leipzig) 20:368–373, 1968.

69. Cooper, A. J. "Neurosis" and disorders of sexual potency in the male. *Journal of Psychosomatic Research* 12:141–144, 1968.

70. Bivin, G. D., and Klinger, M. P. *Pseudocyesis*. Bloomington: Principia Press, 1937.

71. Murray, J. L., and Abraham, G. E. Pseudocyesis: A review. *Obstetrics and Gynecology* 51:627–631, 1978.

72. Yen, S. C. C., Rebar, R. W., and Quesenberry, W. Pituitary function in pseudocyesis. *Journal of Clinical Endocrinology and Metabolism* 43:132–136, 1976.

73. Zarate, A., Canales, E. S., and Soria, J. Gonadotropin and prolactin secretion in human pseudocyesis. *Annals of Endocrinology* (Paris) 35:445–450, 1974.

74. Brown, E., and Barglow, P. Pseudocyesis: A paradigm for psychophysiological interactions. *Archives of General Psychiatry* 24:221–229, 1971.

75. Bliss, E. L. Anorexia Nervosa. In A. M. Freedman, H. I. Kaplan, and B. J. Sadock (eds.), *Comprehensive Textbook of Psychiatry—II* (2nd ed.). Baltimore: Williams & Wilkins Co., 1975. Pp. 1655–1659.

76. Beaumont, P. J. V., Veardwood, C. J., and Russell, G. F. M. The occur-

rence of the syndrome of anorexia nervosa in male subjects. *Psychological Medicine* 2:216–231, 1972.

77. Boyar, R. M., Katz, J., Finkelstein, J. W., Kapen, S., Weiner, H., Weitzman, E. D., and Hellman, L. Anorexia nervosa: Immaturity of the 24-hour luteinizing hormone secretory pattern. *New England Journal of Medicine* 291:861–865, 1974.

78. Vigersky, R. A., Loriaux, D. L., Andersen, A. E., Mecklenburg, R. S., and Vaitukaitis, J. L. Delayed pituitary hormone response to LRF and TRF in patients with anorexia nervosa and with secondary amenorrhea associated with simple weight loss. *Journal of Clinical Endocrinology and Metabolism* 43:893–900, 1976.

79. Bradlow, H. L., Boyar, R. M., O'Connor, J., Zumoff, B., and Hellman, L. Hypothyroid-like alterations in testosterone metabolism in anorexia nervosa. *Journal of Clinical Endocrinology and Metabolism* 43:571–574, 1976.

80. Katz, J. L., Boyar, R., Roffwarg, H., Hellman, L., and Weiner, H. Weight and circadian luteinizing hormone secretory pattern in anorexia nervosa. *Psychosomatic Medicine* 40:549–567, 1978.

81. Pinderhughes, C. A., Grace, E. B., and Reyna, L. J. Psychiatric disorders and sexual functioning. *American Journal of Psychiatry* 128:1276–1283, 1972.

A great mystique surrounds the topic of the sexual impact of pharmacologic substances: Historically, many have pursued the search for an aphrodisiac but have met only varying degrees of satisfaction. Although the twentieth century has been a time of tremendous expansion of our *pharmacopoeia therapeutica*, the elusive aphrodisiac has not been found. Instead, clinicians realize that many pharmacologic agents may be potent inhibitors of sexual function. Regrettably, little systematic research has been done to establish the mechanisms of such effects. In this chapter, knowledge of the sexual side effects that drugs may produce is presented along with suggestions for approaches the clinician may use in patient management.

Before discussing specific drugs and their influences on sexuality, a few general observations are in order. The effects that any pharmacologic agent will have vary greatly from person to person. This variability is due to biologic factors such as absorption rate, rate of metabolism, body weight, rate of excretion, dosage, duration of use, and interaction with other drugs, and to nonbiologic factors such as compliance with a medication schedule and patient suggestibility. An extensive literature exists describing the placebo effect, which is one manifestation of the suggestibility phenomenon. In light of these complicated facts, this chapter should be read as a guide to the *potential* sexual effects of drug use, rather than as an infallible predictor of such changes.

In most instances, the research that has been conducted regarding drug effects on sexual response focuses on the male. Clearly, this represents the prevalent bias of current scientific thought, but it also reflects the fact that it is easier to assess sexual functioning in the male because erection and ejaculation are more visible than lubrication and orgasm in the female.

Effects of Prescribed Drugs on Sexual Function

Drugs Used in the Treatment of Hypertension

Diuretic Agents. The *thiazide diuretics* are widely used as part of a combination drug program in the treatment of hypertension. Their basic action is to increase the renal excretion of sodium and chloride, which is accompanied by an osmotic diuresis of water. The specific antihypertensive effect of these drugs may also result from a reduction in the resistance of peripheral circulation via a relaxation of vascular smooth muscle [1], but the exact mechanism is unsubstantiated.

The fact that these agents are typically used concomitantly with other blood pressure–lowering medications complicates the analysis of their effects on sexual function. Nevertheless, clinical observation indicates that approximately 5 percent of men using thiazide diuretics on a chronic basis experience disturbances of potency that are attributable to the drug. Ejaculation is not known to be affected by diuretics. Although the mechanism of impotence associated with use of the thiazides is unclear, in some instances it may be due to the hyperglycemic effect of these drugs (a side effect that can unmask latent diabetes [2]), whereas in other cases it may be related to the potassium depletion (hypokalemia) that commonly accompanies use of the thiazides [1, 3].

Ethacrynic acid and *furosemide*, two nonthiazide diuretics that are similar pharmacologically, have also been observed to be associated with impotence in about 5 percent of men using these drugs chronically. The theoretic roles of hyperglycemia and hypokalemia may be applicable to these drugs as well, although probably not in the majority of cases. When a patient develops sexual difficulties because of diuretic-induced hypokalemia, a trial of potassium supplementation may produce rapid amelioration of the problem.

Spironolactone is a competitive antagonist of aldosterone that conserves potassium and exhibits an antihypertensive effect. It is sometimes used in the treatment of refractory edema, alone or in combination with other diuretics. This drug causes decreased libido, impotence, and gynecomastia in men and menstrual irregularity and breast tenderness in women [4–6]. These effects appear to be somewhat dose-dependent, in that they are not common in persons using 100 mg or less per day but occur much more often at higher doses [4, 5, 7]. In one study, two-thirds of healthy young men given 400 mg per day of spironolactone developed gynecomastia within 24 weeks of use, and 22 percent reported decreased libido [7]. Alterations in sperm quality were observed during this study as well. The depressed libido and potency seen in men as well as the menstrual abnormalities in women using spironolactone reverse promptly on cessation of drug use. While the gynecomastia caused by spironolactone usually recedes with time after the drug is stopped, this is not always the case.

The specific mechanisms of these effects are not completely understood. In rats, spironolactone interferes with the production of testosterone by affecting a necessary enzyme system, which leads to decreased testosterone in circulation [4]. Some studies with this drug in humans have not found a similar drop in testosterone levels, suggesting that possibly an antiandrogenic effect at the tissue receptor level accounts for the changes described above [5]. However, a recent report described lowered testosterone and elevated blood estradiol levels in six men treated with spironolactone; the changes were attributable to increases in the metabolic clearance rate of testosterone and greater peripheral conversion of testosterone to estradiol [8]. Finally, the finding that spironolactone possesses significant progestational activity [9] may also explain the observed problems of libido, since progesterone is generally believed to be a sexual inhibitor.

Non-Diuretic Blood Pressure–Lowering Agents. Alpha-methyldopa exerts a weak antiadrenergic effect by inhibiting enzyme pathways that are important in brain and peripheral tissue metabolism. It is currently one of the most widely employed of drugs used to treat hypertension, but unfortunately it is also a common inhibitor of sexual function. At dosage levels below 1.0 gm per day, decreased libido and/or impotence occurs in 10 to 15 percent of men, and depressed libido and/or impaired arousal occurs in a like proportion of women. At dosage levels of 1.0 to 1.5 gm per day, 20 to 25 percent of men and women using this drug experience sexual difficulties; at dosages of 2 gm per day or more, approximately 50 percent of persons using this medication experience significant disruptions in sexual function [10–13]. At the higher dosage levels, some women report loss of orgasm as well as decreased arousability, and some men experience delayed ejaculation. The cause of these problems is not clear at present, but it may relate to both catecholamine depletion in the central nervous system and the production of a "false" neurotransmitter [1], which may have a direct effect on the peripheral nerves that control the processes of erection and vaginal vasocongestion. Alpha-methyldopa does not affect circulating testosterone levels in men [10]. The depression of libido may be partly due to the generalized drowsiness and easy fatigability that is often a side effect of this drug; depression may also occur as a consequence of the use of alpha-methyldopa [14] and lead indirectly to sexual difficulties. These side effects of alpha-methyldopa are promptly reversible within one to two weeks after discontinuing use of the drug, although it should be recognized that on some occasions the precipitation of a sexual problem by a biologic factor will lead to enough anxiety that removing the offending agent will not always end the problem; in such cases, psychotherapy oriented toward reducing or eliminating the anxiety may be required to restore normal sexual functioning. Because alpha-methyldopa increases circulating prolactin concentrations, it can sometimes cause either gynecomastia or galactorrhea [15].

Guanethidine is an antiadrenergic drug that blocks the release of norepinephrine from sympathetic nerve endings. Because of its antiadrenergic properties, its primary effect sexually is one of inhibition of ejaculation in the male, which is a dose-dependent phenomenon. At doses above 25 mg per day, approximately 50 to 60 percent of men have retarded ejaculation or inability to ejaculate [16, 17]. Although it has sometimes been thought that guanethidine does not cause impotence, erectile difficulties do occur in a somewhat lower proportion of men using this drug. In a series of 22 men using guanethidine and a thiazide diuretic to control their blood pressure, 3 men (13.6 percent) experienced impotence and 13 men (59.1 percent) reported diminished libido [17]. The mechanism of action here may be a reflection of the inhibited responses or may be simply the psychogenic reaction to disruption of ejaculation. Systematic studies of the effects of guanethidine on female sexual response have not been carried out to date, but it is not unreasonable to assume that sexual problems may be encountered in women using this drug.

Hydralazine is currently thought to exert its antihypertensive effects via direct relaxation of the smooth muscle of arterioles. Except at very high dosage levels, hydralazine does not appear to cause impairment of sexual functioning. However, at dosages above 200 mg per day, approximately 5 to 10 percent of men report decreased libido, sometimes accompanied by impotence. This loss of libido may be the result of a syndrome resembling systemic lupus erythematosus that can develop at high doses with this drug [18], or it may be due to a pyridoxine deficiency that has been described in association with the use of hydralazine [19].

Reserpine and other rauwolfia alkaloids deplete stores of catecholamines in many tissues, including the brain, and produce a marked sedative effect. This sedative effect can be strong enough to lower libido indirectly, or it may be complicated—even at very low dosages—by the occurrence of a clinically significant depression. When such a depression occurs, a high percentage of affected patients will have sexual dysfunction as well as depressed libido. Reserpine is also a potent endocrine agent and causes elevated prolactin levels, which may at times lead to gynecomastia or galactorrhea [20].

Propranolol is a beta-adrenergic blocking agent that is used primarily in the treatment of cardiac arrhythmias but has recently enjoyed a broader range of uses, including the treatment of hypertension. Although some authors have claimed that no sexual problems are attributable to the use of this drug, more recently several instances of propranolol-induced impotence have been reported [17, 21, 22]. Because propranolol and hydralazine are relatively free of sexual side effects, these agents may be useful in the management of hypertension in patients who are experiencing deleterious sexual effects with other medication programs. However, because propranolol blocks cardiac responses during exercise by lowering heart rate and cardiac output, the drug should be used cautiously when given to patients who are prone to developing congestive heart failure.

Clonidine is a newer antihypertensive agent that acts by a central mechanism decreasing sympathetic outflow [23]. Although there have been claims that it is free of sexual side effects, current evidence indicates that 10 to 20 percent of men using this agent experience impotence or diminished libido [24]. In a recent study of 28 men who were using clonidine in combination with a thiazide diuretic, 5 (17.9 percent) were impotent and 4 (14.3 percent) had decreased libido [17]. Clonidine is known to be a potent suppressor of both plasma catecholamines and insulin via interaction with alpha-adrenergic receptors, leading to hyperglycemia and impaired glucose tolerance [25]. The possible effects such metabolic alterations have upon sexual function is not clear at the present time.

Brief mention should be made of two additional antihypertensive drugs that have been recently introduced. *Metoprolol* is a beta-adrenergic blocking agent quite similar to propranolol. Common side effects include tiredness, dizziness, and depression [26]. Although sexual dysfunction is infrequent with this drug except in the case of patients who become depressed, Peyronie's disease has been reported with metoprolol use [27]. *Prazosin* lowers blood pressure by peripheral vasodilation and causes impaired libido in approximately 15 percent of men and women, but impotence occurs infrequently with this drug, and it may be a useful alternative therapeutic agent for patients experiencing sexual difficulties with other blood pressure–lowering regimens.

Ganglionic blocking agents such as pentolinium and mecamylamine, which are used infrequently in the United States, cause sexual problems in a large number of the patients receiving them. Urinary retention resulting from parasympathetic blockade may also be a side effect of such drugs.

General Considerations in the Management of Hypertension. The treatment of hypertension is a major public health problem in this country, with one of the biggest difficulties being poor patient compliance with medication programs [28, 29]. This problem occurs partly because high blood pressure is a "silent" disease—people with hypertension often do not feel ill [30, 31], and frequently the annoying side effects of their medications may seem worse than the condition that requires treatment. While this dilemma obviously requires a multidimensional solution, including effective patient education, it is also possible that better patient management would be beneficial in this regard. Knowledge by health-care professionals of the possibilities of sexual impairment as a consequence of drug use by hypertensive patients may be one step toward better management. The following recommendations are pertinent:

1. Before starting any patient on a medication program to regulate his or her blood pressure, obtain a baseline history of sexual functioning. This history will be important in helping to decide if subsequent reports of sexual symptoms are drug-related or not, and it will also give the patient an indication of the fact that it is permissible to talk about sexual function.
2. Attempt to individualize drug selection on the basis of common sense as well as medical guidelines. For example, do not select reserpine for a patient with a past history of depression, and do not choose guanethidine for a man who is trying to impregnate his wife.
3. There can be no absolute rules concerning the information a patient should be given about possible drug-associated side effects. Although there is the chance that informing a man of the possible occurrence of impotence will create pressures and expectations that may lead to impotence quite apart from any drug effect, in general it appears more sensible to be forthright in such pretreatment discussions. One can present the information in a manner that says, "If this problem occurs with you, just let me know and we can easily make an adjustment in your medications to restore things to normal." The key is having the patient realize that drug-related sexual problems he or she may experience are reversible.
4. When sexual symptoms arise during a patient's use of antihypertensive drugs, do not assume automatically that they are a result of these drugs. Inquire about other medications or illicit drugs the patient may be using. Be sure the problem is not a reflection of marital difficulties, alcohol use, or an intercurrent illness. Find out if the time sequence of drug use and appearance of the symptom appears to be logical from a physiologic viewpoint—for example, did the symptom appear shortly after a new drug was added or a dosage

Table 13-1. Sites of Action of Antihypertensive Medications	
	Drugs Acting Centrally Alpha-methyldopa Clonidine Sedatives and tranquilizers
	Drugs Acting at the Autonomic Nerve Ganglia Pentolinium Mecamylamine
	Drugs Acting at Nerve Endings Guanethidine Reserpine Rauwolfia alkaloids
	Adrenergic Receptor Blocking Agents Alpha-blocking: Phenoxybenzamine Beta-blocking: Propranolol Metoprolol
	Nonadrenergic Vasodilating Agents Hydralazine Minoxidil Prazosin
	Volume Changes and Renal Action Thiazide diuretics Furosemide Ethacrynic acid Spironolactone

raised? Be alert to the possibility that psychological factors underlie the sexual dysfunction.

5. Reversal of sexual problems associated with the use of an antihypertensive drug can be achieved by eliminating the offending drug entirely (while substituting another medication to maintain adequate control of the blood pressure) or by reducing the dosage of the drug in question and either adding a new agent or increasing the dosage of another drug the patient is already using. The use of combination drug programs to control blood pressure is common and convenient, since it allows for the selection of medications that work by different mechanisms of action and thus are less likely to be synergistic in their side effects (see Table 13-1).

6. Be certain to inquire about sexual problems at each followup visit. Such inquiry will aid in determining the dosages of particular drugs that can be well tolerated and will be helpful in detecting sexual

difficulties before they discourage the patient from seeking or continuing treatment.

Lack of patient compliance with medication programs that will effectively control blood pressure is currently viewed as a major public health concern [28]. More careful attention to the sexual side effects of antihypertensive drugs will surely be of assistance in helping to improve patient compliance and consequently to lessen the morbidity and mortality rates of hypertension.

Hormones

Androgens do not ordinarily increase libido or potency in men with normal endogenous testosterone production, although in men with testosterone deficiencies, androgen treatment can often restore libido and potency to baseline levels. The administration of exogenous androgens suppresses the hypothalamic-pituitary-gonadal axis in men, so that testicular atrophy accompanied by severe depression of spermatogenesis may result from the use of moderate or high androgen doses on a chronic basis. This effect can be a problem for male athletes who use anabolic steroids in large quantities, since these drugs are weakly androgenic and will frequently lead to infertility. Some normal men who have been given testosterone report mild increases in libido, but this finding appears to be principally due to the subjects' expectations of the drug, since double-blind studies have not identified such an effect. Nevertheless, androgen has sometimes been recommended as an adjunct to psychotherapy because of this possible action; it would appear more sensible to utilize an inert placebo to obtain the same effect without having to contend with the other possible risks associated with androgen use. Since some of the androgens in the circulation of the male are metabolized to estrogens, gynecomastia may result from the use of these hormones. Prostatic hypertrophy and possible exacerbation of prostatic cancer are also risks associated with androgen use [32].

In women, high doses of androgen increase libido [33, 34], but this effect is limited by the side effects that accompany its use: Hirsutism, acne, clitoral hypertrophy, and sodium retention are particularly troublesome. If androgen is used by a woman while she is pregnant, there is a significant risk of virilization of a female fetus, depending on timing, duration, and dosage of drug use.

Estrogens used by men (e.g., in the treatment of prostatic carcinoma) produce a prompt reduction or obliteration of libido and almost invariably result in impotence. This effect is probably attributable to depression of testosterone production [35]. Impairment of ejaculation is another common result of estrogen use; when ejaculation does occur, the volume of seminal fluid is significantly reduced. Spermatogenesis is disrupted, gynecomastia is common, especially at moderate or high doses, and facial hair growth often decreases substantially. Estrogens used by women do not typically exert a direct effect on libido, although this is not always the case (see Chaps. 5 and 15). When an estrogen deficiency exists, estrogen replacement therapy supports vaginal lubrication, the integrity of the vaginal mucosa, and maintenance of breast tissue mass.

Antiandrogens are substances that oppose the pharmacologic effects of androgens. The synthetic steroid compound *cyproterone acetate* is the prototype of the antiandrogens. This drug acts by competitive inhibition of androgens at all androgen target organs, including the brain, resulting in the "shutting down" of the hypothalamic-pituitary-testicular axis because the cyproterone acetate molecule is recognized falsely as being equivalent to testosterone. Cyproterone acetate reduces libido, impairs erectile capacity, and decreases the ability to be orgasmic in men. These are not side effects but the therapeutic effects of the drug, which is used in Europe as a treatment for deviant sexuality or sex criminals [36]. These effects appear after one week of drug use but increase in severity for up to three or four weeks, after which time a steady state is reached. Sperm production is markedly lowered by administration of this drug, which will typically induce a temporary sterility within six to eight weeks after it is begun [36]; in fact, research is currently being conducted attempting to isolate the sexual and reproductive consequences of the antiandrogens to provide a male contraceptive agent. Gynecomastia may occur in association with cyproterone acetate use. All these effects appear to be reversible upon cessation of drug use. The changes in libido, erection, and ejaculation reverse within one or two weeks, whereas the gynecomastia and infertility may require as long as four to six months to normalize. When the use of this drug is combined with psychotherapy, it is often possible to maintain improved patterns of sexual behavior even after discontinuing the medication. At the present time, however, the drug is not approved for clinical use in the United States. There are a number of difficult ethical questions that need to be answered in conjunction with such a drug, as well as the questions of physical safety and side effects that are still being investigated.

Medroxyprogesterone acetate (MPA) is another type of antiandrogen that is currently used for treating male precocious puberty and sex-offending behavior. MPA lowers production of testosterone [37, 38] and libido; the effects on pituitary function appear to be most specific for gonadotropin suppression, although the pituitary-adrenal axis is also affected [39]. Long-acting MPA can cause a dramatic reduction in sexual fantasies in pathologic psychosexual states such as obsessive pedophilia [40].

The use of *corticosteroids* on a long-term basis has not been carefully studied from the viewpoint of sexual effects. However, the fact that this class of hormones is extensively used to treat a wide variety of chronic diseases makes it a matter of some clinical relevance. A chronic daily dose greater than the equivalent of 20 mg of cortisol is sufficient to suppress the hypothalamic-pituitary-adrenal axis, but a higher dose leads to more frequent occurrence of many of the side effects of corticosteroids. The complications most likely to have impact on sexual function include hyperglycemia and the precipitation of previously latent diabetes mellitus, increased susceptibility to infections (including vaginitis), muscle weakness and muscle atrophy, depression and other mental disturbances [41], and suppression of pituitary gonadotropin secretion [42]. Doses of 30 mg per day of prednisone have been reported to depress spermatogenesis without affecting other testicular function [43], and variable effects on the ovary have been reported [42, 44]. Consideration must also be given to the primary disease process that requires prolonged corticosteroid treatment, since chronic illness alone can decrease libido and exert deleterious effects on sexual responsiveness in both men and women. ACTH or synthetic corticotropin analogues lower circulating testosterone levels in adult males [45, 46].

Tranquilizers, Sedatives, and Hypnotics

Drugs used to lower anxiety are difficult to assess in terms of their effects on sexual function, because reductions in anxiety typically enhance sexual performance, whereas sedation usually diminishes sexual responsiveness and libido. In addition, these drugs have not been studied systematically in reference to their sexual side effects.

Meprobamate was historically the first tranquilizer to gain widespread clinical use, although it is no longer as commonly prescribed. Its pharmacologic properties are similar to the barbiturates in many regards. The drug appears to have specific effects on the limbic system and therefore may directly alter libido or sexual functioning, although few data are available on this point.

Currently, the benzodiazepine compounds *chlordiazepoxide* and *diazepam* are the most frequently used tranquilizers in this country. Both drugs share sedative, antianxiety, and muscle-relaxing properties. Either drug may produce increases or decreases in libido, which may be attributable to reduced anxiety and sedation, respectively. Impotence may occur in association with the use of chlordiazepoxide or diazepam, but it seems to occur only at high dosage levels and then infrequently. However, to the extent that any sexual dysfunction is primarily a reflection of anxiety, these drugs may have a salutary effect sexually by lessening the underlying anxiety. While minor menstrual abnormalities and impaired ovulation have been reported to result from the use of benzodiazepines [47], these observations have not been confirmed by subsequent studies [48, 49]. Galactorrhea has been noted in some patients taking benzodiazepine compounds [50]. One report indicates an increased risk of congenital malformation associated with the use of meprobamate or chlordiazepoxide during the first trimester of pregnancy [51].

The *barbiturates* are used as hypnotics, sedatives, and anticonvulsive agents. They produce a central nervous system depression and also depress the activity of peripheral nerves and both skeletal and smooth muscle. Barbiturates can inhibit the action of androgen on sexual differentiation of the brain [52] and, in high doses, can suppress the release of pituitary gonadotropins. In women who abuse barbiturates, menstrual abnormalities are common; chronic barbiturate use alters circulating levels of both testosterone and estrogen by stimulating the induction of liver enzymes that metabolize these hormones. Barbiturates may sometimes lower sexual inhibitions and in this sense may enhance sexual function, but more commonly barbiturate users describe depressed libido, impotence, or loss of orgasmic responsiveness associated with drug use [53]. However, it appears that many persons who use barbiturates on a chronic therapeutic basis experience no alteration in sexual function.

Methaqualone is a nonbarbiturate hypnotic that recently has achieved a reputation as an enhancer of sexual experience among illicit users. Little objective study of this compound has been carried out, but it is clear from published survey data that the effects of methaqualone are highly variable, with some respondents indicating adverse sexual effects associated with its use [54].

Drugs Used to Treat Psychiatric Disorders

The *phenothiazines* are widely used in the treatment of psychotic disorders and have led to a revolution in the care of patients with chronic schizophrenia, permitting many individuals to function outside of an institutional setting. These drugs are also employed in treating a variety of other psychiatric disorders and may be useful in controlling nausea and vomiting and in the treatment of intractable hiccups.

Phenothiazines produce a sedative effect on both emotions and motor activity and are active at all levels of the nervous system. Chlorpromazine, the prototype of this class of agents, has strong adrenergic blocking activity and weaker peripheral cholinergic blocking activity [55]. It is also endocrinologically active, causing elevations in circulating prolactin and depression of gonadotropin secretion by its action at the hypothalamus [50, 56, 57]. Therefore, this drug can block ovulation, cause menstrual irregularities, induce galactorrhea or gynecomastia, and decrease testicular size. Despite these effects, sexual dysfunction is not a common accompaniment to the use of phenothiazine medications. When impotence occurs, it is usually at doses equivalent to 400 mg per day of chlorpromazine or greater. Decreased libido is found more frequently (in approximately 10 to 20 percent of patients) and may be a reflection of the overall sedative action of these drugs. Hypersexual behavior due to an underlying psychiatric disturbance will often abate with phenothiazine therapy. Inhibition of ejaculation, presumably because of autonomic disruption, has been a frequent side effect of thioridazine [58–60] and has also been reported with other phenothiazines [60]. The antihistaminic properties of some phenothiazines may lead to a decrease in vaginal lubrication in response to sexual arousal. Phenothiazines also potentiate the action of a variety of other drugs, including alcohol, barbiturates, and narcotics, so that sexual side effects may be magnified in persons using these combinations of drugs.

Haloperidol is a nonphenothiazine drug that is useful in the treatment of a variety of psychotic disorders; it is particularly efficacious in the Gilles de la Tourette syndrome (motor tics, spasmodic movements of the entire body, and compulsive use of obscenities). Galactorrhea and gynecomastia are common side effects that are probably attributable to the increase in prolactin caused by this drug as a result of blocking dopamine in the central nervous system [61]; impotence occurs in 10 to 20 percent of men using this drug [62]; and menstrual irregularities also occur. Interestingly, haloperidol increases testosterone production in men when given in low doses but suppresses testosterone when high doses are used [63].

Monoamine oxidase inhibitors (MAO inhibitors) are used in the treatment of depression and, less frequently, in the treatment of hypertension. Following the inhibition of monoamine oxidase, levels of dopamine and norepinephrine are elevated in the brain and other tissues, but it is not clear if these biochemical changes are the sole cause of therapeutic effectiveness. Autonomic side effects that are dose-related are common with these drugs, with delayed ejaculation or loss of ability to ejaculate affecting 25 to 30 percent of the men using MAO inhibitors and impotence occurring in approximately 10 to 15 percent of men receiving these drugs in moderate to high doses. These effects typically are reversible within several weeks after discontinuance of the drug. There are indications that MAO inhibitors may decrease testosterone production in the male [64].

The *tricyclic antidepressants* (imipramine, amitriptyline, and related compounds) are highly efficacious in the treatment of depression. In considering the sexual side effects of this class of drugs as well as those of the MAO inhibitors, it should be remembered that depressed libido and impaired sexual functioning are frequent findings in depression, probably occurring in a majority of patients [65]. In most instances, successful treatment of the mood disorder will result in amelioration of the sexual difficulties. However, in approximately 5 percent of depressed patients, primarily those who continue to be sexually functional despite their depressed state, the tricyclic compounds cause a paradoxic disturbance of sexual functioning at the very time when the depression is lifting [66, 67]. It is likely that this reaction is attributable primarily to atropinelike effects sometimes produced by these drugs: dry mouth, constipation, dizziness, tachycardia, urinary retention, and impotence [68, 69]. In such instances, the sexual symptoms will sometimes subside when the drug dosage is reduced or if there is a change to a different tricyclic compound. Inhibition of ejaculation may also occur with tricyclic antidepressants [68, 70].

Lithium carbonate is a newer drug used in the treatment of mania and hypomania as well as for the treatment of bipolar manic-depressive illness. It is known to have a variety of endocrine effects, including a tendency to induce mild goiter and minimal hypothyroidism [71], interference with antidiuretic hormone action [71, 72], and suppression of serum testosterone levels in adult men [73]. It is difficult to assess the specific effects of this drug on sexual behavior and sexual function, both because it has not been subjected to systematic study and because mania itself can produce a wide spectrum of changes in sexuality, including both hypersexual and hyposexual behaviors [74]. Nevertheless, because of the endocrine changes associated with the use of lithium, it is quite probable that in some individuals this drug will be associated with impotence.

Miscellaneous
Prescription Drugs

Anticholinergic drugs are used primarily in the treatment of gastrointestinal disorders such as peptic ulcer disease and irritable colitis. The inhibition of acetylcholine that makes these drugs therapeutically useful in the gastrointestinal tract also results in inhibition of the parasympathetic nervous system, leading to impairment of reflex vasocongestion in the penis (which ordinarily produces and maintains erection). Because of this effect, impotence is a frequent side effect in men receiving this type of medication. Women may experience decreased vaginal lubrication and interference with sexual arousal as a result of the use of anticholinergics because these phenomena are partly dependent on vasocongestive changes occurring in vaginal tissues. *Cimetidine,* a histamine antagonist used in the management of duodenal ulcer disease, has also been reported as a cause of impotence [75]. Gynecomastia is a frequent side effect of this drug, which also impairs sperm production and alters the hypothalamic-pituitary-gonadal axis [76].

Clofibrate, used to lower serum cholesterol or triglycerides, diminishes libido and impairs potency in some patients by unknown mechanisms. *Disulfiram* has been reported as an occasional cause of impotence [60], but it is not clear if this is actually a drug effect or if it reflects the high incidence of potency problems in alcoholic men (see Chap. 10). *Digitalis* and other cardiac glycosides can cause impotence and gynecomastia [77]; the mechanism of action may be related to the finding that digoxin lowers circulating levels of testosterone [78], although this effect may have more to do with chronic illness and altered circulatory dynamics than with drug use alone. *Antihistamines* can produce depressed libido in either men or women as a result of their sedative effects, and vaginal lubrication may be significantly decreased while antihistamines are being used.

L-Dopa is extremely useful in the treatment of patients with parkinsonism. When this drug first became clinically available, it was the subject of considerable interest, not only because it dramatically relieved the tremors, paralysis, and motor disturbances of this disorder but also because initial reports pointed toward a possible aphrodisiac action associated with the drug [79, 80]. More careful observation and analysis have revealed, however, that although L-dopa is highly active in an endocrine sense, inhibiting prolactin and raising circulating growth hormone levels, it does not raise testosterone levels in man [81]; the probable explanation for the improved libido in patients receiving L-dopa is the alleviation of a frustrating and incapacitating chronic illness.

Nonprescription Drugs and Sexual Function

Alcohol

Alcohol and its effects on sexuality have been the subject of considerable conjecture for centuries. In *Macbeth*, Shakespeare reported that "it provokes the desire but it takes away the performance" (act 2, scene 3, 1.34). Since that time, research has primarily substantiated the bard's observation. Farkas and Rosen [82] gave alcohol in three different doses to college-age men and measured the increase in penile tumescence that occurred in response to erotic films. They found that blood alcohol concentrations well below levels of intoxication produced a marked suppression of erection. Similarly, Wilson and Lawson [83] administered varying doses of alcohol (ranging from 0.3 to 4.3 ounces of 80-proof alcohol) to university women and found a significant negative effect on vaginal pulse pressure in response to watching an erotic film. Other studies have obtained similar findings in both animals and humans [84, 85]. The probable basis for the suppressing effect of alcohol is that alcohol acts as a depressant to the central nervous sytem, thus interfering with pathways of reflex transmission of sexual arousal. In addition to these acute effects of alcohol use, which certainly occur in situations that correspond to social drinking patterns, alcohol has also recently been shown to lower circulating testosterone and luteinizing hormone levels in healthy young men [86, 87].

The acute effects of alcohol on sexuality are more complex than the preceding facts imply, however. Some researchers have suggested that alcohol has a "disinhibition" effect—that is to say, it lowers certain sexual inhibitions a person may ordinarily have, so that in some people the feelings of relaxation and increased openness to sex may combine to facilitate sexual response. In one study, 68 percent of women and 45 percent of men queried reported that alcohol enhanced their sexual pleasure [88], which can be seen as substantiation of the "disinhibition" theory. More recently, data from a series of interviews conducted at the Masters & Johnson Institute revealed that fewer than 35 percent of women claimed that alcohol had a positive effect on their sexual experience, whereas approximately 55 percent reported that alcohol detracted from their sexual feelings. It is not surprising that widespread differences in individual responses were noted here, since only a portion of the attributed "drug effect" may actually come from the pharmacologic activity—including central nervous system depression—that alcohol is known to possess. The expectations of the user and the setting of alcohol use are both important ingredients in defining the perception of effects that an individual will note [84]. In addition, if a person is able to use just enough alcohol to overcome anxieties or guilt associated with sex, but not enough to impede sexual performance, the net effect may be a salutary one. If, however, this balance is exceeded, the person involved may be too drunk to care very much.

Cigarettes

Although cigarette smoking is a common practice widely acknowledged to be linked with a number of health problems, very little systematic study has been conducted concerning the impact of smoking on sexual function. There is recent evidence indicating an association between smoking and an early onset of menopause [89] and cancer of the cervix [90], but a report suggesting that plasma testosterone may be suppressed by cigarette smoking [91] has not been substantiated by another study that found that acute cigarette smoking correlated with increased plasma testosterone concentrations [92]. Our own studies in both clinical and research populations fail to reveal a difference in circulating testosterone levels between smokers and nonsmokers; in addition, a lower incidence of cigarette smoking was found in 246 men with impotence than in age-matched men with normal potency. The experimental animal literature regarding the effects of nicotine or smoking on sex and fertility, reviewed in reference 93, is generally inconclusive and methodologically imprecise. Of signal importance, however, is the extensive set of data indicating that smoking during pregnancy is associated with decreased birthweight [94–100], an increased risk of spontaneous abortion [99, 100], and elevated perinatal mortality [97, 100, 101].

Marihuana

Considerable controversy has surrounded the issue of the effects of marihuana on sex. There are numerous reasons why this is so. Although marihuana is an illegal drug, in many circles its use is the norm rather than the exception, and nonusers may be under pressure to experiment in order to be accepted socially. In this regard, one of the reasons frequently cited for initiating the use of marihuana is its reputation as an enhancer of sexual feelings and experiences, so that the user often has positive expectations of an enjoyable drug effect. It is difficult to separate the expectations from the actual drug effect except under rigorous research conditions (e.g., a double-blind drug-placebo administration experiment), which have not been used to date. When such a project was proposed, in a format similar to the alcohol experiments mentioned previously that measured penile tumescence in response to visual erotic stimuli, it was stopped because of political pressures [102]. The research that has been done thus far has been difficult to interpret because of many issues of methodology that are difficult to solve or to control for [103], including the fact that many people who use marihuana also use other drugs, such as alcohol and tobacco, as well as psychoactive substances. It may be helpful to look at the biologic and behavioral aspects of the effects of marihuana on sex separately in order to gain a clear understanding of the variables involved.

Animal studies have shown that marihuana or its active ingredients can decrease copulatory behavior in male rats [104], inhibit spermatogenesis [105, 106], and depress circulating levels of testosterone [106–108]. Marihuana has also been reported to suppress LH and prolactin in female rodents [109] and to have an antiovulatory effect in both rodents and primates [110–112]. The weight of such evidence, even after making appropriate allowances for methodologic differences in interspecies studies, leaves little doubt that marihuana is endocrinologically active.

In studies in men, chronic marihuana use was reported to be associated with the development of gynecomastia [113], although further research has not substantiated this finding. However, both acute administration [114] and chronic, frequent marihuana use [115] have been shown to depress circulating levels of testosterone in healthy young men (see Fig. 13-1). Although one carefully designed study did not find a suppression of morning testosterone levels during three weeks of daily marihuana use [116], a similar study design that extended over a longer period of drug use showed significant decreases in testosterone beginning with the fifth week of daily marihuana use (see Fig. 13-2) [117].

The depression of testosterone is not, of course, always significant in terms of either biologic function or behavior. Nevertheless, some men who are chronic marihuana users have been found to be impotent and to experience a return to potency within a few weeks after discontinuing use of the drug [115]. Furthermore, inhibited spermatogenesis also has been observed in association with chronic marihuana use [115, 118].

Studies of acute marihuana use by women who were either postmenopausal or who had previously had their ovaries removed surgically demonstrated that marihuana lowers pituitary gonadotropin levels by approximately 35 percent, indicating that the effect of marihuana is centrally mediated [119]. In studies of chronic marihuana use by healthy women aged 18 to 30, users were found to have somewhat shorter menstrual cycles than nonusers, although LH and FSH levels were not significantly different between the two groups. Interestingly, testosterone levels were higher in the women who used

Figure 13-1. Plasma testosterone levels in men (ages 18–28) who had never used marihuana ("controls") and in men who had used marihuana at least 4 days per week for a minimum of 6 months. (From Kolodny, Masters, Kolodner, and Toro [115]. Reprinted, by permission, from *The New England Journal of Medicine* 290:873, 1974.)

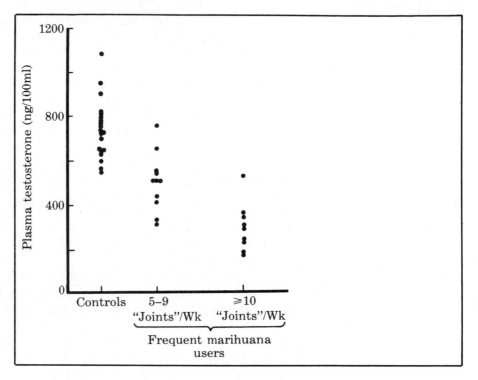

marihuana chronically (probably reflecting the adrenocortical contribution to testosterone synthesis), and prolactin levels were significantly lower [120].

Behavioral studies have shown consistently that marihuana use correlates strongly with sexual activity. For example, Goode reported that 72 percent of 389 students who had tried marihuana were sexually experienced, whereas 66 percent of the 150 students he surveyed who had never used marihuana were virgins [121]. Marihuana use has also been reported to correlate with number of sexual partners, frequency of sexual activity, and satisfaction with sex. However, these correlations do not imply a cause-and-effect relationship. In fact, it should be recognized that there is a high correlation between drug use in general and a wide variety of attitudes and behaviors, so that marihuana use and sexual experience may both be characteristics of a substantial group of youths and young adults who hold to a particular set of values that

Figure 13-2. Plasma testosterone levels (mean ± S.E.M.) in 20 young adult males using marihuana during a 94-day controlled experiment conducted at the Neuropsychiatric Institute of the University of California at Los Angeles. (Data from R. C. Kolodny, P. Lessin, and S. Cohen.)

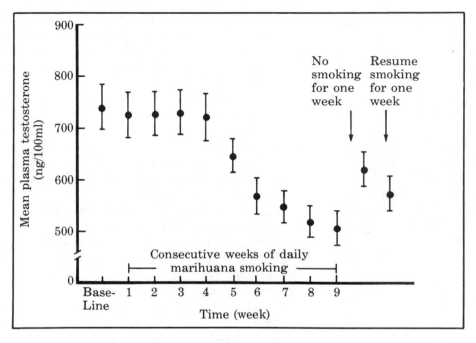

are viewed by certain segments of our society as nontraditional and threatening.

Five years of interviewing subjects at the Masters & Johnson Institute has resulted in a data base of information about the effects of marihuana on sex in 800 men and 500 women between the ages of 18 and 30. Briefly summarized, the majority of both men (83 percent) and women (81 percent) indicated that marihuana enhanced the enjoyment of sex for them. However, the responses to specific questions regarding how this effect occurred were revealing. For example, most men denied that marihuana increased their sexual desire, increased the firmness of their erection, made it easier to get or maintain erections, gave them a greater degree of control over ejaculation, or increased the intensity of orgasm. Similarly, the majority of women stated that marihuana did not increase their interest in sex, increase their arousability, increase the amount of vaginal lubrication, increase the intensity of orgasm, or allow them to be orgasmic more frequently. Instead, both men and women attributed the enhancing effect of marihuana on sex to factors such as an increased sense of touch, a greater degree of relaxation (both physically and mentally), and being more in tune with one's partner. Most people said that if their sexual partner was not "high" at the same time they were, the effect was unpleasant or dyssynchronizing, rather than enhancing.

In this same series of interviews, it was found that while fewer than 10 percent of a control group of men who had never used marihuana and a group who used marihuana once or twice a week experienced potency disorders, almost one-fifth of the men using marihuana on a daily basis were impotent [117]. No statistically significant relationship was found between sexual dysfunction and chronic, intensive marihuana use by women.

What is very clear, out of all this, is that marihuana is a drug that heightens suggestibility. Alterations in time perception and in the perception of tactile sensations are frequently reported, but these changes may not correspond to actuality. Thus the marihuana user may well be perceiving an enhancing effect of this drug on sex, but in reality, sexual performance may be unaltered or even impaired. In instances in which marihuana relaxes inhibitions and loosens ordinary restraints on sexual behavior, people who are normally very anxious or guilty regarding sex may benefit. In some people, of course, the relaxation produced by this drug progresses rapidly to somnolence, which is not an ideal state for sexual activity.

Heroin and Methadone

Drug addicts have long been known to experience disruptions in sexual function, but the cause of such problems has been obscure. On the one hand, a wide variety of theoretical intrapsychic factors relating to the significance of "mainlining" as a substitute for sex have been discussed; Chessick has suggested that the intensely pleasurable sensation of intravenous injection of heroin constitutes a "pharmacogenic orgasm" which is related to a feeling of increased ego mastery and decreased libidinal needs [122]. On the other hand, practical factors involved in addictive behavior, such as preoccupation with use of the drug, decreased social interaction, and the exhausting daily search for drugs or money to buy drugs, may be viewed as significant behavioral components of diminished sexual activity or interest in sexual activity [123]. More recently, however, a clearer understanding of some of the biologic factors involved in drug addiction has emerged to help explain the sexual difficulties of the person addicted to drugs.

Azizi and his colleagues demonstrated lowered serum testosterone in male heroin and methadone addicts [124]; this finding has since been substantiated by others [125–128]. Heroin addiction also lowers pituitary gonadotropin levels in serum [125, 128]. Partly because of methodologic differences, other investigations presented somewhat different findings. Cushman found that of 19 men addicted to heroin, 12 reported impaired libido, 10 were impotent, and 15 had a delayed ejaculation time [129]. However, mean plasma testosterone levels did not differ significantly among these addicts, methadone-maintained addicts, former addicts who were not using drugs, and a normal control group. Cicero and coworkers described serum testosterone levels in methadone users that were 43 percent lower than normal, but found no such effect in heroin addicts [130]. They reported that libido was suppressed in 100 percent of heroin addicts and 96.5 percent of methadone users and also noted a high frequency of potency problems and retarded ejaculation or failure to ejaculate in both drug-using groups. Mintz and his colleagues reported that both heroin and methadone use are related to sexual problems, but found that men on methadone experienced fewer sexual difficulties than while they were using heroin [131]. From these studies, it is clear that heroin and methadone are capable of exerting an active endocrine effect that may predispose to the development of sexual inadequacy.

Although fewer studies have been done with female addicts, Bai and coworkers [132] reported that decreased libido was seen in 60 percent of women in their series, along with the following findings: amenorrhea (45 percent), infertility (90 percent), galactorrhea (25 percent), and reduction in breast size (30 percent). Santen, Bilic, and colleagues [133] showed that narcotic addiction in women is frequently associated with amenorrhea, which is the result of alteration of hypothalamic mechanisms controlling the cyclicity of gonadotropin release.

Medical management of the drug addict who is attempting rehabilitation, whether through a methadone program, psychotherapy, or some other avenue, can be facilitated by some practical considerations. Many addicted women resort to prostitution as a means of supporting their drug habit [134]. They may subsequently have negative feelings toward sex that reflect guilt, loss of self-esteem, or hostility toward men—all issues that will need to be dealt with actively. Poor nutrition is a common finding in addicts and may be contributing to sexual problems. Adequate dietary recommendations are an important part of the treatment plan. If sexual problems persist in the ex-addict, one should recognize that this may predispose to a return to drug use as a means of coping with these problems (lowering desire, reducing anxiety, bolstering self-esteem, and achieving a false sense of mastery of one's life). Attempting to identify the cause of the problem and, when possible, to provide counseling to both sexual partners may often be a useful approach. One should remember, too, that cessation of drug use will not restore sexual and reproductive function to normal immediately; endocrine or psychological problems may persist for months before improving. An open, supportive, educational environment will be optimal in such circumstances.

Amphetamines

Little objective study has been conducted to assess the effects of amphetamine use on sexuality. Bell and Trethowan studied 14 amphetamine users and noted some degree of "sexual abnormality" in 13 of them [135], but most of these abnormalities preceded the use of amphetamines. These authors and others [136] have generally concluded that amphetamine use leads to an increase in libido, but this conclusion is inferential. The fact that amphetamine users report a higher rate of "promiscuity" than nonusers [137] is unlikely to be a drug effect and more realistically reflects personality variables that may predispose to drug abuse. A detailed survey of drug-sex practices in Haight-Ashbury [54] indicates that highly experienced polydrug users are unlikely to choose amphetamines to enhance sexual functioning.

Miscellaneous Drugs

Cocaine is reputed to possess sexually stimulating properties, including those of increasing desire, improving firmness and durability of erections, and intensifying orgasm for both men and women. However, 14 of 39 men reported loss of erection associated with cocaine use [54]. Priapism has also occurred as a result of cocaine use. Research involving the sexual effects of this drug is extremely scanty, and it is not possible to draw any conclusions at this time.

Amyl nitrate is a rapid-acting vasodilator that achieved notoriety as an aphrodisiac that would intensify the orgasmic experience for both men and women [138]. The drug is inhaled and produces tachycardia and local vasodilation; headaches and hypotension are frequent side effects, and syncope, S-T segment depression of the electrocardiogram, and other cardiovascular effects may also occur. These effects are not necessarily innocuous, and the drug should not be used recreationally by persons with cardiovascular, ocular, or cerebrovascular disease.

Lysergic acid diethylamide (LSD) and related psychedelic compounds have been purported to act as aphrodisiacs, but the scanty research literature fails to substantiate this view. Piemme points out that "taking LSD to initiate sexual relations is useless because the user can't remain focused on what he started to do" [139]. In interviews at the

Masters & Johnson Institute with 85 men and 55 women who had used LSD on three or more occasions, fewer than 15 percent of each sex claimed that LSD enhanced sexual participation.

Conclusion

Although drug use has been pursued for centuries as a means of increasing sexual interest and enjoyment, there is little objective data to support the existence of a true aphrodisiac. Drug effects are highly variable, both from person to person and for the same person at different times, and it is certain that subjective sexual perceptions may be widely altered as a result of drug use. All health-care professionals should be familiar with the possible deleterious effects that pharmacologic agents may have on sexual function, since these effects may influence both the patient's quality of life and his or her compliance with a treatment program.

References

1. Page, L. B., and Sidd, J. J. Medical management of primary hypertension: Part II. *New England Journal of Medicine* 287:1018–1023, 1972.
2. Breckenridge, A., Welborn, T. A., Dollery, C. T., and Fraser, R. Glucose tolerance in hypertensive patients on long-term diuretic therapy. *Lancet* 1:61–64, 1967.
3. Costrini, N. V., and Thomson, W. M. *Manual of Medical Therapeutics* (22nd ed.). Boston: Little, Brown and Co., 1977.
4. Loriaux, D. L., Menard, R., Taylor, A., Pita, J. C., and Santen, R. Spironolactone and endocrine dysfunctions. *Annals of Internal Medicine* 85:630–636, 1976.
5. Stripp, B., Taylor, A. A., Bartter, F. C., Gillette, J. R., Loriaux, D. L., Easley, R., and Menard, R. H. Effect of spironolactone on sex hormones in man. *Journal of Clinical Endocrinology and Metabolism* 41:777–781, 1975.
6. Levitt, J. I. Spironolactone therapy and amenorrhea. *Journal of the American Medical Association* 211:2014–2015, 1970.
7. Caminos-Torres, R., Ma, L., and Snyder, P. J. Gynecomastia and semen abnormalities induced by spironolactone in normal men. *Journal of Clinical Endocrinology and Metabolism* 45:255–260, 1977.
8. Rose, L. I., Underwood, R. H., Newmark, S. R., Kisch, E. S., and Williams, G. H. Pathophysiology of spironolactone-induced gynecomastia. *Annals of Internal Medicine* 87:398–403, 1977.
9. Schane, H. P., and Potts, G. O. Oral progestational activity of spironolactone. *Journal of Clinical Endocrinology and Metabolism* 47:691–694, 1978.
10. Kolodny, R. C. Effects of alpha-methyldopa on male sexual function. *Sexuality and Disability* 1:223–228, 1978.
11. Newman, R. J., and Salerno, H. R. Sexual dysfunction due to methyldopa (letter). *British Medical Journal* 4:106, 1974.
12. Laver, M. C. Sexual behaviour patterns in male hypertensives. *Australian and New Zealand Journal of Medicine* 4:29–31, 1974.

13. Page, L. B.   Advising hypertensive patients about sex. *Medical Aspects of Human Sexuality* 9(1):103–104, 1975.
14. McKinney, W. T., Jr., and Kane, F. J., Jr.   Depression with the use of alpha-methyldopa. *American Journal of Psychiatry* 124:80–81, 1967.
15. Steiner, J., Cassar, J., Mashiter, K., Dawes, T., Fraser, T. R., and Breckenridge, A.   Effects of methyldopa on prolactin and growth hormone. *British Medical Journal* 1:1186–1188, 1976.
16. Money, J., and Yankowitz, R.   The sympathetic-inhibiting effects of the drug Ismelin on human male eroticism, with a note on Mellaril. *Journal of Sex Research* 3:69–82, 1967.
17. Kolodny, R. C.   Antihypertensive Drugs and Male Sexual Function. Presented at the Eleventh National Sex Institute, Washington, D.C., April 1, 1978.
18. Perry, H. M., Jr.   Late toxicity to hydralazine resembling systemic lupus erythematosus or rheumatoid arthritis. *American Journal of Medicine* 54:58–72, 1973.
19. Raskind, N. H., and Fishman, R. A.   Pyridoxine-deficiency neuropathy due to hydralazine. *New England Journal of Medicine* 273:1182–1185, 1965.
20. Turkington, R. W.   Prolactin secretion in patients treated with various drugs: Phenothiazines, tricyclic antidepressants, reserpine, and methyldopa. *Archives of Internal Medicine* 130:349–354, 1972.
21. Miller, R. A.   Propranolol and impotence (letter). *Annals of Internal Medicine* 85:682–683, 1976.
22. Warren, S. C., and Warren, S. G.   Propranolol and sexual impotence (letter). *Annals of Internal Medicine* 86:112, 1977.
23. Pettinger, W. A.   Clonidine, a new antihypertensive drug. *New England Journal of Medicine* 293:1179–1180, 1975.
24. Nickerson, M., and Ruedy, J.   Antihypertensive Agents and the Drug Therapy of Hypertension. In L. S. Goodman and A. Gilman (eds.), *The Pharmacologic Basis of Therapeutics* (5th ed.). New York: Macmillan Co., 1975.
25. Metz, S. A., Halter, J. B., and Robertson, R. P.   Induction of defective insulin secretion and impaired glucose tolerance by clonidine. *Diabetes* 27:554–562, 1978.
26. Metoprolol. *Medical Letter on Drugs and Therapeutics* 20:97–98, 1978.
27. Yudkin, J. S.   Peyronie's disease in association with metoprolol (letter), *Lancet* 2:1355, 1977.
28. Sheps, S. G., and Kirkpatrick, R. A.   Subject review: Hypertension. *Mayo Clinic Proceedings* 50:709–720, 1975.
29. Blackwell, B.   Patient compliance. *New England Journal of Medicine* 289:249–252, 1973.
30. Weiss, N. S.   Relation of high blood pressure to headache, epistaxis, and selected other symptoms: The United States Health Examination Survey of Adults. *New England Journal of Medicine* 287:631–633, 1972.
31. Page, I. H.   Hypertension: A symptomless but dangerous disease (editorial). *New England Journal of Medicine* 287:665–666, 1972.
32. Guinan, P. D., Sadoughi, W., Alsheik, H., Ablin, R. J., Alrenga, D., and

Bush, I. M. Impotence therapy and cancer of the prostate. *American Journal of Surgery* 131:599–600, 1976.

33. Schon, M., and Sutherland, A. M. The role of hormones in human behavior: III. Changes in female sexuality after hypophysectomy. *Journal of Clinical Endocrinology and Metabolism* 20:833–841, 1960.

34. Waxenberg, S. E., Drellich, M. G., and Sutherland, A. M. The role of hormones in human behavior: I. Changes in female sexuality after adrenalectomy. *Journal of Clinical Endocrinology and Metabolism* 19:193–202, 1959.

35. Kent, J. R., Bischoff, A. J., Arduno, L. J., Mellinger, G. T., Byar, D. P., Hill, M., and Kozbur, X. Estrogen dosage and suppression of testosterone levels in patients with prostatic carcinoma. *Journal of Urology* 109:858–860, 1973.

36. Laschet, U., and Laschet, L. Antiandrogens in the treatment of sexual deviations of men. *Journal of Steroid Biochemistry* 6:821–826, 1977.

37. Rivarola, M. A., Camacho, A. M., and Migeon, C. J. Effect of treatment with medroxyprogesterone acetate (Provera) on testicular function. *Journal of Clinical Endocrinology and Metabolism* 28:679–684, 1968.

38. Kirschner, M. A., and Schneider, G. Suppression of the pituitary-Leydig cell axis and sebum production in normal men by medroxyprogesterone acetate (Provera). *Acta Endocrinologica* 69:385–393, 1972.

39. Meyer, W. J., III, Walker, P. A., Wiedeking, C., Money, J., Kowarski, A. A., Migeon, C. J., and Borgaonkar, D. S. Pituitary function in adult males receiving medroxyprogesterone acetate. *Fertility and Sterility* 28:1072–1076, 1977.

40. Pinta, E. R. Treatment of obsessive homosexual pedophilic fantasies with medroxyprogesterone acetate. *Biological Psychiatry* 13:369–373, 1978.

41. Nielsen, J. B., Drivsholm, A., Fischer, F., and Brøchner-Mortensen, K. Long-term treatment with corticosteroids in rheumatoid arthritis. *Acta Medica Scandinavica* 173:177–183, 1963.

42. Sakakura, M., Takebe, K., and Nakagawa, S. Inhibition of luteinizing hormone secretion induced by synthetic LRH by long-term treatment with glucocorticoids in human subjects. *Journal of Clinical Endocrinology and Metabolism* 40:774–779, 1975.

43. Mancini, R. E., Lavieri, J. C., Muller, F., Andrada, J. A., and Saraceni, D. J. Effect of prednisone upon normal and pathologic human spermatogenesis. *Fertility and Sterility* 17:500–513, 1966.

44. David, D. S., Grieco, M. H., and Cushman, P. Adrenal glucocorticoids after twenty years: A review of their clinically relevant consequences. *Journal of Chronic Diseases* 22:637–711, 1970.

45. Beitins, I. Z., Bayard, F., Kowarski, A., and Migeon, C. J. The effect of ACTH administration on plasma testosterone, dihydrotestosterone and serum LH concentrations in normal men. *Steroids* 21:553–588, 1973.

46. Irvine, W. J., Toft, A. D., Wilson, K. S., Fraser, R., Wilson, A., Young, J., Hunter, W. M., Ismail, A. A. A., and Burger, P. E. The effect of synthetic corticotropin analogues on adrenocortical, anterior pituitary and tes-

ticular function. *Journal of Clinical Endocrinology and Metabolism* 39:511–529, 1974.

47. Whitelaw, M. J. Menstrual irregularities associated with use of methaminodiazepoxide. *Journal of the American Medical Association* 175:400–401, 1961.

48. Schwartz, E. D., and Smith, J. J. The effect of chlordiazepoxide on the female reproductive cycle as tested in infertility patients. *Western Journal of Surgery in Obstetrics and Gynecology* 71:74–76, 1963.

49. Greenblatt, D. J., and Shader, R. I. *Benzodiazepines in Clinical Practice.* New York: Raven Press, 1974.

50. Kleinberg, D. L., Noel, G. L., and Frantz, A. G. Galactorrhea: A study of 235 cases, including 48 with pituitary tumors. *New England Journal of Medicine* 296:589–600, 1977.

51. Milkovich, L., and Van Den Berg, B. J. Effects of prenatal meprobamate and chlordiazepoxide hydrochloride on human embryonic and fetal development. *New England Journal of Medicine* 291:1268–1271, 1974.

52. Gorski, R. A. Barbiturates and Sexual Differentiation of the Brain. In E. Zimmermann and R. George (eds.), *Narcotics and the Hypothalamus.* New York: Raven Press, 1974. Pp. 197–210.

53. Masters, W. H., and Kolodny, R. C. Unpublished data, 1977.

54. Gay, G. R., Newmeyer, J. A., Elion, R. A., and Wieder, S. Drug-Sex Practice in the Haight-Ashbury or "The Sensuous Hippie." In M. Sandler and G. L. Gessa (eds.), *Sexual Behavior: Pharmacology and Biochemistry.* New York: Raven Press, 1975. Pp. 63–79.

55. Byck, R. Drugs and the Treatment of Psychiatric Disorders. In L. S. Goodman and A. Gilman (eds.), *The Pharmacological Basis of Therapeutics* (5th ed.). New York: Macmillan Co., 1975. Pp. 152–200.

56. Kleinberg, D. L., Noel, G. L., and Frantz, A. G. Chlorpromazine stimulation and L-dopa suppression of plasma prolactin in man. *Journal of Clinical Endocrinology and Metabolism* 33:873–876, 1971.

57. Meltzer, H. Y., and Fang, V. S. The effect of neuroleptics on serum prolactin in schizophrenic patients. *Archives of General Psychiatry* 33:279–286, 1976.

58. Kotin, J., Wilbert, D. E., Verburg, D., and Soldinger, S. M. Thioridazine and sexual dysfunction. *American Journal of Psychiatry* 133:82–85, 1976.

59. Shader, R. I. Sexual dysfunction associated with thioridazine hydrochloride. *Journal of the American Medical Association* 188:1007–1009, 1964.

60. Story, N. L. Sexual dysfunction resulting from drug side effects. *Journal of Sex Research* 10(2):132–149, 1974.

61. Rubin, R. T., Poland, R. E., O'Connor, D., Gouin, P. R., and Tower, B. B. Selective neuroendocrine effects of low-dose haloperidol in normal adult men. *Psychopharmacology* 47:135–140, 1976.

62. Kolodny, R. C. Unpublished data, 1978.

63. Rubin, R. T., Poland, R. E., and Tower, B. B. Prolactin-related testosterone secretion in normal adult men. *Journal of Clinical Endocrinology and Metabolism* 42:112–116, 1976.

64. Urry, R. L., Dougherty, K. A., and Cockett, A. T. K. Age-related changes in male rat reproductive organ weights and plasma testosterone concen-

trations after administration of a monoamine oxidase inhibitor. *Fertility and Sterility* 27:1326–1334, 1976.

65. Woodruff, R. A., Murphy, G. E., and Herjanic, M.   The natural history of affective disorders: I. Symptoms of 72 patients at the time of index hospital admission. *Journal of Psychiatric Research* 5:255–263, 1967.

66. Simpson, G. M., Blair, J. H., and Amuso, D.   Effects of antidepressants on genito-urinary function. *Diseases of the Nervous System* 26:787–789, 1965.

67. Kolodny, R. C.   Unpublished data, 1977.

68. Nininger, J. E.   Inhibition of ejaculation by amitriptyline. *American Journal of Psychiatry* 135:750–751, 1978.

69. Blackwell, B., Stefopoulos, A., Enders, P., Kuzma, R., and Adolphe, A.   Anticholinergic activity of two tricyclic antidepressants. *American Journal of Psychiatry* 135:722–724, 1978.

70. Couper-Smartt, J. D.   A technique for surveying side-effects of tricyclic drugs with reference to reported sexual effects. *Journal of International Medicine* 1:473–476, 1973.

71. Baldessarini, R. J., and Lipinski, J. F.   Lithium salts: 1970–1975. *Annals of Internal Medicine* 83:527–533, 1975.

72. Singer, I., and Rotenberg, D.   Physiology in medicine: Mechanisms of lithium action. *New England Journal of Medicine* 289:254–260, 1973.

73. Sanchez, R. S., Murthy, G. G., Mehta, J., Shreeve, W. W., and Singh, F. R.   Pituitary-testicular axis in patients on lithium therapy. *Fertility and Sterility* 27:667–669, 1976.

74. Spalt, L.   Sexual behavior and affective disorders. *Diseases of the Nervous System* 36:644–647, 1975.

75. Wolfe, M. M.   Impotence on cimetidine treatment (letter). *New England Journal of Medicine* 300:94, 1979.

76. Van Thiel, D. H., Gavalen, J. S., Smith, W. I. Jr., and Paul, G.   Hypothalamic-pituitary gonadal dysfunction in men using cimetidine. *New England Journal of Medicine* 300:1012–1015, 1979.

77. Navab, A., Koss, L. G., and La Due, J. S.   Estrogen-like activity of digitalis. *Journal of the American Medical Association* 194:30–32, 1965.

78. Stoffer, S. S., Hynes, K. M., Jiang, N., and Ryan, R. J.   Digoxin and abnormal serum hormone levels. *Journal of the American Medical Association* 225:1643–1644, 1973.

79. Hyyppä, M., Rinne, U. K., and Sonninen, V.   The activating effect of L-Dopa treatment on sexual functions and its experimental background. *Acta Neurologica Scandinavica* 46 (Suppl. 43):223–224, 1970.

80. Bowers, M. B., Van Woert, M., and Davis, L.   Sexual behavior during L-dopa treatment for Parkinsonism. *American Journal of Psychiatry* 127:1691–1693, 1971.

81. Sinhamahapatra, S. B., and Kirschner, M. A.   Effect of L-DOPA on testosterone and luteinizing hormone production. *Journal of Clinical Endocrinology and Metabolism* 34:756–758, 1972.

82. Farkas, G. M., and Rosen, R. C.   Effect of alcohol on elicited male sexual response. *Journal of Studies on Alcohol* 37:265–272, 1976.

83. Wilson, G. T., and Lawson, D. M.   Effects of alcohol on sexual arousal in women. *Journal of Abnormal Psychology* 85:489–497, 1976.

84. Wilson, G. T. Alcohol and human sexual behavior. *Behaviour Research and Therapy* 15:239–252, 1977.
85. Briddell, D. W., and Wilson, G. T. The effects of alcohol and expectancy on male sexual arousal. *Journal of Abnormal Psychology* 85:225–234, 1976.
86. Gordon, G. G., Altman, K., Southren, A. L., Rubin, E., and Lieber, C. S. Effect of alcohol (ethanol) administration on sex-hormone metabolism in normal men. *New England Journal of Medicine* 295:793–797, 1976.
87. Mendelson, J. H., Mello, N. K., and Ellingboe, J. Effects of acute alcohol intake on pituitary-gonadal hormones in normal human males. *Journal of Pharmacology and Experimental Therapeutics* 202:676–682, 1977.
88. Athanasiou, R., Shaver, P., and Tavris, C. Sex. *Psychology Today* 4:37–52, 1970.
89. Jick, H., Porter, J., and Morrison, A. S. Relation between smoking and age of natural menopause. *Lancet* 1:1354–1355, 1977.
90. Williams, R. R., and Horm, J. W. Association of cancer sites with tobacco and alcohol consumption and socioeconomic status of patients. *Journal of the National Cancer Institute* 58:525–547, 1977.
91. Briggs, M. H. Cigarette smoking and infertility in men. *Medical Journal of Australia* 1:616–617, 1973.
92. Dotson, L. E., Robertson, L. S., and Tuchfeld, B. Plasma alcohol, smoking, hormone concentrations and self-reported aggression: A study in a social-drinking situation. *Journal of Studies on Alcohol* 36:578–586, 1975.
93. Sterling, T. D., and Kobayashi, D. A critical review of reports on the effect of smoking on sex and fertility. *Journal of Sex Research* 11:201–217, 1975.
94. Miller, H. C., Hassanein, K., and Hensleigh, P. A. Fetal growth retardation in relation to maternal smoking and weight gain in pregnancy. *American Journal of Obstetrics and Gynecology* 125:55–60, 1976.
95. Pirani, B. B. K. Smoking during pregnancy. *Obstetrical and Gynecological Survey* 33:1–13, 1978.
96. Rush, D. Examination of the relationship between birthweight, cigarette smoking during pregnancy and maternal weight gain. *Journal of Obstetrics and Gynaecology of the British Commonwealth* 81:746–752, 1974.
97. Butler, N. R., Goldstein, H., and Ross, E. M. Cigarette smoking in pregnancy: Its influence on birthweight and perinatal mortality. *British Medical Journal* 2:127–130, 1972.
98. Davies, D. P., Gray, O. P., Ellwood, P. C., and Abernathy, M. Cigarette smoking in pregnancy: Association with maternal weight gain and fetal growth. *Lancet* 1:385–387, 1976.
99. Kline, J., Stein, Z. A., Susser, M., and Warburton, D. Smoking: A risk factor for spontaneous abortion. *New England Journal of Medicine* 297:793–796, 1977.
100. Fielding, J. E., and Russo, P. K. Smoking and pregnancy. *New England Journal of Medicine* 298:337–339, 1978.
101. Meyer, M. B., and Tonascia, J. A. Maternal smoking, pregnancy complications, and perinatal mortality. *American Journal of Obstetrics and Gynecology* 128:494–502, 1977.

102. Holden, C. House chops sex-pot probe. *Science* 192:450, April 1976.
103. Kolodny, R. C. Research Issues in the Study of Marijuana and Male Reproductive Physiology in Humans. In J. R. Tinklenberg (ed.), *Marijuana and Health Hazards*. New York: Academic Press, 1975. Pp. 71–81.
104. Merari, A., Barak, A., and Plaves, M. Effects of $\Delta^{1(2)}$-tetrahydrocannabinol on copulation in the male rat. *Psychopharmacologia* 28: 243–246, 1973.
105. Dixit, V. P., Sharma, V. N., and Lohiya, N. K. The effect of chronically administered cannabis extract on the testicular function of mice. *European Journal of Pharmacology* 26:111–114, 1974.
106. Collu, R., Letarte, J., Leboeuf, G., and Ducharme, J. R. Endocrine effects of chronic administration of psychoactive drugs to prepubertal male rats. I: Δ^9-tetrahydrocannabinol. *Life Sciences* 16:533–542, 1975.
107. Harmon, J. W., Locke, D., Aliapoulos, M. A., and MacIndoe, J. H. Interference with testicular development with Δ^9-tetrahydrocannabinol. *Surgical Forum* 27:350–352, 1976.
108. Smith, C. G., Moore, C. E., Besch, N. F., and Besch, P. K. Effect of Delta-9 tetrahydrocannabinol (THC) on secretion of male sex-hormone in rhesus monkey. *Pharmacologist* 18:248, 1976.
109. Chakravarty, I., Sheth, A. R., and Ghosh, J. J. Effect of acute Δ^9-tetrahydrocannabinol treatment on serum luteinizing hormone and prolactin levels in adult female rats. *Fertility and Sterility* 26:947–948, 1975.
110. Nir, I., Ayalon, D., Tsafriri, A., Cordova, T., and Lindner, H. R. Suppression of the cyclic surge of luteinizing hormone secretion and of ovulation in the rat by Δ^1-tetrahydrocannabinol. *Nature* 243:470–471, 1973.
111. Besch, N. F., Smith, C. G., Besch, P. K., and Kaufman, R. H. The effect of marihuana (delta-9-tetrahydrocannabinol) on the secretion of luteinizing hormone in the ovariectomized rhesus monkey. *American Journal of Obstetrics and Gynecology* 128:635–642, 1977.
112. Fernandez, E. O., Asch, R. H., Smith, C. G., and Pauerstein, C. J. Effect of antigonadotropins during the luteal phase of the rhesus monkey: Danazol and Δ^9-tetrahydrocannabinol. *Fertility and Sterility* 29:239, 1978.
113. Harmon, J., and Aliapoulos, M. A. Gynecomastia in marihuana users. *New England Journal of Medicine* 287:936, 1972.
114. Kolodny, R. C., Lessin, P., Toro, G., Masters, W. H., and Cohen, S. Depression of Plasma Testosterone with Acute Marihuana Administration. In M. C. Braude and S. Szara (eds.), *The Pharmacology of Marihuana*. New York: Raven Press, 1976. Pp. 217–225.
115. Kolodny, R. C., Masters, W. H., Kolodner, R. M., and Toro, G. Depression of plasma testosterone levels after chronic intensive marihuana use. *New England Journal of Medicine* 290:872–874, 1974.
116. Mendelson, J. H., Kuehnle, J., Ellingboe, J., and Babor, T. F. Plasma testosterone levels before, during, and after chronic marihuana smoking. *New England Journal of Medicine* 291:1051–1055, 1974.
117. Kolodny, R. C. Endocrine and Sexual Effects of Marihuana Use in Men. Presented at the annual meeting of the International Academy of Sex Research, Stony Brook, New York, September 1975.

118. Hembree, W. C., Zeidenberg, P., and Nahas, G. G. Marihuana Effects Upon Human Gonadal Function. In G. G. Nahas (ed.), *Marihuana: Chemistry, Biochemistry and Cellular Effects.* New York: Springer-Verlag, 1976.

119. Kolodny, R. C., Lessin, P., Masters, W. H., and Toro, G. Unpublished data, 1976.

120. Dornbush, R. L., Kolodny, R. C., Bauman, J. E., and Webster, S. K. Human Female Chronic Marijuana Use and Endocrine Functioning. Presented at the eighth annual meeting of the Society for Neuroscience, St. Louis, Missouri, November 7, 1978.

121. Goode, E. Drug use and sexual activity on a college campus. *American Journal of Psychiatry* 128:1272–1276, 1972.

122. Chessick, R. D. The "pharmacogenic orgasm" in the drug addict. *Archives of General Psychiatry* 3:545–556, 1960.

123. DeLeon, G., and Wexler, H. Heroin addiction: Its relation to sexual behavior and sexual experience. *Journal of Abnormal Psychology* 81:36–38, 1973.

124. Azizi, F., Vagenakis, A. G., Longcope, C., Ingbar, S. H., and Braverman, L. E. Decreased serum testosterone concentration in male heroin and methadone addicts. *Steroids* 22:467–472, 1973.

125. Mirin, S. M., Mendelson, J. H., Ellingboe, J., and Meyer, R. E. Acute effects of heroin and naltrexone on testosterone and gonadotropin secretion: A pilot study. *Psychoneuroendocrinology* 1:359–369, 1976.

126. Mendelson, J. H., Mendelson, J. E., and Patch, V. D. Plasma testosterone levels in heroin addiction and during methadone maintenance. *Journal of Pharmacology and Experimental Therapeutics* 192:211–217, 1975.

127. Mendelson, J. H., and Mello, N. K. Plasma testosterone levels during chronic heroin use and protracted abstinence: A study of Hong Kong addicts. *Clinical Pharmacology and Therapeutics* 17:529–533, 1975.

128. Brambilla, F., Sacchetti, E., and Brunetta, M. Pituitary-gonadal function in heroin addicts. *Neuropsychobiology* 3:160–166, 1977.

129. Cushman, P., Jr. Plasma testosterone in narcotic addiction. *American Journal of Medicine* 55:452–458, 1973.

130. Cicero, T. J., Bell, R. D., Wiest, W. G., Allison, J. H., Polakoski, K., and Robins, E. Function of the male sex organs in heroin and methadone users. *New England Journal of Medicine* 292:882–887, 1975.

131. Mintz, J., O'Hare, K., O'Brien, C. P., and Goldschmidt, J. Sexual problems of heroin addicts. *Archives of General Psychiatry* 31:700–703, 1974.

132. Bai, J., Greenwald, E., Caterini, H., and Kaminetzky, H. A. Drug-related menstrual aberrations. *Obstetrics and Gynecology* 44:713–719, 1974.

133. Santen, R. J., Sofsky, J., Bilic, N., and Lippert, R. Mechanism of action of narcotics in the production of menstrual dysfunction in women. *Fertility and Sterility* 26:538–548, 1975.

134. Winick, C., and Kinsie, P. M. *The Lively Commerce: Prostitution in the United States.* Chicago: Quadrangle Books, 1971.

135. Bell, D. S., and Trethowan, W. H. Amphetamine addiction and disturbed sexuality. *Archives of General Psychiatry* 4:74–78, 1961.

136. Angrist, B., and Gershon, S. Clinical effects of amphetamine and

L-DOPA on sexuality and aggression. *Comprehensive Psychiatry* 17:715–722, 1976.

137. Greaves, G. Sexual disturbances among chronic amphetamine users. *Journal of Nervous and Mental Disease* 155:363–365, 1972.

138. Everett, G. M. Amyl Nitrate ("Poppers") as an Aphrodisiac. In M. Sandler and G. L. Gessa (eds.), *Sexual Behavior: Pharmacology and Biochemistry*. New York: Raven Press, 1975. Pp. 97–98.

139. Piemme, T. E. Sex and illicit drugs. *Medical Aspects of Human Sexuality* 10(1):85–86, 1976.

14   Sex and the Handicapped

A paradox of most modern health-care systems is that the philosophic emphasis on a holistic approach to patient care exists in sharp contrast to the often narrowly selective way in which such services are provided. This discrepancy between the ideal and the actual is extraordinarily visible in programs designed for the handicapped: Until very recently, attention to the sexual concerns of handicapped people has focused largely on the issue of reproduction and has ignored or minimized the emotional and social consequences of various types of disabilities. In part, this lack of attention has derived from cultural and social attitudes that equate sexuality with youth, vigor, and physical attractiveness. The limited scope and success of research in this area has also contributed to lack of involvement on the part of health-care professionals, who quickly discovered that even if they were interested in this phase of patient care, there was little physiologic information to draw on and even less in the way of satisfactory guidelines for counseling. Physicians infrequently took the time to talk with handicapped patients about their sexual concerns and sometimes reacted negatively to other members of the health-care team who tried to initiate such discussions, implying that it was better to leave the subject alone than to produce additional problems or anxieties.

Such attitudes, however, have begun to change. The impetus for this transformation has been partly social (increasing recognition that sexuality is a birthright of all people, young or old, man or woman, healthy or ill), partly political (the young adult handicapped population has become more outspoken and better organized), and partly the result of growing professional interest in and comfort with the subject of sexuality. As a consequence, sexual health is now more commonly viewed as an appropriate concern. However, it is important to recognize that health-care professionals cannot restore the sexual health of their patients; in addition to correcting physical or metabolic problems amenable to treatment, they may act as catalysts in the process of helping patients to understand their sexuality, to take responsibility for their sexuality, and to make sexual choices in their lives based on information and on freedom from fear and ignorance [1].

It is the aim of this chapter to discuss the general strategies of approaching the subject of sex and the handicapped, supplementing this overview with a core of background information about several types of disabilities that may be likely to create sexual problems. The conceptual emphasis is on ways in which health-care professionals may contribute to the sexual health of patients by a commitment to a truly holistic approach that integrates attention to the emotional and social aspects of sexuality with the physical aspects of sexual function.

Formulating a General Approach
Background Factors

Persons who wish to provide counseling or information about sexuality to the handicapped must begin by deciding whether their own comfort with sexuality is sufficient for this role. Without adequate professional comfort with the subject, it is all too easy to embarrass, mislead, or frighten disabled patients who may be particularly sensitive to perceptions of their altered sexuality. Of course, there is a major difference between personal and professional comfort with sexuality; individuals who have received no training in methods of obtaining a sexual history may feel awkward or unsure about how to proceed, which is no reflection on their sexuality as such. However, there are instances in which personal discomfort with sexual matters (for instance, being unable to discuss sex without feeling ill at ease, or having personal attitudes toward sex that are highly condemnatory of certain types of sexual behavior) might preclude the possibility of dealing with this area in a professionally beneficial fashion. Physicians who want to examine their attitudes about sexuality and obtain exposure to the ideas of others on this subject may wish to participate in sexual attitude reassessment programs, which are widely available through hospitals and universities [2–4].

Cole has itemized some of the negative reactions he encountered on the part of members of the rehabilitation team to the idea of counseling handicapped patients with sexual problems, as follows [5]:

1. The discussion of sex should be deferred to someone else who may be more effective, so the patient will not be hurt.
2. The discussion of sex should be left to knowledgeable specialists.
3. Rehabilitation is oriented toward achieving a better state of health, and sex is different from health.
4. Only handicapped people who are employed and act responsibly should have assistance with their sexuality, because they need it more than the others.
5. The topic of sexuality may be a distraction from other more important aspects of rehabilitation.

These reactions reflect both personal and professional difficulties with sexuality, but they also indicate a reluctance on the part of health professionals to perceive sex as an integral part of clinical care.

In addition to having the necessary personal and professional comfort with sexuality as a legitimate area of health care, physicians should examine their attitudes toward the handicapped, since these views will be important determinants of the proficiency and sensitivity of their counseling. Sexual problems of the handicapped are often undiscovered or ignored because health-care professionals avoid the issue. While this avoidance undoubtedly reflects the minimal professional education about sexuality that has been typical of the past, it may also point to an attitude that deprecates the worth or rights of the handicapped person and that simultaneously imposes an arbitrary order of priorities on that person's life—priorities that place little value on sexuality and maximal value on other issues in rehabilitation, such as occupational security, being able to transfer from bed to wheelchair, or being able to dress oneself. Some professionals who are adept in providing sex counseling or other services to particular patient populations may have difficulty in extending their range of expertise: for example, the person who is comfortable and effective in working with spinal cord–injured patients may be uncomfortable and less successful dealing with the blind, with adolescents who have cystic fibrosis, or with some other specialized population of patients. It is not unprofessional to recognize that people have different professional talents and preferences; it is unprofessional to persist in trying to provide a full range of services to a population of patients with whom one's objectivity and openness are impaired, whether because of discomfort, too much sympathy, unrealistic expectations, or other dynamics.

It must also be recognized that personal prejudices and preferences may also be highly relevant to management of sexual concerns for the handicapped. Attitudes toward sex roles, for example, will be likely to have an impact on the advice that is offered to patients and their families or partners; attitudes toward the age group or ethnic group that the patient fits into may likewise color the physician-patient relationship. It is unrealistic to believe that health-care professionals are able to be truly value-neutral in every possible clinical situation that might present itself, but it is necessary to be aware of personal preferences, ingrained attitudes, and professional biases that may alter the objectivity required under such circumstances.

Another aspect of significance to this discussion is the background knowledge of the physician or counselor who shows interest in the sexual health and sexual problems of disabled patients. Depending on the plan of medical management and the level of skill required by the situation (for example, is the physician interested in identifying problems and initiating appropriate referral, or is the objective to provide diagnosis and treatment as well as problem identification?), it is important for the physician becoming involved in this aspect of health care to have a knowledge base that integrates the relevant biomedical facts with data from the psychosocial domain. Although many researchers approach these subsets of knowledge as though they were separate and independent of one another, in actuality they are remarkably intertwined and interdependent. The relevant point here, however, is that a clear view of one's professional competence (including, but not limited to, knowledge, training, and proficiency) must be called upon to determine if a clinical situation is suitable for one's level of expertise. The person who may be quite knowledgeable in working with the sexual problems of diabetics may be lacking important insights that are needed for dealing with the sexual concerns of patients with muscular dystrophy or the deaf.

Assessment of Sexual Problems

The evaluation of sexual difficulties produced by a handicap should be carried out in a systematic fashion. However, the widely different requirements of clinical situations that will be encountered suggest the need for a general analysis of actual and potential sexual problems, since it is probable that resourceful, sensitive management may prevent some sexual difficulties that might otherwise occur. The primary categories that should be examined in this initial assessment of the patient are as follows:

1. *Demographic data*: age, sex, educational background, occupation, and marital status.
2. *Origins of the handicap*: physical, mental, or combined.
3. *Time course of the handicap:* congenital or acquired; antedating or subsequent to establishing patterns of dating or other corresponding social skill attainment; antedating or subsequent to coital experience.
4. *Limitations associated with the handicap*: motor, sensory, coordination, social, cognitive, or multiple limitations.
5. *Adjustment to the handicap*: coping abilities, acceptance, motivation for rehabilitation, self-esteem, affect, body image, denial, repression, or other ego-defense mechanisms.
6. *Relevant sexual history*: prehandicap patterns of sexual activity (if

applicable), including difficulties or dysfunctions, sexual orientation, sexual satisfaction, estimate of libido, range of sexual behaviors, sexual attitudes and values, reproductive history; posthandicap patterns of sexual activity, as above; current sexual relationship; current and future sexual expectations (including reproductive goals), worries, and problems.

7. *Relevant medical history*: concurrent illnesses or drugs that may affect sexuality.

8. *Social resources*: family support system, marital relationship, friends or peer group, others (clergy, health-care professionals, etc.).

This brief outline must be applied to individual patients in a flexible fashion, but it will permit a reasonable assessment of the sexual problems that are already present or that are likely to arise in association with a handicap. Details of many of these categories are discussed later in this chapter or in other chapters in this book.

It must be emphasized that a preliminary evaluation of the sexuality of a handicapped person may be based on a relatively brief interview and review of medical records. It is often possible to gather such data from an interview lasting half an hour or less; marathon questioning periods usually are neither necessary nor beneficial to the situation (however, when a consultant specializing in sexual problems has been called in specifically to assess the patient and to formulate a management plan simultaneously, this observation does not apply). Needless to say, the requirements for initial assessment will vary considerably depending on factors such as the setting (a hospital spinal cord injury unit, an outpatient neurology clinic, and a sex counseling center are obviously different situations); the overall health, strength, and attention span of the patient; the job responsibilities of the physician; and the age, comfort, and gender of the patient. At times, the evaluation is most wisely conducted over a series of briefer interviews; on other occasions, such an assessment would be incomplete without obtaining information from the spouse or sexual partner of the handicapped person.

There is a difference between gathering the data required for the assessment of sexual problems, as described above, and letting the patient know that health-care professionals are concerned with his or her sexual status and are willing to discuss this topic. Although the simple act of eliciting information required for evaluation gives a respectability and importance to the subject of sexuality (and thus may be therapeutic in an indirect way), there are more complicated considerations that enter the picture of clinical management. Only a few of these considerations can be discussed here.

The first point to examine is the question of who should bring up the subject. Does it matter if a woman talks about sexuality with a male patient or if a man talks with a female patient about sexuality? Is it best to handle such discussions only on a same-sex basis? In the context of working with handicapped patients, the probable answer is that in the course of discussions about sexuality, the knowledge and professional competence of the health-care professional are usually far more important than his or her gender. In situations of increasing complexity (particularly involving psychosocial difficulties creating or compounding sexual problems), it may be better if the counselor or therapist is of the same sex, but this is not an absolute rule. When a patient expresses difficulty in talking with a professional of the opposite gender about sexuality, or when such difficulty is judged to be present—although the context of each case must be individually assessed—there is probable reason to consider a change in format. On the other hand, it has not appeared to be of major consequence to counseling situations or to psychotherapy dealing with sexual problems if the ages of patient and professional are closely matched or are divergent in either direction.

A second point to consider is one of timing: When is it best to initiate discussions of sexuality with handicapped patients and when is it most appropriate to extend the discussions from the level of factual education to the level of specific suggestions? There is no satisfactory answer that will always apply, because so many different aspects of the individual patient's situation are relevant. Just as physical recuperation from surgery or injury requires widely different times and circumstances, adjustment to the changes in life brought about by physical handicaps varies widely from person to person. Congenital disabilities such as blindness or deafness are also influenced by the maturity of the affected person, so that what might be an appropriate approach for a particular 12-year-old girl would be too much for a different 20-year-old boy. Despite these facts, it is often reasonable to be guided by the patient's requests in these matters, realizing that alleviating sexual concerns (or at least dealing with them openly) may contribute to the overall rehabilitation of the patient. A corollary of this observation is the necessity of not projecting nonexistent sexual problems onto patients with handicaps, which requires being carefully attuned to the patient's sensitivities and needs [6, 7]. What is a problem for one person may not be felt as a problem by another; this is a case in which overzealous and well-meaning professionals may create difficulties where there were none in the beginning. In fact, it is important to recognize that for some disabled people (just as for some able-bodied people), sexual activity ranks very low on the list of personal priorities. Such people should never be intimidated into sexual behavior nor forced to participate in discussions or educational sessions that may be aesthetically or morally uncomfortable for them.

Patients who have recently become handicapped may require a period of psychological adjustment to the impact of their disability. If discussion of sexuality is initiated during a period of denial on their part, it is unlikely to be very productive. This is one reason why it is important to leave the topic of sexuality open for discussion at various times: Changing physical, psychological, or social circumstances may create new or unforeseen difficulties (or give rise to unexpected successes) that may benefit from further consideration.

A third point is how to bring up the subject of sexuality. Health-care professionals who follow the suggestions made in the preceding section on assessment will find that frequently their patients indicate interest in subsequent discussion during the gathering of this limited sexual information. Other patients will provide a logical point of departure by describing worries, problems, or questions that require further thought and dialogue. At other times, however, it is necessary to reintroduce the topic as a potential subject for discussion in a nondemanding, nonthreatening fashion [7]. General statements such as "Many people with a disability like yours have questions about their sex lives" may provide an opening gambit that is neither too personal nor too ambiguous. It is important to realize that in some instances a patient's concerns for confidentiality may limit his or her willingness to enter into such discussions; this may be particularly true in hospital settings where there is little conversational privacy around the patient's bed.

All members of the health-care team who work with the handicapped should possess the attitudes, information, and skills that allow people to acknowledge a problem and to explore it in an atmosphere of permission [1]. Openness in initiating and following through on discussions of sexuality with disabled patients sets the stage for different levels of intervention that can be coordinated with the overall plan for rehabilitation and patient management. At the simplest level of intervention, physicians who inquire about potential sexual problems acknowledge the existence of a sensitive area that may be of concern to the patient and affirm by active, supportive listening the importance of this dimension of life and its relations to health care. The patient often benefits from this opportunity by being allowed to ventilate anxieties that have been previously internalized and unspoken. These anxieties are sometimes dissipated and frequently are diminished in intensity by being brought out into the open.

For each additional type of intervention that may be used, it is best to remember that the possibility of referral to a specialist skilled in dealing with problems of human sexuality may be appropriate. Each level of intervention consists of component parts that ideally are handled in continuity and coordination with the overall rehabilitation effort, so that even when referral has been made, interested physicians should follow the progress of their patients and thus provide a link to the general management plan.

Education is the next level of intervention that may be utilized. It is most effective to provide educational services to the patient and his or her spouse or sexual partner, since the partner's knowledge and attitudes will be important determinants of the cooperation that may exist in their sexual relationship. The spouse or partner may have specific fears that may be quieted by the appropriate facts; the spouse or partner may also provide valuable insights into problems, behaviors, or needs of the handicapped person.

Educational counseling may be approached in many different ways. Private discussions typically facilitate a transition from the shame and stigma associated with both the handicap and the spectre of sexual difficulties to an attitude of realistic acceptance and acknowledgment of physiologic limitations and emotional strengths. Such discussions may be supplemented with the use of appropriate educational materials, including diagrams, photographs, pamphlets or books, slides, movies, recordings, or models. An educational strategy that offers many advantages is the patient's participation in either individual or group discussions with a peer counselor who has lived with the same type of physical handicap and is in a good position to understand both the practical problems that may arise and the reactions of the handicapped patient. Additional education approaches that are potentially useful include participation in group discussions with other handicapped individuals and attendance at sexual attitude reassessment workshops [2–4]. Appropriate educational content includes (but is not limited to) information about sexual anatomy and physiology, reproductive anatomy and physiology, the psychology of sexual relationships and sexual communication, and the range of human sexual behavior. Depending on the specific population of patients included in such programs, information about contraception, mechanical sexual aids, and other topics (e.g., catheter care, massage techniques, use of erotic materials) may also be usefully dealt with.

Education is not a simple therapeutic intervention; many forms of psychotherapy draw heavily on educational techniques for their impact. Therefore, physicians should recognize that in many instances, sex education for the handicapped leads to the suggestion of specific approaches that may be tried to minimize or eliminate sexual problems. Although it is easy to attribute every sexual problem of a handicapped person to the physical limitations of his or her condition (e.g., neurologic deficit, anatomic abnormality), it is necessary to remember that psychosocial stresses may precipitate problems that are not organic in nature but may seem to be so at first glance. A classic example of this situation is illustrated by the following case:

A 24-year-old paraplegic man, whose physical condition was the result of poliomyelitis, had been unable to engage in coitus because of difficulties with erection. He had no difficulty in finding sexual partners and responded to fellatio with erection and ejaculation. His physician erroneously attributed the impotence to the effects of polio on his nervous sytem. After a brief course of sex therapy (8 hours), he was able to overcome his primary difficulties of performance anxiety and making sex into work (which he felt was necessary to compensate for his impaired physical status) and had no difficulty in obtaining and maintaining normal erections.

Physical difficulties may be amplified by factors such as guilt, anxiety, depression, or poor self-esteem. Sexual problems may also arise from ineffective interpersonal communications, rigid sex role stereotypes, or goal-oriented sex values. Therefore, it is likely that education alone may require supplementation by techniques of counseling that permit more specific attention to such matters (see Chaps. 19–22). It is helpful to realize that if a physical handicap is superimposed on a marital relationship that had significant preexisting problems, this additional strain may jeopardize the continuance of the marriage. Although it is true that sometimes people will be drawn together by major obstacles in their lives and will prevail by virtue of determination, hard work, and luck, one should strongly consider the potential place of marriage counseling as a component of the rehabilitation effort when it seems appropriate.

For many patients with physical handicaps, practical suggestions are needed that aim at maximizing the ease and satisfaction of sexual activity while acknowledging the patient's physical limitations. Although relevant approaches will be discussed in subsequent sections of this chapter, it is necessary for those undertaking such counseling to have a realistic view of the sexual and reproductive prognosis of their patients. When the patients react to their disabilities in a fatalistic way, it is all too easy to respond by promising them great potential in the future—but regrettably, their sexual future may be more limited than multidimensional. This responsibility to provide accurate and realistic objectives or prognostic statements implies either a proficiency in technical information relevant to each clinical situation (e.g., urology, neurology, neuroendocrinology) or ready access to other health-care specialists who can contribute such information. Under most circumstances, it also requires additional time spent in patient interviewing to obtain a more detailed sexual and psychosocial history.

The promotion of sexual health for the handicapped will entail suggestions for both attitudinal change and the mechanical aspects of sexual activity. It is important that such suggestions, which are aimed at improving sexual satisfaction and self-esteem, do not have the opposite effect. People should not be coerced into types of sex that they find morally objectionable or that they are displeased with for other reasons. (This point is applicable to the partner of the handicapped person as well. At times, under the guise of "therapy" or "rehabilitation," a partner may be pushed into facets of sexual involvement that he or she does not really want to try.) Although it is admittedly difficult at times to differentiate between people who limit their range of sexual options because of ignorance, misinformation, fear, or guilt, and people who reject certain choices on moral or aesthetic grounds, this point is of such central importance to patient management that it is worth extra time and attention. Sometimes the dilemma may be solved by consultation with an interested member of the clergy; sometimes the situation requires reassessment with the passage of time and additional patient contact.

When progressing to the point of suggesting attitudinal revisions or alternative forms of sexual activity available to the handicapped, one should recognize that the same approach will not suit each patient. Matters of age, education, life-style, and prior sexual knowledge and experience, as well as a host of medical and psychological factors, must all be brought into the formulation of adequate advice. Within the boundaries defined by such variables, the central task of the professional is to emphasize the sexual options open to the handicapped person that permit intimacy, participation, and personal satisfaction. In some situations—particularly those involving men with disabilities resulting in impotence and loss of the ability to ejaculate—emphasis must be placed on the creative and gratifying alternatives to coitus that are available. These alternatives are predicated on the idea that sex is not a matter of genital union (or even genital stimulation) alone: kissing, massage, fantasy, manual stimulation of the breasts or genitals, oral-genital stimulation, and use of vibrators or other mechanical aids are among some of the varied possibilities. Even when physical disabilities make sexual intercourse difficult, variations in position and technique may allow for enjoyable coitus. These matters are examined in detail in a book entitled *Sexual Options for Paraplegics and Quadriplegics* [8].

Guidelines that are useful for professionals and patients in dealing with the sexuality of the physically handicapped have been suggested by Anderson and Cole [9]:

A stiff penis does not make a solid relationship, nor does a wet vagina.
Urinary incontinence does not mean genital incompetence.
Absence of sensation does not mean absence of feelings.
Inability to move does not mean inability to please.
The presence of deformities does not mean the absence of desire.
Inability to perform does not mean inability to enjoy.
Loss of genitals does not mean loss of sexuality.

Such conceptualizations can be useful to the physician who is trying to foster empathic communication with handicapped patients on the subject of sexuality.

When sexual difficulties do not respond to counseling in a fashion commensurate with the physical progress of the patient in other aspects of a rehabilitation program, or when sexual problems appear to be increasing in severity or in their impact on the handicapped patient, referral to a competent sex therapist is in order. Enthusiastic and accurate discussion, education, and advice will not substitute for effective psychotherapy that combines necessary physiologic data with a focus on the appropriate psychosocial dynamics of each clinical situation.

A final word is in order about the general strategy of patient management in regard to the sexual health of the handicapped: The potential of a multidisciplinary team approach that integrates the skills and knowledge of physicians, psychologists, social workers, rehabilitation personnel, nurses, clergy, and handicapped peer counselors is immense. Such a team can prepare effective educational programs at the hospital or community level, can coordinate consultation and referral, and can provide an optimal environment for professional growth as well.

Sex and the Spinal Cord–Injured Patient

Despite a burgeoning literature on the sexual consequences of spinal cord injury, remarkably little knowledge exists that permits a meaningful prediction of the sexual capabilities subsequent to such an injury. This fact is due as much to lack of understanding of the neurophysiologic determinants of sexual response as it is to the complex variables that have to do with recovery, adaptation, and coping.

When vertebral dislocation or fracture causes squeezing or shearing of the spinal cord, necrosis and hemorrhage occur in variable degrees; only in rare circumstances is the cord actually cut in two [10]. The anatomic pathology and the associated limitation of function may vary considerably and combine to determine the permanence and degree of clinical manifestations [10], including the sexual manifestations, of spinal cord injury. For several weeks after the acute injury, there is typically a condition of "spinal shock" (suppression of reflex activity below the level of the spinal cord lesion), which includes atonic paralysis of bladder and rectal sphincters as well as sensory loss [11]. Priapism may be observed in some cord-injured males during this phase as a result of venous stasis [10]. As the spinal shock dissipates, reflex activity begins to return to the lower extremities. Bowel and bladder function may improve somewhat, and flexor and extensor spasm may occur with tactile stimulation. This pattern of changes, highly simplified here, is one reason why it is not possible to predict subsequent sexual function during the first few weeks after a spinal cord injury has occurred. However, physical impairments persisting six months or more after the injury are likely to be permanent [10].

Male Sexual Function after Spinal Cord Injury

Numerous studies have described the effects of spinal cord injury on male sexual functioning, with particular attention to the man's ability to achieve erections, to ejaculate, and to conceive [12–21]. These studies are difficult to interpret because of methodologic factors including variability in subject selection, poorly described diagnostic criteria for determining the level and extent of the spinal cord lesion, incomplete data collection, lack of ample documentation of premorbid sexual function, and other reasons. Nevertheless, if these limitations are kept in mind, some general observations drawn from the reports may be helpful indicators of the overall situation.

Bors and Comarr [12] reported that of 529 patients with spinal cord or cauda equina injury, 93 percent with complete upper motor neuron lesions could achieve reflexogenic erections (erections occurring with tactile stimulation to the genitals or surrounding skin), and 4 percent could ejaculate. Ninety-nine percent of men with incomplete upper motor neuron lesions experienced erections that were usually reflexogenic, and nearly one-third of the men in this group were capable of ejaculation. For men with complete lower motor neuron lesions, 26 percent attained psychogenic erection (erections arising from cognitive stimuli rather than direct physical stimulation), and 18 percent in this category could ejaculate. Ninety percent of men with incomplete lower motor neuron lesions were sometimes capable of erection, and 70 percent could ejaculate. Subjects were categorized as having upper motor neuron lesions if there was clinical evidence of reflex activity mediated by sacral segments; subjects without such sacrally mediated reflex activity were judged to have lower motor neuron involvement. In a later publication from the same center [13], based on a separate study of 150 patients with spinal cord injury, these findings were substantiated and it was stated that, in general, patients with incomplete lesions have a better sexual prognosis than those with complete lesions. In addition, the findings indicated that patients with complete upper motor neuron lesions have a higher rate of erection than patients with complete lower motor neuron lesions, but patients in the former group experience ejaculation and orgasm less frequently. The studies of Talbot [14, 15] generally are in agreement with the preceding observations. Talbot found that the level of the spinal cord lesion was of importance in determining the sexual sequelae: Approximately three-quarters of men with lesions above T-12 continued to have erections, whereas only half of those with lower lesions experienced erections [14]. Although the specific estimates differ considerably from one report to another, most authors confirm this relationship between the level of the lesion and subsequent erectile function.

The distinction between reflexogenic and psychogenic erections in men with spinal cord injury, which originated more than three decades ago, may be an artificial and misleading categorization in some ways. It is difficult to explain how, neurologically speaking, psychogenic erections can occur in men who are unable to have reflexogenic erections or in men with complete upper motor neuron lesions. It is also misleading to consider the percentages that have been carefully gathered by the workers cited above as implying that the quality (or frequency) of the erections experienced by most spinal cord–injured men is equivalent to that of other men. Reflexogenic erections are often extremely brief in duration and do not usually produce pleasurable physical sensations for the man (although gratification may occur for other reasons, such as realization of the presence of the erection or participation in pleasurable activity with a partner). Psychogenic erections, which may persist longer than reflexogenic ones, are not always complete erections and also are usually independent of tactile or temperature sensory awareness of the genitals.

At a level of considerable practicality to many men with spinal cord injuries, sufficient erection is attained for coitus by only about 15 to 25 percent of the cord-injured [14, 19–21], and in these men coital frequency is usually markedly reduced compared to pre-injury patterns. Likewise, the ability to ejaculate normally is lost by more than 90 percent of spinal cord-injured males; the prognosis appears better for men with incomplete lesions and for those with lesions of the lower motor neurons [12–14, 19]. As many authorities point out [9, 16, 20], the sensation of orgasm may or may not accompany ejaculation when it does occur. Ejaculation may sometimes occur in a retrograde fashion in these men as well [8, 9].

There is considerable confusion in the literature on the subject of "cognitional" or "phantom" orgasms that have been reported by paraplegic or quadriplegic men. Money was the first to draw the analogy between sexual responsiveness in some cord-injured men and the phantom limb sensations long known to clinicians wherein a person who has undergone amputation continues to perceive physical sensations that are interpreted as coming from the missing limb [16]. The analogy is not a useful one, however, for most purposes. In actuality, orgasm is a total body response, not limited to the genital region or even requiring the presence of genitals to occur. The cord-injured male can be observed to demonstrate the cardiovascular, pulmonary, and neuromuscular changes of the human sexual response cycle, including those changes seen during the orgasmic phase; these changes may occur in parts of the body uninvolved by the cord injury even when ejaculation does not take place. On the other hand, men who are coached in techniques such as sensory amplification ("thinking about a physical stimulus, concentrating on it, and amplifying the sensation . . . to an intense degree" [8]) and are told this may lead to a "mental orgasm" [8] will often label their experiences as orgasms when in fact none of the physiologic manifestations of orgasm occur. Although in one sense the distinction may be purely a semantic one, it is important to realize that orgasms can occur without ejaculation in some cord-injured men (although this is not a frequent phenomenon), and such orgasms are not only mental.

Men with spinal cord injuries above the fourth thoracic vertebra may experience excessive activation of the autonomic nervous system during sexual arousal. This condition, known as autonomic dysreflexia, is usually marked by a sudden, pounding headache due to a rapid increase of blood pressure [8]. Flushing, sweating, and cardiac arrhythmias may also accompany autonomic dysreflexia, which may be caused by an elevation of catecholamines [21]. Spasticity accompanying sexual arousal is usually not of major consequence, although for certain patients with severe degrees of spasticity it may be a limiting factor.

Female Sexual Function after Spinal Cord Injury

The extensive literature about sexual functioning in men with spinal cord injuries is not matched by a corresponding degree of study of the cord-injured woman. The focus of studies on women with paraplegia or quadriplegia has been primarily on menstruation, conception, and problems of pregnancy and delivery. This differential attention to sexuality should be viewed in historical perspective, however; as female sexuality has become increasingly accepted as a legitimate subject for public and professional interest, a number of authors have addressed the subject in more depth [22–25]. The fact that the great majority of spinal cord-injured patients are male is another reason for the lack of thorough investigation of the sexual capabilities of spinal cord-injured women.

No reliable statistics have been reported on the percentage of women who remain able to experience orgasm after a spinal cord injury. There is no basis for judging whether or not a percentage comparable to that found in cord-injured men would apply, but it is clear from clinical experience that a substantial number of women who had previously been orgasmic with coitus lose this ability. This finding may partly reflect a decrease in vaginal lubrication and diminished pelvic vasocongestion associated with sexual activity and arousal. Because of the impaired pelvic vasocongestion, the orgasmic platform usually does not form during the plateau stage of the female sexual response.

This observation was extended by a unique opportunity for evaluation in the Masters & Johnson Institute's physiology laboratory of a woman who participated in studies of the sexual response cycle while in good health and was subsequently studied three years later, 12 months after a spinal cord injury sustained in an automobile accident. This subject's pre-injury responses were typical of the normal responses described in Chapter 1, but an interesting feature of her description of her own sexuality was that she derived little erotic pleasure or excitation from breast stimulation. After her injury (a complete lower motor neuron lesion at T-12), however, she lost all pelvic sensations and gradually found that her breasts became increasingly sensitive to erotic stimulation. By six months after her injury, she began to experience what she identified as orgasms as a result of breast stimulation. When this subject was monitored in the laboratory setting during breast stimulation, it was noted that cardiopulmonary responses to sexual excitation and orgasm were normal and changes observed in the breasts and nipples were normal, but there was no significant degree of pelvic vasocongestion or vaginal lubrication. However, in the late portion of the plateau phase of the response cycle (identified by the breast changes that occurred), the lips of this woman's mouth became engorged to twice their normal size. At the moment of orgasm, a pulsating wave was observed in her lips and the swelling then dissipated rapidly—in a manner almost identical to the pattern seen with the dissipation of the orgasmic platform formed at the outer portion of the vagina in non-cord-injured women. This case apparently illustrates not only the ability to transfer erotic zones from one region of the body to another (a phenomenon already observed by several authors in relation to the spinal cord–injured) but also the transfer of a physiologic erotic reflex from its ordinary location (in this case, the noninnervated vagina) to a remote but physiologically similar location. It is obvious that this fortuitous opportunity requires followup and more detailed neurophysiologic evaluation of women with cord injuries.

The woman with a spinal cord injury may be less limited in her possibilities for heterosexual participation because intercourse is more easily possible for her than it is for many cord-injured men. This reflects the fact that women do not require specific pelvic vasocongestive changes to achieve intercourse (although some cord-injured women may need to use artificial lubrication to facilitate the mechanics of penile insertion and thrusting). In addition, the psychologic reaction to assuming a physically dependent or passive role during sexual activity, including coitus, is often easier for women than for men because of previous patterns of socialization [23].

Spasticity usually does not interfere with sexual activity in cord-injured women [23, 24], although Romano and Lassiter point out that if adductor spasm is severe, intromission may be impossible [23]. Several patients seen by Griffith and Trieschmann experienced a temporary reduction of spasticity immediately after orgasm [24] in a fashion similar to that described in men [3]. Autonomic dysreflexia and fractures during intercourse have also been noted in isolated instances among women with spinal cord injuries [24].

Other Considerations   Fertility is impaired in most men with spinal cord injuries, although the mechanism of this effect is not fully understood [8, 19, 26–29]. While spermatogenesis is frequently diminished, in some instances a mild degree of oligospermia or the presence of normal sperm counts and motility is quite compatible with conception; in such cases, mechanical problems of retrograde ejaculation or inability to ejaculate coupled with erective difficulties are most problematic. Intrathecal injections of neostigmine (Prostigmin) [28] and electric stimulation of the prostate and seminal vesicles [29] have been tried in order to obtain semen specimens for purposes of artificial insemination, with generally poor results.

Although there has been confusion about the hormonal production of spinal cord–injured men, two recent studies indicate that testicular and pituitary integrity are remarkably normal. Kikuchi and coworkers [30] studied 15 cord-injured men aged 21 to 41; in this group 11 men were paraplegic and 4 were quadriplegic. They found that serum testosterone, estradiol, LH, and FSH levels were normal in 14 of the 15 subjects; normal hormonal responses to testicular stimulation with human chorionic gonadotropin were also observed. Claus-Walker and colleagues [31] studied men who had complete cervical cord transections resulting in quadriplegia; these patients were studied during various stages of paralysis ranging from the acute injury to a stabilized stage of quadriplegia. They found that the mean testosterone level in the first two months after injury was significantly below the mean testosterone concentration in healthy men matched for age (450 ng per 100 ml versus 799 ng per 100 ml for healthy men). During the period from 9 to 30 weeks after injury, mean testosterone values increased to 594 ng per 100 ml, and by 9 to 18 months after injury they had risen to 698 ng per 100 ml. Evaluation of circulating levels of thyroxine, growth hormone, and parathyroid hormone in these same patients indicated that the steady state production of these hormones, as well, was not diminished except by the original trauma to the nervous system and by subsequent medications and changes in life patterns.

The relative integrity of circulating levels of testosterone in cord-injured males provides a biologic explanation for the preservation of libido that is generally seen under these circumstances. Nevertheless, many practical factors may conspire to diminish libido, including the absence of genital sensations (since impulses beginning in the genitals may direct attention to sexual needs [32]), lack of strength and stamina, concern with the messiness of sexual activity (attention to bladder and bowel function, for example), self-consciousness about body-image [25], depression, fears of performance, and concerns about the reaction of spouse or partner. These considerations apply to the cord-injured woman as well as the man, although the sparse literature on this subject implies that libido remains relatively intact for this group as well.

Women experience little reduction in fertility as a result of spinal cord injury; reports of successful term pregnancies and vaginal deliveries are common [33, 34]. However, pregnancy may be complicated by urinary tract infection, autonomic dysreflexia, and anemia, and the risk of premature labor is increased as well [24]. Labor is typically initiated in a normal fashion, and caesarean section is not usually required except when other complications exist. Contraceptive choice for the cord-injured woman is somewhat complicated by the heightened risk of thrombophlebitis associated with oral contraceptives (which may be additive or synergistic with the predisposition to such abnormalities in the cord-injured), the physical dexterity required to insert a diaphragm properly [23], and the small risk that an intrauterine device may perforate the uterus without being felt [25]. For the cord-injured woman who wishes to preserve subsequent fertility potential, the preferable mode of contraception is the use of foam (ideally accompanied by the simultaneous use of a condom by the male partner); however, use of an intrauterine device chosen particularly for a low rate of perforation, coupled with periodic gynecologic examinations to monitor the position of the device, is a medically acceptable alternative. Surgical contraception for the male partner (vasectomy) or for the cord-injured woman (tubal ligation) is an ideal method if future procreation is not a goal.

Considerable professional assistance can be offered to spinal cord–injured men and women by a professional who has an open, honest, and sensitive approach to counseling them in regard to their sexuality. Common sense, accurate information, and willingness to enter a dialogue are among the essential ingredients required. The advice that is given must be adequately individualized to suit the medical facts and the personality and relationship requirements of each situation. Many practical pointers, including details of catheter care, coital positioning, hygiene, and nongenital sex, are discussed and depicted photographically in *Sexual Options for Paraplegics and Quadriplegics* [8], which is suitable for direct patient education.

Sex and the Mentally Retarded

Although this chapter deals primarily with the subject of sex and the physically handicapped, a brief discussion of the large group of individuals designated as mentally retarded can also serve to illustrate the central importance of sex to the lives of all people. In the past, and persisting into the present, the sexual needs and behaviors of the retarded have been stereotyped by society at large, and by the health-care professions in particular, according to a picture based less on fact than on myth. Overlooking the fact that not all mentally retarded persons are alike in learning capacity, emotional stability, social skills, or other important variables, this stereotype depicts the retarded as ignorant about sex and as either asexual or totally impulse-ridden [35].

Research into the sexuality of the mentally retarded has been very sparse, and a large number of methodologic issues have created difficulty in assessing what little is known. For example, in many previous studies it is difficult to tell whether the effects of mental retardation, rather than the effects of institutionalization, are being observed. Furthermore, most researchers have not evaluated separately those people with mental retardation due to organic pathology (e.g., inborn errors of metabolism, chromosomal abnormalities, cranial anomalies, fetal infections, and birth injuries) who, although only a minority of the overall cases of retardation, are often institutionalized and may also have other manifestations of central nervous system damage such as seizures, motor disabilities, or sensory deficits.

Keeping such limitations in mind, it is helpful to examine the data reported by Gebhard concerning sexual behavior in mentally retarded men interviewed for projects at the Institute for Sex Research [36]. Of 84 subjects ranging in age from 11 to their 40s, 46 had IQ scores between 61 and 70; 23 between 51 and 60; 13 between 41 and 50; and 2 between 31 and 40. A control group was made up of 477 normal men who had never been convicted of a crime, imprisoned, or sent to a mental institution. Fewer of the retarded subjects had engaged in prepubertal heterosexual play (40 percent) than subjects in the control group (52 percent), but a larger percentage (50 percent) reported prepubertal homosexual play than control subjects (41 percent). Only 3.6 percent of the retarded subjects had had sexual contacts in childhood with adult males, a rate remarkably similar to control subjects (3.7 percent). Almost half the retarded subjects had engaged in prepubertal masturbation, as compared to one-third of the control subjects, but the incidence of masturbation after puberty was identical in the two groups. For every postpubertal age group, the frequency of masturbation was less for retarded men than in the control group. Homosexual fantasy and dreams occurred more frequently in the retarded men than in the controls, and 57 percent of the retardates compared to 34 percent of the never-married control subjects described homosexual experience; however, the major age range of such activity was from the time of puberty to age 15, with a steadily diminishing incidence thereafter. The retarded men interviewed in this study had had less premarital heterosexual petting experience or coital experience than the controls, but this difference, like the apparently greater rate of homosexual contact, may simply reflect the effect of institutionalization on this sample. In fact, there does not seem to be a great deal of difference between the retarded men and the control subjects that cannot be explained circumstantially.

There is evidence that the timing of sexual maturation in the mentally retarded correlates with IQ [37], but there is much confusion about overall rates of fertility. Although some conditions that can cause mental retardation are clearly associated with impaired fertility, the majority of retarded persons have no biologic limitation to their procreative status. This fact creates obvious problems in advocating more tolerant attitudes toward the sexual behavior of the retarded, since the possibility of undesired pregnancy is high. The issues of provision of contraception services for the retarded, the efficacy and safety of contraception services for the retarded, and the ethics of sexual participation by the retarded, along with important aspects of institutional and community attitudes on these subjects, are discussed in detail in a book entitled *Human Sexuality and the Mentally Retarded* [38], to which interested readers are referred.

Since many of the mentally retarded are capable of developing a reasonable store of sex information, particularly when educational materials are presented to them in language they can comprehend and in a repetitive manner, contraceptive advice and information related to other aspects of sexual behavior may be taught with some effectiveness. The following general points are useful:

1. The intrauterine device offers the greatest range of usefulness for contraception in sexually active postpubertal females who are mentally retarded. For a limited number of mildly retarded women in whom no medical contraindications exist (see Chap. 15) and for whom regular parental or institutional supervision is available, oral contraceptives may be an efficacious alternative. Consideration should also be given, on an individual basis, to the possibility of tubal ligation to provide maximum protection against pregnancy.

2. It is unrealistic to expect sexually active postpubertal males who are mentally retarded to remember to use a condom regularly in their

heterosexual contacts; until such time as other safe and effective male contraceptive techniques are available (long-acting injectable contraceptives, for example), vasectomy appears to be the only contraceptive modality that should be recommended for retarded males. (Before undertaking methods of sterilization that are largely irreversible, such as tubal ligation or vasectomy, one must give careful consideration to the ethical and legal aspects of such approaches. Interest in this subject has been considerable in recent years; professionals working in such situations are strongly urged to keep abreast of appropriate laws and court decisions in order to provide adequate protection for the rights of the mentally retarded, who are not usually judged as competent to give informed consent to such therapeutic procedures.)

3. Many parents of mentally retarded children or adolescents and many health-care professionals working with the retarded feel threatened, frightened, offended, or ambivalent about masturbatory behavior in this population. These persons, who occupy such important roles in the lives of the retarded, must be given effective education regarding the normalcy and naturalness of masturbation. As Sol Gordon has said, "[Masturbation] becomes a compulsive, punitive, self-destructive form of behavior largely as a result of suppression, punishment, and resulting feelings of guilt" [39].

4. The retarded can usually be taught that genital sexual behavior is conducted in privacy in our contemporary culture. However, institutions for the mentally retarded usually do not provide appropriate privacy for sexual purposes, setting up a paradox that reflects the overall discomfort with the sexuality of any population that is considered "special." It is strongly recommended that whenever possible, institutional administrations consider responsible measures to allow for maximum dignity and participation in all facets of life, including the sexual, for their populations.

Blindness and Sex

It is obvious that there are important aspects of visual cues to sexual feelings and sexual behavior. When the sensory input derived from vision is not available to people, either through congenital blindness or acquired blindness, there may be a variety of consequences to sexuality. Unfortunately, there is little systematic research in this area on which to rely.

Evidence from studies in animals indicates that light perception acts on the pineal gland and the brain as an important regulator of reproductive status in both females and males in a variety of species. In humans, congenitally blind girls reach menarche at an earlier age than normally sighted girls [40]. However, menstrual irregularities are common in blind women, with the cycle sometimes becoming irregular in women with blindness acquired in adulthood, years after normal cycling has been established [41]. According to von Schumann, 52 of 54 men whose blindness antedated puberty experienced impaired potency, although libido was not disturbed [41]. Fitzgerald reported that 6 of 35 recently blind men became completely impotent following loss of vision, while 5 other men in this group either decreased or stopped sexual activity [42]. However, he noted that medical explanations existed for these changes: Five of the six men became impotent as a result of diabetes or multiple sclerosis, and the other subjects with altered sexuality were significantly depressed.

Children who are blind have special needs for receiving carefully tailored sex education pertaining to the anatomy, physiology, and psychology of sex. The use of anatomic models may be of particular assistance in such programs; in Scandinavia, live models have been used for this purpose [43]. When congenital blindness coexists with other developmental abnormalities, socialization processes that are important in the subsequent development of sexual relationships may be severely limited. For persons whose general health and intelligence are normal and blindness is an isolated problem, parental attitudes and input from education will be important determinants of how childhood and adolescent interpersonal skills are learned. In all cases of congenital blindness, visual cues that ordinarily contribute to assessment of physical attractiveness and the activation of eroticism are missing and become replaced, to varying degrees, by ancillary sources of interpersonal communication.

When blindness first occurs in adulthood, various aspects of its effect on the patient must be considered. In many instances of nontraumatic blindness, the cause of the loss of vision (e.g., diabetes, multiple sclerosis, or brain tumor) may cause sexual dysfunction. However, the reaction to adult-onset blindness may include depression, impaired self-esteem, feelings of helplessness, and social withdrawal, all of which may contribute to the genesis of sexual problems. Clinical management should begin by careful attention to distinguishing between organic and psychogenic sexual dysfunction; in cases in which a primary organic etiology can be eliminated, treatment of depression if it exists and supportive counsel that recognizes the patient's right to grieve while emphasizing an early return to social activities is helpful. In some instances, psychotherapy may be beneficial.

Sexuality in the Deaf   The impact of impaired hearing on sexuality has been largely overlooked by health-care professionals. Congenital deafness creates major obstacles to the development of language and learning skills. It is not surprising that the pervasive importance of speech and hearing to communication frequently leads to limitations on the deaf child's psychosocial growth, a problem that may be compounded by the isolation of deaf children from their families by placement in residential schools [44]. The problem is dramatized by the following observations by two specialists in education for the deaf:

Understanding such abstract concepts as maleness, femaleness, parenting, relationships, and reproduction becomes secondary when one has to struggle with the basic labelling of one's body parts. For example, the average hearing child, upon hearing a word several hundred times, usually can integrate that word into his/her vocabulary. The deaf child, because of the nature of the impairment, is denied this verbal repetition and ultimately the word itself. For the deaf child, the integration of just one word into the vocabulary requires that someone point out, show, demonstrate again and again what is being taught [45].

Relatively little attention has been devoted to the development of sex education courses for the deaf. Because deaf people can at best comprehend only one-quarter of speech content by lip-reading, and since only 10 percent of 18-year-old deaf students can read at or above an eighth-grade level [45], it is apparent that specialized materials and programs must be devised to overcome the limitations to the acquisition of sexual knowledge that characterize this population. There has been opposition to such an approach, however, both by parents of deaf children—who are dealing simultaneously with guilt over their child's deafness and a strong desire for education designed to lead to an economically independent life for the deaf—and by educators for the deaf, many of whom have chosen to ignore the sexual needs of this special population by assuming a moralistic posture. Even in residential school programs where sex education is formally taught, there is often a problem, since few of the nation's teachers of the deaf have been prepared in their own professional training to assume such a role [46].

Deafness does not impair libido or physical responsiveness to sexual activity. However, the sexual ignorance of many deaf persons, coupled with relative deficits in the realm of social skills and communication, may predispose to the development of marital and sexual problems. Although little research has been done in this area, the impact of deafness on self-esteem and body-image appears to be a fruitful direction for future study. There are indications that homosexual behavior may be more prevalent among deaf students at a residential school than heterosexual behavior; this subject also requires a closer look.

Deafness that first occurs in adolescence or adulthood poses different problems for the affected person. Developmental handicaps are not present, but a pattern of social isolation, reactive depression, and a sense of helplessness may frequently occur. Sexual problems may originate in this context, although the difficulties are often of a relatively transient nature.

Providing health-care services or counseling to the deaf is a complex task in light of the communications barrier that exists. The Fitz-Geralds point out that without the availability of interpreting services, the deaf person feels linguistically cut off from health-care professionals but often will feign understanding to avoid the appearance of ignorance [45, 47]. Ideally, health-care workers skilled in sign language and trained in working with the deaf, as well as deaf peer counselors, will grow in numbers as recognition of this requirement and interest in this area spread.

Concluding Comments

There has been little discussion in this chapter of the effects that handicaps, whether physical or mental, may have on personal relationships. In fact, this subject is too complex to permit a meaningful examination in this text. However, it is naive to believe that marriage is always advisable for handicapped people, and it is overly optimistic to think that the occurrence of a major handicap such as quadriplegia does not frequently result in marked disruption of some marriages and the dissolution of others. Many patients with handicaps can benefit from attention to their sexual concerns by provision of education, attitudinal support, diagnostic services, and suggestions for practical assistance. The formulation of such suggestions depends on knowledge of the patient's sexual values, medical condition (including drugs being used and concurrent illnesses), psychological health, and social situation (including partner availability), as well as the use of a considerable dose of common sense. Suggestions may involve ways of participating in nongenital sex play (such as massage, kissing, breast stimulation); masturbatory techniques (particularly suited to the person without a partner: Males may wish to use an artificial vagina or special adapter for a vibrator [43], females may use a vibrator or other source of friction applied to the external genitals or breasts); oral-genital stimulation; or various positions for coitus. The use of a waterbed may facilitate the sense of active participation in sex play, since when one partner thrusts, the fluid wave produces physical motion for the handicapped person that can provide a counterthrusting; however, getting onto and off a waterbed may pose problems for some quadriplegics or other persons with severe motor impairment.

Attention to details such as the state of bladder function (it is usually advisable for persons with any bladder impairment to empty the bladder prior to sexual activity) and the presence and positioning of catheters (catheters may be doubled back over the penis to permit intercourse) [8, 43] is essential. Mechanical assistance during sexual positioning (using pillows or braces to provide proper support and balance and to provide easier access to the genitals) can be of assistance to amputees, the spinal cord-injured, or persons with multiple sclerosis. But in the final analysis, the attitude of the handicapped person toward sex is often of much greater significance than the mechanical details alone.

It is necessary to realize that disabilities are indeed disabling—that is to say, many people with conditions such as those described in this chapter experience permanent disruptions of their sexuality that preclude a return to prior sexual capabilities. There is an unfortunate tendency accompanying the enthusiasm with which some health-care workers emphasize the possible benefits that may accrue from sexual counseling of the handicapped: communicating the unduly optimistic and simplistic view that all handicapped people can lead enjoyable sex lives. This dishonest and misleading posture can be avoided by approaching sexual health and rehabilitation in precisely the same way that other aspects of health care are provided: with objectivity, sensitivity, and attention to the needs of each individual.

References

1. Cole, T. M., and Cole, S. S.   The handicapped and sexual health. *SIECUS Report* 4(5):1–2, 9–10, 1976.
2. Halstead, L. S., Halstead, M. M., Salhoot, J. T., Stock, D. D., and Sparks, R. W.   Human sexuality: An interdisciplinary program for health care professionals and the physically disabled. *Southern Medical Journal* 69:1352–1355, 1976.
3. Cole, T. M., Chilgren, R. and Rosenberg, P.   A new programme of sex education and counseling for spinal cord injured adults and health care professionals. *Paraplegia* 11:111–124, 1973.
4. Held, J. P., Cole, T. M., Held, C. A., Anderson, C., and Chilgren, R. A. Sexual attitude reassessment workshops: Effect on spinal cord injured adults, their partners and rehabilitation professionals. *Archives of Physical Medicine and Rehabilitation* 56:14–18, 1975.
5. Cole, T. M.   Reaction of the rehabilitation team to patients with sexual problems. In E. R. Griffith, R. B. Trieschmann, G. W. Hohmann, T. M.

Cole, J. S. Tobis, and V. Cummings, Sexual dysfunctions associated with physical disabilities. *Archives of Physical Medicine and Rehabilitation* 56:8–13, 1975.

6. Diamond, M. Sexuality and the handicapped. *Rehabilitation Literature* 35:34–40, 1974.

7. Hohmann, G. W. Considerations in management of psychosexual readjustment in the cord-injured male. *Rehabilitation Psychology* 19:50–58, 1972.

8. Mooney, T. O., Cole, T. M., and Chilgren, R. A. *Sexual Options for Paraplegics and Quadriplegics.* Boston: Little, Brown and Co., 1975.

9. Anderson, T. P., and Cole, T. M. Sexual counseling of the physically disabled. *Postgraduate Medicine* 58:117–123, 1975.

10. Adams, R. D. Diseases of the Spinal Cord. In M. M. Wintrobe, G. W. Thorn, R. D. Adams, I. L. Bennett, E. Braunwald, K. J. Isselbacher, and R. G. Petersdorf (eds.), *Harrison's Principles of Internal Medicine* (6th ed.). New York: McGraw-Hill Book Co., 1970. Pp. 1720–1727.

11. Coxe, W. S., and Grubb, R. L. Central Nervous System Trauma: Spinal. In S. G. Eliasson, A. L. Prensky, and W. B. Hardin, Jr. (eds.), *Neurological Pathophysiology.* New York: Oxford University Press, 1974. Pp. 284–292.

12. Bors, E., and Comarr, A. E. Neurological disturbances of sexual function with special reference to 529 patients with spinal cord injury. *Urological Survey* 10:191–222, 1960.

13. Comarr, A. E. Sexual function among patients with spinal cord injury. *Urologia Internationalis* 25:134–168, 1970.

14. Talbot, H. S. A report on sexual function in paraplegics. *Journal of Urology* 61:265–270, 1949.

15. Talbot, H. S. The sexual function in paraplegics. *Journal of Urology* 73:91–100, 1955.

16. Money, J. Phantom orgasm in the dreams of paraplegic men and women. *Archives of General Psychiatry* 3:373–382, 1960.

17. Munro, D., Horne, H. W., and Paull, D. P. The effect of injury to spinal cord and cauda equina on the sexual potency of men. *New England Journal of Medicine* 239:903–911, 1948.

18. Tsuji, I., Nakajima, F., Morimoto, J., and Nounaka, Y. The sexual function in patients with spinal cord injury. *Urologia Internationalis* 12:270–280, 1961.

19. Jochheim, K. A., and Wahle, H. A study on sexual function in 56 male patients with complete irreversible lesions of the spinal cord and cauda equina. *Paraplegia* 8:166–172, 1970.

20. Zeitlin, A. B., Cottrell, T. L., and Lloyd, F. A. Sexology of the paraplegic male. *Fertility and Sterility* 8:337–344, 1957.

21. Rossier, A., Ziegler, W., Duchosal, P., and Meylan, J. Sexual function and dysreflexia. *Paraplegia* 9:51–59, 1971.

22. Bregman, S., and Hadley, R. G. Sexual adjustment and feminine attractiveness among spinal cord injured women. *Archives of Physical Medicine and Rehabilitation* 57:448–450, 1976.

23. Romano, M. D., and Lassiter, R. E. Sexual counseling with the spinal-cord injured. *Archives of Physical Medicine and Rehabilitation* 53:568–575, 1972.

24. Griffith, E. R., and Trieschmann, R. B.   Sexual functioning in women with spinal cord injury. *Archives of Physical Medicine and Rehabilitation* 56:18–21, 1975.
25. Cole, T. M.   Sexuality and the Spinal Cord Injured. In R. Green (ed.), *Human Sexuality: A Health Practitioner's Text*. Baltimore: Williams & Wilkins Co., 1975.
26. Bors, E., Engle, E. T., Hollinger, V. H., and Rosenquist, R. C.   Fertility in paraplegic males: A preliminary report of endocrine studies. *Journal of Clinical Endocrinology and Metabolism* 10:381–398, 1950.
27. Comarr, A. E., and Bors, E.   Spermatocystography in patients with spinal cord injuries. *Journal of Urology* 73:172–178, 1955.
28. Guttmann, L., and Walsh, J.   Prostigmin assessment test of fertility in spinal man. *Paraplegia* 9:39–51, 1971.
29. Horne, H. W., Paull, D. P., and Munro, D.   Fertility studies in the human male with traumatic injuries of the spinal cord and cauda equina. *New England Journal of Medicine* 239:959–961, 1948.
30. Kikuchi, T. A., Skowsky, W. R., El-Toraei, I., and Swerdloff, R.   The pituitary-gonadal axis in spinal cord injury. *Fertility and Sterility* 27:1142–1145, 1976.
31. Claus-Walker, J., Scurry, M., Carter, R. E., and Campos, R. J.   Steady state hormonal secretion in traumatic quadriplegia. *Journal of Clinical Endocrinology and Metabolism* 44:530–535, 1977.
32. Silver, J. R., and Owens, E.   Sexual problems in disorders of the nervous system: II. Psychological reactions. *British Medical Journal* 3:532–534, 1975.
33. Comarr, A. E.   Interesting observations on females with spinal cord injury. *Medical Services Journal* (Canada) 22:651–661, 1966.
34. Guttmann, L.   Married life of paraplegics and tetraplegics. *Paraplegia* 2:182–188, 1964.
35. Whalen, R. E., and Whalen, C. K.   Sexual Behavior: Research Perspectives. In F. F. de la Cruz and G. D. LaVeck (eds.), *Human Sexuality and the Mentally Retarded*. New York: Brunner/Mazel, Publishers, 1973. Pp. 221–229.
36. Gebhard, P. H.   Sexual Behavior of the Mentally Retarded. In F. F. de la Cruz and G. D. LaVeck (eds.), *Human Sexuality and the Mentally Retarded*. New York: Brunner/Mazel, Publishers, 1973. Pp. 29–49.
37. Mosier, H., Grossman, H., and Dingman, H.   Secondary sex development in mentally deficient individuals. *Child Development* 33:273–286, 1962.
38. De la Cruz, F. F., and LaVeck, G. D. (eds.). *Human Sexuality and the Mentally Retarded*. New York: Brunner/Mazel, Publishers, 1973.
39. Gordon, S.   A Response to Warren Johnson. In F. F. de la Cruz and G. D. LaVeck (eds.), *Human Sexuality and the Mentally Retarded*. New York: Brunner/Mazel, Publishers, 1973. P. 69.
40. Zacharias, L., and Wurtman, R. J.   Blindness: Its relation to age at menarche. *Science* 144:1154–1155, 1964.
41. Blindness believed to impair sexual function. *Hospital Tribune*, September 24, 1973, p. 35.
42. Fitzgerald, R. G.   Commentary on paper by Gillman and Gordon: Sexual behavior in the blind. *Medical Aspects of Human Sexuality* 7(6):60, 1973.

43. Heslinga, K., Schellen, A. M. C. M., and Verkuyl, A. *Not Made of Stone: The Sexual Problems of Handicapped People.* Springfield, Ill.: Charles C Thomas, Publisher, 1974.

44. Evans, D. A. Experimental deprivation: Unresolved factor in the impoverished socialization of deaf school children in residence. *American Annals of the Deaf* 120:545–552, 1975.

45. Fitz-Gerald, D., and Fitz-Gerald, M. Deaf people are sexual, too! *SIECUS Report* 6(2):1, 13–15, November 1977.

46. Fitz-Gerald, D., and Fitz-Gerald, M. The sex-educator: Who's teaching the teacher sex education? *American Annals of the Deaf* 123:68–72, 1978.

47. Fitz-Gerald, D., and Fitz-Gerald, M. Sexual implications of deafness. *Sexuality and Disability* 1:57–69, 1978.

Sex and Family Planning

Sex and reproduction are not synonymous, but the potential outcome of heterosexual activity includes the possibility of conception whether desired or not. Reproduction by choice rather than by chance is an issue with numerous social and economic ramifications for a world with limited resources. On a scale less global but no less important, undesired pregnancy or unwanted sterility may have a strong impact on the individual psyche and the family unit. Patients who are seen in family planning clinics, in the midst of a pregnancy, or complaining of infertility frequently have questions about sex, although health-care professionals generally underestimate the number of such concerns and spend less time than patients would like in discussing these matters [1]. This failure to discuss issues related to sex may be due in part to the realities of time pressure and lack of professional sex education, but it also reflects the general emphasis on the technologic aspects of reproductive health that has been increasingly apparent in the last two decades.

The issues that relate to family planning and sexuality are extraordinarily complex. This chapter will examine contraception, pregnancy, abortion, and infertility from the viewpoint of their effects on sexuality; however, important elements of a thorough analysis of these subjects will be omitted from the discussion either because insufficient data exist to draw useful conclusions or in order to preserve the flow of clinically relevant thought. In particular, the sociologic, religious, and cross-cultural aspects of family planning are beyond the scope of this text.

Sexual Problems and Family Planning: An Overview

An appreciation of the frequency of sexual problems associated with reproductive health may be gained from the data shown in Table 15-1, which summarizes some of the sexual problems discovered in surveys conducted in a family planning clinic in Los Angeles [1] and an infertility service in London [2]. Thirty-seven percent of the respondents in the family planning clinic indicated that they had sexual concerns for which they wanted help; remarkably, 165 of the 500 couples seen for infertility (37 percent) had sexual problems as well.

Despite the relative frequency of these difficulties (sexual problems may also include many categories not listed in Table 15-1), professionals dealing with such populations have not generally included questions about sexual problems or concerns in their discussions with patients. Although it is difficult to imagine how appropriate contraceptive advice can be given without knowledge of the sexual preferences and patterns a person has, it appears that many physicians, nurses, and counselors

Table 15-1. Occurrence of Sexual Problems in a Family Planning Clinic and an Infertility Program

| | Sexual Problem | Percentage of Occurrence | |
		Family Planning Clinic[a] (N = 578)	Infertility Program[b] (N = 500 couples)
♀	Infrequent orgasm or difficulty in achieving orgasm	35	8
	Dyspareunia	23	13
	No orgasm	10	8
	Vaginismus	10–11	No data
♂	Impotence	9	6
	Premature ejaculation	20	2
	Retarded ejaculation	4–5	No data
♀,♂	Loss of libido	15	4

[a]Data from Golden, Golden, Price, and Heinrich [1].
[b]Data from Steele [2].

regard such discussions as unwanted or unnecessary. Similarly, while it seems obvious that counseling for infertility cannot be effectively offered without knowledge of coital timing and frequency, disorders of ejaculation, dyspareunia, and other aspects of sexuality, in actual practice such information is not always obtained.

It is important to remember that pregnancy, contraception, abortion, and infertility mean different things to different people, depending partly on time and circumstance, personal and family values, social customs and taboos, economic considerations, and a host of other variables. To some women, pregnancy is an affirmation of femininity, whereas to others it is an intrusion that is viewed as diminishing physical attractiveness; understandably, there are likely to be different attitudes toward sex during pregnancy in these two groups. Because of the importance of such individual variables, counseling must be specifically oriented to the needs of each woman, man, or couple seeking advice.

Contraception

The current era of contraceptive technology has had major impact on sexual behavior and reproductive patterns throughout the world [2–6]. The fear of unwanted pregnancy was a strong constraint on sexual practices before the advent of efficacious, available, economical types of contraceptive methods, but these very elements have led to new problems that did not previously exist. For example, some adolescent girls report feeling pressured into sexual intercourse because pregnancy is no longer an issue [7]; in another direction, there are clearly instances in which disagreement by a couple over contraceptive practice (e.g., which method should be used, who should be responsible) may create sexual problems as well as other difficulties for their relationship. Both the psychology of contraceptive use and the biomedical aspects of this facet of family planning have important ramifications on sexual functioning and sexual behavior. Before the sexual problems and advantages that may be associated with various contraceptive methods are examined, brief summaries of their relative effectiveness and medical safety will be given.

Efficacy and Safety of Contraceptive Methods

Evaluating the effectiveness of a contraceptive technique in terms of the prevention of pregnancy might seem to be a straightforward task. However, there is much disagreement among researchers on the precise pregnancy rates that occur in association with various contraceptive methods. This disagreement occurs partly because there is a difference between the theoretical effectiveness of a technique (how it *should* work when used correctly and consistently, without human error or negligence) and the actual effectiveness that occurs in real life, when inconsistent use or improper technique combines with the intrinsic failures of the method [8]. Methodological problems arise from comparing studies done in populations with differing characteristics that influence reproductive patterns, including factors such as age, prior reproductive history, future reproductive goals, socioeconomic level, cultural milieu, health status, and coital rates. Even the duration of use of a given contraceptive method may alter its effectiveness: A longer duration of use correlates positively with lower pregnancy rates for users of diaphragms [9] and intrauterine devices [10].

Despite such difficulties, it is possible to arrive at an approximation of contraceptive effectiveness in actual use by combining data from a large number of research studies. Unless otherwise specified, pregnancy rates are given in terms of 100 woman-years of exposure.*

*Failure rates per 100 woman-years are computed using the Pearl formula:
$$\frac{\text{number of pregnancies}}{\text{number of months of exposure}} \times 1200$$

There are other difficulties in assessing the safety of various contraceptive methods. Widespread differences exist in the data compiled by different investigators studying the relationship of a certain contraceptive modality to a possible side effect; even in instances in which there is unanimity of opinion, the question of safety remains a relative one. The possibility of adverse effects resulting from the use of a particular contraceptive method must be compared to the medical risks that would accrue from pregnancy if no contraception or a less effective contraceptive approach were used. In addition, in certain special populations (such as adolescents or patients with certain types of illnesses) the increased risk of maternal mortality may be another consideration.

To illustrate the difficulty of evaluating known contraceptive risks, it may be useful to examine the data regarding the mortality rate for women aged 20 to 34 years due to pulmonary embolism or cerebral thrombosis. Nonusers of oral contraceptives have a mortality risk of 0.2 per 100,000 healthy married nonpregnant women, compared to 1.5 per 100,000 for users of oral contraceptives. Stated another way, women of this age who use birth control pills have a 7.5 times greater risk of death due to thromboembolic phenomena than nonusers. However, if death rates of this age group attributable to pregnancy, delivery, and the puerperium are examined, one finds a total mortality risk of 22.8 per 100,000 pregnancies. Another perspective may be gained by comparing the risk of death from pulmonary embolism or cerebral thrombosis in this same group of women using birth control pills (1.5 per 100,000) with the risk of death from an automobile accident (4.9 per 100,000) or from cancer (13.7 per 100,000). Clearly, the known adverse effects of a contraceptive can be interpreted in many different ways from such data. In the practical management of patients, the evaluation is even more complex because social, psychological, and economic considerations must be weighed with knowledge about medical risk. There are no easy equations to aid in such decisions.

Sterilization. VASECTOMY. The highest degree of contraceptive protection that is attainable except by absolute abstention is associated with surgical techniques to prevent pregnancy. Vasectomy is the simplest and safest form of surgical contraception: The failure rate is a very low 0.15 [11]. Failures of this method are due primarily to unprotected coitus before sperm disappear from the ejaculate [12, 13] and recanalization of the severed vas [14–16]. In addition, there is a possibility of mistaking a blood vessel for the vas deferens, thus cutting the wrong structure, and there is the very rare occurrence of a double vas defer-

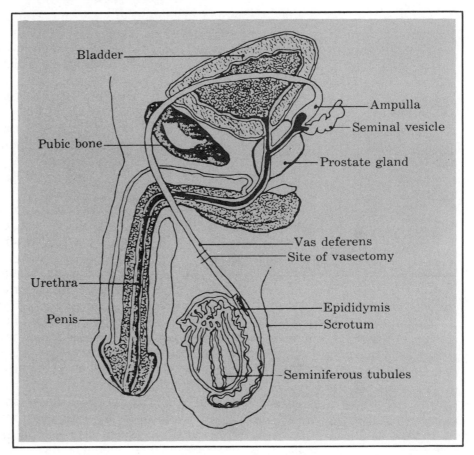

Figure 15-1. Site of vasectomy. (From *Population Reports*, Series D, Number 1, the Population Information Program, the Johns Hopkins University, Baltimore, MD 21205.)

ens on one side of the body, which would allow subsequent transport of sperm into the ejaculate if the situation were not detected and all three vasa severed [12, 13].

Figure 15-1 shows the site at which a vasectomy is done. Typically, the operation is performed under local anesthesia, although general anesthesia may be used when physical problems of the scrotum are present that may complicate the surgery or when the patient is allergic to local anesthetics [12]. The primary significant complications of vasectomy, based on a review of 24 studies involving 24,961 patients, were hematoma (1.6 percent); infection, including skin infections, ligature abscess, vasitis, and/or cellulitis (1.5 percent); epididymitis (1.4 percent);

and granuloma formation (0.3 percent) [13]. Swelling, pain, and skin discoloration due to bruising are common minor side effects that occur in about half of all men after such surgery. Ice packs applied postoperatively [11] and the use of a well-fitted athletic support may reduce postoperative discomfort.

Since the vasectomy does not produce immediate postoperative sterility (viable sperm may persist in the ejaculate for weeks or months after surgery), it is advisable for a couple to use another contraceptive method until two consecutive semen specimens have shown the complete absence of sperm cells. This disadvantage of the procedure is a relatively minor one when viewed in the perspective of the overall safety and effectiveness of the method.

Although followup of men who have undergone vasectomies has failed to indicate any health problems attributable to this surgery, several questions have been raised in recent years about medical safety. It has now been conclusively shown that vasectomy does not alter pituitary function or testosterone production on either a short-term or a long-term basis [17, 18]. Many men develop sperm-agglutinating antibodies sometime after having a vasectomy; this is a natural consequence of absorption of the antigenic material of spermatozoa into body tissues, an event that would not occur if the vasa were intact. Despite widespread research on this phenomenon, no health problems can be attributed to the presence of sperm-agglutinating antibodies in men. In fact, studies at the Masters & Johnson Institute have shown that most nonvasectomized men with circulating sperm-agglutinating antibodies have normal fertility [19].

Perhaps the major drawback of vasectomy is the problem of reversibility. A small proportion of men who have undergone vasectomy later decide that they would like their fertility restored. Reasons for this request include remarriage after divorce or death of the wife, death of a child, and improved economic circumstances [20, 21]. At the present time, surgical reversal of vasectomy by an anastomosis procedure (vasovasotomy) offers uncertain success in the restoration of fertility. Reports of the reappearance of sperm in the ejaculate indicate a 40 to 90 percent success rate for this operation, but if functional success is defined in terms of subsequent conception, a rate of 20 to 60 percent is attained [22]. The use of an operating microscope in newer surgical approaches performed by highly experienced surgeons offers promise for maximal results in this situation.

A controversial and experimental technique for retaining the option to reproduce after vasectomy is the utilization of frozen semen storage to preserve specimens produced prior to the time of surgery. Preliminary reports indicate that the use of such specimens in artificial insemination has a modestly lower rate of conception than with fresh semen and thus far has not proved to be associated with increased rates of congenital anomalies or abortions [23–25]. Caution should be utilized in regard to this option until more recent research is available. Legal and ethical issues related to the use of frozen, stored semen have not yet been subjected to careful scrutiny.

TUBAL METHODS. Female sterilization can be achieved by a number of different operative procedures. Simple tubal ligation (tying the fallopian tubes to prevent the sperm and egg from meeting) is infrequently done today because of unsatisfactory effectiveness. Instead, tubal ligation is usually supplemented by either crushing (the Madlener technique); resection (the Pomeroy technique, fimbriectomy, or—less often used—salpingectomy), division and burial (the Irving technique); or resection and burial (cornual resection or the Uchida technique) [26]. Some of these methods are depicted in Figure 15-2; the range of failure rates reported in the literature is summarized in Table 15–2.

Laparotomy for tubal ligation is not usually necessary unless another indication for abdominal surgery is present or there is technical difficulty or danger to the patient from pelvic pathology [27]. Laparoscopy (use of an instrument inserted through the abdominal wall to visualize the inside of the peritoneum) and approaches through the vaginal cul-de-sac (culdoscopy) or uterus (hysteroscopy) have offered generally safer and more convenient alternatives. In the United States, tubal electrocoagulation and division by laparoscopy, with or without excision of a segment of the tubes, is the most commonly used technique for female sterilization. The failure rate for this procedure is less than 1 percent. Electrocoagulation by hysteroscopy does not require an incision and can be done easily on an outpatient basis, but this procedure has a high failure rate (11–35%) and a risk of uterine burns or perforation [26].

The use of clips or bands to occlude the fallopian tubes offers the potential of later reversal of sterility combined with a high rate of efficacy [28, 29]. Experimental work with the insertion of plugs that can block the uterine end of the fallopian tubes also offers the potential of reversibility. The introduction of chemical agents into the tubes to produce fibrosis or blockage has not yet achieved a satisfactory rate of effectiveness, and safety is uncertain [26].

The most common cause of failure of tubal occlusion is when the

Figure 15-2. Frequently used methods of tubal ligation. (From *Population Reports*, Series C, Number 7, the Population Information Program, the Johns Hopkins University, Baltimore, MD 21205.)

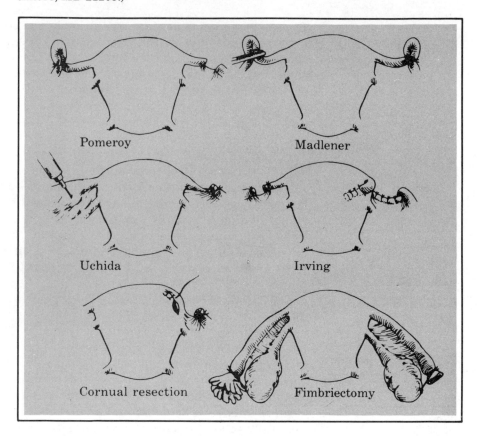

Pomeroy

Madlener

Uchida

Irving

Cornual resection

Fimbriectomy

Table 15-2. Failure Rates for Tubal Occlusion Methods

Technique	Percentage of Failure
Simple tubal ligation	20
Madlener technique (ligation and crushing)	1–2
Pomeroy technique (ligation and resection)	0–0.4
Ligation and fimbriectomy	0
Ligation and salpingectomy	0–1.9
Irving technique (ligation with division and burial)	0
Uchida technique (ligation with resection and burial)	0

woman is pregnant at the time of surgery [30]. Other reasons for failure include recanalization of the tube, incomplete ligation or coagulation, and misidentification of another structure as the tube. Complications of tubal surgery include the risk of the anesthetic method, the possibility of bleeding or infection, perforation of the uterus or bowel, and burning of an internal structure (with electrocautery). The overall rate of complications with laparoscopic sterilization ranges from one to six percent [30]. With culdoscopic sterilization, minor rectal perforation or bleeding complications each occurs in about 0.5 percent of patients, while anesthetic risk is minimized by the use of a local agent [31].

Although Green estimates that 20 percent of women who have had tubal sterilization may be able to have the procedure reversed [27], women considering such surgery should realize that current methods of tubal occlusion are largely permanent. Since both a higher degree of operative safety and a better chance for reversibility are associated with vasectomy, both the man and the woman should be carefully counseled and advised of these facts when a couple is inquiring about the advantages of a surgical method of contraception.

Oral Contraception. Few advances in medical technology have had the broad social impact of the development of effective birth control pills. The historical background of this story has been interestingly recounted by two scientists who played a personal role in the development and evaluation of oral contraceptives [32]. At present, after two decades of clinical experience, there is considerable controversy among scientists, feminists, and consumer advocates about the use and safety of these agents, with the arguments often generating more heat than understanding.

Birth control pills that are currently available are of two types: a combination of synthetic estrogen and progestogen, and a "minipill" with progestogen only in low dosage. This discussion will focus on combination oral contraceptives, unless otherwise specified. Birth control pills prevent pregnancy primarily by interfering with the normal cyclic output of FSH and LH from the pituitary gland, both by a hypothalamic effect on gonadotropin-releasing factor and by a separate pituitary action. The differences in circulating gonadotropin levels between birth control pill users and nonusers are shown in Figure 15-3.

Birth control pills also produce changes in cervical mucus that inhibit the penetration of sperm and may influence both the tubal and the uterine environment, further impairing the chances of conception. Of the nonsurgical methods for contraception, birth control pills are

Figure 15-3. (A) Mean gonadotropin levels during one complete menstrual cycle in a group of women not using oral contraceptives. (B) Mean gonadotropin levels during one complete menstrual cycle in a group of oral contraceptive users. Note the absence of a midcycle LH or FSH peak.

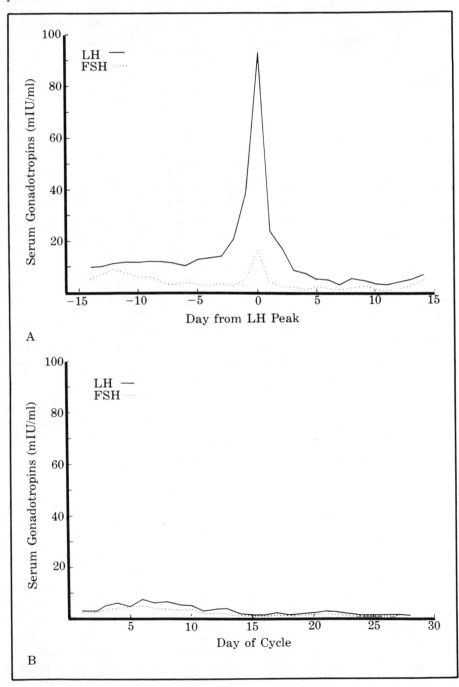

clearly the most effective: The failure rate for combination oral contraceptives is 1 per 100 woman-years of use, while the minipill has a failure rate of 2 to 3 per 100 woman-years.

Many side effects are encountered in women using birth control pills. The difficulty is in evaluating the extent to which these troublesome symptoms are actually due to the pill, since many occur spontaneously in women. Several investigations have been conducted to attempt such determinations by examining side effects with placebo pills* [33, 34], but there can be few firm conclusions drawn on the basis of available data. One of these studies found that a larger percentage of women gained weight while taking a placebo than while using birth control pills [33]. Another problem in assessing health risks due to oral contraceptives is allowing for the problems that would occur as a result of unwanted pregnancy, either aborted or carried to term, that is prevented by their use. The principal side effects that are attributed to the use of birth control pills are listed in Table 15-3.

CARDIOVASCULAR EFFECTS. There is now solid evidence that shows an increased risk of thromboembolic problems for women using birth control pills [35–40]. Although the exact mechanism of this phenomenon is not clear, abnormalities in coagulation mechanisms [41], in lipid levels [42, 43], and in the intimal lining of arteries and veins may be involved. Both the morbidity and the mortality risk of deep-vein thromboembolism and thrombophlebitis appear to be approximately two to four times greater for women using oral contraceptives than for nonusers.

Recent evidence has documented a specific association between oral contraceptive use and the occurrence of myocardial infarction. Mann and Inman studied 153 women with fatal myocardial infarctions occurring before the age of 50 in a matched-case study [44]. There was a significant correlation between the use of oral contraception and myocardial infarct, with a stronger association with increasing age. Beral has analyzed mortality trends in women 15 to 44 years old in 21 different countries, identifying an increase in cardiovascular mortality of

---

*Studies of this type have been questioned on ethical grounds, since use of a placebo birth control pill necessarily provides no contraception, thus placing the woman at risk for possible unwanted conception. Although in some studies of this type, women were told to use an alternative method of contraception, many did not, since they believed their "pills" were satisfactory protection. The most proper approach to this ethical dilemma appears to us to be the use of a test group of women who have undergone tubal ligations; in this context, the side effects of placebo versus actual birth control pills could be monitored without risk of pregnancy, although, since other risks *would* be present, all women participating would need to give prior informed consent.

Table 15-3. Side Effects
of Combination Oral
Contraceptives

Major Effects	Minor Effects
Thrombophlebitis	Nausea
Pulmonary embolism	Vomiting
Cerebral thrombosis and hemorrhage	Diarrhea
	Constipation
Myocardial infarction	Abdominal cramps
Gallbladder disease	Breakthrough bleeding
Retinal thrombosis	Spotting
Optic neuritis	Rise in blood pressure
Hepatic tumors	Vaginitis (especially moniliasis)
Cholestatic jaundice	Change in menstrual flow
Migraine headaches	Amenorrhea during or after treatment
Hypertension	Edema
Glucose intolerance	Chloasma or melasma
	Rash
	Weight change (increase or decrease)
	Breast changes (tenderness, enlargement, galactorrhea)

three to five times in users of oral contraception [45]. The results of such investigations point toward a significant increase in the risk of myocardial infarction for women over the age of 35 who use birth control pills, especially when other risk factors such as cigarette smoking, diabetes, obesity, or hypercholesterolemia exist [46]. However, as Jaffe points out, these medical risks are still exceedingly small as absolute events and when viewed as relative to the risks of childbirth, except in the case of women over age 40 [47].

Oral contraceptives have been linked to strokes, cerebral ischemia, and a variety of neuro-ophthalmic sequelae [48–52]. Women suffering from migraine headaches may be predisposed to such adverse effects with birth control pills, and their migraine pattern may be exacerbated. A small number of women using oral contraceptives develop hypertension [53, 54] and a larger number develop minimal increases in both systolic and diastolic pressures that remain within the normal range. These changes may be due to sodium retention and alterations of the renin-aldosterone system and are reversible within a few months after discontinuing the pill [55].

EFFECTS ON THE GASTROINTESTINAL SYSTEM. Minor side effects of oral contraceptives involving the gastrointestinal system such as nausea, cramping, diarrhea, or constipation tend to decrease after the first few cycles in which the pill is used [32, 56]. Alteration of liver function tests occurs commonly in women using oral contraceptives [52, 57], but these changes rarely lead to clinical manifestations. In some women cholestatic jaundice develops; this rare event is usually due to a previous history of familial jaundice, chronic liver disease, or jaundice during pregnancy [57]. An increased incidence of gallbladder disease has been documented in association with birth control pills [58, 59], and interestingly, estrogen use by men has also been shown to cause gallbladder abnormalities [60]. In addition, there is an increased risk of developing liver cell adenomas in women using oral contraceptives; 20 to 25 percent of these tumors may rupture, causing intra-abdominal hemorrhage and sometimes leading to shock [61].

ENDOCRINE EFFECTS. Amenorrhea and/or anovulation may occur following the use of oral contraceptives, but it is unusual for these problems to persist for more than three months. Persistent amenorrhea accompanied by galactorrhea after use of the pill may be associated with a high rate of prolactin-secreting pituitary tumors [62]. For women who fail to ovulate after using birth control pills, clomiphene citrate often restores normal function. (It should be kept in mind that some women who have anovulatory menstrual cycles that they are not aware of before using the pill may be discovered to be anovulatory when they want to have children and have stopped the use of oral contraceptives. In this substantial group, it is erroneous to attribute the infertility to use of the pill.)

Oral contraceptives alter carbohydrate metabolism, although characteristically the fasting blood sugar level is not greatly influenced [63–66]. Women who have had gestational diabetes appear to be at a higher risk for developing abnormal glucose tolerance patterns while using birth control pills. Diabetic women may find that their insulin requirement is increased while using birth control pills. It is not known at present whether women who develop carbohydrate intolerance during the use of oral contraceptives are at greater risk for maturity-onset diabetes later in life.

The estrogenic component of oral contraceptives elevates the circulating proteins that bind cortisol, thyroxine, and testosterone. As a result, measurement of these hormones in serum or plasma may show an elevation that does not correspond to a functional overactivity of the adrenals, the thyroid, or the ovaries. Birth control pills may also cause an increase in circulating prolactin, which can sometimes cause galactorrhea [67, 68].

EFFECTS ON REPRODUCTION. There is now increasing evidence that the use of birth control pills by a pregnant woman can cause a variety of birth defects in the developing fetus. Nora and Nora described a pattern of multiple anomalies and an increased incidence of congenital heart defects in association with such maternal exposure [69]. Janerich and coworkers found that 14 percent of 108 mothers of children with congenital limb-reduction defects (the absence of an arm or leg or part of an arm or leg) had exposure to exogenous sex steroid hormones during pregnancy, whereas only 4 percent of a control group of mothers of normal children had similar exposure [70]. In another study, the inadvertent use of oral contraceptives after conception by 278 women was found to be associated with a rate of 21.5 per 1,000 for cardiovascular birth defects [71]. The range of congenital anomalies that may be produced by birth control pills is described by the acronym VACTERL (V for vertebral, A for anal, C for cardiac, T for tracheal, E for esophageal, R for renal, and L for limb). It is not yet clear what the separate or combined roles of the estrogenic and progestational components of birth control pills are in this regard, and not all researchers accept the thesis of an increased risk of teratogenicity [72]. Birth control pills taken during pregnancy can also cause masculinization of the female fetus [73].

There is no solid evidence linking prior use of oral contraceptives to abortion or miscarriage, or to a higher incidence of chromosomal disorders in offspring of pregnancies following the use of birth control pills. If pregnancy occurs while oral contraceptives are being used, there is a higher risk of ectopic pregnancy.

RISK OF NEOPLASIA. It is extraordinarily difficult to assess the possible carcinogenicity of oral contraceptives given current conflicting evidence and serious methodological hindrances. Undoubtedly, one of the reasons for this problem is that there may be a long period of latency between exposure to a known carcinogen and the appearance of detectable signs of cancer. Studies that evaluate the risks of estrogen exposure to postmenopausal or perimenopausal women (see Chap. 5) do not provide reliable data to answer concerns about the use of oral contraceptives for a number of different reasons. In addition to the uncertainty about birth control pills causing cancer, there is also the question of whether these agents may increase the growth or development of certain neoplasias that are thought to be hormone-sensitive (for example, breast carcinoma).

Several thorough review articles are available that evaluate previous research and clinical findings in this area of controversy [74–76]. There is fair agreement that users of oral contraceptives are less likely to develop benign tumors of the breast than nonusers. It is also generally agreed that use of sequential birth control pills is associated with an increased risk of endometrial carcinoma (which contributed to the sequential pills being withdrawn from the market), but this same risk does not apply to combination oral contraceptives. Most studies have been unable to demonstrate a convincing correlation between use of birth control pills and breast cancer [77, 78], although there have been conflicting reports regarding the use of estrogen replacement therapy. No conclusion can be reached at present about the possible relationship between cancer of the cervix and use of the birth control pill, but this should not be viewed as evidence of safety in this regard.

OTHER CONSIDERATIONS. Although there are sound theoretical reasons for believing that combination birth control pills with low doses of an estrogenic component are less likely to produce adverse effects such as thromboembolic phenomena, hypertension, or altered carbohydrate tolerance, this hypothesis has not been substantiated as yet. It is helpful to keep in mind the fact that most currently available oral contraceptives have far less hormonal potency than those in use 10 or more years ago, so that if this theory proves to be correct, many complications of birth control pills may actually be on the decline at present.

The minipill (a microdose progestogen-only contraceptive that is taken on a daily basis, even during menstruation) has a much lower rate of side effects than combination oral contraceptives, since no estrogen component is present. The mechanism of pregnancy prevention for the minipill is uncertain, since ovulation is blocked only in some cycles; changes that affect tubal motility, alter the physiochemical nature of cervical mucus, or interfere with implantation of the fertilized ovum in the endometrium have been cited as possible explanations for effectiveness [79]. The primary problem with the use of the minipill is lack of regularity of the menstrual cycle and other menstrual disturbances. Spotting and breakthrough bleeding occur in 25 to 50 percent of women using the minipill. The length of the menstrual cycle may vary considerably; the most typical change is toward a cycle of short duration (12 to 16 days), although some users may experience the opposite effect, which may lead to anxiety about possible pregnancy. These problems cause many women to discontinue use of this method of contraception and contribute to a failure rate of 3 to 4 per 100 woman-years of use [79].

The advantages of combination birth control pills are many when a highly effective form of reversible contraception is desired, in spite of the numerous side effects that may occur. Since many of the side effects listed in Table 15-3 are also complications of pregnancy, a perspective that balances the individual needs of each woman with her medical history and current health status is necessary to formulate an informed decision about contraception. The following conditions are generally contraindications to the use of combination oral contraceptives:

1. Thromboembolic disorders, past or present.
2. Myocardial infarction, past or present.
3. Chronic liver disease causing impaired liver function or acute hepatic disorders.
4. Known or suspected breast carcinoma.
5. Known or suspected uterine tumors.
6. Known or suspected gallbladder disease.
7. Preexisting lipid abnormality.
8. Undiagnosed abnormal genital bleeding.
9. Known or suspected pregnancy.
10. Women over age 40 with coronary risk factors.

In addition, diabetes mellitus, hypertension, and a history of migraine headaches constitute relative contraindications to the use of birth control pills, although when patients with these disorders have the need for absolutely effective contraception, oral contraceptives may be cautiously employed under individual circumstances of careful clinical management.

Intrauterine Devices. Since 1960, increasing interest has focused on the contraceptive properties of a device inserted into the uterine cavity. A huge variety of shapes, sizes, and materials have been used for these intrauterine devices (IUDs); some examples are shown in Figure 15-4. The mechanism of action whereby pregnancy is prevented in a highly effective manner (the failure rate is 2 to 4 per 100 woman-years) is not known at present, although the most popular explanation is an interference with implantation of the fertilized ovum [80]. It is also likely that an inflammatory response, including an abundance of macro-

Figure 15-4. Different types of IUDs. (*A*) Lippes Loop. (*B*) Copper T. (*C*) Cu-7. (*D*) Dalkon Shield (removed from market). (*E*) Saf-T-Coil. (From *Population Reports*, Series B, Number 2, the Population Information Program, the Johns Hopkins University, Baltimore, MD 21205.)

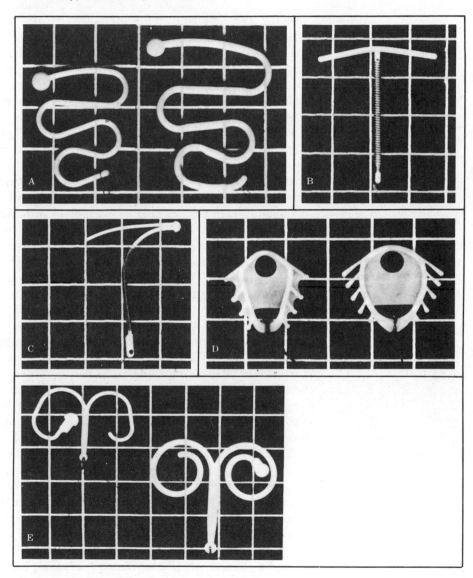

phages, renders the endometrial cavity hostile to sperm and to the blastocyst. Despite this excellent rate of effectiveness, problems with IUDs—their rate of expulsion from the uterus, a high rate of bleeding, pain, infection, or other complications—may lead to removal.

Approximately 5 to 20 expulsions occur for each 100 insertions. The primary risk here is that an expelled device will be unnoticed, leaving the woman unknowingly exposed to pregnancy. The rate for voluntary removal for all reasons ranges from 3.6 to 34.8 per 100 users during the first year of use [80]. Uterine perforation is a serious but rare risk of IUDs; the Dalkon Shield was removed from the market because of a number of deaths from septic abortion resulting from pregnancy with the device in place. Women using IUDs also have a substantially increased risk of contracting acute pelvic inflammatory disease.

According to Green [27], if pregnancy occurs with an IUD in place it is advisable to remove the device, since removal is associated with a smaller risk of abortion (30 percent) than if the device is left in place (abortion risk: 50 percent). This approach also lowers the risk of septic abortion. If pregnancy occurs with the IUD in place, there is greater than a 5 percent chance that it may be ectopic. Congenital defects are not increased in the children of women who have used IUDs.

Copper-containing devices have become popular in the past few years and are highly efficacious [81–83]. IUDs containing slow-release progesterone are also being used currently, offering the advantages of lessening menstrual blood loss, relieving dysmenorrhea in some women, and having a low rate of perforation [84]. Both the copper and the progesterone devices are often more easily tolerated by nulliparous women.

The IUD is well suited to women who want a highly effective contraceptive method that requires no active participation on their part and is easily and promptly reversible. It may be particularly appropriate for patients who cannot use oral contraceptives for medical reasons and for the mentally retarded or psychiatrically ill. The following contraindications pertain: (1) known or suspected pregnancy; (2) active pelvic infection; (3) congenital anomalies of the uterus; (4) severe cervical stenosis; (5) coagulation disorders or use of anticoagulant drugs. Other relative contraindications include women with severe dysmenorrhea or hypermenorrhea, whose problems may be exacerbated by most IUDs (progesterone devices may be tried in these patients); women with valvular heart disease (because seeding of bacteria from the insertion may cause bacterial endocarditis); and women using immunosuppressive agents, including corticosteroids, or having diseases that suppress normal immunity (such as leukemia or lymphoma), since the increased risk of infection carries potentially serious consequences in such patients [84].

Barrier Methods. The barrier methods of contraception are all free of systemic side effects. Increasing attention has been paid to these agents by women who are unwilling to assume the risks of birth control pills or intrauterine devices. The barrier methods—diaphragm, cervical cap, condom, foam, cream, jelly, and vaginal suppositories—can also be incorporated into sexual activity as a shared responsibility between partners.

The *diaphragm* should never be used by itself, since it does not prevent all sperm cells from reaching the cervical os. When the diaphragm is used in combination with a spermicidal cream or jelly, the actual failure rate ranges from 6 to 20 per 100 woman-years of use [85]. However, when proper insertion and usage criteria (Fig. 15-5) are followed by women experienced in the use of a diaphragm, the failure rate can be reduced to 2.4 per 100 woman-years of use [9]. Allergic reactions, vaginal irritation, or infection rarely complicate the use of diaphragms. Pelvic pathology involving or impinging on the vagina (fistulas, cystocele or rectocele, lacerations, congenital anomalies, complete uterine prolapse, severe retroversion or anteflexion of the uterus), severe distaste in regard to touching the genitals, or inability to learn or remember to use the diaphragm are contraindications.

The *cervical cap* is infrequently used in the United States. This device is inserted directly over the cervix, where it is held in place by suction and blocks the passage of sperm into the uterine cavity. Unlike the diaphragm, it can be left in place during the entire menstrual cycle except during menstruation, and it is unlikely to slip out of position during intercourse as the vagina undergoes alterations in size and shape (see Chap. 1). The cervical cap is most effectively used in combination with a spermicidal agent. The effectiveness is comparable to that of the diaphragm [85].

The *condom* is the only currently available nonsurgical method of contraception used by the male, other than coitus interruptus. Effectiveness is difficult to assess; in the majority of studies, failure rates range between 10 and 20 per 100 years of condom use [86]. The major cause of failure is inconsistent use. A benefit of the condom is its relatively high success in protecting against coital transmission of venereal disease.

Vaginal foams, jellies, creams, and other spermicidal agents when

Figure 15-5. Proper use of a diaphragm. (A) The rim of the diaphragm is pinched between the fingers and thumb. (B) Alternatively, a plastic introducer may be used to insert a diaphragm. The rim is hooked over the Y-shaped tip of the introducer and the opposite rim is stretched over the calibrated notch, which matches the size of the diaphragm. (C) The cervix is felt through the dome of the diaphragm to check proper placement. (D) A finger is hooked under the forward rim to remove the diaphragm. (From *Population Reports*, Series H, Number 4, the Population Information Program, the Johns Hopkins University, Baltimore, MD 21205.)

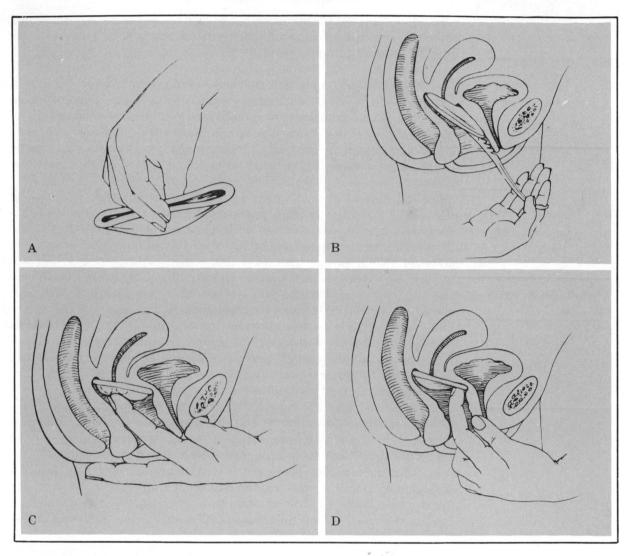

used by themselves are less effective than a diaphragm used with one of these agents. These products have a duration of effectiveness that lasts for about one hour; they need to be reinserted for repeated coital activity. The reported failure rates in a number of selected studies range from less than 2 to almost 40 per 100 woman-years, with a major reason for failure being inconsistency in use, as with the condom [8]. Because the chemical formulations of many of these spermicidal products have changed in the past decade, additional research is required to determine current efficacy.

Miscellaneous Methods of Contraception. In *coitus interruptus*, the man withdraws the penis before intravaginal ejaculation occurs. This may be a frustrating form of contraception, since it decidedly interferes with the spontaneity of sexual interaction, but it is nevertheless widely used. The effectiveness of coitus interruptus is approximately 15 to 40 percent. Since there may be viable sperm cells in the pre-ejaculatory fluid, it is obvious that pregnancy may occur even when intravaginal ejaculation does not take place. If ejaculation begins before the penis is completely withdrawn, or if drops of semen are deposited in the vaginal orifice by spurting from the withdrawn penis, pregnancy may also occur.

Douching is a poor method of contraception, since sperm may quickly penetrate the cervical mucus where they are unaffected by douching. The failure rate is more than 40 percent.

While *breast feeding* is biologically and psychologically advantageous for a variety of reasons [87, 88], it does not confer a high degree of contraceptive protection. Women may ovulate prior to their first post-delivery menstrual period, and studies of nursing mothers who have resumed menstrual cycling show a high rate of pregnancy, ranging from 16.2 to 100 percent [88].

Various *rhythm methods* of contraception depend on periodic abstinence during times of the menstrual cycle when fertility is most likely. So-called calendar rhythm methods require the identification of safe days for having intercourse by inferring from past menstrual length when ovulation will occur. Usual estimates predict that this will happen 12 to 16 days before the next menstrual flow begins. For three days before this time (and sometimes one day afterward), intercourse is not allowed. The temperature method utilizes a daily recording of basal body temperature to pinpoint the time of ovulation. Increasing progesterone levels at ovulation presumably cause an elevation of body temperature, as measured upon awakening each morning. Typical examples of ovulatory and anovulatory patterns are shown in Figure 15–6. Intercourse is generally precluded from the cessation of menses until two to four days after the temperature rise. If no temperature rise is detected during a complete menstrual cycle, devotees of this method must observe total coital abstinence. The Billings Ovulation Method is

Figure 15-6. Basal body temperature
charts. (*A*) Typical ovulatory pattern
(note sharp temperature rise at day
16). (*B*) Typical anovulatory pattern.

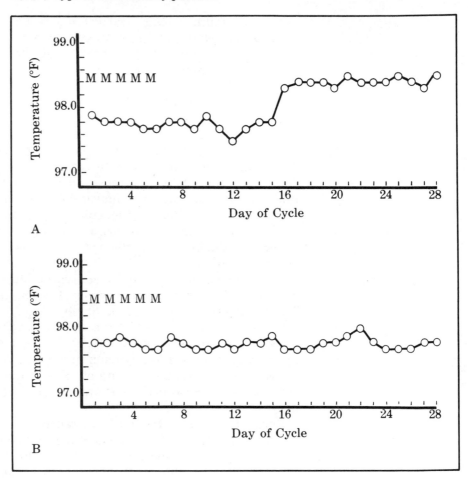

based on changes that occur in the cervical mucus and is the most
recent of the rhythm methods. At this time, lack of research data
precludes comment about its utility.

The rhythm methods have been subjected to considerable controversy because they are the only approaches to contraception recognized as "natural" by the Roman Catholic Church. Research on their
efficacy has been confused by inaccurate reporting of results and comparatively low levels of coital activity in some of the study populations
[89]. The calendar method is not very effective because menstrual

cycles are more variable than its theoretical model assumes: Failure rates ranging from 14.4 to 47 per 100 woman-years have been reported [89]. Temperature methods are inaccurate because they are difficult to interpret even when obtained accurately [90], and because in approximately 20 percent of ovulatory cycles the basal temperature chart does not indicate ovulation [91]. When intercourse is permitted in both the preovulatory and postovulatory phases of the cycle, failure rates are approximately 10 to 20 per 100 woman-years, but when coitus is restricted to the postovulatory phase only (as shown by the temperature chart), failure rates then drop to 0.3 to 6.6 per 100 woman-years [89]. A two-year pilot study of the Billings Method, recently reported [92], requires verification.

Postcoital methods of contraception include the use of hormones, IUD insertion, or therapeutic abortion. These methods may be used in emergency situations (such as rape, leakage of a condom, or rupture of a diaphragm) as well as in circumstances in which contraceptive protection was omitted during coitus and pregnancy prevention is desired. These methods should not be used for contraception on other than an acute, special situation basis. Morris and van Wagenen used diethylstilbestrol in their initial studies with rape victims [93]. Current treatment regimens, which should be started within 24 hours after unprotected coitus when possible and within 72 hours to ensure effectiveness, include diethylstilbestrol, 50 mg daily for 5 days; ethinyl estradiol, 5 mg daily for 5 days; or conjugated estrogens, 20 to 25 mg daily for 3 days [94]. Postcoital estrogens appear to work by interfering with implantation [94, 95]. The effectiveness of postcoital estrogens is extremely high: When estrogens are used within the time schedule outlined above, fewer than one percent of the cases usually result in pregnancy [94]. Unfortunately, about 10 percent of pregnancies that result despite the use of postcoital estrogens are ectopic, perhaps because estrogens may not be effective in blocking extrauterine implantation. The primary side effects of postcoital estrogen use are nausea (sometimes accompanied by vomiting), breast tenderness, and minor alterations in the menstrual cycle. Vomiting usually responds to antiemetic therapy, but at times injectable estrogens need to be given if tablets are vomited [95]. These estrogens, including diethylstilbestrol, are extremely unlikely to have any lasting effect on the recipient or on a fetus resulting from pregnancy, as long as therapy is instituted within the first few days after unprotected coitus [94]. Postcoital contraception using estrogens and progestogens in combination [94, 95] or progestogens alone has also been utilized.

A more recent approach to postcoital contraception involves the insertion of a copper-containing IUD. Since these devices are easier to insert in nulliparous women and the contraceptive effect begins quickly, if the copper IUD is inserted before implantation occurs, this is a highly effective alternative to the use of hormones. The risks and contraindications of IUD use were discussed earlier in this chapter.

Therapeutic abortion may be considered as a form of postcoital contraception in the sense that it has been recommended as a backup to other contraceptive modalities if failure occurs. The issues involved here are not so much medical as they are personal. Individual factors, including those of religious, economic, psychological, and medical significance, will determine the potential applicability of this alternative.

Sexual Effects of Contraceptive Techniques

Sterilization Procedures. Female sterilization procedures are remarkably free of adverse sexual effects. In a small percentage of cases, particularly in surgery involving the vaginal approach, dyspareunia may result due to granulation formation, adhesions around the uterus, or postoperative infection or hemorrhage. When intercourse is resumed too quickly after colpotomy or culdoscopy, spotting or heavier bleeding from the vagina may occur. Occasionally, women who have undergone tubal occlusion procedures develop diminished libido and depressed sexual arousability on a psychological basis. This pattern may occur in situations in which permanent sterility was not strictly voluntary, but a decision imposed on the woman by her husband or by health or economic circumstances. This reaction may also be seen in women who discover at some point after the operation that they want another pregnancy or that they do not feel the same way about sex, knowing that their reproductive capacity has been negated. For some women, particularly those from backgrounds of extreme religiosity, sex is considered to be unnatural or sinful when the possibility of reproduction is terminated.

Vasectomy does not interfere with sexual function on a physiologic basis except in extremely rare instances in which complications such as hemorrhage, infection, or surgical error produce permanent testicular damage. Following vasectomy, the sensations of ejaculation and the amount of the ejaculate are unaltered, and there is no impairment in the production of testosterone. On the other hand, in some men, concerns about the sexual effects of vasectomy may lead to difficulty on a psychogenic basis. Men who incorrectly regard this procedure as a form of castration or who equate masculinity with the ability to reproduce may have difficulties with erection or ejaculation following vasectomy. Adverse psychological and sexual sequelae have been noted in men with hypochondriasis, concerns about their masculinity, and preexisting sexual difficulties [97]. In one study it was concluded that "the strongest contraindication for a vasectomy is disagreement with one's wife over its advisability" [98]. Rodgers and Ziegler have found that a relative decrease in marital harmony in some couples after the man has undergone a vasectomy may be due to the fact that the husband expected special recognition or gratitude from his wife in return for having had the surgery [99].

A small number of men choosing vasectomies do so primarily because they believe that it allows them an advantage in extramarital sexual activity by making them "safe" partners and indicating their sensitivity to contraception as a politicized issue. Although these men do not typically have sexual difficulties, they may become less interested in sex with their wives if they begin an active pattern of extramarital sex or expand a previously established frequency of such activity. Another small subgroup of men who believe that a vasectomy will improve their sexual function may experience subsequent difficulties if they find that their expectations are not met. Some men who have been well adjusted to a vasectomy may experience impotence (usually transient) if they divorce and subsequently remarry, particularly if they and their new spouse would like to have children.

The wife or sexual partner of a man who has had a vasectomy may react negatively if she did not participate in making the decision or disapproved of the choice. Some women react negatively because they believe that engaging in sex solely for pleasure is wrong. Infrequently, a woman who is sexually "turned on" by the idea of risking pregnancy may become disinterested in sex or sexually unresponsive if either she or her husband undergoes sterilization.

Before a sterilization procedure is performed for either a man or a woman, both the patient and his or her spouse or sexual partner should be interviewed and a determination made of psychological suitability. If sexual difficulties are present in a man considering vasectomy, it is advisable to obtain competent evaluation by a sex therapist to ascertain the advisability of such an operation as opposed to the possibility of first entering psychotherapy. Many men and women will benefit from the opportunity to ask questions and receive information about the sexual aspects of such surgery, and it is likely that preventive counseling of this type may minimize the occurrence of sexual problems after the operation has been performed.

Oral Contraception. A large research literature is available on the subject of female sexuality as affected by birth control pills. Assessing these reports is extraordinarily difficult because all women using the pill are not in similar cultures, of similar ages, or in similar health, to name several important variables that contribute to dimensions of sexuality. In addition, there are major methodological issues that range from lack of appropriate control groups, imprecise instruments for assessment, unsophisticated statistical analyses, and small sample size, to other aspects such as not controlling for marital status, parity, or socioeconomic differences.

It is certainly true that oral contraceptives may have a decided effect on the sexuality of a particular woman. At times, this effect is attributable to purely physiologic factors, whereas in other instances, the alteration is a result of psychosocial elements alone. Women with chronic vaginitis, breast tenderness, galactorrhea, hirsutism, acne, headaches, or other physical changes resulting from the pill may understandably experience diminished libido or lowered sexual responsivity as a consequence of these problems. But physical changes may also be quite positive from the viewpoint of enhancing sexuality and body-image: In an appreciable number of women, use of the pill decreases dysmenorrhea, improves acne or hirsutism, makes the menstrual cycle more predictable, and reduces the amount of menstrual flow. This point has been largely ignored in the publicity about oral contraceptives, but it is clear that there are beneficial side effects as well as those that are adverse.

From the psychosocial viewpoint, women who expect to find lowered sexual interest or responsiveness from using the pill may very well find that this becomes a self-fulfilling prophecy. Women who feel a conflict between wanting children and using contraception may also experience sexual problems, as may those unmarried women who are concerned that the use of birth control pills puts them into an unvirtuous position of preparing for what they consider to be illicit sex (this attitude is frequent among teenagers). Similarly, women whose religion prohibits the use of oral contraception may experience emotional turmoil and subsequent sexual difficulties because of their choice. Psychosocial factors may contribute to sexual enjoyment as well: Many women report improved libido or sexual responsiveness after beginning birth control pills because of decreased fear of pregnancy or because the method of contraception is independent of sexual activity, thus preserving the spontaneity and intimacy of their sexual interactions.

One question that is as yet unsettled in relation to the use of birth control pills is their possible causative relationship to depression. The methodological issues here are as complex as those relating to sexuality and are further compounded by solid evidence that depression is more common in women than in men [100, 101]. Some investigators claim that depression or other mood alterations caused by oral contraceptives lead to sexual disinterest and other sexual problems [102–104], but there are also reports indicating that oral contraceptives may improve mood or depression [105]. It is a mistake to assume that a woman who becomes depressed while using birth control pills always does so because of pharmacologic properties of these hormones.

Under certain specific physiologic conditions, the risk of sexual side effects from oral contraceptives may be increased. Such conditions would include the infrequent instance of a woman who develops diabetes (as opposed to mildly impaired carbohydrate tolerance) as a result of the pill, women who develop neurologic sequelae of the pill (including strokes), and women who experience a diminution in vaginal lubrication, leading to dyspareunia. Some women using the pill appear to develop a state of estrogen insufficiency; in this group, discontinuing the use of oral contraceptives will usually solve the associated sexual problems.

On balance, it appears that there are as many women using birth control pills who experience enhanced sexuality from a variety of factors as there are women who experience decreased libido or impairment of sexual functioning [106, 107]. Most women using oral contraceptives do not experience significant alterations in either sexual behavior, sexual interest, or sexual enjoyment.

Intrauterine Devices. Intrauterine devices share with oral contraceptives the advantages of high effectiveness in preventing pregnancy and independence from sexual activity, so that sexual spontaneity or mood is not impaired by attention to contraceptive needs. The IUD may interfere with sex by causing dyspareunia for the woman due to improper positioning or pelvic inflammatory disease; infrequently, dyspareunia in the male partner is associated with the tail or string attached to the IUD that protrudes from the cervix into the vagina, irritating the penis during coital thrusting. Abdominal cramping or profuse menstrual flow of prolonged duration, both commonly associated with the use of IUDs, may have a deleterious effect on sexual interaction as well.

Barrier Methods. Sexual difficulties involved with the use of the diaphragm are related primarily to matters of convenience. For example, either partner may experience loss of arousal while time is being taken to insert and check the device, if unanticipated sex play occurs. Either partner may find the method unaesthetic, including the fact that the woman touches her genitalia to insert the device. Occasionally the diaphragm may become dislodged during sex play because of improper insertion, a poor fit, or expansion of the interior of the vagina and movement of the uterus during sexual excitation, which can cause interruption and consternation to both partners as well. There is a tendency to fit women with a mildly retroverted uterus with a diaphragm that is too small because the uterus fills the cul-de-sac; expansion of the cul-de-sac during sexual excitation allows the device to fall from behind the pubic symphysis [108]. Even a well-fitted and properly inserted diaphragm may become dislodged when the woman is astride the man or with multiple mounting (when the penis slips out of the vagina during plateau levels of arousal and is then reinserted) [108].

The diaphragm may cause dyspareunia for the woman if it is too large. Some men complain that they have altered penile sensations associated with coitus when a diaphragm is in place. However, one advantage of the use of a diaphragm is that during menstrual flow, it provides a "reverse barrier" that contains the flow during sexual activity.

The cervical cap is not liable to displacement due to expansion of the vagina during sexual activity and is not likely to be noticed by the male partner during coitus.

The condom is enjoying a new era of interest, including attention to details of sexual aesthetics. Lubricated condoms are likely to facilitate intercourse if insufficient vaginal lubrication is a problem. Condoms are now sold in a variety of colors and shapes, including some with external ridges, bumps, or other features that supposedly provide additional stimulation to the woman during intercourse. Many men are unhappy with the loss of tactile sensation in the penis while wearing a condom; some men have marked difficulty maintaining an erection while trying to put on the device. The condom is not a good contraceptive choice for a man with potency problems, since it calls for increasing attention to the presence or absence of erection and thus may seriously heighten performance anxiety and "spectatoring" (see Chap. 20). However, the use of a condom may sometimes permit more satisfactory control for mild cases of premature ejaculation. One other sexual disadvantage of the condom is the fact that unless the penis is removed from the vagina before postejaculatory detumescence occurs, there may be spillage of semen into the vagina or on the labia. This necessitates rather prompt withdrawal after ejaculation, which may interfere with the intimacy of the moment.

The use of vaginal creams, foams, or jellies may require interrupting the spontaneous flow of sexual activity, but insertion of these chemicals (and application of a condom to the erect penis) may be made a part of sexual play. The use of intravaginal spermicides may produce aesthetic discomfort or physical distaste for cunnilingus. Both women and men sometimes complain that these agents provide too much vaginal lubrication and diminish sensation. Rarely, allergic reactions can cause dyspareunia. Vaginal suppositories that effervesce after insertion may cause burning sensations for either the female or male.

Miscellaneous Methods of Contraception. Coitus interruptus has obvious sexual disadvantages that pertain to the degree of vigilance that must be exercised to avoid intravaginal ejaculation. This technique may be highly frustrating to the woman as well as the man when she is nearing orgasm just as he suddenly removes the penis from the vagina.

Breast feeding may be a turn-on for the man (milk flow often occurs during sexual arousal in a nursing mother), or it may have the opposite effect. Soreness of the nipples and perineum and fatigue may contribute to impaired sexuality during the first postpartum months. Changing roles for first-time parents may either enhance or inhibit their sexual interaction.

Couples who use one of the rhythm methods of contraception may experience sexual problems because the need for periods of abstinence places unusual pressure to have sexual activity on infertile days, independent of mood, interpersonal relationship, or other elements. Fear of pregnancy may also lead to difficulties. However, it should be stressed that in spite of the calendar restrictions imposed by this method of contraception and its less than high effectiveness, most couples using rhythm methods do not experience sexual distress.

There are no reliable data currently available delineating the effects of postcoital methods of contraception on sexuality. Clinically, it has been apparent that some people with sporadic sexual activity may rely primarily on postcoital measures to prevent or terminate pregnancy. Health-care professionals should avoid moralistic postures about such practices in their interactions with patients.

Unfortunately, the controversies surrounding the legitimacy of induced abortions have been transposed to political, legal, economic, and religious arenas. There is a paucity of information describing the im-

pact that abortion or failure to obtain an abortion that is medically
induced may have on subsequent sexuality. Babikian points out: "The
majority of papers published after 1967 stress the point that induced
abortions performed in a medical setting produced little if any sequelae
and that patients who were psychiatrically ill before abortion did
poorly, whereas patients who were psychiatrically healthy did well"
[109]. From a clinical perspective, this general observation might be
extended to say that adverse sexual consequences attributable to induced abortion *per se* are extremely unusual. When sexual problems
arise in this context, they are most frequently caused by factors such as
lack of support and understanding on the part of the man responsible
for the impregnation, fear of a subsequent unwanted pregnancy, or
conflict over the pregnancy. It is difficult to believe that the abortion
procedure itself, rather than the unwanted pregnancy, would frequently be the cause of psychosexual problems.

Sex and Infertility

The term *family planning* is usually taken to be synonymous with
contraception, but an important aspect is the provision of health care
services directed toward reversing unwanted infertility. Approximately
10 percent of couples in the reproductive years are unable to have
children. For many of these couples, the psychological, social, and economic consequences of being childless unwillingly are considerable.
This discussion will focus specifically on sexual difficulties sometimes
associated with infertility.

Infertility of Sexual
Etiology

An adequate investigation of infertility must always include evaluation
of the reproductive status of both partners, because infertility is attributable to male factors in 35 to 40 percent of cases [110, 111], and in a
significant number of couples, relative subfertility in both the man and
the woman combine to produce lack of conception. If only one partner is
studied, lessened diagnostic accuracy is compounded by inefficiency
from the viewpoint of time, and unnecessary and expensive testing may
be undertaken as well.

The importance of evaluating both partners is particularly germane
from the viewpoint of gathering historical information related to sexual
function and the timing and frequency of sexual activity. If only one
partner is interviewed, the existence of a sexual problem as the primary cause of infertility may be easily overlooked due to denial, deception, misperception, or inaccuracy of response. The opportunity to question both partners individually and together provides a much higher

degree of veracity in regard to the presence or absence of sexual problems.

Since conception can only occur when an egg is fertilized by a sperm cell, lack of intravaginal ejaculation will almost always preclude pregnancy. This problem is most dramatically encountered in men with ejaculatory incompetence—inability to ejaculate within the vagina despite the presence of normal erection (see Chap. 20)—which may first be discovered during an investigation for infertility, although typically one or both partners already realize that coital ejaculation does not occur. Such a couple may present by asking for artificial insemination using the husband's sperm or, if the man has never ejaculated, may wish to be evaluated for possible physical causes. (On rare occasions, congenital absence of the ejaculatory ducts precludes the emission of any seminal fluid, although sperm production in the testes is normal and sexual function, including orgasmic response, is otherwise intact [112].) Ejaculatory incompetence may sometimes be situational in the sense that the man is able to ejaculate intravaginally only when he believes there is no chance of pregnancy occurring.

Ejaculatory incompetence may sometimes be confused with retrograde ejaculation (see Chap. 9). In the latter condition, men experience orgasm during intercourse but the seminal fluid is propelled posteriorly into the bladder, whereas in ejaculatory incompetence there is no coital orgasm. The diagnosis of retrograde ejaculation may be made by examination of a postcoital urine specimen that documents the presence of sperm. Retrograde ejaculation may be a result of diabetes mellitus, neurologic disease, the use of certain antihypertensive drugs, or surgery affecting the innervation of the bladder or the anatomic integrity of the bladder sphincter. Premature ejaculation rarely affects fertility except in severe cases in which ejaculation consistently occurs before the penis is inserted intravaginally.

Impotence may cause infertility when intercourse is impossible or when intercourse occurs rarely or not at all during the fertile phase of the menstrual cycle. At times, impotence due to organic causes such as Klinefelter's syndrome, alcoholism, or hypopituitarism may also be associated with functional sterility. These cases are not frequent causes of infertility in most series, however, and more often impotence occurs while fertility (as measured by sperm count and other parameters such as morphology and motility) is normal.

Impotence may be the cause of an unconsummated marriage, which may also be due to vaginismus, lack of sexual knowledge, or a combination of these factors. Jeffcoate estimates that 5 percent of women seeking treatment for infertility have not consummated their marriage [113], but this figure appears to overestimate the prevalence of this problem seen in clinical populations in the United States. More frequently, vaginismus may contribute to infertility by producing dyspareunia, leading to avoidance of intercourse and sometimes to secondary impotence in the man who is anxious about injuring or hurting his partner. Although vaginismus is usually of psychogenic origin (see Chap. 21), at times it originates from a physical lesion such as an abscess near the vaginal opening.

Problems of coital frequency may also lead to infertility. If intercourse occurs infrequently because either or both spouses have little interest in sex, the chances of conception are statistically lowered. In addition to the lessened chance of infrequent intercourse occurring at the fertile phase of the menstrual cycle, the motility and longevity of spermatozoa are adversely affected by infrequent ejaculation [111]. On the other hand, for some couples sexual behavior at the opposite end of the frequency spectrum produces relative infertility for a different reason: Ejaculation on a daily basis or more often tends to lower the sperm count and diminish fertility [114]. This observation is of particular relevance to the man who frequently engages in extramarital sexual activity or who may be unaware of the fact that frequent masturbation lowers the sperm count. The impact of frequent ejaculation is decidedly greater on men with marginal fertility; normal sperm counts generally are not lowered into the infertile range by daily ejaculation, although ejaculation several times a day may produce relative infertility [114]. Some couples enthusiastically but incorrectly have intercourse several times a day while they are attempting to conceive; in these instances, infertility is usually reversed promptly after a reduction in the frequency of ejaculation is suggested.

Errors in sexual technique may also contribute to infertility. The intravaginal use of artificial lubricants is a sometimes overlooked cause of infertility due to the weakly spermicidal nature of these preparations. Frequent douching may create an intravaginal environment that is hostile to sperm survival. In rare cases couples may engage in intraurethral coitus, with the male inserting the penis into the female's urethra rather than the vagina, causing marked dilatation of the urethral meatus. In other cases, improper coital positioning reduces the number of spermatozoa that reach the cervical os. Although not specifically related to sexual techniques, conditions that produce increased scrotal temperature, such as wearing excessively tight underwear or taking frequent hot tub baths or saunas, affect spermatogenesis and may diminish fertility [115].

At times, stress and anxiety produced by sexual problems may cause infertility by blocking ovulation. This is a nonspecific response to stress that has been observed under a variety of conditions [116]. Some investigators believe that infertility due to psychogenic causes occurs relatively frequently [117–120], but few systematic data have been collected in this regard. This diagnosis is difficult to make because in 15 to 20 percent of infertile couples no organic etiology is found by present testing methods [110, 111], but this cannot be taken to mean that the problems must therefore be psychogenic.

Sexual Problems
Caused by Infertility

Infertility is rarely an expected problem. Most couples anticipate being able to have children when they plan to, and the frustration and disappointment of not conceiving over a period of many months or years frequently leads to temporary psychosexual problems. The average time required for pregnancy to occur in normal couples not using contraception is 5.3 months [110]. After one month of unprotected coitus, 25 percent of couples conceive; 63 percent conceive by the end of six months, and 80 percent conceive after one year of intercourse without use of contraception [111]. For this reason, infertility is usually only diagnosed after a couple has attempted conception unsuccessfully for one year or longer.

Prior to seeking medical evaluation or assistance, couples contending with infertility may be caught in crosscurrents of negative emotions. Pressures may be felt from peers and family in reference to having children; spouses may blame each other for the failure to conceive; implicit or explicit demands for more frequent sexual activity may create an onerous situation of diminished spontaneity, increased pressure, and lessened enjoyment and intimacy; and guilt over prior sexual behavior or other areas may be aroused. Many women become particularly despondent during menstruation, since menstrual flow signals lack of success in achieving a pregnancy. Men may falsely equate their virility with the ability to father a child and thus experience anxiety or depression because of this association in their minds.

Diminished libido and impaired sexual arousal are noted by a majority of women with infertility [121]. These changes may be attributable in part to depression or a diminished sense of self-esteem, but a considerable contribution is made iatrogenically as well. Many diagnostic or therapeutic strategies of an infertility program place specific time demands on when intercourse should or should not occur, thus creating a situation in which sexual activity is mandated by the calendar rather than by feelings. For example, the basal body temperature chart is frequently kept for months to identify the timing or occurrence of ovulation. It is usually suggested that intercourse occur in a pattern concentrated around the day of ovulation. After months of following such a schedule without success, it is no wonder that sexual activity may begin to be work rather than fun for the couple. Other iatrogenic factors that may interfere with sexuality include the performance of multiple pelvic examinations during testing and treatment evaluation, which many women find embarrassing or uncomfortable, and transient dyspareunia resulting from diagnostic procedures such as a hysterosalpingogram (x-ray of the uterus and fallopian tubes) or endometrial biopsy.

Many women also report a decreased frequency of orgasm in association with infertility [2, 121, 122]. This reaction may result from a loss of self-esteem related to reproductive inadequacy, increased marital tensions, changes in patterns of sexual activity, diminished spontaneity of sexual interaction, preoccupation with thoughts of having a baby, or depression. When sex becomes highly focused on the goal of reproduction, couples often dispense with aspects of sexual play that they have previously enjoyed in an effort to "get down to business," with the result being a hurried, unimaginative, and often emotionally detached experience. Under these circumstances, it is not surprising that sexual responsivity diminishes.

Some men being evaluated for infertility have difficulty in producing a masturbatory semen specimen for examination, reflecting the anxieties and pressures of the diagnostic situation as well as a reluctance to discover that the reproductive problem is theirs rather than their wife's. Inability to ejaculate or transient impotence may occur when a Sims-Huhner test (a postcoital evaluation of the ability of spermatozoa to penetrate and survive in cervical mucus, performed at the time of ovulation) is scheduled; the principal reason for this difficulty is the pressure to perform at a specific time on a specific date. Although difficulties of this sort may sometimes be attributable to deeper-seated problems such as fear of pregnancy or the suppressed wish not to have children, in most instances these sexual problems reflect immediate stress rather than other psychodynamic factors.

During the treatment phase of an infertility program, occasional impotence is commonly encountered. This reaction may relate to diminished libido, increased sexual pressures being placed on the husband by his wife, loss of spontaneity brought about by the need to follow medical advice regarding the timing of intercourse, depression, loss of self-esteem, and general marital tension that sometimes occurs because of the frustration of not achieving a pregnancy.

Couples who are childless because of repeated miscarriage or spontaneous abortion often avoid any sexual activity once a pregnancy occurs because of fear that coitus, orgasm, or even sexual arousal may cause the pregnancy to abort. This is an ungrounded assumption in many cases.

For couples attempting to conceive by the use of artificial insemination, whether the husband's semen or donor semen is used, the frequency of sexual activity often plummets from previous levels. Similarly, for many couples being treated for infertility there is relatively little sexual contact after ovulation is past, since reproduction is no longer possible.

The physician should be aware of the impact that infertility may have on people's lives. Many potential problems can be prevented by providing advice about participating in infertility evaluation and treatment that emphasizes positive strategies for coping with the stresses that may arise. Specific suggestions should always include the importance of open communication within the couple, since verbalizing anxieties or tension may help to reduce significantly the magnitude of these difficulties. The benefits of sharing noncoital physical closeness and intimacy should also be pointed out, since infertile couples frequently become so oriented toward their reproductive goal that they stop most noncoital physical contact. Offering reassurance to the couple concerning the normality of their frustrations and attendant sexual difficulties can also be of great value, although such reassurance is best conveyed by a continuing attitude of professional concern rather than simply being stated at one point in time and never addressed again. Providing education that dispels myths about sexuality and reproductive anatomy and physiology can also be of marked benefit in counseling infertile couples.

Many couples seek treatment or further diagnostic services for infertility for long periods of time—frequently for two years or longer. It is often advisable to suggest in such circumstances that taking time off from the pursuit of medical services may have beneficial effects on both the couple's relationship and their chance for conception, since eliminating the stresses of frequent scrutiny of ovulatory patterns, the timing of intercourse, and similar details may actually enhance the odds that conception will occur. Consideration should also be given to referral for psychological evaluation of those couples in whom no physical or metabolic abnormality is identified as the cause of infertility and in whom personality problems, psychosocial immaturity, or other emotional difficulties seem to be present.

Sex and Pregnancy

Remarkably little research has been conducted to evaluate the effects of pregnancy on sexuality. Only one study has been designed in a prospective fashion, involving interviews conducted with 111 pregnant women and, in 79 cases, their husbands [123]. Additional methodological strengths of this investigation included the use of a series of personal interviews conducted by a male-female team and the availability of detailed data concerning the prior obstetric history and health status of the study population.

In the first trimester of pregnancy, marked variation was observed in sexual behavior patterns and sexual responsiveness. Women who experienced nausea and vomiting during this time reported diminished interest in sex and a reduced rate of sexual activity, but some women reported an increase in libido. In the second trimester, however, 82 of the 101 women interviewed described heightened sexuality both in terms of libido and physical responsivity. By the third trimester, a marked reduction in coital activity was noted, accompanied by increased fatigue and diminished libido. Twenty of 101 women interviewed in the third trimester felt that their husbands had lost interest in them sexually, which they attributed to either their altered physical appearance, concern for their physical comfort, or fear of injuring the fetus.

By the third postpartum month, the 24 women who were breast-feeding their babies reported a discernibly higher interest in sexual activity, whereas 47 of the 77 women who did not breast-feed experienced little sexual desire. The nursing mothers indicated that breast-feeding sometimes induced sexual excitation and, on three occasions in the group, orgasm. Some of these women felt guilty about what they perceived as an unnatural form of eroticism.

Interviews with the husbands of 79 of the women who were studied revealed that they gradually withdrew from initiating sexual activity with their wives toward the end of the second trimester or early in the third trimester of pregnancy. Although in most instances the men gave no consistent reason for their withdrawal of sexual interest (the most frequently cited reason was fear of injury to the wife or fetus), most of the wives involved suspected that their husbands were reacting to their loss of physical attractiveness. Twelve of the 79 men turned to extramarital sex during this time.

Solberg and coworkers interviewed 260 postpartum women regarding their sexual behavior during pregnancy [124]. Interviews were conducted by male medical students, and the women were asked to recall monthly coital frequencies at different phases of their pregnancy, creating a problem with inaccuracy of recall. These investigators found a gradual and persistent decline in the frequency of intercourse for each chronological stage of pregnancy. Twenty-eight percent of women reported decreased interest in sex during the first trimester of pregnancy as compared to the year preceding the pregnancy; for the second trimester, 44 percent reported diminished sexual interest; and by the ninth month of pregnancy, 75 percent of the sample indicated a decrease in libido. As pregnancy reached the last trimester, positions for intercourse other than the man-on-top became preferred, and in the last month of pregnancy, the side-by-side position was most frequently used.

Morris provided data on a cross-sectional sample of 110 pregnant women in Thailand who were interviewed by public health nurses about their coital activity during the preceding week [125]. In addition to the statistical problems inherent in a cross-sectional study (and the fact that there were only 12 and 11 women interviewed during the eighth and ninth months, respectively), this type of methodology overestimates the frequency of reports of no intercourse. Morris concluded that coital frequency diminishes progressively as pregnancy lengthens.

In contrast, Falicov [126] reported a decline in first-trimester sexual interest, frequency, and enjoyment, but observed an increase in these parameters during the second trimester prior to a drop late in pregnancy. Kenny found relatively constant levels of sexual behavior during the first two trimesters in a sample of 33 women [127].

Tolor and DiGrazia conducted a cross-sectional study involving 216 women who were pregnant or six weeks postpartum [128]. They found that the median frequency of intercourse during pregnancy was highest in the second trimester; a marked decrease in coital activity was observed in the last trimester. Likewise, women in the second trimester reported the largest percentage having "considerable interest" or "very high interest" in sex at any stage during pregnancy.

Taken as a group, these studies document the sharp decrease in sexual interest and activity that occurs during the last three months of pregnancy. Although Solberg's data indicate a steady decline in coital frequency beginning much earlier in pregnancy [124], other reports indicate either heightened frequency in the second trimester [123, 126, 128] or no decline during this time [127].

It is important to realize that many factors apart from the biology of gestation interact to determine sexual behavior patterns during pregnancy. How a woman feels about parenthood, the quality (or absence) of her marriage, culturally derived expectations, preexisting sexual attitudes, and other individual considerations are undoubtedly of major consequence. The presence of medical complications in the mother (diabetes, hypertension, or other chronic diseases) or concern about miscarriage or genetic abnormalities in the fetus will also influence the sexual component of her life.

There are a number of practical questions related to sexual activity during pregnancy. Women who are habitual aborters have been thought to be at risk for the termination of pregnancy as a result of uterine contractions during coital orgasm [129]. Because there is physiologic evidence that uterine contractions may be more intense with noncoital orgasms both in nonpregnant and in pregnant women [123], it appears judicious to advise women who have repeatedly encountered difficulty in maintaining a pregnancy to avoid sexual stimulation to orgasm, no matter what the source. Similarly, if vaginal bleeding occurs during the third trimester, intercourse should be avoided.

There is speculation about whether orgasm in the third trimester may sometimes be associated with premature delivery [130–133]. It appears clinically that female orgasm late in the third trimester may initiate labor at times or may at least have a close temporal association to the onset of labor. Whether or not this mechanism is involved in premature delivery cannot be ascertained with certainty from present data, but a recent study indicates that there was no association between coitus, orgasm, or other sexual experiences and the onset of labor in 25 women delivering premature infants [133]. This same study also showed that among 155 pregnant women, being orgasmic was associated with lower rates of early deliveries, and masturbation was consistently associated with a lower risk of prematurity through all stages of pregnancy.

The timing of return to coital activity in the postpartum period is a matter of practical concern to both wife and husband. The matter may be complicated by a slow-healing episiotomy, granulation tissue, persistent vaginal bleeding, postpartum depression, or (for couples having a first child) difficulties in adjusting to parenthood. The husband may feel neglected or may resent the intrusion of a baby he feels to be vying for affection from his wife in competition with him. Although many couples can resume intercourse within a few weeks after delivery, it is important to individualize advice on this matter. Attention should be devoted to the psychological state of both husband and wife, taking into account, for example, birth of a stillborn baby or a child with a congenital anomaly. Even highly educated people may blame such tragedies on themselves; sexual guilt is often the specific result of such an occurrence.

Postpartum reproductive care should not be regarded as complete without discussing the possible need for contraception with a couple or providing them with information about contraceptive alternatives, if desired. This is also a good time to let patients know that opportunities exist for sexual counseling, if it should be required.

References

1. Golden, J. S., Golden, M., Price, S., and Heinrich, A.   The sexual problems of family planning clinic patients as viewed by the patients and the staff. *Family Planning Perspectives* 9:25–29, 1977.
2. Steele, S. J.   Sexual Problems Related to Contraception and Family Planning. In S. Crown (ed.), *Psychosexual Problems: Psychotherapy, Counseling and Behavioral Modification*. New York: Grune & Stratton, 1976. Pp. 383–401.
3. Venning, G. R.   Family planning and populations policies in developed and less developed countries. *Clinics in Endocrinology and Metabolism* 2:589–606, 1973.
4. Brackett, J. W., and Ravenholt, R. T.   World fertility, 1976: An analysis of data sources and trends. *Population Reports*, Series J, No. 12, November 1976.
5. Paige, K. E.   Sexual pollution: Reproductive sex taboos in American society. *Journal of Social Issues* 33:144–165, 1977.
6. Zelnik, M., and Kantner, J. F.   Sexual and contraceptive experience of young unmarried women in the United States, 1976 and 1971. *Family Planning Perspectives* 9:55–71, 1977.
7. Sorenson, R. C.   *Adolescent Sexuality in Contemporary America*. New York: World Publishing Co., 1973.
8. Belsky, R.   Vaginal contraceptives: A time for reappraisal? *Population Reports*, Series H, No. 3, January 1975. Pp. H37–H56.
9. Vessey, M., and Wiggins, P.   Use-effectiveness of the diaphragm in a selected family planning clinic population in the United Kingdom. *Contraception* 9:15–21, 1974.
10. Tietze, C.   Evaluation of intrauterine devices (ninth progress report of the cooperative statistical program). *Studies in Family Planning* 1:1–40, July 1970.
11. Davis, J. E.   Vasectomy. *American Journal of Nursing* 72:509–513, 1972.
12. Wortman, J., and Piotrow, P. T.   Vasectomy: Old and new techniques. *Population Reports*, Series D, No. 1, December 1973.
13. Wortman, J.   Vasectomy: What are the problems? *Population Reports*, Series D, No. 2, January 1975.
14. Blandy, J. P.   Male sterilization. *Nursing Times* 63:142–144, 1972.
15. Leader, A. J., Axelrad, S. D., Frankowski, R., and Mumford, S. D.   Complications of 2,711 vasectomies. *Journal of Urology* 111:365–369, 1974.

16. Klapproth, H. J., and Young, I. S. Vasectomy, vas ligation and vas occlusion. *Urology* 1:292–300, 1973.

17. Wieland, R. G., Hallberg, M. C., Zorn, E. M., Klein, D. E., and Luria, S. S. Pituitary-gonadal function before and after vasectomy. *Fertility and Sterility* 23:779–781, 1972.

18. Varma, M. M., Varma, R. R., Johanson, A. J., Kowarski, A., and Migeon, C. J. Long-term effects of vasectomy on pituitary-gonadal function in man. *Journal of Clinical Endocrinology and Metabolism* 40:868–871, 1975.

19. Kolodny, R. C., and Bauman, J. Unpublished observations, 1977.

20. Kar, J. K. Surgical correction of post-vasectomy sterility. *Journal of Family Welfare* 15:50–53, 1969.

21. Pardanani, D. S., Kothari, M. L., Pradhan, S. A., and Mahendrakar, M. N. Surgical restoration of vas continuity after vasectomy: Further clinical evaluation of a new operation technique. *Fertility and Sterility* 25:319–324, 1974.

22. Bradshaw, L. E. Vasectomy reversibility: A status report. *Population Reports*, Series D, No. 3, May 1976.

23. Sherman, J. K. Synopsis of the use of frozen human semen since 1954: State of the art of human semen banking. *Fertility and Sterility* 24:397–412, 1973.

24. Tyler, E. T. The clinical use of frozen male semen banks. *Fertility and Sterility* 24:413–416, 1976.

25. Steinberger, E., and Smith, K. D. Artificial insemination with fresh or frozen sperm: A comparative study. *Journal of the American Medical Association* 223:778–783, 1973.

26. Wortman, J. Tubal sterilization: Review of methods. *Population Reports*, Series C, No. 7, May 1976.

27. Green, T. H. *Gynecology: Essentials of Clinical Practice.* Boston: Little, Brown and Co., 1977.

28. Hulka, J. F., Omran, K. F., Phillips, J. M., Jr., Lefler, H. T., Jr., Lieberman, B., Lean, H. T., Pat, D. N., Koetsawang, S., and Madrigal Castro, V. Sterilization by spring-clip: A report of 1,000 cases with a 6-month follow-up. *Fertility and Sterility* 26:1122–1131, 1975.

29. Brenner, W. E., Edelman, D. A., Black, J. F., and Goldsmith, A. Laparoscopic sterilization with electrocautery, spring-loaded clips, and silastic bands: Technical problems and early complications. *Fertility and Sterility* 27:256–266, 1976.

30. Wortman, J., and Piotrow, P. T. Laparoscopic sterilization: II. What are the problems? *Population Reports*, Series C, No. 2, March 1973.

31. Wortman, J. Female sterilization using the culdoscope. *Population Reports*, Series C, No. 6, May 1975.

32. Goldzieher, J. W., and Rudel, H. How the oral contraceptives came to be developed. *Journal of the American Medical Association* 230:421–425, 1974.

33. Goldzieher, J. W., Moses, L. E., Averkin, E., Scheel, C., and Taber, B. Z. A placebo-controlled double-blind crossover investigation of the side-effects attributed to oral contraceptives. *Fertility and Sterility* 22:609–623, 1971.

34. Aznar-Ramos, R., Giner-Velasquez, J., Lara-Ricolde, R., and Martinez-

Manautou, J. Incidence of side-effects with contraceptive placebo. *American Journal of Obstetrics and Gynecology* 105:1144–1149, 1969.

35. Inman, W. H. V., and Vessey, M. P. Investigation of deaths from pulmonary, coronary, and cerebral thrombosis and embolism in women of childbearing age. *British Medical Journal* 2:193–199, 1968.

36. Vessey, M. P., and Doll, R. Investigation of relation between use of oral contraceptives and thromboembolic disease: A further report. *British Medical Journal* 2:651–657, 1969.

37. Sartwell, P. E., Masi, A. T., Arthes, F. G., Green, G. R., and Smith, H. E. Thromboembolism and oral contraceptives: An epidemiologic case-control study. *American Journal of Epidemiology* 90:365–380, 1969.

38. Collaborative Group for the Study of Stroke in Young Women. Oral contraception and increased risk of cerebral ischemia or thrombosis. *New England Journal of Medicine* 288:871–878, 1973.

39. Collaborative Group for the Study of Stroke in Young Women. Oral contraceptives and stroke in young women: Associated risk factors. *Journal of the American Medical Association* 231:718–722, 1975.

40. Greene, G. R., and Sartwell, P. E. Oral contraceptive use in patients with thromboembolism following surgery, trauma, or infection. *American Journal of Public Health* 62:680–685, 1972.

41. Varvalho, A. C. A., Vaillancourt, R. A., Cabral, R. B., Lees, R. S., and Colman, R. W. Coagulation abnormalities in women taking oral contraceptives. *Journal of the American Medical Association* 237:875–878, 1977.

42. Wynn, V., Doar, J. W. H., and Mills, G. L. Some effects of oral contraceptives on serum-lipid and lipoprotein levels. *Lancet* 2:720–723, 1966.

43. Hazzard, W. R., Spiger, M. J., Bagdade, J. D., and Bierman, E. L. Studies on the mechanism of increased plasma triglyceride levels induced by oral contraceptives. *New England Journal of Medicine* 280:471–474, 1969.

44. Mann, J. I., and Inman, W. H. W. Oral contraceptives and death from myocardial infarction. *British Medical Journal* 2:245–248, 1975.

45. Beral, V. Cardiovascular disease mortality trends and oral contraceptive use in young women. *Lancet* 2:1047–1052, 1976.

46. Hennekens, C. H., and MacMahon, B. Oral contraceptives and myocardial infarction (editorial). *New England Journal of Medicine* 296:1166–1167, 1977.

47. Jaffe, F. S. The pill: A perspective for assessing risks and benefits. *New England Journal of Medicine* 297:612–614, 1977.

48. Cole, M. Strokes in young women using oral contraceptives. *Archives of Internal Medicine* 120:551–555, 1967.

49. Salmon, M. L., Winkelman, J. Z., and Gay, A. J. Neuroophthalmic sequelae in users of oral contraceptives. *Journal of the American Medical Association* 206:85–91, 1968.

50. Masi, A. T., and Dugdale, M. Cerebrovascular diseases associated with the use of oral contraceptives. *Annals of Internal Medicine* 72:111–121, 1970.

51. Altshuler, J. H., McLaughlin, R. A., and Neuberger, K. T. Neurological catastrophe related to oral contraceptives. *Archives of Neurology* 19:264–273, 1968.

52. Elgee, N. J.   Medical aspects of oral contraceptives. *Annals of Internal Medicine* 72:409–418, 1970.
53. Laragh, J. H., Dealey, J. E., Ledingham, J. G. G., and Newton, M. A.   Oral contraceptives, renin, aldosterone, and high blood pressure. *Journal of the American Medical Association* 201:918–922, 1967.
54. Crane, M. G., Harris, J. J., and Winsor, W.   Hypertension, oral contraceptive agents, and conjugated estrogens. *Annals of Internal Medicine* 74:13–21, 1971.
55. Weir, R. J., Briggs, E., Mack, A., Naismith, L., Taylor, L., and Wilson, E.   Blood pressure in women taking oral contraceptives. *British Medical Journal* 1:533–535, 1974.
56. Murad, F., and Gilman, A. G.   Estrogens and Progestins. In L. S. Goodman and A. Gilman (eds.), *The Pharmacologic Basis of Therapeutics* (5th ed.). New York: Macmillan Co., 1975. Pp. 1423–1450.
57. Weindling, H., and Henry, J. B.   Laboratory test results altered by "The Pill." *Journal of the American Medical Association* 229:1762–1768, 1974.
58. Boston Collaborative Drug Surveillance Programme. Oral contraceptives and venous thromboembolic disease, surgically confirmed gallbladder disease, and breast tumours. *Lancet* 1:1399–1404, 1973.
59. Bennion, L. J., Ginsberg, R. L., Garnick, M. B., and Bennett, P. H.   Effects of oral contraceptives on the gallbladder bile of normal women. *New England Journal of Medicine* 294:189–192, 1976.
60. The Coronary Drug Project Research Group. Gallbladder disease as a side effect of drugs influencing lipid metabolism. *New England Journal of Medicine* 296:1185–1190, 1977.
61. Edmondson, H. A., Henderson, B., and Benton, B.   Liver-cell adenomas associated with use of oral contraceptives. *New England Journal of Medicine* 294:470–472, 1976.
62. Van Campenhout, J., Blanchet, P., Beauregard, H., and Papas, S.   Amenorrhea following the use of oral contraceptives. *Fertility and Sterility* 28:728–732, 1977.
63. Wynn, V., and Doar, J. W. H.   Some effects of oral contraceptives on carbohydrate metabolism. *Lancet* 2:715–719, 1966.
64. Spellacy, W. N., Buhi, W. C., Birk, S. A., and McCreary, S. A.   Studies of chlormadinone acetate and mestranol on blood glucose and plasma insulin: I. Six-month oral glucose tolerance test. *Fertility and Sterility* 22:217–223, 1971.
65. Spellacy, W. N., Buhi, W. C., Birk, S. A., and McCreary, S. A.   Studies of chlormadinone acetate and mestranol on blood glucose and plasma insulin: II. Twelve-month oral glucose tolerance test. *Fertility and Sterility* 22:224–228, 1971.
66. Wingerd, J., and Duffy, T. J.   Oral contraceptive use and other factors in the standard glucose tolerance test. *Diabetes* 26:1024–1033, 1977.
67. Dericks-Tan, J. S. E., and Taubert, H.-D.   Elevation of serum prolactin during application of oral contraceptives. *Contraception* 14:1–8, 1976.
68. Frantz, A. G.   Prolactin. *New England Journal of Medicine* 298:201–207, 1978.
69. Nora, J. J., and Nora, A. H.   Birth defects and oral contraceptives. *Lancet* 1:941–942, 1973.

70. Janerich, D. T., Piper, J. M., and Glebatis, D. M. Oral contraceptives and congenital limb-reduction defects. *New England Journal of Medicine* 291:697–700, 1974.

71. Heinonen, O. P., Slone, D., Monson, R. R., Hook, E. B., and Shapiro, S. Cardiovascular birth defects and antenatal exposure to female sex hormones. *New England Journal of Medicine* 296:67–70, 1977.

72. Ambani, L. M., Joshi, N. J., Vaidya, R. A., and Devi, P. K. Are hormonal contraceptives teratogenic? *Fertility and Sterility* 28:791–797, 1977.

73. Voorhess, M. L. Masculinization of the female fetus associated with norethindrone-mestranol therapy during pregnancy. *Journal of Pediatrics* 71:128–131, 1967.

74. Drill, V. A. Oral contraceptives: Relation to mammary cancer, benign breast lesions, and cervical cancer. *Annual Review of Pharmacology* 15:367–385, 1975.

75. Rinehart, W., and Felt, J. C. Debate on oral contraceptives and neoplasia continues; answers remain elusive. *Population Reports*, Series A, No. 4, May 1977.

76. Lipsett, M. B. Estrogen use and cancer risk. *Journal of the American Medical Association* 237:1112–1115, 1977.

77. Vessey, M. P., Doll, R., and Jones, K. Oral contraceptives and breast cancer: Progress report of an epidemiologic study. *Lancet* 1:941–944, 1975.

78. Ory, H., Cole, P., MacMahon, B., and Hoover, R. Oral contraceptives and reduced risk of benign breast diseases. *New England Journal of Medicine* 294:419–422, 1976.

79. Rinehart, W. Minipill: A limited alternative for certain women. *Population Reports*, Series A, No. 3, September 1975.

80. Huber, S. C., Piotrow, P. T., Orlans, B., and Kommer. G. IUD's reassessed: A decade of experience. *Population Reports*, Series B, No. 2, January 1975.

81. Measham, A. R., and Villegas, A. Comparison of continuation rates of intrauterine devices. *Obstetrics and Gynecology* 48:336–340, 1976.

82. Cooper, D. L. Modified insertion techniques for Copper 7, Copper T and Progestasert intrauterine contraceptive devices. *Contraception* 15:75–85, 1977.

83. Oster, G., and Salgo, M. P. The copper intrauterine device and its mode of action. *New England Journal of Medicine* 293:432–438, 1975.

84. Rao, R. P., and Scommegna, A. Intrauterine contraception. *American Family Physician* 16(5):177–185, 1977.

85. Wortman, J. The diaphragm and other intravaginal barriers: A review. *Population Reports*, Series H, No. 4, January 1976.

86. Dumm, J. J., Piotrow, P. T., and Dalsimer, I. A. The modern condom: A quality product for effective contraception. *Population Reports*, Series H, No. 2, May 1974.

87. Jelliffe, D. B., and Jelliffe, E. F. P. "Breast is best": Modern meanings. *New England Journal of Medicine* 297:912–915, 1977.

88. Buchanan, R. Breast-feeding: Aid to infant health and fertility control. *Population Reports*, Series J, No. 4, July 1975.

89. Ross, C., and Piotrow, P. T. Birth control without contraceptives. *Population Reports*, Series I, No. 1, June 1974.

90. Lenton, E. A., Weston, G. A., and Cooke, I. D. Problems in using basal body temperature recordings in an infertility clinic. *British Medical Journal* 1:803–805, 1977.

91. Moghissi, K. S. Accuracy of basal body temperature for ovulation detection. *Fertility and Sterility* 27:1415–1421, 1976.

92. Klaus, H., Goebel, J., Woods, R. E., Castles, M., and Zimny, G. Use-effectiveness and analysis of satisfaction levels with the Billings ovulation method: Two-year pilot study. *Fertility and Sterility* 28:1038–1043, 1977.

93. Morris, J. M., and van Wagenen, G. Compounds interfering with ovum implantation and development: III. The role of estrogens. *American Journal of Obstetrics and Gynecology* 96:804–815, 1966.

94. Rinehart, W. Postcoital contraception: An appraisal. *Population Reports*, Series J, No. 9, January 1976.

95. Haspels, A. A. Interception: Post-coital estrogens in 3016 women. *Contraception* 14:375–381, 1976.

96. Yuzpe, A. A., and Lancee, W. J. Ethinylestradiol and dl-norgestrel as a postcoital contraceptive. *Fertility and Sterility* 28:932–936, 1977.

97. Ziegler, F. J. Vasectomy and adverse psychological reactions. *Annals of Internal Medicine* 73:853, 1970.

98. Ferber, S., Tietze, C., and Lewit, S. Men with vasectomies: A study of medical, sexual, and psychosocial changes. *Psychosomatic Medicine* 29:354–366, 1967.

99. Rodgers, D. A., and Ziegler, F. J. Psychological Reactions to Surgical Contraception. In J. T. Fawcett (ed.), *Psychological Perspectives on Population*. New York: Basic Books, Publishers, 1973. Pp. 306–326.

100. Radloff, L. Sex differences in depression. *Sex Roles* 1:249–265, 1975.

101. Woodruff, R. A., Jr., Goodwin, D. W., and Guze, S. B. *Psychiatric Diagnosis*. New York: Oxford University Press, 1974.

102. Huffer, V., Levin, L., and Aronson, H. Oral contraceptives: Depression and frigidity. *Journal of Nervous and Mental Disease* 151:35–41, 1970.

103. Lewis, A., and Hoghughi, M. An evaluation of depression as a side effect of oral contraceptives. *British Journal of Psychiatry* 115:697–701, 1969.

104. Grant, E. C. C., and Pryse-Davies, J. Effect of oral contraceptives on depressive mood changes and on endometrial monoamine oxidase and phosphatases. *British Medical Journal* 3:777–780, 1968.

105. Glick, I. D. Psychotropic Action of Oral Contraceptives. In T. M. Itil, G. Laudahn, and W. M. Hermann (eds.), *Psychotropic Action of Hormones*. New York: Spectrum Publications, 1976. Pp. 155–167.

106. Bragonier, J. R. Influence of oral contraception on sexual response. *Medical Aspects of Human Sexuality* 10(10):130–143, 1976.

107. Gambrell, R. D., Bernard, D. M., Sanders, B. I., Vanderburg, N., and Buxton, S. J. Changes in sexual drives of patients on oral contraceptives. *Journal of Reproductive Medicine* 17:165–171, 1976.

108. Johnson, V. E., and Masters, W. H. Intravaginal contraceptive study: Phase I. Anatomy. *Western Journal of Surgery, Obstetrics, and Gynecology* 70:202–207, 1962.

109. Babikian, H. M. Abortion. In A. M. Freedman, H. I. Kaplan, and B. J.

Sadock (eds.), *Comprehensive Textbook of Psychiatry*. Baltimore: Williams & Wilkins Co., 1975. P. 1499.

110. Shane, J. M., Schiff, I., and Wilson, E. A. *The Infertile Couple: Evaluation and Treatment*. Clinical Symposia, Vol. 28, No. 5. Summit, N.J.: CIBA Pharmaceutical Co., 1976.

111. Behrman, S. J., and Kistner, R. W. (eds.). *Progress in Infertility* (2nd ed.). Boston: Little, Brown and Co., 1975.

112. Masters, W. H. Unpublished data, 1978.

113. Jeffcoate, N. *Principles of Gynecology*. London: Butterworth & Co., 1975. P. 586.

114. Lampe, E. H., and Masters, W. H. Problems of male fertility: II. Effect of frequent ejaculation. *Fertility and Sterility* 7:123–127, 1956.

115. Robinson, D., and Rock, J. Intrascrotal hyperthermia induced by scrotal insulation: Effect on spermatogenesis. *Obstetrics and Gynecology* 29:217–223, 1967.

116. Peyser, M. R., Ayalon, D., Harell, A., Toaff, R., and Cordova, T. Stress-induced delay of ovulation. *Obstetrics and Gynecology* 42:667–671, 1973.

117. MacLeod, A. W. Some psychogenic aspects of infertility. *Fertility and Sterility* 15:124–134, 1964.

118. Sandler, B. Infertility of emotional origin. *Journal of Obstetrics and Gynaecology of the British Commonwealth* 68:809–815, 1961.

119. Benedek, T., Ham, G. C., Robbins, F. P., and Rubenstein, B. B. Some emotional factors in infertility. *Psychosomatic Medicine* 15:485–498, 1953.

120. Smith, J. A. Psychogenic factors in infertility and frigidity. *Southern Medical Journal* 49:358–362, 1956.

121. Debrovner, C. H., and Shubin-Stein, R. Sexual problems in the infertile couple. *Medical Aspects of Human Sexuality* 9(1):140–150, 1975.

122. Elstein, M. Effect of infertility on psychosexual function. *British Medical Journal* 3:296–299, 1975.

123. Masters, W. H., and Johnson, V. E. *Human Sexual Response*. Boston: Little, Brown and Co., 1966.

124. Solberg, D. A., Butler, J., and Wagner, N. N. Sexual behavior in pregnancy. *New England Journal of Medicine* 288:1098–1103, 1973.

125. Morris, N. M. The frequency of sexual intercourse during pregnancy. *Archives of Sexual Behavior* 4:501–507, 1975.

126. Falicov, C. J. Sexual adjustment during first pregnancy and postpartum. *American Journal of Obstetrics and Gynecology* 117:991–1000, 1973.

127. Kenny, J. A. Sexuality of pregnant and breast-feeding women. *Archives of Sexual Behavior* 2:215–229, 1973.

128. Tolor, A., and DiGrazia, P. V. Sexual attitudes and behavior patterns during and following pregnancy. *Archives of Sexual Behavior* 5:539–551, 1976.

129. Javert, C. T. Role of the patient's activities in the occurrence of spontaneous abortion. *Fertility and Sterility* 11:550–558, 1960.

130. Goodlin, R. C., Keller, D. W., and Raffin, M. Orgasm during late pregnancy: Possible deleterious effects. *Obstetrics and Gynecology* 38:916–920, 1971.

131. Goodlin, R. C., Schmidt, W., and Creevy, D. D.   Uterine tension and heart rate during maternal orgasm. *Obstetrics and Gynecology* 39:125–127, 1972.

132. Wagner, N. N., Butler, J. C., and Sanders, J. P.   Prematurity and orgasmic coitus during pregnancy: Data on a small sample. *Fertility and Sterility* 27:911–915, 1976.

133. Perkins, R. P.   Sexual behavior and response in relation to complications of pregnancy. *American Journal of Obstetrics and Gynecology* 134:498–505, 1979.

Forcible rape is usually a crisis of immense proportions: The psychological and physical traumas of the rape victim require sensitive, competent medical care both acutely and on a long-range basis. Rape has been characterized as a crime that degrades, dehumanizes, and violates the victim's sense of self [1, 2], yet it remains a poorly understood phenomenon from numerous perspectives. In the past decade, public and professional attention has begun to focus on the needs of the rape victim, with one result being the emergence of rape as a legitimate health-care concern. However, since rape is a legally defined crime rather than a medical diagnosis, health-care professionals must be familiar with basic legal aspects of sexual assault—aspects which, in their practical ramifications, may prove as stressful to the rape victim as the act of rape itself [2–4]. Similarly, the social and emotional consequences of sexual assault must be understood from a broad perspective if the health-care community is to provide adequate service to rape victims.

Although rape can occur in a homosexual context and although there are instances in which women have committed rape, this chapter deals exclusively with heterosexual rape in which the victim is female. Our usage of the word *rape* by itself refers principally to forcible rape; statutory rape, attempted rape, or other varieties of sexual assault are specifically mentioned when these situations are included in the discussion. It should be noted that laws relating to sexual assault in general and rape in particular are undergoing considerable revision in many jurisdictions; readers are urged to be familiar with the current situation in their own location.

The health-care professional who has contact with the rape victim must be skilled in observing and assessing the individual's physical and psychological needs, integrating data about each victim and her individual circumstances into a matrix of general knowledge about the rape situation. Necessary medical services must be combined with compassionate understanding of the stressful situation, with acute management strategies aimed at minimizing the long-term problems for the rape victim.

Social Aspects

Systematic collection of data about the social nature of rape behavior is sparse [5–7]; the available information has been gathered primarily by men, who have often brought their own biases into the analysis and interpretation of data. For example, the older literature includes many studies conducted by men who viewed the woman as the instigator of rape, implying that the female victim behaved in such a way as to invite or encourage sexual assault. This attitude is based on a number of misconceptions, including the assumptions that women secretly enjoy rape; that all women fantasize about being raped; that women instigate rape by their style of dress or by certain provocative mannerisms; and that a woman cannot be raped unless she wants to be [1–6, 8–10]. Other false assumptions include the idea that women frequently make false accusations of rape and the belief that women who are sexually assaulted are predominantly those with "bad" reputations. In view of these negative and discrediting attitudes toward rape victims, it is not surprising that some recent authors tend to regard rape as a reflection of societal prejudice toward women and their worth as human beings [1, 4, 8–10].

Various attempts have been made to categorize men who may commit rape. Gebhard describes five major groups [11]: (1) men with defects of intellect or thought processes (the mentally retarded, psychotics, and men who are seriously intoxicated with alcohol or drugs); (2) men with defects of socialization or learning; (3) men with defective personality development (men who are basically amoral, sometimes known as sociopaths); (4) men with neurosis or with certain deviant patterns (these men tend to commit assaultive rapes, motivated by a subconscious sadistic component); and (5) normal men (generally involved in statutory rape). However, it is important to note that investigations of convicted rapists are limited in their generalizability by several facts. Only a fraction of the rapes committed are ever reported to legal authorities; of these, only a minority of cases result in conviction [4, 5, 7–9]. Since it is likely that rapists who are convicted may be less intelligent and less affluent than those who are neither apprehended nor convicted, and since not all convicted rapists are willing to participate in assessment programs [7], inferences about the social causes of rape or about the personal motivations of rapists are seriously limited.

In an effort to document patterns of forcible rape, Amir studied 646 cases obtained through police records in Philadelphia [12]. He concluded that most rapes occur in the home, rather than in alleys or parks; most rapes are planned, rather than being impulsive acts; and most rapes occur within a context of physical violence rather than sexual passion. Many of the rapists Amir studied carried out the act not as a means of sexual gratification but as one of many behaviors demonstrating membership in or allegiance to a group in which antisocial acts were expected. More recently, Abel and coworkers have shown that sexual arousal for some rapists is dependent primarily on aggression and physical violence [13], rather than upon sexual satisfaction alone. Although Amir's work aided in dispelling the mythology that surrounds rape, rape is still frequently misconstrued as being primarily a sexual encounter: The focus is too often on the sexual rather than on the violent aspects of the act [1, 7, 8, 10]—again, a bias that appears to reflect male prejudice.

Groth, Burgess, and Holmstrom have analyzed descriptions of rape assaults obtained from both offenders and victims [14]. On the basis of clinical and statistical data about 133 convicted rapists and 92 adult rape victims, they stated:

One of the most basic observations one can make about rapists is that they are not all alike. Similar acts are performed for different reasons or different acts serve similar purposes. Our clinical experience with convicted offenders and with victims of reported sexual assault has shown that in *all* cases of forcible rape three components are present: power, anger, and sexuality. The hierarchy and interrelationships among these three factors, together with the relative intensity with which each is experienced and the variety of ways in which each is expressed, may vary, but there is sufficient clustering to indicate distinguishable patterns of rape. We have found that either power or anger dominates and that rape, rather than being primarily an expression of sexual desire, is, in fact, the use of sexuality to express issues of power and anger. Rape, then, is a pseudo-sexual act, a pattern of sexual behavior that is concerned much more with status, aggression, control, and dominance than with sensual pleasure or sexual satisfaction. It is sexual behavior in the service of nonsexual needs and, in this sense, is clearly a sexual deviation [14].

These authors characterized forcible rape as falling under two major categories: power rape, in which the rapist seeks to intimidate and control his victim, and anger rape, in which the rapist unleashes his rage on the victim "to retaliate for perceived wrongs or rejections he has suffered at the hands of women" [14]. Subdivisions of these typologies were also identified: The power-assertive rapist perceives sexual assault as a means of expressing his virility and dominance; the power-reassurance rapist uses the act of rape to resolve doubts about his sexual adequacy; the anger-retaliation rapist seeks revenge by degrading and humiliating women; and the anger-excitation rapist derives sexual excitement from inflicting pain and punishing his victim. In their overall series, power rapes outnumbered anger rapes 65 to 35 percent [14].

Women in our society are predisposed in certain ways to victimization: While men are usually socialized to equate masculinity with aggressiveness, women have traditionally been conditioned to accommodate themselves to others. Until recently, this social role was extended to sexual encounters, where females were usually taught to be passive and unassertive. In this regard, women have internalized the psychological characteristics of defenseless victims—they have never been taught to defend themselves against acts of aggression. However, the outcome of active resistance to rape is problematic: While Giacenti and Tjaden reported that 319 of 915 sexually assaulted women were able to interrupt the rape by physically fighting, fleeing, or screaming or by outside intervention [15], other writers express concern that resistance may provoke the attacker to inflict further injury [4, 7, 8, 15, 16]. In addition, the prevalent cultural stereotypes and misconceptions about rape have led many females to accept the belief that rape can be prevented by their avoidance of potentially dangerous or compromising situations [6, 10, 17].

Rape is not always an assault by a stranger; it may occur in any type of male-female relationship. Thus, rape can be committed against friends, lovers, neighbors, and relatives; it can also occur in a professional or business context. Rape is not always committed by one person acting alone: Amir found that in 276 of the 646 rapes he examined (43 percent), females were victims of more than one assailant [12]. Rape has no boundaries defined by age, health, or physical appearance—there have been reports of rape involving victims as young as 5 months or as old as their nineties [18, 19]. In spite of its universality, rape remains a phenomenon that is only poorly understood. The lack of systematic, unbiased studies of the social aspects of rape will be remedied only by the expenditure of research dollars and the multidisciplinary collaboration of interested scientists and scholars.

Legal Aspects

Rape can be defined as sexual assault with penile penetration of the vagina when mutual consent is lacking. If sexual assault is limited to penile contact with a location other than the vagina, or if the offender uses another body part (his fingers or tongue, for example), a dildo, or some other object to achieve vaginal penetration, the crime would not be classified as rape [20]. Instead, it is likely that such assaults would be categorized as attempted rape, sodomy, or carnal abuse—acts that are generally punished by prison sentences considerably less severe than those prescribed for rape. The specific terminology of the legal definition of rape varies from statute to statute, with recently enacted laws modifying, in some instances, more archaic criteria that have contributed to the perpetuation of rape as a social problem. In most jurisdictions there is a stipulation that actual or threatened force must be present in order to constitute rape [7, 8, 21]. Such a condition does not apply in circumstances in which consent is fraudulently obtained or when the victim is legally incapable of giving consent because of age, mental status, or other considerations. Nevertheless, in jurisdictions that require the presence of force, whether threatened or real, the rape victim may be in a situation in which she cannot obtain prosecution. Similarly, although in some districts penile contact with the labia is sufficient grounds for rape when there is no mutual consent to this contact, most courts require some degree of vaginal penetration—no matter how slight—before the charge of rape can be brought against the assailant. The occurrence of ejaculation is not a necessary condition to meet the legal definition of rape in any jurisdiction.

Brownmiller summarized the requirements that must typically exist in order for rape to be successfully prosecuted in courts across the United States in 1977:

The perpetration of an act of sexual intercourse with a female, not one's wife, against her will and consent, whether her will is overcome by force or fear resulting from the threat of force, or by drugs or intoxication; or when because of mental deficiency, she is incapable of exercising rational judgment, or when she is below an arbitrary "age of consent" [8].

There is currently heated debate about whether a husband can be convicted of raping his wife; it is interesting to note that marriage does not exempt either party from conviction for other acts of violence perpetrated upon a spouse.

Once rape has been reported to the legal authorities, a complex legal process is set in motion. The frightening implications of this system undoubtedly contribute to estimated statistics indicating the large number of women who fail to report a rape: Such estimates range from 50 to 90 percent of all women who have been raped [5, 7, 8, 18]. Other factors that contribute to underreporting include fear of further humiliation; desire to avoid shame or embarrassment to self and others; concern about possible recriminations from the rapist; uncertainty about procedures for entering a formal complaint; and fear that the rapist—even if reported—will not be apprehended, or if apprehended, will go unpunished [5, 7, 8, 22]. These are legitimate concerns and are symptomatic of the fact that for some women, the most painful aspect of the rape experience comes from their confrontation with the criminal justice system. Other problems contribute to difficulties in determining accurate statistics about rape. MacNamara and Sagarin summarize this less discussed area:

From another direction, a difficulty in arriving at reliable statistics on forcible rape derives from the possibility that some girls, discovered *in flagrante delicto* or finding themselves spurned by a former date, have cried rape when they had been quite willing partners to the act. Some charges of rape against black men by white women seem to be very clear examples of voluntary sex the discovery of which embarrassed the female partner. . . . According to *Uniform Crime Reports*, the FBI has concluded that in the 1970s one out of every five reports to the police of forcible rape proves upon investigation to be unfounded [20].

If the victim seeks medical treatment without first reporting the incident to the police, many hospitals and clinics insist on notifying legal authorities. In most jurisdictions, the examining physician has a legal obligation to report a rape because it is classified as a felony [18]. Institutions and physicians may also routinely report cases of suspected or alleged rape to protect themselves against later charges of negligence.

After the crime is reported, the police arrive to interrogate the victim; they then file a report of the victim's account of the incident. When the first priority is medical attention, questioning may be initially brief, followed by a detailed report at a later time. This encounter with the police can be a negative experience for many victims of sexual assault, as in the following dramatic description:

Victims report being leered at, humiliated, and harassed by the policemen they call for help. To many women, the police often seem more interested in explicitly sexual details than in catching the rapist. "Are you a virgin?" "Did you like it?" "Did you climax?" "What were you wearing?" are police questions repeated by rape victims throughout the nation—in urban, suburban, and rural areas alike. Women are often asked things like "How long were you on the floor?" "What verbal response did you make during the rape?" "Did his language excite you?" "How much prior sexual experience have you had?" Such questions have little to do with finding the rapist and much more with human curiosity or satisfying the officers' vicarious sexual urges [7].

Fortunately, special police units have been set up in many locations to handle cases involving sexual assault; these units usually include specially trained personnel, with a policewoman assigned to each case.

If the rape victim decides to attempt prosecution, she rapidly discovers that this process is largely outside her control, since it is the state rather than the victim that brings charges [7, 8]. Unless substantial evidence is available to corroborate the victim's allegation, many district attorneys choose not to proceed on charges of rape. The subsequent passage of a case through the legal system thus depends on information from several sources: the report of the interrogating police officer (and his or her testimony about the victim's appearance and presumed state of mind); evidence gathered during the medical examination; and statements of the victim herself. It is unfortunate that health-care providers may be called upon to assist in the legal investigation of rape in ways that may increase the victim's discomfort or anxiety about the rape situation and its aftermath.

Although many women view the legal process of prosecution as an exercise in futility [2, 5, 7, 8, 22], an increasing number of rape cases are being reported and brought to trial each year [7, 20]. The trial is likely to be a stressful experience for the victim, even under the best of conditions; typically, the woman may be made to feel that she is on trial, rather than the accused man. In court proceedings, the rape victim is placed under stress in a variety of ways, since it is thought that stress will aid in the quest for truth [21]. This attitude stems from a view of women as being devious or evil, a view that still influences our legal system. Such thinking underlies the assumption that females frequently fabricate complaints of rape [2, 7, 8]. These fallacies permeate a society that has chosen to cast woman in the role of willing victim, subtle instigator, or seductress—stereotyped notions that are reinforced by the equally erroneous belief that every man can be entrapped into sexual play.

Rape is the only violent crime for which corroboration remains mandatory in most jurisdictions [7, 21]. The requirement of corroboration indicates that a female's testimony is considered to be less credible than that of a male. Corroboration—defined as "evidence independent of the mere assertion of the fact" [23]—is not simply supporting evidence that might be used to strengthen the prosecutor's case; it is primary evidence that is required to prove that the act of rape occurred [8, 21]. The corroboration requirement aids in protecting the defendant; unfortunately, it sometimes results in the rape victim being the unintended victim of the law.

The law considers the issue of consent at the time of the incident to be the primary factor in determining the guilt of the accused [7, 8, 10, 17, 21]. Consequently, most jurisdictions demand that the victim demonstrate a high degree of resistance to the attack. As Burgess and Holmstrom have shown, a significant number of rape victims may be physically or psychologically paralyzed by the threat of attack and are therefore unable to resist; alternatively, they may choose compliance as a way of getting through the rape situation quickly and with minimal physical trauma [24]. In assessing the legal parameters of consent, the victim's background, past behavior, past sexual relationships, and relationship to the offender have all frequently been used as evidence to refute or undermine the female's credibility. According to Slovenko and Brownmiller, the moral character of the victim may be used as a defense in a rape case under the assumption that an unchaste female or one with a questionable sexual history is likely to have consented [8, 25]. Kalven and Zeisel found that the jury often weighs evidence concerning the woman's prior sexual behavior in reaching a verdict in charges of rape [26]. In addition, the complainant's credibility may be questioned if the jury feels that she failed to notify legal authorities promptly. The complainant who bathes and changes her clothing soon after the rape incident or who presents a calm exterior following the attack is also handicapped when evidence must be presented in a rape trial.

The complexities of our legal system of checks and balances exist not to thwart victims of crimes but to protect the accused who is innocent of wrongdoing. This dilemma is addressed in the following passage:

[In cases where consent is at issue,] in the absence of any other evidence that would show whether the sex act had been a willing encounter or a rape, some have asked, "Why isn't her word as good as his?" This is a logical question, and if the persons were meeting in a family gathering, a social group, a therapy session, or elsewhere, one would say that her word must be as good as his, and sometimes—if she is a person who has shown herself to be believable—it may be better. But in a criminal case, when the evidence is neatly balanced, one cannot convict solely on the contested word of the victim. If the jury feels that complainant and defendant are equally believable (although one must be lying), it has no choice: it must find the man not guilty. To act otherwise would erode the principle of presumption of innocence and abandon the concept of guilt beyond a reasonable doubt.... [20]

A recent study sheds light on a previously consternating fact: In many cases of well-documented rape, no medical evidence of the presence of spermatozoa or seminal fluid can be identified. Groth and Burgess noted a relatively high rate of sexual dysfunction in convicted rape offenders during episodes of rape; 16 percent of the rapists were impotent and 15 percent were unable to ejaculate [27]. Therefore, failure to detect laboratory evidence such as microscopic identification of spermatozoa or prostatic acid phosphatase in vaginal secretions [28] does not rule out the possibility of vaginal penetration having occurred.

Several states have recently amended their laws concerning mandatory corroboration in regard to rape. In some instances, the requirement of medical evidence such as physical trauma or semen to verify the victim's testimony has been eliminated. Other changes include a prohibition of the use of evidence pertaining to the victim's prior sexual behavior, except under defined circumstances [7, 21, 29]. With increasing public awareness of and attention to the inequities of the legal system as it pertains to victims of sexual assault, it is likely that many more changes will be made.

Medical Aspects

Medical management of the rape victim includes the immediate care of physical injuries, the conduct of a medical examination, attention to the possibility of venereal disease or pregnancy, and emotional support to alleviate both acute and long-term psychological trauma [3, 7, 18, 19, 30, 31]. The manner in which these matters are handled in terms of medical competence and the preservation of personal dignity of the rape victim varies widely from hospital to hospital, depending in part on the personnel involved and their knowledge and attitudes about rape.

Some hospitals refuse to treat rape victims because of concern about legal entanglements ensuing from such cases—including accusations of negligence and incomplete evidence—and the wish to avoid the necessity of hospital personnel giving testimony during trials [7, 10, 23]. In other hospitals there are well-developed programs for managing rape cases [31]. Nevertheless, remarkably little formal education has traditionally been offered to physicians to prepare them for treating such patients.

The Hospital Environment

From the moment the rape victim arrives at the hospital, she becomes involved in a process that can potentially intensify her emotional reactions and heighten her feelings of depersonalization. She is thrust into an institutional setting, confronted with unfamiliar procedures and routines, and exposed to a multitude of hospital personnel. On admission, rape victims should be considered high-priority patients. Their needs differ from the needs of most other emergency room patients in that they have just experienced a crisis situation with profound emotional and psychological consequences. All hospital personnel who come into contact with rape victims have a responsibility to help reduce the trauma and anxieties of the situation by fostering prompt, nonjudgmental, and effective medical and psychological care. This care begins with providing an environment of safety, an attitude of acceptance and emotional support, and the assurance of confidentiality [3, 23, 31–33]. Toward this end, health-care professionals should avoid using legal language ("When did the alleged incident occur?"); such terminology only serves to intimidate the victim and to disparage the authenticity of her statements.

Promptly after admission, the rape victim must be given information related to her subsequent treatment, including a description of the procedures that will be followed, their purposes and risks, and alternative choices that she has. Any questions raised by the victim should be answered fully and openly. In this way, the victim is better able to make decisions about her treatment and to view herself as an active, effective person who is able to cope with the situation [2, 3, 23, 31, 33]. Informed consent regarding all aspects of diagnosis and treatment should be obtained in writing from the woman who has been sexually assaulted; in cases involving minors, written consent must be obtained from a parent or legal guardian.

The Medical Examination

The purpose of the medical examination is, first and foremost, the welfare of the patient; only secondarily is it meant to gather documentary evidence. *This examination does not determine whether or not rape occurred.* However, since evidence obtained from this examination may be used to refute or corroborate points of law, thorough and accurate medical records must be kept.

Obtaining a History. In the initial assessment of the rape victim's status, a careful history should be obtained. Whenever possible, information regarding the sexual assault should be documented with the victim's actual statements. Toward this end, details about the events surrounding the rape should be elicited, including data pertaining to the following factors [3, 19, 23]:

1. Time, place, and circumstances of the rape.
2. Identification (if known) and description of the assailant(s).
3. Types and amount of sexual contact.
4. Types and degree of physical force or injury.
5. Types of coercion or threatened force, including use or presence of weapons.
6. Presence or absence of witnesses.
7. Types and degree of resistance employed by the victim.
8. Postrape behavior, including behavior that might alter or remove evidence (such as a change of clothing, douching, bathing, or urinating).

A thorough medical and sexual history is also necessary to aid in the treatment of the rape victim. This history should include the date of last menses, a full menstrual history, information about contraceptive use, any previously diagnosed venereal disease, and the date and type of the last sexual contact prior to the rape.

Physical Examination. Assessment of the signs and symptoms of physical injury is mandatory. Common types of physical trauma include nongenital areas, such as the head and neck, extremities, breasts, and rectum; the range of severity of such injuries varies from minor bruises to internal hemorrhage, concussions, stab wounds, and fractures. Gynecologic injuries include abrasions or lacerations of the external genitalia, the perineum, and the urethra; in cases involving sadistic behavior, rupture of the cul-de-sac, broad ligament damage, or injuries to the cervix or uterus may be encountered [3, 19, 30].

A thorough general physical examination should always be conducted to assess trauma. A pelvic examination is performed to determine the extent of internal injuries, to obtain possible evidence of semen in or around the vagina, to obtain necessary cultures for venereal disease testing, and to ascertain whether pregnancy exists. Unfortunately, the pelvic examination is often conducted in an insensitive and demeaning fashion. It is important for health-care professionals to remember that what they view as a routine minor procedure may take on entirely different dimensions for the patient—and in the context of rape, it is likely that this additional invasion of privacy may be especially unwelcome and distasteful. The rape victim often needs an unusual degree of professional reassurance, acceptance, and understanding in regard to the pelvic examination.

The pelvic examination should be conducted in such a way that the patient has control over its pace and can stop any aspect of the procedure if it is uncomfortable to her. With sensitivity to the patient's feelings and dignity, it is possible to minimize the trauma and anxiety involved. False promises ("This won't hurt at all") should never be made. Instead, the physician and nurse, working as a team, should discuss with the patient the procedures that will be performed, their intention of being gentle, the possibility that some discomfort may occur, and their willingness to slow down or halt the procedure at the patient's request.

LABORATORY DIAGNOSTIC TESTING AND COLLECTION OF EVIDENCE. The pelvic examination should include smears obtained from the vulva, the vagina, and the cervix as well as microscopic review of washings of any dried secretions on the thighs, perineum, or buttocks. Fluid from the posterior fornix should be examined for sperm, for gonococci, and for seminal fluid by measurement of prostatic acid phosphatase [28, 34,

35]. A urine sample should be collected for a pregnancy test, and a blood sample should be taken. These specimens should be labeled and submitted to the clinical laboratory with appropriate security measures, using signed receipts [34, 35].

Scrapings from beneath the fingernails may be used as evidence and should be collected separately; combings of the victim's pubic hair, using a new comb and a clean paper towel, should be placed in a plastic bag or test tube and labeled. These scrapings and combings may aid in the identification of the rapist [34, 35]. A few pubic hairs from the victim herself should also be obtained, placed in a separate container, and labeled, in order to allow precise identification of the victim's hair pattern to differentiate it from the rapist's.

Preventing Venereal Disease. The risk of venereal disease resulting from rape is of unknown magnitude but requires attention. When prophylactic treatment is desired, the drug of choice is procaine penicillin G given by intramuscular injection in a dose of 4.8 million units divided into two sites; efficacy is increased by the use of probenecid (1.0 gm taken orally just before the injection), since this agent reduces urinary excretion of penicillin [36]. Other types of penicillin, such as benzathine penicillin or penicillin with aluminum monostearate, are not effective in protecting against syphilis and gonorrhea simultaneously and therefore should not be used in treating rape victims. For women who are allergic to penicillin and are not pregnant, tetracycline (0.5 gm given orally four times a day for 15 days) may be used.

When antibiotics are given, they may disrupt the normal bacterial balance of the vagina, creating an overgrowth of unaffected organisms and resulting in nonvenereal discharge and discomfort. If the rape victim is unaware of this possibility, the experience of a vaginal discharge may cause her undue alarm.

Serologic tests for syphilis and cultures for gonococci will determine only if venereal disease was already present at the time of rape. Therefore, it is essential for the welfare of the victim that these diagnostic tests be repeated approximately four to six weeks after the emergency preventive measures and again at a six-month interval. It is important to note that rape victims should have two negative cultures for gonorrhea as part of the followup treatment before they can be considered to be cured. If the culture remains positive, a course of retreatment is required.

While the gram-stain is frequently used for detecting gonorrhea, it is not as reliable as properly obtained cultures plated on Thayer-Martin medium. Cultures should be routinely taken from the cervix, urethra, and rectum in rape cases; throat cultures should also be obtained if oral-genital contact occurred during the assault.

Preventing Rape-Induced Pregnancy. If there is a risk of pregnancy as a consequence of the rape, emergency preventive measures should be discussed in detail with the victim. The pregnancy test performed shortly after a rape will determine only if the woman was already pregnant when the assault occurred. The options available to prevent or terminate an unwanted pregnancy include (1) the use of postcoital hormonal contraception, such as diethylstilbestrol or other estrogens (see Chap. 15); (2) prompt insertion of an intrauterine device (also discussed in Chap. 15); (3) menstrual extraction; and (4) abortion (if pregnancy occurs). In the absence of medical contraindications to these methods, the rape victim's preference should be the primary basis for the choice that is made. Needless to say, personal and religious values may enter into this decision; consultation with a clergyman may be of assistance when there is a conflict between religious teachings and the desire to prevent conception as a result of rape.

Psychological Considerations	In the emergency management of rape victims, sedatives or tranquilizers may be administered to alleviate, at least in part, the severe emotional stress of the situation. Such an approach may be beneficial, but it does not remove the underlying trauma; at times, these drugs may actually precipitate a heightened state of agitation and excitability. Emotional support from health-care professionals, significant others, or rape crisis center personnel is of critical importance during the initial postrape phase.

The type of counseling to be given should be flexible enough to accommodate differences in age, education, social and cultural background, marital status, and personality in rape victims; there is no single best approach. Empathy is more useful than sympathy; sensitivity is more valuable than outrage; active communication is more constructive than merely adopting a receptive attitude; specific suggestions are more helpful than broad generalities. The rape victim should be given an opportunity to identify and ventilate her feelings in a supportive environment—although for some women, denial or the need for privacy may outweigh the benefits of lengthy dialogue in the early postrape stage. When possible, the woman should be reassured about the appropriateness of the way she reacted to the events surrounding the rape and the way in which she behaved afterward; such reassurance may contribute to the preservation or restoration of her self-esteem and may help to eliminate personal feelings of guilt. An important aspect of the counseling effort is the identification of potential resource persons who can help each rape victim to deal with the emotional aftermath of the situation; whenever possible, a relative or close friend should be enlisted in the initial support process.

Recommendations for followup care, including counseling, should be made (in writing, if necessary). Some authorities suggest that all rape victims receive specific followup counseling or psychotherapy. As Massey explains, "Many deep-seated feelings, both conscious and unconscious, may be aroused and even the most innocent victim may have difficulty handling her feelings alone. Friends and relatives are of unquestioned supportive value, but a few sessions with an objective and trained individual may be of great preventive value from an emotional point of view" [37].

Psychosocial Consequences of Rape: The Aftermath

Rape changes the way the victim feels about herself, others, and the world around her [3, 7, 38, 39]. Metzger, herself a victim of rape, describes the rape victim's reaction as a total loss of self leading to a sense of emptiness and isolation from self and society [1]. The fact that rape is often followed by isolation—both psychological and social—is acknowledged by many authors [4, 6, 8–10].

Descriptions of stress reaction patterns found in a variety of circumstances can be applied to the reactions of rape victims. The general schema is as follows [3, 38, 39]:

1. The impact phase [38] or acute-reaction phase [39] can range from a few days to several weeks in duration. During this period the rape victim may exhibit gross anxiety, disorganization, shock, and disbelief.
2. The posttraumatic or "recoil" phase is a time of outward adjustment that may encompass denial of the impact of the rape experience [38]. Emotional awareness and expression undergo a limited degree of reorganization; the victim appears superficially to be well integrated, while denial or suppression is occurring on a deeper level [39].
3. The posttraumatic reconstitution phase is a period of integration and resolution, sometimes marked by recurring depression and the need to talk, during which the rape victim attempts to resolve her conflicting feelings [38]. She may develop coping mechanisms that lessen self-esteem or are psychologically costly in other ways, even though they may assist the integration of the rape experience [39].

Burgess and Holmstrom found that a certain reaction pattern was typically described by rape victims. They designated this symptom cluster as the *rape trauma syndrome*, involving an immediate stage with major disruption of life-style, accompanied by emotional and physical symptoms, and a long-term stage of reorganization [3]. In the acute phase, somatic complaints such as general body soreness, genital discomfort, sleep disturbances, and altered eating patterns are common, while emotional reactions include humiliation, self-blame, a desire for revenge, and wide variations in mood. In the long-term phase of the rape trauma syndrome, behavioral changes may be characterized by recurring nightmares and the appearance of various fears or phobias.

As a consequence of rape, some women avoid any type of involvement with men in either social or sexual situations. There has been speculation that in some victims exhibiting this reaction, rape may contribute to subsequent homosexuality [40]. Anxiety, depression, and phobic responses to situations reminiscent of the rape may persist for many years and may alter the victim's reaction to subsequent sexual encounters.

Women who have been raped may face a variety of sexual problems as a consequence. In some instances, the rape victim has an aversion to all sexual activity (see Chap. 22). This phobic response may occur abruptly after the rape encounter or may develop gradually. Women may also experience difficulties with sexual arousal or sexual activity, including impaired vaginal lubrication, loss of genital sensations, pain during intercourse, vaginismus, and loss of orgasmic facility. The underlying causes of such responses are often complex, involving diminished self-esteem, guilt, fear of rejection by the sexual partner, anger toward men in general, depression, and feelings of learned helplessness reinforced by the rape experience. Statistics are not currently available to document the incidence and frequency of sexual difficulties following rape.

The impact of the rape experience on the victim's sexual partner can also be depicted in both its acute and its long-range effects. In either instance, the partner's reactions influence the long-term adjustment of the rape victim in many ways. The woman who is deprived of emotional support from her partner appears particularly vulnerable to the adverse consequences of rape. The realization that the partner's reactions can be as complex as those of the victim will lead to a better understanding of the aftermath of the rape situation for all concerned.

Like the rape victim, the partner may initially feel anger and a wish for revenge [38]. The emotions that form the basis of this anger take on significance as time passes. While some partners react as though they have been personally attacked and view the woman as an extension of themselves, others react with disgust and revulsion—as though the woman were guilty of complicity in the rape and had been soiled or despoiled by the experience [9]. Some men react very defensively; others respond with sympathy and kindness. Even when they attempt to be sensitive, understanding, and supportive, men can never really appreciate the emotional trauma that the female rape victim has experienced.

In coping with the rape situation, regardless of their emotional and psychological reactions, partners may experience sexual difficulties. These problems are most commonly manifested as impotence, although diminished sexual interest or disturbed ejaculation may also be encountered.

Counseling
Implications

Counseling is necessary to aid the rape victim and her partner in accepting the situation and understanding how it can affect them as individuals and in their relationship with each other. Immediate post-rape crisis counseling for the rape victim is crucial; some form of counseling should generally be continued for a period of time following the rape as well. Although the act itself and its associations vary from victim to victim, forcible rape is almost invariably a degrading, depersonalizing experience that evokes a wide range of feelings and behaviors long after the acute-reaction phase has passed. The rape victim needs to be acknowledged without judgment as an individual who has endured a crisis situation. She should initially be offered emotional support and should be encouraged to verbalize her feelings about the experience; through active listening, the counselor can achieve a better understanding of the person and the event before a course of action is formulated and discussed with the victim.

In counseling the rape victim, the following aspects of the situation must be carefully considered: (1) the victim's current physical and emotional status; (2) the circumstances of the rape and the victim's reactions to it; (3) the reactions of significant others to the situation, as perceived by the victim; (4) the victim's current resources for emotional support and counseling; and (5) the victim's prior experience with crisis situations and her characteristic method and patterns of coping with stress. Assessment of these factors will provide the counselor with information about the complexity of the situation and the particular needs of the individual. It will also provide the victim with reassurance that the counselor is interested in helping her. More specifically, it will aid the counselor in deciding what type of counseling is appropriate [41] and whether referral should be made. All information communicated to the counselor should be considered privileged and should not be released without the informed consent of the victim (this includes reports to legal authorities).

To meet the needs of the rape victim during both the acute and the long-term phases of counseling, the health-care counselor must create a climate in which the victim feels free to talk about the events leading up to, during, and immediately following the rape. The victim should be allowed to feel that she is in control of the counseling situation; the professional's attitude should be reassuring rather than patronizing so that feelings of helplessness will not be perpetuated in the victim. The role of the counselor is to aid the victim in restoration of her emotional, social, physical, and sexual well-being. One way in which this can be accomplished is by helping the rape victim to examine specific aspects of these areas that may be producing conflict as a result of the rape experience, and to decide on a specific course of action for each problem—whether it be to seek further medical care, social support, psychotherapy, or legal counsel.

The literature on rape presents guidelines, suggestions, and descriptions of therapeutic techniques and procedures that have proved to be valuable in counseling the rape victim. Burgess and Holmstrom detail their mode of counseling in the book *Rape: Victims of Crisis*, based on a long-range study of rape victims [3]. They employ a short-term issue-oriented therapy model with the primary goal of attempting to isolate problems that rape victims experience as a consequence of being raped. The rape victim is seen as a "customer" whose crisis needs and counseling requests are listened to and met without judgment and with full acceptance of the victim as a "normal" person whose life has been temporarily disrupted [3]. Crisis and counseling requests are differentiated; the authors outline various categories corresponding to different types of requests, which gives the counselor a basis on which to proceed with a plan of action [3]. Other discussions of counseling the rape victim suggest the importance of flexibility in approach and of providing long-term support for integration of the stress experience [33, 41].

Rape Crisis Centers   Most rape crisis centers are organized, staffed, and equipped with the following objectives [7, 9, 10, 23]:

1. To provide the rape victim with immediate information regarding

the medical examination, police interrogation, and court procedures (this information is generally available through a 24-hour "hot line" service).

2. To provide escort service to accompany the rape victim to the hospital or clinic, police department, or courts, if she wishes it.
3. To provide followup counseling services to rape victims, either through group therapy or by referral to individual counselors.
4. To work toward improvement in the handling of rape cases by police and hospital personnel.
5. To keep the news media informed of any changes in rape-related legislation.
6. To educate the public by providing volunteers to speak on rape and rape prevention.

Health-care professionals should be aware of and familiar with rape crisis programs, centers, and personnel in their community so that they can make use of these resources as the need arises.

Concern about rape is currently being focused at two different levels. At the societal and governmental level, there are efforts to change social legislation; at the grass-roots level, there are efforts to redefine social attitudes toward rape and its victims through programs instituted by women's groups, crisis centers, colleges and universities, hospitals, and social service agencies. Although each program has its own guidelines, procedures, and target areas, their common goal is to effect positive change in attitudes toward rape in our society. It is hoped that additional studies of social and psychological factors associated with sexual assault [42] will combine with appropriate treatment programs for rapists [43] to reduce the frequency of this violent crime.

References

1. Metzger, D.   It is always the woman who is raped. *American Journal of Psychiatry* 133:405–408, 1976.
2. Hilberman, E.   Rape: The ultimate violation of the self. *American Journal of Psychiatry* 133:436, 1976.
3. Burgess, A. W., and Holmstrom, L. L.   *Rape: Victims of Crisis*. Bowie, Md.: Robert J. Brady Co., 1974.
4. Griffin, S.   Rape: The all-American crime. *Ramparts* 10:26–35, September 1971.
5. Schultz, L. G. (ed.).   *Rape Victimology*. Springfield, Ill.: Charles C Thomas, Publisher, 1975.
6. Medea, A., and Thompson, K.   *Against Rape*. New York: Farrar, Straus and Giroux, 1974.
7. Gager, N., and Schurr, C.   *Sexual Assault: Confronting Rape in America*. New York: Grosset & Dunlap, 1976.

8. Brownmiller, S. *Against Our Will: Men, Women and Rape*. New York: Simon & Schuster, 1975.

9. Horos, C. V. *Rape: The Private Crime, a Social Horror*. New Canaan, Conn.: Tobey Publications, 1974.

10. Connell, N., and Wilson, C. (eds.). *Rape: The First Sourcebook for Women*. New York: New American Library, 1974.

11. Gebhard, P. H., Gagnon, J. H., Pomeroy, W. B., and Christenson, C. V. *Sex Offenders: An Analysis of Types*. New York: Harper & Row, 1965. Pp. 197–206.

12. Amir, M. *Patterns in Forcible Rape*. Chicago: University of Chicago Press, 1971.

13. Abel, G. G., Barlow, D. H., Blanchard, E. B., and Guild, D. The components of rapists' sexual arousal. *Archives of General Psychiatry* 34:895–903, 1977.

14. Groth, A. N., Burgess, A. W., and Holmstrom, L. L. Rape: Power, anger, and sexuality. *American Journal of Psychiatry* 134:1239–1243, 1977.

15. Giacenti, T. A., and Tjaden, C. The crime of rape in Denver. Unpublished report to the Denver Anti-Crime Council, 1973. Cited in A. W. Burgess and L. L. Holmstrom, Coping behavior of the rape victim, *American Journal of Psychiatry* 133:413–418, 1976.

16. Report of District of Columbia Task Force on Rape. Reprinted in L. G. Schultz (ed.), *Rape Victimology*, Springfield, Ill.: Charles C Thomas, Publisher, 1975. Pp. 339–373.

17. Weis, K., and Borges, S. Victimology and rape: The case of the legitimate victim. *Issues in Criminology* 8:71–115, 1973.

18. Hayman, C. R. Sexual assault on women and girls. *Annals of Internal Medicine* 72:277–278, 1970.

19. Massey, J. B., Garcia, C.-R., and Emich, J. P. Management of sexually assaulted females. *Obstetrics and Gynecology* 38:29–36, 1971.

20. MacNamara, D. E. J., and Sagarin, E. *Sex, Crime, and the Law*. New York: The Free Press, 1977. Pp. 26–64.

21. Hibey, R. A. The trial of a rape case: An advocate's analysis of corroboration, consent, and character. *American Criminal Law Review* 11:309–334, 1973. Reprinted in L. G. Schultz (ed.), *Rape Victimology*, Springfield, Ill.: Charles C Thomas, Publisher, 1975.

22. Nadelson, C. C. Rapist and victim. *New England Journal of Medicine* 297:784–785, 1977.

23. Hilberman, E. *The Rape Victim*. Baltimore: American Psychiatric Association, Garamond/Pridemark Press, 1976.

24. Burgess, A. W., and Holmstrom, L. L. Coping behavior of the rape victim. *American Journal of Psychiatry* 133:413–418, 1976.

25. Slovenko, R. *Psychiatry and Law*. Boston: Little, Brown and Co., 1973. Pp. 59–60.

26. Kalven, H., and Zeisel, H. *The American Jury*. Chicago: The University of Chicago Press, 1971.

27. Groth, A. N., and Burgess, A. W. Sexual dysfunction during rape. *New England Journal of Medicine* 297:764–766, 1977.

28. Schumann, G. B., Badawy, S., Peglow, A., and Henry, J. B. Prostatic acid

phosphatase: Current assessment in vaginal fluid of alleged rape victims. *American Journal of Clinical Pathology* 66:944–952, 1976.

29. *American Bar Association Journal* 61:464–465, 1975. (No author; section of article "House of Delegates Redefines Death . . .", pp. 463–473.)

30. Hayman, C. R., and Lanza, C. Sexual assault on women and girls. *American Journal of Obstetrics and Gynecology* 109:480–486, 1971.

31. McCombie, S., Bassuk, E., Savitz, R., and Pell, S. Development of a medical center rape crisis intervention program. *American Journal of Psychiatry* 133:418–421, 1976.

32. Sager, C. J. Standardizing medical procedures in examining victims of rape. *Medical Tribune* Jan. 21, 1976. Pp. 18, 19, 32.

33. Schaefer, J. L., Sullivan, R. A., and Goldstein, F. L. Counseling sexual abuse victims. *American Family Physician* 18(5):85–91, 1978.

34. North Carolina Memorial Hospital Emergency Room. Guidelines for Care of the Victims of Rape, Sexual Assault. In E. Hilberman, *The Rape Victim*, Baltimore: American Psychiatric Association, Garamond/Pridemark Press, 1976. Pp. 80–86.

35. Suspected Rape. Technical Bulletin No. 14. Chicago: American College of Obstetricians and Gynecologists (ACOG), July 1970; revised April 1972.

36. *Physicians' Desk Reference* (31st ed.). Oradell, N.J.: Medical Economics Company, 1977.

37. Mathis, J. L. Rape. In D. W. Abse, E. M. Nash, and L. M. R. Louden (eds.), *Marital and Sexual Counseling in Medical Practice*. Hagerstown, Md.: Harper & Row, 1974. P. 410.

38. Notman, M. T., and Nadelson, C. C. The rape victim: Psychodynamic considerations. *American Journal of Psychiatry* 133:408–413, 1976.

39. Sutherland, S., and Scherl, D. Patterns of response among victims of rape. *American Journal of Orthopsychiatry* 40:503–511, 1970.

40. Grundlach, R. Sexual molestation and rape reported by homosexual and heterosexual women. *Journal of Homosexuality* 2:367–384, 1977.

41. Evans, H. I. Psychotherapy for the rape victim: Some treatment models. *Hospital and Community Psychiatry* 29:309–312, 1978.

42. Rada, R. T. (ed.). *Clinical Aspects of the Rapist*. New York: Grune & Stratton, 1978.

43. Abel, G. G., Blanchard, E. B., and Becker, J. V. An integrated treatment program for rapists. In Rada, R. T. (ed.), *Clinical Aspects of the Rapist*. New York: Grune & Stratton, 1978. Pp. 161–214.

Homosexuality

Few topics in human sexuality have received as much attention in the past five years as has homosexuality. Dozens of books, hundreds of journal articles, and thousands of newspaper stories have dealt with various aspects of this subject. To be certain, this is partly a reflection of prevalent cultural biases and discomfort; at the same time, there has been an increasing degree of research attention to and clinical recognition of homosexuality, indicating at least a beginning step toward regarding the health-care needs of homosexuals as legitimate and proper. In parallel fashion, increasing attention has been devoted to the civil liberties and economic rights of homosexuals, and in some jurisdictions the homosexual community is gaining impetus as a political force.

The term *homosexuality* does not describe a unitary population any more than the term *heterosexuality* can be taken to predict the personality, behavior, or pathology of persons whose sexual activity occurs exclusively with persons of the opposite gender. Unfortunately, both scientific and societal misperceptions and biases have conspired to produce a stereotypic view of homosexuality that assumes that all homosexuals are alike and labels them as abnormal. It is important for health-care professionals to recognize the dangers of such sweeping generalizations; homosexual men and women constitute as diverse a group as heterosexuals from the viewpoints of occupation, education, life-style, personality characteristics, and physical appearance.

Homosexual behavior is depicted in the art, literature, and histories of the most ancient civilizations; its legal and social acceptability has varied with time, culture, and circumstances. Readers interested in detailed discussions concerning the history of homosexuality are referred to the References [1–3]. Cross-cultural aspects of homosexuality are discussed by Ford and Beach, who found that 49 out of 76 societies approved some form of homosexuality [4], and also by Marshall and Suggs [5].

There is considerable diversity in the way homosexuality is defined in the scientific literature. Some authors restrict the term to describing sexual contact between persons of the same sex, whereas others extend the definition to include sexual desire or fantasy as well as overt sexual behavior. Marmor and Green state, "As a working definition, homosexuality can best be described as a strong preferential attraction to members of the same sex" [6].

Kinsey and coworkers devised a numerical scale for describing a person's sexual orientation on the basis of both behavior and fantasy [7]. This seven-point heterosexual-homosexual rating scale (Table 17-1) emphasizes the continuity of the spectrum of sexual orientation, with

Table 17-1. The Kinsey Heterosexual-Homosexual Rating Scale		
0	Exclusively heterosexual
1	Predominantly heterosexual: only incidentally homosexual
2	Predominantly heterosexual: more than incidentally homosexual
3	Equally heterosexual and homosexual
4	Predominantly homosexual: more than incidentally heterosexual
5	Predominantly homosexual: only incidentally heterosexual
6	Exclusively homosexual

Source: Based upon Kinsey, Pomeroy, and Martin [7].

some persons living their entire lives in a single category while others shift along the spectrum from time to time. Although it is not a sophisticated form for analyzing sexual orientation, this simple quantitative model has some utility as a research tool and a clinical descriptor.

Kinsey and his associates gathered cumulative estimates of the incidence of homosexuality by recording interview data from 5,300 white males and 5,940 white females. Their samples were not randomly selected nor were they representative of a balanced cross-section of the population, but they provide the most extensive statistical data available to date. According to these workers, 4 percent of white males were exclusively homosexual from puberty on; 10 percent were predominantly homosexual for at least three years between the ages of 16 and 55; and 37 percent had at least one homosexual experience leading to orgasm after the time of puberty [7]. Primarily or exclusively homosexual behavior in females was approximately half of that found in males, according to the Kinsey data [8]. More recently, Gebhard estimated that the cumulative incidence of overt homosexual experience for the adult female population as a whole is between 10 and 12 percent [9]. Although changing attitudes in the past 30 years may have contributed to the number of persons now willing to identify themselves as homosexual, it is not clear whether there has been an actual shift in the incidence of homosexuality.

Theories of Etiology

There has been much historical conjecture concerning the origins of homosexuality. That there is no current agreement may simply reflect the need for the development of knowledge that satisfactorily explains the origins of heterosexuality, which is equally enigmatic at the present time. Nevertheless, a brief summary of the various research and clinical viewpoints will be provided here.

Biologic
Considerations

Many homosexuals claim that their sexual orientation is the result of biologic forces over which they have no control or choice. Although a report by Kallman in 1952 postulated a genetic origin for homosexuality based on a study of concordance for sexual orientation among identical and nonidentical twins [10], subsequent studies have not supported this claim [11, 12].

More recently, interest has revived in the investigation of hormonal factors that may play a role in the development of human sexual behavior. Animal research has shown that hormonal manipulations can produce variations in adult sexual behavior that appear to be commensurate with homosexuality [13–16]. Several studies in humans indicated that there were differences in the urinary excretion of sex hormone metabolites between heterosexual and homosexual men [17, 18]; that homosexual men excreted lower amounts of urinary testosterone than heterosexual men [19]; and that circulating testosterone levels were lower in young men who were exclusively or almost exclusively homosexual than in age-matched heterosexual men [20]. Subsequent studies have produced conflicting results, however. A number of reports have failed to demonstrate a difference between circulating testosterone concentrations in homosexual and heterosexual men [21–25], whereas a confirming report has also appeared [26]. Some investigators have found other endocrine differences between homosexual and heterosexual men, including higher levels of estradiol in male homosexuals [24], higher levels of luteinizing hormone in male homosexuals [27–29], and differences in serum lipid concentrations and urinary hormone metabolite patterns [30]. One report that found no difference in total plasma testosterone between homosexual and heterosexual men found significantly lower free plasma testosterone in homosexual subjects, accompanied by elevated circulating gonadotropins [29]. A similar controversy exists in regard to the hormonal status of homosexual women: Although some reports describe elevated levels of testosterone in the urine [19] and blood [31] of homosexual women as compared to heterosexual controls, other reports have failed to find any differences [32–34]. The methodological issues in such studies and the possible explanations for the discrepancies in results are concisely reviewed elsewhere [35, 36].

The possibility of hormonal mechanisms influencing sexual behavior in humans is not simply a theoretical exercise. Information gained from instances of excesses or deficiencies of prenatal androgen (see the discussion in Chap. 2 of the adrenogenital syndrome and testicular feminization, for example) and research into the effects of prenatal exposure to female hormones [37] indicate the probability that important aspects of sexual orientation and other components of behavior may be susceptible to early hormonal influence.

Psychosocial Considerations

Classic psychoanalytic theory views the determinants of adult homosexuality as disordered parent-child relationships or as disruption of the normal process of psychosexual development [38]. Freud, drawing on his background in biology, postulated an innate bisexuality in the human psyche, paralleling the early embryologic bisexuality of the human fetus [39]. Freud believed that elements of this innate bisexuality contributed to the universal presence of latent homosexual tendencies that might be activated under certain pathologic conditions. These classic analytic concepts were derived from clinical impression rather than from research data. Later analysts have moved away from the idea of innate psychic bisexuality and have focused instead on ways in which childhood and adolescent experiences may lead to subsequent homosexuality. However, it is interesting to note that Freud, who wrote relatively little about homosexuality, took a rather neutral stance on the subject in a letter to the mother of a homosexual son:

Homosexuality is assuredly no advantage, but it is nothing to be ashamed of, no vice, no degradation, it cannot be classified as an illness; we consider it to be a variation of the sexual development. Many highly respected individuals of ancient and modern times have been homosexuals, several of the greatest men among them (Plato, Michelangelo, Leonardo da Vinci, etc.). It is a great injustice to persecute homosexuality as a crime and cruelty, too [40].

A number of investigators have examined the family backgrounds of homosexuals in an attempt to elucidate theories of the cause of homosexuality. Bieber and coworkers examined questionnaire data provided by 77 psychoanalysts on 106 homosexual and 100 heterosexual male patients [41]. A parental pattern consisting of a close-binding, seductive, overindulgent mother who was dominant over the detached, ambivalent, or hostile father was found to characterize the histories of many of the homosexual subjects. Bene studied a group of 83 homosexual men and 84 married men who were presumed to be heterosexual; she found that the homosexual subjects more frequently had poor relationships with their fathers, who tended to be ineffective and poor role-models [42]. At the same time, there was no evidence that the homosexual men were more strongly attached to or overprotected by their mothers than heterosexual men. Other studies have also documented disturbed parental relationships in association with homosexuality [43, 44]. However, Greenblatt found that fathers of homosexual men were good, generous, dominant, and underprotective, while mothers were free of excessive protectiveness or dominance [45]. Siegelman reported that for groups of homosexuals and heterosexuals who were low on neuroticism, no differences in family relationships could be seen [46]. Siegelman's findings are compatible with the view stated by Hooker: "Disturbed parental relations are neither necessary nor sufficient conditions for homosexuality to emerge" [47].

In recent years, investigators have increasingly come to accept the view stated by Marmor in 1965, that homosexuality is "multiply determined by psychodynamic, sociocultural, biological, and situational factors" [48]. Green theorizes that children who consistently show atypical sex-role behavior are more likely than other children to develop a homosexual orientation as adults [49]. In support of this concept, Whitam found that male homosexuals described childhood patterns showing interest in dolls, cross-dressing, preference for girls as playmates, preference for being in the company of adult women rather than men, being regarded as a "sissy" by other boys, and childhood sexual interest in boys rather than girls significantly more frequently than male heterosexuals [50].

The search for a "cause" of homosexuality continues to be hindered both by methodological difficulties and by lack of homogeneity in the homosexual population. Before a more reliable taxonomy of human sexual behavior in general is developed, efforts to determine the origins of homosexual behavior are likely to be futile.

Psychological Adjustment of Homosexuals

Until very recently, homosexuality was viewed as an emotional disorder. This belief was partially a reflection of early research done on the subject that was conducted principally among populations of psychiatric patients and prisoners—hardly environments where one could expect to find psychologically healthy individuals. Nevertheless, the view that homosexuality is a disease is still held by some professionals [51, 52].

Hooker provided one of the first balanced studies assessing the psychological concomitants of homosexuality in 1957 [53]. In this investigation, 30 homosexuals and 30 heterosexuals (neither psychiatric patients nor prisoners) were matched by age, education, and IQ. The subjects were given a variety of psychological tests, the results of which were shown to a panel of expert clinical psychologists who were asked to rate each subject's personality adjustment and to identify each subject's sexual orientation from their analysis of the test results. The personality ratings for homosexual and heterosexual subjects were not significantly different, and the judges were unsuccessful in identifying subjects' sexual orientation at better than a chance level.

Saghir and coworkers conducted an extensive set of investigations on male and female homosexuality [54–57]. An important innovation of their research was in comparing homosexual subjects (male or female) with unmarried heterosexual controls, since the prevalence of certain psychiatric illnesses is higher in single persons [56]. They reported that "there was little difference demonstrated in the prevalence of psychopathology between a group of 89 male homosexuals and a control group of 35 unmarried men" [56]. In their sample of homosexual women, these workers found "slightly more clinically significant changes and disability" than among the heterosexual controls, primarily reflected in an increased rate of alcoholism and attempted suicide [57]. In both populations, however, the majority of homosexual subjects were well-adjusted, productive persons [56, 57].

In keeping with the data derived from such studies, the American Psychiatric Association officially removed the designation of homosexuality as a mental disorder in 1974. A category of "sexual orientation disturbance" was added to include persons conflicted by their sexual orientation.

The Homosexual Patient

If current estimates of the prevalence of homosexuality are accurate, most physicians deal with homosexual patients on a daily basis. The present climate of social, political, and economic forces creates pressures for homosexuals that may be compounded by the attitudes of health-care workers. Personal biases—whether stemming from ignorance, religious beliefs, or other sources—should not impinge on the right of any person, regardless of sexual orientation, to obtain competent, objective professional services in a dignified manner, including the right to obtain necessary services without having to contend with gratuitous attempts to alter one's sexual orientation.

Medical Aspects

Relatively little attention has been devoted to the medical epidemiologic ramifications of homosexuality until recently [58]. As Ritchey and Leff point out, seeking an examination for venereal disease requires an admission of sexual preference, and the reaction of health-care personnel to this fact may deter the homosexual from obtaining future care [59]. However, a relatively high rate of venereal disease in homosexual men has been documented by several screening programs. Judson and coworkers found that 48 of 419 men (11.5 percent) screened in Denver homosexual steam baths had asymptomatic gonorrhea, and 6 men (1.4 percent) had early syphilis [60]. Ritchey found 4 new cases of early syphilis and 13 cases of gonorrhea in an outreach program to control venereal disease among homosexuals [61]. Because the primary lesion in syphilis in homosexual men may be oropharyngeal or rectal, it may go unnoticed by the patient and may only present as fulminant secondary syphilis. Similarly, homosexual men who engage in anal intercourse should have rectal cultures obtained to detect gonorrhea in addition to urethral and pharyngeal cultures.

Schmerin, Gelston, and Jones reported on an increasing occurrence of amebiasis among male homosexuals who had not traveled outside the New York area [62]. They pointed out that anal intercourse followed by oral-genital sex or oral-anal contact is the probable mechanism for transmission of the infecting organism. Two cases of venereal transmission in homosexual men of multiple enteric pathogens, resulting in amebiasis, shigellosis, and giardiasis, have also been reported recently [63]. The increased incidence of a variety of colonic and rectal disorders in homosexual men has been termed the "gay bowel syndrome" by Sohn and Robilotti [64].

Other studies indicate that homosexuality may predispose to the development of hepatitis B infection. In a study of male homosexuals, 51.5 percent had serologic evidence of hepatitis B, as contrasted with only 20.4 percent among male heterosexuals [65]. A correlation was found between patterns of sexual behavior and the occurrence of serologic evidence of hepatitis B, with higher rates in those with involvement in anal intercourse primarily and those with large numbers of sexual partners. A similar survey conducted in England has confirmed these findings [66]. However, it should be pointed out that sexual transmission of hepatitis B can also occur in heterosexuals [58].

Anal intercourse among homosexual or heterosexual couples can result in infections or trauma that may require medical or surgical intervention [67, 68]. *Condyloma acuminata* were noted in 51.5 percent of the patients seen by Sohn and Robilotti, who also found nonspecific proctitis in 12 percent, anal fistulas in 11.5 percent, and perirectal abscesses in 6.9 percent of 260 male homosexuals [64]. *Chlamydia trachomatis* has been isolated from the throat and rectum of homosexual men [69]. The use of a dildo by homosexual women may result in laceration of the vagina, if done injudiciously. However, the sexual practices of homosexual men and women do not create any special health hazards that are not present at least in certain situations for heterosexuals.

Psychological and
Sociological Aspects

Homosexuals may have problems related to the social, legal, or economic pressures that they face. These problems frequently include the following categories: discovering one's homosexuality; parental rejection; encountering discrimination at school, at work, or in seeking housing; relationship problems; difficulties attendant upon leading a double life; and a sense of religious guilt [70]. Additional conflicts may arise from peer group pressures or political ideology: DeFries describes the fact that some feminist college students have been vulnerable to confusion over their sexual identity, and terms this situation pseudohomosexuality [71].

Homosexuals may experience any of the emotional problems that are seen in heterosexual populations. However, they are sometimes uniquely pressured to change the direction of their sexual orientation. Unless the individual wishes to change, such alteration should not be undertaken [72, 73]. In fact, therapists are increasingly beginning to realize that some homosexuals seek treatment in order to enhance their sexuality—a realization at marked variance with the therapists' previous practice of attempting to eradicate homosexual behavior.

The emotional stability and personal maturity of homosexuals is no different from that of heterosexuals [53, 56, 57, 74–76]. Unfortunately, a number of popular misperceptions about the nature of homosexuality are still widely accepted; for example, it is generally believed that homosexual men are effeminate and homosexual women are masculine and that homosexuals make occupational choices on the basis of their sexual orientation. While these specific stereotypes may not result in serious consequences, other myths about homosexuality—such as the incorrect notion that homosexual men frequently molest children [77]—may be much more harmful to social acceptance, occupational freedom, and civil liberties.

A recent report by Bell and Weinberg provides a large amount of statistical data concerning homosexuality and the behavior of homosexuals [78]. In this study, conducted in the San Francisco area, 686 homosexual men and 293 homosexual women were interviewed. The data led the authors to the delineation of five different homosexual typologies based on sexual experience: (1) close-coupled (living in a quasi-marriage), (2) open-coupled (living in a quasi-marriage but continuing to have a large number of other sexual partners), (3) functional (not coupled, having a large number of sexual partners, with little regret over homosexuality and few sexual problems), (4) dysfunctional (not coupled, having a large number of sexual partners, but with many sexual problems and significant regret about their homosexuality), and (5) asexual (not coupled, having low levels of sexual activity—with frequent sexual problems—and relatively low levels of sexual interest) [78]. The overall diversity of the group of study subjects was highly apparent, both from a socioeconomic and from a psychological perspective. The following statement summarizes one of the authors' conclusions:

It would appear that homosexual adults who have come to terms with their homosexuality, who do not regret their sexual orientation, and who can function effectively sexually and socially, are no more distressed psychologically than are heterosexual men and women. Clearly, the therapist who continues to believe that it is by fiat his or her job to change a homosexual client's sexual orientation is ignorant of the true issues involved. What is required, at least initially, is a consideration of why a particular person's homosexuality is problematic and to examine the ways in which his or her life-style can be made more satisfying [78].

Masters and Johnson have recently described a detailed research program focusing on homosexuality from the perspectives of both the physiology of sexual response and the results of participation in sex therapy [79]. In their physiologic studies, 94 homosexual men (age range, 21 to 54) and 82 homosexual women (age range, 20 to 54) were investigated during sexual activity in the laboratory in a fashion analogous to the methods employed for heterosexual men and women in *Human Sexual Response*. When the observations of homosexual male and female subjects were compared with data from a subset of subjects previously reported in *Human Sexual Response*, there were only minor differences in the rates of functional efficiency of sexual response cycles (see Table 17-2). Masters and Johnson summarized their findings as follows:

Not only is there no quantitative difference in capacity for orgasmic attainment when comparing men and women of different sexual preferences: There also is no significant difference found when comparing the functional facility of the two genders. . . . The central thesis developed from this research program is that no real difference exists between homosexual men and women and heterosexual men and women in their physiologic capacity to respond to similar sexual stimuli. . . . It is reasonable to speculate that, when absorbed, this finding should lead to significant modification in current cultural concepts [79].

Table 17-2. Summary Comparison of Failure Rates in Manipulative Stimulation by Gender and Preference in Homosexuals and Heterosexuals

	Sexual Preference							
	Homosexual				Heterosexual			
Gender and Type of Stimulation	Observed Cycles	Functional Failures	Failure Incidence	Failure Percentage	Observed Cycles	Functional Failures	Failure Incidence	Failure Percentage
Male[a]								
Masturbation	126	1	1:126.0	0.79	502	4	1:125.5	0.80
Partner manipulation	195	2	1:97.5	1.02	562	5	1:112.4	0.89
Fellatio	217	1	1:217.0	0.46	146	1	1:146.0	0.68
Total	538	4	1:134.5	0.75	1210	10	1:121.0	0.83
Female[b]								
Masturbation	211	2	1:105.5	0.95	812	4	1:203.0	0.49
Partner manipulation	306	2	1:153.0	0.65	1004	8	1:125.5	0.80
Cunnilingus	192	1	1:192.0	0.52	159	2	1:79.5	1.26
Total	709	5	1:141.8	0.71	1975	14	1:141.1	0.76

[a]Homosexual males, N = 94; heterosexual males, N = 343.
[b]Homosexual females, N = 82; heterosexual females, N = 338.
Source: Masters and Johnson [79].

Masters and Johnson described two different clinical situations in which homosexuals were treated. In one group, homosexual men and women who were sexually dysfunctional were treated in the dual-sex therapy team format for the specific dysfunctions of impotence or anorgasmia, respectively. In 57 impotent homosexual men, the overall failure rate after five years of followup was 10.5 percent [79]. Similarly, in 27 nonorgasmic female homosexuals, the overall treatment failure rate after five years of followup was 11.1 percent [79]. There were relatively few differences in techniques of sex therapy for the reversal of sexual dysfunction in homosexual and heterosexual couples.

In a second clinical group, homosexual men and women who wished to convert or revert to heterosexual functioning were treated. In contrast to more traditional psychotherapeutic approaches to this situation, relatively good outcomes were found (see Table 17-3). These results must be interpreted cautiously, since clients who were treated were a highly motivated group [79]; but it is clear that homosexuals who are dissatisfied with their sexual orientation may turn to health-care professionals with greater confidence about the prospects of obtaining effective treatment than they could have done in the past.

Gender and Complaint	N	F	IFR(%)	TR	OFR (%)
Male					
Conversion	9	2	22.2	1	33.3
Reversion	45	9	20.0	3	26.7
Male total	54	11	20.4	4	27.8
Female					
Conversion	3	0	0	0	0
Reversion	10	3	30.0	1	40.0
Female total	13	3	23.1	1	30.8
Male and female total	67	14	20.9	5	28.4

Table 17-3. Male and Female Homosexual Dissatisfaction: Treatment Failure Statistics

N = number of clients; F = initial treatment failures; IFR = initial failure rate; TR = treatment reversals; OFR = overall failure rate.
Source: Masters and Johnson [79].

For homosexuals who want to convert or revert to heterosexual function, a number of psychotherapeutic approaches have been employed with varying degrees of success [79–83]. Some argue that sexual orientation is essentially irreversible in adults, although behavior may still be changed [84]. In any event, it is clear that physicians and other health-care professionals must no longer stigmatize homosexuals or deprive them of needed services. There is no justification for a health-care system that penalizes people on the basis of their sexual choices.

References

1. Karlen, A. *Sexuality and Homosexuality: A New View.* New York: W. W. Norton and Co., 1971.
2. Rowse, A. L. *Homosexuals in History.* New York: Macmillan, 1977.
3. Bullough, V. L., and Bullough, B. *Sin, Sickness and Sanity—A History of Sexual Attitudes.* New York: New American Library, 1977.
4. Ford, C. S., and Beach, F. A. *Patterns of Sexual Behavior.* New York: Harper and Row, Publishers, 1951.
5. Marshall, D. S., and Suggs, R. C. *Human Sexual Behavior, Variations in the Ethnographic Spectrum.* Englewood Cliffs, N. J.: Prentice-Hall, 1972.
6. Marmor, J., and Green, R. Homosexual Behavior. In J. Money and H. Musaph (eds.), *Handbook of Sexology.* New York: Elsevier/North Holland Biomedical Press, 1977. Pp. 1051–1068.
7. Kinsey, A. C., Pomeroy, W. B., and Martin, C. E. *Sexual Behavior in the Human Male.* Philadelphia: W. B. Saunders Co., 1948.
8. Kinsey, A. C., Pomeroy, W. B., Martin, C. E., and Gebhard, P. H. *Sexual Behavior in the Human Female.* Philadelphia: W. B. Saunders Co., 1953.

9. Gebhard, P. H. Incidence of Overt Homosexuality in the United States and Western Europe. In *National Institute of Mental Health Task Force on Homosexuality: Final Report and Background Papers.* DHEW Publication No. (HSM) 72-9116. Washington, D.C.: Department of Health, Education and Welfare, 1972. Pp. 22–29.

10. Kallman, F. J. Comparative twin study on the genetic aspects of male homosexuality. *Journal of Nervous and Mental Disease* 115:283–298, 1952.

11. Davison, K., Brierley, H., and Smith, C. A male monozygotic twinship discordant for homosexuality. *British Journal of Psychiatry* 118:675–682, 1971.

12. Ranier, J. C., Mesnikoff, A., Kolb, L. C., and Carr, A. Homosexuality and heterosexuality in identical twins. *Psychosomatic Medicine* 22:251–259, 1960.

13. Dörner, G. Hormonal induction and prevention of female homosexuality. *Journal of Endocrinology* 42:163–164, 1968.

14. Dörner, G., and Hinz, G. Induction and prevention of male homosexuality by androgen. *Journal of Endocrinology* 40:387–388, 1968.

15. Dörner, G. *Hormones and Brain Differentiation.* Amsterdam: Elsevier Scientific Publishing Company, 1976.

16. Edwards, D. A. Neonatal administration of androstenedione, testosterone, or testosterone propionate: Effects on ovulation, sexual receptivity and aggressive behavior in female mice. *Physiology and Behavior* 6:223–228, 1971.

17. Margolese, M. S. Homosexuality: A new endocrine correlate. *Hormones and Behavior* 1:151–155, 1970.

18. Margolese, M. S., and Janiger, O. Androsterone/etiocholanolone ratios in male homosexuals. *British Medical Journal* 3:207–210, 1973.

19. Loraine, J. A., Ismail, A. A. A., Adamopoulos, D. A., and Dove, G. A. Endocrine function in male and female homosexuals. *British Medical Journal* 4:406–408, 1970.

20. Kolodny, R. C., Masters, W. H., Hendryx, J., and Toro, G. Plasma testosterone and semen analysis in male homosexuals. *New England Journal of Medicine* 285:1170–1174, 1971.

21. Birk, L., Williams, G. H., Chasin, M., and Rose, L. I. Serum testosterone levels in homosexual men. *New England Journal of Medicine* 289:1236–1238, 1973.

22. Tourney, G., and Hatfield, L. M. Androgen metabolism in schizophrenics, homosexuals, and normal controls. *Biological Psychiatry* 6:23–36, 1973.

23. Brodie, H. K. H., Gartrell, N., Doering, C., and Rhue, T. Plasma testosterone levels in heterosexual and homosexual men. *American Journal of Psychiatry* 131:82–83, 1974.

24. Doerr, P., Kockott, G., Vogt, H. J., Pirke, K. M., and Dittmar, F. Plasma testosterone, estradiol, and semen analysis in male homosexuals. *Archives of General Psychiatry* 29:829–833, 1973.

25. Friedman, R. C., Dyrenfurth, I., Linkie, D., Tendler, R., and Fleiss, J. L. Hormones and sexual orientation in men. *American Journal of Psychiatry* 134:571–572, 1977.

26. Starká, L., Šipová, I., and Hynie, J.   Plasma testosterone in male transsexuals and homosexuals. *Journal of Sex Research* 11:134–138, 1975.

27. Kolodny, R. C., Jacobs, L. S., Masters, W. H., Toro, G., and Daughaday, W. H.   Plasma gonadotropins and prolactin in male homosexuals. *Lancet* 2:18–20, 1972.

28. Doerr, P., Pirke, K. M., Kockott, G., and Dittmar, F.   Further studies on sex hormones in male homosexuals. *Archives of General Psychiatry* 33:611–614, 1976.

29. Rohde, W., Stahl, F., and Dörner, G.   Plasma basal levels of FSH, LH and testosterone in homosexual men. *Endokrinologie* 70:241–248, 1977.

30. Evans, R. B.   Physical and biochemical characteristics of homosexual men. *Journal of Consulting and Clinical Psychology* 39:140–147, 1972.

31. Gartrell, N. K., Loriaux, D. L., and Chase, T. N.   Plasma testosterone in homosexual and heterosexual women. *American Journal of Psychiatry* 134:117–119, 1977.

32. Griffiths, P. D., Merry, J., Browning, M. C. K., Eisinger, A. J., Huntsman, R. G., Lord, E. J. A., Polani, P. E., Tanner, J. M., and Whitehouse, R. H.   Homosexual women: An endocrine and psychological study. *Journal of Endocrinology* 63:549–556, 1974.

33. Eisinger, A. J., Huntsman, R. G., Lord, J., Merry, J., Polani, P., Tanner, J. M., Whitehouse, R. H., and Griffiths, P.   Female homosexuality. *Nature* 238:106, 1972.

34. Kolodny, R. C., and Masters, W. H.   Unpublished data, 1977.

35. Meyer-Bahlburg, H. F. L.   Sex hormones and male homosexuality in comparative perspective. *Archives of Sexual Behavior* 6:297–325, 1977.

36. Meyer-Bahlburg, H. F. L.   Sex hormones and female homosexuality: A critical examination. *Archives of Sexual Behavior* 8:101–120, 1979.

37. Yalom, I. D., Green, R., and Fisk, N.   Prenatal exposure to female hormones. *Archives of General Psychiatry* 28:554–561, 1973.

38. Brill, A. A.   *Freud's Contribution to Psychiatry*. New York: W. W. Norton and Co., 1962.

39. Stoller, R. J.   The "bedrock" of masculinity and femininity: Bisexuality. *Archives of General Psychiatry* 26:207–212, 1972.

40. Historical notes: A letter from Freud. *American Journal of Psychiatry* 107:786–787, 1951.

41. Bieber, I., Dain, H. J., Dince, P. R., Drellich, M. G., Grand, H. G., Grundlach, R. H., Kremer, M. W., Rifkin, A. H., Wilbur, C. B., and Bieber, T. B.   *Homosexuality: A Psychoanalytic Study*. New York: Basic Books, Publishers, 1962.

42. Bene, E.   On the genesis of male homosexuality: An attempt at clarifying the role of the parents. *British Journal of Psychiatry* 111:803–813, 1965.

43. West, D. J.   Parental figures in the genesis of male homosexuality. *International Journal of Social Psychiatry* 5:58–97, 1959.

44. Evans, R. B.   Childhood parental relationships of homosexual men. *Journal of Consulting and Clinical Psychology* 33:129–135, 1969.

45. Greenblatt, D. R.   Semantic Differential Analysis of the "Triangular System" Hypothesis in "Adjusted" Overt Male Homosexuals. Doctoral dissertation, University of California, 1966.

46. Siegelman, M.   Parental background of male homosexuals and hetero-sexuals. *Archives of Sexual Behavior* 3:3–18, 1974.

47. Hooker, E.   Parental relations and male homosexuality in patient and nonpatient samples. *Journal of Consulting and Clinical Psychology* 33:140–142, 1969.

48. Marmor, J. (ed).   *Sexual Inversion.* New York: Basic Books, Publishers, 1965.

49. Green, R.   *Sexual Identity Conflict in Children and Adults.* New York: Basic Books, Publishers, 1974.

50. Whitam, F. L.   Childhood indicators of male homosexuality. *Archives of Sexual Behavior* 6:89–96, 1977.

51. Socarides, C. W.   Homosexuality and medicine. *Journal of the American Medical Association* 212:1199–1202, 1970.

52. Ellis, A.   The right to be wrong. *Journal of Sex Research* 4:96–107, 1968.

53. Hooker, E.   The adjustment of the male overt homosexual. *Journal of Projective Techniques* 21:18–31, 1957.

54. Saghir, M. T., and Robins, E.   Homosexuality: I. Sexual behavior of the female homosexual. *Archives of General Psychiatry* 20:192–201, 1969.

55. Saghir, M. T., Robins, E., and Walbran, B.   Homosexuality: II. Sexual behavior of the male homosexual. *Archives of General Psychiatry* 21:219–229, 1969.

56. Saghir, M. T., Robins, E., Walbran, B., and Gentry, K.   Homosexuality: III. Psychiatric disorders and disability in the male homosexual. *American Journal of Psychiatry* 126:1079–1086, 1970.

57. Saghir, M. T., Robins, E., Walbran, B., and Gentry, K. A.   Homosexuality: IV. Psychiatric disorders and disability in the female homosexual. *American Journal of Psychiatry* 127:147–154, 1970.

58. Vaisrub, S.   Homosexuality: A risk factor in infectious disease (editorial). *Journal of the American Medical Association* 238:1402, 1977.

59. Ritchey, M. G., and Leff, A. M.   Venereal disease control among homosexuals: An outreach program. *Journal of the American Medical Association* 232:509–510, 1975.

60. Judson, F. N., Miller, K. G., and Schaffnit, T. R.   Screening for gonorrhea and syphilis in the gay baths: Denver, Colorado. *American Journal of Public Health* 67:740–742, 1977.

61. Ritchey, M. G.   Venereal disease among homosexuals (letter). *Journal of the American Medical Association* 237:767, 1977.

62. Schmerin, M. J., Gelston, A., and Jones, T. C.   Amebiasis: An increasing problem among homosexuals in New York City. *Journal of the American Medical Association* 238:1386–1387, 1977.

63. Mildvan, D., Gelb, A. M., and William, D.   Venereal transmission of enteric pathogens in male homosexuals: Two case reports. *Journal of the American Medical Association* 238:1387–1389, 1977.

64. Sohn, N., and Robilotti, J. G.   The gay bowel syndrome: A review of colonic and rectal conditions in 200 male homosexuals. *American Journal of Gastroenterology* 67:478–484, 1977.

65. Szmuness, W., Much, I., Prince, A. M., Hoofnagle, J. H., Cherubin, C. E., Harley, E. J., and Block, G. H.   On the role of sexual behavior in the

spread of hepatitis B infection. *Annals of Internal Medicine* 83:489–495, 1975.

66. Lim, K. S., Wong, V. T., Fulford, K. W. M., Catterall, R. D., Briggs, M., and Dane, D. S. Role of sexual and non-sexual practices in the transmission of hepatitis B. *British Journal of Venereal Diseases* 53:190–192, 1977.

67. Neumann, H. H. Urethritis caused by anal coitus. *Medical Aspects of Human Sexuality* 10(5):73–74, 1976.

68. Swerdlow, H. Trauma caused by anal coitus. *Medical Aspects of Human Sexuality* 10(7):93–94, 1976.

69. Goldmeier, D., and Darougar, S. Isolation of *Chlamydia trachomatis* from throat and rectum of homosexual men. *British Journal of Venereal Diseases* 53:184–185, 1977.

70. Lawrence, J. C. Gay peer counseling. *Journal of Psychiatric Nursing and Mental Health Services* 15:33–37, 1977.

71. DeFries, Z. Pseudohomosexuality in feminist students. *American Journal of Psychiatry* 133:400–404, 1976.

72. Money, J. Bisexual, homosexual, and heterosexual: Society, law, and medicine. *Journal of Homosexuality* 2:229–233, 1977.

73. Davison, G. C. Homosexuality and the ethics of behavioral intervention: I. Homosexuality, the ethical challenge. *Journal of Homosexuality* 2:195–204, 1977.

74. Siegelman, M. Adjustment of male homosexuals and heterosexuals. *Archives of Sexual Behavior* 2:9–25, 1972.

75. Siegelman, M. Adjustment of homosexual and heterosexual women. *British Journal of Psychiatry* 120:477–481, 1972.

76. Siegelman, M. Adjustment of homosexual and heterosexual women: A cross-national replication. *Archives of Sexual Behavior* 8:121–125, 1979.

77. Newton, D. E. Homosexual behavior and child molestation: A review of the evidence. *Adolescence* 13:29–43, 1978.

78. Bell, A. P., and Weinberg, M. S. *Homosexualities—A Study of Diversity Among Men and Women.* New York: Simon & Schuster, 1978.

79. Masters, W. H., and Johnson, V. E. *Homosexuality in Perspective.* Boston: Little, Brown and Co., 1979.

80. Hatterer, L. J. *Changing Homosexuality in the Male.* New York: McGraw-Hill Book Co., 1970.

81. Birk, L. Group therapy for men who are homosexual. *Journal of Sex and Marital Therapy* 1:29–52, 1974.

82. Rogers, C., Roback, H., McKee, E., and Calhoun, D. Group psychotherapy with homosexuals: A review. *International Journal of Group Psychotherapy* 26:3–27, 1976.

83. Latham, J. D., and White, G. D. Coping with homosexual expression within heterosexual marriages: Five case studies. *Journal of Sex and Marital Therapy* 4:198–212, 1978.

84. McConaghy, N. Is a homosexual orientation irreversible? *British Journal of Psychiatry* 129:556–563, 1976.

Transsexual individuals persistently feel a discordance or incongruity between their anatomic sex and their psychological orientation, a dilemma that they frequently describe as being trapped in the wrong body. Increasing awareness of the phenomenon of transsexualism and a willingness by the medical profession to pursue procedures leading to sex reassignment have coupled over the past two decades to generate considerable publicity about this subject. As a result, many individuals with widely divergent disorders have sought clinical assistance with requests for sex-change procedures. Nevertheless, transsexualism is not a disorder of recent vintage: Documentation of mythologic references to transsexualism and real persons suffering from this disorder extends back over thousands of years [1].

Although Harry Benjamin believed that he had coined the term transsexualism in 1953, the word had previously been introduced by Cauldwell in 1949 in a case description of a girl who wanted to be a boy [2]. Transsexualism became a focus of public attention via the case of Christine Jorgensen in Denmark in 1953, although it is interesting to note that the case was reported in the *Journal of the American Medical Association* as "Transvestism, Hormonal, Psychiatric and Surgical Treatment" [3], since there was not a distinction at that time between transsexualism and transvestism [4].

Although more has been written about transsexual men who want to undergo medical and surgical treatment to alter their anatomy and appearance to be congruent with their feeling of being women, there are in fact significant numbers of transsexual women who wish to undergo the reverse process. Reliable prevalence figures regarding the transsexual phenomenon are not available, although Pauly estimates the figure as 1 in 100,000 for male transsexuals and 1 in 130,000 for female transsexuals [5]. Among patients contacting gender-identity clinics or other centers that treat this disorder, there is a marked preponderance of men. Whether this reflects a differential rate of distribution between the biologic sexes or other factors, such as the relative ease of male-to-female genital reassignment surgery compared to female-to-male operations, is not known at present. Children and adolescents of either sex also may evidence inappropriate gender behavior that ranges from isolated cross-dressing to a picture that appears identical to that of the adult transsexual, including verbalization of the desire to change into the opposite sex [6–8].

Other situations may sometimes be confused with transsexualism. Transvestites dress in the clothing of the opposite sex as a means of obtaining sexual arousal, but they usually do not want a permanent change of anatomy or appearance. However, it is not unusual to obtain histories from male transsexuals of sexual arousal brought about by wearing women's clothes [9, 10]; there is considerable conflicting opinion over how to classify such persons. Buhrich and McConaghy contend that transvestism and transsexualism are two discrete syndromes, reporting that transsexuals cross-dress more fully, evidence homosexual rather than heterosexual interest, have a feminine gender identity, and desire sex reassignment surgery, while transvestites report heterosexual interest, cross-dress partially, and typically show fetishistic arousal [11]. However, these authors also believe that a subgroup of transsexual men may have elements of transvestite experience in their histories [10]. In contrast, Stoller [12], Hoenig and coworkers [13], and Baker [14] regard sexual arousal during cross-dressing as antithetical to the diagnosis of transsexualism.

At times, patients with other psychopathology may claim to want sex reassignment surgery, but careful evaluation will often reveal the lack of a consistent history and the presence of other personality or adjustment problems. In this vein, it is now clear that many patients requesting sex-change surgery are quite conversant with the relevant literature and may fabricate stories that they believe will facilitate their acceptance for surgical reassignment [15]. The mystery and drama of change-of-sex surgery and the intense publicity transsexualism has received in recent years combine to attract a variety of confused, maladjusted, and vulnerable persons to the promise of "a new life"; it has been estimated that for every applicant for whom surgery is indicated, there are at least nine others for whom it is not [16].

The effeminate male homosexual and the very masculine lesbian may sometimes request sex-revision surgery; while most authorities would not undertake such a procedure, there is currently disagreement on this point. It is not unusual for transsexuals to live in the homosexual subculture as a matter of social and sexual adaptation [17], and this may further confuse diagnostic precision. Meyer and Hoopes note as well that some homosexuals, feeling stigmatized by their sexual orientation, may attempt to camouflage it under the rubric of transsexualism [8]. Most homosexuals requesting sex-reassignment surgery will not have a long-standing desire for such a change.

Theories of Etiology

A number of authorities believe that a prenatal neuroendocrine influence provides a predisposition for the subsequent development of transsexualism [18–20]. However, endocrine studies of transsexualism are relatively few in number. Starká and coworkers reported that plasma testosterone levels in male transsexuals were lower than in normal men [21] and subsequently found plasma testosterone in transsexual women to be significantly higher than in normal women [22]. Other workers have found basal hormone levels in transsexual men and women to be generally within the normal range [19, 23–25]. Recently, Seyler and coworkers have shown that despite normal basal hormone levels, transsexual women exhibit abnormal gonadotropin secretory responses when given synthetic gonadotropin-releasing factor, showing a pattern that is intermediate between normal women and men [19]. These disparate bits of evidence require further investigation before a reasonable conclusion can be drawn.

Although transsexualism has been reported in isolated instances as associated with brain tumors [26, 27], with asymmetric enlargement of the sella turcica (suggesting the presence of a pituitary tumor) [28], and with both the 47,XYY karyotype [29, 30] and the 47,XXY karyotype characteristic of Klinefelter's syndrome [31], there is no decisive evidence indicating that these are other than chance occurrences. Pauly, in reviewing 80 cases of female transsexualism reported in the literature, noted that there is only a single report of a chromosome abnormality (XO/XX mosaicism [32]) associated with this disorder and observed that in 95 percent of cases where data were available, no significant physical abnormalities were found [33].

Psychological etiologies of transsexualism have been considered by a number of authors. Stoller, who restricts his discussion to the prototypical transsexuals whose histories reveal consistent opposite-sex behavior from early childhood on, believes that a particular parent-child relationship is the principal force in determining subsequent transsexualism [34, 35]. In the development of classic male transsexualism, he postulates a mother with a strong bisexual personality component who is unhappy or depressed and usually married to a distant, passive man. The mother is, in a sense, rejuvenated by the birth of a beautiful son, and their ensuing interaction has been described as follows:

[The mother's] desire for loving completeness with this son is profound; in her joy at holding in her arms a cure for her sadness, she finds herself unable to let go. And so, usually skin-to-skin, in the most loving embrace, she keeps her infant against her body and psyche for months and then for years. An excessively close, blissful symbiosis develops [34].

Stoller also believes that in addition to this extensive physical intimacy, the mother reinforces behavior that she perceives as feminine; this reinforcement is unopposed because the father is absent.

Stoller has theorized a different etiologic pattern for female transsexualism [35]. In these cases, he believes that the mother is typically depressed and psychologically distant from the family; the father, who is quite masculine, does not provide sufficient psychological support for his wife's depression and does not encourage the development of his daughter's femininity. The daughter, who is not perceived by her parents as beautiful or graceful and who is not cuddly as an infant, begins to show masculine interests and behavior as early as age 3 or 4. The daughter is propelled into a position of becoming a substitute male and ameliorating her mother's depression; she is encouraged in masculine behavior, which elicits love, approval, and improvement of the mother's health and family solidarity. Stoller also suggests that, in contrast with male transsexualism, the phenomenon of female transsexualism may be allied to female homosexuality [35].

Other authors perceive transsexualism as a severe defensive maneuver to counterbalance profound early identity conflict [36, 37]. Taking a more pragmatic approach, Meyer and Hoopes describe the genesis of transsexualism in terms of unconscious parental reinforcement of cross-sex behavior during early childhood, creating ambivalence and conflict about gender identity [8]. Despite all these theories, it is safe to say that there is no current certainty regarding the etiology of transsexualism: Research now in progress studying the longitudinal development of children with atypical gender identity or sex-role behavior may shed light on this topic.

Treatment

Psychotherapy of adult transsexuals has been unsuccessful in resolving the basic distress of feeling trapped in the wrong body. However, a high percentage of transsexuals may have other psychological problems, including depression, poor self-esteem, and guilt, that may be improved by counseling or psychotherapy. Derogatis and his colleagues have recently done a detailed study of the psychological profile of male transsexuals, finding that they have a characteristic symptom constellation consisting of elevated levels of depression and anxiety with significant self-depreciation, agoraphobic behaviors, and a prominent degree of alienation from other people [38]. Pauly notes that a high incidence of alcoholism and depression is seen in female transsexuals, with 14 of 80 cases he reviewed having a history of suicide attempts, although he suggests that these problems may be secondary to the underlying gender-identity problem coupled with the frustrations of not receiving adequate medical or social acceptance [33]. The importance of adequate attention to such problems has been generally ignored in the literature about transsexualism.

The successful management of the transsexual patient requires the participation of a knowledgeable team of specialists from behavioral, medical, and surgical disciplines. This does not mean that surgical intervention is always required or advisable; individual assessment must be used to determine which transsexuals will be likely to benefit from a sex-revision operation. Although some authors favor a liberal approach and would provide surgery to a wide range of candidates requesting such change [10, 29, 40], others are less willing to operate in cases that do not conform more closely to the classic transsexual pattern [12, 16, 41]. The need for caution is underscored by clear evidence that some patients professing a desire for sex-change surgery may be helped by relatively brief psychotherapy [41, 42].

The differential diagnosis of transsexualism is complicated by many variables. It now appears that the largest percentage of people contacting gender-identity programs to request change-of-sex surgery are not transsexuals at all, making apparent the necessity of detailed diagnostic procedures carried out by experienced personnel. It is unfortunate that increasing publicity about and interest in transsexualism have resulted in more than a few cases of permanent surgery being undertaken to treat individuals who were inappropriately diagnosed as transsexual.

Presurgical Management

After the initial evaluation of a transsexual has been completed, it is necessary to defer any positive decision in regard to surgery until a trial period of one to two years of living in a cross-gender role has been completed [8, 42–44]. During this time, the transsexual patient begins appropriate hormone therapy, assumes the dress of the opposite sex, and begins other cosmetic procedures that may be required.

The transsexual man is placed on a regimen of estrogens to promote feminization, while a transsexual woman is begun on testosterone therapy to induce masculinization. For the male transsexual taking daily estrogens, breast growth occurs, skin texture becomes softer, muscle strength diminishes, and the distribution of subcutaneous fat assumes a feminine pattern [43]. These are gradual changes that require months of hormone therapy. Libido decreases early in the course of treatment and growth of body hair diminishes, but preoperative electrolysis is required to eliminate facial and unwanted body hair.

Since estrogen therapy does not typically raise voice pitch, the male transsexual may wish to take voice lessons to learn to speak in a more feminine fashion. A detailed report has been made describing preoperative training in feminine skills for the male transsexual using techniques that include modeling, behavioral rehearsal, and videotape feedback [45].

Transsexual women usually require testosterone injections to suppress menstruation, increase facial and body hair growth, and deepen the voice. The hormone regimen frequently causes hypertrophy of the clitoris, but generally there is not any appreciable change in breast size. Both male and female transsexuals often report a psychological boost after beginning hormone therapy, but often there is subsequent disappointment when the observed physical changes are not as dramatic as those the patient expected. Surgery may be required to adjust breast size in transsexuals of either sex.

Prior to and during the phase of hormone therapy, before the patient begins assuming the outward appearance of the opposite gender in dress, behavior, and name, it is mandatory for the patient to obtain proper legal counsel. In some jurisdictions, a biologic male dressed in women's clothes is breaking the law; attention must also be devoted to matters of identity and changing records such as a birth certificate, driver's license, occupational license, and educational records; necessarily, if the transsexual is married, there are also legal aspects that require attention. These matters have been reviewed elsewhere [46–49].

The trial period of living, working, and dressing in the cross-gender role serves several purposes. First, this period provides a time for further assessment of the transsexual's coping abilities and general psychological health. Second, if the patient is unable to contend with pressures encountered in this phase, or wavers in his or her conviction about wanting surgery, it can be decided that surgery is unlikely to be beneficial. Third, the testing period allows the patient to determine whether he or she is making a decision that is comfortable and correct. Finally, this time is a rehearsal period during which the transsexual must undergo a careful process of socialization and learning so that postsurgical behavior will be reasonably consistent with appearance.

Surgery

The most common practice in male-to-female transsexual surgery is a single-stage procedure, although some surgeons prefer to perform the castration surgery first, followed in a second stage by penectomy and construction of an artificial vagina. In some techniques, penile skin can be used for the construction of the labia and a portion of the vagina [50–53]. In the two-stage procedure, a split-thickness skin graft from the thigh or buttock is generally used. In either operation, the dimensions of the newly created vagina are preserved by wearing a vaginally inserted form for several months to prevent constriction. Claims by some surgeons that a portion of tissue from the glans of the penis can be retained to form a functional clitoris are unsubstantiated and misleading, although the male-to-female transsexual may express interest in such a technique.

The complications that may occur after sex-reassignment surgery are varied. Malloy and coworkers reported that in 17 male transsexuals, one case each of meatal stenosis, osteitis pubis, hematoma formation, prostatitis, and vaginal stenosis were encountered [52]. Markland and Hastings estimate that use of a split-thickness skin graft of penoscrotal skin in a one-stage operation fails in 10 to 20 percent of cases because of inadequate perineal dissection or flap necrosis or infection, causing either introital stenosis or loss of vaginal depth [54]. They have devised an operation using a segment of sigmoid colon to create an artificial vagina for cases in which prior surgery has been unsuccessful. Jayaram and coworkers note an increasing incidence of surgical complications in male-to-female transsexuals, including postoperative bleeding and infection, loss of vaginal lining, vaginal stenosis, meatal stenosis, and urethral-vaginal fistula [55]. They also report a number of undesirable cosmetic results, including redundant labia, scanty labia, urinary meatus placed too high, gaping vagina, retained corpora cavernosa, and the vaginal orifice being positioned too posteriorly in relation to the labia (see Fig. 18-1). Many patients in their series had multiple complications or undesirable features. Nevertheless, although it is important that the patient understand the limits of the procedure that will be done and its possible complications, the results of male-to-female transsexual surgery are generally functionally and cosmetically adequate [8, 51, 53].

The female-to-male transsexual may undergo bilateral mastectomy with preservation of the nipples and often chooses to have a hysterectomy and ovariectomy as well. However, there is no current operation that produces an artificial penis that is functional for both urination and sexual activity [56]. The surgical techniques that have been used include creation of a tubed flap of abdominal skin and the use of labial and perineal tissue; both methods are difficult and cosmetically lacking [57]. Noe and colleagues recently reported on a series of 25 female-to-male transsexuals who underwent such surgery; half their patients

Figure 18-1. Undesirable postsurgical results in four male-to-female transsexuals. (From B. N. Jayaram, O. H. Stuteville, and I. M. Bush, Complications and undesirable results of sex-reassignment surgery in male-to-female transsexuals, *Archives of Sexual Behavior* 7:337–345, 1978.)

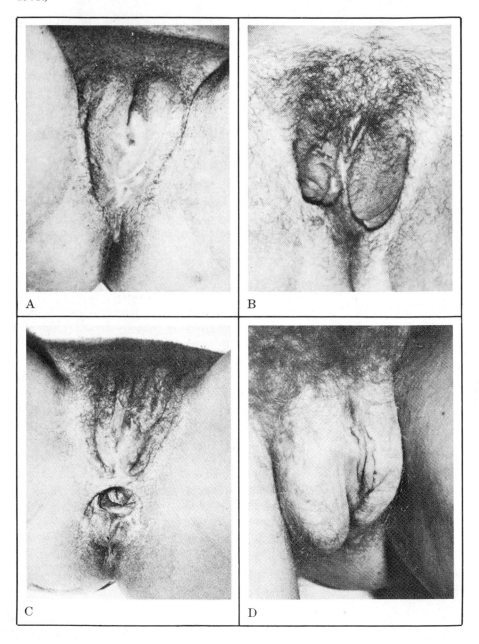

who underwent phalloplasty had complications, including 7 who required regrafting after partial loss of a skin graft and 2 who experienced dehiscence of the tube [57]. Of 10 patients who had testicular prostheses implanted, 6 experienced infection and 3 subsequently had to have the prostheses removed. Even when techniques are employed that can permit intercourse to occur by the use of mechanical aids [58], it is important to keep in mind that the penis will have no sensation at all. For this reason, along with the technical difficulties and expense of surgery, many female-to-male transsexuals decide to forego the construction of a malelike phallus. It is possible that further experience with the inflatable penile prosthesis [59] may allow a better functional result for female-to-male transsexuals who wish to have phalloplasty done. In such instances, testicular implants may also be used, with the scrotum fashioned from the labia.

Transsexual surgery is not a cure for this disorder but is merely a rehabilitative procedure that may facilitate a sense of emotional well-being. Although most patients have been initially pleased with the change of anatomic sex produced by the operation, surgery does not ameliorate the psychopathology that is present: Some transsexuals have attempted suicide, become severely depressed, had psychotic episodes, or wanted restorative surgery done after their change-of-sex operation. A recent report describes a 23-year-old male-to-female transsexual who experienced psychotic decompensation 3 days after surgery [60]. The possibility of such problems underscores the importance of careful screening and evaluation of the patient before the decision is made to utilize surgery as part of the treatment program and the marked need for adequate pre- and postoperative counseling [61].

Postsurgical
Considerations

Followup studies of transsexuals after surgery have been lacking in many regards. Benjamin reported on 51 male-to-female transsexuals followed for an average of five to six years: One-third of the group achieved a good outcome, while 14 percent had an unsatisfactory course [62]. Pauly comments that virtually all female-to-male transsexuals have been reported as showing considerable improvement after surgery, but this assessment is subject to question because "it is quite unlikely that someone is going to publish an example of a surgically treated transsexual having done poorly, in view of the controversial nature of the procedure" [33]. However, Van Putten and Fawzy described a patient who developed a paranoid psychosis five years after sex-reassignment surgery [63]. Stürup reports generally satisfactory results observed in followup on 10 cases in Denmark [64], noting that problems of family relations and stigmatization are likely to produce severe long-range stress. Several studies are now in progress with the objective of systematic followup assessment.

There are few guidelines available for counseling the families of transsexual patients. When the transsexual has children there is a particularly strong need for providing age-appropriate counseling or psychotherapy; Money and Walker point out that ideally, the transsexual should postpone sex reassignment until the children are at least in their adolescent years [65]. Education and advice must also be given to parents, siblings, and significant others in the transsexual's life. Discussion of these topics is beyond the scope of this text.

Conclusion

Much about the transsexual phenomenon is unknown at present. Despite the poor results achieved by the use of psychotherapy in patients with transsexualism, several developments are worthy of note. Barlow and his colleagues reported successful gender-identity change in a 17-year-old male transsexual treated by an intensive behavior modification program [66]. A similarly successful gender identity change has also been achieved in a 14½-year-old female transsexual by individual and milieu therapy [67]. If others can achieve similar results with transsexual patients in psychotherapy, it is possible that an entirely different approach to the management of this disorder may evolve. Green, Newman, and Stoller have described a program for treating boyhood transsexualism, working with the boy and his parents in an effort to alter gender-role behavior in the direction of masculinity [7]. If additional research data become available identifying characteristics of children at risk for subsequent transsexualism, it may be possible to move toward the development of effective prevention programs.

At the present time, it has become faddish to be in favor of surgery for transsexualism, as though this were an issue of civil rights. It is important to remember that transsexualism is an illness, rather than a normal expression of human sexuality. What appears to be most necessary is a moratorium on surgery performed without extensive research evaluation, both preoperatively and postoperatively, to determine the parameters of treatment that are most beneficial to the patient. With collaborative, multi-institutional studies and continuing efforts to determine the etiology of this disorder, it may be possible to offer patients more than a cosmetic cure.

References

1. Bullough, V. *Sexual Variance in Society and History*. New York: John Wiley & Sons, 1976.

2. Cauldwell, D. Psychopathia transexualis. *Sexology* 16:274–280, 1949.

3. Hamburger, C., Stürup, G. K., and Dahl-Iversen, E. Transvestism, hormonal, psychiatric and surgical treatment. *Journal of the American Medical Association* 152:391–396, 1953.

4. Bullough, V. L., and Bullough, B. *Sin, Sickness, and Sanity: A History of Sexual Attitudes.* New York: New American Library, 1977. P. 243.

5. Pauly, I. B. Female transsexualism: Part I. *Archives of Sexual Behavior* 3:487–507, 1974.

6. Newman, L. E. Transsexualism in adolescence: Problems in evaluation and treatment. *Archives of General Psychiatry* 23:112–121, 1970.

7. Green, R., Newman, L. E., and Stoller, R. J. Treatment of boyhood "transsexualism": An interim report of four years' experience. *Archives of General Psychiatry* 26:213–217, 1972.

8. Meyer, J. K., and Hoopes, J. E. The gender dysphoria syndromes: A position statement on so-called "transsexualism." *Plastic and Reconstructive Surgery* 54:444–451, 1974.

9. Buhrich, N., and McConaghy, N. Can fetishism occur in transsexuals? *Archives of Sexual Behavior* 6:223–235, 1977.

10. Buhrich, N., and McConaghy, N. Two clinically discrete syndromes of transsexualism. *British Journal of Psychiatry* 133:73–76, 1978.

11. Buhrich, N., and McConaghy, N. The discrete syndromes of transvestism and transsexualism. *Archives of Sexual Behavior* 6:483–495, 1977.

12. Stoller, R. J. Male transsexualism: Uneasiness. *American Journal of Psychiatry* 130:536–539, 1973.

13. Hoenig, J., Kenna, J., and Youd, A. Social and economic aspects of transsexualism. *British Journal of Psychiatry* 117:163–172, 1970.

14. Baker, H. J. Transsexualism—Problems in treatment. *American Journal of Psychiatry* 125:1412–1417, 1969.

15. Fisk, N., quoted in "Open forum: Selected proceedings of the Fourth International Conference on Gender Identity." *Archives of Sexual Behavior* 7:402, 1978.

16. Prince, V. Transsexuals and pseudotranssexuals. *Archives of Sexual Behavior* 7:263–272, 1978.

17. Levine, E. M. Male transsexuals in the homosexual subculture. *American Journal of Psychiatry* 133:1318–1321, 1976.

18. Ihlenfeld, C. L. Thoughts on the treatment of transsexuals. *Journal of Contemporary Psychotherapy* 6:63–69, 1973.

19. Seyler, L., Jr., Canalis, E., Spare, S., and Reichlin, S. Abnormal gonadotropin secretory responses to LRH in transsexual women after diethylstilbestrol priming. *Journal of Clinical Endocrinology and Metabolism* 47:176–183, 1978.

20. Dörner, G., Rohde, W., Seidel, K., Haas, W., and Schatt, G. On the evocability of a positive oestrogen feedback action on LH secretion in transsexual men and women. *Endokrinologie* 67:20–25, 1976.

21. Starká, L., Šipová, I., and Hynie, J. Plasma testosterone in male transsexuals and homosexuals. *Journal of Sex Research* 11:134–138, 1975.

22. Šipová, I., and Starká, L. Plasma testosterone values in transsexual women. *Archives of Sexual Behavior* 6:477–481, 1977.

23. Kolodny, R. C. Unpublished observation, 1979.

24. Jones, J. R., and Samimy, J.   Plasma testosterone levels and female transsexualism. *Archives of Sexual Behavior* 2:251–256, 1973.

25. Migeon, C. J., Rivarola, M. A., and Forest, M. G.   Studies of Androgens in Male Transsexual Subjects: Effects of Estrogen Therapy. In R. Green and J. Money (eds.), *Transsexualism and Sex Reassignment*. Baltimore: Johns Hopkins University Press, 1969. Pp. 203–211.

26. Blumer, D.   Transsexualism, Sexual Dysfunction, and Temporal Lobe Disorder. In R. Green and J. Money (eds.), *Transsexualism and Sex Reassignment*. Baltimore: Johns Hopkins University Press, 1969. Pp. 213–219.

27. Wålinder, J.   *Transsexualism: A Study of Forty-Three Cases*. Göteborg, Sweden: Scandinavian University Books, 1967.

28. Lundberg, P. O., Sjövall, A., and Wålinder, J.   Sella turcica in male-to-female transsexuals. *Archives of Sexual Behavior* 4:657–662, 1975.

29. Wagner, B.   Ein transsexueller mit XYY syndrom. *Nervenarzt* 45:548–551, 1974.

30. Buhrich, N., Barr, R., and Lam-Po-Tang, P. R. L. C.   Two transsexuals with 47-XYY karyotype. *British Journal of Psychiatry* 133:77–81, 1978.

31. Davidson, P. W.   Transsexualism in Klinefelter's syndrome. *Psychosomatics* 7:94–98, 1966.

32. James, S., Orwin, A., and Davies, D. W.   Sex chromosome abnormality in a patient with transsexualism. *British Medical Journal* 3:29, 1972.

33. Pauly, I. B.   Female transsexualism: Part II. *Archives of Sexual Behavior* 3:509–526, 1974.

34. Stoller, R. J.   Gender Identity. In A. M. Freedman, H. I. Kaplan, and B. J. Sadock (eds.), *Comprehensive Textbook of Psychiatry: II*. Baltimore: Williams & Wilkins Co., 1975. Pp. 1400–1408.

35. Stoller, R. J.   Etiological factors in female transsexualism: A first approximation. *Archives of Sexual Behavior* 2:47–64, 1972.

36. Person, E. S., and Ovesey, L.   The Psychodynamics of Male Transsexualism. In R. M. Friedman, R. L. Richart, and R. L. Vande Wiele (eds.), *Sex Differences in Behavior*. New York: John Wiley & Sons, 1974. Pp. 315–325.

37. Socarides, C.   A psychoanalytic study of the desire for sexual transformation (transsexualism): The plaster-of-Paris man. *International Journal of Psychoanalysis* 51:341–349, 1970.

38. Derogatis, L. R., Meyer, J. K., and Vazquez, N.   A psychological profile of the transsexual: I. The male. *Journal of Nervous and Mental Disease* 166:234–254, 1978.

39. Fisk, N. M.   Five spectacular results. *Archives of Sexual Behavior* 7:351–369, 1978.

40. Money, J.   Open forum. *Archives of Sexual Behavior* 7:390–391, 1978.

41. Morgan, A. J., Jr.   Psychotherapy for transsexual candidates screened out of surgery. *Archives of Sexual Behavior* 7:273–283, 1978.

42. Kirkpatrick, M., and Friedman, C. T. H.   Treatment of requests for sex-change surgery with psychotherapy. *American Journal of Psychiatry* 133:1194–1196, 1976.

43. *An Outline of Medical Management of the Transsexual: Endocrinology,*

Surgery, Psychiatry. Baton Rouge, La.: Erickson Educational Foundation, 1973.

44. Green, R., and Money, J. (eds.). *Transsexualism and Sex Reassignment*. Baltimore: Johns Hopkins University Press, 1969.

45. Yardley, K. M. Training in feminine skills in a male transsexual: A pre-operative procedure. *British Journal of Medical Psychology* 49:329–339, 1976.

46. Presser, C. S. Legal problems attendant to sex reassignment surgery. *Journal of Legal Medicine* 5(4):17–24, April 1977.

47. Holloway, J. P. Transsexuals: Legal considerations. *Archives of Sexual Behavior* 3:33–50, 1974.

48. *Legal Aspects of Transsexualism and Information on Administrative Procedures* (3rd ed.). Baton Rouge, La.: Erickson Educational Foundation, 1973.

49. Belli, M. M. Transsexual surgery: A new tort? *Journal of the American Medical Association* 239:2143–2148, 1978.

50. Pandya, N. J., and Stuteville, O. H. A one-stage technique for constructing female external genitalia in male transsexuals. *British Journal of Plastic Surgery* 26:277–282, 1973.

51. Granato, R. C. Surgical approach to male transsexualism. *Urology* 3:792–796, 1974.

52. Malloy, T. R., Noone, R. B., and Morgan, A. J. Experience with the 1-stage surgical approach for constructing female genitalia in male transsexuals. *Journal of Urology* 116:335–337, 1976.

53. Wesser, D. R. A single stage operative technique for castration, vaginal construction and perineoplasty in transsexuals. *Archives of Sexual Behavior* 7:309–312, 1978.

54. Markland, C., and Hastings, D. Vaginal reconstruction using bowel segments in male-to-female transsexuals. *Archives of Sexual Behavior* 7:305–307, 1978.

55. Jayaram, B. N., Stuteville, O. H., and Bush, I. M. Complications and undesirable results of sex-reassignment surgery in male-to-female transsexuals. *Archives of Sexual Behavior* 7:337–345, 1978.

56. *Guidelines for Transsexuals*. Baton Rouge, La.: Erickson Educational Foundation, 1976.

57. Noe, J. M., Sato, R., Coleman, C., and Laub, D. R. Construction of male genitalia: The Stanford experience. *Archives of Sexual Behavior* 7:297–303, 1978.

58. Noe, J. M., Laub, D. R., and Schulz, W. The External Male Genitalia: The Interplay of Surgery and Mechanical Prostheses. In J. K. Meyer (ed.), *Clinical Management of Sexual Disorders*. Baltimore: Williams & Wilkins Co., 1976. Pp. 252–264.

59. Puckett, C. L., and Montie, J. E. Construction of male genitalia in the transsexual using a tubed groin flap for the penis and a hydraulic inflation device. *Plastic and Reconstructive Surgery* 61:523–530, 1978.

60. Childs, A. Acute symbiotic psychosis in a postoperative transsexual. *Archives of Sexual Behavior* 6:37–44, 1977.

61. Lothstein, L. M. The psychological management and treatment of hos-

pitalized transsexuals. *Journal of Nervous and Mental Disease* 166:255–262, 1978.

62. Benjamin, M.   *The Transsexual Phenomenon*. New York: Julian Press, 1966.

63. Van Putten, T., and Fawzy, F. I.   Sex conversion surgery in a man with severe gender dysphoria: A tragic outcome. *Archives of General Psychiatry* 33:751–753, 1976.

64. Stürup, G. K.   Male transsexuals: A long-term follow-up after sex reassignment operations. *Acta Psychiatrica Scandinavica* 53:51–63, 1976.

65. Money, J., and Walker, P. A.   Counseling the Transsexual. In J. Money and H. Musaph (eds.), *Handbook of Sexology*. Amsterdam: Excerpta Medica, 1977. Pp. 1289–1301.

66. Barlow, D. H., Reynolds, E. J., and Agras, W. S.   Gender identity change in a transsexual. *Archives of General Psychiatry* 28:569–576, 1973.

67. Davenport, C. W., and Harrison, S. I.   Gender identity change in a female adolescent transsexual. *Archives of Sexual Behavior* 6:327–340, 1977.

19

Concepts of Sex Therapy

Until the last decade the treatment of sexual problems was largely regarded as the domain of psychiatry [1], with the general theoretic assumption being that sexual dysfunction was a symptom of a deeper personality conflict that required therapeutic identification and resolution. Traditional approaches to the patient with a sexual problem, utilizing a psychoanalytic or psychoanalytically-oriented model, were of lengthy duration and were often unsatisfactory in outcome [2, 3]. The publication in 1970 of *Human Sexual Inadequacy* [4] documented the existence of an effective approach to the psychotherapy of sexual difficulties in a rapid treatment format. This chapter will discuss the essential characteristics of that therapy model.

Background

The data reported in *Human Sexual Inadequacy* in 1970 grew out of a research program that was conceptualized in 1958 and implemented in 1959. At that time, the expertise generally required in the treatment of sexual disorders was severely lacking. "It seemed that sexually dysfunctional patients were being treated with professional insight drawn either from the psychotherapist's own sexual experience—good, bad, or indifferent as it may have been—or from anecdotal material provided by previous patients" [5].

Since 1970, many professionals have modified or extended the treatment program described in *Human Sexual Inadequacy* from the viewpoint of style, format, and content of therapy. Numerous publications have described or reviewed these approaches [1, 3, 6–20]. At the same time, the availability of additional clinical material and followup data, information gained in teaching, and input from other professionals (both theoretical and practical) has contributed to an evolution of the sex therapy program at the Masters & Johnson Institute. In most instances, the changes that have occurred represent modest refinements of the original procedures or techniques rather than marked departures from previous practice. This represents, in a sense, an affirmation of the utility and soundness of the original conceptual model.

Integrating Biologic and Psychosocial Information

One of the central premises of sex therapy is the necessity for recognizing the importance of the anatomic and physiologic components of sexual function and sexual behavior and integrating this information with the knowledge and skills requisite for good psychotherapy. The effective incorporation of both biologic and psychosocial knowledge into sex therapy accomplishes the following: (1) it assists in the initial evaluation of patients to eliminate those whose sexual dysfunction is attributable solely to an organic etiology, for whom a course of psychotherapy would be unwarranted; (2) it provides a means for assessing improvement in sexual functioning during sex therapy; (3) it allows the therapists to formulate suggestions that take into account dimensions of the health status and physical condition of their patients, as well as their psychological patterns (also giving the therapists a clearer view of how physical and psychosocial facts interact in determining feelings and behavior); and (4) it provides a data base from which many questions related to sexual anatomy or physiology may be answered. Gathering specific information about the anatomic and physiologic background of each case is done by conducting a thorough medical history, physical examination, and laboratory evaluation of both sexual partners. The laboratory tests routinely conducted on each person for this purpose are listed below.

Both Males and Females

Complete blood count
Urinalysis
VDRL
Serum thyroxine
Phosphorus
Iron
Total protein
Albumin
Glucose
Blood urea nitrogen (BUN)
Creatinine
Sodium

Potassium
Cloride
Uric acid
Calcium
Cholesterol
Triglycerides
Total bilirubin
Alkaline phosphatase
SGOT
SGPT
LDH
CPK

Females Only

Pap smear
Vaginal culture
Serum estrogens

Males Only

Serum testosterone

Since on many occasions a sexually dysfunctional person has blamed the difficulty on a medical problem, which usually allows him or her to feel less threatened and less responsible for doing something about it, it is important to have accurate information to assist in determining the role of organic contributors to the distress. The relevance of this approach is even more apparent once it is recognized that in some cases of sexual dysfunction, the cause is primarily ignorance of sexual physiology [4].

Sex as a Natural Function

Another concept underlying the direct therapy of sexual dysfunction is the view that sex is a natural function [4]. Although it is clear that human sexual *behavior* depends heavily on social learning and personality dynamics in addition to organic factors such as hormonal status, it is equally clear that the reflexes of human sexual response are present from the moment of birth. To define sex as *natural* means that just as an individual cannot be taught how to sweat or how to digest food, a man cannot be taught to have an erection, nor can a woman be taught how to lubricate vaginally. Because the reflex pathways of sexual functioning are inborn does not mean that they are immune from disruption due to impaired health, cultural conditioning, or interpersonal distress.

Many patients undertake sex therapy believing that they will be taught the desired sexual responses. This is a mistaken assumption. It is usually possible to identify the obstacles to effective sexual functioning that are present in an individual situation and that have removed sex from its natural context, and to suggest ways of removing or circumventing these obstacles. When this process is accomplished, natural function takes over promptly in most instances. This partially explains the dramatic changes that may be seen in patients with sexual dysfunction of marked chronicity in a brief but intensive therapy experience.

Although sexual responsivity is a natural psychophysiologic process, many learned behaviors or attitudes may be maladaptive from the viewpoint of sexual functioning—that is, they may interfere with rather than enhancing (or at least leaving undisturbed) the natural set of sexual reflexes. For example, people who have learned that the more they work at something, the better they get (or the more success they attain) are apt to find that working at sex produces more problems than it solves, because it diminishes spontaneity and introduces pressure into the situation [21]. Because it appears that elements such as cultural conditioning, childhood attitudes toward sex, ineffective communications, and a host of other circumstances may lead to sexual dysfunction (see Chaps. 20 and 21), one of the most important conceptual departures from traditional psychiatric thought that Masters and Johnson emphasized was the fact that sexual dysfunctions are not necessarily symptoms of underlying personality conflict or psychopathology. Both the practical and the theoretic ramifications of this position were very real: The former facilitated the development of a rapid treatment approach, while the latter disputed the view of psychoanalysts who avoided dealing with sexual symptoms, which they regarded as (1) simply surface manifestations of deeper problems that required attention, (2) useful motivators to the continuance of therapy, and (3) likely either to relapse or to be replaced by other symptoms, if the underlying problems were not adequately resolved.

In spite of the impressive results of numerous variations of direct, time-limited approaches to treating sexual dysfunction, there is still controversy on the question of how often sexual difficulties occur independently of personality disorders, psychoneuroses, or psychosis. Maurice and Guze [22] found that the majority of 20 couples they evaluated who had been treated for sexual dysfunction by Masters and Johnson were free of associated psychiatric disorders, and concluded that "sexual dysfunction may be seen in the absence of associated psychiatric disorders." On the other hand, O'Connor and Stern classified 65 percent of 96 patients with sexual problems as having character disorders, 33 percent as neurotic, and 2 percent as schizophrenic [17]. Such disagreement may be attributable in part to differing diagnostic criteria and patient populations.

Fears of Performance

Closely allied to the view that sexual dysfunction may exist independently of intrapsychic conflict was recognition of the importance of fears of sexual performance as a significant element in the genesis or perpetuation of sexual difficulties. Anxiety about sexual performance or responsivity may affect both men and women, although the immediate result of such performance anxieties in men—loss of erection—is for obvious reasons more visible and more limiting within the context of a typical sexual encounter. Fears of performance may lead to diminished interest in sex (avoidance), loss of self-esteem, attempts to control the anxiety by working hard to overcome it (with an added loss of spontaneity further compounding the problem), and alterations in the nonsexual aspects of a relationship. In addition, fears of performance characteristically lead to one or both partners' assuming a spectator role in their sexual interaction: They observe and evaluate their own or their partner's sexual response as a means of relieving performance anxieties by seeing if everything is okay. The almost preordained result of this spectator role is a reduction in the degree of involvement in the sexual activity, brought about by the distraction of watching and assessing the physical response patterns. The loss of intimacy that also occurs in such a situation, which is like having a third party in the bedroom to rate the sexual progress and activity, usually combines with the elements of distraction, heightened expectations, preexisting fears, and lessened personal involvement to dampen the sexual reflexes to the point where natural responsiveness is difficult if not impossible. (It is interesting to note that some people *without* performance anxieties may experience a heightened degree of sexual excitation or sense of involvement by assuming a spectator role, such as by watching themselves and their partner in a mirror during sexual activity. The presence or subsequent introduction of fears of performance thus appears to be the crucial variable.)

Because the spectator role usually associated with fears of performance further handicaps the possibility for a natural, relaxed, spontaneous sexual encounter, the resulting sexual failure reinforces the preexisting performance anxieties, and a self-perpetuating cycle is established. Identifying the presence of such a maladaptive pattern and providing insight into the dynamics of the situation as well as specific guidance for means of overcoming the dilemma is a central task of sex therapy. In particular, pointing out how each sexual partner contributes to such a pattern, directly or indirectly, is a necessary part of such an approach. For example, performance anxieties may arise from misperceptions of one partner's sexual expectations; they may also arise from a direct comment made in relation to sexual activity ("Were you tired tonight, dear?" or "You're not as young as you used to be"). The woman who experiences difficulty in becoming sexually aroused or in being orgasmic is just as susceptible to fears of performance and assuming the spectator's role as is the impotent male. Finally, educating each partner about the particular sexual anxieties and vulnerabilities of the other may be required to help the situation. The partners may be unwittingly fueling each other's anxieties and apprehensions as much by their omissions as by their commissions.

Principles of Conjoint Therapy

The preceding discussion illustrates one reason for working with couples in the treatment of sexual dysfunction: Frequently the behaviors, attitudes, or anxieties of one person have decided impact on the sexual function and satisfaction of his or her partner. This was one element in the early recognition of the fact that there is no such thing as an uninvolved partner in a committed relationship in which there is any form of sexual distress. The meaning of this general observation has been misunderstood and misapplied, however. It is important to recognize that no implication of causality is necessarily inherent in such a view [5], since it is often clear that the origins of one person's sexual difficulties may have preceded the relationship that presents for treatment by years. In addition, sexual problems may occur for a large number of reasons that are unrelated to the functional partner, including such common etiologies as depression, drug use, medical illness, or extramarital sexual involvement. The sexually functional partner is then typically involved in the problem to the extent that the sexual difficulty creates other problems in nonsexual areas of the relationship.

The utility of the conjoint therapy model extends in many directions, only a few of which will be addressed here. In individual therapy, the nonparticipating partner in a sexual relationship is sometimes placed in a difficult position in the process of assimilating therapeutic suggestions into a real-life situation. In addition, because sexual difficulties often derive from or are associated with poor communication patterns, to address only one component (the sexual) while avoiding scrutiny of the other (communication processes in general) is to misread the ways in which these components influence each other. Although effective sexual response cannot be taught, effective means of communication *can* be taught and frequently serve as a direct catalyst in the establishment of a pleasurable and satisfying sexual interaction.

Participation by the couple in therapy also provides a means of accurately assessing the expectations that each partner has of the other in both sexual and social dimensions. At times these expectations may be central to the sexual dysfunction and require open discussion or demonstration of how they may be adversely affecting the partner. The man who has difficulty controlling his speed of ejaculation may be pushed into impotence by his perception that his partner expects long periods of thrusting that he is unable to provide (this can occur whether or not the woman actually has such expectations). In either case, it is essential that this situation be explored with both partners, and this example serves to illustrate the extent to which both people are involved in the sexual distress, although one may be functioning in quite a normal fashion. A similar situation may develop when a woman feels that her partner expects her to be orgasmic in every coital experience in order to prove how proficient he is. The pressure to perform that arises from such expectations, real or imagined, may destroy the spontaneity of the situation and result in her loss of orgasmic return.

Bias, memory lapse, or deliberate deception in conversations with the therapy team are far less likely to occur when both partners are present. In a sense, the conjoint therapy format has a built-in means of validation of information, which is helpful far more often than might be imagined. For example, the impotent man who is still contending with fears of performance may describe having poor-quality erections in a touching experience, only to be interrupted by his surprised partner who reports enthusiastically that he had a firm erection for quite a while. Obviously, in such a situation the man's anxiety level has altered his perception of the actual occurrence, and his partner is providing more objective information. This objectivity is possible because it is the physical event rather than the feelings associated with the event that is the fact in question. Similarly, many women are quite unsure of their degree of vaginal lubrication, whereas their partners can often provide information on this point. These brief examples simply serve to highlight input that would be missing from an individual therapy setting and would therefore detract from the accuracy of assessment that a therapist might make.

Finally, one partner may raise a question that the other person has but is reluctant to ask. At times it may be surprising how critical such a question or the problem raised in the question is. A parallel principle is utilized by obtaining separate histories from the man and the woman; material volunteered by one partner may provide an important key to problems that ostensibly involve the other partner. For example, a man who described impotence that had begun abruptly three years earlier denied any stressful occurrences in his life within the months prior to the onset of his dysfunction. His wife remembered that he had been passed over for a major promotion at work, while his best friend won the new job. Because this man's self-esteem was closely related to his perception of his success and competence in his profession, this information was vital to the treatment of the impotence, but it might never have been elicited from the husband alone.

When the conjoint model is used, the emphasis is continually placed on the fact that it is the *relationship* that is in therapy. This attitude reduces the likelihood that the sexually dysfunctional partner will be seen as the patient while the functional partner regards himself or herself as another therapist, which can create multiple therapeutic difficulties.

Dual-Sex Therapy Teams

Equally as important as treating the relationship rather than singling out either individual as the patient is the use of a male-female therapy team in the treatment of sexual difficulties. In *Human Sexual Inadequacy* it was noted that the dual-sex therapy team provided each partner with "a friend in court as well as an interpreter," a statement that requires clarification. The concept of the friend in court was not intended to convey the idea of an advocate who—as a lawyer might—would defend his or her client against the opposition. Instead, the role of each cotherapist may be conceptualized as providing a same-sex listener whose ability to understand and relate to the feelings and behaviors being described is broader than that of an opposite-sex listener. Similarly, the male or female cotherapist, in theory, is better able to explain concepts or facts to the same-sex client and the therapist of the opposite sex.

A woman who has been trying for years to explain to her husband that she needs communication and the sharing of feelings outside the bedroom before she is comfortable moving into a sexual situation may be immeasurably aided by the female cotherapist's developing such information both to the woman's husband and to her male cotherapist, who will then be able to amplify on this area from the male viewpoint in discussion that the husband might otherwise summarily dismiss. Such discussions might involve specifically sexual information as well as essentially nonsexual information.

It is imperative that neither cotherapist become an advocate for one partner, since this will usually be at the expense of the other partner. The cotherapy team necessarily shares a responsibility toward the relationship under treatment. To uphold this responsibility it may at times be necessary to confront one or both clients with evidence of maladaptive behavior, but it is essential that the definition of what is maladaptive emanate from the goals of the couple and not from those of the therapists, since patterns that may be interpreted as maladaptive for one couple may constitute a valuable and gratifying coping mechanism for another. Therefore, such confrontation must be done in a manner that clearly points to what is best for the relationship by terms previously or concurrently established by the partners in the relationship.

Another way of conceptualizing the role of the cotherapy team is to regard the team as holding up a mirror to the present relationship. Although this may be achieved in a variety of ways, it allows people to look at how they are perceived by others in what they say and what they do, giving them a chance to get a glimpse of themselves (the reflection in the mirror) in a way that may be more objective than their self-perception has been:

A man who is an important West Coast executive is being seen with his wife, who is nonorgasmic and very uninterested in sex. He is very articulate and precise. She has a difficult time expressing herself and does so in an uncertain manner. Early in therapy she is adamant in stating that he must not care much about her because he ignores whatever she says. He completely denies this, claiming that he always listens carefully to her and incorporates her feelings into his decisions. She is on the verge of tears with frustration and anger, and says, "I'm just trying to explain how I feel." He answers, "That's irrelevant." The male therapist repeats these words several times, until the husband realizes how accurate his wife's perception was. He states at the conclusion of therapy that that interchange gave him a first glimpse of how he was subjugating his wife. The woman is orgasmic with intercourse for the first time in her life during the course of therapy.

To function in this mirroring manner, reflecting the content or style of a relationship, the cotherapists must make it clear that they are doing so in a nonblaming, nunjudgmental way. Rather than pointing an accusing finger, what they are saying is, "This is how you come across to me. Is this what you mean to say? Is this how you want to act?" The effectiveness of this approach is considerable. This method of reflective teaching may be extended by replaying a tape recording to allow a couple to hear how they sound and to get a clearer view of their communicative interaction.

The dangers of an individual therapist counseling a couple have been enumerated by Lederer and Jackson [23]; they include the possibilities of the therapist taking sides with one spouse, the therapist becoming judgmental and blaming one spouse, the therapist concluding that the couple is mismatched and overtly contributing to the dissolution of the marriage, and the therapist viewing one spouse as "sicker" and therefore elevating the "well" spouse to the role of assistant therapist. In addition to these dangers, it is far more difficult for an individual therapist to recognize and cope with counter-transference than for a cotherapy team to do so. The individual therapist is also limited and biased by his or her own sexuality and sexual experience; inadvertently, such bias and limitations will become apparent in the therapy setting without the balancing forces made possible by the dual-sex therapy team approach.

In *Human Sexual Inadequacy*, Masters and Johnson described briefly the fact that transference is always present in the client-therapist relationship but stressed the need to minimize the importance of the transference phenomenon. It is necessary to understand that a rapid treatment format does not allow time to develop the classic transference interaction and insights. Furthermore, therapeutic emphasis on the classic patterns of transference would obviously distract the focus of therapy from the relationship between the client-couple to relationships between the individual client and either or both cotherapists. Clients with prior experience in analytically oriented psychotherapy often demand, overtly as well as covertly, a chance to nurture and discuss transference dynamics; this frequently slows progress in therapy because it diminishes attention to communication processes and sharing of feelings within the client-couple relationship.

It is helpful to recognize the distinction between a full working-through of transference and ways in which elements of the transference relationship may be utilized in acute situations. A good example of the use of transference within the rapid treatment format is the approach to the reversal of vaginismus by client education and instruction in the use of a series of graduated vaginal dilators. It is usually necessary to foster an extraordinary degree of trust on the part of the female client toward the therapist who is performing the pelvic examinations and initially introducing the smallest dilators into use. For a day or two, as the woman is gaining confidence in her ability to overcome a situation that had previously been painful and frustrating, her partner's participation in the use of dilators is typically kept at a minimum. Deliberate development of this aspect of a transference relationship has been found to be highly effective in allowing prompt reversal of the vaginismus so that the couple can focus on their sexual interaction without fear of vaginal spasm interfering. Of course, a transition period is then needed to downplay the transference; this transition is usually accomplished by repeatedly stressing to the woman the extent to which she has been the one who changed and the one who brought about the change. Emphasis is placed on the catalytic role played by the cotherapists in such a situation.

Closely directed transference, then, is employed on a regular basis by the cotherapy team as a means of setting the stage for a couple to develop a more effective focus on their own interaction. Needless to say, this technique must be individualized on the basis of the needs and personalities of the individuals in each client relationship. While such techniques do not involve the full development and working-through of transference in the classic sense, there is significant therapeutic attention directed to transference phenomena.

That the dual-sex therapy team's functions of educating, modeling, and providing both overt and covert permission to be sexual are parentlike is beyond dispute. This aspect undoubtedly constitutes one of the strengths of the therapy format. In fact, some people view this as further evidence of the use of transference dynamics that are purposely directed toward permitting individuals to reduce guilt feelings associated with sex. Open discussions and the nonjudgmental attitudes of the therapists, combined with their aura of authority, certainly lessen such guilt. However, the differences between the cotherapists' roles and parental roles are so wide that this explanation seems of only limited usefulness. In particular, the care taken by the cotherapy team not to impose values or moral postures on the couple in treatment contrasts sharply with parental roles. In addition, it is not up to the therapy team to make decisions for a couple or for an individual, though they are frequently asked to do so; it is certainly not the therapists' right to be punitive; and it is extremely important that neither therapist become emotionally invested in the lives or experiences of the people they are treating.

The Rapid Treatment Format

Although a number of authors contend that there are few conceptual differences in sex therapy done on a weekly basis rather than a daily basis [1, 7, 8, 14, 16], and claims have been made for a similar outcome for these two approaches [7, 11, 14, 16], the Masters & Johnson Institute continues to employ a daily treatment format over a two-week period. This format provides for a degree of day-to-day continuity that appears to be beneficial in certain aspects of sex therapy such as anxiety reduction, understanding of therapeutic suggestions, and rapidity of attention to treatment crises. However, it is also necessary to note that since most couples participating in this treatment program do so during a period of social isolation (living in a hotel rather than at home; not going to work; not seeing family or friends socially, in order to devote time and energy to therapy), it is difficult to ascertain the specific contribution of the time framework as opposed to the other changes in life-style that occur.

There is something to be said for the value of treating people in the situation of their daily lives, including the stresses of work, time commitments, family obligations, and other elements of reality; if therapy is successful in this context, there will be no need to transpose what has occurred on a "vacation" under more or less special circumstances (e.g., no distractions from children, lots of time together, little element of physical fatigue) back to the home environment. On the other hand, there are good precedents in medical practice (for example, use of a diabetic teaching unit for live-in patients to receive a comprehensive and intensive educational exposure and participation) that illustrate the fact that the rapid, intensive approach is also highly beneficial and may succeed where a less intensive experience fails because of diminishing interest, distraction from other sources, or lack of seeing relatively quick results. A most important part of the sex therapy experience is the interaction within the relationship that occurs during the time when the partners are not with their therapists. The intensity of a daily therapy process catalyzes the focus of energies and attention on the relationship in both its sexual and nonsexual dimensions. A common problem encountered by clinicians who see couples on a weekly basis is that often excuses are found to avoid focusing this interaction outside of the therapy sessions. The Institute's clinical experience, which is not rigidly controlled from a research viewpoint, indicates that there is a modest loss of efficacy when either the daily treatment format or the social isolation component is not used.

History-Taking and Initial Assessment

History-taking is typically accomplished in one day, with each client being interviewed separately. After a brief introductory discussion involving both cotherapists and the couple, the first history is obtained on a same-sex basis—that is, the male cotherapist interviews the male client and the female cotherapist interviews the female client. During this session, which typically lasts from 1½ to 2½ hours, a detailed psychosocial history is obtained in addition to an in-depth examination of the sexual history. The clients are then given a lunch break, after which a second interview is done with the male cotherapist interviewing the woman and the female cotherapist interviewing the man. These second histories are typically shorter and are supplementary to the initial history; they do not cover the same ground except in instances in which clarification or verification is needed. Data collection at the outset of therapy is completed by the performance of a complete physical examination for each client and by obtaining a blood sample for laboratory evaluation.

After the histories have been obtained and the physical examinations have been done, the cotherapists meet to exchange information and to formulate a rational approach to the problems and personalities of the couple with whom they are working. Based on this exchange of information, a series of preliminary answers are reached concerning the following questions:

1. What are the specific sexual dysfunctions?
2. What are the etiologies of these dysfunctions?
3. What are the major nonsexual problems of the couple?
4. What are the major sexual problems of the couple apart from the specific dysfunctional states?

5. What, if any, psychopathology exists in either individual and how might this influence therapy?
6. What, if any, physical problems exist in either individual and how might these influence therapy?
7. What degree of motivation for therapy does each individual have?
8. Are there any areas of information that one individual requests be withheld from his or her partner?
9. Are there major discrepancies in historical information?
10. What are the objectives each individual has in terms of therapy? Are these objectives realistic?
11. Is a rapid, intensive psychotherapy program suitable for this couple?

Most frequently, the answers to these questions are readily apparent. At times, however, additional information may be needed before going on. This information may be gained by further individual interviewing or by conjoint interviewing, depending on the situation. Infrequently, the needed information can only be obtained during the course of subsequent therapy, since accurate assessment of such factors as motivation, psychopathology, and interactional dynamics cannot always be obtained from history-taking alone.

It must be stressed that the preliminary formulations reached after one day's interviewing are not viewed as final. Errors may arise through the cotherapists' incorrect interpretation of historical data, lack of clear comprehension of historical fact, or omission of questioning in areas of significance. Likewise, incorrect answers may have been given by the clients either because of misunderstanding of a question, faulty recollection, deliberate deception, or an attempt to provide what they believed the interviewer "wanted" to hear. In the course of treatment, objectives may change, new problems may surface, and degrees of motivation may fluctuate. Nevertheless, it is helpful to examine each question in some detail to comprehend more fully the wide variety of approaches that may be used at the time of the roundtable discussion.

Identifying the specific sexual dysfunction(s) is not always as simple as it sounds. For example, it may not be clear if the husband of a woman with severe vaginismus is impotent or if the wife of a man with premature ejaculation is nonorgasmic with intercourse. Sexual aversion occasionally may be mistakenly diagnosed as impotence, vaginismus, or dyspareunia. Individuals with a low sex drive may be using a dysfunctional label as an excuse to avoid sexual activity that they perceive as tedious; while this is clearly not an aversive situation, their partner may be thoroughly convinced that impotence or dyspareunia is present. For obvious reasons, establishing accurate diagnoses is imperative to allow an appropriate focus in therapy. This is most often done through a careful and detailed history obtained from both partners.

Once the specific dysfunctional diagnoses are established, assessment of the etiologic possibilities is necessary. Although it is not always possible to establish the precise etiology of a sexual dysfunction—and certainly this may be more difficult early in therapy than after additional time has passed when the therapists have the opportunity to observe the results of a therapeutic trial—it usually is possible to attribute the sexual distress(es) to organic or psychogenic processes with a high degree of accuracy. Of course, there are frequently times when elements that are both organic and psychogenic are acting together to produce the dysfunctional state. An example of this would be the impotent male whose difficulty in erective functioning began as a manifestation of a side effect of an antihypertensive drug he was using, but who subsequently developed such a strong fear of performance that the impotence persisted even after the drug was stopped. Likewise, a woman with dyspareunia due to irritation of remnants of the hymen may develop vaginismus as a protective response; even after the cause of the dyspareunia is corrected, the vaginismus may continue on a purely psychogenic basis. The importance of establishing an etiologic diagnosis as accurately as possible lies in the need to provide appropriate treatment methods, such as hormone replacement in thyroid or gonadal deficiencies, changes in medications that may be adversely affecting sexual functioning, and even surgical intervention when required, at the same time as or prior to psychotherapeutic intervention. If a necessary medical treatment is omitted, even the most sensitive and supportive psychotherapeutic approach understandably may produce a high level of frustration in the couple being treated.

Major Nonsexual Problem Areas

Identifying the major nonsexual problems of a couple is of critical importance to the initial focus of therapy. When a significant degree of hostility or distrust exists, it would be foolish to proceed with an emphasis on the sexual interaction alone. Many times, long-standing patterns of overt and covert hostility derive from frustration over lack of sexual gratification, but it is not unusual to encounter instances in which it appears that hostility in other areas of life has carried over to the sexual relationship with severely detrimental impact. Examples of areas of conflict that might precipitate sexual distress if not resolved include disagreements about child-rearing, problems with in-laws, conflicts between professional and personal priorities, financial troubles, and major cultural or religious differences. When hostility is a significant problem, whatever its origin, early therapeutic attention must be directed toward dissipating this maladaptive behavior. The means of implementing this early goal of therapy must of course be tailored to the individuals in the relationship.

Communication. Difficulty in communication between two people in a relationship constitutes the most frequently seen nonsexual problem at the Masters & Johnson Institute. Almost invariably, poor communicative interaction in areas apart from sex portends a less than fully satisfactory sexual interaction. Because sexual matters have been given a multitude of cultural and religious taboos, even couples who have relatively effective communication in other spheres of their lives are often reluctant to verbalize their sexual feelings, needs, and fears except in a perfunctory way. For the couple whose communication skills are lacking in areas with less emotionally charged impact, effective sexual communication may be next to impossible, forcing them into stereotyped patterns of behavior and response.

Double Standard. Relationships that may be regarded as "double-standard" in terms of one person consistently making decisions for both or overruling the other are problems that typically have sexual ramifications. Most frequently seen is the double standard by which the man is regarded (by himself and perhaps also by his wife) as infallible or is privileged by virtue of his masculinity in ways that his wife would never dream of claiming for herself. Occasionally, however, the scripts are reversed. While this situation often is recognized by the subjugated partner in a double-standard relationship, it is not always seen as a problem. Indeed, if both individuals are satisfied with the arrangement, it is certainly not the position of the therapists to attempt to alter this, except in cases in which it specifically and directly conflicts with effective sexual functioning. The double standard may be so valuable to the relationship, in fact, that it is necessary to continue it in the sexual interaction, although this situation is infrequent. For example, a woman who derives her sexual pleasure totally from her perception of her husband's satisfaction may be most gratified when he ejaculates rapidly; both partners may believe that this indicates how exciting and attractive he finds her to be. Not every person is interested in regularity of orgasmic response; in such an instance, tampering with the

highly gratifying sexual interaction that both individuals enjoy would
be of questionable value and would entail the risk of causing many
problems.

The double-standard relationship is usually detrimental to sexual
satisfaction, however, because it inevitably diminishes one person's
self-esteem in order to create and perpetuate the double standard.
Thus, the person serving as the lesser half of the double-standard
relationship may actually perceive himself or herself as less intelligent,
less creative, less deserving, less attractive, and less important than the
partner in all spheres of their existence together. These attitudes eventually carry over into a person's concept of self as a sexual being and
often result in that individual's trying to satisfy or at least accommodate the sexual needs of the partner at his or her own expense.

Deceit. Deliberate deceit in a relationship is a problem encountered
with less frequency than those mentioned above, but when it occurs in
major proportions it may have the most devastating results of all.
Dishonesty may be used sexually to assure the partner that everything
is all right when it really isn't, or it may serve as a means of attempting
to provide gratification for the partner by telling the partner what he or
she is thought to want to hear—for example, a woman may pretend to
be orgasmic or to be orgasmic simultaneously with her partner for
either reason. Deception over extramarital or extra-relationship sexual
involvement is not infrequent; however, sometimes it is done at the
request of a partner who may say, "If you are ever involved sexually
with someone else, I don't mind as long as I don't know about it." Other
examples of sexual dishonesty would include the individual within a
heterosexual relationship who is actively involved in homosexual functioning but professes fatigue or lack of interest with regard to his or her
heterosexual partner, or the person in a homosexual relationship prac-
ticing similar deceit about concurrent heterosexual activity. A more
subtle form of sexual deception is seen when a person acquiesces to a
particular type of sexual activity that he or she finds distasteful, solely
to please the partner; the attempt at providing gratification is often
misdirected because the partner might find alternative, mutually
agreeable avenues of sexual activity if the other person's distaste were
known.

Deceit that is not really directed toward sexual matters is particularly harmful when it involves misrepresentation of the commitment
one person has to another. Of course, even with a good sexual relation-

ship people not uncommonly dissolve relationships because of other problems. Occasionally when a couple comes to St. Louis for treatment, it becomes apparent that one of the two clients has no interest in maintaining the relationship and may be attempting to use participation in therapy as a means of ending the involvement. That person may hope that therapy will "fail" and thus give him or her an excuse to withdraw from the relationship while blaming the "failure" on the partner. The person may make active attempts to undermine therapy, whether specifically for this reason or in an attempt to punish the partner. The motivation behind such attitudes is varied, but in the two or three cases each year in which this is observed at the Masters & Johnson Institute it often appears to be related to legal problems of obtaining a divorce. Thus, a woman may wish to demonstrate that she has made every reasonable effort to maintain her marriage in order to obtain a better financial settlement, or a husband may come to St. Louis for the sole purpose of obtaining custody of the children in divorce proceedings. Needless to say, the legal interpretations made by such persons are often as misdirected as their deceptive behavior.

Deliberate misrepresentation may be a manifestation of the best intentions and may actually be evidence of commitment to a relationship. Thus, a person who is afraid that his or her spouse will leave or be very hurt by knowledge of that person's sexual experience prior to marriage may attempt to conceal this information, even to the point of lying. Similarly, embarrassment or concern about what constitutes "normal" sexual behavior may motivate deception. At times, this may not contribute significantly to the current sexual situation, particularly if the embarrassed or worried individual is satisfied by reassurance offered privately. Childhood or adolescent homosexual encounters often fit into such a category. Not surprisingly, once the person is convinced of the frequent occurrence and normalcy of such experiences, he or she often raises the subject to the spouse and is usually relieved to find a comfortable acceptance of the situation. However, other types of sexual concerns—rape, incest, transvestism, to mention a few—may have deeper and more lasting ramifications that require detailed therapeutic attention beyond the merely supportive.

Sexual Problem Areas Other Than the Specific Dysfunction

At least as important as diagnosing the sexual dysfunction affecting a couple is developing a detailed understanding of the sexual problems within their relationship that may or may not be related to the dysfunctional state. Such problems can be grouped into three broad categories:

attitudinal, informational, and behavioral. Since a full discussion of these areas would require an entire book, only those problems seen with relative frequency will be mentioned.

Attitudinal. Many people have been given such negative conditioning about sex as children that even in adulthood they are unable to outgrow the attitude that sex is dirty, sinful, or demeaning. The genesis of this negative conditioning, whether derived from parental attitudes, teachings absorbed in school or church, or cultural input, is less important than the end result: a state of constraint, defensiveness, guilt, and anxiety about sexual behavior and sexual feelings.

Informational problems can be highlighted by pointing to the appearance in the 1950s and 1960s of numerous "marriage manuals," which purported to explain "correct" sexual techniques. For some, the information about anatomy, positions for sexual activity, and varieties of sexual activity was valuable; for others, the rigid guidelines of technique or suggestions of what was normal or good became more a burden than a help. Men were instructed to find and stimulate their female partner's clitoris, usually without regard to how irritating direct clitoral pressure might be; admonitions were given to allow ample time for "warming up" the female in foreplay, without allowance for the possibility that a woman might be interested in intercourse before the male had completed his step-by-step stimulative routine. However, probably the greatest disservice of such books was the pronouncement of the goal of mutual orgasm as the pinnacle of sexual proficiency. An entire generation of diligent readers strove to achieve this magical moment in the belief that merging two orgasms into one would vastly enhance the experience—often tempting one hapless partner into faking orgasm in order to allow the other his or her moment of actualization. Somewhere along the way, however, common sense brought out the facts that pushing for orgasm often prevented it from happening, trying to coordinate timing often resulted in distraction from the physical sensations, and experiencing mutual orgasm frequently meant being so involved in one's own feelings that perception of the partner's orgasm was minimal or nonexistent.

The concept of a master plan for sex permeated our culture in many other ways. Rigidity in sexual roles was mistakenly seen as a source of strength: The man should initiate sexual activity (although his wife might obliquely hint at her desire by preparing a candlelit meal, wearing perfume, putting on an enticing nightgown rather than her usual housedress); the man should provide the proper amount of foreplay; the man should have an erection, select a position, insert the penis, provide the thrusting, and ejaculate at the moment when his partner was reaching the height of her orgasm. A variation on this scheme was the simpler view that it was the wife's role to service her husband, even if he paid no attention to the intricacies just outlined and even if she had no interest in the event. Many other ancillary conditions accompanied these rigid lines of thought: Sexual fantasies were viewed as bad, oral-genital contact was seen as dirty or perverted, contraception was not to be discussed, sexual activity was to occur at night, in the dark, and preferably under the covers.

Needless to say, cultural generalizations have their limitations. The preceding description is not meant to imply complete uniformity of attitude or behavior in the United States, but is rather a typical composite history as related by couples who were married prior to the early 1960s. Regional, religious, and ethnic factors would of course influence the individual details of this description. But when this tableau is placed alongside the cultural messages about sex implicit in keeping contraceptives behind the drugstore counter, not allowing *Playboy* magazine to be on open shelves, and even the more recent attempt to market vaginal spray deodorant products commercially, it is easy to see how a multiplicity of deeply ingrained taboos about sex have permeated our lives.

Clinically, such attitudinal problems may be expressed in a variety of ways. One or both partners may be embarrassed to appear before the other in the nude. Sexual fantasies may be equated with infidelity, sin, or even mental disorders. Masturbation may be looked upon as degrading. Commonly, a woman will expect her partner to know when she is in the mood for sex, what kind of stimulation she wants, and when she is ready for intercourse without her having to provide him with any information. Some men will be frightened by a woman who attempts to initiate sex play or to be innovative during sexual interaction. The list of such problems could continue for many pages, but the point here is that recognition of these attitudinal contributions to sexual dissatisfaction prior to the roundtable allows them to be identified, discussed, and placed in perspective early in the course of therapy. If this is not done, they will often confound progress toward a resolution of the specific dysfunction(s) under treatment.

Informational. Informational problems that contribute to sexual distress apart from the specific sexual dysfunction are commonplace. It is interesting to note that couples in their early twenties seem to be no less frequently afflicted with such problems than older couples; the so-called sexual revolution has apparently not succeeded in alleviating the widespread lack of accurate information. The type of problem encountered is generally related to the anatomy or physiology of sex. Common examples include:

1. Uncertainty about the location of the clitoris.*
2. A woman not recognizing her own orgasm.
3. Belief that the capacity for sexual functioning is lost with aging.
4. Belief that the male must ejaculate every time he has intercourse or every time he has an erection.
5. Belief that the amount of vaginal lubrication is proportional to the woman's sexual excitation.
6. Belief that sexual activity must cease as soon as the male has ejaculated.

Although these informational problems are usually easy to correct, it must be recognized that they have often contributed to more complex patterns of sexual behavior that may not be so quickly altered. In such cases, providing accurate information is not the entire answer; an attempt to correct all factual inaccuracies during the roundtable is almost never indicated.

Selected informational issues may serve as useful focal points for other concepts to be presented in the roundtable, and correcting misinformation may help to increase the self-esteem of one or both clients. As an example of the latter, a woman might describe a sexual response pattern of gradually building neuromuscular tension and pelvic congestion that rapidly dissipates and produces a feeling of relaxation and well-being, while complaining that she has never been orgasmic. With an understanding of what she expects the orgasmic experience to be, it is possible to provide the couple with reassurance that the woman probably *has* been orgasmic: A brief explanation of the varied sensations and intensities of orgasm would usually suffice to show that this response might not always be recognized, and would allow both the male and female to feel that their sexual difficulties were not as bad as they had believed them to be. Discussion of this point during the roundtable would typically be brief and open-ended, with the assurance

---

*A married couple in their mid-twenties reported using frequent clitoral stimulation. When asked to identify the clitoris during a conjoint physical examination, the husband proudly pointed to a large freckle on the lower portion of his wife's left labia minora.

that information concerning the anatomy and physiology of sexual response would be presented to the couple in an integrative fashion in the days ahead. A supportive approach would be taken, stressing that many women are unaware of having been orgasmic and clearly stating that such misunderstanding need not be a major therapeutic concern. Although the couple may totally accept the factual information that is provided, patterns and pressures that may have arisen in the relationship out of concern over lack of orgasmic response may not dissipate immediately. Therefore, it is imperative for the therapists to continually reinforce the corrected information while dealing with the associated problems.

Of course, attempts by the cotherapy team to correct misinformation may not always be accepted by the clients. A man may refuse to believe that his wife can be aroused unless there is a marked degree of vaginal lubrication. A woman may be quite certain that her husband's premature ejaculation is a conscious attempt to punish her. A person who has received a previous professional assessment of a problem indicating a particular etiology (for example, an unresolved oedipal complex or latent homosexuality) either for self or partner may be reluctant to accept an alternative explanation. This also influences the planning of the roundtable, since often it would be a mistake to force the issue at this early time. The passage of several days of therapy allows the cotherapy team the opportunity to establish their expertise in the couple's view, while simultaneously getting to know the couple better. Both factors are of major importance in deciding when and how to approach issues involving previously held erroneous beliefs.

Behavioral. Behavioral difficulties concerning sex that may not relate to a specific dysfunction are common and require recognition and consideration prior to the roundtable. At times, these behavioral problems spring directly from the attitudinal problems already discussed (for example, a woman always waiting for her husband to initiate sexual play). Other types of difficulties may not be directly related to either attitudinal or informational problems. A situation often encountered clinically is the existence of a major discrepancy between the two clients' levels of sexual appetite. When one person desires a high frequency of sexual activity and the other is content with sexual contact once every few weeks, many frustrations and defensive behavior patterns usually arise. Although this dilemma is more often seen in a relationship where the man desires a markedly greater frequency than the woman, it is not uncommon to see these roles reversed. Usually this problem is mentioned only briefly in the roundtable, with acknowledgment of how frustrating it can be and a statement to the effect that once people learn effective communication skills, it is remarkable how quickly the difficulties disappear. It is pointed out that both partners can usually find a comfortable middle ground that allows less frustration and less sense of sexual pressure.

A different but related behavioral problem is presented when a person uses sex or the withholding of sex as a means of obtaining his or her way. The idea of coercive sex is certainly not new, since it was plainly portrayed by the Greek playwright Aristophanes in his *Lysistrata* (411 B.C.). Sex, forced sex, or sexual avoidance may be used as a means of punishment, a bargaining point, a conciliatory ploy, or a reward or reinforcement in a variety of situations that, if repeatedly employed, often produce major problems in a relationship. As will be discussed in Chapter 22, the net result of such behaviors may be a strongly negative conditioning of one partner who is constantly subjected to sexual demands closely tied to a set of rules imposed by the other partner.

When husband and wife disagree over reproductive goals—one strongly wishing a child and the other opposed—the potential for sexual and nonsexual problems is high. Similar problems may arise from conflict over the issue of responsibility for contraception. With the recent frequency of reports of possible adverse effects of a variety of contraceptives used by women, this has become a more substantial issue. In either type of problem, withdrawal from sexual activity is a frequent defensive maneuver by one or both partners.

Yet another area of behavioral conflict occurs when one person objects to a specific type of sexual activity while the other person voices a strong desire for that activity. Differing views of oral-genital sex commonly present in this manner. Extramarital sex may also be a polarized issue; sometimes one partner may press the other to participate in "swinging" or bisexual activity against the other's wishes. It is important to keep in mind the individual nature of each couple's difficulties, but failure to plan general approaches to such problems would seriously undermine later therapeutic effectiveness.

One final type of behavioral difficulty will be mentioned because it is encountered so frequently. The expression of general dissatisfaction with sex may take the form of complaints about "routinized" sexual activity or may be voiced as concern about one's own or partner's "poor technique." Adequate information about the details of such problems must have been elicited during history-taking to provide a sound basis for the roundtable discussion. Such difficulties often stem from ineffective communication, and open exploration of each partner's perception of the situation during the roundtable may provide impetus for spontaneous resolution of the distress. At times, individual perceptions are so biased that one well-meaning partner deliberately avoids that which the other desires out of imagined preferences that have been catalogued over the years. For instance, a man who was asked by his partner on one occasion to stop performing cunnilingus on her may have mistakenly believed that this was a permanent injunction against oral stimulation, whereas his partner was simply turning down one activity at a particular time. As many such imagined preferences and prejudices become ritualized, it is no wonder that sexual activity for some couples may become little more than a mechanical routine.

Identification of Neuroses and Psychoses

Sexual dysfunction was once viewed almost exclusively as a surface manifestation of deeply rooted neurotic or psychotic processes. Current behavioral theory has moved away from this position with the strong support of clinical evidence. Although 86 percent of couples seen at the Masters & Johnson Institute between 1971 and 1977 had undergone prior psychotherapy for a minimum of six months, in most cases treatment was directed at their specific sexual problem rather than an associated psychiatric disorder. Nevertheless, approximately 8 percent of the people seen in this time period had a diagnosable psychiatric illness according to the classification and criteria of Woodruff, Goodwin, and Guze [24].

In the evaluation prior to the roundtable, identification of patterns of stress reaction, psychoneurotic disorders, and psychotic disorders is of critical importance. The stresses of continuing sexual frustration are not the same for all individuals and to a large extent reflect the priority each person places on sexual actualization or gratification and the extent to which his or her coping mechanisms diminish or resolve the frustration without altering the problem. For some people, total abstinence from sexual activity represents actualization. However, this is simply one end of the spectrum; for most individuals, sexual gratification is not easily put aside without consequent sexual frustration. This form of stress commonly threatens self-esteem and may simultaneously pose the risk of loss of love from a significant other. In a situation of continuing stress, ego defense mechanisms are activated quite normally to allow optimal adaptation to the stress without behavioral decompensation. No matter how well integrated the individual, neurotic or even psychotic symptoms may develop if exposure to stress exceeds personal tolerance levels.

Identifying the defense mechanisms that predominate in the behavior patterns of two individuals within a relationship is extremely important for the roundtable. Some measure of insight into both sexual and nonsexual difficulties may be reached if these patterns are described in practical terms explaining how the defenses are being employed and what responses they have evoked in the other partner. The most commonly encountered defenses include intellectualization, emotional insulation, avoidance, rationalization, projection, compensation, sublimation, and repression. Overlooking the extent to which such defense mechanisms are operant in a given couple may lengthen the amount of time needed in therapy and will reduce the effectiveness of any therapeutic approach.

Coleman defines a key factor in the development of psychoneurotic disorders as "intolerable anxiety aroused when vulnerable aspects of the personality are placed under stress and the basic adequacy and worth of the self are threatened" [25]. Many of the defenses that the neurotic uses to cope with the stressful situation may succeed in reducing the anxiety but are nonintegrative in the sense that they do not alleviate the source of stress. Thus, the impotent man who avoids any sexual opportunity succeeds in diminishing anxiety but does not relieve his sexual frustration. Similarly, a woman experiencing dyspareunia may compensate by frequent masturbation but may experience further loss of self-esteem as she perceives herself as increasingly unable to function "normally."

One goal of therapy is to decrease stress simultaneously with increasing the couple's adaptive capabilities; this is generally compatible with the neurotic personality except for those so rigid that they refuse to change their defenses or perceptions, fearing loss of their "protection" against the world.

Although there is no clear line of demarcation between the neuroses and the psychoses, two features may serve to represent the Institute's definition of psychosis: severe personality decompensation and major distortion in perception of reality. If psychopathology of this magnitude exists, a rapid treatment approach to sexual dysfunction is rarely warranted. Similarly, assessment must be made of the neurotic personality in terms of that person's capacity to deal with the stresses that are inherent in any therapeutic setting and that are clearly magnified by an intensive treatment approach involving three other people. This assessment has not always been made accurately: Approximately one in every 300 persons treated has a major psychiatric crisis during therapy. In such situations, individual psychiatric evaluation and treatment is immediately instituted, with hospitalization if required.

Physical Problems

Evaluating the presence of physical problems that may influence therapy is a matter of more than theoretical significance. Problems such as arthritis or obesity may obviously limit the range of possible coital positions (see Chap. 10); the existence of genital disorders may necessitate modifications in patient management (see Chaps. 8 and 9); and the presence of problems such as neurologic limitations or postsurgical scarring requires careful planning on the part of the therapy team.

Motivation

Assessing the degree of motivation each person brings to therapy is admittedly a difficult task. At times, clients' statements about their motivation turn out to be incongruent with their subsequent behavior, while at other times, persons professing ambivalence either about their motivation for therapy or their commitment to the relationship evidence high levels of motivation and commitment as therapy progresses. Motivation is not to be confused with expectations—it is often easier to work with persons who are somewhat skeptical about the potential outcome of therapy than with those who believe all their problems will suddenly be solved. Furthermore, clients with low levels of motivation are not arbitrarily rejected; rather, early recognition of their minimal enthusiasm allows the therapists to utilize appropriate approaches and particular strategies that may serve to improve motivation as therapy proceeds.

Special Requests Regarding Confidentiality

There are occasional situations in which one client requests that a particular piece of personal historical information not be revealed to his or her partner. It is up to the therapists to decide whether they wish to work under this agreement; it is often possible to work with a couple under such circumstances without any lost effectiveness. Our standard approach to this situation is to explain to the person making the request that the information will be held confidential unless disclosure of such material appears crucial to successful outcome of therapy, at which point this determination will be made known to him (or her) privately, along with an explanation of why the therapists believe that the information merits full disclosure and discussion. In any event, no violation of client confidentiality is permitted—if the client agrees to the sharing of the material in question, therapy continues, but if he or she still insists that the information be withheld from the partner, therapy is terminated with no disclosure of the protected information.

Conflicting
Information

Determining whether there are significant discrepancies in the historical facts related by both clients is important for a number of reasons. Such discrepancies frequently point to areas of conflict within the relationship—for example, the wife may be certain her husband has had an affair, while he states vehemently that he has not—or indicate major differences between the two clients' values or personalities. It is necessary to pay particular attention to the areas of such discrepancies during subsequent therapy and to avoid drawing inferences or reaching conclusions based on insufficient information.

Objectives

Identifying the objectives each client has in terms of therapy is one of the central tasks of the therapists, both to indicate directions that therapy should take and to assess whether the clients' goals are realistic or not. The therapists must guard against imposing their own values and objectives on clients; in order to do this, they must be skilled in listening to the clients and eliciting statements that adequately describe the clients' goals. Sometimes the clients' goals are so disparate that they cannot be resolved, necessitating a termination of therapy; in other instances, the clients' goals may be unattainable, and the therapists must point this out. This situation is illustrated by a case in which the male wanted to be able to ejaculate a number of times in an hour: He was not satisfied with the explanation that psychotherapy could not alter the physiology of his refractory period, and he decided to pursue his goal by other means.

Presentation of
Assessment and
Proposed Treatment

Determining whether a rapid, intensive form of sex therapy is suitable for a given couple is not always an easy task. Certain situations—an unresolved medical problem, uncontrolled mania, or psychosis—may preclude such an approach, while in other cases, the decision must be based on criteria that are less easily defined. In these situations, individual assessment must be made on the basis of the persons involved, their previous therapy experiences, and the likelihood that sex therapy may be helpful. There is no simple formula for making such a determination.

On the day following history-taking, the cotherapists and clients meet together in a roundtable session that allows the therapy team to provide their assessment of the situation to the couple, including information related to the origin of the sexual problem(s), the specific pertinent diagnoses, the prognosis, and an overview of the approaches that will be used to solve the difficulty. From this session on, the primary format for sex therapy is a four-way dialogue that includes education, examination of attitudes, modeling, and use of a wide range of psychotherapeutic techniques as required by each situation.

The focus of the therapy process is on the present, rather than on an attempt to analyze or examine past behaviors or feelings. Typically, concepts that are utilized in the treatment of committed relationships include, in addition to those discussed earlier in this chapter, the following attitudes:

1. The need to adopt a nonblaming, open-minded attitude of neutrality or openness toward partner as well as self; this involves not using past behaviors or feelings to predict the present or future.
2. The need to assume responsibility for oneself, rather than assigning this responsibility to someone else.
3. The need to communicate effectively with one's partner, both sexually and nonsexually (this includes both verbal and nonverbal forms of communication and encompasses the ability to solve problems together through a process of relationship negotiation as well as the ability to exchange information).
4. The need to be aware of one's feelings and needs.
5. The facts that sex does not simply mean intercourse or orgasm; that sex can be fun, rather than work; and that sex can be a highly effective means of interpersonal communication.

Although these concepts have been only briefly summarized here, they are actually discussed in considerable detail with each couple, including elaboration of examples of how difficulties in these areas have either led to, maintained, or compounded the sexual and relationship difficulties in the couple presenting for therapy. Since in the majority of cases a sexual dysfunction is accompanied by other problems that require attention (many of which have traditionally been regarded as marital discord, while some pertain more directly to one individual, such as a phobia, depression, or neurosis), sex therapy is certainly not restricted to dealing with sexual problems alone.

Beginning Treatment: Sensate Focus

Following the roundtable session, unless other major issues such as overwhelming hostility are present, specific techniques are suggested for approaching sexual interaction. Such suggestions pertain to activity that the client couple will pursue in the privacy of their home or hotel;

patients are never observed in sexual activity. In the beginning, couples are instructed to abstain from intercourse or genital stimulation, both as a means of reducing performance pressures and as an opportunity to initiate new patterns of nonverbal communication and sensory awareness. They are instructed to take turns touching one another's bodies—avoiding the breasts and genitals—to establish a sense of tactile awareness by noticing textures, contours, temperatures, and contrasts (while doing the touching) or to be aware of the sensations of being touched by their partner. They are carefully instructed that sexual excitation is not the purpose of this exercise (although it may occur); instead, their attention should focus on their own physical sensations and should minimize cognitive processes. As Masters and Johnson have explained:

In order to achieve optimum effect, sensate focus should be used as a means of physical awareness by the partner doing the touching and not specifically or solely for the sensual pleasure or even sexual excitation of the partner being touched. . . . By specifically structuring the sensate focus opportunities at the onset of therapy, it is usually possible to significantly reduce the constraints imposed by old habit patterns of sexual interaction. Concomitantly, removing stereotyped expectations of what sexual interaction "should be" often leads to an awakening of spontaneous natural response that has long been forgotten and was sometimes never recognized [5].

The sensate focus techniques form a framework for a progressive integration of nonverbal skills, newly acquired perspectives on sexual anatomy and physiology, and anxiety reduction, while restructuring maladaptive habit patterns to more useful ones. The couple gradually moves through various levels of sensate focus that progress from nongenital touching to touching that includes the breasts and genitals; touching that is done in a simultaneous, mutual format rather than by one person at a time; and touching that extends to and allows for the possibility of intercourse. Sensate focus has sometimes been misinterpreted as comprising the entirety of sex therapy. In actuality, sensate focus is simply a component of a much more comprehensive psychotherapeutic armamentarium.

Further discussion of the psychotherapeutic approach to the treatment of sexual dysfunction, including the delineation of specific techniques used, is included in the two chapters that follow.

References

1. Levine, S. B. Marital sexual dysfunction: Introductory concepts. *Annals of Internal Medicine* 84:448–453, 1976.
2. Marmor, J. Frigidity, Dyspareunia, and Vaginismus. In A. M. Freed-

man, H. I. Kaplan, and B. J. Sadock (eds.), *Comprehensive Textbook of Psychiatry* (2nd ed.). Baltimore: Williams & Wilkins Co., 1975. P. 1522.

3. LoPiccolo, J., and Heiman, J. Cultural values and the therapeutic definition of sexual function and dysfunction. *Journal of Social Issues* 33(2):166–183, 1977.

4. Masters, W. H., and Johnson, V. E. *Human Sexual Inadequacy*. Boston: Little, Brown and Co., 1970.

5. Masters, W. H., and Johnson, V. E. Principles of the new sex therapy. *American Journal of Psychiatry* 133:548–554, 1976.

6. Brady, J. P. Behavior therapy and sex therapy. *American Journal of Psychiatry* 133:896–899, 1976.

7. Kaplan, H. S. *The New Sex Therapy*. New York: Brunner/Mazel, Publishers, 1974.

8. Annon, J. S. *The Behavioral Treatment of Sexual Problems: Brief Therapy*. New York: Harper & Row, 1976.

9. Annon, J. S. *The Behavioral Treatment of Sexual Problems: Intensive Therapy*. Honolulu, Hawaii: Enabling Systems, 1975.

10. Hartman, W. E., and Fithian, M. A. *The Treatment of Sexual Dysfunction*. Long Beach, Calif.: Center for Marital and Sexual Studies, 1972.

11. Lobitz, W. C., and LoPiccolo, J. New methods in the behavioral treatment of sexual dysfunction. *Journal of Behavior Therapy and Experimental Psychiatry* 3:265–271, 1972.

12. LoPiccolo, J., and Lobitz, W. C. The role of masturbation in the treatment of orgasmic dysfunction. *Archives of Sexual Behavior* 2:153–164, 1972.

13. McGovern, L., Stewart, R., and LoPiccolo, J. Secondary orgasmic dysfunction: I. Analysis and strategies for treatment. *Archives of Sexual Behavior* 4:265–275, 1975.

14. Caird, W., and Wincze, J. P. *Sex Therapy: A Behavioral Approach*. Hagerstown, Md.: Harper & Row, 1977.

15. Zussman, L., and Zussman, S. Continuous Time-Limited Treatment of Standard Sexual Disorders. In J. K. Meyer (ed.), *Clinical Management of Sexual Disorders*. Baltimore: Williams & Wilkins Co., 1976.

16. Schmidt, C. W., and Lucas, J. The Short-Term, Intermittent, Conjoint Treatment of Sexual Disorders. In J. K. Meyer (ed.), *Clinical Management of Sexual Disorders*. Baltimore: Williams & Wilkins Co., 1976.

17. O'Connor, J. F., and Stern, L. O. Results of treatment in functional sexual disorders. *New York State Journal of Medicine* 72:1927–1934, 1972.

18. Fordney-Settlage, D. S. Heterosexual dysfunctions: Evaluation of treatment procedures. *Archives of Sexual Behavior* 4:367–387, 1975.

19. Barbach, L. G. *For Yourself: The Fulfillment of Female Sexuality*. New York: Doubleday, 1975.

20. Heiman, J., LoPiccolo, L., and LoPiccolo, J. *Becoming Orgasmic: A Sexual Growth Program for Women*. Englewood Cliffs, N.J.: Prentice-Hall, 1976.

21. Johnson, V. E., and Masters, W. H. Contemporary influences on sexual response: I. The work ethic. *Journal of School Health* 46:211–215, 1976.

22. Maurice, W. L., and Guze, S. B. Sexual dysfunction and associated psychiatric disorders. *Comprehensive Psychiatry* 11:539–543, 1970.

23. Lederer, W. J., and Jackson, D. D. *Mirages of Marriage*. New York: Norton, 1968.
24. Woodruff, R. A., Goodwin, D. W., and Guze, S. B. *Psychiatric Diagnosis*. New York: Oxford University Press, 1974.
25. Coleman, J. C. *Abnormal Psychology and Everyday Life* (3rd ed.). Chicago: Scott, Foresman and Co., 1964. P. 193.

20

Male Sexual Dysfunction

Sexual function involves the activation of a variety of inborn reflex responses that are ordinarily integrated into a psychosocial matrix. The basic physiologic mechanisms of normal sexual function may be impaired by a variety of factors of organic or psychogenic origin. An understanding of these conditions is facilitated by a classification that distinguishes sexual dysfunctions (marked by impaired physiologic response) from other sexual problems (marked by alterations or conflicts in behavior, attitude, or feelings, but not accompanied by impaired sexual function in a physiologic sense). To be sure, sexual problems—such as guilt about participation in sexual activity—may lead to subsequent sexual dysfunction; and sexual dysfunction—such as impotence—may create ancillary sexual problems. In this chapter, the two categories of male sexual dysfunction, disorders of erection and disturbances of ejaculation, are considered from the viewpoints of etiology, diagnosis, and treatment.

Impotence

Impotence is the inability to obtain or maintain an erection of sufficient firmness to permit coitus to be initiated or completed [1]. Impotence may be classified as either primary or secondary: The male with primary impotence has never been able to have intercourse, whereas the male with secondary impotence is experiencing erectile dysfunction after a previous period of normal function. Isolated, transient episodes of inability to obtain or maintain an erection are normal occurrences that do not warrant diagnostic evaluation or treatment; such erectile failure is usually attributable to fatigue, distraction, inebriation, acute illness, or transient anxiety. However, a persistent pattern of impaired erectile function is indicative of the presence of a sexual dysfunction that requires diagnostic and therapeutic attention.

Etiology

Approximately 10 to 15 percent of men affected by impotence appear to have a primarily organic basis for their sexual dysfunction [1–4]. The most common organic causes of impotence are listed in Table 20-1; specific details of the relevant pathophysiology, natural history, and treatment of these conditions can be found in previous chapters. When impaired erectile function occurs as a result of physical or metabolic causes, it is common for psychological or behavioral changes to develop over time in reaction to the dysfunction; such changes may themselves affect sexual function so that even if the primary organic cause is discovered and successfully treated, sexual difficulties may persist on a psychogenic basis.

Similarly, although 85 to 90 percent of patients with impotence

Table 20-1. Classification of the Physical Causes of Secondary Impotence

Anatomic Causes	Thiazide diuretics
Congenital deformities	Thioridazine
Hydrocele	*Endocrine Causes*
Testicular fibrosis	Acromegaly
Cardiorespiratory Causes	Addison's disease
Angina pectoris	Adrenal neoplasms (with or without Cushing's syndrome)
Coronary insufficiency	Castration
Emphysema	Chromophobe adenoma
Myocardial infarction	Craniopharyngioma
Pulmonary insufficiency	Diabetes mellitus
Rheumatic fever	Eunuchoidism (including Klinefelter's syndrome)
Drug Ingestion	Feminizing interstitial-cell testicular tumors
Addictive drugs	Hyperprolactinemia
Alcohol	Infantilism
Alpha-methyldopa	Ingestion of female hormones (estrogen)
Amphetamines	Myxedema
Antiandrogens (cyproterone acetate)	Thyrotoxicosis
Atropine	*Genitourinary Causes*
Barbiturates	Cystectomy
Chlordiazepoxide	Perineal prostatectomy (frequently)
Chlorprothixene	Peyronie's disease
Cimetidine	Phimosis
Clofibrate	Priapism
Clonidine	Prostatitis
Digitalis (rarely)	Suprapubic and transurethral prostatectomy (occasionally)
Guanethidine	Urethritis
Imipramine	*Hematologic Causes*
Marihuana	Hodgkin's disease
Methantheline bromide	Leukemia, acute and chronic
Monoamine oxidase inhibitors	Pernicious anemia (with combined systems disease)
Nicotine (rarely)	
Phenothiazines	
Propranolol	
Reserpine	
Spironolactone	

Sickle cell anemia

Infectious Causes

Elephantiasis

Genital tuberculosis

Gonorrhea

Mumps

Neurologic Causes

Amyotrophic lateral sclerosis

Cerebral palsy

Cord tumors or transection

Electric shock therapy

Multiple sclerosis

Myasthenia gravis

Nutritional deficiencies

Parkinsonism

Peripheral neuropathies

Spina bifida

Sympathectomy

Tabes dorsalis

Temporal lobe lesions

Vascular Causes

Aneurysm

Arteritis

Sclerosis

Thrombotic obstruction of aortic bifurcation

Miscellaneous Causes

Chronic renal failure

Cirrhosis

Obesity

Toxicologic agents (lead, herbicides)

---

appear to have a primarily psychogenic origin for their dysfunction, physical or metabolic factors may contribute to the difficulty as well in a significant number of instances. Some men with sexual dysfunction that is already marginal may be pushed into frankly dysfunctional status by the onset of illness, by the use of sexually depressing drugs, or by physical changes (including aging) that would not ordinarily be sufficient grounds for impotence. There is currently no means of identifying men who are particularly susceptible to the subsequent development of impotence or other sexual problems.

The psychogenic causes of impotence may be conceptualized as falling into four major categories: developmental, affective, interpersonal, and cognitional. The most common elements of these categories are summarized in Table 20-2. It must be stressed that such etiologies are conjectural in that they have not been rigorously studied from a research viewpoint; they are based on clinical impression. No inference is made that all men, or even many men, with similar histories will be impotent. In fact, it appears that quite the opposite is true: Men frequently overcome potentially negative background factors that might appear to place them at substantial risk for the development of sexual

Table 20-2. Major Categories of Psychogenic Impotence

Developmental Factors

Maternal or paternal dominance

Conflicted parent-child relationship

Severe negative family attitude toward sex (often associated with religious orthodoxy)

Traumatic childhood sexual experience

Gender identity conflict

Traumatic first coital experience

Homosexuality

Affective Factors

Anxiety (particularly fears of performance, anxiety about size of penis)

Guilt

Depression

Poor self-esteem

Hypochondria

Mania

Fear of pregnancy

Fear of venereal disease

Interpersonal Factors

Poor communications

Hostility toward partner or spouse

Distrust of partner or spouse

Lack of physical attraction to partner or spouse

Divergent sexual preferences or sex value systems (regarding types of sexual activity, time of sexual activity, frequency of sexual activity, etc.)

Sex role conflicts

Cognitional Factors

Sexual ignorance

Acceptance of cultural myths

Performance demands

Miscellaneous Factors

Premature ejaculation

Isolated episode of erectile failure (often due to fatigue, inebriation, acute illness, or transient anxiety)

Iatrogenic influences

Paraphilias

difficulties. This phenomenon may be a reflection of the remarkable extent to which sex is a natural function.

Masters and Johnson described overt mother-son sexual encounters over a prolonged period of time (extending from childhood until beyond the time of puberty) as a factor of significance in some cases of primary impotence [1]. Undue dominance by one parent may create a sense of inadequacy leading to erectile problems because of either lack of an effective male figure with whom to identify (in cases of maternal dominance) or the impossibility of measuring up to the seemingly omnipotent father (in cases of paternal dominance). Other aspects of development that may be implicated in the genesis of impotence include restrictive, rigid, negative attitudes toward sex impressed upon the child in the home environment, frequently found in association with religious orthodoxy; traumatic childhood sexual experiences, including punishment for masturbation or participation in sex play with other children; gender identity conflict; traumatic first attempts at intercourse; and homosexuality.

Sometimes merging with such developmental factors in the occurrence of impotence are a number of intrapsychic or affective elements that may also arise independently. Anxiety, guilt, depression, and poor self-esteem are often intertwined in cases of sexual dysfunction; it may be virtually impossible to determine the temporal sequence that led to the difficulty. In some situations these components may arise only after the onset of impotence; nevertheless, therapeutic attention should be focused on such problems when they are present, regardless of the cause that initially precipitated the dysfunction. Phobias related to sexual functioning are infrequently seen but are important determinants of therapeutic strategy, while the paraphilias—conditions in which sexual arousal is impossible without a particular stimulus (dressing in women's clothes, being spanked or humiliated, or wearing rubber garments, for example), either fantasized or in actuality—are thought to be rare but are of indeterminate frequency.

The importance of interpersonal factors in the genesis of sexual dysfunction has been widely acknowledged in the last decade but had previously received little attention. Most cases of impotence involve these factors either as contributors to or original causes of the problem or as ramifications of the guilt, frustration, and anger that may be generated by the sexual dysfunction over time. The ego-defense mechanisms that both men and women frequently employ to cope with impotence (including rationalization, projection, emotional insulation, intellectualization, sublimation, avoidance, and denial of reality) are likely to create relationship difficulties that require direct therapeutic intervention.

Iatrogenic influences can lead to impotence in a number of different ways [1]. In each instance, the common element is that a respected health-care professional plays a causative role in the development of erectile disturbances. This may come about through direct statements or through the omission of an anticipated statement; by misperceptions on the part of the patient about instructions or explanations he is given; by the perpetuation of myths by a respected authority; or by undue anxiety or overinterpretation on the part of the professional. At times, impotence may occur iatrogenically in the context of treating another problem, such as infertility, heart disease, or prostatic disorders requiring surgery. Impaired erectile function may be the result of injudicious or incompetent sex therapy, developing either in situations in which the male has no prior history of dysfunction or when the male is under treatment for ejaculatory difficulties. Iatrogenic impotence can also occur when men misinterpret articles or books they have read about sexuality.

An interesting category of psychogenic impotence that has only recently been recognized is aptly described by the term *widower's syndrome*. In this disorder, generally involving men over the age of 50, there is characteristically a prolonged period of little or no sexual activity in conjunction with a lengthy and eventually fatal physical illness of the wife. During this protracted illness—cancer being the most frequent variety—the male often becomes a caretaker of his spouse, providing increasing physical and psychological ministration to his partner as she becomes more and more severely debilitated and dependent on him. The husband may be frustrated by the lack of sexual outlet but avoids sexual contact with his sick wife except on infrequent occasions. His combined sense of conjugal duty and guilt over his wife's illness is usually sufficient to restrain him from seeking extramarital sexual involvement; a few men in this category may seek out the services of a prostitute, an experience that typically proves unsatisfactory and tends to engender more guilt. After his wife finally dies and he observes what he considers to be an appropriate mourning period, the widower's first attempt at resuming sexual activity with a partner ends in erectile failure, a situation that is as embarrassing as it is frustrating. From this point on, his performance anxieties are mobilized; in general, no matter how alluring or cooperative his subsequent partner(s) may be, he continues to be locked into a cycle of performance pressures, spectatoring, and subsequent erectile insecurity. Variants of the widower's syndrome may occur in men whose histories are not precisely the same as the one just outlined—for example, impotence is not uncommon after divorce as well as after sudden death of a spouse—but the underlying dynamics of these situations appear to be different from the specifics of the widower's syndrome.

Diagnostic
Considerations

Normal penile erections do not usually occur unless there are reasonably intact anatomic, neurologic, circulatory, and hormonal support mechanisms. For this reason, ascertaining whether an impotent man experiences erections under any special set of circumstances is an important aspect of the process of differential diagnosis. The initial objective is to determine whether impaired erectile function is due primarily to psychogenic factors or to physical ones; the sexual history is the most useful single indicator of this.

Historical Clues for Determining the Etiology of Impotence. If a man achieves erections under certain conditions but not others, the likelihood is high that the impotence is psychogenic [1–4]. Thus, the impotent man who experiences erections with masturbation, during homosexual activity, during extramarital sex, in response to reading or looking at erotic materials, or with certain types of sexual activity (fellatio, sadomasochistic sex, or wearing particular items of clothing, for example) is unlikely to have a physical or metabolic explanation for his difficulties. For the same reason, the common history of the man who has no difficulty achieving a firm erection, only to lose it promptly upon attempting vaginal insertion, is strong evidence for a psychogenic problem.

Similarly, the presence of a firm erection at the time of awakening indicates that the capacity for normal erectile response is present physiologically. The clinical significance that can be placed on self-reports of morning erections is limited, however. Some men may be unaware of such erections, even though they are present. In other circumstances, it is the pattern of the relative frequency of morning erections viewed in the context of each man's history that is most important. A report of infrequent (or absent) morning erections is of no diagnostic assistance if the patient had a similar pattern prior to the onset of erectile difficulties. However, if a man has noticed a significant reduction in the frequency of his awakening with an erection since the onset of impotence, the possibility of an organic etiology is suggested. If firm erections are frequently present on awakening, it is unlikely that an organic cause for impotence exists.

The history will also reveal important information about the onset and progression of impotence that will aid in the diagnostic process. Impotence resulting from organic causes typically begins in an insidious fashion, becoming slowly and progressively more troublesome. In contrast, psychogenic impotence is likely to be of sudden onset—at times, the patient may be able to identify the specific date on which his difficulties began. However, some organic causes of impotence, such as trauma (postsurgical or neurological injury) or drug use, can lead to impotence abruptly, so this point of differentiation needs to be balanced carefully with other bits of clinical and historical evidence.

There may be a temporal association between the onset of psychogenic impotence and a stressful event. A man may first experience difficulty with erections after finding out that his wife has had an affair, after the death of a parent or child, after a divorce, or after a stressful change at work. If the patient is not seen until long after the onset of his dysfunction, he may not remember the temporal relationship at all, but his partner may recall the association if queried. Although the stressful event initially impairs sexual responsiveness, subsequent anxieties and fears of performance become the perpetuating mechanism, so that when there is recovery from the stress, sexual function may continue to be impeded.

Although organic impotence most frequently follows a progressively downhill course, psychogenic impotence may mimic this pattern. This may be the case when continued frustration, diminishing self-esteem, and interpersonal problems lead to a pattern of avoidance of sexual activity as a means of coping; libido may or may not be reduced in such situations. Likewise, when depression occurs in reaction to sexual difficulties, the dysfunctional state may progressively deteriorate until appropriate treatment is instituted.

It is important to recognize that impotence is not synonymous with the absence of erections. Many impotent men experience erections that are quite firm but are only transient; other men have a pattern of impaired penile rigidity, but are able to obtain or maintain a partial degree of erection. Care should be used in interpreting the clinical significance of such variations. Although a patient who is able to have intercourse with one woman but not another is probably psychogenically impotent, there is also the possibility that the degree and firmness of his erections are the same with both women, but that differences between the women in vaginal size, muscle tone [5], and physical cooperation lead to differences in the man's ability to have intercourse. The temporal association of the onset of impotence with a major psychological stress may be related to the onset of a medical problem that was precipitated by the stress, rather than being indicative of a purely psychogenic origin of the dysfunction. Certain types of organic impotence may be episodic, rather than persistent and worsening; for example, the impotence caused by multiple sclerosis follows such a waxing and waning course. For such reasons, more reliable methods for differential diagnosis are desirable, and even when the history appears compatible with a psychological origin of sexual dysfunction, careful assessment of physical factors should also be conducted.

Impotence of long standing may have obscure origins. It is frequently impossible to determine with any hope of accuracy the specific mechanism (or mechanisms) that precipitated erectile failure. Nevertheless, evaluation of the patient's current physical and psychological status is important in determining the best course of treatment.

The Physical Examination As a Source of Diagnostic Information. The utility of a thorough physical examination in evaluating possible organic etiologies of impotence is considerable. Assessment of the signs of systemic disease is at least as important as diagnostic attention to the genitourinary tract. Detecting subtle organic impairments that may be relevant to erectile failure requires specific attention to the vascular and neurologic examination in a more detailed fashion than is usually attendant upon a general physical examination. When the history is suggestive of a physical or metabolic cause underlying a potency disorder, the inability to detect concrete evidence of disease by the physical examination is not sufficient reason to decide that the problem must be psychological; in such cases and in other instances when information obtained from the history and physical examination is inconclusive, it is necessary to employ more specific testing to complete the diagnostic process.

Diagnostic Testing for Organic Causes of Impotence. At the present time, psychogenic impotence is usually diagnosed by a process of exclusion after organic factors have been eliminated from consideration. The following methods, selectively applied, may be helpful in pinpointing specific organic etiologies of impotence.

All impotent men with equivocal histories should undergo an oral glucose tolerance test (Table 20-3) after adequate dietary preparation (including at least 300 gm of carbohydrates daily for three days) for the detection of diabetes mellitus, which appears to be the single most

Table 20-3. Criteria for
Abnormal Oral Glucose
Tolerance Test[a]

	Level of Plasma Glucose	
Time (min)	U.S. Public Health Service (100 gm oral glucose)	Fajans and Conn (1.75 mg/kg oral glucose)
0	127 mg/dl (1 point)	110 mg/dl
60	195 mg/dl (½ point)	185 mg/dl
120	138 mg/dl (½ point)	138 mg/dl
180	127 mg/dl (1 point)	
Criteria:	Equal or exceed at least three values; or total 2 points or more	Equal or exceed all three values

[a]Values are given as plasma glucose; for older patients, 10 mg/100 mg/decade over age 50 should be added to the criteria for the upper limits of normal.
Source: Adapted from N. V. Costrini and W. M. Thompson (eds.), *Manual of Medical Therapeutics* (22nd ed.), Boston: Little, Brown, 1977.

common disease causing erectile failure. Even in men with no other symptoms that suggest the presence of diabetes, an increased rate of abnormal carbohydrate tolerance has been found [1, 6]. Detecting diabetes does not automatically imply that it is the cause of impotence, since diabetic men may also be impotent for psychogenic or other organic reasons [1, 5, 7, 8], but the presence of diabetes coupled with a history suggestive of an organic process indicates the need for further testing to evaluate neurologic and circulatory mechanisms.

Men with impotence accompanied by low libido or with a history compatible with an organic origin of dysfunction should have a measurement of circulating testosterone concentrations. The blood sample should be obtained in the early morning hours (between 7:00 and 10:00 A.M.) because there is a diurnal variation in testosterone levels that makes it difficult to interpret low values obtained at other hours. Subnormal levels of testosterone may indicate the presence of hypogonadism (see Chap. 6) and, depending on the clinical context, may require further diagnostic testing. If no medical contraindications exist, a trial of testosterone replacement therapy is warranted for a period of two to four months when a low testosterone value is found. If improvement in the potency problem does not occur during this time and no other medical explanation of the dysfunction is present, it is possible that the depressed testosterone level was a result of psychological stress [9]; a course of sex therapy should then be recommended.

The use of laboratory testing for impotent men must be viewed within a context of the expense of such procedures. Modern laboratory methods permit economical screening profiles that include assessment of a spectrum of biochemical parameters that may be of diagnostic assistance. Evaluation of the fasting blood sugar, liver function, serum electrolytes, lipid levels, thyroid function, and a complete blood count (CBC) may be useful. More specialized endocrine testing may be helpful in certain cases of hypogonadism; specifically, measurement of LH, FSH, and prolactin may be used in differentiating between hyper- and hypogonadotropic hypogonadism.

If an impotent man is using a drug that may be contributing to his sexual problem (see Chap. 13), it is advisable to discontinue the medication—and if necessary, to change to a different treatment program with less likelihood of impairing erectile response—for a period of one or two months to observe possible improvement in sexual functioning. Since it is common for sexual difficulties to have multiple determinants [1, 2, 4], it is helpful to avoid the use of potentially compromising pharmacologic agents during a course of sex therapy, as well.

One of the most promising techniques to be developed for the diagnostic assessment of impotence is the physiologic monitoring of erection patterns during sleep. Based on observations showing that normal men have periodic reflex erections during the sleep cycle, the measurement of nocturnal penile tumescence (NPT) derives its usefulness from the fact that men with organic impotence have impaired erections or no erections at all during sleep, whereas men with psychogenic impotence have normal erection patterns [1, 5, 8]. Presumably, the removal by the state of sleep of anxiety, internal conflicts, or other psychological factors that may impede erection during wakefulness allows normal body reflex pathways to take over and produces measurable episodes of penile tumescence. In an extensive series of investigations conducted in a sleep research laboratory, Karacan and his colleagues have analyzed NPT patterns in various groups of men with and without potency disorders [5, 8, 10–14]. These workers utilized simultaneous electroencephalograph (EEG) tracings with continuous measurements of changes in penile circumference during sleep.

From the findings of these studies, a simplified instrument has been developed to measure NPT patterns outside the sleep research laboratory. This device records changes in penile circumference during sleep that permit evaluation of the organic versus psychogenic origins of impotence. Although further systematic study is required to determine whether the reliability of this simplified instrument is comparable to the more complete data obtained from a sleep research laboratory, it is an accessible and more economical method of diagnostic screening that holds significant potential. Questions that need to be answered in regard to either technique include the validity of NPT measurements in depressed patients (since depression is known to interfere with normal sleep patterns [15]) and the effects of drugs on erections associated with sleep.

The NPT tracing does not distinguish between various types of organic impotence, although it appears to discriminate successfully between psychogenic and organic forms of impotence most of the time. It is usually necessary, if organic impotence is documented, to perform additional diagnostic studies to determine the exact mechanism leading to impotence, since this may have important implications for treatment. Techniques that may be useful in this regard include arteriography [16] or penile pulse and blood pressure measurements [17, 18] to assess vascular competency and cystometrography [19] or direct neurophysiologic testing [20, 21] to evaluate the neurologic factor.

Cases of impotence arising primarily from organic causes must be medically or surgically managed in accord with principles that have been extensively discussed in previous chapters. In some instances, the patient and his sexual partner may benefit from ancillary counseling or psychotherapy aimed at improving depression, self-esteem, communication patterns, or other aspects of psychosocial health; however, when physical or metabolic conditions preclude the possibility of coital functioning, this fact must be pointed out to the couple and alternative suggestions for sexual expression should be discussed. In selected cases, consideration may be given to the implantation of a penile prosthetic device to permit participation in intercourse (see Chap. 9).

The Treatment of Psychogenic Impotence

In cases of psychogenic impotence or in situations in which a significant component of psychosocial difficulty contributes to the etiology or perpetuation of impotence, sex therapy is indicated if counseling attempts have not reversed the dysfunction. As discussed in the preceding chapter, sex therapy ideally includes both the impotent man and his partner, since therapeutic cooperation of the partner appears to be an important determinant of the outcome of therapy. The partner's presence during therapy sessions provides an opportunity for observation of patterns of communication within the relationship as well as a source of information about sexual function and related behavior occurring between therapy sessions.

The psychotherapeutic approach to impotence shares certain common features with the approach to the treatment of any sexual dysfunction. These features include the following points (summarized here, but amplified and developed extensively during the early phases of psychotherapeutic intervention) [1]:

1. It is not useful to blame one's partner or oneself for the occurrence of a sexual problem.
2. There is no such thing as an uninvolved partner when sexual difficulties exist.
3. Sexual dysfunctions are common problems and do not usually indicate psychopathology.
4. It is not always possible to be certain of the precise origin of a sexual dysfunction, but treatment can frequently proceed successfully even when such knowledge is lacking.
5. In general, cultural stereotypes about how men and women should behave or function sexually are misleading and counterproductive.
6. Sex is not something a man does to a woman or for a woman; it is something a man and woman do together.
7. Sex does not only mean intercourse; apart from procreative purposes, there is nothing inherent in coitus that makes it always more exciting, more gratifying, or more valuable than other forms of physical contact.
8. Sex can be a form of interpersonal communication at a highly intimate level; when sexual communications are not satisfactory, it often indicates that other aspects of the relationship might benefit from enhanced communication as well.
9. Using past feelings or behaviors to predict the present is not likely to be helpful, since such predictions tend to become self-fulfilling prophecies or may limit the freedom to change.
10. Developing awareness of one's feelings and the ability to communicate feelings and needs to one's partner sets the stage for effective sexual interaction.
11. Assuming responsibility for oneself rather than delegating this responsibility to one's partner is often an effective means of improving the sexual relationship.

The specific aspects of treating impotence by sex therapy, beyond the general approaches indicated above, depend in large part on the historical details of each case; factors such as the etiology of the dysfunction, the presence or absence of other dysfunctions or sexual problems, the status of the relationship, and intrapsychic dynamics are all important determinants of specific strategies that may be employed.

Most cases of impotence are characterized by fears of performance, a debilitating set of sexual anxieties that arise when the male is unable to obtain or maintain a normal erection and begins pressuring himself to improve his functioning [1]. Sometimes the partner contributes to such anxieties—either purposely (by making demands or derogatory remarks, for example) or inadvertently (by pretending that nothing is wrong or by attempting to be supportive)—and may compound the difficulties. A careful analysis of the ways in which performance anxieties are complicating the couple's sexual interaction is an early component of treatment, which should be followed by continuing attention to specific ways of reducing such anxieties and altering associated maladaptive behavior patterns (such as goal-setting or being a spectator; see Chap. 19).

The first approach to reducing performance anxieties is achieved at the outset of therapy by prohibiting any direct sexual activity. The couple is told that after a therapeutic plan has been formulated, the therapists will make specific suggestions for reestablishing sexual activity to facilitate learning. The second approach to anxiety reduction is in the process of identification and verbalization. Bringing the man's anxieties into the open, assuring him that such concerns are quite common, acquainting the wife or partner with the problems that the impotent man has been facing, and offering hope that such problems can be overcome allows a dialogue to develop that may materially reduce the intensity of pressures to perform and simultaneously facilitate the establishment of therapeutic rapport.

The third—and usually the most important—approach to anxiety reduction involves introduction of the principles of sensate focus. Early in therapy, the couple is instructed to participate in semistructured touching opportunities that will permit them to focus on their sensual awareness without any need to perform sexually. In fact, at the initial level of sensate focus, touching the genitals or female breasts is "off limits"; the intent is to become attuned to one's body and physical sensations and to avoid blocking such awareness by too much thinking, talking, or goal-setting. Further details of the instructions that patients are given regarding sensate focus techniques are discussed in the following chapter.

Not surprisingly, when a man who has been unable to obtain erections largely because of fears of performance has these fears eliminated because no sexual performance or response is expected, erections frequently occur during the early stages of sensate focus. When this happens, it may be reassuring to the couple for several reasons: The man's confidence in himself is improved, both partners receive concrete evidence that the therapists are accurate in their analysis of the situation, and the sense of hopelessness that either or both partners feel subsides. If erections do not occur in this early stage of treatment, it is not a bad prognostic sign nor does it necessarily indicate that the man is doing something wrong. While he may not be successful in eliminating his "spectatoring" or while he may actually be trying too hard to elicit a sexual response, it is more likely that the difficulty in such a situation is the man's inability to actually focus on his physical sensations and to reduce his cognitional activity or preconceived expectations.

Although the unique feature of sex therapy may seem to be the use of sensate focus exercises, other elements of therapy are of significant concurrent importance. Thus attention is given throughout the therapy program to verbal communication skills (including the ability to resolve interpersonal conflicts or problems), education about sexual anatomy and physiology, attitude change, and other aspects of psychological management. In some cases marriage counseling is the predominant theme of therapy; in other cases, improving self-esteem, reducing guilt, modifying maladaptive ego-defense mechanisms, and altering problems of imagery are some areas likely to receive a major degree of therapeutic focus.

The impotent man must understand that it is impossible to will an erection to occur, since erections are reflex responses.* Most impotent men understand this point intellectually because it is supported by their own experience, but nevertheless find it extremely difficult to stop trying to produce an erection by a variety of mental or physical gymnastics. As therapy progresses, they will often find that erection occurs at just the time when they are not thinking about it or trying to make it happen. A great deal of time and ingenuity may be required on the part of the therapists in order to assist the impotent man in altering his

---

*Recent research indicates that some men can be trained to use biofeedback techniques to produce erections; the applicability of this finding to the treatment of impotence is unclear at present. Anxiety and difficulty in being aware of body sensations—problems that affect many impotent men—are likely to impede learning by biofeedback techniques.

tendency to set sexual goals or expectations which, if not met, define failure in his mind.

A closely associated problem is that many men with erectile problems try to rush their sexual performance once they get an erection, out of fear that they will promptly lose it. The effect, of course, is that of mobilizing anxiety by increasing performance pressure, and the usual result is the prompt loss of erection. When this problem is present, once a pattern of erection has been established in the stage of sensate focus touching that includes the genitals, the woman may be advised to deliberately stop stroking or fondling the penis when a firm erection occurs, so that the erection recedes and the man has an opportunity to see that it will return with further touching.

Throughout the course of therapy, both partners should be reminded that fears about sexual functioning may be reduced but will never be entirely eliminated. Every man has occasional times when his erectile response is slow or absent; although these episodes may be frustrating, they are not indicative of a return to a state of impotence.

Some men will continue to have difficulty obtaining or maintaining an erection even though most aspects of therapy are proceeding well. In these instances, the problem is usually related to the fact that the man is continuing to slip into a spectator role during sexual activity. The most effective solution to this problem, once sensate focus has progressed to the stage of mutual touching, is for the man to focus his attention on some aspect of his partner's body whenever he becomes aware of watching himself or trying to gauge his own responsiveness. If he can lose himself (cognitionally) in the process of becoming sensually involved with his partner, it takes away the pressure for performance and returns some of the spontaneity that is lost in the spectator role. When this technique does not work, the man should verbalize his feelings or anxieties to his partner and alter the pattern of sexual activity that led to the difficulty—for example, he might say, "I'm watching my response, so I'd just like to hold you for a while."

When adequate erectile function has been attained in situations of caressing and non-goal-oriented touching, the couple is asked to extend the principles of sensate focus to include genital contact, possibly progressing to penile insertion. The woman is advised to be the one to insert the penis, using a position with the woman astride the man. This approach reduces pressure on the man, since he does not need to decide when it is time to insert, and since the woman in this position is most easily able to place the penis properly for initiating vaginal containment; thus two potential sources of distraction for the impotent man are largely eliminated. Following a premise that has been discussed at length during prior phases of therapy, the man is told that he may lose his erection at some point during sexual play, but is simultaneously reminded that erections, being reflex responses, characteristically wax and wane.

The treatment statistics reported in *Human Sexual Inadequacy* showed a failure rate of 40.6 percent for primary impotence and 30.9 percent for secondary impotence [1]. Between 1971 and 1977, 19 cases of primary impotence were treated at the Masters & Johnson Institute with 4 failures, for a failure rate of 21.1 percent. In the same time period, 288 cases of secondary impotence were treated with 42 failures, for a failure rate of 14.6 percent. It is likely that as more effective diagnostic methods become available and further delineation of the mechanisms causing impotence takes place, there will be commensurate gains in treatment outcome.

Premature Ejaculation Although premature ejaculation is a common sexual dysfunction, there is no precise definition of this problem that is clinically satisfactory at present, partly because of the relative nature of the timing of ejaculation in the context of the female partner's sexual response cycle. If the man's rapid ejaculation limits his partner's ability to reach high levels of sexual arousal or orgasm, a problematic situation exists. However, in some couples rapidity of ejaculation does not impede the coital responsiveness of the woman; thus, it does not appear warranted to label this pattern arbitrarily as a sexual dysfunction.

The subjective nature of evaluating the length of time a man is able to participate in coitus without ejaculating is further complicated by sociocultural and personality factors [1, 3, 22]. Kinsey, Pomeroy, and Martin reported that 75 percent of the men they studied ejaculated within 2 minutes of vaginal containment [23], but these data may have been influenced by their belief that rapid ejaculation was a biologically superior trait as well as by the fact that their study was conducted more than three decades ago. The timing of rapid ejaculation may simply reflect a primary focus on the sexual gratification of the male, an attitude that seems to predominate in men from low socioeconomic levels or with limited education [1, 24, 25]. However, this double standard regarding sex ("Sex is for the man's pleasure, not for the woman's") may be found cutting across cultural and socioeconomic lines.

Severe cases of premature ejaculation are easy to diagnose because they are marked by a pattern of ejaculation occurring before, during, or shortly after insertion of the penis into the vagina. In men with a less virulent problem of ejaculatory rapidity, premature ejaculation has been defined as the inability of the male to control ejaculation long enough to satisfy his partner in at least 50 percent of their coital opportunities, when there is no female dysfunction [1]; or inability of the male to exert voluntary control over the ejaculatory reflex [3]. LoPiccolo suggests that it is easier to define what is not premature ejaculation: "Both husband and wife agree that the quality of their sexual encounters is not influenced by efforts to delay ejaculation" [26]. Despite the difficulty of formulating a precise definition of premature ejaculation that will be applicable in all cases, as a practical matter it is not very complicated to decide when lack of ejaculatory control is problematic.

Etiology

There is no reliable research documentation of the cause (or causes) of premature ejaculation. Ejaculation is a reflex phenomenon regulated by neurologic and possibly endocrine pathways; nevertheless, clinical evidence indicates that there is a strong learned component to the process as well. Common historical patterns have been found in men with long-standing histories of premature ejaculation, with the central feature being early coital experiences in which the men ejaculated rapidly [1]. Typical histories included first coital experiences under circumstances of fear of being discovered (such as in the back seat of a car, in a teenager's home while parents were away, or in a motel) or encouragement for rapid ejaculation from a prostitute interested in quick turnover of customers. In effect, the man became conditioned to fast ejaculation, and in subsequent (more relaxed) sexual opportunities he was often unable to alter the pattern that had been established. Viewed from this perspective, premature ejaculation is seen as a primarily psychophysiologic disorder.

Past theories of organic origins of premature ejaculation usually identified prostatic or other genitourinary inflammation as the cause; however, more recent examination of large series of patients has not supported such a view [1, 3, 22]. Some authors have suggested that relationship problems, unconscious hostility toward or fear of women, or hidden female sexual arousal problems are processes underlying premature ejaculation [3, 22, 27], but these dynamics appear infrequently in couples seen at the Masters & Johnson Institute.

Treatment

The general principles of sex therapy outlined earlier apply to the couple for whom premature ejaculation is a problem. The therapeutic approach is optimal when working with the couple, since premature ejaculation is usually a matter of sexual distress to the woman in addition to being a male dysfunction. The woman may harbor resentment or hostility toward her partner as a result of the long-term sexual frustration she has experienced and the lack of intimacy that has characterized their sexual relationship. The latter situation is found particularly if the man has persistently tried to overcome his ejaculatory difficulty by mental distraction (such as counting backwards or thinking about work), shortening the time of noncoital sex play, or using other techniques to limit his arousal; such well-meant but ineffective practices may simply convince the woman of her partner's selfishness.

After thorough psychosexual histories are obtained, treatment begins with an explanation of the evolution of the problem of premature ejaculation. The therapists carefully delineate the fact that the man has not been capable of voluntarily controlling the timing of ejaculation, and they stress that this situation does not automatically equate with selfishness, fear, or hostility. The couple is told that rapid ejaculation is a common sexual problem that has an excellent prognosis with short-term therapy.

With concurrent attention to relationship dynamics and the existence of other sexual problems, the couple is then given basic information about the physiology of ejaculation (see Chap. 1). They are informed that although the precise neurophysiologic events that trigger ejaculation in the male are not known, a program of reconditioning the ejaculatory reflex response can be easily undertaken. Because performance anxiety typically develops in men with premature ejaculation, particularly when their partners are dissatisfied sexually, early attention is devoted to techniques of anxiety reduction in a manner similar to that outlined earlier in this chapter.

When genital touching is to be incorporated into sensate focus opportunities, the woman is instructed in the use of a specific physiologic method for reducing the tendency for rapid ejaculation. In this procedure, known as the "squeeze technique," the woman puts her thumb on the frenulum of the penis and places her first and second fingers just above and below the coronal ridge on the opposite side of the penis (Fig. 20-1) [1]. A firm, grasping pressure is applied for 4 seconds and then abruptly released. The pressure is always applied in a front-to-back fashion, never from side to side. It is important that the woman use the pads of her thumb and fingers and avoid pinching the penis or scratching it with her fingernails. For unknown neurophysiologic reasons, this maneuver reduces the urgency of ejaculatory tension and, used with

Figure 20-1. The squeeze technique
used to treat premature ejaculation.
(*A*) Anatomic landmarks of the erect
penis. (*B*) and (*C*) The thumb is placed
on the frenulum; the first two fingers
are placed just above and below the
coronal ridge. The squeeze is always
done in an anterior-posterior fashion,
not from side to side.

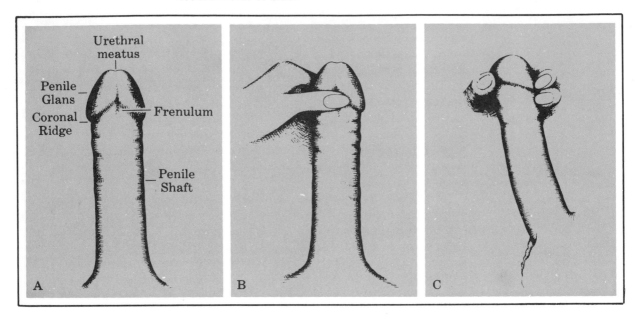

consistency, reconditions the pattern of ejaculatory timing to improve
control surprisingly well. The squeeze technique works considerably
less effectively when the man attempts to apply it to himself.

The woman is encouraged to use the squeeze technique every few
minutes during a touching opportunity, regardless of whether the man
feels that ejaculation is fast approaching or imminent. If she has mis-
givings about the mechanical or artificial nature of this procedure, she
should be reassured that it will lead to later spontaneity and that it is a
means of improving her own opportunities for sexual enjoyment by
facilitating the man's control. The specific degree of pressure that
should be used in the process of squeezing is proportional to the degree
of erection present: With a full erection, a firm squeeze should be used,
whereas when the penis is flaccid, only a moderate squeeze is employed.
Both the man and woman can be reassured that the squeeze technique
is not painful when properly applied (assuming that there are no abnormalities of the penis or urethra, such as infection, ulceration, rashes,
or anatomic deformities); a sense of pressure but not discomfort is
experienced. The sensation is similar to that achieved by squeezing the
distal portion of the thumb between the other thumb and first two
fingers with an anterior-to-posterior pressure. The couple should be

warned that the squeeze may cause a transient decrease in the firmness of the erection—usually between 10 and 25 percent—but this does not mean that the squeeze is being incorrectly applied.

After several days of practice in using the squeeze technique, if no other sexual problems are present and the man is gaining confidence, the couple is instructed to transfer this procedure to the coital situation. Since intravaginal penetration or containment is a very different sensation for the man from noncoital play, it is quite possible that he will ejaculate rapidly on the first attempt or two. Such an occurrence has no prognostic significance, and the couple should be warned of this possibility in advance. The emphasis is on the overall process of reconditioning the ejaculatory reflex, not on gains from one sexual episode to the next.

The woman is asked to mount the man and to use the squeeze technique three to six times before attempting insertion. She should employ a squeeze just before inserting the penis into the vagina, and after vaginal containment is achieved she should hold still so that both she and her partner can focus on their physical sensations. The man must be instructed to abstain from active thrusting during this process. After a short interval of intravaginal containment of the penis, the woman should move off the penis, apply the squeeze again, and reinsert, this time beginning a slow thrusting pattern. If the man feels that ejaculation is approaching, he signals the woman so that she can again dismount and use the squeeze technique. If containment continues for approximately 4 or 5 minutes, the couple can move to a more rapid thrusting pattern and the man can be allowed to ejaculate. When improved ejaculatory control is attained in this fashion, another version of the squeeze technique applied to the base of the penis (the "basilar squeeze"; see Fig. 20-2) is taught so that intercourse need not be interrupted by repeated dismounting in order to apply a squeeze.

Most men have considerable improvement in control over ejaculation prior to the end of the two-week program of sex therapy, typically experiencing 10 to 15 minutes of intravaginal containment with active thrusting. In general, couples need to continue the use of the squeeze technique for three to six months after the intensive phase of therapy to achieve a permanent reconditioning of the ejaculatory response. In *Human Sexual Inadequacy* a failure rate of only 2.7 percent was reported in a series of 186 men with premature ejaculation [1]; other workers describe excellent therapeutic outcomes as well [28–30]. From 1971 to 1977, an additional 246 men with premature ejaculation were treated at the Masters & Johnson Institute with 12 failures, for a

Figure 20-2. The basilar squeeze
technique used in the treatment of
premature ejaculation. (*A*) Arrows
indicate the areas where pressure is
applied at the base of the penis. (*B*)
Pressure may be applied in either a
posterior-anterior or an anterior-
posterior fashion, but not laterally.

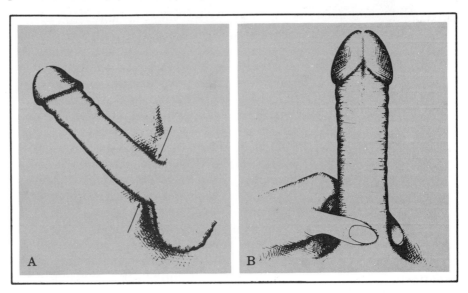

failure rate of 4.9 percent. This increase in the failure rate is probably
primarily a reflection of the fact that in more than two-thirds of these
cases, premature ejaculation coexisted with secondary impotence.

**Ejaculatory
Incompetence**

The male sexual dysfunction that is least frequently encountered in
clinical populations (and is presumed to be of correspondingly low prevalence) is ejaculatory incompetence, or the inability to ejaculate intravaginally [1]. Men with this disorder rarely have difficulty with
erection and typically are able to maintain a firm erection during
lengthy episodes of coitus. The functional problem may be conceptualized as being the opposite of premature ejaculation.

Although secondary ejaculatory incompetence is sometimes seen
(loss of the ability to ejaculate intravaginally after a previous history of
normal coital ejaculation), the most common form of ejaculatory incompetence is primary (never having been able to ejaculate intravaginally). There is variability in the pattern of noncoital ejaculation: Some
men with ejaculatory incompetence can ejaculate with solitary masturbation, others can ejaculate by noncoital partner stimulation (manual or oral), while still others are unable to ejaculate by any means. In a
small percentage of cases, ejaculatory incompetence may be situational, occurring with one partner but not another [31].

Etiology

Organic causes of ejaculatory incompetence include congenital anatomic lesions of the genitourinary system, spinal cord lesions, damage to the lumbar sympathetic ganglia, and use of drugs that impair sympathetic tone, such as guanethidine [22]. The phenothiazines may also delay or prevent ejaculation. However, most instances of ejaculatory incompetence are of psychogenic origin.

Etiologic factors that may be seen include the effects of severe religious orthodoxy during childhood, which instills attitudes of sex as sinful, the genitals as unclean, and the act of masturbation to ejaculation as evil and destructive. Hostility toward or rejection of the spouse, homosexuality, fear of pregnancy, the desire not to have children, and specific psychosocial trauma (the discovery by a man that his wife has been having an affair or has been raped, for example) have also been described as important in the development of ejaculatory incompetence [1, 3, 22].

Treatment

It is important to explain the etiology of the dysfunction carefully to both partners, since the woman's attitudes toward her partner's failure to ejaculate may be quite negative, particularly if she wants to have children and perceives her husband as willfully preventing conception. Since the woman will be called upon to play an active role in the reversal of ejaculatory incompetence, neutralizing initial hostilities or distrust is a necessary early therapeutic concern.

The sensate focus exercises are employed in a fashion similar to that used in the treatment of impotence: The goal is to facilitate the man's awareness of his own physical sensations, improve nonverbal communication patterns, and eliminate the pressure to perform. When genital touching occurs, the woman is encouraged to stimulate the penis in a deliberate and demanding fashion, with the man communicating to her information about timing, pressure, and types of stimulating motions that he finds most arousing sexually. The first objective is for the woman to induce ejaculation by manual stimulation. Once this has been accomplished, sex play in the female-astride position is recommended. The woman stimulates her partner to a high degree of sexual excitation; as the man approaches the stage of ejaculatory inevitability, the woman inserts the penis into the vagina rapidly, continuing penile stimulation as she inserts. If the man does not ejaculate after a brief period of vigorous thrusting, the woman dismounts and returns to manual stimulation of the penis, reinserting the penis as ejaculation becomes imminent.

A single occasion of intravaginal ejaculation is usually all that is required to reverse the dysfunction permanently. After several successful episodes, the couple's confidence is firmly established. In cases in which intravaginal ejaculation has not occurred despite repeated attempts with therapeutic suggestion and analysis, the woman should bring the man to ejaculation by the use of manual stimulation, in a position that allows the ejaculate to spurt onto the external female genitalia. As the man becomes more comfortable seeing his ejaculatory fluid in genital contact with his partner, intravaginal ejaculation may occur more easily.

Throughout the treatment of the couple in whom ejaculatory incompetence is present, emphasis must be placed on effective patterns of communication. In instances of patients who do not respond to sex therapy, referral for in-depth individual therapy may be beneficial. In a series of 17 cases reported in *Human Sexual Inadequacy*, the failure rate was 17.6 percent [1]. An additional 58 cases of ejaculatory incompetence were treated at the Masters & Johnson Institute between 1971 and 1977 with 15 failures, giving a failure rate of 25.9 percent.

Mixed Dysfunctions

It is not surprising that combinations of sexual dysfunctions may exist in the same man, since common etiologic factors appear to underlie many of these disorders. The most frequently encountered combination is premature ejaculation and impotence; indeed, it appears that anxiety over sexual performance resulting from rapid ejaculation is a cause of impotence. Much less frequently, ejaculatory incompetence may coexist with impotence.

In treating these conditions, it is generally necessary to deal initially with the erectile failure and to institute appropriate management of the ejaculatory dysfunction only after security has been gained in erectile function. The exception to this strategy is the instance in which a man ejaculates prematurely while the penis is flaccid; in this situation, the squeeze technique must be used to provide ejaculatory control before adequate erections can be attained.

There has been a remarkable improvement in the efficacy of clinical approaches to the treatment of male sexual dysfunction following the techniques briefly outlined in this chapter. As additional passage of time permits increased clinical and research experience to accumulate, it is hoped that even further therapeutic inroads will be made.

References

1. Masters, W. H., and Johnson, V. E. *Human Sexual Inadequacy*. Boston: Little, Brown and Co., 1970.

2. Levine, S. B.   Marital sexual dysfunction: Erectile dysfunction. *Annals of Internal Medicine* 85:342–350, 1976.

3. Kaplan, H. S.   *The New Sex Therapy*. New York: Brunner/Mazel, 1974.

4. Reckless, J., and Geiger, N.   Impotence as a Practical Problem. *Disease-a-Month*, May 1975. Chicago: Year Book Medical Publishers, 1975.

5. Karacan, I., Salis, P. J., Ware, J. C., Dervent, B., Williams, R. L., Scott, F. B., Attia, S. L., and Beutler, L. E.   Nocturnal penile tumescence and diagnosis in diabetic impotence. *American Journal of Psychiatry* 135:191–197, 1978.

6. Goldman, J. A., Schechter, A., and Eckerling, B.   Carbohydrate metabolism in infertile and impotent males. *Fertility and Sterility* 21:397–401, 1970.

7. Kolodny, R. C., Kahn, C. B., Goldstein, H. H., and Barnett, D. M.   Sexual dysfunction in diabetic men. *Diabetes* 23:306–309, 1974.

8. Karacan, I., Scott, F. B., Salis, P. J., Attia, S. L., Ware, J. C., Altinel, A., and Williams, R. L.   Nocturnal erections, differential diagnosis of impotence, and diabetes. *Biological Psychiatry* 12:373–380, 1977.

9. Kreuz, L. E., Rose, R. M., and Jennings, J. R.   Suppression of plasma testosterone levels and psychological stress. *Archives of General Psychiatry* 26:479–482, 1972.

10. Karacan, I., Goodenough, D. R., Shapiro, A., and Starker, S.   Erection cycle during sleep in relation to dream anxiety. *Archives of General Psychiatry* 15:183–189, 1965.

11. Karacan, I., Hursch, C. J., and Williams, R. L.   Some characteristics of nocturnal penile tumescence in elderly males. *Journal of Gerontology* 27:39–45, 1972.

12. Karacan, I., Hursch, C. J., Williams, R. L., and Littell, R. C.   Some characteristics of nocturnal penile tumescence during puberty. *Pediatric Research* 6:529–537, 1972.

13. Karacan, I., Hursch, C. J., Williams, R. L, and Thornby, J. I.   Some characteristics of nocturnal penile tumescence in young adults. *Archives of General Psychiatry* 26:351–356, 1972.

14. Karacan, I., Williams, R. L., Thornby, J. I., and Salis, P. J.   Sleep-related tumescence as a function of age. *American Journal of Psychiatry* 132:932–937, 1975.

15. Hawkins, D. R., and Mendels, J.   Sleep disturbance in depressive syndromes. *American Journal of Psychiatry* 123:682–690, 1966.

16. Michal, V., Kramář, R., Popischal, J., and Hejhal, L.   Arterial epigastricocavernous anastomosis for the treatment of sexual impotence. *World Journal of Surgery* 1:515–520, 1977.

17. Gaskell, P.   The importance of penile blood pressure in cases of impotence. *Canadian Medical Association Journal* 105:1047–1051, 1971.

18. Abelson, D.   Diagnostic value of the penile pulse and blood pressure: A Doppler study of impotence in diabetics. *Journal of Urology* 113:636–639, 1975.

19. Ellenberg, M.   Impotence in diabetes: The neurologic factor. *Annals of Internal Medicine* 75:213–219, 1971.

20. Lundberg, P. O.   Sexual Dysfunction in Patients with Neurological Dis-

orders. In R. Gemme and C. C. Wheeler (eds.), *Progress in Sexology*. New York: Plenum Press, 1977. Pp. 129–139.

21. Ertekin, C., and Reel, F.   Bulbocavernous reflex in normal men and in patients with neurogenic bladder and/or impotence. *Journal of the Neurological Sciences* 28:1–15, 1976.

22. Levine, S. B.   Marital sexual dysfunction: Ejaculation disturbances. *Annals of Internal Medicine* 84:575–579, 1976.

23. Kinsey, A. C., Pomeroy, W. B., and Martin, C. E.   *Sexual Behavior in the Human Male*. Philadelphia: W. B. Saunders Co., 1948.

24. Caird, W., and Wincze, J. P.   *Sex Therapy: A Behavioral Approach*. New York: Harper & Row, 1977.

25. Rainwater, L.   *And the Poor Get Children*. Chicago: Quadrangle Books, 1960.

26. LoPiccolo, J.   Direct Treatment of Sexual Dysfunction in the Couple. In J. Money and H. Musaph (eds.), *Handbook of Sexology*. New York: Elsevier/North Holland Biomedical Press, 1977. Pp. 1227–1244.

27. Levine, S. B.   Premature ejaculation: Some thoughts about its pathogenesis. *Journal of Sex and Marital Therapy* 1:326–334, 1975.

28. Yulis, S.   Generalization of therapeutic gain in the treatment of premature ejaculation. *Behavior Therapy* 7:355–358, 1976.

29. Kaplan, H. S., Kohl, R. N., Pomeroy, W. B., Offit, A. K., and Hogan, B.   Group treatment of premature ejaculation. *Archives of Sexual Behavior* 3:443–452, 1974.

30. Kilmann, P. R., and Auerbach, R.   Treatments of premature ejaculation and psychogenic impotence: A critical review of the literature. *Archives of Sexual Behavior* 8:81–100, 1979.

31. Munjack, D. J., and Kanno, P. H.   Retarded ejaculation: A review. *Archives of Sexual Behavior* 8:139–150, 1979.

Until relatively recent times, women were generally regarded as less sexual beings than men. Some medical authorities were convinced that women were incapable of sexual arousal, while others believed that the responsive female ejaculated at the moment of orgasm. Freud regarded sexual desire as a masculine trait; the notion of penis envy as a universal developmental fact in females and the subsequent conceptualization of mature female sexuality as being demonstrated only by vaginal (rather than clitoral) orgasm were central elements of his thinking. As Gould has observed, these beliefs led Freud into seeing all personality traits as determined by such theories:

Freud postulated that man is the aggressor and all active traits are rightfully male, whereas passive traits are female. The masculine nature was defined as objective, analytical, tough-minded, intellectual, rational, aggressive, independent, active and confident. The feminine nature was thought to embody opposing traits, such as subjectivity, emotionality, irrationality, illogical thinking, empathy, sensitivity, intuition, receptivity, passivity, and dependency. . . . Freud made it clear in one of his last statements ("Analysis Terminable and Interminable") that woman must come to accept her secondary status and compensate for her lack of a penis by having a baby and a husband; but something is always lacking. Man has to overcome his castration fear, which can reflect itself in passive traits; but, if successful, man emerges as a complete human being; the woman can never achieve this [1].

The work of later psychiatrists such as Karen Horney and contributions made by sex researchers including Kinsey and his colleagues combined with changing cultural values to produce a current view of female sexuality that is markedly different. The evolution of public and scientific attitudes toward female sexuality has been expertly reviewed by several authors [2–4]. It is clear that while changes have occurred, many myths and misperceptions related to female sexuality abound; these misperceptions may serve as important factors in the genesis of female sexual dysfunction. However, this chapter specifically focuses on the clinical aspects of female sexual dysfunctions and does not attempt a broad cultural or political analysis of such problems.

Vaginismus

Vaginismus is a condition of involuntary spasm or constriction of the musculature surrounding the vaginal outlet and the outer third of the vagina (Fig. 21-1). This psychophysiologic syndrome may affect women of any age, from the time of earliest attempts at sexual activity to the geriatric years, and may vary considerably in severity. The most dramatic instances of vaginismus often present as unconsummated marriages, since penile insertion into the vagina may not be possible

Figure 21-1. (*A*) Normal female pelvic
anatomy. (*B*) Vaginismus, showing
involuntary constriction of outer
third of vagina. (From Masters and
Johnson [5].)

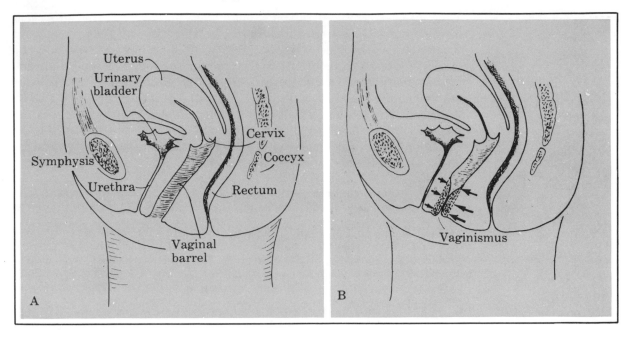

due to spasm, resistance, and attendant pain; at the other end of the
clinical spectrum are cases in which coitus is possible but painful. The
frequency of vaginismus in the general population is unknown.

Although the woman with vaginismus may be quite fearful of sexual
activity, thus limiting her overall sexual responsivity, more commonly
women with vaginismus have little difficulty with sexual arousal.
Vaginal lubrication occurs normally, noncoital sexual activity may be
pleasurable and satisfying, and orgasmic responsiveness is often intact.
Women with vaginismus usually have normal libido and are distressed
by their inability to participate pleasurably in coitus.

Etiology

Vaginismus may arise from a natural protective reflex to pain
originating from any lesion of the external genitalia or vaginal introitus. The percentage of cases of vaginismus that are initially attributable to organic problems of this type is not certain; one difficulty is that
repeated episodes of such pain may produce a conditioned response so
that even if the original lesion heals spontaneously or is eliminated by
proper medical therapy, the vaginismus may remain. Thus a woman

who initially experiences vaginismus in association with a poorly healed episiotomy may continue to be dysfunctional after the perineal and vaginal tissues have healed normally. Transient or subacute vaginismus in association with pelvic pathology often does not require psychotherapy, but chronic vaginismus, even if it is attributable to organic processes, usually requires such treatment. Among the frequent organic causes of vaginismus are hymenal abnormalities, including remnants of the hymen that are stretched during attempts at vaginal penetration; genital herpes or other infections that cause ulcerations near the opening of the vagina or on the labia; obstetric trauma; and atrophic vaginitis.

More commonly, however, no organic process can be implicated as the cause of vaginismus. In these cases, a variety of psychosocial factors may be operative. There appears to be more than a chance association between a background of negative conditioning to sex fostered by intense childhood and adolescent exposure to religious orthodoxy and the later occurrence of vaginismus. It should be emphasized that the development of vaginismus (or any sexual dysfunction) from this background has little to do with the specific theological content of religious upbringing; rather, the major difficulty seems to stem from the rigid, often punitive thinking that regards sex as dirty, sinful, and shameful. This background pattern is frequently encountered in women with unconsummated marriages, and indicates that they have difficulty in making the psychic transition from viewing sex as evil (premaritally) to viewing sex as good (upon marriage). Interestingly, women from such backgrounds often marry men of similar upbringing, and a high incidence of primary impotence has been found among such couples when the woman has vaginismus [5].

Vaginismus may also stem from a severely traumatic sexual experience. Although this etiology is seen most typically in the case of women who were raped during childhood or adolescence, the occurrence of rape at any age may precipitate a subsequent pattern of secondary vaginismus, even when previous sexual function had been well established. Vaginismus may also occur as a consequence of traumatic sexual experiences other than rape: Incest, repeated sexual molestation as a child, or a pattern of psychologically painful sexual episodes at any age may predispose to this condition.

Other factors that may be important in the genesis of vaginismus include homosexual orientation, traumatic experience with an early pelvic examination, pregnancy phobia, venereal disease phobia, or cancer phobia. The precise role of negative maternal conditioning in regard to menstruation, reproduction, and sex has not been carefully explored but may sometimes be a factor in the subsequent development of vaginismus.

Diagnostic Considerations

Vaginismus may present in a number of different ways. As previously mentioned, vaginismus is frequently seen clinically in the context of an unconsummated marriage. Vaginismus may also be present in cases of unconsummated marriage that appear to result from primary impotence: The actual difficulty in such a situation may be compounded by the constrictive resistance of the vagina to accepting the erect penis. When the severity of vaginismus is moderate or mild, coitus may be possible but is characteristically painful; cases of this variety may therefore present as dyspareunia without either the woman or her partner being aware of the origins of the pain associated with intercourse. In a smaller number of cases, vaginismus may be discovered to be the cause of secondary impotence. In this situation, the man may have developed impotence as a result of not wanting to hurt his partner; alternatively, the anxiety provoked by being unable to achieve vaginal penetration may trigger performance fears and push the man into the spectator role, as discussed in the two preceding chapters. Vaginismus may also be found occasionally in cases that ostensibly present as problems of low female libido (see Chap. 22).

The histories of women with vaginismus may contain clues to the appropriate diagnosis. In addition to facts pertaining to the possible etiologies mentioned previously, a careful history should be obtained regarding vaginal penetration occurring under any circumstances. Women with severe vaginismus are typically unable to use a vaginal tampon during menstruation. A history may be obtained of pain associated with the insertion of a finger into the vagina or pain related to attempts at inserting other objects, such as a vaginal speculum (during a pelvic examination), a diaphragm, a contraceptive foam applicator, or a vaginal suppository prescribed for the treatment of an infection. A specific history regarding the woman's previous experience with pelvic examinations, including her perceptions of the physician's manner, should be carefully elicited. Additional historical facts related to menstruation (including age at onset, menstrual difficulties, and attitudes toward menstruation), contraception, pregnancy, therapeutic abortion, pelvic trauma, and masturbatory patterns may be of help in pointing toward the correct diagnosis.

Even in situations in which the history is strongly suggestive of the possibility of vaginismus, the diagnosis can be established with certainty only by a carefully conducted pelvic examination. Because many women with vaginismus are fearful of such examinations, in part because of their concerns over any vaginal penetration and in part due to their frequent history of insensitive and traumatic prior pelvic examinations, the female cotherapist discusses the objectives and methods of the diagnostic pelvic examination with the woman extensively before it is performed. In this session, the patient is allowed to ventilate her anxieties and concerns but at the same time is given reassurance that the examination will be unhurried, gentle, and restricted to obtaining information relevant to establishing the diagnosis of vaginismus; thus a speculum will not be used as part of this examination. Furthermore, and most important, the patient is assured that she will be in control of the examination from start to finish, as described below.

At the Masters & Johnson Institute, the diagnostic pelvic examination for detecting vaginismus is performed in the context of a general physical examination. The examining physician proceeds methodically but in an unhurried manner; at each phase of the examination, the physician tells the woman what will be done next ("I'm going to examine your ears"), shows her any piece of equipment that will be used ("This instrument is called an otoscope; it shines a light into the ear canal so I can see the inside of the ear"), and tells her what was found ("Your ears look completely normal"). In this fashion, as the physician examines each body system, the patient becomes accustomed to the pace of the examination and has an opportunity to ask questions. Throughout the examination, a chaperone is present; if the physician is not a woman, the female cotherapist is also present.

The pelvic examination is performed using knee supports rather than heel stirrups, allowing a greater degree of physical comfort on the part of the patient. The patient should not be hurried or pressured, and should never be told, "This won't hurt at all," because such a promise is impossible to keep; instead, the examiner can assure the patient, "I'll be as gentle as possible." Realistic statements made in a factual and sensitive manner will contribute to the female patient's comfort level but should never be assumed to dispel all anxiety or fear that is present.

The patient is again reminded that she is in control of the examination. If she wishes the examiner to stop and wait, to go more slowly, or to answer a question, the examiner should do so. This practical demonstration to the patient that she will not be forced into anything or taken by surprise is an important element of the examination process.

The examination begins by simple inspection of the external

genitalia. Often at this point in the examination it is possible to detect spasm about the vagina and rigidity in the muscles along the interior of the thighs or along the perineum. A determination must be made by observation of the patient as to whether such muscular rigidity is the result of voluntary muscle guarding; if this is the case, the patient may be adducting her thighs or may be drawing away from the end of the examining table. If voluntary guarding occurs, the patient must be relaxed by further discussion or by the use of techniques such as breathing exercises, since vaginismus—an involuntary response— cannot be diagnosed in the presence of voluntary guarding.

The examiner should next allow the patient to see his or her gloved hand and should explain that the lips of the vagina will be gently moved apart. It is important for the examiner to proceed quite slowly, allowing the woman to become accustomed to the physical contact and to realize that nothing is being hurried or sprung on her by surprise. After examination and palpation of the external genitalia, including the labia, the clitoris, and the urethral meatus, the next step will be insertion of a single examining finger into the vaginal outlet. The physician should coat the gloved examining finger liberally with a lubricant and show this to the patient. Next, the examining finger is rested gently, with a minimum of pressure, at the vaginal orifice, and the patient is asked if this is uncomfortable (never "Does this hurt?").* If discomfort is attendant upon this maneuver, the physician inquires as to whether the finger should be removed or whether the discomfort is diminishing to a tolerable level. If significant discomfort persists (which would be quite unusual under these circumstances), the female cotherapist talks with the patient to induce a further degree of relaxation. If no significant discomfort is present, the examining finger is very gradually inserted into the vagina to a depth of approximately 1 to 2 inches. Insertion should be accomplished quite slowly, never in a sudden fashion. It is generally advisable to exert a slightly posterior pressure with the examining digit rather than simply inserting directly forward, which may be more uncomfortable.

The diagnosis of vaginismus can be made if involuntary spasm or constriction of the musculature surrounding the outer portion of the vagina is detected. If this diagnosis is made, it is not usually necessary to go on to a more detailed pelvic examination at this time, including

---

*The connotation of the words "hurt" and "pain" in the context of this pelvic examination is counterproductive; speaking in terms of "discomfort" allows the woman to feel better able to handle the situation and reduces the element of fear.

deep palpation, insertion of a speculum, and obtaining Pap smears or vaginal cultures. These procedures can be performed a day or two later in the treatment process, once the patient has been educated about her condition and active treatment has begun.

Because many patients who may have vaginismus are extremely fearful of having a pelvic examination, some physicians conduct such an examination under general anesthesia. Although this procedure may be helpful in detecting organic pathology that would otherwise be difficult to identify, the muscle relaxation induced by anesthesia makes it impossible to diagnose vaginismus even if it is present.

Treatment

The basic principles of conjoint sex therapy discussed in Chapter 19 provide the overall matrix for the treatment of vaginismus. Unique features of the therapeutic approach to this dysfunction are presented here.

Information about the diagnosis of vaginismus, including a description of its anatomy, probable etiology, and prognosis, are presented to the couple in the round-table session following history-taking. Specific areas of impact that the condition of vaginismus may have brought about are discussed in detail, and emphasis is placed on the involuntary nature of the vaginismus reflex, since often the man has perceived his partner as willfully precluding coital participation. An outline of the overall treatment plan is presented.

Immediately following this session, a second pelvic examination is performed. At this time, with the woman's consent, her husband or partner is present in the examining room so that the nature of the involuntary constriction about the vagina can be demonstrated to both partners. The woman is encouraged to watch the examination in a mirror held by a medical assistant.

The purpose of this examination is to introduce the use of a series of graduated plastic dilators (Fig. 21-2), which will be used to reprogram the maladaptive muscular constriction of the vaginismus response. The physician begins by teaching the woman a paradoxical approach to relaxation of her pelvic musculature. The woman is told to deliberately tighten her pelvic muscles as intensely as she can, to maintain this tightness for 3 or 4 seconds, and then to let go. The contrast between deliberate, *intense* voluntary muscle constriction and the unavoidable degree of relative relaxation that occurs when the woman is no longer straining to hold her pelvic muscles in contraction is the simplest and most effective way of providing an active means for the woman to gain a degree of pelvic relaxation. The usefulness of this maneuver is high-

Figure 21-2. Plastic dilators used in
the treatment of vaginismus. The
dilators (from smallest to largest) are
nos. 1, 1½, 2, 3, 4, and 5.

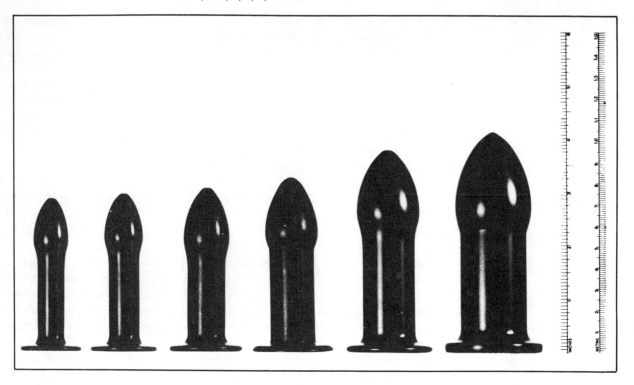

lighted by the fact that many women with vaginismus have repeatedly
tried to relax their pelvic musculature by other means, without success.

Once the woman has been able to practice this "tensing and letting
go" cycle for a minute or two, she is shown the smallest size plastic
dilator and is urged to hold it and inspect it. Most women with vaginismus do not believe that they will be able to accept even this smallest
dilator comfortably; an unhurried manner together with reassurance
that, as with the previous pelvic examination, she will control the
timing and action often is beneficial at this point. The physician gently
places a gloved and well-lubricated finger at the vaginal introitus. The
woman is asked to deliberately tighten the muscles around the vagina
and is then told to let go. As muscular relaxation occurs, the tip of the
examining finger is slowly inserted intravaginally (the patient is still
watching the procedure in the mirror) and is simply held in place. The
woman is asked if she is experiencing discomfort; if no discomfort is

present, the examining finger is withdrawn and the woman is then shown the plastic dilator again, pointing out that it is smaller in diameter than the examining finger. With her agreement, she is then asked to tighten the muscles around the vagina once again, hold the contraction for 3 or 4 seconds, and let go. At this point, the well-lubricated plastic dilator, which was held just above the examining finger, is gently and slowly slid over the top of the finger into the introitus just as the finger is withdrawn with a slight posterior pressure. The dilator is inserted at a slight angle, with its tip aimed toward the coccyx. It is important to move the dilator very slowly and gently, rather than abruptly pushing it into the vagina. If the woman experiences any discomfort—the female cotherapist is maintaining a dialogue with her to check on this point—she is again asked to tighten her muscles and then let go. Following this general approach, it is almost always possible to insert the smallest size (No. 1) dilator within a minute or two.

Many women with vaginismus are astounded when they look in the mirror and realize that the dilator is entirely within the vagina except for its base. The woman is given a chance to talk about this, including discussion with her partner, and is then asked to reach down and touch the base of the dilator and to move it gently intravaginally. She is reminded of the technique for muscle relaxation and is asked to use this again several times; finally, she is asked to withdraw the dilator completely.

Following this procedure, the woman is asked to insert the dilator herself. Additional lubrication is put on the dilator, if necessary. The woman is told to sit up on the examining table or to use whatever position is most comfortable for her. She is told how to angle the dilator and is reminded to tighten her vaginal muscles for 3 or 4 seconds immediately before attempting insertion; the dilator should be just at the vaginal opening at this time. More than 90 percent of the time, the woman is able to accomplish intravaginal insertion of the dilator easily. This procedure is then repeated several times to allow her to gain confidence and experience.

Depending on the severity of vaginismus, the emotional state of the woman, and the ease with which she is able to insert the No. 1 dilator, she may then be asked to attempt insertion of the No. 1½ dilator. In some cases, this is not done on this same day. In any event, the woman is given the dilators she has used in the examination room to take with her. She is asked to insert the dilator approximately four times during the day, leaving it in place intravaginally for 10 to 15 minutes before removing it. She is reminded to lubricate it thoroughly prior to insertion, never to try to force the dilator in, and to use the vaginal tightening exercise in conjunction with insertion. She is also asked to insert the dilator just before bedtime and to attempt to fall asleep with the dilator in place. If this is uncomfortable and prevents her from falling asleep, she should simply remove the dilator.

The couple also is given instruction in beginning sensate focus techniques, as discussed earlier, and is given counseling in regard to verbal communication skills. The use of vaginal dilators is an adjunct to the psychotherapy program in which the couple is participating. Therapeutic focus remains on the relationship; care must be taken not to single out the female client as the patient and make it seem that the male client is an assistant therapist.

On subsequent days of therapy, the female cotherapist ascertains how the woman is progressing in the use of the dilators. If this is proceeding smoothly, introduction of the next size dilator is undertaken; if any problems exist, the manner in which the woman is inserting the dilators is rechecked by direct observation in the examination room. Typically, women with vaginismus are able to move progressively from the No. 1 to the No. 4 dilator within a period of five or six days. When a No. 2 dilator can be used comfortably by the woman, a pelvic examination using a pediatric speculum or a narrow-bladed adult (Pederson) speculum should be conducted to obtain further diagnostic information, including a Pap smear and vaginal culture. Needless to say, any pelvic pathologic condition that is detected should be appropriately treated; this may necessitate slowing the progression in the use of vaginal dilators or the progression of sensate focus exercises. Depending on the dynamics of each case, the male partner may be asked to assist the woman in inserting the vaginal dilators as therapy progresses.

By the time the woman is able to insert the No. 4 dilator comfortably, and assuming that the man is having reasonably normal erective function, the couple is able to make the transition to coitus. The female-superior position (Fig. 21-3) is always suggested for this purpose, to allow the woman the greatest degree of freedom of motion and control. The couple is reminded that the dilators are made of inflexible plastic; in contrast, the penis, even when fully erect, has a greater degree of pliability. The woman is instructed to insert the penis just as she has been doing with the dilators, including the use of an artificial lubricant applied to the penis if she wishes. Although for some couples the memory of past difficulties in attempts at coitus flood in to create temporary problems, for most the techniques for relaxed intimacy without perfor-

Figure 21-3. The female-superior coital position. (From Masters and
Johnson [5].)

mance demands learned through the sensate focus exercises set the
stage for uneventful coitus without difficulty.

Necessarily, particular issues related to either the etiology of the
vaginismus or to marital discord, negative sexual attitudes, poor self-
esteem, or similar factors must be dealt with during the daily
psychotherapy program. A description of these methods is beyond the
scope of this text. However, it is important to view the approach to the
patient with vaginismus as one that combines accurate diagnosis,
psychophysiologic intervention, and appropriate psychotherapeutic
techniques, rather than as a simple mechanical treatment program.
With this type of combined approach, vaginismus can be reversed in all
motivated patients except those who have an irreversible organic pathologic condition underlying the problems.

In *Human Sexual Inadequacy*, experience was reported with 29 cases
of vaginismus treated without failure. Between 1971 and 1977, an additional 54 cases of vaginismus were treated with a single failure, giving a
failure rate of 1.9 percent.

Orgasmic Dysfunction   Prior to 1970 and the publication of *Human Sexual Inadequacy*, the
term *frigidity* was used to describe a wide variety of female sexual
difficulties. Because this term was lacking in diagnostic precision—it

was variably applied to women who were uninterested in sex, women who never experienced orgasm, and women who purportedly experienced clitoral instead of vaginal orgasms (a distinction that is now known to be erroneous)—and because of the negative, disparaging connotations toward women that it implies, most recent authors have abandoned its use. Although there is no uniform agreement on the precise diagnostic terminology to be used in reference to women who do not experience orgasm, many professionals have adopted the classification suggested by Masters and Johnson [5].

Primary orgasmic dysfunction (primary anorgasmia) is defined as the condition of a woman who never has attained orgasm under any circumstances. The classification of *situational orgasmic dysfunction* (situational anorgasmia) applies to women who have achieved orgasm on one or more occasions, but only under certain circumstances—for example, women who are orgasmic during masturbation but not with stimulation by their partner. Women who are orgasmic by many means but are nonorgasmic during intercourse are described in a subcategory of situational orgasmic dysfunction known as *coital orgasmic inadequacy* (coital anorgasmia). *Random orgasmic dysfunction* refers to women who have experienced orgasm in different types of sexual activity but only on an infrequent basis. *Secondary orgasmic dysfunction* describes women who were regularly orgasmic at one time but no longer are.

There is some controversy at the present time regarding the number of women who are anorgasmic. However, the available data are in good agreement. Kinsey and his colleagues reported that 10 percent of married women never experienced coital orgasm [6]. Chesser found that 10 percent of 3,705 married British women rarely experienced orgasm, while 5 percent never experienced orgasm during intercourse [7]. Fisher reported that approximately 6 percent of married women never experienced orgasm [8]. Levine and Yost reported that 5 percent of patients seen in a general gynecologic clinic had never been orgasmic with a sexual partner, while 17 percent had difficulty reaching orgasm with a partner [9]. From a clinical perspective, women who are unhappy about lack of orgasmic responsiveness are far more likely to seek treatment than women who are nonorgasmic but do not feel dissatisfied sexually.

Etiology

Much less is known about organic factors causing female sexual dysfunction than is the case with male sexual dysfunction. Conditions that affect the nerve supply to the pelvis (for example, multiple sclerosis, spinal cord tumors or trauma, amyotrophic lateral sclerosis, nutritional deficiencies, or diabetic neuropathy) or conditions that impair the vascular integrity of vaginal circulation (abdominal aneurysm, thrombotic obstruction, arteritis, or severe arteriosclerosis) are sometimes responsible for loss of orgasmic responsiveness. Endocrine disorders (Addison's disease, Cushing's syndrome, hypothyroidism, hyperthyroidism, hypopituitarism, or diabetes mellitus) may likewise interfere with female sexual response and usually are correctable by appropriate medical treatment of the underlying disorder. Gynecologic factors, including the impact of extensive surgical procedures, chronic vaginal infections, and congenital anomalies, were discussed in Chapter 8. Many chronic illnesses impair orgasmic responsiveness indirectly by affecting libido and general health.

Analysis of a large series of cases of orgasmic dysfunction seen at the Masters & Johnson Institute indicates that 95 percent or more are psychogenic in origin. Undoubtedly, this figure reflects characteristics of this particular clinical population, but it underscores the necessity for an appropriate psychotherapeutic approach.

It is frequently difficult to trace the etiology of orgasmic dysfunction because so many women have been exposed to negative cultural conditioning in regard to sexuality. Until recently, the prevailing message most women received throughout childhood, adolescence, and adulthood was that sexuality was to be repressed. While the male has had society's blessing in becoming sexual and exploring his own sexuality, females were expected to be "good"—that is, to postpone sexual feelings or sexual participation until after marriage. The growing girl was traditionally permitted to develop only simulated facets of her sexuality, namely, those aspects having to do with symbolic romanticism and rehearsals of maternalism. To these cultural limits must be added the constraints imposed by rigid social scripting in which the male has been expected to initiate both courtship and sexual behavior; the female has been inadvertently placed into a chronic role of the relatively passive partner in both social and sexual aspects of development.

As cultural patterns change, there is often a divergence between actual behavior and the accepted cultural norm. Many women have been caught in a dichotomous situation in which current behaviors that appear acceptable to their peers, are widely discussed in the media, and may even come to be statistically normative, create internal conflicts because they are appreciably different from learned attitudes and values that originated in an earlier cultural and social environment. Although it appears that most women are flexible enough to adapt to such changing patterns, for others such conflicts prove to be major obstacles to relaxed sexual enjoyment.

Aside from the broad cultural influences on female sexuality just mentioned, a number of specific developmental factors appear to have relevance to orgasmic dysfunction. Childhood exposure to a home environment of rigid religious orthodoxy and its attendant negative attitudes toward nudity and sex is a frequently recurring theme in women with orgasmic inadequacy. Traumatic sexual experiences during childhood or adolescence, such as incest or rape, may also be associated with orgasmic dysfunction. However, it must be emphasized that sexual dysfunction in adulthood does not uniformly follow from such developmental histories; why one person copes successfully with potentially negative influences and another person develops long-range sequelae is not well understood.

Affective factors may also be implicated in the etiology of orgasmic dysfunction. Although guilt related to sexual practices may be a residual hallmark of developmental conditioning, as discussed previously, guilt may also be a result of other dynamics reflecting either intrapsychic or interpersonal processes. Anxiety has been less widely recognized as a contributor to sexual dysfunction in women than in men; however, women are frequently victims of performance anxieties that arise not only from their self-perceptions but from the demands placed on them by their partners. The man who attempts to measure his own virility by the frequency or intensity of his partner's orgasmic responses may be contributing significantly to her fears of performance. Anxiety may also be related to physical attractiveness, worry about a partner's sexual adequacy (particularly in relation to impotence, in which case the woman may view the man's dysfunction as a sign of her own inability to excite him sexually), or concern over loss of control.

In a small number of women who have never been orgasmic, anxiety related to fear of loss of control during orgasm results in deliberate blocking of sexual arousal. Such women may voice concern about becoming convulsive during orgasm, being incontinent, losing consciousness, or having other manifestations that they equate with illness or embarrassment. These women often have low self-esteem and view themselves as incompetent, dependent on others, and unable to control their own lives.

Depression is a frequent cause of impaired orgasmic responsiveness. The precise cause of altered sexual function in depression is not known; since libido is typically decreased in depressed women, it may be difficult to determine if a true orgasmic inadequacy is present. Depression may be a cause of secondary orgasmic dysfunction but is unlikely to be the principal factor in primary orgasmic dysfunction; similarly, depression is unlikely to account for situational orgasmic problems.

In many instances, orgasmic dysfunction stems from interpersonal factors that include ineffective communication, hostility toward the partner or spouse, distrust of the partner or spouse, and divergent sexual preferences. The importance of communication as a means of interpersonal relating cannot be stressed too highly; the consequences of poor communication patterns include frustration, feeling hurt, anger, disinterest, and withdrawal. Many women with sexual problems have not been able to communicate their preferences for a particular type of touch, position, or timing related to sex to their partner. This inability to communicate may result from lack of learned facility in sexual communications, a feeling that it is improper for the woman to tell the man what she might like, or fear that the man will be offended by such suggestions.

Boredom or monotony in sexual practices may be an important element in the genesis of secondary orgasmic dysfunction. Women who are orgasmic by masturbation but not in sexual activity with their partner may be so because of anxieties or, probably at least as frequently, because the partner controls the initiation, timing, and type of sexual activity that occurs.

In some cases, sexual ignorance appears to be a major element of orgasmic dysfunction. Many women are unfamiliar with their own anatomy or have no idea of what type of sexual activity is pleasurable for them. In other instances, misconceptions about personal hygiene or male sexual needs become dominant elements dictating a woman's sexual behavior patterns.

Diagnostic Considerations

Care must be taken to identify any organic factors contributing to orgasmic dysfunction. Dyspareunia should always be carefully evaluated in a systematic fashion [5, 10], since organic lesions are frequently missed on a cursory pelvic examination. A detailed medical and surgical history, accompanied by a complete physical examination and appropriate laboratory testing, will assist in the diagnosis of systemic disease that may impair sexual responsivity. Every woman with a history of secondary orgasmic dysfunction and a close relative with diabetes mellitus should have an oral glucose tolerance test. Evaluation of steroid hormone status is most likely to be beneficial for patients with depressed libido or with vaginal atrophy.

In cases in which male sexual difficulties coexist with lack of female orgasmic responsiveness, it is not always possible to make a precise diagnosis. For example, the partner of a man with premature ejaculation cannot be diagnosed as having coital orgasmic dysfunction, since rapidity of ejaculation seriously hinders her opportunity for exploring coital patterns of sexual arousal. However, if the woman remains unable to have orgasms during intercourse after the man's ejaculatory control has been improved, then the diagnosis may be correctly applied. Similarly, a woman whose partner is impotent may be handicapped in her sexual responsivity in proportion to both the man's dysfunction and her own loss of spontaneity or sense of responsibility for overcoming his distress.

Some women are unsure about whether or not they have ever experienced orgasm. In some instances, the history may reveal enough precise information—for instance, a pattern of sexual arousal culminating in rhythmic, pulsating contractions of the vagina and a general sense of relaxation and tension release—to determine that orgasm has occurred. In other cases, the woman's description of her past sexual response patterns is quite inconclusive. While it has been said that if a woman isn't sure if she has ever been orgasmic, then she probably hasn't, this generalization is not always accurate. Some women have expectations of orgasm as an earth-shattering event; in these cases, which may reflect the unrealistic portrayals of female sexuality in many popular movies and books, the woman may in fact be orgasmic frequently, yet not realize that she is.

A detailed history of each woman's ability to be orgasmic by self-stimulation is important from both diagnostic and therapeutic perspectives. Facility with masturbatory orgasm but lack of orgasm occurring with a partner points to the likelihood of interpersonal factors being of primary importance. If a woman has not been orgasmic with self-stimulation or has never attempted masturbation, it is more likely that attitudinal problems exist that require therapeutic attention.

It may be difficult to determine whether low libido accompanying orgasmic dysfunction is etiologically important (for example, as a symptom of depression, drug use, or chronic illness) or whether it has been a secondary reaction to a long-standing pattern of sexual frustration. Claims of low interest in sex may also indicate pervasive guilt associated with sexual activity or performance anxieties.

Additional aspects of each clinical situation that require careful diagnostic assessment to permit a rational formulation of treatment plans include information about the following factors:

1. Contraceptive practices and reproductive goals.
2. Sexual responsiveness in other relationships.
3. Quality of the present relationship.
4. Sexual attitudes of both partners.
5. Concurrent psychopathology.
6. Previous experiences in psychotherapy.
7. Self-esteem.
8. Body-image.

Treatment

The basic principles of sex therapy described in the two preceding chapters apply directly to the treatment of the nonorgasmic woman. Because of differences in the socialization of men and women in our culture in regard to sex, it is usually important to encourage the nonorgasmic woman to think of herself as a sexual being—in effect, to give her permission to be sexual. Stereotypes that relegate women to a secondary role in sexual activity are discussed at length, with the therapists pointing out where these stereotypes have influenced the particular woman developmentally as well as identifying any current constraints on sexual attitudes or behavior that originate from such cultural conditioning. Thus the woman who has been taught to believe that men have a greater sexual capacity than women is informed that physiologically the reverse is true, because there is no refractory period following orgasm in women (see Chap. 1). It is equally important as a part of therapy to correct misconceptions that men have about female sexuality, which is most effectively accomplished in the context of the conjoint therapy model. In this format, both the male and female client have an opportunity to see the female cotherapist openly discussing sexual matters in a knowledgeable fashion; this provides an effective model for the female client and reinforces the concept that women can think or talk about sex.

Necessarily, many details of treatment depend on the histories, personalities, and objectives of the patients. The discussion here will focus on the components of therapy that are usually applicable; elaboration of techniques used on a case-by-case basis will be presented in a future publication.

It is important to identify each couple's sexual value system and to approach therapy within the boundaries of what is acceptable to them. Although attitudinal change may be requisite to therapeutic progress in some cases, therapists should refrain from imposing arbitrary values on their clients and should recognize the dimensions of each couple's moral and sexual values. Thus a woman who feels that masturbation is "dirty" but wants to change this feeling may be counseled in ways to become comfortable with self-stimulation, but a woman who objects to masturbation on moral grounds should never be urged to masturbate as a requirement of therapy.

Education is employed to provide accurate information related to sexual anatomy and physiology. Many women, as well as their partners, are uncertain about aspects of their own sexual anatomy. Some women do not know or are uncertain about where the clitoris is; even when the anatomy is familiar to them, they may not understand changes that occur during the sexual response cycle. Discussing the facts that direct clitoral manipulation may be uncomfortable, that vaginal lubrication waxes and wanes naturally, and that nongenital accompaniments of sexual arousal such as tachycardia, sweating, or carpopedal spasm are normal may be directly beneficial in certain cases.

Education is also directed at informing both the woman and her partner about patterns of female orgasm. In particular, it must be stressed that the intensity of orgasm may vary considerably from time to time; the search for a body-shaking, explosive orgasm is likely to block the acceptance of any less dramatic response as authentic. Similarly, it is usually helpful to address the erroneous notion of vaginal versus clitoral orgasms by explaining that all female orgasms, regardless of the source of stimuli, have the same physiologic manifestations.

Education should encompass a thorough explanation of sexual anatomy and physiology without artificially separating the biologic components of sexuality from psychosocial factors. Therefore, it should be pointed out that regardless of how the body is responding, the way in which physical sensations are integrated into the subjective emotional experience of each person has a great deal to do with what is perceived as pleasurable. Factors such as mood, interfering or preoccupying thoughts, and physical discomfort due to feelings such as fatigue, soreness, or hunger, all contribute to the perception of the quality of a sexual experience.

Anxiety reduction is accomplished by several different approaches. Encouraging couples to verbalize their concerns about sex allows for a modest degree of anxiety reduction by the simple process of ventilation. Sensate focus exercises are employed to remove performance pressures, increase communication skills (which typically lowers anxiety by improving both competence and self-confidence), and induce physical relaxation. In addition, because anxiety may result from irrational labeling of a behavior, situation, or feeling as negative or dangerous [11], interventions that have been termed *cognitive relabeling* [12] are sometimes used successfully. For example, labeling a sexual encounter as a failure if it does not result in orgasm—and simultaneously reinforcing feelings of personal inadequacy by this labeling process—can obviously lead to anxiety in anticipation of sexual activity. Helping the woman learn that a sexual experience may be enjoyable even if orgasm does not occur is likely to contribute to a reduction in anxiety and a subsequent increase in sexual responsivity.

Anxieties about sex often derive from the notion that sex is in a category completely apart from all other aspects of our lives. The process of cognitive relabeling can be facilitated by using analogies drawn from nonsexual aspects of life to indicate the unrealistic nature of many expectations women (and men) have about sex. For example, if a couple is concerned because the wife is not "ready" for sex just when her partner is, they might be asked if they only sit down to a meal when both have an equal appetite. The nonsexual analogy might be developed further by stating: "If one of you is hungry and the other isn't, you might join each other at the table; then, if your appetite develops, you are free to decide if you wish to have a meal." Many women are concerned that even a slight degree of physical intimacy (a hug, a kiss, cuddling) will be taken by the man as a signal to progress to intercourse. In this situation, the woman might be asked if it isn't ever possible to have a bowl of soup or a salad without having to eat a complete dinner; the concept behind such examples, of course, is to highlight the inflexibility and irrationality of certain maladaptive sexual beliefs while pointing out that common-sense principles that the patient often uses on her own can be equally applicable to sexual situations.

Since anxiety and depression may reflect an attitude of learned helplessness (feeling that one has no control over one's life), anxiety may be decreased by helping the woman to assume a more active responsibility for herself and helping her partner to give her room to accomplish this. When this is done in the context of an attitude of neutrality—not predicting present feelings or behaviors on the basis of the past—it allows many women to break away from old conditioned anxieties and find that they can make substantive changes in how they feel about themselves.

As mentioned previously, sensate focus provides a framework for reducing anxiety, increasing awareness of physical sensations, and transferring communications skills from the verbal to nonverbal domains. While one important aspect of these processes derives from specifically altering previous sexual habit patterns by initially prohibiting genital or breast stimulation, another facet of significance involves specific skills in nonverbal communication that are taught to the couple. When touching progresses to the stage of including genital exploration, each person is told to rest a hand lightly on the partner's hand to provide nonverbal cues about the touching (see Fig. 21-4). By a slight pressure, the wish for a firmer or gentler touch can be conveyed without having to break the mood by talking. In addition, this exercise facilitates the concept of sex as a matter of mutual participation—not something the man does "to" or "for" the woman.

Using such nonverbal messages, a hand can be moved from one spot to another without meaning "I don't like that"; instead, the unspoken message is simply "Right now, I'd prefer a change." The man is relieved of the (usually unwanted) responsibility of having to know what kind of touch at what location and for how long is "right"; the woman is able to explore her own sensations without having to make anything happen.

In some cases, it is beneficial to suggest that the woman might explore her own body without the presence of her partner to become more aware of her own physical sensations. This suggestion usually is made deliberately in the context of exploration rather than as a suggestion to masturbate, since the goal is not to produce orgasm but to identify interesting or pleasurable sensations. As the woman becomes more knowledgeable about her own body, she is better able to convey her feelings and needs to her partner. In this regard, it must be stressed to both patients that it is not the man's job to make his partner orgasmic, although this is frequently the attitude couples have prior to beginning therapy. A man is no more able to make a woman orgasmic than he is able to make her digest her food. Orgasm is a natural psychophysiologic response to the buildup of neuromuscular sexual excitation; when the body is allowed to function in a positive emotional matrix (unencumbered by anxiety, anger, or excessive cognition), orgasm will occur spontaneously.

In the case of a woman with primary orgasmic dysfunction, it may be helpful to suggest the use of a vibrator to provide her with an opportunity to experience orgasm so that she has a frame of reference for this experience. Except for this situation, however, the use of vibrators in sex therapy is problematic for several reasons. First, the intensity of physical stimulation delivered by the vibrator cannot be duplicated by the man. Second, the use of the vibrator may alarm the woman if she perceives it as unnatural. Third, use of the vibrator may have a distancing effect on the couple—either or both partners may view it as

Figure 21-4. Two versions of the hand-riding technique used as a means of nonverbal communication during certain stages of sensate focus. The person being touched may indicate preferences for changes in tactile pressure, tempo, or position by this technique.

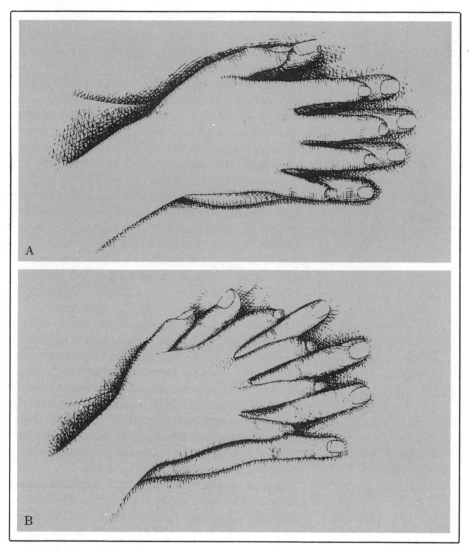

reducing their intimacy. Finally, repeated use of a vibrator over time may result in a degree of either psychological or physical dependency on this device as the only possible source of orgasmic release.

A major objective of therapy is to assist both clients in seeing that sexual arousal develops spontaneously and is usually hindered by goal-setting. If the couple can learn to interact sexually by focusing on their feelings, communicating openly together, and avoiding routinized patterns, orgasm is likely to occur. In fact, women often are told that orgasm may occur when they least expect it; the fact being, of course, that pushing to reach orgasm is much more likely to inhibit overall sexual responsiveness.

As therapy progresses, most women will experience orgasm from manual stimulation as a part of the sensate focus exercises. A transition to coital play is then made, retaining the basic themes of sensate focus: Explore feelings without a goal, communicate openly, assume responsibility for yourself, not for your partner. The female-superior position is utilized and the woman is told to play with the penis around the external genitalia, rubbing or stroking the penis against the labia, the clitoris, and the perineum to elicit feelings and explore sensations. The woman is asked to insert the penis into the vagina only if she feels ready for this (both mentally and physically); thus, "having intercourse" is not "assigned." If she decides to insert, she first is asked to notice the sensations of containment alone and then is encouraged to experiment with a variety of coital movements. It is specifically suggested that she try slow, shallow thrusting, with the penis only partially inserted in the vagina; this type of thrusting pattern, often ignored in favor of vigorous and deep thrusting, is more likely to be pleasurable to the woman because of the formation of the orgasmic platform at the outer third of the vagina.

The man is told to continue touching during intercourse, with guidance from his partner as to what feels pleasurable. Clitoral stimulation may be employed during coitus as a means of additional sensory input to facilitate orgasmic responsiveness. Depending on the individual circumstances of each case, the woman may be asked to experiment with fantasy during sexual play, particularly if she has difficulty freeing herself from distracting thoughts.

Using these methods, an overall failure rate of 20.8 percent in a series of 342 women with orgasmic dysfunction was reported in *Human Sexual Inadequacy* [5]. Between 1971 and 1977, a series of 388 anorgasmic women were treated at the Masters & Johnson Institute with an overall failure rate of 28.1 percent. Additional treatment approaches are currently being used at a number of centers [13–21], but there is a definite need for controlled studies with adequate sample sizes to determine the specific efficacy and applicability of these strategies.

References

1. Gould, R. E. Socio-Cultural Roles of Male and Female. In A. M. Freedman, H. I. Japlan, and B. J. Sadock (eds.), *Comprehensive Textbook of Psychiatry: II*. Baltimore: Williams & Wilkins Co., 1975. Pp. 1460–1465.

2. Sherfey, M. J. *The Nature and Evolution of Female Sexuality*. New York: Random House, 1972.
3. Gordon, M., and Shankweiler, D. P. Different equals less: Female sexuality in recent marriage manuals. *Journal of Marriage and the Family* 33:459–466, 1971.
4. LoPiccolo, J., and Heiman, J. Cultural values and the therapeutic definition of sexual function and dysfunction. *Journal of Social Issues* 33(2):166–183, 1977.
5. Masters, W. H., and Johnson, V. E. *Human Sexual Inadequacy*. Boston: Little, Brown and Co., 1970.
6. Kinsey, A. C., Pomeroy, W. B., Martin, C. E., and Gebhard, P. *Sexual Behavior in the Human Female*. Philadelphia: W. B. Saunders Co., 1953.
7. Chesser, E. *The Sexual, Marital and Family Relationships of the English Woman*. London: Hutchinson's Medical Publications, 1956.
8. Fisher, S. *The Female Orgasm*. New York: Basic Books, Publishers, 1973.
9. Levine, S. B., and Yost, M. A., Jr. Frequency of sexual dysfunction in a general gynecological clinic: An epidemiological approach. *Archives of Sexual Behavior* 5:229–238, 1976.
10. Abarbanel, A. R. Diagnosis and Treatment of Coital Discomfort. In J. LoPiccolo and L. LoPiccolo (eds.), *Handbook of Sex Therapy*. New York: Plenum Press, 1978. Pp. 241–259.
11. Ellis, A. *Reason and Emotion in Psychotherapy*. New York: Lyle Stuart, 1962.
12. Goldfried, M. R., and Davidson, G. C. *Clinical Behavior Therapy*. New York: Holt, Rinehart and Winston, 1976. Pp. 158–185.
13. Kaplan, H. S. *The New Sex Therapy*. New York: Brunner/Mazel, Publishers, 1974.
14. LoPiccolo, J., and Lobitz, W. C. The role of masturbation in the treatment of orgasmic dysfunction. *Archives of Sexual Behavior* 2:153–164, 1972.
15. Caird, W., and Wincze, J. P. *Sex Therapy: A Behavioral Approach*. Hagerstown, Md.: Harper & Row, 1977.
16. Barbach, L. G. *For Yourself: The Fulfillment of Female Sexuality*. New York: Doubleday, 1975.
17. Sotile, W. M., and Kilmann, P. R. Treatments of psychogenic female sexual dysfunction. *Psychological Bulletin* 84:619–633, 1977.
18. Munjack, D., Cristol, A., Goldstein, A., Phillips, D., Goldberg, A., Whipple, K., Staples, F., and Kanno, P. Behavioural treatment of orgasmic dysfunction: A controlled study. *British Journal of Psychiatry* 129:497–502, 1976.
19. Wolman, C. S. Therapy groups for women. *American Journal of Psychiatry* 133:274–278, 1976.
20. Leiblum, S. R., Rosen, R. C., and Pierce, D. Group treatment format: Mixed sexual dysfunctions. *Archives of Sexual Behavior* 5:313–322, 1976.
21. Kilmann, P. R. The treatment of primary and secondary orgasmic dysfunction: A methodological review of the literature since 1970. *Journal of Sex and Marital Therapy* 4:155–176, 1978.

22

Sexual Aversion and Inhibited Sexual Desire

Not all sexual problems are dysfunctions, since the term *dysfunction* refers to an altered state of physiologic responsivity. In this chapter the focus is on two nondysfunctional diagnostic categories that are characterized by impeded initiatory sexual behavior or impeded sexual receptivity. While sexual aversion is an infrequently encountered disorder, its highly dramatic nature and potential responsiveness to treatment make it a topic of interest; on the other hand, inhibited sexual desire is a problem that presents commonly to clinicians.

Sexual Aversion

Sexual aversion is a consistent negative reaction of phobic proportions to sexual activity or the thought of sexual activity. Although it may be situational—occurring only with a particular partner or only in a heterosexual context—the typical case of sexual aversion involves a pervasive negative reaction to all aspects of sexual contact with another person. In some instances, the phobic nature of the response is manifested physiologically by profuse sweating, nausea or vomiting, diarrhea, or palpitations, but in other instances the phobic components are internalized and do not appear in this manner. Sexual aversion may occur in either males or females, but the preponderance of cases involves women.

Sexual aversion is neither a situation of aesthetic distaste for sex in general nor an intense dislike of a specific type of sexual activity. The diagnosis cannot be made unless there is a consistent phobic component to the reaction. For instance, although it is common to hear that a person regards oral-genital sex as repugnant, shameful, or unnatural, while being able to participate without difficulty in coital activity, such a pattern must be differentiated from the reaction encountered in the person with sexual aversion. The person with sexual aversion experiences irrational, overwhelming anxiety at the thought of sexual contact. Often a kiss, a hug, or a touch may precipitate such a response, unless it occurs under circumstances in which the prospect of progression to further levels of sexual involvement is incontrovertibly absent. As may be seen with other types of phobias, the anticipation of the dreaded situation is often more intensely anxiety-provoking than the actual situation itself: Some persons with the syndrome of sexual aversion report having greater difficulty with undressing and touching in a sexual context than they do with participation in intercourse. In fact, patterns of sexual arousal are apt to be largely intact in persons with sexual aversion, so that it is not unusual to discover that men with sexual aversion are fully potent and able to ejaculate or that women with sexual aversion experience orgasm.

Cases of sexual aversion may present in the guise of either a low frequency of sexual activity or a lack of interest in sex. It is common for patients to deal with phobias by assiduously avoiding the fear-provoking stimulus, which in this instance results in withdrawal from all sexual interaction. In many cases of sexual aversion, coitus occurs only once or twice a year, and even then the circumstances of sexual activity may be "special," involving either a deliberate lowering of sexual inhibitions by the use of alcohol or an extremely reluctant and guilt-laden concession to maintaining a marriage in the face of threats of separation or divorce. Despite the avoidance of sexual situations with a partner, solitary sexual stimulation is not usually anxiety-provoking in persons with sexual aversion and libido may be variably affected.

Most cases of sexual aversion are antedated by a period of relatively normal sexual functioning, which may be brief or may last a decade or more. Sexual aversion is most likely to affect men and women under the age of 40. There is not a dramatically increased frequency of psychiatric disorders in persons with sexual aversion, and these individuals are often relatively successful and mature in other facets of their lives, including their role as parents and their occupational performance.

Sexual aversion must be distinguished from anxiety neurosis, which is characterized by free-floating anxiety and anxiety attacks with cardiorespiratory symptoms unrelated to a specific and consistent stimulus. While the self-esteem of people with sexual aversion may be lessened, perhaps reflecting their acknowledgement of loss of autonomy in being unable to overcome their aversion, in some instances self-esteem and ego strength are remarkably intact. However, if self-esteem is sufficiently impaired, it is not unusual to find that the person with sexual aversion gives a history of sporadic depression. In some cases sexual aversion coexists with a sexual dysfunction such as impotence, vaginismus, or orgasmic dysfunction.

Etiology

A variety of etiologic factors have appeared to be important in the series of 116 cases of sexual aversion seen at the Masters & Johnson Institute from 1972 to 1977. Severely negative parental sexual attitudes are frequently associated with sexual aversion not preceded by an interval of normal sexual participation. Cases of this type are sometimes marked by a history of childhood sexual trauma, such as incest or sexual assault. Probably the failure of parents to provide an accepting, sensitive, supportive environment for the child who has been sexually abused is more central to the subsequent development of sexual aversion than the sexual experience itself. In one case we treated, a woman's mother sent her news clippings from her home-town newspaper describing cases of rape and sexual assault from the time she left home to attend college until well into her marriage.

Certain problems of adolescent sexuality may be causally related to sexual aversion. It is common to find that the person with sexual aversion had severe difficulty with either body-image or self-esteem, or both, during adolescence. Such problems—including the boy who is gravely concerned about gynecomastia, the girl troubled by hirsutism or failure of breast development, and the teenager contending with obesity or serious acne—often lead to avoidance of exploration or experimentation with sexual activity and may, in fact, severely limit dating behavior. Sexual trauma occurring during adolescence (rape, incest, or painful early coital experience) may lead to an association between sex and exploitation or pain and may thus serve as the precipitator of sexual aversion as a protective posture. Similarly, a pregnancy scare during adolescence may so traumatize the individual that the avoidance of sexual activity is the simplest and easiest way to preserve a sense of personal autonomy while also assuaging the usual guilt and conflict by "paying the price" of sexual abstention.

Many cases of sexual aversion appear to have arisen on a conditioned basis. It is not unusual in such cases to discover that the spouse or partner of the person with sexual aversion has constantly pressured him or her into sexual activity or has made sexual activity a form of payment for some other desired objective, whether behavioral or material (e.g., "I'll have sex with you if you do the dishes this week"). A pattern of this sort, when repetitively experienced, is a powerful reinforcer of the association of sex with an unpleasant set of feelings ("I'm being coerced," "I'm being used"), and since avoidance reduces the discomfort in such interactions, the development of anxiety over sexual activity may continue even long after the negative conditioning process has been changed. The avoidance of negative consequences, whether real or presumed, leads to maintenance of the avoiding behavior and confirms the person's self-assessment and resultant labeling. In this sense, it appears that sexual aversion is frequently a learned condition—a matter that is quite consistent with modern learning theory.

Sexual aversion can also develop from overzealous attempts at "working at" sex. The man who assiduously tries to make his partner orgasmic and never succeeds, or the woman who tries persistently and rather rigidly to cure her partner's impotence and fails in the attempt, may subsequently develop a distaste for sexual interaction that eventually progresses to a true phobic state. Similarly, the person who is repeatedly traumatized, psychically or physically, by the pattern of sexual activity with his or her partner (or a series of partners) may understandably develop sexual aversion.

Less frequently, sexual aversion occurs after sexual assault in adulthood or is associated with other phobias (including phobias related to cancer, pregnancy, or venereal disease). In a few cases, sexual aversion has been found in association with other intrapsychic pathology, such as obsessive-compulsive neurosis, character disorders, or anxiety neurosis. In men, sexual aversion has been seen in association with major lifelong conflicts in sexual identity: In this instance, fear and avoidance of sexual activity may provide an excellent means for the man to cope with his internal anxieties regarding broader issues of his sexuality. Men who regard themselves as homosexual but have had little or no sexual contact with another person of either sex may sometimes be found in this latter group—in our society, the male often believes himself to be homosexual if he is not sexually active with the opposite sex, in effect, a self-classification by exclusion.

Treatment

The diagnosis of sexual aversion can only be established via history-taking, with the consistency of the phobic component of this disorder the key to making the diagnosis. Treatment of sexual aversion requires, first and foremost, motivation on the part of the patient to wish to change. Although it may sound contradictory, many persons who are terrified of sexual contact recognize that there is potential gratification and intimacy involved in sex if they can overcome their fears. This is quite analogous to the businessman with a phobia toward airplanes who recognizes the utility of air travel and so seeks treatment. Of course, there are times when individuals with sexual aversion achieve secondary gains by maintaining their distress; in such instances, there may ostensibly be motivation for change, but simultaneously there may be severe resistance to psychotherapy because of ancillary motivations to maintain the status quo.

The treatment process that has proved to be highly successful in cases of sexual aversion involves many of the principles discussed in earlier chapters. After a thorough psychosexual and relationship history is obtained, the first task of the therapists is to delineate and explain to the couple the pertinent etiologic factors. Often, this discussion may lead to insights on the part of either or both clients which will be of signal importance in altering previous behaviors within the relationship. As part of this discussion, the cooperation of the partner of the person with sexual aversion must be enlisted, since it will, in general, be necessary to place this spouse or partner's interests secondary to those of the person with aversion during the early phases of treatment. Specifically, the person with sexual aversion must be put in rather complete control (temporarily) of all situations involving sexual activity as therapy begins. In some cases it is imperative to neutralize the partner's guilt induction behavior before progressing to the procedures described below.

Nowhere in the treatment of sexual difficulties does our methodology dovetail more closely with the fundamental techniques of behavior modification than in the treatment of sexual aversion. However, even in this situation there are differences as well as major similarities. The therapists begin by prohibiting any sexual activity by the couple except what they will be instructed to undertake as part of the therapeutic suggestions. Then, beginning on the day after history-taking, a carefully structured, finite progression of sensate focus tasks is assigned. The idea is to permit the person with sexual aversion to lower his or her anxiety at a particular level of sexual interaction by knowing that there will be no sudden progression to another more involved or more threatening level and by gaining comfort with that specific type of sexual contact. The emphasis throughout this process is on acknowledging the presence of anxiety (without making the person feel foolish or incompetent for being anxious), recognizing that there is motivation to overcome the anxiety (hence a willingness to take some risk in tolerating exposure to limited amounts of anxiety for finite, controllable time periods), and reminding both partners that what is unfamiliar is often uncomfortable; as familiarity increases, comfort levels usually increase as well.

In some cases it is necessary to begin sensate focus prior to the stage that consists of generalized nude body touching, without touching the breasts or genitals. This may be done either by altering the degree of nudity (for example, suggesting that the person with sexual aversion might wear an open shirt or blouse but be otherwise undressed) or by limiting the range of touching (for example, the first assignment might be to touch only the head, neck, and upper extremities). Restrictions of these types are usually not required, however, since the precise instructions accompanying the sensate focus assignment make it plain that the person with sexual aversion will be the one to decide during the exercise exactly how much anxiety he or she is able to tolerate. Although it might appear appealing to begin in severe cases by using *in vitro* desensitization procedures (having the person with aversion first construct an imagery hierarchy of graded anxiety-provoking situations to build up some tolerance [1] before undertaking the *in vivo* situation), this method slows the progress of therapy, may at times actually intensify the terror of the real-life contact, and has not seemed necessary in our experience.

Both partners are told in considerable detail that the purpose of the sensate focus experience is to develop awareness of the physical sensations associated with touching or being touched, without any expectation of sexual arousal or any need for sexual performance. Working with the concepts of neutrality (not predicting what one's feelings or responses will be on the basis of the past, thus being open to change) and vulnerability (being willing to take a risk, knowing one's partner will not knowingly take advantage of the situation) discussed in Chapters 19 and 21, the partners are asked to participate in the sensate focus exercise allowing the person with sexual aversion to initiate the activity and to decide when to stop the activity for reasons of anxiety, fatigue, satiation, or disinterest. The one with sexual aversion is typically told to begin by touching his or her partner and to concentrate on an awareness of the physical sensations associated with this. It is emphasized that the touching is not designed primarily for the pleasure of the person being touched, but rather that the touching should reflect the interests of the person doing the touching. In some cases it is easier for the person with sexual aversion to touch than to be touched, while in other cases the reverse is true. There does not appear to be any prognostic importance to this, and we routinely assign, as part of the same sensate focus session, a second segment in which the person with sexual aversion is touched by his or her partner, following the ground rules outlined above. In either situation (as in all cases where sensate focus is used), both partners are told that it is the responsibility of the person being touched to notify the partner if any discomfort occurs as a result of the touching.

Certain details of the sensate focus progression must necessarily be carefully individualized to fit each case. It is not the aim to eliminate all anxiety at a particular stage of sensate focus before moving on to the next (this is one difference from systematic desensitization), but it is often necessary for a couple to repeat the sensate focus exercise two or three times at a particular level before moving farther, to allow for a sufficient degree of anxiety reduction and concomitant sense of mastery and increasing confidence.

During this phase of therapy, including not simply the sensate focus experience without genital touching but also subsequent stages of sensate focus involving the breasts and genitals, it is common to find several problems occurring. The first is that anxiety may surface unexpectedly and disproportionately in particular situations (remember that phobias are not generally rational phenomena): This must be met by acknowledgement of the anxiety as a fact, acceptance of its existence, but a firm reminder of the motivation to change, coupled with encouragement that as risks are undertaken (primarily the risk of tolerating measured doses of anxiety), the likelihood of positive change is enhanced. A second problem that is encountered almost invariably at some point in the treatment of sexual aversion is that the partner, impressed that progress is being made and that the aversive individual is trying emphatically to change, nevertheless pushes too fast or for too much sexual contact, in direct violation of the therapists' request (reiterated repeatedly on a daily basis) to allow the person struggling with sexual aversion to set the tempo for sexual activity. Such episodes often create a microcosm of the maladaptive relationship dynamics important in the genesis of sexual aversion: Rapid confrontation and resolution of the situation is mandatory to validate the positive reinforcement the sexually aversive person is getting from the therapists and from feelings of self-actualization.

Despite such problems and problems of resistance to therapy that are beyond the scope of this discussion, it is noteworthy that seven or eight sessions after beginning treatment, there is usually considerable lessening of the phobic component of sexual aversion, although there may continue to be vague feelings of discomfort or disinterest in overtly sexual situations. In many cases, by this point the natural psychophysiologic sexual responsiveness of the patient, previously severely bridled by the dimensions of the phobia, now proceeds spontaneously and without encumbrance—at times, much to the surprise of the partner, who may suddenly find more demand for sexual activity than he or she can keep up with. Because patients with sexual aversion are not usually sexually dysfunctional, it is rarely difficult for the couple to make the transition from noncoital to coital sexual activity.

Simultaneously with the assignment of a series of sensate focus exercises, careful assessment and development of verbal communication patterns within the dyad must be undertaken in most cases. The process of development of new communication skills provides a convenient and concrete matrix for altering maladaptive patterns of the relationship, as well as helping the couple to clarify ancillary issues of either a sexual or nonsexual nature that may previously have created tensions for them. In addition, therapeutic attention in certain cases must be devoted to such areas as body-image, self-esteem, or sexual fantasy.

The primary objectives in treating the person with sexual aversion are extinction of the aversive consequences and reconditioning of the ways in which sexual activity is experienced. Extinction is more difficult to attain when there is a particularly strong element of pain or fear in the original learning; if learning has been reinforced over a prolonged time; if reinforcement has been intermittent; if there is generalization of reinforcement from other similar situations; or if the person's memory of the original circumstances precipitating anxiety is strong [2]. In spite of these problems, the therapy outcome of cases of sexual aversion has been highly gratifying.

Between 1972 and 1977, a total of 116 cases of sexual aversion were treated at the Masters & Johnson Institute. In one instance, the couple withdrew from therapy during the first week. In 85 cases of female sexual aversion, there were eight treatment failures (failure rate: 9.4 percent); in 31 cases of male sexual aversion, there were two treatment failures (failure rate: 6.5 percent). Thus, the overall failure rate for the treatment of sexual aversion was 7.6 percent.

Inhibited Sexual Desire

The degree to which human sexual desire reflects instinctual drives as opposed to a learned set of responses is unclear at present. It appears realistic to view libido as a complexly determined phenomenon combining certain aspects of biologic (instinctual) components, probably mediated largely by hormonal stimuli, with elements of psychosocial conditioning. Viewed in this context, it is uncertain whether there are any people who are truly asexual in the sense of never having feelings of sexual desire; however, clinicians are well aware that some people repress or suppress their sexual feelings so thoroughly that it may appear, from a practical standpoint, that they have no sexual desire.

The frequency of impaired libido in the general population is not known. Frank and colleagues recently found that 35 percent of women and 16 percent of men in a group of relatively well-adjusted and well-educated married couples reported disinterest in sex [3]. Steele noted that 20 percent of 500 couples seen because of infertility showed loss of libido [4]. No operational definition of either loss of libido or disinterest in sex was offered by these authors. Lief stated that 32 of 115 patients (27.8 percent) seen at the Marriage Council of Philadelphia were given the primary diagnosis of inhibited sexual desire, with a rate among female patients (37%) approximately twice that observed in males (18.7 percent) [5].

Low libido may be the result of either organic processes or psychosocial factors. Although low libido is likely to be a sexual problem when a marked discrepancy exists between the levels of sexual interest of two persons in a marriage or long-term sexual relationship, there are certainly instances in which an acceptable accommodation is made to such a divergence and no problem results. For example, a person with low libido may agree to participate in sexual activity when his or her partner requests this, regardless of the person's general lack of interest. Alternatively, in some couples a workable solution is reached by allowing—or even encouraging—the partner with higher libido to pursue sexual activity outside the relationship. Most frequently, however, when only one person in the relationship has little desire for sexual activity, the situation is viewed as problematic by both partners. Inhibited sexual desire is not synonymous with disparate levels of sexual interest in a relationship. For example, if one partner desires intercourse on a daily basis and the other prefers a twice-a-week coital frequency, while a problem may be present, inhibited sexual desire is not the correct diagnostic category.

Etiology

A variety of organic conditions that may lower libido are listed in Table 22-1. It should be understood, in reading this list, that almost any chronic disease process may potentially inhibit sexual desire, but this does not always mean that this effect is directly attributable to biochemical change or tissue pathology. Psychosocial adaptation to chronic disease may have an adverse impact on sexuality for reasons quite apart from physical factors, as discussed in further detail in other chapters in this book. Differentiating between organic and psychosocial etiologies of lowered libido is often a difficult process involving a large measure of clinical judgment rather than precise laboratory testing.

This is true partially because libido is a more elusive phenomenon than erection, ejaculation, or female orgasm. While these physiologic responses are quantifiable and rather easily identified, there are no completely accurate measures of libido. Commonly, clinicians assess libido by asking about the frequency of sexual activity, but this is partly influenced by social and environmental factors such as the availability of a sexual partner or privacy for sexual activity. A person may have considerable interest in sex but have no available partner; conversely, the fact that a person participates frequently in sexual activity does not always indicate that his or her sex drive is intact. Sexual desire is based in part on the context of the relationship in which it occurs: If boredom, hostility, distrust, lack of physical attractiveness, or other influences

Table 22-1. Organic Conditions Causing Diminished Libido

Conditions That Typically Lower Libido	Conditions That Sometimes Lower Libido
Addison's disease	Acromegaly
Alcoholism	Amyloidosis
Chronic active hepatitis	Anemia
Chronic renal failure	Brain tumors
Cirrhosis	Cerebrovascular disease
Congestive heart failure	Chronic obstructive pulmonary disease
Cushing's syndrome	Collagen diseases
Drug addiction	Drug ingestion:
Drug ingestion:	Alcohol
Antiandrogens (in men)	Alpha-methyldopa
Estrogen (in men)	Antihistamines
Feminizing tumors (in men)	Barbiturates
Hemochromatosis	Clofibrate
Hyperprolactinemia (in men)	Clonidine
Hypopituitarism	Diphenylhydantoin
Hypothyroidism	Marihuana
Kallmann's syndrome	Monoamine oxidase inhibitors
Klinefelter's syndrome	Phenothiazines
Male climacteric	Propranolol
Myotonic dystrophy	Reserpine
Parkinson's disease	Spironolactone
Pituitary tumors	Hyperaldosteronism
Tuberculosis	Hyperthyroidism
	Hypoglycemia
	Hypokalemia
	Malabsorption
	Malignancy
	Multiple sclerosis
	Nutritional deficiencies
	Parasitic infestation
	Prostatitis
	Sarcoidosis
	Wegener's granulomatosis

are present, desire may be lowered for sexual activity with that particular partner, but may or may not be lowered in a more general sense.

When inhibited sexual desire is purely situational—that is, when interest in sexual activity with one specific partner is affected while desire for sexual activity with other partners or in other contexts (such as masturbation) is intact—it is always an indication of a psychosocial etiology. Although organic factors may depress libido to varying degrees in different persons or in a varying manner in the same person at different times, most physical or metabolic causes of inhibited sexual desire are characterized by a general level of consistency and persistence.

Men or women with inhibited sexual desire may be quite functional sexually or may have concomitant difficulty in mechanisms of sexual arousal or orgasm. At times, inhibited sexual desire occurs secondarily as a means of coping with a preceding dysfunction: In effect, by developing a low interest in sexual activity, the person avoids the unpleasant consequences of sexual failure such as embarrassment, loss of self-esteem, and frustration. Viewing this pattern in a different context, when sexual activity is not gratifying or is actually a negative experience, a process of negative conditioning can occur that leads to a drop in libido. However, some persons with inhibited sexual desire are relatively unfettered in their sexual responsiveness, being quite capable of normal patterns of erection or vaginal lubrication and having no difficulty with orgasm, once having begun participation in an episode of sexual activity. While this situation allows for rapid diagnosis of the problem as inhibited sexual desire, when sexual dysfunction coexists with low libido it is often quite difficult to determine which is the primary disorder.

Inhibited sexual desire is a state marked by a simultaneously low level of sexual receptivity and initiatory sexual behavior. Clinically, more problems arise because of impeded receptivity, since being repeatedly unreceptive to a partner's sexual overtures is likely to be taken as rejection and leaves the partner who desires sexual activity feeling frustrated and alone; at the same time, the person who is unreceptive may feel guilty about not being willing to meet the partner's need. Sometimes this sense of guilt is deliberately induced by the partner who expects or demands sexual activity as compensation for some positive action ("I took care of the kids today, didn't I?", or "I did everything you wanted, now pay me back"), which results in marital friction and increases the problem. Lack of initiatory sexual behavior is often construed as a problem if it is the man who seems uninterested in initiating sexual contact, since our society has generally cast the male in the role of sexual aggressor or initiator.

In addition to instances of inhibited sexual desire arising for reasons already mentioned (e.g., organic factors; as a secondary reaction to sexual dysfunction; as a result of negative conditioning), low libido may stem from other etiologies. Inhibited sexual desire frequently occurs as a result of depression (see Chap. 12). In this context, appropriate therapy of the depression characteristically results in improved libido. Low levels of sexual desire may also be seen following traumatic experiences such as sexual assault or incest. Inhibited sexual desire may arise because of fears or inhibitions that are not of phobic proportions but nevertheless impinge upon the freedom to be sexual: These include hygienic concerns; fear of pregnancy or venereal disease; fear of losing control (either physically or mentally) during sexual arousal; fear of disturbing sexual imagery with themes such as incest, homosexuality, sadomasochism, or adultery; and fear of rejection by one's partner.

Interpersonal difficulties of many varieties are frequently related to inhibited sexual desire. For obvious reasons, persons in conflict with each other are likely to have diminished feelings of sexual attraction for each other or may simply find that a large portion of their sexual energies are drained by other problems of their relationship. Couples contending with difficulties such as hostility, deceit, poor communication, and lack of respect or affection may therefore experience impairment in libido. Sometimes it is apparent that one partner uses lack of sexual receptivity as a weapon for punishing his or her partner, either consciously or subconsciously. This is a possibility in situations in which the person professing lack of libido engages in relatively frequent masturbatory activity, although the psychodynamics of this pattern are complicated and may reflect other factors as well. Since avoidance of sexual activity with a particular partner is not always equivalent to inhibited sexual desire, the clinician must be circumspect in assessing the individual circumstances of each case.

Intrapersonal problems ranging from poor self-esteem to negative body-image, guilt about sexuality, neuroticism, depersonalization of sex, and suppressed or repressed sexuality may lead to lowered libido. In this category, negative childhood conditioning about sex is likely to be a particularly frequent component of the problem in cases of inhibited sexual desire that have been present from early adulthood on. Although guilt concerning sexuality may arise from numerous sources, it is particularly relevant for the clinician to consider the potential contribution of rigid religious input that characterizes sexual pleasure as sinful. Denial of sexual interest is one ego defense that may assuage the guilt; denial also may be operating in persons frightened by their sexuality or internally conflicted for other reasons. Kaplan notes that the anxiety and conflicts associated with inhibited sexual desire are usually "more tenacious and profound than those associated with orgasm and excitement phase disorders," and that patients with inhibited sexual desire tend to be "more injured, more vulnerable, and, therefore, more rigidly defensive" than patients with sexual dysfunctions [6].

An aspect of everyday life that is often overlooked in textbook discussions of sexuality is the presence of stress from other sources that may influence sexual feelings or limit sexual behavior. Men or women living with high levels of stress often have lowered libido; although a modest portion of this reduction in libido may stem from alterations in circulating levels of testosterone attributable to stress [7], it is likely in this situation that the major factor in lowered sexual interest is the additional cost in emotional and cognitive terms of coping with the stress. Thus, it is easy to see how libido may be impaired in a man who has been fired from his job and is struggling with the economic and practical realities of finding new employment; similarly, if a child is stricken by serious medical illness, the parents may be living with a stressful situation that markedly reduces their interest in sexual activity.

Treatment

With the exception of cases of inhibited sexual desire resulting from depression or attributable to organic factors such as drug use or illness, most patients with this difficulty require an intensive psychotherapeutic approach. As with the treatment of sexual aversion, unless the person with low libido is interested in attempting to change, therapy is quite unlikely to be beneficial and may actually be a negative experience. For this reason, in the assessment of couples in which the person with inhibited sexual desire has been "brought" for help, rather than seeking counseling autonomously or together with his or her partner, it is important to determine the level of motivation that exists prior to recommending or undertaking any treatment procedures.

Judging such motivation is often a complex problem, since it is not unusual to find rather coercive elements in the circumstances leading to presentation of the couple: In a marriage troubled by inhibited sexual desire, the spouse with intact libido may threaten separation or divorce unless something is done to improve the sexual relationship. Because less emphatic requests for help commonly go unheeded by the person with low sexual interest, it is not advisable to turn such a couple away from therapy if their mutual cooperation can be elicited. On the other hand, it is necessary to be reasonably certain that the therapists do not become party to a coercive pattern: Unless the person with inhibited sexual desire genuinely wishes to overcome this difficulty, ethical as well as practical problems would undoubtedly arise in the context of treatment.

When possible, it is advisable to begin therapy of a couple in which one partner has inhibited sexual desire by outlining the etiology of their problem and helping them gain insight into their situation. Realistically, however, it is not always possible to determine the precise etiology with any certainty, particularly in instances of inhibited sexual desire that has been present for long periods of time (five years or more). It is advisable to avoid overly interpretive license in this regard. Instead, when the etiology of the problem is unclear, this fact can be made apparent to patients, who can also be advised that successful treatment is contingent on the alteration of current attitudes, expectations, and behaviors rather than on an analysis of past events and their significance.

It is critical to orient the therapeutic focus to the relationship, rather than singling out one partner as "sick" and the other as "healthy." Many times, the person with relatively normal libido in a relationship with a person with inhibited sexual desire experiences an artificial amplification of libido, sometimes to the point of becoming preoccupied with sexual thoughts and sexual feelings. This phenomenon reflects the frustrations of not having something one wants rather than a true hypersexuality, in a manner analogous to the person who is on a starvation diet becoming preoccupied by thoughts of food. The person with inhibited sexual desire does not realize this, however, and may be overwhelmed by his or her partner's seemingly constant interest in sex. A usual result of successful therapy is that as the libido of the person with inhibited sexual desire increases, the sexual appetite and interests of the partner moderate somewhat. In this sense, there is a degree of complementarity in the sexual relationship.

Although treatment must always be individualized to the background and needs of each couple, certain priorities are typically present in the early phases of therapy dealing with inhibited sexual desire. It is important to identify for the couple ways in which the expectations of both partners preordain patterns of sexual behavior. Frequently, such expectations are directly or indirectly transmitted from one partner to the other, resulting in stereotypic, rather than spontaneous, behavior.

This situation is dealt with most effectively by use of the concept of neutrality, combined with specific attention to communication skills.

Among commonly encountered expectations that may be deleterious to the couple's sexual interaction are three recurring themes that require particular attention. The first and probably the commonest of these themes is the idea on the part of the person with inhibited sexual desire that gratification or pleasure from sexual activity is contingent upon his or her initial sexual interest. Such a belief confuses the state of receptivity with the state of arousal: In the absence of definite interest in a sexual encounter, this person believes himself or herself to be unreceptive. The fact is that, given a chance, sexual interest and arousal may develop rather quickly in a situation unfettered by guilt, anxiety, or coercion. Stated another way, if the person who initially feels uninterested in sexual activity allows himself or herself to experience the sexual situation, that person's feelings may change quite positively. This is analogous to a person who is not hungry sitting down in a restaurant with a partner who is hungry; by virtue of entering into the situation and watching the partner eat, the other person's appetite for food may be activated and he or she may go on to partake of—and enjoy—a meal.

A second type of expectation that frequently requires attention is the set of sex-role stereotypes that most people have acquired. Even for persons who philosophically find these culturally imbued stereotypes meaningless, there is often a surprising lack of personal comfort in behaving in ways that do not adhere to the ordinary sex-role norms. The sexual script that society has written dictates that the male should initiate sexual activity and show rapid evidence of his sexual arousal; for a man with lackluster libido, there may be instantaneous alarm if sexual overtures are made by his female partner in violation of the accepted and expected roles. Fortunately, this area is usually easily amenable to improvement with support and encouragement from the therapists and with the use of sensate focus exercises in which one partner is specifically assigned the task of initiating the touching opportunity. An ancillary issue related to the matter of sex-role expectations and the initiation of sexual behavior is the way in which a couple views their sexual interaction along the dominance-submission continuum. When frequency of sexual activity is an issue, as it is almost by definition for a couple in which one person has inhibited sexual desire, ordinary views of mutuality and togetherness may be lost sight of in a distorted perception of who is doing what to whom. Sexual activity may become an arena for a power struggle, with matters of assertiveness, receptivity, compliance, cooperation, and gratification magnified to dimensions appropriate to a battlefield. Therapeutic attention must be carefully directed to the attitudes and feelings (both real and expected) surrounding this view of the sexual interaction, and specific interventions must be made, often with the use of communication techniques, to modify this type of difficulty.

The concept of vulnerability is one means of handling problems of this sort. Vulnerability is perceived and discussed as a unique attribute of a committed relationship; being vulnerable is implicit in the act of telling one's partner what one is afraid of, worried about, or unsure of, knowing that the partner might use this information against one. People avoid such vulnerability in their general interpersonal relationships, since there is little likelihood that such a pattern of honest and open communication is in their best interests. But in a committed relationship, the basic knowledge of commitment may be translated another way: Each person agrees to behave in the best interests of the relationship and specifically avoids *deliberately* hurting the partner. For this reason, being vulnerable becomes a way of drawing upon the strength of the relationship to deal with a problem or concern; the relationship cannot be stronger than the freedom (or lack of freedom) both partners have to admit their vulnerability in an active fashion.

A third expectation commonly found in people with inhibited sexual desire is the idea that sexual activity must progress inexorably to culminate in coitus and orgasm. This attitude, aptly hinted at linguistically by the term "foreplay," creates a situation of little autonomy—that is, if a person begins touching, kissing, or caressing, to stop is to leave things incomplete, to be a failure. Since so many values in our culture are encapsulated by ideas such as "Finish what you start" and by accolades to the worthiness of perseverance and hard work, the person with low libido may feel trapped sexually. On the other hand, if the person "tries out" a sexual situation to see if his or her feelings are activated, he or she is then compelled (either by the partner or by a personal internal view of things) to "go all the way."

The therapeutic remedy for this dilemma is made up of several components. There is direct, repeated discussion of this expectation with the couple, encouraging both partners to identify and verbalize their feelings about it. When sensate focus is introduced, it is specifically structured so as to remove the goals of either sexual arousal or intercourse as having any immediate relevance. As sensate focus progresses, both partners are encouraged to participate in sexual activity only so long as they are not bored, tired, or uncomfortable with it, with specific attention devoted to means of clarity in communicating, verbally and nonverbally, what is comfortable as opposed to what is not. The sense of sexual freedom is fostered by making it apparent to both partners that one of them cannot be responsible for the other person's sexual turn-on.

As therapy progresses, it may be useful to explore other areas such as the role of self-stimulation in increasing sexual responsivity or the use of fantasies to augment sexual feelings. Such techniques must be employed selectively, as they will not be useful in all cases and may sometimes create more of a stumbling block than a help. When inhibited sexual desire is accompanied by a specific sexual dysfunction such as impotence or female anorgasmia, other methods may be simultaneously incorporated into therapy (see Chaps. 20 and 21), since it is quite likely that as sexual function improves, libido will improve as well.

For many patients with inhibited sexual desire, the idea of nudity is uncomfortable because it signals for them an automatic beginning to sexual activity. The suggestion may be made that nudity be tried (in the privacy of their home) apart from sexual activity in order to overcome this association. However, since it is important to help such patients see that there need not be an artificial separation of closeness, affection, touching, and sex, it is helpful to foster the creation of a free-flowing relationship in which either partner can initiate sexual contact, knowing that both partners are free to participate or to stop as their feelings dictate. The emphasis, as in dealing with other types of sexual problems, is on establishing a focus on physical sensations without labeling them as good or bad: With attention to clarity of communication, both verbally and nonverbally, a sexual opportunity becomes a time of shared feelings and mutual exploration rather than a mechanical excursion.

Careful attention should be given to environmental factors that delimit sexual interest. Certain environmental cues may automatically lower sexual desire because of their association with previous unhappy patterns: For example, if having the television set turned on in the bedroom has previously signified one partner's disinterest in sex, it might be advisable to remove the television from the bedroom indefinitely. Very real environmental problems, such as having little privacy at home because of children moving freely about the house, may be partly solved by putting a lock on the bedroom door. Practical solutions can often be found to similar types of problems by discussing these matters objectively and examining the range of available options.

Except when inhibited sexual desire is the result of organic problems or a corollary of depression, treating the person with low libido individually is far less likely to be successful than working with the couple. For couples who are reasonably motivated to work together toward the restoration of libido, satisfactory therapeutic outcomes are the rule rather than the exception.

References

1. Husted, J. R.   Desensitization procedures in dealing with female sexual dysfunction. *Counseling Psychologist* 5:30–37, 1975.
2. Dollard, J., and Miller, N. E.   *Personality and Psychotherapy.* New York: McGraw-Hill Book Co., 1950. Pp. 162–163.
3. Frank, E., Anderson, C., and Rubinstein, D.   Frequency of sexual dysfunction in "normal" couples. *New England Journal of Medicine* 299:111–115, 1978.
4. Steele, S. J.   Sexual Problems Related to Contraception and Family Planning. In S. Crown (ed.), *Psychosexual Problems.* New York: Grune & Stratton, 1976. Pp. 383–401.
5. Lief, H. I.   Inhibited sexual desire. *Medical Aspects of Human Sexuality* 11(7):94–95, 1977.
6. Kaplan, H. S.   Hypoactive sexual desire. *Journal of Sex & Marital Therapy* 3:3–9, 1977.
7. Kreuz, L. E., Rose, R. M., and Jennings, J. R.   Suppression of plasma testosterone levels and psychological stress. *Archives of General Psychiatry* 26:479–482, 1972.

23

The Paraphilias

The vocabulary of contemporary sexology is in a state of flux attributable in part to advancing knowledge arising from research data and clinical experience. At the same time, there is growing recognition of a high degree of cultural relativism in defining what is "normal," particularly in regard to sexual behavior. As a result, considerable attention is being given to the interplay of diagnostic nomenclature, stigmatization, and humanistic concern. These factors combine to make it a matter of perplexity how to discuss the spectrum of sexual behaviors without making value-laden statements—either unintentionally or by design—through the choice of language used to label such behaviors. The choice of the relatively neutral word *paraphilia*—derived from Greek roots meaning "alongside of" and "love"—to describe the category of sexual behaviors previously labeled perversions, deviations, or aberrations, is an attempt to minimize such difficulties.

The dilemma shared by psychiatry and sexology today in discussion of this area can be highlighted by the following description:

Perversion, the erotic form of hatred, is a fantasy, usually acted out but occasionally restricted to a daydream. . . . It is a habitual, preferred aberration necessary for one's full satisfaction, primarily motivated by hostility. . . . The hostility in perversion takes form in a fantasy of revenge hidden in the actions that make up the perversion and serves to convert childhood trauma to adult triumph. . . . [This] trauma of childhood . . . actually occurred and is memorialized in the details of the perversion. My hypothesis is that a perversion is the reliving of actual historical sexual trauma . . . and that in the perverse act the past is rubbed out. This time, trauma is turned into pleasure, orgasm, victory. But the need to do it again—unendingly, eternally again in the same manner—comes from one's inability to get completely rid of the danger, the trauma [1].

In sharp contrast, the following view is also widely held:

Since the concept of sexual deviation not only fails to meet quantitative and qualitative scientific criteria but also has harmful effects, it should be dropped from the nomenclature. In fact, the concept of sexual deviation as a scientifically identifiable entity is a major anachronism. . . . To classify behavior in terms of degree of conformity to cultural biases would not be a meritorious or constructive activity, particularly when such activity serves merely to pronounce some of society's members as "unfit" and justify the intervention in their lives by presumably "more fit" professional persons [2].

The variety of forms of expression of human eroticism is great; defining what is sexually normal is highly problematic in any operational sense. It is impossible to obtain completely accurate statistics describing sexual behavior, since even under optimal circumstances of questionnaire administration or personal interviewing (optimal in terms of guarantees of anonymity and confidentiality) there are problems such as faulty recall, deliberate falsification, or omission of information. The more a person perceives his or her behavior as unusual, the greater the anxiety or guilt that is likely to be associated with a behavior or fantasy; and the more a behavior or fantasy conflicts with accepted cultural standards, the less the researcher is likely to delineate true prevalence statistics in a given population.

The problem of determining what is sexually normal is complicated by an additional factor in clinical situations. It is quite probable that consequential differences exist between the group of persons who seek treatment and those who do not; inferences about sexual normality drawn from a clinical population are thus likely to be biased in important ways. Therefore, in discussions that deal with the boundaries differentiating normal from abnormal, it is best to be circumspect and to acknowledge openly the state of our ignorance.

Money believes that the pathognomonic feature of all paraphilias is dependence of sexual arousal on a fantasy different from those involving only a consenting partner of the opposite sex [3]. Stoller has defined sexual deviation as "a preferred, habitual, compelling method of achieving sexual gratification other than by willing genital intercourse between human male and female" [4]. In both of these views, the element of consent between sexual partners is a critical component in defining what is not a paraphilia or deviation; however, there may be situations of sexual behavior such as sadism, masochism, or urophilia between consenting adults that would be regarded by most authorities as aberrant if they comprise the only means by which sexual arousal can be obtained. Therefore, a distinction must be drawn between behavior that occurs occasionally—as a means of experiencing a variety of sexual activities—and behavior that is repeated with a high degree of consistency as an exclusive or almost exclusive means of erotic gratification. The element of mutual consent is not necessarily the determining criterion.

Money also distinguishes between benign and pathologic paraphilias by utilizing the concept of mutual consent [3]. However, physical harm may result from situations in which mutual consent is present (again, cases of sadomasochism are the best example) as well as from paraphilias that do not require the participation of a partner (and thus have no requisite for consent), as evidenced by bizarre instances of autoerotic self-strangulation [5] or self-mutilation [6].

Such a discussion emphasizes the difficulty of attempting to formulate a single operational definition of paraphilia. This difficulty is compounded by the need to differentiate between persons who never enact their sexual fantasies (who may, of course, incorporate their fantasy content into masturbatory imagery or use the act of thinking about their fantasy as a stimulus during sexual activity with a partner), persons who enact their fantasies only in isolated instances, and persons who do so on a regular basis. It is doubtful that all such individuals are equivalent; further, it is likely that most persons have sexual fantasies, at least occasionally, that diverge from culturally defined normative behavior.

There are other difficult questions in this area that require thought and attention beyond the scope of this volume. For example, what are the ethical ramifications of attempting intervention in sexual behaviors generally regarded as abnormal [7, 8]? Who should determine which societal norms and legal sanctions require adherence and which do not? Should paraphiliac behavior that violates the law be regarded as a psychiatric disorder requiring treatment, or as a criminal act requiring punishment? Finally, on a level perhaps even more philosophical but probably central to answering the preceding queries, to what extent is paraphilia a reflection of biopsychosocial determinism and to what extent is it a matter of free will?

Paraphilias Requiring Particular Acts
Exhibitionism

Exhibitionism is the deliberate exposure of sex organs under inappropriate conditions with the intention of evoking a response in the observer [9]. Although sexual excitation is usually produced in the performer by the act of exhibitionism, it is not invariably present even if desired; further, although exhibitionism has been generally regarded as a paraphilia exclusive to males [4, 10, 11], there are isolated reports of female genital exhibitionism [9]. If exhibitionism occurring as a result of organic brain disease or psychosis is excluded, most cases involve the deliberate attempt to obtain sexual gratification via the act of exposure and the unwilling viewer's response. The exhibitionist may or may not masturbate coincidentally with exposing himself—in a significant percentage of cases, the exhibitionist may be impotent or have other sexual problems in heterosexual relations [4]; in some cases, the exhibitionist is impotent even during the act of genital exposure [11].

Mohr and his colleagues found that the peak incidence of exhibitionism occurs in the twenties, with only rare occurrence after age 40

[10]. Smukler and Schiebel, in a more recent report, described an age range of 17 to 54 (average age, 29) in a series of 41 male exhibitionists [11]. These workers found that the typical exhibitionist "is married, has above average intelligence, holds a satisfactory job and does not present evidence of severe psychopathology" [11].

The exhibitionist often follows a particular pattern of behavior leading up to his genital exposure (for example, returning to the same street corner or using his automobile, ostensibly to permit a quick getaway), and this partially accounts for the fact that apprehension by the police is more likely with this paraphilia than with others. Stoller hypothesizes that the need to risk being caught may be a part of the syndrome [4].

Most authorities suggest that exhibitionists are usually outwardly passive, shy, or dependent [4, 10–13]. There is also general consensus on the fact that exhibitionists are unlikely to commit rape or to progress to other forms of paraphiliac behavior. However, multiple paraphilias may coexist in the same person, and cases of exhibitionism combined with other forms of aberrant sexual behavior are not unusual [14, 15].

Voyeurism

The voyeur obtains sexual gratification by observing others engaged in sexual activity or in the act of undressing. Although the usual pattern of voyeurism is clandestine sexual looking and involves males observing females [4], neither of these features is absolute [16]. For example, homosexual males may practice voyeurism by surreptitiously looking at other males; similarly, the voyeur may arrange an episode of sexual activity that he can observe with the consent of the participants (sometimes his wife, sometimes a prostitute). The voyeur may be either sexually functional or dysfunctional in heterosexual situations. As with exhibitionism, the impulse for voyeurism may dissipate over the years for reasons that are not known.

Obscene Telephone Calling

The twentieth century has contributed at least one new category to the group of paraphilias by the ubiquitous availability of the telephone in our society. Persons making obscene telephone calls as a means of sexual excitement and gratification (the act is usually accompanied by masturbation leading to orgasm) do so—as the hackneyed phrase goes—"in the comfort and safety of their own home," temporarily insulated from the realities of the world and able to invoke an idealized visual imagery that circumvents the need for face-to-face confrontation and interaction. The aura of mystery induced by one-sided anonymity (the caller knows the name and phone number of the person being called) and the surprised response of the recipient of the call enhance the caller's freedom to boast, threaten, or flatter, making such calls a haven of psychosexual security for the caller. Although the overwhelming majority of obscene telephone callers are male, the following case illustrates the fact that females may become involved as well:

A 22-year-old woman reported that at age 18, while living in her own apartment, she began to receive calls from a stranger who gave detailed descriptions of his sexual anatomy and masturbatory activity. She became sexually excited during the first such call and masturbated to orgasm after getting off the phone. The next few evenings, she incorporated fantasies about the phone caller into masturbatory activity. When the man called again three or four days later, she was deliberately seductive and asked to meet him. The caller voiced concern that she was attempting his apprehension by the authorities through such an invitation; to "prove" her good intentions she began to describe, in great detail, her anatomic features and masturbatory proclivities. Although they never met, he called her several more times, with marked sexual excitement generated on her part by each call. Between calls and after the calls ceased (approximately six weeks after they had begun), the woman became increasingly preoccupied with fantasies about these calls. In contrast, sexual activity with three different sexual partners produced far less gratification. Finally, she initiated a telephone conversation of similar nature with a man she had seen briefly at her place of employment. She was multiply orgasmic during this call and began regularly repeating the pattern: Her calls were always directed toward men she could identify (but who were not familiar with her voice) and were always done in the evening after an elaborate ritual of bathing, drinking wine, and dressing in a particular robe. She continued to make such calls once or twice a week for three years, stopping only when she became engaged to be married. She rarely experienced orgasm during heterosexual activity unless she fantasized about her calls.

Sadomasochism

Sadism is the derivation of sexual arousal from the infliction of pain on another; in masochism, the person derives sexual arousal from having pain inflicted upon himself or herself. Since elements of sadistic or masochistic pleasure probably exist in all people, there is some semantic difficulty in defining boundaries for appropriate terminology: Is the biting, scratching, squeezing, or teasing that facilitates sexual responsivity different in kind from more obvious forms of sadomasochism such as spanking, bondage, or whipping? At one extreme are sadists who inflict their attacks on unwilling partners (e.g., rape, lust murder, torture) and masochists who derive pleasure from being subjected to dramatic and seemingly bizarre acts of enslavement, humiliation, bondage, and physical abuse; at the opposite extreme, persons may participate in well-staged episodes of mild (or even symbolic) sadistic or masochistic behavior in which only minimal amounts of discomfort are generated while gratification derives primarily from a combination of fantasy, experimentation, and security in knowing that one's partner understands the rules and will not transgress prearranged limits.

An extensive portion of pornographic literature is devoted to themes of a sadomasochistic nature [1]; magazines, equipment catalogues, and "social clubs" catering to a sadomasochistic clientele seem to be flourishing. Perhaps this reflects a search for sexual satisfaction in a society where the increasing discussion and visibility of eroticism creates a sense of something being missed, and imposes a requirement to go beyond commonly accepted standards of behavior to gain greater return. On the other hand, the visibility of sadomasochistic paraphernalia and pornography may be more a matter of rhetoric and vicarious practice than actual behavior.

Instances of extreme sadomasochism are seen infrequently by clinicians. Psychiatrists working with the courts may encounter such situations in the group described as criminal sex offenders. Coroners and specialists in forensic medicine also come into contact with unusual cases of this nature: Litman and Swearingen estimate that there are approximately 50 bondage deaths in the United States annually [17]. The extent to which sadism contributes to instances of sexual abuse of children or rape has not been determined, but is likely to be consequential.

Transvestism

Stoller defines transvestism as "a condition in which a man becomes genitally sexually excited by wearing feminine garments" [4]. Both Stoller [4, 18] and Person and Ovesey [19] point out that a fetishistic element is prominent in many but not all instances of transvestism; some transvestites use cross-dressing as a means of diminishing anxiety about gender identity and gender role [19]. Transvestism is to be distinguished from transsexualism, where a change of anatomic sex is desired and cross-dressing does not typically produce genital excitation, and is also traditionally differentiated from homosexual cross-dressing, since most transvestites are clearly heterosexual in their preferences.

The typical transvestite begins cross-dressing in childhood or adolescence, although usually he does not exhibit effeminate behavior. In adulthood, there is also a general picture of unremarkable masculinity in everyday life—the transvestite typically pursues cross-dressing in relative privacy. In contrast to this pattern is the small subgroup of transvestites who cross-dress while frequenting bars or social clubs: These men may seek homosexual contact (often unbeknownst to their prospective "partners") while masquerading as women. The transvestite may limit his behavior to cross-dressing or may use wigs, makeup, and other devices to produce a dramatic transformation in outward appearance from male to female. Many transvestites involve their wives in their cross-dressing behavior; with a tolerant partner, cross-dressing may become a prominent theme of sexual interaction.

Transvestism coexists with other paraphilias—including fetishism, exhibitionism, and masochism—quite commonly. An indeterminate number of transvestites are impotent except when cross-dressing. Transvestism has been reported in association with manic-depression [20] and as a form of symptom passing from father to son [21]. No prevalence data are currently available.

Paraphilias Related to Particular Objects
Fetishism

In fetishism, sexual arousal occurs principally in response to an object or body part that is not primarily sexual in nature. The fetish object is generally used during masturbation or incorporated into sexual activity with another person in order to produce sexual excitation. Often the fetishist collects such objects; in some cases, the behavior involves stealing the objects, which appears to contribute an added sense of risk and mystery. Stoller points out:

What seems important is that while the fetish may formerly have belonged to a person (for instance hair or shoes), it is clearly sensed as separate from that person. It is not simply an object that substitutes for a person, with the implication that the original owner of the fetish object would be preferred if he or she were present. On the contrary, the fetish is *preferred* to the owner. It is safe, silent, cooperative, tranquil, and can be harmed or destroyed without consequence [4].

In some men and women, sexual arousal to the point of orgasm can occur only in response to the fetish object (real or fantasized). In others, sexual response occurs in situations without the fetish object but is of considerably lower intensity or gratification. The following case example illustrates this point:

A married 26-year-old male medical student reported becoming sexually aroused by wearing tight-fitting rubber garments. This pattern had begun in his early teenage years and had been his sole means of masturbation. Sexual activity with his wife was unimpeded from a functional viewpoint, but his involvement and level of responsivity was much less in person-to-person sex than in his fetishistic behavior. He sought treatment because of depressive symptomatology, which dissipated rapidly upon the discovery of his sexual unhappiness. After "confessing" his dilemma to his wife and finding her agreeable to incorporating rubber garments into their sexual relationship, he decided he did not wish further treatment.

Pedophilia

Pedophilia (literally, "love of children") describes adults who have a need for sexual contact with preadolescent children [4, 10]. Although Mohr and colleagues believe that immature gratification is a hallmark of pedophilia, with the nature of the sexual act generally corresponding "to the maturity expected at the age of the victim rather than at the age of the offender" [10], there is considerable variability in this finding. In fact, the many cases of pedophilia involving oral-genital sex or actual or attempted coitus seem to refute this belief. Similarly, Stoller's contention that pedophilia occurs only in males [4] is probably valid only if conditioned upon a particular definition of the behavior in terms of a repeated, compulsive need. Women who have sexual relations with young boys are apt to be charged with an offense other than pedophilia (such as "contributing to the delinquency of a minor"—a puzzling statement in itself, since the presumption seems to be that sexual activity is a form of delinquency). Furthermore, since it is customary to consider incest involving a child as a variety of pedophilia [4, 10, 22], it is certainly well documented that incest occurs between mothers and their preadolescent sons and daughters.

Mohr and coworkers report that 4 percent of pedophilia victims are age 3 or under, while 18 percent are age 4 to 7 and 40 percent are between the ages of 8 and 11 [10]. They also found that incestuous pedophilia accounted for only 15 percent of cases, and that the victim is a total stranger to the pedophile in only 10.3 percent of cases [10]. While there may be methodological artifacts in these data, it appears quite likely that the last observation is generally accurate.

Pedophiles are frequently married and are quite likely to have marital and sexual difficulties. Difficulty in sexual functioning with an adult partner may be a major motivating factor in pedophilic behavior: the pedophile obtains a greater sense of security through mastery and control of sexual contact with a child. Alcohol abuse is another factor that figures prominently in a number of cases of pedophilia [23]; customary inhibitions may be lowered, facilitating sexual behavior that would otherwise be objectionable.

Miscellaneous Paraphilias Involving Particular Objects

It is not our intention to offer a complete catalogue of all the existing paraphilias. Categories such as bestiality (zoophilia), involving sexual contact with an animal, and necrophilia, involving sexual contact with a corpse, are unlikely to be encountered by most clinicians and are so poorly studied that little can be said about them. Instances of hypersexuality—usually labeled as satyriasis in males and nympho-mania in females—are incorrectly classified as paraphilias, although Stoller does so by creating a special category for them and describ-ing them in terms of practices involving "degraded heterosexual objects," emphasizing the dehumanizing aspect of sex with an unend-ing series of partners [4]. Since this argument, attractive as it may at first appear, loses substance in the recognition that even marital sex can occur in a highly depersonalized context (and certainly this pattern is common among both heterosexual and homosexual singles), there appears to be no convincing evidence that hypersexual states should be regarded as paraphilias.

Treatment of the Paraphilias

The literature describing treatment approaches to the paraphilias is rather fragmentary: Most reports discuss results obtained in a small number of cases, have no formal control group, or fail to provide specific criteria for evaluating outcome. Only brief mention will be made of the range of therapeutic techniques that have been utilized, since this area appears to be under current reappraisal.

Aversion therapy is a type of treatment used to produce a reduction in an undesired behavior via a conditioned emotional response, by suppression of a punished response, or by the development of an avoidance response [24]. Aversion therapy methods have included the use of electric shock and chemical induction of nausea and vomiting, usually in combination with exposure to photographs depicting the undesired behavior [24–28]. There are substantive ethical problems associated with the use of aversion techniques, which, combined with their low level of effectiveness in treating the paraphilias, makes these methods generally a poor treatment choice.

Other behavior modification techniques that have been used to treat the paraphilias include positive conditioning of desired behavior [29, 30], systematic desensitization [31, 32], and biofeedback and penile plethysmography [15]. A promising method that utilizes principles of aversion therapy without electric shock or other physical harm is a technique known as covert sensitization: The subject imagines aversive scenes (such as being caught by the police or being discovered by family members) immediately after being confronted with a sexually arousing scene, either visually or by fantasy [14, 33, 34]. Another novel approach offering some promise is the use of boredom in the reduction of undesired sexual interests via a procedure involving verbalizing such fantasies while engaging in prolonged masturbatory episodes [35].

Both hypnosis and psychotherapy have been employed with varying degrees of success in the treatment of paraphilias [36–38]. In addition, combined approaches utilizing pharmacologic therapy (in particular, with the use of antiandrogens such as cyproterone acetate or medroxyprogesterone acetate [see Chap. 13]) and psychotherapy or behavior modification have been gathering proponents and appear to offer a high degree of efficacy [39–43]. However, there is no single approach that will suit all such cases. At the moment, we can only hope for the future development of a greater understanding of these behavioral patterns.

References

1. Stoller, R. J. *Perversion: The Erotic Form of Hatred.* New York: Pantheon Books, 1975.
2. Tallent, N. Sexual deviation as a diagnostic entity: A confused and sinister concept. *Bulletin of the Menninger Clinic* 41:40–60, 1977.
3. Money, J. Paraphilias. In J. Money and H. Musaph (eds.), *Handbook of Sexology.* New York: Elsevier/North Holland Biomedical Press, 1977. Pp. 917–928.
4. Stoller, R. J. Sexual Deviations. In F. A. Beach (ed.), *Human Sexuality in Four Perspectives.* Baltimore: Johns Hopkins University Press, 1977. Pp. 190–214.
5. Walsh, F. M., Stahl, C. J., III, Unger, H. T., Lilienstern, O. C., and Stephens, R. G., III. Autoerotic Asphyxial Deaths: A Medicolegal Analysis of Forty-Three Cases. In C. H. Wecht (ed.), *Legal Medicine Annual 1977.* New York: Appleton-Century-Crofts, 1977. Pp. 157–182.
6. Money, J., Jobaris, R., and Furth, G. Apotemnophilia: Two cases of self-demand amputation as a paraphilia. *Journal of Sex Research* 13:115–125, 1977.
7. Kolodny, R. C. Ethical Issues in the Prevention of Sexual Problems. In C. B. Qualls, J. P. Wincze, and D. H. Barlow (eds.), *The Prevention of Sexual Disorders.* New York: Plenum Press, 1978. Pp. 183–196.
8. Masters, W. H., Johnson, V. E., and Kolodny, R. C. (eds.). *Ethical Issues in Sex Therapy and Research.* Boston: Little, Brown and Co., 1977.
9. Hollender, M. H., Brown, C. W., and Roback, H. B. Genital exhibitionism in women. *American Journal of Psychiatry* 134:436–438, 1977.
10. Mohr, J. W., Turner, R. E., and Jerry, M. B. *Pedophilia and Exhibitionism.* Toronto: University of Toronto Press, 1964.
11. Smukler, A. J., and Schiebel, D. Personality characteristics of exhibitionists. *Diseases of the Nervous System* 36:600–603, 1975.
12. Mathis, J. L. The exhibitionist. *Medical Aspects of Human Sexuality* 3(6):89–101, 1969.
13. Rickles, N. K. *Exhibitionism.* Philadelphia: J. B. Lippincott Co., 1950.
14. Brownell, K. D., and Barlow, D. H. Measurement and treatment of two

sexual deviations in one person. *Journal of Behavior Therapy and Experimental Psychiatry* 7:349–354, 1976.

15. Rosen, R. C., and Kopel, S. A. Penile plethysmography and biofeedback in the treatment of a transvestite-exhibitionist. *Journal of Consulting and Clinical Psychology* 45:908–916, 1977.

16. Smith, R. S. Voyeurism: A review of the literature. *Archives of Sexual Behavior* 5:585–608, 1976.

17. Litman, R. E., and Swearingen, C. Bondage and suicide. *Archives of General Psychiatry* 27:80–85, 1972.

18. Stoller, R. J. The term "transvestism." *Archives of General Psychiatry* 24:230–237, 1971.

19. Person, E., and Ovesey, L. Transvestism: New perspectives. *Journal of the American Academy of Psychoanalysis* 6:301–323, 1978.

20. Ward, N. G. Successful lithium treatment of transvestism associated with manic-depression. *Journal of Nervous and Mental Disease* 161:204–206, 1975.

21. Krueger, D. W. Symptom passing in a transvestite father and three sons. *American Journal of Psychiatry* 135:739–742, 1978.

22. Peters, J. J. Children who are victims of sexual assault and the psychology of offenders. *American Journal of Psychotherapy* 30:398–421, 1976.

23. Rada, R. T. Alcoholism and the child molester. *Annals of the New York Academy of Sciences* 273:492–496, 1976.

24. Bancroft, J. *Deviant Sexual Behavior.* Oxford: Clarendon Press, 1974.

25. Bancroft, J., and Marks, I. Electric aversion therapy of sexual deviations. *Proceedings of the Royal Society of Medicine* 61:796–799, 1968.

26. Fookes, B. H. Some experiences in the use of aversion therapy in male homosexuality, exhibitionism, and fetishism-transvestism. *British Journal of Psychiatry* 115:339–341, 1969.

27. Marks, I. M., and Gelder, M. G. Transvestism and fetishism: Clinical and psychological changes during faradic aversion. *British Journal of Psychiatry* 113:711–730, 1967.

28. Gaupp, L. A., Stern, R. M., and Ratlieff, R. G. The use of aversion-relief procedures in the treatment of a case of voyeurism. *Behavior Therapy* 2:585–588, 1971.

29. Jackson, B. T. A case of voyeurism treated by counterconditioning. *Behavior Research and Therapy* 7:133–134, 1969.

30. Stoudenmire, J. Behavioral treatment of voyeurism and possible symptom substitution. *Psychotherapy* 10:328–330, 1973.

31. Stevenson, J., and Jones, I. H. Behavior therapy technique for exhibitionism: A preliminary report. *Archives of General Psychiatry* 27:839–841, 1972.

32. Bond, I. K., and Hutchinson, H. E. Application of reciprocal inhibition therapy to exhibitionism. *Canadian Medical Association Journal* 83:23–25, 1960.

33. Barlow, D. H., Leitenberg, H., and Agras, W. S. The experimental control of sexual deviation through manipulation of the noxious scene in covert sensitization. *Journal of Abnormal Psychology* 74:596–601, 1969.

34. Callahan, E. J., and Leitenberg, H. Aversive therapy for sexual devia-

tion: Contingent shock and covert sensitization. *Journal of Abnormal Psychology* 81:60–73, 1973.

35. Marshall, W. L., and Lippens, K. The clinical value of boredom: A procedure for reducing inappropriate sexual interests. *Journal of Nervous and Mental Disease* 165:283–287, 1977.

36. Alexander, L. Psychotherapy of sexual deviation with the aid of hypnosis. *American Journal of Clinical Hypnosis* 9:181–183, 1967.

37. Roper, P. The use of hypnosis in the treatment of exhibitionism. *Canadian Medical Association Journal* 94:72–77, 1966.

38. Bastani, J. B. Treatment of male genital exhibitionism. *Comprehensive Psychiatry* 17:769–774, 1976.

39. Tennent, G., Bancroft, J. H. J., and Cass, J. The control of deviant sexual behavior by drugs: A double-blind controlled study of benperidol, chlorpromazine and placebo. *Archives of Sexual Behavior* 3:261–271, 1974.

40. Van Moffaert, M. Social reintegration of sexual delinquents by a combination of psychotherapy and anti-androgen treatment. *Acta Psychiatrica Scandinavica* 53:29–34, 1976.

41. Walker, P. A. The Role of Antiandrogens in the Treatment of Sex Offenders. In C. B. Qualls, J. P. Wincze, and D. H. Barlow (eds.), *The Prevention of Sexual Disorders*. New York: Plenum Press, 1978. Pp. 117–136.

42. Laschet, U., and Laschet, L. Antiandrogens in the treatment of sexual deviations of men. *Journal of Steroid Biochemistry* 6:821–826, 1975.

43. Money, J., Wiedeking, C., Walker, P. A., Migeon, C., Meyer, W., and Borgaonkar, D. 47,XYY and 46,XY males with antisocial and/or sex offending behavior: Antiandrogen plus counseling. *Psychoneuroendocrinology* 1:165–178, 1975.

24

Practical Management
of Sexual Problems

This chapter focuses on the clinical needs of the office practitioner who is not a specialist in sex therapy. Such a discussion is firmly in the mainstream of modern medical care, since it is clear that most patients with sexual problems do not require sex therapy. Despite this observation, it is important to distinguish between patients who need such a specialized approach and those likely to respond to simpler interventions. The chapter is organized around a number of pivotal themes, including how to establish the existence of a sexual problem, differentiating organic from psychogenic etiologies of sexual disorders, defining workable time-limited treatment formats, and deciding how and when to make a referral.

Diagnosis and Assessment
History-Taking

Identifying the existence of a sexual problem is dependent both on eliciting information from the patient and on being alert to the possible sexual implications that certain symptoms portend. If the practitioner does not regularly inquire about sexual difficulties in his or her patients, many problems will be missed because the patient is likely to be reluctant to volunteer such information. Reasons patients give for not initiating discussions about sex with their physician include embarrassment, not wanting to waste the physician's time with trivial matters, concern that the physician is uninterested or uninformed about sex, and fear that nothing can be done to improve a sexual problem. Although some physicians voice concern about embarrassing their patients by querying them about sexual matters, if this is done in a routine, comfortable fashion as part of the review of systems, such questions are unlikely to elicit any more embarrassment than those about bowel or bladder function.

Inquiring About Sexual Difficulties. For purposes of general information-gathering as part of a routine office visit, a short series of questions about sexuality can be asked in the space of two or three minutes. These questions include the following:

1. Are you currently active sexually? If so, what is the approximate frequency of sexual activity?
2. Are you satisfied with your sex life? If not, why not?
3. [For men] Do you have difficulty obtaining or maintaining an erection? Do you have any difficulty with the control of ejaculation?
4. [For women] Do you have any difficulty becoming sexually aroused?

Do you ever experience pain during intercourse? Do you have difficulty being orgasmic?
5. Do you have any questions or problems related to sex that you would like to discuss?

With this brief set of questions, it is likely that more than 95 percent of sexual problems in a clinical practice will be detected. The remaining 5 percent will only surface at a later time because of either denial; initial reluctance of the patient to discuss sex (combined with the sense of being "caught by surprise" by such questions, particularly if the patient has never been questioned by a physician in this fashion; such patients frequently return for another visit to admit to their initial hesitancy after rehearsing or even writing down a description of their sexual problems or questions); fear of shocking the physician or eliciting his or her disapproval; or, finally, not having considered this subject in any detail.

Defining the Dimensions of the Problem. Necessarily, when responses to such questions indicate the existence of an area of sexual concern, the next task of the physician is to gather further information to define the dimensions of the problem or problems and to assist the process of diagnosis. Therefore, questions about the onset, duration, and temporal sequence of a sexual disorder are in order; these should be followed by an attempt to identify the precipitating pattern(s), if any, that are causally linked with the sexual difficulty. Thus, the man who complains of impotence of two years' duration might be asked about conditions under which he has normal erections (during masturbation? with a prostitute? while reading erotic materials?) as well as about possible causes of his problem (Are you using any drugs? How frequently do you use alcohol? How do you and your wife get along in general?).

It is important to remember that defining a sexual problem is a relative matter: What counts most of all is the patient's perception of whether a given state is bothersome or not. While a coital frequency of three times a week may be perceived as a woefully hyposexual state by one person, abstinence from sexual activity may be the desirable norm for someone else. The physician must refrain from imposing his or her own definitions and sexual values on patients.

In determining the dimensions of a sexual problem, it is helpful to consider the impact such a problem has on the patient's life as well as the ways in which the patient has reacted to or coped with his or her problem. Is the marital relationship a solid one or is it troubled on many fronts? Is the patient hypochondriacal and prone to overdramatize all symptoms or difficulties? Is the patient depressed or troubled by poor self-esteem, negative body-image, or lack of assertiveness? In some cases, a sexual problem stands in relative isolation from other facets of the patient's life; in other cases, the sexual difficulty may be intricately interwoven with other interpersonal difficulties, psychological problems, or medical conditions. As a general rule, the more complicated the circumstances of the sexual problem and the more central it is to the patient's existence (creating anxiety, depression, or social isolation, for example), the greater the need for appropriate treatment and the more likely the patient is to require sex therapy or psychiatric care.

Identifying Specific Sexual Dysfunctions. The identification of specific sexual dysfunction either accompanying or causing sexual problems is an integral part of patient assessment and, for obvious reasons, determines to a major degree the direction of subsequent therapeutic efforts. Treating a man for impotence when the actual (unrecognized) problem is inhibited sexual desire is unlikely to be productive; similarly, treating a woman for general disinterest in sex when she actually has vaginismus is also an example of a needless diagnostic error. Vaginismus is unique among the sexual dysfunctions in that it is the only one that can only be definitively diagnosed by evidence found at the physical examination. The other sexual dysfunctions—impotence, premature ejaculation, ejaculatory incompetence, and anorgasmia—must all be diagnosed on the basis of historical information. Specific discussion of the natural history of these dysfunctions and lines of inquiry to be followed in taking a sex history are given in Chapters 20 and 21.

Once the office practitioner has identified the existence of a sexual problem and made a preliminary assessment of the dimensions of this problem, it is often advisable to schedule a followup visit for the purpose of eliciting more detailed historical information prior to instituting treatment. This allows the physician an unhurried opportunity to gather relevant information and gives the patient a certain degree of comfort from knowing that the physician considers the problem important enough to discuss in more than passing detail. Of course, the practitioner who is uninterested in treating patients with sexual problems has the option of making an immediate referral at this point, without acquiring further historical data. For the followup visit, it is worth considering the possibility of meeting separately with the patient and his or her sexual partner, if the sexual partner is willing to come in, since valuable information and perspectives may be gained by discussions with the partner or spouse.

Assessing Categories of Etiology. The sexual history is unsurpassed as a source of information for differentiating between organic and psychogenic etiologies of sexual problems. While additional data gleaned from the physical examination or laboratory assessment will provide further input to making such a distinction, it is the details of the history that usually provide the most important diagnostic clues. With this in mind, the following points bear particular attention.

Most organically induced sexual problems are persistent and progressively worsening, as opposed to psychogenic problems, which may more frequently be episodic or situational. Although there are a few exceptions to the first part of this statement, most notably including sexual problems associated with diseases such as multiple sclerosis that are marked by periods of exacerbation and remission or by conditions of fluctuating metabolic status (labile diabetes mellitus, for example, or periodic paralysis), in general, the observation holds true. It is important to realize that cases of psychogenic sexual disorders may be both persistent and progressive, particularly as the affected individual becomes more enmeshed in a matrix of compounding performance anxieties, self-doubts, and maladaptive defenses.

Sexual problems such as impotence or secondary ejaculatory incompetence usually have an abrupt onset when the origin is psychogenic. In most cases in which the problem is caused by organic factors, such disorders tend to develop gradually over a period of time. There are numerous exceptions to both of these generalizations. When sexual problems are precipitated by such organic factors as injury or surgery or when they reflect the impact of drug use, a sudden onset of disturbed sexual function is typically seen. Likewise, in some cases of sexual problems that are strictly psychogenic, the development of the problem is gradual, either as a result of negative conditioning over time, deterioration of the quality of a dyadic relationship, or the development of psychopathology.

When a sexual problem appears only in a situational context (e.g., with one partner but not another, or with coitus but not with masturbation), the probability is strong that the problem is psychogenic. Psychogenic sexual difficulties also are frequently correlated temporally with other stressful events in a person's life, although it may require extensive history-taking to uncover the precise origin of the problem.

In general, it is easier to determine the etiology of sexual problems of short duration than to define the precipitating causes of a problem that has existed for many years. This may partly reflect the fact that it is not unusual for a sexual problem that started for rather simple reasons to be maintained and to evolve through a series of more complex stages, including denial, increasing anxiety, attempts to improve or overcome the situation (characteristically amplifying the anxiety, if unsuccessful), and eventually, a sense of helplessness or guilt, often accompanied by avoidance or withdrawal. By the time the practitioner sees a patient who has been contending with a sexual problem for many years, it may not be realistic to attempt to determine the specific sequence of previous events; this does not necessarily mean that treatment attempts are predestined to fail, since many cases in this category will respond positively to therapeutic strategies that draw largely on an adequate delineation of the current status of the sexual problem.

Some sexual problems are so clearly of psychogenic origin that they do not ordinarily require any investigation of the physical or metabolic status of the patient. Conditions such as the paraphilias, incest, deficits in sex information, sexual guilt, and sexual aversion might be included in this category. For patients with sexual dysfunctions, dyspareunia, disorders of gender identity, or inhibited sexual desire, a careful physical examination has the potential of documenting specific organic conditions that will explain the genesis of the sexual difficulty and will suggest the most appropriate approach to treatment. Disturbances in sexual behavior or sexual function due to psychiatric illness generally require treatment for the specific psychiatric condition rather than sex counseling or sex therapy (see Chap. 12).

Assessing Patient Motivation. It is tempting to assume that whenever a sexual problem is identified, the patient wishes to be relieved of the burden of it, but this is not always the case. Some patients prefer their dysfunctional or problematic state for reasons that are primarily masochistic; other patients use their sexual distress as a means of obtaining other benefits from their spouse or partner. It is important to assess the patient's motivation for participating in a treatment program, since the likelihood of therapeutic success is diminished if the patient is unmotivated or poorly motivated. For example, some patients would be happy to be cured by a pill or "shot" but have little interest in investing their time, effort, or money in psychotherapy. Other patients indicate their low level of motivation by repeatedly missing or canceling appointments, refusing to request the participation of their partner or spouse in treatment, or deliberately disregarding therapeutic suggestions.

The Physical
Examination

The importance of the physical examination as a source of diagnostic information is second only to that of historical material. While it is obvious that detailed examination of the genitalia is necessary to gather needed diagnostic data, it is also mandatory to conduct a thorough general physical examination to obtain information about systemic illness that may impede sexual function. For example, dermatologic signs such as spider angiomata (suggestive of liver disease), hirsutism in women (sometimes associated with Cushing's syndrome, adrenal tumors, or ovarian tumors), hyperpigmentation (a striking feature of Addison's disease), and acanthosis nigricans (often associated with malignant disease such as gastric adenocarcinoma) may assist in the diagnostic process. Examination of the eyes may uncover evidence of a variety of disorders, including thyroid disease (exophthalmos, lid lag, Stellwag's sign), hyperlipidemia (xanthelasma), multiple sclerosis (optic papillitis, atrophy of the optic disks, nystagmus), diabetes (diabetic microaneurysms or more advanced diabetic retinopathy, including hemorrhages, exudates, dilatation of veins, and neovascularization), and neurosyphilis (the Argyll Robertson pupil, which is small, irregular, and reacts to accommodation but not to light; optic atrophy may also be seen).

In addition to providing diagnostic information, the general physical examination is also a potential source of practical data relevant to sexual counseling. For instance, advising arthritic patients about coital positioning is more sensibly undertaken after determining which joints are affected and the degree to which the ordinary range of motion is impaired. Similarly, answering patients' concerns about the normality of their anatomic appearance (such as queries about penile size) is hardly possible without direct observation of these features.

A detailed genitourinary examination and a thorough general physical examination should be supplemented by neurologic and vascular examinations in most patients with sexual dysfunction. Impaired neurologic function and vascular insufficiency are not likely to be detected by routine clinical laboratory investigation, although either category may be associated with sexual difficulties that may be reversible with appropriate treatment. A hasty check of patellar and ankle jerk reflexes does not constitute a complete neurologic exam: Testing should include assessment of the cranial nerves; evaluation of coordination, movement, sensation, and motor strength; eliciting of deep tendon, superficial, and pathologic reflexes; and observation of patterns of speech, comprehension, memory, and judgment. Similarly, a cursory perusal of peripheral pulses is not an adequate examination of the peripheral vascular system: Testing should include inspection of skin color, hair growth and distribution, and venous filling in the extremities, with special attention to signs of ulceration, atrophy, and skin temperature; palpation of peripheral pulses with auscultation of the femoral arteries; and palpation of the epigastrium to detect an expansile, pulsating tumor (if an abdominal aortic aneurysm is suspected).

Laboratory Testing of Patients with Sexual Problems

Those patients whose sexual and medical histories are consistent with a possible organic etiology for their sexual difficulty should undergo routine laboratory testing of hematologic, biochemical, and endocrine parameters. For practical purposes, this group includes men with impotence or reduced libido and women with orgasmic dysfunction, dyspareunia, or impaired libido. For all these patients, a complete blood count, urinalysis, serologic test for syphilis, and chemistry screening profile (including evaluation of blood sugar, hepatic and renal function, and electrolytes) are indicated. Men with impotence or reduced libido should have serum or plasma testosterone measured (this should be done between 7:00 A.M. and 10:00 A.M. to control for diurnal variation); if the testosterone level is low, the test should be repeated along with a determination of serum LH and prolactin. As discussed in Chapter 6, hypogonadism may result from hyperprolactinemia; if hyperprolactinemia is documented (in either males or females), radiologic studies should be performed to determine whether a pituitary tumor is present.

Estrogen determinations in women are clinically useful only in restricted circumstances; in suspected cases of estrogen deficiency, blood concentrations of estrogens may be measured but must be interpreted in the context of physical signs and the patient's symptoms. Measurements of cortisol, thyroxine, ACTH, and TSH seem indicated only when the history or physical examination point toward the likelihood of adrenal or thyroid disease, or when the sexual history is strongly suggestive of an organic etiology that is not detected by other tests.

We believe that oral glucose tolerance testing is advisable in the case of men with secondary impotence and women with secondary orgasmic dysfunction. Such testing should certainly be done on patients with a family history of diabetes mellitus in a parent, sibling, grandparent, or child.

Special Studies on Patients with Sexual Problems. The monitoring of patterns of nocturnal penile tumescence has already been considered as a means of differentiating between psychogenic and organic impotence (see Chap. 20), but methodological issues render these data difficult to interpret in some instances. Schiavi reports that psychological factors may sometimes impede sleep-associated erections and also notes that some men with proved organic impotence occasionally have an episode of full erection during sleep [1]. This observation is consistent with reports from patients with spinal cord injuries or diabetes who infrequently experience relatively normal erections and are clearly impaired sexually because of their underlying physiologic lesion.

Specialized testing may be employed to determine the integrity of peripheral circulation if vascular disease is suspected as the possible cause of sexual dysfunction. Arteriography can be useful in delineating the location of arterial obstruction and will also demonstrate the extent of collateral circulation around the obstruction. Phalloarteriography, a special angiographic approach for radiographic visualization of the arterial supply of the penis, offers particular relevance in selected cases [2]. Thermometry and thermography provide indirect assessments of arterial circulation. Radioactive substances may also be used to assess local blood flow and changes in blood flow with exercise and pharmacologic manipulation. A noninvasive technique for measuring penile blood pressure using a digital cuff and a portable ultrasound Doppler system offers diagnostic utility as well [3]. Venous occlusion may be studied either radiographically or by the use of ultrasound, plethysmography, or intraluminal pressure readings. Studies of the physiologic measures of sexual arousal and its disturbances in women are comparatively lacking. Abel and coworkers describe the use of vaginal photoplethysmography during sleep to demonstrate changes in vaginal blood volume and pulse pressure, but the diagnostic significance of these findings is uncertain [4].

A detailed discussion of neurologic evaluation techniques is beyond the scope of this chapter. Such testing includes the study of cerebrospinal fluid, electroencephalography, neuroradiology (including computerized transaxial tomography), radioactive brain scans, myelography, nerve conduction velocity, and nerve or muscle biopsy. If neurologic disease is suspected, a neurologist should be consulted for proper evaluation; similarly, it is advisable to consult with a urologist if specialized urodynamic studies or other urologic assessments are indicated.

At the present time, psychological testing does not appear to offer much diagnostic or prognostic assistance in the management of patients with sexual problems.

Office Treatment of Sexual Problems

Practitioners must define their approach to the management of sexual problems on the basis of a number of factors, including their level of knowledge and skill in the area of sex education or counseling, the time they have available, and their professional interest. For some physicians it is inefficient or uncomfortable to talk with patients about sexual concerns, while for others the process of sex counseling is challenging or is viewed as an integral part of health-care delivery. The decision to treat patients should not be made without considerable attention to the quality of services that can be provided—a point applicable to all facets of health care—but the interested, well-informed, and sensitive physician can contribute significantly to solving the sexual problems patients are likely to experience.

Certain sexual problems should always be referred to a specialist for treatment. These include all cases of transsexualism or severe gender ambivalence, all cases of sexual aversion, and all cases of primary impotence. Except in rare instances, cases of primary orgasmic dysfunction, paraphilia, incest, child sexual abuse, ejaculatory incompetence, and low libido of long duration likewise require referral for specialized treatment. On the other hand, the informed nonspecialist will frequently be successful in treating patients with dyspareunia; premature ejaculation; secondary impotence; sexual problems attendant upon illness, drugs, or surgery; concerns about sexual normality; and deficits in sex information.

In deciding whether to treat or to refer, it is helpful to assess several points in addition to the basic sexual dilemma. Generally speaking, sexual dysfunctions that have been present for long periods of time are more recalcitrant to treatment than those of shorter duration. Cases complicated by marital discord, psychiatric illness, or severe problems of body-image, self-esteem, or denial are also difficult and may require intensive therapy. On the other hand, the age of the patient is unrelated to treatment outcome: Younger patients do not necessarily have a better outcome than patients who are middle-aged or in their geriatric years.

It is usually advisable for the nonspecialist in sex therapy to define limits to the duration of treatment that he or she undertakes in advance of beginning any counseling approach. While each practitioner must develop individual criteria in this regard, we believe referral is indicated if significant progress is not made by the end of six counseling sessions, as the likelihood of helping the patient decreases dramatically thereafter. This aspect of deciding when to refer depends in part on the specific level of intervention that is being utilized: In some instances, it becomes clear after a short period of time that the patient requires psychotherapy rather than sex education or counseling.

Primary care physicians and medical specialists who are not sex therapists or psychiatrists are probably able to provide effective treatment for patients with sexual problems in 80 percent or more of the cases encountered in their practices. All health-care professionals can initiate a first level of treatment by giving patients an opportunity to ventilate in an atmosphere of supportive listening—the efficacy of this simple but powerful strategy should never be underestimated. The next level of treatment involves patient education, which can be accomplished by the use of personal discussion, books, movies, or other standard educational techniques. Education is not restricted to matters of anatomy and physiology; patients may benefit from simple reassurance about the normality of their sexual feelings or sexual behavior, or they may need information about particular topics such as contraception, sexual function after a heart attack, and other similar concerns.

Education and counseling are not always easily distinguishable. In general, the counselor provides patients with suggestions about ways of dealing with particular problems or encourages patients to develop their own solutions after evaluating a range of available options, while the educator provides information rather than suggestions. Both in educating and in counseling patients, for reasons that are both ethical and related to the risk of impairing the outcome of the interaction by discomfiting the patient, it is important to avoid imposing one's personal values onto the patient. Identifying the patient's own value matrix is not always an easy task, but the more extensive the counseling or psychotherapy, the more such definition must be undertaken.

Some sexual problems can be managed with counseling that is restricted to simple levels. Introduction of the squeeze technique may lead to a rapid resolution of premature ejaculation (although this is certainly not always the case); vaginismus may be promptly reversed following the use of vaginal dilators and supportive encouragement; secondary impotence may improve after performance anxieties are identified and discussed. Why some people experience rapid amelioration of their sexual difficulties while others fail to respond to the same suggestions is only poorly understood at present. Unfortunately, there are no reliable predictors of which patients will be successful in a given type of treatment.

Several matters of treatment format deserve brief discussion. It is generally advantageous to treat the couple with sexual problems rather than to treat the individual alone (see Chap. 19), but such an approach is not always feasible or necessary. When sexual difficulties include problems in interpersonal behavior or communication or when marital discord is prominent, therapy for the couple is particularly important. If this is impossible, group therapy may be a suitable alternative approach. It is usually difficult to treat sexual problems when patients are seen infrequently. Most office practitioners find that appointments on a once-a-week basis are adequate for management of such cases; if appointments are less frequent, a number of problems—including poor compliance with counseling suggestions and poor recall of information—can conspire to reduce treatment effectiveness. While the use of a dual-sex therapy team offers both theoretic and practical advantages in the management of sexual difficulties (as discussed in Chap. 19), individual therapists can often achieve satisfactory treatment outcomes [5–9]. However, the physician may sometimes find it advantageous to work in a dual-sex counseling or therapy team with another physician or a psychologist, social worker, or nurse.

As in all aspects of medical care, it is necessary in sex counseling to set appropriate treatment objectives that are realistic and congruent with the patient's desires. Once this has been done, it is important to formulate a specific treatment plan rather than simply to assume that talking with the patient will automatically provide effective management. For example, the physician working with an impotent man may decide to follow the steps in management depicted in Figure 24-1. In setting appropriate and realistic treatment objectives, it should be realized that sex counseling cannot usually retrieve broken marriages: If nonsexual issues of marital conflict are prominent in the case of a couple in treatment, consideration should be given to appropriate referral to a qualified marriage counselor. The interrelationship between sex therapy and marital therapy has been discussed by other authors [10, 11].

Sex counseling may fail for a variety of reasons ranging from poor patient motivation to incompetent management. Some professionals misunderstand or misapply treatment techniques such as sensate focus, forgetting that a single technique is no panacea for a broad range of maladaptive patterns. Other professionals overextend the limits of their skills and undertake treatment of patients with complex problems

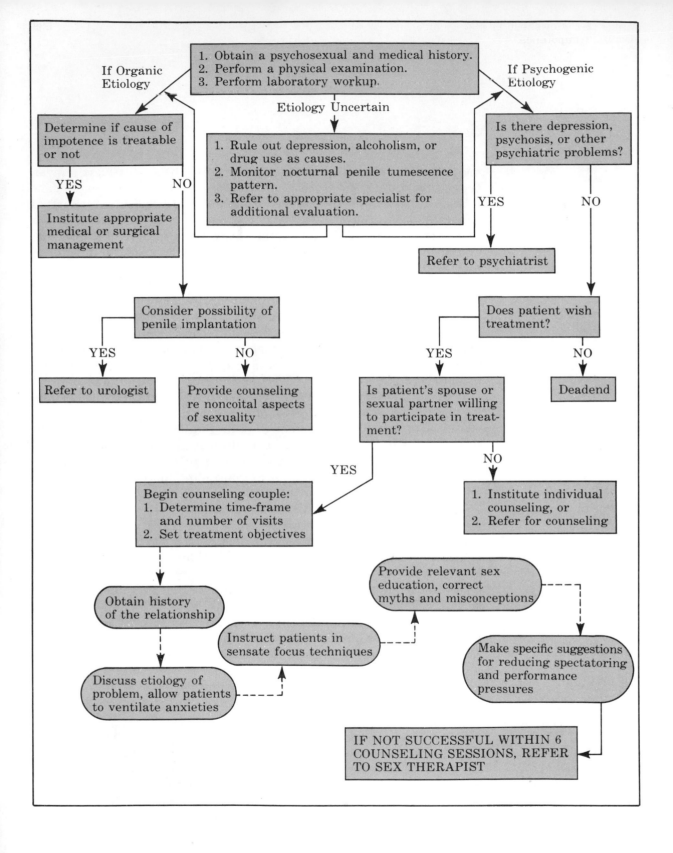

Figure 24-1. Flowsheet for management of a case of
secondary impotence.

599

requiring intensive psychotherapy. Unfortunately, it is all too easy to
assume that sex counseling or sex therapy depends more upon "gim-
micks" and psychological tricks than careful attention to technique,
assessment, and flexibility. When this is coupled with the unfortunate
view that the physician must be all things to all people, it is easy to see
how pressures are created that undermine the quality of care that the
patient receives.

The physician who provides his or her patients with sex education
and sex counseling can accomplish a great deal. In many instances, the
judicious use of sex education contributes to the prevention of future
difficulties. Counseling may also prevent or minimize the occurrence of
sexual problems, as demonstrated in areas such as pre- and postsurgical sex counseling for patients undergoing prostatectomy, hysterectomy, or mastectomy; counseling of cardiac patients; and counseling for
sexually active teenagers. With routine attention to sexual health concerns, physicians and other health-care professionals can have a decided impact on the quality of their patients' lives. This is the essential
message of this book.

References

1. Schiavi, R. C. Some problems in the differential diagnoses of erectile
   disorders. *Sexuality and Disability* 2:66–70, 1979.
2. Michal, V. and Pospíchal, J. Phalloarteriography in the diagnosis of
   erectile impotence. *World Journal of Surgery* 2:239–248, 1978.
3. Engel, G., Burnham, S. J., and Carter, M. F. Penile blood pressure in the
   evaluation of erectile impotence. *Fertility and Sterility* 30:687–690, 1978.
4. Abel, G. G., Murphy, W. D., Becker, J. V., and Bitar, A. Women's vaginal
   responses during REM sleep. *Journal of Sex & Marital Therapy* 5:5–14,
   1979.
5. Kaplan, H. S. *The New Sex Therapy.* New York: Brunner/Mazel, Publishers, 1974.
6. Prochaska, J. O., and Marzilli, R. Modifications of the Masters and
   Johnson approach to sexual problems. *Psychotherapy: Theory, Research
   and Practice* 10:294–296, 1973.
7. Mathews, A., Bancroft, J., Whitehead, A., Hackmann, A., Julier, D., Bancroft, J., Gath, D., and Shaw, P. The behavioural treatment of sexual
   inadequacy: A comparative study. *Behaviour Research and Therapy*
   14:427–436, 1976.
8. McCarthy, B. W. A modification of Masters and Johnson sex therapy
   model in a clinical setting. *Psychotherapy: Theory, Research and Practice*
   10:290–293, 1973.
9. Kohlenberg, R. J. Directed masturbation and the treatment of primary
   orgasmic dysfunction. *Archives of Sexual Behavior* 3:349–356, 1974.
10. Sager, C. J. The role of sex therapy in marital therapy. *American Jour-
    nal of Psychiatry* 133:555–558, 1976.
11. Olson, D. (ed.). *Treating Relationships.* Washington, D.C.: Graphic
    Press, 1976.

Index

in feminizing adrenocortical
tumors, 149
in fertile eunuchs, 123
in handicapped persons, 361, 362
history-taking in, 513–515, 588, 589,
590
in homosexuals, 456
in hyperaldosteronism, 149–150
and hypogonadism, 517
in hypopituitarism, 124, 151, 152,
153, 155, 411
iatrogenic, 512
and infertility, 411–412, 414
in Kallmann's syndrome, 122
in Klinefelter's syndrome, 38, 119,
411
laboratory testing in, 515–518, 593,
594
in Leriche syndrome, 179
libido in, 516
in manic males, 304
in multiple sclerosis, 233, 257, 258,
515
in muscular dystrophy, 259–260
after myocardial infarction, 169
in obesity, 251
organic causes of, 507, 508, 513,
514, 515–518
and orgasmic dysfunction in females, 548
after ostomy surgery, 245, 248, 249
pathogenesis of, 129–131
penile prosthesis in, 134–135, 222,
227
after penile trauma, 222
in Peyronie's disease, 219, 224
physical examination in, 515
in poliomyelitis, 260
and premature ejaculation, 528,
530
primary and secondary, 507, 523
after prostatectomy, 216, 217–218,
222
in prostatic carcinoma, 218
psychological considerations in,
131–134, 216, 217–218, 222, 227,
507–513, 514, 515, 517, 518–523
with pulmonary disease, 264
reactions of women to, 133

in rectal carcinoma, 273
in renal failure, 235
with retrograde ejaculation, 221
after sphincterotomy, 222
after stroke, 255
in temporal lobe lesions, 253
and testicular tumors, 290, 291
and testosterone levels, 22
in thyroid disorders, 142, 143, 144
treatment of
in diabetes, 131–135
failure in, 523
in office, 595, 596, 597
psychotherapeutic approach to,
131–134
sensate focus instructions in,
520–523
sex therapy in, 518–523
after urethral injury, 222
in vaginismus, 411, 412, 535, 536
after vasectomy, 405
in widower's syndrome, 512–513
Incest, 72, 535, 546
and depression, 302
fantasies of, 94
libido after, 568
and pedophilia, 582
Incompetence, ejaculatory. See
Ejaculatory incompetence
Infancy
gender-identity formation in,
64–68
hormone status in, 59–60
masturbation in, 62–63
parent-child bonding in, 63–64
sexuality in, 62–68
stages of psychosexual development in, 60–61, 62
witch's milk phenomenon in, 60
Infarction, myocardial. See Myocardial infarction
Infections
in Addison's disease, 146
and clitoral pain, 193
in Cushing's syndrome, 148
cystitis, 140, 186, 187, 213–214
in diabetes
in females, 139, 140
in males, 135